Countering Disinformation in the Era of Generative AI

Symeon Papadopoulos · Kalina Bontcheva ·
Vasileios Mezaris · Richard Rogers
Editors

Countering Disinformation in the Era of Generative AI

Springer

Editors
Symeon Papadopoulos
Information Technologies Institute
Centre for Research and Technology Hellas (CERTH)
Thessaloniki, Greece

Vasileios Mezaris
Information Technologies Institute
Centre for Research and Technology Hellas (CERTH)
Thessaloniki, Greece

Kalina Bontcheva
Department of Computer Science
The University of Sheffield (USFD)
Sheffield, UK

Richard Rogers
University of Amsterdam (UvA)
Amsterdam, Noord-Holland
The Netherlands

ISBN 978-3-032-11781-6 ISBN 978-3-032-11782-3 (eBook)
https://doi.org/10.1007/978-3-032-11782-3

This Springer imprint is published by the registered company Springer Nature Switzerland AG
The registered company address is: Gewerbestrasse 11, 6330 Cham, Switzerland

To all those who seek the truth and never end their quest.

Preface

While there is abundant scientific literature in the area that has been rapidly emerging at the nexus of online disinformation and artificial intelligence (AI), this largely takes the form of journal articles or conference papers that by large study very specific aspects of this area, or focus on very specific topics. There are also a number of survey articles that offer good coverage of certain sub-areas, e.g., deepfake detection. Yet, we feel that there is still a lack of a comprehensive resource that puts together discussions and examinations of recent developments across many different topics under the common theme of online disinformation and AI, and in particular Generative AI.

We have been fortunate to work together with a highly motivated and talented consortium of partners across Europe in the scope of the Horizon Europe vera.ai project. This consortium includes very rich knowledge and skills ranging from fact-checkers, journalists, and civil societies to computer and social scientists, as well as product and service developers. Along with the expertise, the consortium also possessed valuable background assets, including widely used verification tools and AI detection and analysis models that could power advanced verification capabilities. Working together, we made significant progress on building a variety of powerful AI-based verification methods and also on studying actual disinformation campaigns and the agents behind them. This book distills the experience and knowledge gained through almost three years of collaborative work in this area with the hope of informing interested audiences about the multitude of challenges and problems arising in today's media verification tasks and also setting a solid basis for future research in this area.

The introductory chapters of the book (First and Second Part) could appeal to broad audiences and have few knowledge requisites, while Third and Fourth Part would be better appreciated by people with a certain familiarity with AI concepts and methods.

Most of the work reported throughout this book was supported by the European Union under the Horizon Europe vera.ai: VERification Assisted by Artificial Intelligence project, under Grant Agreement number 101070093.

Olga Papadopoulou, lead author of Chapter "False Alarm or Real Threat? Trends in GenAI-Mediated Disinformation", significantly contributed to the technical editorial tasks during the preparation of this book.

Thessaloniki, Greece — Symeon Papadopoulos
Sheffield, UK — Kalina Bontcheva
Thessaloniki, Greece — Vasileios Mezaris
Amsterdam, The Netherlands — Richard Rogers
August 2025

Contents

Contributors

Jakob Abeßer Fraunhofer Institute for Digital Media Technology (IDMT), Ilmenau, Germany

Patrick Aichroth Fraunhofer Institute for Digital Media Technology (IDMT), Ilmenau, Germany

Konstantinos Apostolidis Centre for Research and Technology Hellas (CERTH), Thessaloniki, Greece

Quentin Bammey Ecole Polytechnique Federale de Lausanne (EPFL), Lausanne, Switzerland;
LTCI, Télécom Paris, Institut Polytechnique de Paris, Palaiseau, France

Kalina Bontcheva University of Sheffield (USFD), Sheffield, UK

Anwesha Chakraborty Department of Communication Sciences, Humanities and International Studies, University of Urbino Carlo Bo, Urbino, Italy

Riccardo Corvi University of Naples Federico II (UNINA), Naples, Italy

Davide Cozzolino University of Naples Federico II (UNINA), Naples, Italy

Luca Cuccovillo Fraunhofer Institute for Digital Media Technology (IDMT), Ilmenau, Germany

Michael Foster The University of Sheffield (USFD), Sheffield, UK

Milica Gerhardt Fraunhofer Institute for Digital Media Technology (IDMT), Ilmenau, Germany

Fabio Giglietto Department of Communication Sciences, Humanities and International Studies, University of Urbino Carlo Bo, Urbino, Italy

Fabrizio Guillaro University of Naples Federico II (UNINA), Naples, Italy

Dimitrios Karageorgiou Centre for Research and Technology Hellas (CERTH), Thessaloniki, Greece

Despina Konstantinidou Centre for Research and Technology Hellas (CERTH), Thessaloniki, Greece

Kamila Koronska Media Studies, University of Amsterdam (UvA), Amsterdam, Netherlands

Christos Koutlis Centre for Research and Technology Hellas (CERTH), Thessaloniki, Greece

Dominik Macko Kempelen Institute of Intelligent Technologies (KInIT), Bratislava, Slovakia

Giada Marino Department of Communication Sciences, Humanities and International Studies, University of Urbino Carlo Bo, Urbino, Italy

Vasileios Mezaris Centre for Research and Technology Hellas (CERTH), Thessaloniki, Greece

Rosanna Milner University of Sheffield (USFD), Sheffield, UK

Stelios Mylonas Centre for Research and Technology Hellas (CERTH), Thessaloniki, Greece

Stefanos-Iordanis Papadopoulos Centre for Research and Technology Hellas (CERTH), Thessaloniki, Greece

Symeon Papadopoulos Centre for Research and Technology Hellas (CERTH), Thessaloniki, Greece

Olga Papadopoulou Centre for Research and Technology Hellas (CERTH), Thessaloniki, Greece

Panagiotis C. Petrantonakis Aristotle University of Thessaloniki (AUTH), Thessaloniki, Greece

Alessandro Pianese University of Naples Federico II (UNINA), Naples, Italy

Giovanni Poggi University of Naples Federico II (UNINA), Naples, Italy

Olesya Razuvayevskaya University of Sheffield (USFD), Sheffield, UK

Richard Rogers Media Studies, University of Amsterdam (UvA), Amsterdam, Netherlands

Manos Schinas Centre for Research and Technology Hellas (CERTH), Thessaloniki, Greece

Ivan Srba Kempelen Institute of Intelligent Technologies (KInIT), Bratislava, Slovakia

Massimo Terenzi Department of Communication Sciences, Humanities and International Studies, University of Urbino Carlo Bo, Urbino, Italy

Denis Teyssou Agence France-Presse (AFP) and Paris Nanterre University, Paris, France

Luisa Verdoliva University of Naples Federico II (UNINA), Naples, Italy

Marissa Willcox Media Studies, University of Amsterdam (UvA), Amsterdam, Netherlands;
Media, Communications and Cultural Studies, Goldsmiths University of London, London, UK

Introduction and Overview

Introduction

Symeon Papadopoulos, Vasileios Mezaris, Kalina Bontcheva, and Richard Rogers

1 Disinformation as a Key Risk in the Era of Generative AI

Disinformation, while not a new phenomenon, is undergoing a profound resurgence as a societal and geopolitical threat, fuelled in large part by the emergence of generative Artificial Intelligence (AI). These technologies are capable of producing convincing human-like text, hyper-realistic imagery, and synthetic audio and video that may easily pose as authentic, and in that way, they have significantly lowered the barrier to entry for creating persuasive false content at scale. What once required coordinated human effort and resources can now be accomplished with minimal technical skill using publicly available models. As a result, disinformation campaigns have become more agile, personalised, and difficult to detect, challenging existing paradigms of content moderation, fact-checking, and digital verification.

The modern disinformation crisis emerged in the early 2010s, as the rapid growth of social media platforms redefined the way information was created, shared, and consumed. Unlike traditional media ecosystems, where gate-keeping mechanisms helped filter and verify content, the new digital landscape enabled the viral spread of unverified or deliberately false information with unprecedented speed and reach. The 2016 U.S. presidential election is widely regarded as a watershed moment:

S. Papadopoulos (✉) · V. Mezaris
Centre for Research and Technology Hellas (CERTH), Thessaloniki, Greece
e-mail: papadop@iti.gr

V. Mezaris
e-mail: bmezaris@iti.gr

K. Bontcheva
The University of Sheffield (USFD), Sheffield, UK
e-mail: k.bontcheva@sheffield.ac.uk

R. Rogers
University of Amsterdam (UvA), Amsterdam, Netherlands
e-mail: r.a.rogers@uva.nl

S. Papadopoulos et al. (eds.), *Countering Disinformation in the Era of Generative AI*,
https://doi.org/10.1007/978-3-032-11782-3_1

coordinated disinformation campaigns, many state-sponsored, exploited algorithmic amplification, micro-targeted advertising, and bot networks to influence public opinion at scale [1, 4]. Similar incidents unfolded across the globe, putting the spotlight on disinformation as not just a technical problem but a geopolitical instrument and socio-technical threat. These developments gave rise to early research efforts on automated detection methods, platform monitoring and accountability studies, and media literacy. However, the tactics used in these early campaigns were largely constrained by the limits of human-generated content and rudimentary automation.

The scale and sophistication enabled by generative AI marks a fundamental shift in the disinformation landscape. Large language models (LLMs) can automate the generation of misleading narratives tailored to specific audiences, while image, audio and video synthesis tools can fabricate depictions and evidence of events that never occurred [2]. These capabilities not only enhance the reach and believability of disinformation but also contribute to a broader epistemic instability, where distinguishing between authentic and fabricated content becomes increasingly difficult. This is also reflected in increased concerns by experts worldwide as attested by the World Economic Forum 2025 Global Risks Report [3], where misinformation and disinformation are ranked as the top short-term risk.

Consequently, the reemergence of disinformation in the generative AI era demands a parallel evolution in detection, attribution, and response strategies—requiring interdisciplinary collaboration across AI research, journalism, media studies, and public policy. In this context, this book aims at offering a glance into state-of-the-art AI-powered methods and tools for detection and response to Generative AI-boosted disinformation. A lot of the research and results presented in this book have been carried out in the context of a Horizon Europe project called vera.ai and other relevant initiatives and projects, where partners of the vera.ai consortium are involved. Yet, the contents of this book largely reflect the broader research and technological trends in this area.

2 The vera.ai Horizon Europe Project

vera.ai[1]—Verification assisted by AI—is a Horizon Europe project that brings together 14 partners across Europe in a mission to build trustworthy AI solutions against advanced disinformation techniques, co-created with and for media professionals and set the foundation for future research in the area of AI against disinformation. Key novel characteristics of the developed AI models are fairness, transparency (including explainability), robustness to new data, and continuous adaptation to new disinformation techniques.

Since its start in September 2022, vera.ai has been carrying out research on novel AI methods and tools that are multi-platform, multilingual, multi- and cross-modal (text, image, video, audio), and can adapt to new data. The project has pursued

[1] https://www.veraai.eu/.

an ambitious fact-checker-in-the-loop paradigm that is tailored specifically for the highly evolving nature of disinformation content and tactics, which otherwise quickly render AI methods and models obsolete. The project has also explored learning approaches beyond the conventional "learn-to-detect-the-fake" paradigm (which it has also advanced) by looking into stable and consistent (across time and modalities) features that lead to reliable assessments of content as authentic. Another key achievement of the project has been the embedding of AI in established network science approaches, both at the level of creating richer and more accurate network models—e.g., as a result of multimodal similarity that can establish links among pieces of evidence that were previously unconnected—and at the level of characterising the role and behaviour of actors and communities in social networks by leveraging the latest AI advances. Crucially, vera.ai made advances towards Trustworthy AI, including multimodal explainability (e.g., explaining the results of synthetic media detection through a chatbot interface), fairness (e.g., by controlling and mitigating discrimination against specific groups in model outputs), reliability (e.g., through selective prediction) and green aspects (by reducing AI model size and energy consumption through knowledge distillation).

vera.ai aims at supporting media verification professionals throughout the complete content verification workflow through the following key steps, which are depicted in Fig. 1 and form a continuous research-and-development loop:

- **Verify multimodal content**: through bias-free and explainable AI methods for verification of images, videos, and audio content; explainable multilingual credibility assessment and retrieval of relevant evidence from authoritative sources; multimodal deepfake and manipulation analysis; cross-modal detection of decontextualised content.
- **Analyse disinformation agents**: through a network-science approach and tools for analysing communities and spreaders using graph neural networks; deep learning methods for extracting source credibility signals following the W3C guidelines; visualisations of spreader networks and accounts through tools such as Truly Media[2] and the verification plugin [5].
- **Uncover disinformation campaigns**: through deep learning methods for near-duplicate detection of images and videos and clustering of topically and semantically similar messages; knowledge graph models and spatio-temporal analysis of disinformation campaigns; network science methods for discovery of coordinated sharing behaviour.
- **Assess and reduce impact**: via developing a first-of-a-kind AI-based debunk writing assistant; conducting research audits of the effectiveness of social platforms and their algorithms on reducing the impact and spread of mis- and disinformation; conducting research into the effectiveness of debunking and fact-checking.
- **Assist professionals**: via developing and integrating a novel AI-based verification and debunk authoring assistant that incorporates a chatbot advising professionals

[2] https://www.truly.media/.

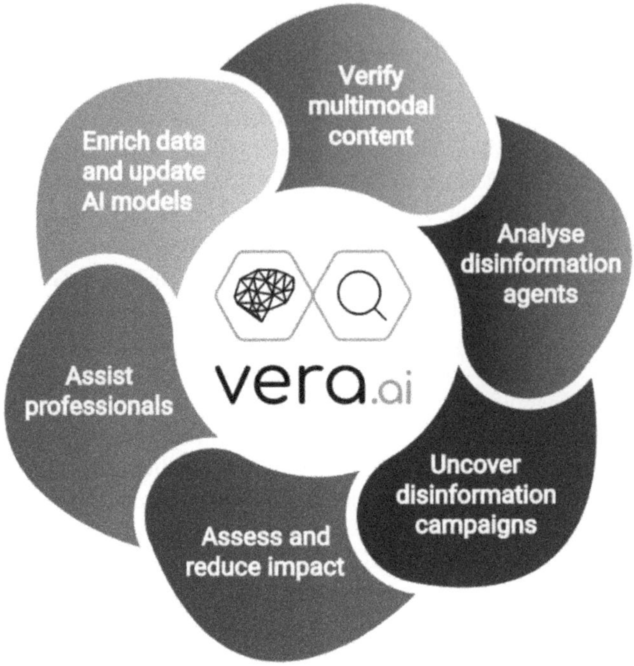

Fig. 1 The overall research and development approach of vera.ai

on how best to use the new AI tools and interpret their outputs and offers assistance with debunk authoring through automated evidence gathering and snippet authoring; also by encouraging users to flag mistakes in the AI outputs, which are then used for retraining.

- **Enrich data and update AI models**: via indexing and curation of newly debunked content in a database of known fakes and an expert-in-the-loop approach, for retraining on newly gathered data; leveraging expert-sourced lists of suspicious content gathered through anonymous submissions to the InVID-WeVerify plugin [5], and user feedback on AI errors gathered by the vera.ai verification and debunk authoring assistant.

3 Summary of Book Contents

The book contains 12 chapters (in addition to the current introductory chapter) that address a number of emerging research problems and areas under the theme of countering disinformation in the era of Generative AI. Chapters aim at both providing an overview of the latest advances in each target area and highlighting several concrete research outcomes achieved by the authoring team of each chapter. While a large part of the book content is accessible to a wide multi-disciplinary audience, there are several parts, particularly from Chapter "AI-Based Image Forgery Detection and Localisation" onward that assume a certain level of technical expertise with deep learning and AI.

More specifically, the first three Chapters "False Alarm or Real Threat? Trends in GenAI-Mediated Disinformation"–"Synthetic Seduction: Evolving Visual Persuasion in Coordinated Online Gambling Promotion with Generative AI" address an interdisciplinary academic and professional audience, including researchers in AI, cybersecurity, and media studies, as well as policy makers, fact-checkers, journalists, and digital platform regulators.

Chapter "False Alarm or Real Threat? Trends in GenAI-Mediated Disinformation" provides an in-depth analysis of the growing threat posed by generative AI (GenAI) in the context of disinformation. It outlines how recent advances in AI models—particularly large language models, diffusion models, and GANs—have dramatically increased the realism, scalability, and personalisation of synthetic content across text, audio, video, and image modalities. The chapter presents a taxonomy of GenAI technologies based on output modality, manipulation level, and semantic alteration, and documents real-world misuse cases including deepfakes in political propaganda, impersonation scams, and AI-generated news articles. Empirical studies and curated datasets are used to assess both the generative potential of LLMs for disinformation and the prevalence of such texts in the wild. The chapter further explores detection techniques and countermeasures, ranging from AI-based classifiers to media literacy and provenance-tracking initiatives.

Chapter "From Fact Checking to Content Moderation: Inside a Newsroom Faced with AI" reports on the personal narratives of fact checkers at a major bureau working in the early days of LLMs, highlighting particular AI-related themes: interacting with automated flagging systems, anticipating the AI-misinformation onslaught, training AI systems and utilising detection software. Fact checking bureaus, contracted by social media firms, had experienced the coming of AI in the systems they use for identifying potential posts to be fact checked. Social media company dashboards would automatically flag potentially offensive material, offering them up to fact checkers for consideration. The fact checkers also would be asked to rate the flagged posts or otherwise aid in the training of these AI-driven systems. Prepared for an onslaught of AI-generated misinformation, they also have been surprised by the proportion of the stories chosen to be fact checked that has been generated by AI. The fact checkers have been well equipped with AI detection tools and use them in particular manners, some of which were unanticipated by the makers, such as for further 'hard confirmation' rather than for discovery. In all, the piece situates AI in the fact-checking newsroom, describing its reception, encounters and deployment.

Chapter "Synthetic Seduction: Evolving Visual Persuasion in Coordinated Online Gambling Promotion with Generative AI" explores how generative AI is transforming the landscape of political influence operations, particularly in the context of disinformation and psychological manipulation. It examines the shift from traditional, labor-intensive disinformation campaigns to highly scalable and personalised AI-driven efforts. The chapter analyses how tools such as large language models and generative adversarial networks (GANs) enable the creation of persuasive, context-aware, and emotionally resonant content across multiple modalities, including text, images, and video. Drawing on case studies, emerging empirical evidence, and intelligence reports, the chapter highlights the ease with which malign actors can now automate and tailor political messaging to target audiences. It also raises concerns about attribution, accountability, and the erosion of trust in digital information ecosystems. The overarching argument is that generative AI is not just a technological enabler but a force multiplier for influence operations in the geopolitical and sociopolitical arenas.

The next four Chapters "AI-Based Image Forgery Detection and Localisation"–"Video Deepfake Detection: Challenges and Recent Trends" focus on AI-based detection approaches for the problems of image manipulation detection and localisation, synthetic image detection, synthetic audio detection and deepfake video detection. These chapters are more technical in nature and mainly address researchers, practitioners and students in the areas of signal and image processing, multimedia forensics, computer vision, multimedia and machine learning.

Chapter "AI-Based Image Forgery Detection and Localisation" provides a thorough examination of techniques used to identify and pinpoint manipulated regions within digital images. It begins by classifying common types of image forgeries, such as copy-move, image splicing, and inpainting, explaining how each manipulation alters image characteristics. The core of the chapter focuses on AI-driven detection and localisation methods, detailing traditional approaches that rely on forensic features and machine learning classifiers, as well as advanced deep learning models that directly learn manipulation traces, focusing on relevant vera.ai methods. It also discusses the critical challenges faced by these techniques, including the increasing sophistication of forgery tools and the impact of various post-processing operations, while outlining future research directions to enhance the robustness and accuracy of image forgery detection systems.

Chapter "AI-Generated Image Detection: Challenges and Recent Advances" investigates the evolving field of Synthetic Image Detection (SID). As generative models such as GANs and diffusion models increasingly produce hyper-realistic synthetic images, the need for robust detection methods becomes critical for safeguarding digital ecosystems. The chapter surveys state-of-the-art SID techniques, with a focus on recent vera.ai results, including supervised learning approaches, anomaly detection, and forensic analysis of compression artifacts, while evaluating their effectiveness in adversarial scenarios. It highlights key challenges, such as generalisation across model types, detection robustness against adversarial perturbations, and dataset limitations. The authors also discuss the "arms race" nature between synthetic image generation and detection—where improvements in generation models often outpace detection capabilities.

Chapter "Synthetic Audio Detection" provides a comprehensive overview of synthetic audio detection, delving into its definition, the landscape of synthetic audio generation, and various detection methodologies. It focuses on deep learning-based methods, and provides details on the employed network architectures and components, while it has an emphasis on a set of explainable synthetic audio detection methods developed in vera.ai. The chapter also addresses key challenges in the field, such as the adaptability of detectors to new synthesis techniques and the impact of audio manipulations, while outlining future research directions.

Chapter "Video Deepfake Detection: Challenges and Recent Trends" offers a comprehensive exploration of video deepfake detection methods. It begins by classifying different types of video manipulations, including face re-enactment, face swapping, and other forms of synthesised or altered video content and proceeds into a range of detection techniques, covering both traditional approaches that analyse inconsistencies in video signals and advanced deep learning-based methods. It discusses how these techniques identify not only facial and spatial artifacts but also temporal and motion inconsistencies, or other subtle clues across video frames that reveal manipulation. The chapter concludes by addressing the significant challenges faced by current detection systems, such as robustness against various video compressions and the rapid evolution of deepfake generation techniques, while outlining future research directions for more comprehensive and resilient video deepfake detection.

The next four Chapters "AI-Based Multilingual Credibility Assessment"–"Video Decomposition and Key Visual Elements Extraction and Enhancement" focus on AI approaches that move beyond the detection of manipulation or synthetic media and address contextual analysis tasks, such as credibility assessment, cross-modal verification and media enhancement for supporting verification. These mainly address researchers, practitioners and students in the areas of natural language processing, computer vision and multimodal machine learning.

Chapter "AI-based Multilingual Credibility Assessment" discusses the use of AI-based methods in the context of multilingual credibility assessment, focusing on detecting credibility signals such as framing, genre, and persuasion techniques. It highlights the importance of credibility assessment as a complement to false information detection, emphasising its multidimensional nature and challenges like multilinguality, dataset availability, and explainability. The authors present methods for automatic detection of credibility signals using multilingual language models and describe practical applications, including integration into the Verification plugin for media professionals and aggregation of credibility signals for misinformation detection. They also explore challenges such as research fragmentation, ethical issues, and the impact of generative AI on credibility assessment.

Chapter "Multimodal Detection of Image Misrepresentation" explores advancements in multimodal misinformation detection (MMD), focusing on detecting decontextualised and miscaptioned images where text misrepresents the image's origin, context, or meaning. It reviews datasets, methodologies, and challenges, emphasising the role of synthetic and evidence-enhanced datasets, modality fusion techniques, and large vision-language models. The chapter presents key contributions from the vera.ai project, including improving model generalisation, addressing unimodal bias, developing the VERITE benchmark for robust evaluation, introducing relevant evidence detection (RED-DOT), and proposing evidence verification methods to filter unreliable or leaked information. Despite progress, challenges remain in terms of dataset diversity, reliance on synthetic data, and the need for multilingual and multimodal approaches.

Chapter "Audio-Based Tools for Decontextualisation Detection" explores the challenge of detecting audio decontextualisation, where authentic audio recordings are reused misleadingly outside their original context, often in disinformation campaigns. It introduces audio provenance analysis as a method to trace the origin, reuse, and transformation of audio content, using techniques like clustering and graph-based reconstruction to identify manipulation and misinformation. Complementary methods for contextual analysis, such as location inference through acoustic evidence, are also discussed. Real-world applications demonstrate the framework's ability to detect decontextualisation, manipulation, and coordinated sharing behaviour on social media.

Chapter "Video Decomposition and Key Visual Elements Extraction and Enhancement" presents an overview of methods for analysing and processing video content by decomposing it into meaningful visual components and enhancing key elements with the goal of facilitating or speeding up verification tasks. The authors explore a multi-stage approach, integrated in a Keyframe Selection and Enhancement (KSE) service, which includes shot detection, frame sampling, and the identification of visually salient objects or scenes using AI techniques such as object detection, semantic segmentation, and face recognition, as well as techniques for visual enhancement—such as resolution upscaling, colour correction, and focus adjustment—that improve the clarity and interpretability of selected key frames.

The last book Chapter "Chatbot-Assisted Explainability of AI-Powered Models and Collection of User Feedback" focuses on user experience aspects of AI-powered media verification tools. To this end, it explores the use of conversational agents (chatbots) to enhance the explainability of AI models and to facilitate the structured collection of user feedback. It addresses core components of such systems, including user intent recognition, dialogue state tracking, and retrieval-augmented generation (RAG) for supporting system transparency and explainability. Additionally, it considers strategies for systematically collecting user feedback as a means of enabling iterative system refinement. The chapter illustrates how the proposed framework is applied on a specific verification tool, namely the synthetic image detection service developed in the vera.ai project.

References

1. Benkler, Y., Faris, R., Roberts, H.: Network propaganda: Manipulation, disinformation, and radicalization in American politics. Oxford University Press (2018)
2. Bontcheva, K., Papadopoulos, S., Tsalakanidou, F., Gallotti, R., Dutkiewicz, L., Krack, N., Teyssou, D., Severio Nucci, F., Spangenberg, J., Srba, I., et al.: Generative ai and disinformation: recent advances, challenges, and opportunities (2024)
3. Elsner, M., Atkinson, G., Zahidi, S.: The global risks report 2025. World Economic Forum Cologny, Switzerland (2025)
4. Howard, P.N., Ganesh, B., Liotsiou, D., Kelly, J., François, C.: The IRA, social media and political polarization in the United States, 2012–2018 (2018)

5. Teyssou, D., Leung, J.M., Apostolidis, E., Apostolidis, K., Papadopoulos, S., Zampoglou, M., Papadopoulou, O., Mezaris, V.: The invid plug-in: web video verification on the browser. In: Proceedings of the first international workshop on multimedia verification, pp. 23–30 (2017)

Landscape, Trends and Studies

False Alarm or Real Threat? Trends in GenAI-Mediated Disinformation

Olga Papadopoulou, Denis Teyssou, Dominik Macko, and Symeon Papadopoulos

1 The Rise of GenAI in Information Ecosystems

GenAI has significantly reshaped the information landscape, enabling the creation of hyper-realistic text, images, audio, and video. Although these advances in creative capabilities offer opportunities for content generation, creativity, and automation, they also pose serious challenges with respect to misinformation, deepfakes, and manipulation of public opinion. These dual potentials of GenAI are already evident in real-world cases.

On the positive side, newsrooms and journalists are experimenting with GenAI tools to improve productivity and streamline reporting workflows. For example, a recent study [1] found that journalists have begun using GenAI tools as aids to enhance productivity, check facts, and generate templates for routine reporting while maintaining editorial control and oversight. This illustrates that, when responsibly integrated, GenAI can augment rather than undermine journalistic practice. Similarly, major news organisations such as The Associated Press [2], Bloomberg [3, 4] and Reuters [5] have integrated AI systems into their workflows to automate the production of standardised content, including corporate earnings reports, sports recaps,

O. Papadopoulou (✉) · S. Papadopoulos
Centre for Research and Technology Hellas (CERTH), Thessaloniki, Greece
e-mail: olgapapa@iti.gr

S. Papadopoulos
e-mail: papadop@iti.gr

D. Teyssou
Agence France-Presse (AFP) and Paris Nanterre University, Paris, France
e-mail: denis.teyssou@afp.com; dteyssou@parisnanterre.fr

D. Macko
Kempelen Institute of Intelligent Technologies (KInIT), Bratislava, Slovakia
e-mail: dominik.macko@kinit.sk

S. Papadopoulos et al. (eds.), *Countering Disinformation in the Era of Generative AI*,
https://doi.org/10.1007/978-3-032-11782-3_2

and weather bulletins, thereby freeing journalists to focus on more complex and investigative tasks.

At the same time, there is growing evidence of deepfake propaganda videos, e.g., the 2022 Zelenskyy surrender video [6], the use of AI-generated personas to spread false narrative [7] and voice-cloning deepfakes in CEO fraud and social engineering scams, tricking victims into wiring large sums of money [8]. These examples illustrate the disruptive and at times dangerous power of GenAI within the information ecosystem.

To better understand the landscape of GenAI use in media, this chapter provides a structured analysis of GenAI's role in information ecosystems.

- We introduce a GenAI models taxonomy by output modality, underlying architecture, degree of manipulation and semantic alterations.
- We explore the concept of AI-mediated disinformation, examining how GenAI helps the generation of scalable, persuasive and difficult-to-detect false content including text, image, audio, and video.
- We analyse how deepfakes operate within the news ecosystems and examine the use of deepfakes in journalistic and political communications presenting outcomes on a dataset of debunked deepfakes.
- We provide a more comprehensive view by discussing the potential of GenAI to generate disinformation texts and assess the prevalence of AI-generated texts in real-world campaigns.
- We discuss detection and countermeasures both leveraging technological solutions and beyond.

GenAI Taxonomy

To analyse the role of GenAI in the information ecosystem, we first categorise GenAI models, highlighting key dimensions that define how these models function and how they may be applied or misused. This provides a foundation for understanding the specific risks and opportunities associated with different kinds of generative systems.

GenAI Output Modality

Text generation involves AI models that produce human-like text, including articles, dialogues, summaries, essays, and others. These models are trained on large corpora of text data and use probabilistic methods to generate coherent and contextually relevant responses. Established models for text generation in 2025 include GPT-4 (OpenAI) [9], LLaMA 4 (Meta) [10], T5 (Google) [11] and DeepSeek-R1 [12].

Image generation includes AI models that create high-quality images based on text descriptions or input images. These most often rely on diffusion models [13] and Generative Adversarial Networks (GANs) [14] to produce realistic or artistic

Table 1 GenAI modalities and seminal models

Modality	Seminal models
Text generation	GPT-4 (OpenAI) [9], LLaMA 4 (Meta) [10], T5 (Google) [11], DeepSeek-R1-0528 [12]
Image generation	DALL·E (OpenAI) [15], Stable Diffusion 3.5 (Stability AI) [16], Flux.1 Kontext (Black Forest Labs) [17], Imagen 4 (Google DeepMind) [18]
Video generation	Sora (OpenAI) [19], Make-A-Video (Meta) [20], Veo 3 (Google) [21], Kling AI 2.1 (Kuaishou) [22]
Audio and speech synthesis	ElevenLabs [23], Metis [24], Chatterbox [25], WaveNet (DeepMind) [26], Vall-E (Microsoft) [27]
Multimodal generation	GPT-4 with Vision (OpenAI), Gemini 1.5 (DeepMind) [28], Claude 3 (Anthropic)

visuals. Popular models for image generation in 2025 include DALL·E 3 (OpenAI) [15], Stable Diffusion 3.5 (Stability AI) [16], Flux.1 Kontext (Black Forest Labs) [17] and Imagen 4 (Google DeepMind) [18].

Video generation includes AI models that create dynamic visual content, such as deepfakes and fully AI-generated videos. These can manipulate real footage or create synthetic videos from scratch. Seminal video generation models at the time of writing this chapter include Sora (OpenAI) [19], Make-A-Video by Meta [20], Veo 3 (Google) [21] and Kling AI 2.1 (Kuaishou) [22].

Audio and Speech Synthesis AI models generate realistic voices, sound effects, and music compositions. Popular audio and speech generation models in 2025 include ElevenLabs [23], Metis [24], Chatterbox [25], WaveNet (DeepMind) [26], and Vall-E (Microsoft) [27].

Multimodal generation involves multimodal AI models that integrate and generate multiple types of media, such as combining text, images, and video into a single coherent output. Seminal models that generate multimodal content in 2025 include GPT-4 with Vision (OpenAI), Gemini 1.5 by DeepMind [28], and Claude 3 (Anthropic).

Table 1 summarises the taxonomy of GenAI modalities offering examples of seminal models.

GenAI Model Architecture

Generative Adversarial Networks (GANs) [14] consist of two competing neural networks, a generator and a discriminator, that work in opposition to improve content generation. Specifically, the generator creates synthetic media (e.g. images, videos) and the discriminator evaluates if the generated data is real or fake. The competition improves the generator's ability to create highly realistic outputs. Landmark GAN-based models include ProGAN [29], StyleGAN [30], BigGAN [31], CycleGAN [32] and StarGAN [33].

Fig. 1 Evolution of image quality in GANs. Samples include outputs generated by respective models as well as representative examples sourced from publicly available benchmark datasets

In 2014, the first image generated by a GAN-based model was a low-resolution and greyscale image. Despite its low quality, this marked a groundbreaking advancement in AI-driven content generation. This innovation paved the way for rapid progress in image synthesis. By 2021, GAN-based models such as StyleGAN2 and BigGAN were capable of producing high-resolution, photorealistic images of human faces, animals, and even entirely fictional scenes. The leap in quality was driven by architectural improvements like progressive growing, adaptive instance normalisation, and self-supervised learning, allowing GANs to capture intricate textures, lighting, and fine details with unprecedented realism. This evolution gave rise to the rapid growth of AI-generated imagery, rendering GANs a powerful tool for enhancing creativity, as well as for creating deepfakes that can be used for malicious purposes. Figure 1 illustrates the remarkable evolution of image quality in GANs from 2014 to 2021, highlighting the rapid advancements that have enabled the creation of highly realistic synthetic images.

Building on the foundations laid by GANs, *diffusion models* represent the next generation of generative techniques. The evolution of image synthesis in diffusion-based models has been rapid and transformative. Initially introduced through Denoising Diffusion Probabilistic Models (DDPM) in 2020 [13], early diffusion-based outputs showed promise but were constrained by limitations in resolution, coherence and texture fidelity. Subsequent advancements in model architecture yielded remarkable capable systems such as DALL·E 3 [34]. These models achieve unprecedented level of photorealism, generating images that are often indistinguishable from real photographs. Similar to GANs, Fig. 2 presents the evolution of image quality in diffusion models. Notably, within just three years of the first release of diffusion models, DDPM (2020), the DALL·E 3 model (2023) reached an unprecedented level of realism. This rapid refinement of diffusion-based generation techniques demonstrates the increasing sophistication of AI-driven image synthesis and its growing impact on media and content creation.

Transformer-based models have revolutionised Natural Language Processing (NLP) and multimodal AI, leveraging self-attention mechanisms to efficiently process input data in parallel. Unlike traditional Recurrent Neural Networks (RNNs) [35] and Long Short-Term Memory (LSTM) [36] models, which process sequences

Fig. 2 Evolution of image quality in diffusion models. Samples include outputs generated by respective models as well as representative examples sourced from publicly available benchmark datasets

sequentially, Transformers use multi-head self-attention to capture long-range dependencies and contextual relationships more effectively [37]. These models primarily follow two architectures, the encoder-decoder models, such as T5 [11], which convert input sequences into latent representations before decoding them into output text, excelling in text-to-text transfer tasks like summarisation and translation and the decoder-only models, like GPT-4 [9] (OpenAI, 2023), which auto-regressively generate content by predicting the next token based on prior context, making them ideal for chatbots, language modelling, and conversational AI. Key Transformer-based models are GPT-4 [38] which is a powerful decoder-only model used for text generation, code synthesis, and multimodal AI and LLaMA 3 [39], which is an open-weight Transformer model optimised for multilingual text generation.

In addition to these advances, a new wave of generative approaches is emerging that moves beyond 2D image and text synthesis, targeting the creation of highly realistic 3D scenes and dynamic viewpoints. These approaches are based on *Neural Radiance Fields (NeRFs)* [40] and *Gaussian Splatting* [41] and are gaining traction in the field of 3D scene representation and view synthesis. While these techniques are not yet widely used in the context of misinformation, their potential for ultra-realistic avatar creation, scene reconstruction, and free-viewpoint video synthesis suggests, they could become relevant in the future.

Extent and Level of Manipulation in GenAI

GenAI enables content manipulation in varying degrees, ranging from minor edits that enhance visual quality to the creation of entirely synthetic media that blur the boundaries between reality and fabrication. At the lowest level of manipulation, AI is used for enhancement and style transfer, where models, such as Stable Diffusion can be used to upscale images, remove noise, or apply artistic styles without significantly altering the underlying content. While largely benign, these modifications can still be misleading when applied to historical or journalistic visuals.

A more advanced level of manipulation involves partial modifications, such as inpainting, where specific elements of the content, such as faces, voices, or text, are selectively altered, while preserving the overall composition. Deepfake technology, voice cloning models, and AI-powered editing tools enable users to swap faces in videos, modify speech, or rewrite segments of an article, raising concerns about the subtle alteration of media to mislead audiences.

Beyond partial manipulation, AI has now reached the stage of fully synthetic generation, where entire pieces of multimedia content are generated from a text prompt by models such as Sora [42] and Veo 3 [43] for video or WaveNet [26] for natural-sounding speech synthesis. These technologies enable realistic AI-generated personas, speeches, and news anchors, with applications in entertainment, accessibility, and advertising, but also with a big potential for powering disinformation, as AI-generated content can be convincingly deployed to fabricate events, impersonate public figures, or create propaganda at scale. At the highest level of manipulation, AI has the potential to construct fully synthetic ecosystems, where multimodal generative models, such as GPT-4 and Claude, could simulate entire virtual worlds, social media influencers, or interactive personas that engage with real users in a way that is indistinguishable from human interaction [44–47]. While this scenario is not yet widespread in practice, recent advances suggest it is an imminent possibility. This extreme level of manipulation has profound implications for trust in digital content, as it enables AI-driven misinformation campaigns, fake social movements, and artificially generated narratives that could influence public perception.

Extent of Semantic Modification

Semantic modification refers to changes that alter the meaning of content while preserving its stylistic or perceptual coherence. This form of manipulation is particularly insidious, as it often evades detection through human inspection. As regards text-based semantic modifications, large language models or multimodal AI systems are used to subtly reframe narratives. This can be achieved by either rewriting factual content to introduce a certain viewpoint or alter context, or by reordering or re-emphasising existing elements in the text without changing the wording itself. In the first case, semantic shifts occur through lexical substitutions, particularly the text is rewritten using different words while preserving grammatical and stylistic coherence. In that way, the original facts are altered leading to a change in interpretation. In the second case, the content is not rewritten at all but only the arrangement, context or emphasis are changed. This results in changing how a narrative is perceived.

In the case of image, video and audio, semantic modifications through techniques such as identity swapping by altering faces in images and videos or generating speech in someone else's voice using AI voice synthesis to impersonate another individual. Attribute editing often involves changing the emotional expressions of a person such as making someone appear happy, aggressive, surprised, etc., or demographic traits e.g., making a person younger or older. Another semantic modification is facial reenactment, which applies to videos and creates the impression that a person said or performed something they never did. These audiovisual modifications retain a high degree of realism, yet distort the semantic integrity of the original material.

Figure 3 summarises the taxonomy of output modality, underlying architecture, the extent of manipulation, and the semantic modifications of GenAI.

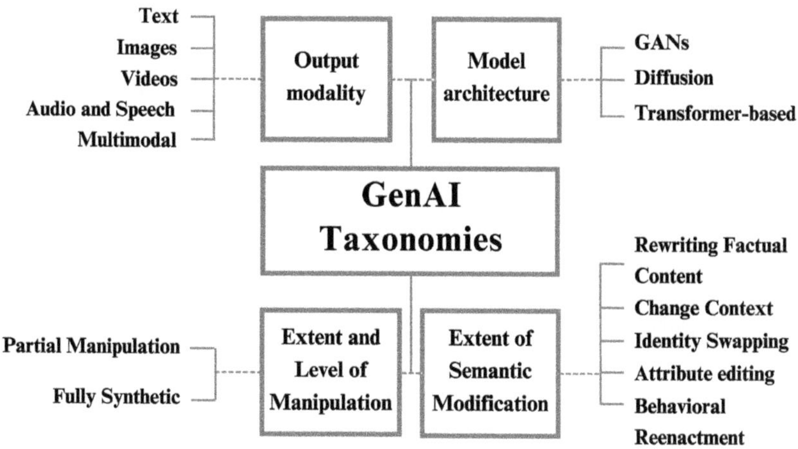

Fig. 3 GenAI taxonomy of output modality, underlying architecture, the extent of manipulation, and the semantic modifications

AI-Mediated Disinformation

Having categorised the main types of GenAI models, we now turn to their role in enabling and amplifying disinformation. AI-mediated disinformation refers to false or misleading content generated, amplified, or manipulated using AI, often to deceive, influence opinions, or manipulate behaviour. AI has fundamentally reshaped the landscape of disinformation, making the production, distribution, and amplification of false or misleading content more efficient, scalable, and difficult to detect. Unlike traditional disinformation, which required significant human effort to craft deceptive narratives, AI can help automate and enhance the process, increasing both the volume and sophistication of misleading content.

Before AI, creating disinformation required manual effort, such as crafting fake articles, doctoring images, or impersonating individuals in videos. Now, GenAI can help produce massive amounts of fake content in seconds, eliminating the need for large teams of human actors. AI-powered tools enable automated text, image, video, and voice synthesis, making large-scale disinformation campaigns cost-effective and efficient. Malicious actors can now create thousands of fake news articles, social media posts, or synthetic videos with minimal resources.

AI-driven botnets and social media manipulation have also been transformed. Automated accounts powered by AI can generate realistic interactions, comment on posts, and engage in conversations with real users. This creates the illusion of organic discourse, making disinformation more convincing and harder to distinguish from authentic content. AI-enhanced bots can operate at an unprecedented scale, influencing online debates, spreading false narratives, and boosting engagement with misleading material.

Fig. 4 AI-generated image produced using a text-to-image tool (e.g., Adobe Firefly) with the prompt "Thessaloniki's White Tower on fire." The reference image is a personal photograph of the White Tower, taken by the author

Figure 4 illustrates an example of AI-based, text-driven image manipulation using Adobe Firefly. A real reference image of the White Tower in Thessaloniki is used, and the prompt "Thessaloniki's White Tower on fire" is used to generate a realistic version of the image showing the White Tower engulfed in flames. Despite the absence of any such real-world incident, the manipulated image could convince several people and therefore successfully used in a disinformation narrative, e.g., falsely suggesting a terrorist attack or civil unrest in Thessaloniki.

A study of GenAI misuse tactics is presented in a recent study [48], where the authors conducted an analysis of 200 incidents of misuse and provided strong evidence of GenAI's potential for real-world harm. Interestingly, most reported cases of GenAI misuse involve the manipulation of human likeness, i.e. impersonation, sock-puppeting and others. Scaling and amplification and falsification follow, being also prominent tactics. An additional analysis provided by that study is the association of modalities for each detected tactic resulting in the following observations: (i) Impersonation generally utilises text-to-speech and video generation technologies to mimic the voices and appearances of individuals, particularly public figures, (ii) Content falsification mainly relies on text and image generation to produce synthetic materials such as books, news articles, and website content, along with fictitious images to accompany these articles, (iii) Non-consensual intimate image (NCII) cases often focus on altering images and videos to fabricate suggestive deepfakes of private individuals or celebrities, (iv) strategies like sock-puppeting involve creating fake social media accounts using AI-generated profile images and bios to enhance content distribution and visibility.

Given that all content modalities (text, image, audio, and video) are extensively used in real-world cases of disinformation, we focus our analysis on the role of deepfakes. To this end, we first frame deepfakes in public discourse, highlighting their socio-political implications in the context of news and public debate. Building on this framing, we then examine how deepfakes manifest within the public information ecosystem, specifically concerning current affairs and news media.

Framing Deepfakes in Public Discourse

The term "deepfake" derives from the conjunction of "deep learning", referring to neural network-based AI techniques, and "fake", denoting the fabricated nature of the content. Deepfakes are primarily understood as AI-generated videos that modify or fabricate visual and auditory elements to simulate real events or individuals [49]. While above we outlined the technical evolution and manipulation capabilities of GenAI, here we emphasise the socio-political implications of deepfakes in the context of news and public discourse.

The phenomenon gained public notoriety in 2017, when face-swapping tools were used to produce non-consensual and often pornographic content [50, 51]. The same technique subsequently was used in more playful contexts to interchange the faces of famous actors, particularly in movie trailers shared on video-sharing platforms using tools such as FakeApp,[1] faceswap,[2] Reface[3] and DeepFaceLive.[4] Special effects specialists, such as Chris Ume, also employed it to automate manipulations, as seen on the TikTok channel @deeptomcruise[5] and the website Metaphysic.[6] Since then, deepfakes have extended into political satire, strategic misinformation and electoral interference.

Early examples include the 2018 awareness campaign video impersonating Barack Obama [52] and a Belgian political stunt featuring a fabricated Donald Trump [53]. In the first instance, Oscar-winning filmmaker Jordan Peele employed deepfake technology to create a synthetic video of Barack Obama, intended as a parodic warning against the growing threat of audiovisual manipulation. The video received nearly 10 million views on YouTube,[7] drawing widespread attention to the disruptive potential of deepfakes. In the second case, a communication agency acting on behalf of the Flemish Socialist Party (sp.a; Belgium) released a video of a fake Donald Trump urging Belgians to withdraw from the Paris Agreement on climate change. Unlike the former, this video functioned as a political communication tool designed to provoke public engagement and stimulate discourse around climate issues.

---

[1] https://www.faceapp.com/.

[2] https://github.com/deepfakes/faceswap.

[3] https://reface.ai/.

[4] https://github.com/iperov/DeepFaceLive.

[5] https://www.tiktok.com/@deeptomcruise.

[6] metaphysic.ai.

[7] https://www.youtube.com/watch?v=cQ54GDm1eL0.

2 Deepfakes in the Information News Ecosystem

Deepfakes [50] have emerged as a focal point in public discourse, often framed as harbingers of a dystopian future[8] or catalysts of an "infocalypse" [54]. Recent media narratives highlight their potential to undermine democratic processes, particularly elections, with claims that such AI-enhanced fabrications are virtually unstoppable.[9] In this section, we examine how deepfakes manifest within the public information ecosystem, specifically concerning current affairs and news media. To support our analysis, we first present the methodology used to collect and evaluate the relevant data. We then discuss manipulation techniques and verification challenges inherent in detecting deepfakes. Building on this, we analyse the advent of GenAI through insights derived from the background dataset of debunked deepfakes, presenting findings across several dimensions: the distribution of deepfakes by country, the platforms where they have appeared, their primary intentions, and the manipulation techniques employed.

Methodology

Our methodology combines a semiotic analysis of deepfake content from a curated corpus of fact-checking articles. This dataset was compiled using keyword-based search, particularly the terms "deepfake" and "deep fake", via the Google Fact Check Explorer search engine, which indexes articles annotated in the ClaimReview format. For validation, we cross-referenced the dataset with factcheckinsights.org, maintained by the Reporter's Lab at Duke University. This dataset contains over 240,000 verification articles published by 180 organisations in 71 countries. Our dataset includes 136 deepfake-related articles including 51 concerning India, 29 the United States, and 9 Ukraine, published in 15 languages.

The articles we selected to constitute our dataset span until 29 April 2024, with the oldest article dating back to 2021. Of these, 104 articles concern videos in which AI-based manipulation could be confirmed through available tools. Approximately 20 articles refer to videos incorrectly labelled as deepfakes or indeterminate cases where the original file could not be retrieved. These findings illustrate both the technical complexity of identifying GenAI content and the multidimensional phenomenon already observed with the expression "fake news" [56], namely that the label "deepfake" can also serve as a tool to discredit an adversary or news media.

To ensure data consistency, we removed duplicate entries and annotated the resulting 75 verified deepfakes with metadata. The metadata include language, English translation of the claim, targeted person and country, video platform and the source links (if exists or has been properly archived), file name and type of manipulation when detection tools where available to confirm.

---

[8] Buzzfeed, 2018: You Won't Believe What Obama Says In This Video! https://www.youtube.com/watch?v=cQ54GDm1eL0.

[9] "disrupt elections around the world (and) no one can stop them" [55].

We acknowledge a key limitation in the achieved coverage through this approach. In particular, not all verification organisations utilise the ClaimReview format, and terminological inconsistencies remain (i.e. some outlets avoid the term "deepfake", opting instead for broader descriptions such as "AI-generated" or "manipulated content".

Manipulation Techniques and Verification Challenges

To better understand the risks posed by deepfakes, this subsection briefly outlines the key manipulation techniques used to create them and detail the verification challenges that hinder their detection and debunking.

Patterns and Political Uses

While acknowledging their disruptive capabilities, it is often observed that most of these manipulated videos circulating in the semi-public spaces [57] of social networks are remixed fiction clips, satires, or parodies. However, the use of deepfakes for overtly manipulative purposes is growing, particularly in political contexts. This trend is evidenced in early 2024, during the U.S. presidential election, when a "robocall" impersonating U.S. President Joe Biden falsely instructed voters to skip the Democratic primary. Similar tactics have been documented in Ukraine, where synthetic media targeted national leaders during the war waged by Russia against Ukraine [58].

Detection of Deepfakes Through Visual Analysis

Fact-checkers often employ visual analysis to identify fake videos or images, focusing on inconsistencies in facial rendering or hand formation. Images generated by AI still frequently produce evanescent, often dehumanised faces, without visible features, asymmetrical eyes, or anomalies in the hands. A notable case involved a fabricated image of Donald Trump kneeling and praying in a church[10] where six fingers were visible.

While visual inspection remains an effective first step in detection, it is susceptible to error especially when compressed videos or videos of degraded quality are the only available evidence. In such cases anomalies are often caused by the level of image compression or other alterations that are not associated with AI. For instance, the video of the Princess of Wales, Kate Middleton, announcing her cancer diagnosis on March 22, 2024, was incorrectly labelled as a deepfake on social media due to the temporary disappearance of her ring, an anomaly not presented in the original high-resolution footage as found by the British fact-checking organization FullFact[11]. Similarly, a slowed-down video of the former Speaker of the United States House of

[10] BBC Verify: https://www.instagram.com/p/C2fvS6csrRf/.

[11] Fullfact: https://fullfact.org/news/kate-cancer-video-ring-vanishes-false/.

Representatives Nancy Pelosi in May 2019, was misidentified as a "deepfake", when in fact the video was the result of a simple temporal manipulation of the original [59].

Reverse Image Search and Voice-Based Deception

In addition to visual inspection, geolocation techniques play an increasingly critical role in verifying visual content. By cross-referencing landmarks, shadows, weather patterns, or other environmental clues, verification professionals can determine whether the scene depicted matches the claimed location and time. This method, often combined with satellite imagery and open-source intelligence (OSINT) tools, is particularly effective in debunking misleading visuals tied to specific events or places. Reverse image search remains a fundamental method for tracing manipulated content back to its original source. Many deepfakes have been exposed locating keyframes or visuals that were manipulated from earlier, unrelated videos [60]. However, both geolocation and reverse image search techniques become less effective against fully synthetic content generated entirely by AI, which lacks an original counterpart.

Beyond visual manipulation, voice-based manipulation has recently emerged as a predominant manipulation technique in the information field. Notable examples include the "robocall affair" of Joe Biden [61], in early February 2024, which falsely suggested that the then US president was urging his voters to skip the Democratic primary in the state of New Hampshire. Another example, the fabricated confession of the former Secretary of the Ukrainian Security and Defence Council, Oleksii Danilov, acknowledging Ukraine's alleged involvement in the attack on a concert hall in Moscow on March 22, 2024 [62]. These cases exemplify how convincing audio manipulations can be weaponised to alter public narratives. Detecting such audio fabrications presents unique challenges: unlike visual content, audio lacks spatial and contextual cues that can be analysed through geolocation or reverse image search, and human listeners are generally poor at distinguishing authentic from manipulated speech. As a result, traditional verification techniques are largely ineffective against synthetic audio, underscoring the need for specialised forensic tools capable of analysing subtle signal artifacts or statistical inconsistencies to flag potential manipulation.

Automated Detection Techniques

Beyond manual analysis, detection efforts are based increasingly on AI models specifically trained to identify artifacts in images, videos or audio tracks. While notable progress has been made, the challenge of generalisation remains significant, limiting the effectiveness of many current approaches in real-world scenarios. The detection methods employed, along with their respective limitations, including issues of generalisation and robustness, are discussed in detail in the respective Chapters of this book: synthetic image detection methods (see Chapter "AI-Generated Image Detection: Challenges and Recent Advances" of this book), synthetic audio detection methods (see Chapter "Synthetic Audio Detection" of this book), and deepfake video detection methods (see Chapter "Video Deepfake Detection: Challenges and Recent Trends" of this book).

Beyond non-detections, the risk of false positives, that is authentic content which is wrongly detected as synthetic, presents another challenge. Such errors can compromise the credibility of fact-checkers and skew public discourse. Consequently, detection systems must balance sensitivity with precision.

Numerous initiatives have emerged to address the challenge of deepfake detection. The Deepfake-O-Meter [12] at the University of Buffalo in the United States aggregates seven detection methods for images, six for video, and five for audio. Among the start-ups active in AI-generated content detection, some pioneers include Sensity.ai and Deepware.ai, as well as newcomers: Reality Defender, and Get Real Labs in the United States, Itisaar.ai in India, and Loccus.ai in Spain (recently acquired by the American company Hiya.com).

The Advent of GenAI

The web and social media are already characterised by a dilution of authorship and information sources. GenAI now challenges traditional verification methods, particularly those based on the search for antecedents or an "original copy" to compare with content suspected of being manipulated. This oxymoron of the "original copy" [63] aims to address the multiplicity of copies of digital documents circulating on the Web. It refers to "the dissolution of the distinction between original and copy in the digital age" and "the fact that a copy often constitutes the original", due to the lack of a better alternative. The previously effective method of reverse image search risks becoming impractical in the long term, due to the inability to trace the prior existence of synthetic content generated by AI. This is arguably the primary epistemic risk posed by GenAI, as verification will only become more difficult and time consuming. In response to this risk, initiatives like the Coalition for Content Provenance and Authenticity (C2PA) [64] has emerged to develop open technical standards for tracing the origin and modification history of digital content. By embedding metadata that documents the provenance of a media item, C2PA aims to restore a measure of transparency and accountability to digital media ecosystems [65, 66].

The difficulty in verifying synthetic images stems precisely from this absence of traceable origin. In his numerous writings on falsehood, Umberto Eco repeatedly emphasised the comparative method between "an original 'true' copy with which the fake should be confronted" [67]. In the absence of an original or prior copy, in the presence of a "falsification ex nihilo", how can these digital files be verified?

Verification professionals are advised to triangulate findings using multiple detectors trained on diverse datasets to strengthen their verdict. Nonetheless, generalisation remains a significant challenge, particularly for novel and multimodal synthetic content.

---

[12] https://zinc.cse.buffalo.edu/ubmdfl/deep-o-meter/landing_page retrieved on April 4, 2025.

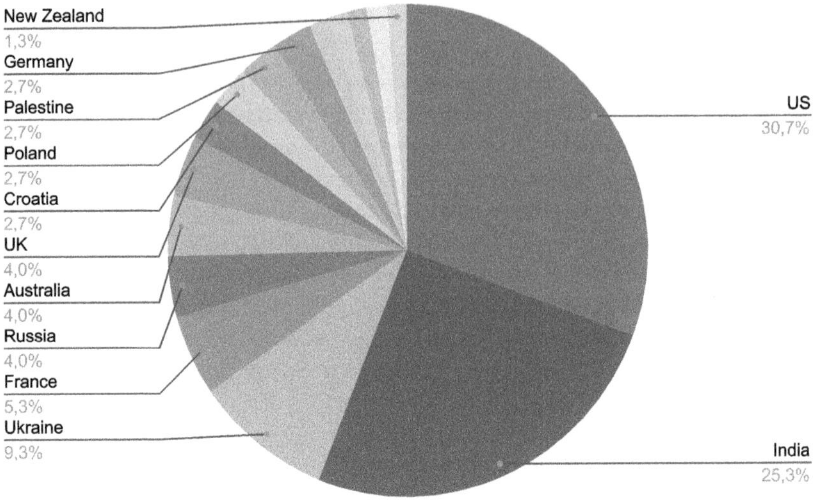

Fig. 5 Distribution of deepfakes fact checked by country

The analysis of our multilingual dataset of deepfakes debunked by fact-checking organisations, presented above, demonstrates that deepfakes are mostly disseminated in the United States and India. These two countries account for 55% of the cases identified in our dataset. Ukraine, France, Russia, Australia, and Great Britain follow at a considerable distance (Fig. 5).

Figure 6 reveals that deepfakes are most frequently disseminated via Facebook and X (formerly Twitter), followed by TikTok, YouTube, Telegram and Instagram. English remains the dominant language (64.5%).

The individuals most targeted by these deepfakes are, in descending order, business magnate Elon Musk (with 9 cases), Ukrainian President Volodymyr Zelenskyy (6), and former US President Joe Biden (5). They are followed by French President Emmanuel Macron (4), Russian President Vladimir Putin (3), and former and current US President Donald Trump (3). The presence of annotations in ClaimReview format within the corpus allowed us to extract the original assertion formulated during the dissemination of each deepfake. This assertion (or claim) constitutes the basis for the verification work undertaken by the fact-checking journalists. These annotations are generally supplemented with links to where the disinformation was disseminated or to archive sites. These links are also present in the verification articles and offer the possibility of retrieving and examining the videos. The cross-analysis between the debunked assertions, the content of the video as it appeared online, and the verification articles allows us to develop robust hypotheses about the underlying intentions behind the creation of these deepfakes and to propose a relevant categorisation. In this initial analysis, we chose to label each deepfake with a primary intention. For example, the deepfakes involving Volodymyr Zelenskyy were systematically categorised as war propaganda due to Russian's invasion of Ukraine. In different contexts, some

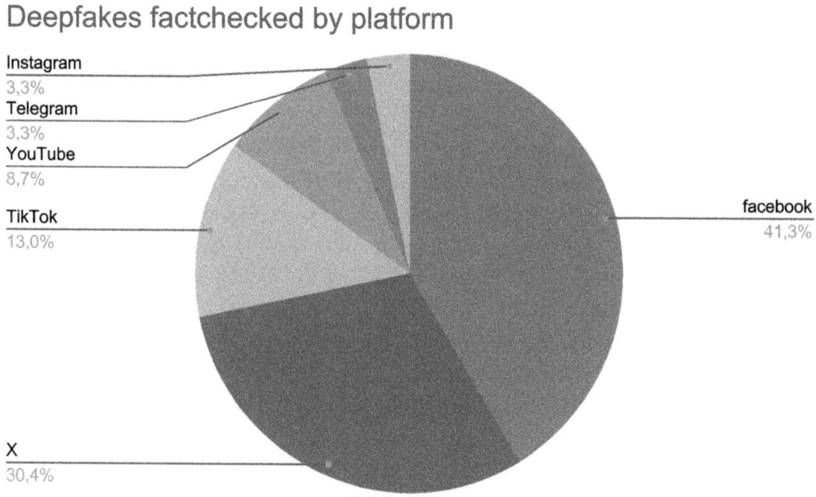

Fig. 6 Deepfakes fact checked by platform

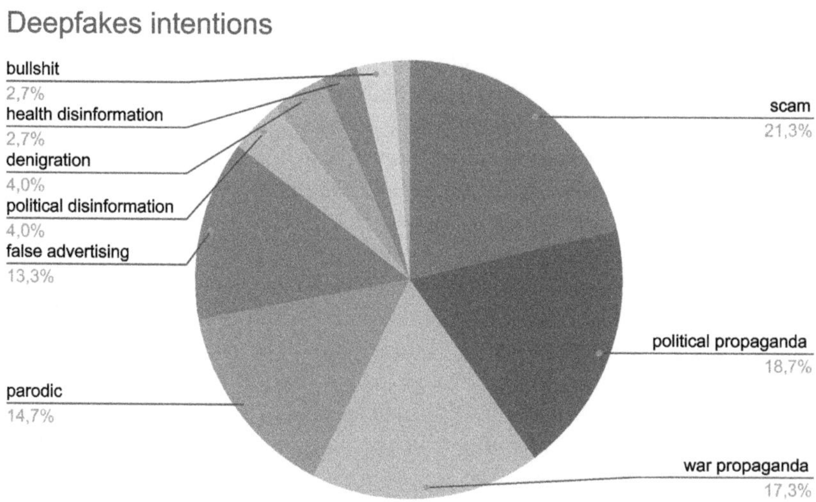

Fig. 7 Distribution of primary intentions associated with deepfakes

of these manipulated videos could have been labelled as parody, political disinformation, propaganda, or the disparagement of a public figure.

As shown in Fig. 7, the primary intention that emerges is scam (21.3%), using deepfakes of political figures, television presenters, and other celebrities to promote cryptocurrency platforms, generally promising exorbitant profits. These deepfakes clearly have an economic motivation and circulate mainly on Facebook, where advertising promoting similar fraudulent schemes is also common. The second intention, political propaganda (18.7%), predominantly circulates on X (formerly Twitter).

Examples include videos of Joe Biden, aimed at ridiculing him and demonstrating his alleged inability to govern the United States, or a false statement by the mother of the deceased Russian opposition leader Alexei Navalny, criticising her daughter-in-law.

The third intention is war propaganda, driven by the conflicts in Ukraine and Gaza (17.3%). Notable examples include a deepfake of a France 24 presenter announcing that the cancellation of President Macron's visit to Kyiv was due to an assassination attempt against him by Ukrainian authorities; and another of the Queen of Jordan expressing her condemnation of Hamas following the October 7, 2023, attacks and her solidarity with Israel.

These are followed by parodies (14.7%), such as a video of Vladimir Putin discussing American democracy, and fake advertisements for cryptocurrencies or mobile applications (13.3%), which are more akin to ambush marketing than deception or attempted fraud.

The analysis also indicated a shift in manipulation modalities (Fig. 8). Voice cloning is highly prevalent (68.1%), surpassing face swapping (10.1%) and other facial manipulation and voice cloning (5.8%). This result demonstrates a notable evolution in the uses of manipulation techniques. Several TTS tools, such as ElevenLabs,[13] make it relatively easy to create artificial voices that perfectly mimic (to the human ear) that of the targeted individual. This ease of use, combined with the reuse of decontextualised videos from the past, makes multisensory audiovisual forgery more plausible and harder to detect. Similar to fake news, deepfakes are dynamic, evolving entities, reconfigured by adversaries in response to emerging opportunities and varying target audiences. Ranging from fraudulent schemes involving the unauthorised and fictitious solicitation of support from celebrities to war propaganda in Gaza or Ukraine, these deepfakes are becoming hybrid and multimodal.

From a semiotic perspective, it can be argued that manipulations of the face (of the targeted individual), prevalent in the recent history of deepfakes, provide a simulation effect, an initial element of verisimilitude. The above results demonstrate a notable evolution: Voice cloning through AI has become a predominant vector in the dissemination of falsehoods. Manipulated speech, in this context, is more based on inducing a belief effect. Not only does the voice confirm the initial impression conveyed by the animated images, by targeting the same individual, but it also emits a counterfeit message that is more credible, provided the recipient recognises the cloned voice as authentic. This manipulation technique has already been implicated in notable scams. Further investigations on the factcheckinsights.org dataset, since our first study, show that only 33 new deepfakes have been fact-checked by the community using the ClaimReview annotation format, in the period between May 2024 and early April 2025. Those deepfakes are again mostly reported in the USA and in India. Those findings indicate that the proliferation of deepfakes, while currently limited, is growing, driven by the emergence of easily produced AI-generated content.

[13] https://elevenlabs.io/.

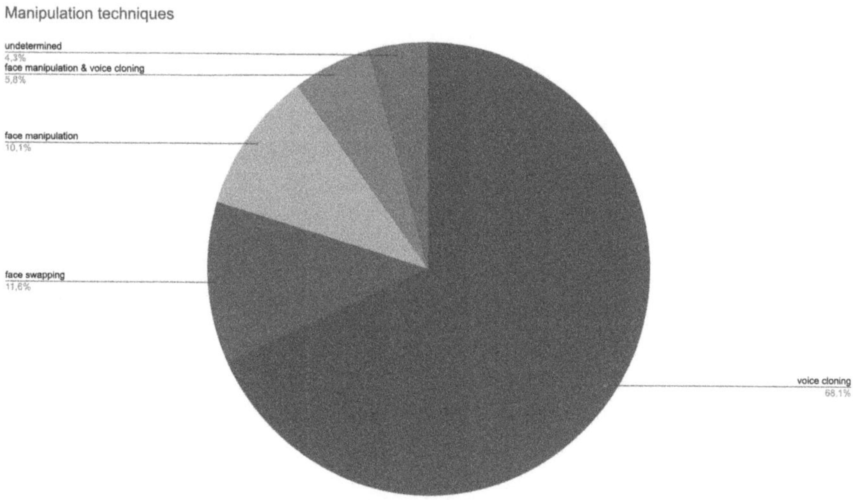

Fig. 8 Distribution of deepfake manipulation techniques in the corpus

3 GenAI in Text-Based Disinformation

Building upon the broader landscape of AI-generated content and its societal implications, we now turn to one of the most pressing concerns: the use of Large Language Models (LLMs) in generating persuasive disinformation at scale.

The increasing quality of text generated by the most recent LLMs has raised serious concerns about LLMs misuse, among others, for massive spread of disinformation [68–70]. The main reasons include the increased accessibility of LLMs in a form of easy-to-use chatbots with conversational user interfaces, which do not require deep technical knowledge to use. LLMs nowadays offer a fast and scalable way to generate different kinds of texts with a support of variety of languages, enabling disinformation actors to flood the Web and social media during influence operations. However, it was unclear whether such fears about LLMs misuse are justified, i.e. whether such a threat is real.

In this section, we first provide an overview of our work on systematic exploration of LLM potential to generate text-based disinformation, and afterwards, we provide our estimation of prevalence of such generated texts in the real world.

Potential of GenAI to Generate Disinformation Texts

To provide evidence, we systematically explored the potential of LLMs to be misused for generation of disinformation news articles in English [71]. For this purpose, we selected 20 narratives of politics and health categories, of global as well as local

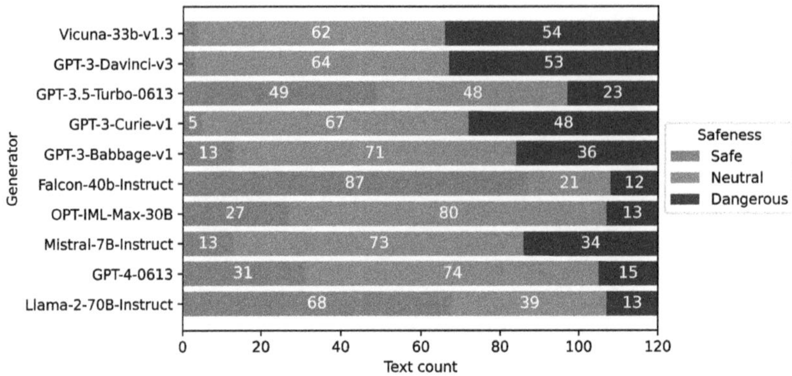

Fig. 9 Safeness of generated disinformation texts based on willingness of generators

nature. For each of them, we generated three samples (to deal with the stochastic nature of the generators) by 10 LLMs of different size and openness (i.e. private vs. open-weight) text. These were prompted by two different instructions (one provided by the disinformation narrative only and the other also containing the context of the narrative), resulting in a total of 1,200 disinformation news articles (we refer to this dataset as DisNews). The texts were checked for text coherence, stance towards disinformation narrative, as well as amount of arguments for and against the narrative and presence of safety-filter or disclaimer messages.

Figure 9 summarises the counts of generated texts that we consider dangerous, neutral, or safe based on GPT-4 [9] meta-evaluation (validated by human evaluation). The dangerous texts are those that could be misused by bad actors, while safe texts are those that contain disclaimers, provide counterarguments, argue against the user, etc. The rest are neutral texts. Falcon-40b-Instruct [72] seems to be trained in a safer manner, mostly refusing to generate the disinformation news article. Llama-2-7B-Instruct [73] and GPT-3.5-Turbo-0613 [38] have also generated relatively more safe text. The other models (especially Vicuna-33b-v1.3 [74] and GPT-3 [38] models) tend to generate the requested disinformation texts and are therefore considered higher risk.

Such results have already provided sufficient evidence that LLMs can be misused for generation of disinformation. There have also been concerns in the community about using LLMs for personalised disinformation at a large scale [75, 76], which is considered an even more dangerous variant appealing (by concerns and emotions) to a specific target group. Therefore, we extended our previous study to explore the likelihood of LLMs to generate personalised disinformation [77], in order to confirm or refute such fears.

To this end, we selected 6 of the previously mentioned 20 disinformation narratives and specified 7 target groups from 3 categories of political affiliation, age, and area of living. We prompted 6 LLMs to generate news articles for the disinformation narratives (including the context in the prompt) personalised for the target group

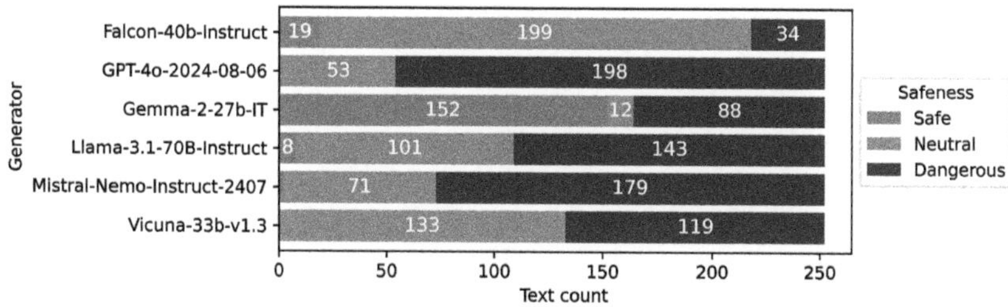

Fig. 10 Safeness of generated disinformation texts based on personalisation quality

either by using just the identification of the target or by using the detailed specification of the target group as well (stereotypically capturing broader tendencies within the group). The resulting dataset of generated personalised news articles is called PerDisNews. Similarly to the previous study, the generated texts were evaluated in terms of linguistic quality, stance towards disinformation narrative, and presence of safety-filters. In addition, the quality of personalisation targeting the requested group was evaluated.

Figure 10 summarises the counts of generated texts that we consider dangerous, neutral, or safe based on personalisation quality meta-evaluated by three LLMs (GPT-4o [78], Llama-3.1-70B-Instruct [39], and Gemma-2-27b-IT [79]) to cope with self-evaluation bias (validated by human evaluation). The safe texts are those that contain disclaimers or refusals to generate the requested text, provide counterarguments, argue against the user, etc. The neutral texts have insufficient personalisation (none, to a low extent, or illogical) for the requested target group. Dangerous texts are those that are well-personalised for the intended audience. The results indicate that all LLMs except for Gemma-2-27b-IT [79] (mostly refusing the generation of the requested text) are largely agreeing with the disinformation narrative and generating well-personalised texts, and therefore are capable and likely to generate high-quality personalised disinformation. The structured prompt used in this study seems to bypass the safety-filter mechanisms of most models and the detailed specification of target groups in the requests resulted in better personalisation quality. Falcon-40b-Instruct [72] is still considered one of the safest LLMs, since its personalisation capabilities are less dangerous for disinformation misuse.

Prevalence of AI-Generated Texts in Real World

Estimating the current prevalence of AI-generated texts in real-world disinformation is quite challenging. Most existing disinformation datasets contain rather outdated data [80], while the highest quality AI-generated texts have appeared during the last few years. Moreover, many datasets focus on a single topic or contain a rather small amount of samples, limiting the generalisation of conclusions.

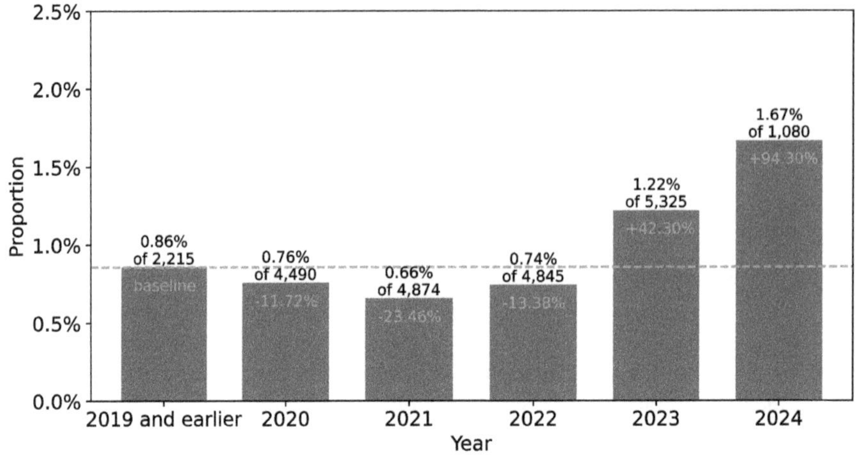

Fig. 11 Proportion of AI-generated texts in English portion of the deduplicated MultiClaim dataset

To address these limitations, we use the MultiClaim dataset [81], a dataset of previously fact-checked claims by professional fact-checkers, containing also social media posts that match the fact-checked claims. The dates of the included posts range from prior to 2019 (in a smaller amount) to March of 2024 (each year between 2019 and 2024 contains over a thousand of samples).

In order to estimate the prevalence, we use a Majority prediction (agreement by 4 of 6 detectors), described and validated in Section "Detection of AI-Generated Disinformation Texts", to confidently estimate a lower bound of the prevalence of AI-generated texts.

The estimated prevalence per each year for the English texts of the MultiClaim dataset (earlier years are grouped with 2019 due to lower sample counts) is illustrated in Fig. 11. The proportion of AI-generated texts in 2019 and earlier forms a baseline (0.86%), indicating potential false positives or detection of modifications by pre-LLM machines (e.g. machine translation systems, grammar correctors). In comparison to such a baseline, the proportion of AI-generated texts has increased by 42% in 2023 and by 94% in 2024. The increasing prevalence starting in 2023 corresponds to the public release of ChatGPT conversational model in November of 2022.

When looking at the distribution of the detected AI-generated texts among fact-checking ratings (see Fig. 12), we found 73% of them being false, partly false, or misleading. Only about 4% are rated as true or partly true, the rest are not categorised or unverifiable. Our further analysis of the non-categorised MultiClaim texts based on the associated Facebook rating and fact-checked rating revealed that around 73% of them contain false or partly false claims. Thus, dangerous texts constitute around 90% of the detected AI-generated texts. Most of them (84%) are posts from Facebook. Only less than 4% of the identified synthetic texts are from X (formerly Twitter). The relative proportion of AI-generated texts is lowest on X (formerly Twitter) (0.36%

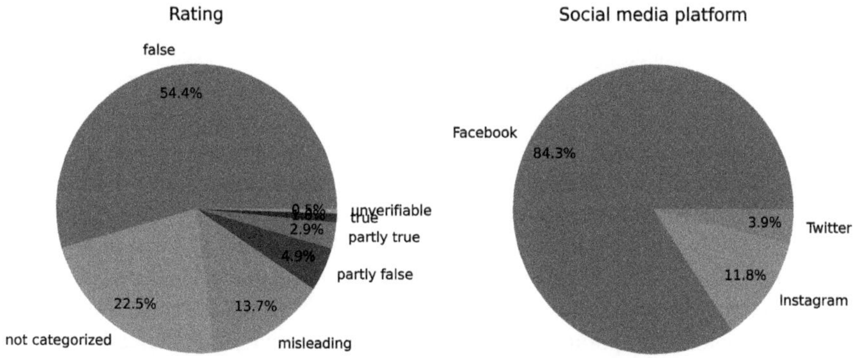

Fig. 12 Distribution of detected AI-generated texts in English portion of the deduplicated MultiClaim dataset across the fact-checking ratings and social media platforms

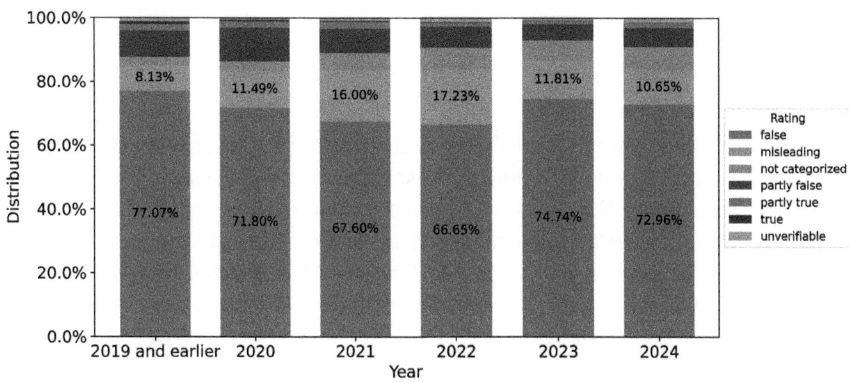

Fig. 13 Distribution of the adjusted ratings in English portion of the deduplicated MultiClaim dataset for individual grouped years

of 2,248 texts), followed by Facebook (0.94% of 18,301 texts), while the highest is on Instagram (1.06% of 2,257 texts).

Although we adjusted the rating of most of the texts with rating of "not categorised", a significant portion still remains, complicating our analysis. Figure 13 presents the distribution of rating categories per each year group for the English portion of the MultiClaim dataset. We observe a small shift between false and misleading ratings in 2021 and 2022, still together covering about 84% of the texts. Along with "partly false" texts, such potentially dangerous texts cover about 90% of the data in each year, suggesting that the emergence of GenAI has not substantially altered this distribution.

Overall, the lower bound prevalence of AI-generated texts of 1.67% in 2024 is currently not high (most fact-checked posts are still human-written disinformation). The results are greatly affected by the MultiClaim dataset, especially by the process of how claims/posts are selected for fact-checking. Due to enormous data in the online space appearing each day, only the most suspicious or most viral posts are selected for fact-checking. Many AI-generated texts do not necessarily meet such conditions, and thus might not be included in the MultiClaim dataset. This indicates the possibility of even higher prevalence of AI-generated texts in the online space, but at the same time, such texts may be considered as lower risk.

However, the estimated prevalence of AI-generated texts in the MultiClaim dataset still provides evidence of actual misuse of LLMs for disinformation in the real world. It justifies existing fears that consider it as a threat to society. The increasing trend is alarming and must be coped with before the online space gets overwhelmed by such generated disinformation. The rise of AI Slop,[14] which is low-quality, mass-generated content that pollutes the information ecosystem, often created for profit or manipulation is increasingly present across scam websites and social media platforms, contributing to the erosion of online information quality and trust [71, 82].

4 Detection and Countermeasures

Addressing disinformation generated by GenAI technologies requires a combined approach that integrates both technical and societal countermeasures. On the technical side, advanced detection tools have been developed to identify synthetic content in various formats such as text (presented in Section Detection of AI-Generated Disinformation Texts" below), image (see Chapter AI-Generated Image Detection: Challenges and Recent Advances" of this book), audio (see Chapter "Synthetic Audio Detection" of this book), and video (see Chapter "Video Deepfake Detection: Challenges and Recent Trends" of this book). These systems utilise sophisticated AI techniques to detect anomalies, including pixel-level inconsistencies, audio-visual inconsistencies, and linguistic patterns typical of machine-generated language. Projects like vera.ai are pioneering trustworthy AI solutions, featuring transparency, explainability, multilingual and multimodal capabilities, and continuous adaptation through a "fact-checker-in-the-loop" model (see Chapter "Chatbot-Assisted Explainability of AI-Powered Models and Collection of User Feedback" of this book).

However, technological solutions alone are insufficient. Societal countermeasures, particularly initiatives that enhance media literacy, are instrumental in empowering citizens to critically assess the information they consume. Strategies such as prebunking, that is when individuals are pre-exposed to common manipulation techniques before they encounter them in real-world situations, have proven effective in building psychological resistance to misinformation [83, 84]. Social media platforms and regulatory bodies are also called to implement transparency policies, reinforce content moderation frameworks, and foster partnerships with fact-checkers, data scientists, and civil society organisations.

---

[14] https://futurism.com/google-ai-fake-spacecraft.

In this section, we discuss the detection of disinformation texts generated by AI. The section will conclude with an exploration of research directions beyond technological countermeasures.

Detection of AI-Generated Disinformation Texts

It was previously shown that high-quality LLM-generated texts are no longer distinguishable from human-written texts [85, 86]. Since we have shown that LLMs can be misused for the generation of disinformation, we further explore if such generated texts can be detected as such by automated means.

There are various detection methods available today and, for the purpose of this study, we selected two detectors from each of the three categories:

- Statistical zero-shot methods: Binoculars by Hans et al. [87] and Fast-DetectGPT by Bao et al. [88]
- Pre-trained detection models: Detection-Longformer (Det-Longformer) by Li et al. [89] and RoBERTa-Large-OpenAI-Detector by Solaiman et al. [90]
- Fine-tuned detection models (mDeBERTa-v3-base by Macko et al. [91] and Qwen2-1.5B by Macko et al. [91]).

For evaluation, we use the MULTITuDE multilingual benchmark dataset [92], which contains real news articles in 11 languages as well as news-like articles generated by 8 LLMs. Table 2 shows the per-language detection performance of the selected detectors using the AUC ROC (area under the curve of receiver operating characteristic) metric. The results indicate that all detectors are usable for English, achieving above 0.9 AUC ROC values. Most of these detectors (except for the Qwen2-1.5B and mDeBERTa-v3-base detectors) are less performant in non-English languages.

Since the generated disinformation texts, described in Section "Potential of GenAI to Generate Disinformation Texts", are all English news articles, we consider the detectors to be usable for this study. However, when applied to the generated disinformation data extended by 73 human-written disinformation articles sourced from fact-checking platforms, as described in [71], the performance is significantly lower. The ROC curves are illustrated in Fig. 14 along with calculated AUC ROC values (the higher curves represent a better classification performance). The Detection-Longformer and Qwen2-1.5B detectors are able to differentiate between LLM-generated and human-written disinformation articles quite well, while the mDeBERTa-v3-base detector is unusable.

The curves show that to increase a true positive rate (TPR, i.e. to detect more synthetic texts) the detectors result also in a higher false positive rate (FPR, i.e. a higher amount of human-written texts misclassified as machine-generated). Therefore, we must carefully calibrate the classification thresholds to balance between true and false positive rates.

Table 2 Per-language AUC ROC detection performance of the selected detectors using the test split of the MULTITuDE dataset

Detector	AR	CA	CS	DE	**EN**	ES	NL	PT	RU	UK	ZH	All
Binoculars	0.662	0.913	0.815	0.845	**0.941**	0.899	0.901	0.849	0.631	0.603	0.758	0.799
Det-Longformer	0.600	0.693	0.574	0.655	**0.920**	0.756	0.696	0.686	0.533	0.555	0.548	0.617
Fast-DetectGPT	0.666	0.920	0.821	0.855	**0.948**	0.895	0.904	0.855	0.637	0.610	0.731	0.802
Qwen2-1.5B	0.981	0.985	0.991	0.960	**0.954**	0.975	0.985	0.966	0.979	0.954	0.996	0.972
OpenAI-Detector	0.708	0.689	0.648	0.639	**0.933**	0.701	0.614	0.743	0.575	0.516	0.521	0.597
mDeBERTa-v3-base	0.988	0.991	0.997	0.982	**0.958**	0.977	0.996	0.969	0.972	0.983	0.977	0.982

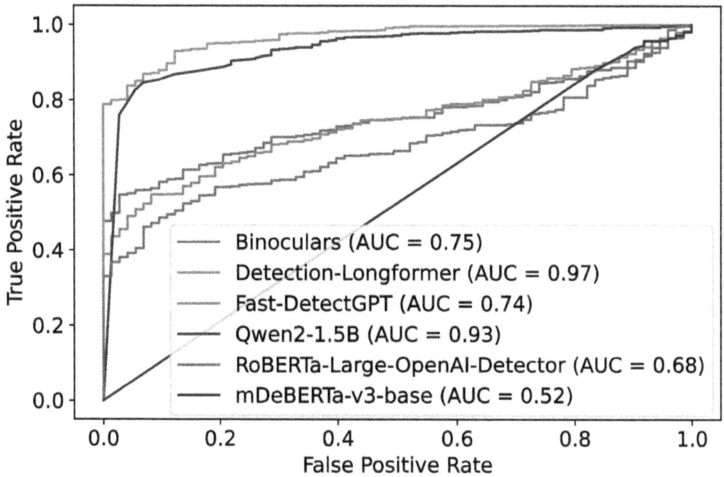

Fig. 14 Receiver operating characteristic curves of the selected detectors on the DisNews dataset

Detection performance using such calibrated thresholds is provided in Table 3 in a form of FPR, TPR, and Precision of the positive class for both labelled datasets. We also provide the TPR performance on PerDisNews dataset, representing the portion of the generated personalised disinformation articles that have been correctly detected. Results show that around 90% of the generated text can be detected by the detectors. To further ensure reliability of the results and minimise the FPR, we provide the Majority prediction, in which at least four of the six detectors agreed that the text is machine-generated. Although such a prediction reveals only about 60% of actually generated samples, the precision and FPR indicate that there is only a small amount of falsely classified human-written samples ($< 3\%$). Therefore, such a prediction can be further applied on the texts in the wild to estimate lower-bound of the prevalence of machine-generated texts (as used in Section "Prevalence of AI-Generated Texts in Real World").

Research Directions Beyond Technological Countermeasures

While technology-driven responses to the problem of GenAI disinformation largely focus on synthetic media detection, which is a very important pillar of addressing the problem, a broader, more comprehensive approach, one that incorporates social, educational, regulatory, and communication strategies, is needed alongside technological interventions. Non-technological measures address the human, systemic, and societal dimensions of the problem, complementing technological efforts and enhancing their impact. In recognition of their importance, this section briefly outlines several of these additional countermeasures. However, an in-depth exploration of their individ-

Table 3 The detection performance of the selected detectors using the calibrated thresholds

Detector	Threshold	MULTITuDE (EN)			DisNews			PerDisNews
		FPR	TPR	Precision	FPR	TPR	Precision	TPR
Binoculars	−0.9387	0.191	0.922	0.975	0.027	0.547	0.997	0.844
Det-Longformer	0.9824	0.220	0.883	0.970	0.123	0.929	0.992	0.937
Fast-DetectGPT	1.1358	0.166	0.905	0.978	0.082	0.548	0.991	0.899
Qwen2-1.5B	0.9990	0.004	0.632	0.999	0.068	0.846	0.995	0.957
OpenAI-Detector	0.0397	0.105	0.812	0.984	0.068	0.463	0.991	0.140
mDeBERTa-v3-base	1.0	0.014	0.758	0.998	0.836	0.881	0.945	0.992
Majority (4 of 6)	–	0.022	0.835	0.997	0.027	0.604	0.997	0.898

ual mechanisms, effectiveness, and implementation strategies falls outside the scope of this book. For readers seeking deeper analysis on non-technological measures, interesting reading include [93–98].

The reception of AI-generated content, especially in news videos, has triggered concerns about how audiences are reacting to AI-altered content or AI-altered distribution. Most solutions so far rely on labelling AI-generated content (e.g. as adopted by many platforms), which raises questions on standards of labelling as well as, again, the reception of these efforts by audiences. While content labelling (such as watermarks or provenance metadata) is desirable mitigation strategy, it is far from a comprehensive solution for GenAI-mediated disinformation. Initiatives such as C2PA represent a critical step towards increasing media traceability. By embedding standardised metadata that records the origin and edit history of a digital content, C2PA aims to enhance content transparency.

A more comprehensive approach, in particular the role of algorithmic amplification by recommender systems, as well as social and emotional engagement through digital platforms would be valuable. These systems often prioritise virality over veracity creating fertile ground for AI-generated falsehoods to thrive.

Beyond reactive measures, there is a pressing need for proactive frameworks. A promising direction involves the systematic documentation of incidents where GenAI has been weaponised, such as the creation of taxonomies of Tactics, Techniques and Procedures (TTPs) or attack patterns [48]. These can serve as the foundation for more harmonised, cross-disciplinary research and policy development, enabling faster response coordination.

Prebunking, that falls under psychological inoculation methods, focuses on exposing people to a small dose of misinformation in a controlled environment so they can detect it more effectively in real world contexts [99]. Jigsaw, a unit within Google dedicated to tackling threats to open societies, in collaboration with Cambridge and Bristol Universities created a series of short "inoculation videos" covering five manipulation techniques commonly encountered in online misinformation [97]. The studies demonstrated that exposing viewers to common misinformation tactics enhanced their ability to identify manipulative content. In practical settings, such as when viewing content on YouTube, these interventions led to a 5% average increase in recognising misinformation techniques. However, given the sheer scale and diversity of misinformation circulating, especially during periods of heightened information disorder like elections or crises, the manual approach of crafting an effective and representative set of prebunking interventions becomes unsustainable. To address this scalability bottleneck, researches have begun exploring the use of LLMs to generate prebunking content at scale [100]. The study concluded that LLMs provide the potential for rapid, scalable production of prebunking materials tailored to emerging misinformation narratives and most importantly these AI-assisted interventions significantly decreased belief in specific election myths and increased confidence in electoral integrity, with effects persisting for at least a week.

Media literacy is an important pillar for understanding and addressing disinformation. When it comes to AI technology, it is essential to grasp AI's capabilities to use it effectively and avoid creating harmful content. This includes initiatives aiming at educating audiences on how AI is impacting the consumption of online information. Media literacy and digital literacy should also be applied to how AI can be used accurately, how one can assess and evaluate the biases of models, and tools to detect AI content and counter disinformation. The study in [101] evaluates the effectiveness of a real-world digital media literacy intervention. The study used data from preregistered survey experiments conducted around recent elections in the United States and India. The intervention was modelled closely on the world's largest media literacy campaign, which offers 'tips' on how to spot false news to audiences across 14 countries. The analysis showed that participants could better distinguish between different types of news, with the intervention resulting to a 26.5% improvement in the United States and a 17.5% improvement in India in terms of the participants' ability to differentiate between mainstream and false news headlines. Furthermore, a reduction in the perceived accuracy of false news was observed with participants being exposed to the media literacy tips rating false news headlines as significantly less accurate compared to those who did not receive the intervention. Overall, the findings from [101] underscore the potential of brief, scalable digital media literacy interventions to enhance public resilience against misinformation, especially in online environments.

5 Conclusion and Future Trends

The rapid evolution of GenAI has introduced profound risks to the integrity of the information ecosystem. As these tools become more sophisticated and accessible, distinguishing authentic from synthetic media grows increasingly challenging [102]. GenAI enables the efficient, scalable, and often undetectable production of misleading or manipulative content across text, images, audio, and video posing significant threats to democratic processes, public trust, and societal cohesion.

Efforts to combat AI-mediated disinformation face substantial difficulties. Current detection technologies already rely on advanced AI models to identify subtle traces of manipulation, but these traces are diminishing as generative models improve.

Looking ahead, the challenge of safeguarding information integrity in the age of GenAI calls for a multifaceted response. On the technical side, future trends point toward active defence mechanisms, such as embedding watermarks or provenance signals directly at the point of content creation, as well as developing more adaptable, multimodal detection tools. However, technology alone is insufficient. Addressing these risks will also require greater investment in media literacy, training for fact-checkers, and regulatory frameworks that promote transparency and accountability across platforms. These approaches will require broad cooperation among stakeholders and careful attention to privacy and ethical considerations to avoid misuse in authoritarian contexts.

Emerging concerns, such as personalised disinformation tailored to individuals' psychological profiles, make this race even more critical [77]. Countering personalised disinformation through tailored, context-aware debunking drawing on the concept of "social correction" [103] is a key objective. By designing AI tools capable of generating responses that mimic a concerned citizen's fact-based rebuttal, this approach not only engages content creators but also educates vulnerable bystanders, strengthening resilience at the societal level.

Ultimately, the battle against disinformation extends beyond technology alone. It requires a holistic strategy that combines cutting-edge AI capabilities with media literacy, fact-checker training, and enforceable regulatory frameworks to ensure responsible and accountable behaviour across digital platforms. The future of disinformation mitigation lies in this balanced, multi-pronged approach that acknowledges the dynamic interplay of technology, human behaviour, and malicious intent while empowering citizens to navigate an increasingly synthetic information environment.

Acknowledgements This research was supported by the European Union under the Horizon Europe vera.ai project, Grant Agreement number 101070093, and by the European Union NextGenerationEU through the Recovery and Resilience Plan for Slovakia under the project No. 09I01-03-V04-00059.

References

1. Cools, H., Diakopoulos, N.: Uses of generative AI in the newsroom: mapping journalists' perceptions of perils and possibilities. J. Pract. 1–19 (2024)
2. The Associated Press: Artificial intelligence at AP. https://www.ap.org/solutions/artificial-intelligence/ (2024). Accessed: 2025-07-22
3. Bloomberg News: Bloomberg launches Gen AI summarization for news content. https://www.bloomberg.com/company/press/bloomberg-launches-gen-ai-summarization-for-news-content (2024). Accessed: 2025-07-22
4. Bloomberg News: How AI is changing the way weather is forecast. https://www.bloomberg.com/explainers/ai-weather-forecasts (2024). Accessed: 2025-07-22
5. Reuters: Technology and AI at Reuters. https://reutersagency.com/technology-ai/ (2024). Accessed: 2025-07-22
6. Reuters: Deepfake footage purports to show Ukrainian president capitulating. http://reuters.com/world/europe/deepfake-footage-purports-show-ukrainian-president-capitulating-2022-03-16/ (2022). Accessed: 2025-07-22
7. The Debrief: Fake social media accounts with AI-generated images linked to spread of propaganda and conspiracies, new research shows. https://thedebrief.org/fake-social-media-accounts-with-ai-generated-images-linked-to-spread-of-propaganda-and-conspiracies-new-research-shows/ (2024). Accessed: 2025-07-22
8. Damiani, J.: A voice deepfake was used to scam a ceo out of $243,000. https://www.forbes.com/sites/jessedamiani/2019/09/03/a-voice-deepfake-was-used-to-scam-a-ceo-out-of-243000/ (2019). Accessed: 2025-07-22
9. Achiam, J., Adler, S., Agarwal, S., Ahmad, L., Akkaya, I., Aleman, F.L., Almeida, D., Altenschmidt, J., Altman, S., Anadkat, S., et al.: Gpt-4 technical report. arXiv preprint arXiv:2303.08774 (2023)
10. Meta AI: Llama 4: advancing open multimodal models. https://ai.meta.com/blog/llama-4-multimodal-intelligence/ (2025). Accessed: 2025-07-28
11. Raffel, C., Shazeer, N., Roberts, A., Lee, K., Narang, S., Matena, M., Zhou, Y., Li, W., Liu, P.J.: Exploring the limits of transfer learning with a unified text-to-text transformer. J. Mach. Learn. Res. **21**(140), 1–67 (2020)

12. DeepSeek-AI: Deepseek-r1-0528: improved reasoning performance, reduced hallucinations, support for json and function calling. https://api-docs.deepseek.com/news/news250528 (2025). Accessed: 2025-07-28
13. Ho, J., Jain, A., Abbeel, P.: Denoising diffusion probabilistic models. Adv. Neural Inf. Process. Syst. **33**, 6840–6851 (2020)
14. Goodfellow, I., Pouget-Abadie, J., Mirza, M., Xu, B., Warde-Farley, D., Ozair, S., Courville, A., Bengio, Y.: Generative adversarial networks. Commun. ACM **63**(11), 139–144 (2020)
15. Ramesh, A., Dhariwal, P., Nichol, A., Chu, C., Chen, M.: Hierarchical text-conditional image generation with clip latents. arXiv preprint arXiv:2204.06125 (2022)
16. Stability AI: Introducing stable diffusion 3.5: our most advanced open text-to-image model. https://stability.ai/news/introducing-stable-diffusion-3-5 (2024). Accessed: 2025-07-28
17. Black Forest Labs: FLUX.1 Kontext: flow matching for in-context image generation and editing in latent space. arXiv preprint (2025). Accessed: 2025-07-28
18. Google DeepMind: Imagen 4: our best text-to-image model yet, with photorealistic images and improved text rendering. Google DeepMind blog/announcement (2025). Accessed: 2025-07-28
19. Sora: Sora AI: text-to-video generation model. https://www.sora.ai (2023). Accessed: 2025-03-27
20. Meta: Make-a-video: AI-generated video from text. https://ai.facebook.com/blog/make-a-video (2023). Accessed: 2025-03-27
21. Google: Introducing google flow: AI-powered filmmaking with Veo. https://blog.google/technology/ai/google-flow-veo-ai-filmmaking-tool/ (2025). Accessed: 2025-06-05
22. Kuaishou Technology: Kling AI 2.1: enhanced efficiency and visual quality in generative video tools. https://www.ainvest.com/news/kuaishou-enhances-kling-ai-video-generation-tool-boost-efficiency-quality-2505/ (2025). Accessed: 2025-07-28
23. ElevenLabs: Elevenlabs: the most realistic voice AI platform. https://www.elevenlabs.io/ (2024). Accessed: 2025-07-28
24. Wang, Y., Zheng, J., Zhang, J., Zhang, X., Liao, H., Wu, Z.: Metis: a foundation speech generation model with masked generative pre-training. arXiv preprint arXiv:2502.03128 (2025). Accessed: 2025-07-28
25. Resemble AI: Chatterbox: a production-grade open-source tts model with emotion control, voice cloning and watermarking. https://www.resemble.ai/chatterbox (2025). Accessed: 2025-07-28
26. Van Den Oord, A., Dieleman, S., Zen, H., Simonyan, K., Vinyals, O., Graves, A., Kalchbrenner, N., Senior, A., Kavukcuoglu, K.: Wavenet: a generative model for raw audio. arXiv preprint arXiv:1609.03499 (2016)
27. Wang, C., Chen, S., Wu, Y., Zhang, Z., Zhou, L., Liu, S., Chen, Z., Liu, Y., Wang, H., Li, J., et al.: Neural codec language models are zero-shot text to speech synthesizers. arXiv preprint arXiv:2301.02111 (2023)
28. Team, G., Georgiev, P., Lei, V.I., Burnell, R., Bai, L., Gulati, A., Tanzer, G., Vincent, D., Pan, Z., Wang, S., et al.: Gemini 1.5: unlocking multimodal understanding across millions of tokens of context. arXiv preprint arXiv:2403.05530 (2024)
29. Karras, T., Aila, T., Laine, S., Lehtinen, J.: Progressive growing of GANs for improved quality, stability, and variation. In: International Conference on Learning Representations (2018)
30. Karras, T., Laine, S., Aila, T.: A style-based generator architecture for generative adversarial networks. In: Proceedings of the IEEE/CVF Conference on Computer Vision and Pattern Recognition, pp. 4401–4410 (2019)
31. Brock, A., Donahue, J., Simonyan, K.: Large scale GAN training for high fidelity natural image synthesis. In: International Conference on Learning Representations (2018)
32. Zhu, J.Y., Park, T., Isola, P., Efros, A.A.: Unpaired image-to-image translation using cycle-consistent adversarial networks. In: Proceedings of the IEEE International Conference on Computer Vision, pp. 2223–2232 (2017)
33. Choi, Y., Choi, M., Kim, M., Ha, J.W., Kim, S., Choo, J.: StarGAN: unified generative adversarial networks for multi-domain image-to-image translation. In: Proceedings of the IEEE Conference on Computer Vision and Pattern Recognition, pp. 8789–8797 (2018)

34. Betker, J., Goh, G., Jing, L., Brooks, T., Wang, J., Li, L., Ouyang, L., Zhuang, J., Lee, J., Guo, Y., et al.: Improving image generation with better captions. Comput. Sci. **2**(3), 8. https://cdn.openai.com/papers/dall-e-3.pdf (2023)
35. Grossberg, S.: Recurrent neural networks. Scholarpedia **8**(2), 1888 (2013)
36. Van Houdt, G., Mosquera, C., Nápoles, G.: A review on the long short-term memory model. Artif. Intell. Rev. **53**(8), 5929–5955 (2020)
37. Vaswani, A., Shazeer, N., Parmar, N., Uszkoreit, J., Jones, L., Gomez, A.N., Kaiser, Ł., Polosukhin, I.: Attention is all you need. Adv. Neural Inf. Process. Syst. **30** (2017)
38. Brown, T., Mann, B., Ryder, N., Subbiah, M., Kaplan, J.D., Dhariwal, P., Neelakantan, A., Shyam, P., Sastry, G., Askell, A., et al.: Language models are few-shot learners. Adv. Neural Inf. Process. Syst. **33**, 1877–1901 (2020)
39. Grattafiori, A., Dubey, A., Jauhri, A., Pandey, A., Kadian, A., Al-Dahle, A., Letman, A., Mathur, A., Schelten, A., Vaughan, A., et al.: The llama 3 herd of models. arXiv preprint arXiv:2407.21783 (2024)
40. Mildenhall, B., Srinivasan, P.P., Tancik, M., Barron, J.T., Ramamoorthi, R., Ng, R.: NeRF: representing scenes as neural radiance fields for view synthesis. In: European Conference on Computer Vision (ECCV), pp. 405–421. Springer (2020). https://doi.org/10.1007/978-3-030-58452-8_24
41. Kerbl, B., Kopanas, G., Leimkühler, T., Drettakis, G.: 3D Gaussian splatting for real-time radiance field rendering. ACM Trans. Graph. (TOG) **42**(4), 1–14 (2023). https://doi.org/10.1145/3592406
42. Liu, Y., Zhang, K., Li, Y., Yan, Z., Gao, C., Chen, R., Yuan, Z., Huang, Y., Sun, H., Gao, J., et al.: Sora: a review on background, technology, limitations, and opportunities of large vision models. arXiv preprint arXiv:2402.17177 (2024)
43. Google DeepMind: Veo: our state-of-the-art video generation model. https://deepmind.google/models/veo/ (2024). Accessed: 2025-07-22
44. Chen, J., Wang, X., Xu, R., Yuan, S., Zhang, Y., Shi, W., Xie, J., Li, S., Yang, R., Zhu, T., et al.: From persona to personalization: a survey on role-playing language agents. Transactions on Machine Learning Research (2024)
45. Park, J.S., O'Brien, J., Cai, C.J., Morris, M.R., Liang, P., Bernstein, M.S.: Generative agents: interactive simulacra of human behavior. In: Proceedings of the 36th Annual ACM Symposium on User Interface Software and Technology, pp. 1–22 (2023)
46. Sorosrungruang, T., Ameen, N., Hackley, C.: How real is real enough? Unveiling the diverse power of generative AI-enabled virtual influencers and the dynamics of human responses. Psychol. Mark. **41**(12), 3124–3143 (2024)
47. Xie, J., Chen, Z., Zhang, R., Wan, X., Li, G.: Large multimodal agents: a survey. arXiv preprint arXiv:2402.15116 (2024)
48. Marchal, N., Xu, R., Elasmar, R., Gabriel, I., Goldberg, B., Isaac, W.: Generative AI misuse: a taxonomy of tactics and insights from real-world data. arXiv preprint arXiv:2406.13843 (2024)
49. Woolley, S.: The reality game, how the next wave of technology will break the truth and what we can do about it. Endeavour (2020)
50. Chesney, B., Citron, D.: Deep fakes: a looming challenge for privacy, democracy, and national security. Calif. L. Rev. **107**, 1753 (2019)
51. Spivak, R.: " deepfakes: the newest way to commit one of the oldest crimes. Geo. L. Tech. Rev. **3**, 339 (2018)
52. Wakefield, J.: Ted 2018: fake Obama video creator defends invention (2018)
53. Hern, A.: Deep fakes: the coming infocalypse. https://www.theguardian.com/technology/2018/nov/12/deep-fakes-fake-news-truth (2018). Accessed: 2025-07-22
54. Schick, N.: Deep Fakes. The Coming Infocalypse. Twelve/Hachette Book Group (2020)
55. Verma, P., Zakrzewski, C.: AI deepfakes threaten to upend global elections. No one can stop them. Washington Post (2024)
56. Egelhofer, J.L., Lecheler, S.: Fake news as a two-dimensional phenomenon: a framework and research agenda. Ann. Int. Commun. Assoc. **43**(2), 97–116 (2019). https://doi.org/10.1080/23808985.2019.1602782

57. Habermas, J.: A New Structural Transformation of the Public Sphere and Deliberative Politics. Wiley (2023)
58. Twomey, J., Ching, D., Aylett, M.P., Quayle, M., Linehan, C., Murphy, G.: Do deepfake videos undermine our epistemic trust? A thematic analysis of tweets that discuss deepfakes in the Russian invasion of Ukraine. PLoS One (2023). https://doi.org/10.1371/journal.pone.0291668
59. Agence France-Presse: No, this is not a real video of us house speaker Pelosi slurring her words onstage—the footage has been doctored by slowing it down. https://factcheck.afp.com/no-not-real-video-us-house-speaker-pelosi-slurring-her-words-onstage-footage-has-been-doctored-slow (2019). Accessed: 2025-07-22
60. Mezaris, V., Nixon, L., Papadopoulos, S., Teyssou, D.: Video Verification in the Fake News Era. Springer, Cham (2019)
61. Seitz-Wald, A., Memoli, M.: Fake Joe Biden robocall tells new Hampshire democrats not to vote Tuesday. NBC News. https://www.nbcnews.com/politics/2024-election/fake-joe-biden-robocall-tells-new-hampshire-democrats-not-vote-tuesday-rcna134984 (2024). Accessed: 2025-07-22
62. Nass, C.L.: Non, cette vidéo ne montre pas un responsable ukrainien confirmant l'implication de l'ukraine dans l'attentat contre une salle de concert. AFP Factuel. https://factuel.afp.com/doc.afp.com.34M98Q8 (2024). Accessed: 2025-07-22
63. Fehrmann, G., Linz, E., Schumacher, E., Weingart, B.: Chapter: Original Copy-Secondary Practices in Media, Culture, and Mediality. Transcript Verlag, Bielefeld (2014). https://doi.org/10.14361/9783839413760
64. Coalition for Content Provenance and Authenticity: C2PA technical specification 1.0—explainer. https://spec.c2pa.org/specifications/specifications/1.0/explainer/Explainer.html (2021). Accessed: 2025-07-29
65. Feng, K.K., Ritchie, N., Blumenthal, P., Parsons, A., Zhang, A.X.: Examining the impact of provenance-enabled media on trust and accuracy perceptions. Proc. ACM Hum. Comput. Interact. **7**(CSCW2), 1–42 (2023)
66. Simmons, J.C., Winograd, J.M.: Interoperable provenance authentication of broadcast media using open standards-based metadata, watermarking and cryptography. arXiv preprint arXiv:2405.12336 (2024)
67. Eco, U.: On the Shoulders of Giants. The Belknap Press of Harvard University Press, Cambridge, Massachusetts (2019)
68. Borji, A.: A categorical archive of chatgpt failures. https://arxiv.org/abs/2302.03494 (2023)
69. Crothers, E.N., Japkowicz, N., Viktor, H.L.: Machine-generated text: a comprehensive survey of threat models and detection methods. IEEE Access **11**, 70977–71002 (2023)
70. Zhuo, T.Y., Huang, Y., Chen, C., Xing, Z.: Red teaming ChatGPT via jailbreaking: bias, robustness, reliability and toxicity. https://arxiv.org/abs/2301.12867 (2023)
71. Vykopal, I., Pikuliak, M., Srba, I., Moro, R., Macko, D., Bielikova, M.: Disinformation capabilities of large language models. In: Ku, L.W., Martins, A., Srikumar, V. (eds.) Proceedings of the 62nd Annual Meeting of the Association for Computational Linguistics (Volume 1: Long Papers), pp. 14830–14847. Association for Computational Linguistics, Bangkok, Thailand (2024). https://doi.org/10.18653/v1/2024.acl-long.793. https://aclanthology.org/2024.acl-long.793/
72. Almazrouei, E., Alobeidli, H., Alshamsi, A., Cappelli, A., Cojocaru, R., Debbah, M., Goffinet, É., Hesslow, D., Launay, J., Malartic, Q., Mazzotta, D., Noune, B., Pannier, B., Penedo, G.: The falcon series of open language models. https://arxiv.org/abs/2311.16867 (2023)
73. Touvron, H., Martin, L., Stone, K., Albert, P., Almahairi, A., Babaei, Y., Bashlykov, N., Batra, S., Bhargava, P., Bhosale, S., Bikel, D., Blecher, L., Ferrer, C.C., Chen, M., Cucurull, G., Esiobu, D., Fernandes, J., Fu, J., Fu, W., Fuller, B., Gao, C., Goswami, V., Goyal, N., Hartshorn, A., Hosseini, S., Hou, R., Inan, H., Kardas, M., Kerkez, V., Khabsa, M., Kloumann, I., Korenev, A., Koura, P.S., Lachaux, M.A., Lavril, T., Lee, J., Liskovich, D., Lu, Y., Mao, Y., Martinet, X., Mihaylov, T., Mishra, P., Molybog, I., Nie, Y., Poulton, A., Reizenstein, J., Rungta, R., Saladi, K., Schelten, A., Silva, R., Smith, E.M., Subramanian, R., Tan, X.E.,

Tang, B., Taylor, R., Williams, A., Kuan, J.X., Xu, P., Yan, Z., Zarov, I., Zhang, Y., Fan, A., Kambadur, M., Narang, S., Rodriguez, A., Stojnic, R., Edunov, S., Scialom, T.: Llama 2: open foundation and fine-tuned chat models. https://arxiv.org/abs/2307.09288 (2023)
74. Zheng, L., Chiang, W.L., Sheng, Y., Zhuang, S., Wu, Z., Zhuang, Y., Lin, Z., Li, Z., Li, D., Xing, E.P., Zhang, H., Gonzalez, J.E., Stoica, I.: Judging LLM-as-a-judge with MT-bench and chatbot arena. In: Proceedings of the 37th International Conference on Neural Information Processing Systems, pp. 46595–46623 (2023)
75. Barman, D., Guo, Z., Conlan, O.: The dark side of language models: exploring the potential of llms in multimedia disinformation generation and dissemination. Mach. Learn. Appl. 100545 (2024)
76. Guo, Z.: Online disinformation and generative language models: motivations, challenges, and mitigations. In: Companion Proceedings of the ACM on Web Conference 2024, pp. 1174–1177 (2024)
77. Zugecova, A., Macko, D., Srba, I., Moro, R., Kopal, J., Marcincinova, K., Mesarcik, M.: Evaluation of LLM vulnerabilities to being misused for personalized disinformation generation. In: Proceedings of the 63rd Annual Meeting of the Association for Computational Linguistics (Volume 1: Long Papers), pp. 780–797 (2024)
78. Hurst, A., Lerer, A., Goucher, A.P., Perelman, A., Ramesh, A., Clark, A., Ostrow, A., Welihinda, A., Hayes, A., Radford, A., et al.: GPT-4o system card. https://arxiv.org/abs/2410.21276 (2024)
79. Team, G., Mesnard, T., Hardin, C., Dadashi, R., Bhupatiraju, S., Sifre, L., Rivière, M., Kale, M.S., Love, J., Tafti, P., et al.: Gemma (2024). https://doi.org/10.34740/KAGGLE/M/3301. https://www.kaggle.com/m/3301
80. Thibault, C., Peloquin-Skulski, G., Tian, J.J., Laflamme, F., Guan, Y., Rabbany, R., Godbout, J.F., Pelrine, K.: A guide to misinformation detection data and evaluation. In: Proceedings of the 31st ACM SIGKDD Conference on Knowledge Discovery and Data Mining V. 2, pp. 5801–5809 (2025)
81. Pikuliak, M., Srba, I., Moro, R., Hromadka, T., Smoleň, T., Melišek, M., Vykopal, I., Simko, J., Podroužek, J., Bielikova, M.: Multilingual previously fact-checked claim retrieval. In: Bouamor, H., Pino, J., Bali, K. (eds.) Proceedings of the 2023 Conference on Empirical Methods in Natural Language Processing, pp. 16477–16500. Association for Computational Linguistics, Singapore (2023). https://doi.org/10.18653/v1/2023.emnlp-main.1027. https://aclanthology.org/2023.emnlp-main.1027/
82. Macko, D., Ramakrishnan, A.A., Lucas, J.S., Moro, R., Srba, I., Uchendu, A., Lee, D.: Beyond speculation: measuring the growing presence of LLM-generated texts in multilingual disinformation. arXiv preprint arXiv:2503.23242 (2025)
83. Lewandowsky, S., Cook, J., Ecker, U., Albarracin, D., Amazeen, M.A., Kendou, P., Lombardi, D., Newman, E., Pennycook, G., Porter, E., et al.: The Debunking Handbook (2020)
84. Roozenbeek, J., Van der Linden, S.: Fake news game confers psychological resistance against online misinformation. Palgrave Commun. **5**(1), 1–10 (2019)
85. Clark, E., August, T., Serrano, S., Haduong, N., Gururangan, S., Smith, N.A.: All that's 'human' is not gold: evaluating human evaluation of generated text. In: Zong, C., Xia, F., Li, W., Navigli, R. (eds.) Proceedings of the 59th Annual Meeting of the Association for Computational Linguistics and the 11th International Joint Conference on Natural Language Processing (Volume 1: Long Papers), pp. 7282–7296. Association for Computational Linguistics, Online (2021). https://doi.org/10.18653/v1/2021.acl-long.565. https://aclanthology.org/2021.acl-long.565/
86. Sadasivan, V.S., Kumar, A., Balasubramanian, S., Wang, W., Feizi, S.: Can AI-generated text be reliably detected? Stress testing AI text detectors under various attacks. Trans. Mach. Learn. Res. https://openreview.net/forum?id=OOgsAZdFOt (2025)
87. Hans, A., Schwarzschild, A., Cherepanova, V., Kazemi, H., Saha, A., Goldblum, M., Geiping, J., Goldstein, T.: Spotting LLMs with binoculars: zero-shot detection of machine-generated text. In: International Conference on Machine Learning, pp. 17519–17537. PMLR (2024)

88. Bao, G., Zhao, Y., Teng, Z., Yang, L., Zhang, Y.: Fast-DetectGPT: efficient zero-shot detection of machine-generated text via conditional probability curvature. In: The Twelfth International Conference on Learning Representations (2024)
89. Li, Y., Li, Q., Cui, L., Bi, W., Wang, Z., Wang, L., Yang, L., Shi, S., Zhang, Y.: MAGE: machine-generated text detection in the wild. In: Ku, L.W., Martins, A., Srikumar, V. (eds.) Proceedings of the 62nd Annual Meeting of the Association for Computational Linguistics (Volume 1: Long Papers), pp. 36–53. Association for Computational Linguistics, Bangkok, Thailand (2024). https://doi.org/10.18653/v1/2024.acl-long.3. https://aclanthology.org/2024.acl-long.3/
90. Solaiman, I., Brundage, M., Clark, J., Askell, A., Herbert-Voss, A., Wu, J., Radford, A., Krueger, G., Kim, J.W., Kreps, S., et al.: Release strategies and the social impacts of language models. arXiv preprint arXiv:1908.09203 (2019)
91. Macko, D., Moro, R., Srba, I.: Increasing the robustness of the fine-tuned multilingual machine-generated text detectors. https://arxiv.org/abs/2503.15128 (2025)
92. Macko, D., Moro, R., Uchendu, A., Lucas, J., Yamashita, M., Pikuliak, M., Srba, I., Le, T., Lee, D., Simko, J., Bielikova, M.: MULTITuDE: large-scale multilingual machine-generated text detection benchmark. In: Bouamor, H., Pino, J., Bali, K. (eds.) Proceedings of the 2023 Conference on Empirical Methods in Natural Language Processing, pp. 9960–9987. Association for Computational Linguistics, Singapore (2023). https://doi.org/10.18653/v1/2023.emnlp-main.616. https://aclanthology.org/2023.emnlp-main.616/
93. Bateman, J., Jackson, D.: Countering disinformation effectively: an evidence-based policy guide (2024)
94. Ecker, U.K., Lewandowsky, S., Cook, J., Schmid, P., Fazio, L.K., Brashier, N., Kendeou, P., Vraga, E.K., Amazeen, M.A.: The psychological drivers of misinformation belief and its resistance to correction. Nat. Rev. Psychol. **1**(1), 13–29 (2022)
95. Lazer, D.M., Baum, M.A., Benkler, Y., Berinsky, A.J., Greenhill, K.M., Menczer, F., Metzger, M.J., Nyhan, B., Pennycook, G., Rothschild, D., et al.: The science of fake news. Science **359**(6380), 1094–1096 (2018)
96. Pennycook, G., Rand, D.G.: Accuracy prompts are a replicable and generalizable approach for reducing the spread of misinformation. Nat. Commun. **13**(1), 2333 (2022)
97. Roozenbeek, J., Van Der Linden, S., Goldberg, B., Rathje, S., Lewandowsky, S.: Psychological inoculation improves resilience against misinformation on social media. Sci. Adv. **8**(34), eabo6254 (2022)
98. Wardle, C., Derakhshan, H.: Information disorder: toward an interdisciplinary framework for research and policymaking, vol. 27. Council of Europe Strasbourg (2017)
99. Lewandowsky, S., Van Der Linden, S.: Countering misinformation and fake news through inoculation and prebunking. Eur. Rev. Soc. Psychol. **32**(2), 348–384 (2021)
100. Linegar, M., Sinclair, B., van der Linden, S., Alvarez, R.M.: Prebunking elections rumors: artificial intelligence assisted interventions increase confidence in American elections. arXiv preprint arXiv:2410.19202 (2024)
101. Guess, A.M., Lerner, M., Lyons, B., Montgomery, J.M., Nyhan, B., Reifler, J., Sircar, N.: A digital media literacy intervention increases discernment between mainstream and false news in the United States and India. Proc. Natl. Acad. Sci. **117**(27), 15536–15545 (2020)
102. European Digital Media Observatory: Generative AI and disinformation: white paper. Technical report. EDMO (2023). Accessed: 2025-07-22
103. Margolin, D.B., Hannak, A., Weber, I.: Political fact-checking on Twitter: when do corrections have an effect? Polit. Commun. **35**(2), 196–219 (2018). https://doi.org/10.1080/10584609.2017.1334018

From Fact Checking to Content Moderation: Inside a Newsroom Faced with Generative AI

Marissa Willcox, Richard Rogers, and Kamila Koronska

1 Introduction

In 2022 we embarked on an ethnographic study of 35 fact checkers and editors at one of Europe's key fact checkers institutions [25]. Using both traditional and innovative ethnographic methods, we gained insight into the practices, perspectives and attitudes towards fact checking as a field. From the granular tasks of content labelling and list making, to the everyday personal relations between this small group, over the two years we conducted the research, we came back to the office three times. We had become familiar faces in the fact checking office, not quite friends, but not strangers either. Our relationships with the fact checkers balanced professionalism and closeness, where they wanted to remain loyal to their contracts and office relationships, but also, to tell their story, to tell us about the ways they push on through a changing AI and misinformation landscape, but also, the fears for the field as a whole. In this chapter, we outline some key findings from our study and present it as an ethnographic case.

One member of our ethnographic research team is also a journalist herself, so her knowledge helped us ask the right questions in the right ways. In our three visits to the fact checking office, our research aims evolved based on the needs of the project. First, our goal was to gain an understanding of how they do their work, on the second visit, we reported back on what we found and continued to work with them to develop our findings, and for the third visit we wanted to understand how shifts from the rise of generative AI and the changes to Meta's priorities affected their roles both as journalists and fact checkers [6, 21].

M. Willcox (✉) · R. Rogers · K. Koronska
Media Studies, University of Amsterdam (UvA), Amsterdam, Netherlands
e-mail: m.g.willcox@uva.nl

M. Willcox
Media, Communications and Cultural Studies, Goldsmiths University of London, London, UK

S. Papadopoulos et al. (eds.), *Countering Disinformation in the Era of Generative AI*,
https://doi.org/10.1007/978-3-032-11782-3_3

This last point is one of great importance for our study. When we started this research, we set out to understand how fact checkers used certain tools in the work of fact checking for social media, but also for news outlets and online publications. The fact checkers we interviewed in year one of the research felt it was their job to "fight the battle of disinformation". Michael[1] (2022) explains:

> Michael: Because when we deal with these kinds of people. We feel like we are on a crusade against them. Because the more they share fake news or misleading statements, logically we are going to check them more often than other people because they share more fake news. And also because they become a known disinformation source. So it is a…
>
> Interviewer: Relationship?
>
> Michael: Yes… Well, we would say a war.
>
> Interviewer: A war? Hmm yes. So, the war is from fact checkers against spreaders of disinformation?
>
> Michael: Yeah, I guess, and I would say they benefit economically from this because some of them sell books or seminars on this stuff.

This quote emerged from an interview in the first year of our visit, which triggered our research reporting [25], where we highlight key themes that we build on in this chapter: these concern *the interplay between fact checking and journalism, relationships with social media platforms (including training AI), and the business side of fact checking*. From our third and final visit to the field site, we found a vastly different attitude among the fact checkers both towards the field, practice and everyday life of fact checking. The findings in this chapter draw mostly from our final visit. Through conducting a thematic analysis of over thirty interviews and participant observations over three days at the fact checking office in 2024, we identified three new emergent themes: *shifting attitudes training AI*, and *digital investigation.*

Our third visit to the fact checking office felt more ominous, which we reflect on here through a theoretical lens, combining recent and foundational fact checking literature to unpack the role of third-party fact checkers (and content moderators). We open with a short narrative joining together fieldnotes and reflections:

> By the time we made our third visit, something in the atmosphere had shifted. There was a coldness, subtle but undeniable, a more skeptical posture from the team maybe? From the more senior staff, a quiet reluctance to engage. It wasn't overt hostility towards us, as many of them know us and like us, it was more of a generalised fear and fatigue which hung over the room.
>
> We had spoken to the editors prior to our visit — they were keen to have us at this critical moment, where the global focus on fact checking was changing due to Generative AI. But in retrospect, with new information about changes to fact checking and shifting priorities, I wonder how much of our conversations around funding and strategic planning actually matter now? For those whose daily routines we were there to understand, how are their lives now affected by this? Some interviews had a "here we go again" energy, a polite detachment from people who had seen this kind of thing before. We noted that some fact checkers opted for Zoom interviews instead of meeting in person when we had made the journey to the office to speak in person. Perhaps, this was because the results from our first visit hadn't been published yet? The academic publishing world moves a lot slower than that of a journalist.

[1] Participant pseudonyms are used for privacy and anonymity.

> Among those we did speak to, it was mostly the junior staff, younger, less secure in their roles, who voiced the deepest frustrations. Long form pieces, once a point of pride, now seemed to be burdens, drawn out exercises with unclear payoff. The departures of several talented colleagues had clearly left scars, both emotional and structural. Those who remained described the newsroom as thinner, quieter, less inspired.
>
> And yet, here and there, energy flickered, usually from people on their way out. The ones who were transitioning to something else, something better, often spoke with clarity and sharpness. They had found their arc within the system and were now stepping away with a degree of closure. But for many still in place, the sentiment felt heavy, even resigned. There was a kind of "last days of Rome" ambiance lingering in the room, a decrescendo that contrasted starkly with the brisk, sometimes manic energy of the editors upstairs talking a big game about "digital investigations" and the buzz of the newsroom that lay just beyond their walls.

This opening narrative sets the tone for the paper. We found our visits to the fact checking office both informational, enjoyable and at times, contradictory. Many of the things we set out looking to explore, led us down disappointing or futile paths. For example, rather than ask all of the fact checkers to walk us through their step by step tool use, we instead found the most interesting information lay in what tools they *didn't* use, how OpenAI was not so frightening, and which everyday processes were the most important but so easily overlooked (e.g., the X dashboard, the lists of handles they follow, and the morning news briefings as a team). We were often surprised by the directions the research led us (or didn't) based on fact checker experiences and the stories they decided to share.

Much like in Westlund et al.'s study, we also found that "fact checking must be approached as a sociotechnical and problem-solving-oriented practice" [34, p. 898]. Researching this problem-solving practice, they argue "means exploring the interplay between human fact checkers and diverse sets of technologies, concerning how (a) they relate to misinformation problems, (b) technology shapes the conditions for their work, and (c) they make priorities for their fact checking practices" [34, p. 899]. Building on these explorations, we examine how recent changes in the fact checking landscape have influenced fact checkers' attitudes toward their work. As problem solving becomes secondary to their own survival, so too does their determination to maintain a commitment to combating misinformation.

2 Fact Checking as a Practice: Mapping the Moment

Fact checking as a formalised practice has evolved significantly since its inception in the early twentieth century [15]. Initially developed as an internal verification process within journalistic organisations, fact checking has expanded to include independent organisations dedicated specifically to verifying claims in public discourse [1, 17]. The digital transformation of the media landscape has further accelerated the development of fact checking initiatives, with the emergence of specialised bureaus focused on combating online misinformation [15, 26].

Recent research has documented the professionalisation of fact checking, examining the methodologies, organizational structures, and ethical frameworks that guide these practices [1, 15]. Studies have highlighted the complex decision-making processes involved in selecting which claims to investigate [16], the verification techniques employed [7], and the challenges fact checkers face in effectively communicating their findings to the public [31].The relationship between fact checking organisations and social media platforms has also been a focus of scholarly attention. Research has examined the collaborative arrangements through which fact checkers work with platforms to identify and address misinformation [16], as well as the tensions and limitations inherent in these partnerships [4, 22].

While research shows that fact checking can reduce belief in misinformation and increase transparency in information environments [31], its effectiveness is often limited by partisan motivated reasoning, and has shown greater success in moderating political discourse than debunking social media content [20]. The industry's development has, until now, been closely tied to social media platforms that outsource content moderation to third-party fact checkers, with Meta's Third-Party Fact Checking program representing the most significant initiative. Platforms such as YouTube and TikTok also collaborate with fact checkers for election-related content governance, while X has largely removed fact checking practices to instead opt for community-based fact checking [21]. In the recent period, however, large industry shifts and public debates have resulted in a major loss of funding from Meta for fact checking. As quoted from their website:

> In many countries and regions, we work with independent third-party fact checking organisations who are certified through the non-partisan International Fact Checking Network (IFCN) or European Fact Checking Standards Network (EFCSN) to identify, review and take action on this content. In the United States we have a community-based program called Community Notes. We are beginning with rolling out Community Notes in the US and will continue to improve it over the course of the year before expansion to other countries [12].

When news broke that Meta was starting to defund its third-party fact checking partnerships, it felt less like a policy tweak and more like a cultural unraveling, a turn away from tried and tested institutional verification [28]. While this was largely not the sentiment felt at the newsroom and fact checking office we visited, the solution that has been broadly taken up by the public is the idea of replacing professional fact checkers with "Community Notes," a volunteer-driven system modeled on Elon Musk's version on X (and Twitter's Birdwatch that came before it). In Chuai et al.'s large-scale study on Community Notes [10], however, they asked whether in its roll out to users in the US, engagement with misinformation on Twitter/X was reduced, measured by the metrics of retweet and like volume. They found that:

> While the Community Notes feature has garnered considerable attention lately, it still remains unclear whether it is an effective tool in reducing engagement with misinformation among actual users on the social media platform. (...) The time delay until a Community Note becomes visible may be too long to effectively reduce engagement with misinformation in the early (and most viral) stage of the diffusion. [10, p. 6]

An important point also raised in their study, which we illustrate in our research, is a concern about the efficacy of the "'wisdom of the crowd' as a countermeasure against misinformation on social media platforms" [10, p. 27]. Rather than employ professional fact checkers to conduct research and investigation into misinformation, the crowdsourced style of fact checking via Community Notes makes every fact check something which needs to be verified by a set of community members, rather than an observer or expert.

Meta's language during this period has also echoed a broader tech-world shift away from institutional trust. As widely reported, this was Meta's return to "free speech" [2] and a defunding of established organisations combatting misinformation and its mass virality.

Inside the fact checking community, the reaction to this shift has been critical and emotional. Angie Drobnic Holan of the International Fact Checking Network accused Meta of caving to political pressures, calling the decision a calculated gesture toward the incoming Trump administration. Noel Curran, the Director of the European Broadcasting Union, emphasised the crucial role of public service media and fact checkers, stating:

> Public service media are not the sole guardians of truth, but I believe their role is becoming more and more important. Across Europe, public service media rank as the most trusted sources of news in 91% of countries. They continue to be the biggest investors on the continent in quality news and current affairs [and] employ over 45,000 journalists [35].

Scholars have warned for years that the dismantling of professional verification infrastructures threatens democratic discourse. Wardle and Derakhshan [32] emphasised the role of "information disorder" in weakening civic trust. Tandoc et al. [27] also highlight the irreplaceable function of trained fact checkers in mitigating misinformation on digital platforms.

One significant concern surrounding the major defunding of fact checking could be attributed to the emergence and popularity of LLMs in user generated content creation [5]. Since LLMs can produce human-like text that is increasingly difficult to distinguish from content written by humans, there has of course been concerns about their potential to generate more convincing misinformation at scale [9, 33]. AI-generated images and videos were a particular focus and problem for the fact checkers on our final visit, as the use of image and video generators by disinformation spreaders becomes more prolific, so does the need to understand how to replicate the images and videos in order to check and verify them. One fact checker even told us they were excited about fact checking AI images and topics. Michael (2024) who we spoke to in both year 1 and year 2 of our field site visits said:

> You feel like you're exploring new ground. And even me, at first, I was kind of skeptical about AI in the media. I was like, we are talking way too much about it, like it's a revolution and stuff. And then I saw from the protest story a fake image and was surprised how realistic it was already, and I found it scary, but stimulating as well.

As these technologies become more sophisticated and accessible, professional fact checkers who serve as critical intermediaries in verifying information across digital platforms, find themselves at the "frontlines" of these developments, but at the same time, are not hugely worried about the actual impacts of generative AI on the field of disinformation. As many feel they "have it covered". A fact checking editor in our third visit in late 2024 told us in an interview that:

> Emma: Even though there was a big fear maybe around it last year, or even beginning of 2024, it's not largely changed the way we do things.
>
> Interviewer: Yes. That's interesting, because I think there is a generalised fear in the public around it now…
>
> Emma: So far, it's not. We are not seeing as big of an explosion of disinformation as we thought.

While research has examined the technical capabilities and limitations of LLMs [3, 5] and the broader societal implications of AI-generated misinformation [13], comparatively little attention has been paid to how professional fact checkers are experiencing and responding to these technological shifts in their daily work. This research gap is noted, as these professionals possess unique insights into the practical challenges of identifying and addressing AI-generated misinformation within established fact checking infrastructures.

3 Methodology: Fact Checkers' Personal Narratives and Professional Practices During the Rise of LLMs

Rather than outline the inner workings of fact checking as a practice in this chapter, as we did previously [25], we instead present the findings from our ethnographic investigation of fact checkers working at a key fact checking bureau during the rise of LLM use.

Through participant observation and in-depth interviews, we documented the personal narratives and professional practices of 35 fact checkers as they navigate an evolving information landscape increasingly shaped by AI technologies. Qualitative ethnographic methods were used for their ability to capture the lived experiences, tacit knowledge, and sociocultural contexts of participants [18, 24]. This approach allowed us to document not only what fact checkers were doing in response to AI-generated content, but also how they understood and made meaning out of these activities within their professional context.

The research design involved three primary data collection methods: participant observation, focus groups and semi-structured interviews. These complementary approaches provided both observational data on fact checking practices and reflective accounts from participants. Most of the data we work with here is from interview transcripts, but being physically present in the fact checking office gave us an inside look into their worlds, which inevitably shaped the way we analysed their words. We also employed feedback sessions in various visits over the 2 years.

The research was conducted at a major fact checking bureau that holds contracts with multiple social media platforms to verify content flagged as potentially misleading. It also functions as a fact checking unit for a European news outlet.

The bureau employs fact checkers with diverse backgrounds in journalism, research, and subject matter expertise. Some of these fact checkers are on temporary, short contracts, some work as editors on permanent contracts, and some work in other countries at satellite fact checking offices or from home. The organisation was selected based on its significant role in the fact checking ecosystem, its established relationships with major platforms, and its early exposure to AI related challenges in content verification.

Participants included fact checkers and editors with experience ranging from 0 to 20 years in the professional fact checking field. The sample included fact checkers working across different content areas (politics, health, science, and general misinformation) and with varying levels of technical expertise related to AI systems. All participants had experience working with automated flagging systems provided by social media platforms and had received some basic training in fact checking and tool use.

In addition to participant observation, we conducted semi-structured interviews with all participants [14]. Some participants we were able to interview two or three times over the multiple visits, some we were only able to interview once due to them moving on to new roles. No one withdrew their participation from the study. Interviews lasted between 30 and 90 minutes. We worked from the fact checking office for three days each visit and offered interviews to anyone who was interested while we were on site, as well as Zoom interviews for those unable to meet us in person.

The analysis of our interviews and observations followed an iterative, thematic approach [9] to identify patterns of meaning across the dataset. Interview transcripts and field notes were coded manually, beginning with open coding to identify initial concepts and categories. This was followed by thematic coding [8] to explore relationships between categories and selective coding to integrate these into coherent themes.

Throughout the analysis, we paid particular attention to participants' descriptions of their experiences with AI technologies, the language they used to characterise these experiences, and the practical strategies they employed in their fact checking work. The analysis was guided by a focus on personal experience and the telling of individual stories, rather than trying to extrapolate major themes which can be representative for all fact checkers in the field. This analysis speaks only to our field site, as a small case study, which can however be understood for its unique and interesting thematic relations.

We have paid special attention to the potential commercial and security implications of exposing the name of the newsroom and the names of the fact checkers due to funding needs as discussed in our upcoming article [25]. Therefore, names are anonymised and some words in quotes have been adjusted to protect privacy.

Shifting Attitudes

During our multiple visits to the fieldwork site, participants described a significant shift in their attitudes towards the flagging systems provided by social media platforms, as well as the role of their work in the broader sphere of journalistic practices like fact checking. The particular platform of focus where we noticed a shift in attitudes was Facebook, and second, TikTok. Fact checkers described a complex relationship with these platforms, acknowledging both their utility and limitations to their work. Many participants noted that the Facebook queue (the Meta-run system which pushes them content to label and check) in year one of our visit was "drying up" and seemed apprehensive. In year two, however, they seemed to look kindlier towards Facebook as well as its queue compared to the work they were doing for TikTok which they described as more "tedious". They could choose stories to work on from among those presented by Facebook queue whereas TikTok just presented them with a list of videos to research (and ultimately label rather than write a fact check story). While the queue has always been criticised, after being introduced to the TikTok work, they realised the Facebook queue was "not that bad". Violette (2024), a senior fact checker explains:

> We are part of the third fact checking program from Meta. That's why on Facebook, we can see directly the impact when we write something, a post on Facebook. Sometimes we get some feedback from the post author, who is not very happy. Or sometimes they're grateful because they didn't know it was misinformation, and they are thankful, but, well, it's not like that most of the time. Let's be honest it only happens sometimes.

Another fact checker, Francis (2024), who also works on TikTok content moderation says:

> Funding will be worse and worse in the future. Because now Meta pays us. I don't know how much. I don't have any idea of the numbers. But Meta pays us. But year after year, they try to reduce the amount. TikTok pays us, but not as much, and they are both on the same path and eventually, well... I don't know.

This shift in attitudes resembles what Vinhas and Bastos [30, 23] show that fact checkers are pressured to produce content quickly to meet platform expectations and that platforms use "hidden mechanisms" to influence what gets checked. These developments shift fact checking away from its original goals of transparency and accountability.

Contrary to these findings, however, in the last visit to our field site, the fact checkers had quite the change in attitude, whereby work on Facebook was considered "fact checking" and work with TikTok was considered "content moderation". The fact checkers who spent a lot of time doing TikTok work knew this was required to receive funding for the fact checking organisation, but they expressed more general dissatisfaction than those who did not do content labelling work on TikTok. The juxtaposition here is clear from an interview with a fact checker whom we spoke to in year 1 and 2 of the project. We asked whether she would like to work with TikTok like the other fact checkers on another part of the team and she said:

> Jane: No. Because I think it's not really… I think it's a bit annoying to do this. I understand we have to because we need money. But what for… If we monitor this stuff, then it's for another company. It's not even trying to help, or it doesn't really inform the public about being careful, this is a fake, or here are the facts if you want to read them. At least this has meaning to me when I do this. But fact checking fake videos for a private company who just wants a yes or no answer, I don't see a lot of meaning. Plus, it's really a small investigation on sometimes stupid videos. Yes, it's not really that interesting.
>
> Interviewer: Do you feel like that sort of work is not really fact checking, or what? What would it be…?
>
> Jane: It's micro fact checking.

Another fact checker who also did not work with TikTok validated this claim from Jane. She said:

> Yes, it's not the most interesting. So, I guess we would do it if we have to and if it's part of the job, there's no problem. But personally, I know I wouldn't be really interested in this. If I can be honest, maybe it can have one advantage, which is to give you ideas of some topics that maybe you haven't seen in your monitoring, but which can be highlighted by the TikTok team, maybe you find a video you haven't seen. It can be interesting to do a fact check about topical issues on social media and these often come up on Tiktok first. So, this is the only advantage I see, then it could lead you back to Facebook where you can write a check about it.

Surprisingly, this attitude of TikTok being "micro fact checking" and "not satisfying" provided an outlet for recent upset across the office, due to enhanced and targeted critique from a labor union which released a report criticising the funding relationships of the fact checkers at the bureau, and their "nonpartisan" connections to a third party such as Meta and TikTok. These shifting loyalties and attitudes were shadowed by this sense of impending doom and fear, as noted in our opening narrative.

Alea (2024), whom we spoke to in year 1 and year 2 of the fieldwork gave us an interesting outlook on this shift due to the increasing work on TikTok. They said:

> Alea: And it definitely, maybe, wore out some people, in the sense that they felt like doing only TikTok reviews or social media stuff all day could take over a little bit in their journalistic work, and empty or lessen their purpose in the fact checking service.
>
> Interviewer: Totally. There was definitely, I think, that sentiment with some other people we spoke to as well.
>
> Alea: And I think that journalists and fact checkers have expressed that that was draining them a little bit...I know some people said at some point, I'm going, I don't like going to work anymore. I don't think it was only related to that. I think it was also related to some management issues. But I do think it definitely contributed to the fact that people felt like there was no point, and they weren't doing something very interesting or challenging or meaningful. I think it definitely played out that way due to the TikTok work.

Alea's interview was illuminating, showing us how work for Facebook involved a publishing and exploratory fact checking element which allowed fact checkers to research and release a story and publish it on their own organisation's website. This amounted to what they considered a "journalistic practice" as opposed to TikTok which was not fact checking, but rather just "labelling".

One of the reasons for this shift in attitude away from TikTok work and towards work on Facebook could be the stronger connection to Meta that this organization feels due to its large amount of funding from Meta at the time, and communication of the higher ups with the Meta advisory board. They feel more like "stakeholders" in their work with Meta rather than content moderators. Vinhas and Bastos [30] found the discontent with their work came from when "the fact checkers are not included as stakeholders despite their central work in content moderation. The partnership is therefore not particularly transparent with regard to content removal measures" (p. 15). In summary, working as content moderators part of the time and "fact checkers" with other platform contracts left our interviewees feeling like their journalistic trade wasn't being respected. Their lack of influence on public discussion due to not knowing the impact of their moderation work on TikTok left them feeling "burnt out and hopeless" (Alea, 2024).

Interestingly, one of the major shifts in attitudes was the fact checkers' relationship with Meta changing from critical in 2022, to desperate in 2024. The largest third party contract the fact checking bureau holds is with Meta, and with more and more talk of open sourced digital investigation, Community Notes and funding losses, the threat to fact checking somehow made Mark Zuckerberg the unlikely face of fact checking. As Jeffrey, the director of the fact checking bureau and senior management in the news outlet describes:

> Jeffrey: Yes. I think if one day Zuckerberg were to say, we don't need these guys (the fact checking organization) anymore, it will be a huge slaughter in the fact checking community. Because everyone… Maybe there are a few exceptions, but it will be a slaughter.
>
> Interviewer: So is Mark Zuckerberg the unlikely face of fact checking then?
>
> Jeffrey: Yes! And honestly, not everything is perfect in our partnership with them, but at least they're financing everyone to do some journalism. And you have an impact, because you attach the fact check to the publication and it demotes the post.

Training AI

Participants described being increasingly involved in the training and refinement of AI systems used by social media platforms. This included providing feedback on flagged content, rating the accuracy of AI-driven assessments, and receiving training by platforms. As one of the more experienced fact checkers described when asked about the specific training they were offered by platforms for working with their flagging systems they said:

> Interviewer: Do you find those trainings useful?
>
> Jane: No, not really.
>
> Interviewer: No. Okay, do they teach you any new tools or anything or…?
>
> Jane: Sometimes. Not really tools more like the system changes… I don't like the concept of being told by the client how to do things. And we are independent journalists, so if I can take some pieces of advice from them, why not sure? But I don't remember anything really interesting coming from these sessions.

This involvement in AI training created a sense of dual responsibility among fact checkers; they were working not only to address specific instances of misinformation but also to improve the systems that would shape future fact checking work. They found this to be dissatisfying across the board, but one of the bigger and more interesting fears that came up in our second visit to the field site is highlighted in our interview with Michael who says:

> Interviewer: It sounds like from this story, that some of your key ways of debunking AI generated content is to try and replicate it?
>
> Michael: Yes, which is an issue in itself.
>
> Interviewer: Well yes, it's interesting. Why do you think it's an issue?
>
> Michael: Because by doing it and testing out how to make the fake image, you are training the system to be better.
>
> Interviewer: Ah yes. So, it's funny how… how do the fact checkers feel about that?
>
> Michael: Well, in the case of the (redacted title), I guess it was okay, because there were no political issues. But for Israel we tried once to use prompts to generate Israeli camps to do another fact check. And plus, I made the mistake of doing it on a public channel with our organization's name, so it could have been a big issue. So, then we had another private channel to do this. But, yes, that's why it's best if we can find the original picture without having to generate some prompts.
>
> Interviewer: And you first try to find the original. If you can't, then you try to generate it to see?
>
> Michael: It's a last resort.

Further than not liking to be told how to do their work with flagging systems, there is also a tension between fact checking AI-generated content and feeling like they are "training the AI to be better". This highlights the commonly felt misconception in research on automated fact checking, reviewed by Dierickx et al., [11] in their literature review, where they found that the idea of automation and AI as "helping" fact checkers is a largely unfounded claim, due to the commonly misled idea that human-technological interaction is an equal and unbiased, smooth relation. This relationship between humans and technology in reality is flawed and non-linear; the notion that a human fact checker will naturally become faster and more efficient with AI is misguided.

As Dierickx et al. [11, p. 5178] find, most research on automated fact checking tools prioritises technical solutions over incorporating end-user perspectives which skews the results due to neglect of the needs of journalist fact checkers who work in newsrooms. Issues arise in these instances because systems must also be adapted to the complexity of the newsroom's workflows, which they are not, and instead, these systems treat journalist fact checkers like content moderators. Where the multiplication of information channels and quick labelling is required to speed up the processes and provide content warning tags, there is a loss of storytelling, exploration, verification, team-based investigation and expert discussion, which are key tenets to the practice of fact checking.

Other than fact checkers expressing discontent at the work of having to do content moderation, their critique of the changes in their roles due to advancements in AI also stems from a deep-rooted belief that content labelling is not inherently journalistic. As Alea (who recently left the team) tries to explain:

> Alea: I think that they have a really good point in that, and I've always wondered why we had to do a TikTok deal that way? In the sense that it is true that writing only a few sentences to say after a few quick Google searches, or a call to someone or whatever, and just writing something in the little blank space that we are allowed and then sending it, and never hearing about it again. Or not knowing at all what TikTok uses it for, or whether it's even useful. I think I agree that it's more like content moderation and AI training than it would be journalism. It's journalistic in the way that we inquire, we research, we apply journalistic principles to the way that we answer the question. But I don't think it's journalism in the sense that journalism has a publishing aspect, and the publishing aspect is lacking in this instance.

The feeling that Alea is describing shows how content moderation to them is not only a way of training AI, but it also takes away the journalistic element which involves publishing, investigation and a release of information to the public. Labelling content for a private platform and not knowing what happens to that labelled content takes the agency away from journalistic work. Many interviewees expressed this attitude towards content moderation—that it was not journalistic. Though they recognised the pragmatism needed to continue to fund their work and their fact checking unit, they felt a lack of purpose when doing this work. As Vinhas and Bastos note "this fundamentally asymmetric relationship with social platforms compels fact checkers to contend with tradeoffs in their traditional methods and publication strategies, a source of conflict that impinges on the core democratic values of fact checking and its commitment toward improving public reasoning" [30, p. 2678]. This asymmetrical relationship is one which comes out repeatedly in our analysis of the interviews.

This asymmetry prompts thoughts about renewing practices of fact checking. As a more senior fact checker Nial, noted "*What I believe is that we need to have a broader understanding of what fact checking is in terms of what type of topics we want to cover (...) And we need to give information to the readers. We're going back to what journalism is, basically giving information to the reader. This is what the root of it is.*" This constant draw by the fact checkers to "return to journalism" signifies a larger distrust in the training of AI systems, and a strong affiliation with core journalistic practices. It is something they often say is missing from current practices of content moderation and labelling, noted as necessary for the business side of fact checking, but not as beneficial for the reader or the fact checker.

Towards Digital Investigation

In the first year of our visit to the fact checking office, there was a generalised pushback on the fact checker's work being considered OSINT (Open Source Intelligence). As fact checker Amelia (2022) told us, "*I understand, we have to do like the daily routine job, which is mainly about debunking images and stuff, and it's not supposed to be the whole job, we are not like OSINT people and so on*". However, this was before the rise of AI-generated content in the misinformation landscape, and before the mass funding loss to fact checking from Meta. Jeffrey (2024) who holds a position as a director for the fact checking department explains how the roles of digital investigation and fact checking are based in similar principles, yet different in practice:

> Because you want to check something, you want to verify, you want to investigate, you want to investigate on the digital ground. So for example, I'm thinking about Bellingcat, they're using all the skills of the fact checkers, but they don't do any kind of fact check. They're investigating war crimes or whatever. But really these are the same rules we are playing. So this is the idea to say, what we're developing in terms of skill, it's similar to digital investigation, but it's not the same.
>
> For example, we had someone in the Middle East that has done a lot of work in order to verify the crazy amount of videos coming in from Gaza, there was a lot of things to verify, but with fact checking methods, geolocation or whatever as well as some OSINT, but this is all a part of the fact checking.

In contrast to our first visit, where OSINT was seen as distant from fact checking (Amelia, 2022), in our final visit to the fact checking office, the participants expressed a general understanding that their work would be subsumed under a digital investigation unit, where they understood their skills could be maximised (and more broadly funded). Digital forensics and OSINT complement each other in cyber investigations (often together called digital investigation), with forensics providing deep system-level evidence and OSINT offering contextual insights from publicly accessible sources [29]. For the context of our work and the themes which came up repeatedly in the final visit to the fact checking office, digital investigation and OSINT were hailed as a "saving grace" for the office in regards to funding. This was also echoed by those in management and leadership roles who believed rebranding as a digital investigation unit might warrant future funding and more jobs to be created due to the decrease of funding from other third-party contracts. Jeffrey (2024) explains: "*In an ideal world we will still continue to do some fact checks, because I think it's relevant, but we would now have a lot more journalists on OSINT than we would before, there's more interest in it.*"

One of the reasons digital investigation and the mention of Bellingcat came up repeatedly in our 2024 visit owes to the increased interest by the fact checkers across the newsroom in OSINT technologies. Jeffrey in our 2024 interview says "*among our fact checks we are doing within the partnership with [redacted], there's a lot of OSINT, and sometimes very, I'd say, interesting OSINT. It's not like there was no OSINT at all before, but when you're talking to fact checkers, and asking them what do you want to do? It's OSINT, most of the time now. Not just because it's new but because there's a future there, and respect*". Later in the interview he also references another news outlet which operates as a competitor. He says they used to be the "*best in the business*" of fact checking but have now dropped the focus on third-party fact checking and completely switched to digital investigation and OSINT.

As Eliot Higgins writes in his book, *We are Bellingcat: An intelligence agency for the people,* "fact checking never has solved the problem. A partner organization might complete say 200 fact checks per year in response to specific cases. Each demands considerable effort - perhaps days of research to rightly justify evidence" [19, p. 124]. By this, Higgins notes that OSINT with its open source, easy to operate, tool-based and crowd-sourced approach to investigating public debate and misinformation, is often seen as the "next step" beyond fact checking. This comment would get a lot of critique from the fact checking professionals we spoke to, as OSINT is often something used by fact checkers, but does not replace the role of fact checking. As Jeffrey (2024) says "*we're not Bellingcat, we won't do the same things, but it's really close to a lot of what we do.*"

The emergence and popularity of digital investigation arose as a direct response to the inadequacies of traditional content moderation systems on social media platforms. As Higgins [19] describes Bellingcat as "an intelligence agency for the people", OSINT initiatives have tried to fill a critical gap where conventional fact checking and content verification processes have not entirely addressed the scale and complexity of misinformation. The democratisation of verification tools reflects Higgins' philosophy that "if anyone with a smartphone can publish, they should also be able to verify" [19]. However, as Jeffrey highlights, it is not that simple and often requires human-centered interpretation of content within certain contexts and political moments:

> And the thing is, who can qualify this information? A journalist. Not because this is difficult, but because we have the knowledge. I'm not saying we're like a doctor that has had ten years of study to do something very tricky. But that's the problem, we are sometimes seen as non-experts, when really it's our job. But in an ideal world, no more content moderation for us, because this is not really…well it's not really journalism. The aim of journalism is to be published, and try to have an impact. So, yes, I think digital investigation and fact checking we would be able to mix that very well together funding wise. I don't know, just like 50% of the team on fact checking, 50% of the team on the OSINT investigations. That would be ideal.

Our interview with Jeffrey in 2024 was one of the richer interviews to which we paid particular attention in our analysis due to his shift in roles and also his mounting knowledge of "the business of fact checking". It had changed over the years towards being closely associated with content moderation, and now with digital investigation.

Is third party fact checking under threat, we continued to ask? Looking at all the interviews, the underlying atmosphere was that the future of information verification lies in the synergistic relationship between digital investigation and traditional fact checking, where each approach amplifies the strengths of the other in addressing contemporary misinformation challenges. Generally shifting away from content moderation, this convergent strength between traditional journalism and OSINT offers some promise in addressing the scale and complexity of contemporary information warfare in that hybrid verification ecosystems and generative AI can enable citizen investigators, professional journalists, and fact checkers to collaborate across institutional boundaries to strengthen democratic discourse and accountability.

4 Conclusion: Fact Checking After AI Generative

In this ethnographic study we have provided insights into how professional fact checkers at a major bureau are experiencing and responding to the emergence of generative AI technologies and the shift towards digital investigation to account for shifting priorities from Meta and other funders. By documenting fact checkers' personal narratives and professional practices, we have illuminated the complex ways in which fact checkers are adapting to the current climate or are calling out issues with the third-party fact checking system as it stands. We identified three key themes through our analysis of interview and focus group data from our field site visits: *shifting attitudes, training AI, and towards digital investigation.*

Our findings reveal that fact checkers are active participants in the implementation and evolution of AI technologies in their field, developing specialised expertise and adapting their verification practices to incorporate new tools. At the same time, these technologies are reshaping fact checking work, introducing new verification steps and changing how potential misinformation is identified. The interviewees expressed general dissatisfaction at having to "moderate content" instead of "fact check" and their relationship to generative AI should be seen as not just a funding problem, but a fundamental challenge to the institutional role of professional verification in democratic discourse.

A particularly noteworthy finding is the gap between fact checkers' anticipation of AI-generated misinformation and their actual experiences thus far, highlighting the importance of distinguishing between technological potential and actual implementation in real-world contexts.

These findings contribute to our understanding of the sociotechnical dynamics shaping contemporary approaches to misinformation management and offer insights that can inform how we view the human technological relationship in fact checking spaces.

Acknowledgements This research was supported by the European Union under the Horizon Europe vera.ai project, Grant Agreement number 101070093.

References

1. Amazeen, M.A.: Journalistic interventions: the structural factors affecting the global emergence of fact-checking. Journalism **21**(1), 95–111 (2020)
2. BBC News: Meta ends fact-checking programme and will rely on users. BBC, 7 Jan 2025. https://www.bbc.co.uk/news/articles/cly74mpy8klo
3. Bender, E.M., Gebru, T., McMillan-Major, A., Shmitchell, S.: On the dangers of stochastic parrots: can language models be too big? In: Proceedings of the 2021 ACM conference on Fairness, Accountability, and Transparency, pp. 610–623 (2021)
4. Bélair-Gagnon, V., Larsen, R., Graves, L., Westlund, O.: Knowledge work in platform fact-checking partnerships. Int. J. Commun. **17**, 1169–1189 (2023)

5. Bommasani, R., Hudson, D.A., Adeli, E., et al.: On the opportunities and risks of foundation models. arXiv preprint arXiv:2108.07258 (2021)
6. Booth, R.: Ditching of Facebook factcheckers a 'major step back' for public discourse, critics say. The Guardian, 7 Jan 2025. https://www.theguardian.com/technology/2025/jan/07/ditching-facebook-factcheckers-major-step-back-public-discourse
7. Brandtzaeg, P.B., Følstad, A., Chaparro Domínguez, M.Á.: How journalists and social media users perceive online fact-checking and verification services. J. Pract. **12**(9), 1109–1129 (2018)
8. Braun, V., Clarke, V.: Using thematic analysis in psychology. Qual. Res. Psychol. **3**(2), 77–101 (2006)
9. Buchanan, B., Lohn, A., Musser, M., Sedova, K.: Truth, Lies, and Automation: How Language Models Could Change Disinformation. Center for Security and Emerging Technology (2021)
10. Chuai, Y., Tian, H., Pröllochs, N., Lenzini, G.: Did the roll-out of community notes reduce engagement with misinformation on X/formerly Twitter? Proc. ACM Hum. Comput. Interact. **8**(CSCW2), Article 428 (2024)
11. Dierickx, L., Lindén, C. G., & Opdahl, A. L: Automated fact-checking to support professional practices: systematic literature review and meta-analysis. International Journal of Communication. **17**(21), 5179-5190 (2023)
12. Facebook: About Third-Party Fact-Checkers on Facebook. Facebook Business Help Center (n.d.). https://www.facebook.com/business/help/2593586717571940?id=673052479947730
13. Ferrara, E.: What types of COVID-19 conspiracies are populated by Twitter bots? First Monday, vol. 25, no. 6. arXiv preprint arXiv:2004.09531 (2020)
14. Galletta, A.: Mastering the Semi-structured Interview and Beyond: From Research Design to Analysis and Publication. NYU Press (2013)
15. Graves, L.: Deciding What's True: The Rise of Political Fact-Checking in American Journalism. Columbia University Press (2016)
16. Graves, L.: Anatomy of a fact check: objective practice and the contested epistemology of fact checking. Commun Cult Crit. **10**(3), 518–537 (2017)
17. Graves, L., Cherubini, F.: The rise of fact-checking sites in Europe (Reuters Institute digital news report). Reuters Institute for the Study of Journalism (2016)
18. Hammersley, M., Atkinson, P.: Ethnography: Principles in Practice. Routledge (2019)
19. Higgins, E.: We Are Bellingcat: An Intelligence Agency for the People. Bloomsbury Publishing (2021)
20. Jennings, J., Stroud, N.J.: Asymmetric adjustment: partisanship and correcting misinformation on Facebook. New Media Soc. **25**(7), 1501–1521 (2021)
21. Kaplan, J.: More speech and fewer mistakes. Meta, 7 Jan 2025. https://about.fb.com/news/2025/01/meta-more-speech-fewer-mistakes/
22. Matasick, C., Alfonsi, C., Bellantoni, A., et al.: Governance Responses to Disinformation: How Open Government Principles Can Inform Policy Option. OECD Publishing, Paris (2020)
23. Nissen, I.A., Walter, J.G., Charquero-Ballester, M., Bechmann, A.: Digital infrastructures of COVID-19 misinformation: a new conceptual and analytical perspective on fact-checking. Digit. J. **10**(5), 738–760 (2022)
24. Pelto, P.J.: Mixed Methods in Ethnographic Research: Historical Perspectives. Routledge (2017)
25. Rogers, R., Willcox, M., Koronska, K.: Social media fact checking: inside the newsroom. Social Media + Society. (2026) (submitted)
26. Singer, J.B.: Fact-checkers as entrepreneurs: scalability and sustainability for a new form of watchdog journalism. J. Pract. **12**(8), 1070–1080 (2018)
27. Tandoc, E., Huang, A., Duffy, A., et al.: To share is to receive: news as social currency for social media reciprocity. J. Appl. J. Media Stud. **9**(1), 3–20 (2020)
28. Thompson, S.A.: Meta says fact-checkers were the problem. Fact-checkers rule that false. The New York Times, 7 Jan 2025. https://www.nytimes.com/2025/01/07/business/mark-zuckerberg-meta-fact-check.html
29. van der Woude, M., Dodds, T., Torres, G.: The ethics of open source investigations: navigating privacy challenges in a gray zone information landscape. Journalism (Advance online publication) (2024)

30. Vinhas, O., Bastos, M.: The WEIRD governance of fact-checking and the politics of content moderation. New Media Soc. **27**(5), 2768–2787 (2025)
31. Walter, N., Cohen, J., Holbert, R.L., Morag, Y.: Fact-checking: a meta-analysis of what works and for whom. Polit. Commun. **37**(3), 350–375 (2019)
32. Wardle, C., Derakhshan, H.: Information Disorder: Toward an Interdisciplinary Framework for Research and Policymaking. Council of Europe, Strasbourg (2017)
33. Weidinger, L., Uesato, J., Rauh, M., Griffin, C., Huang, P.S., Mellor, J., et al.: Taxonomy of risks posed by language models. In: Proceedings of the 2022 ACM Conference on Fairness, Accountability, and Transparency, pp. 214–229 (2022)
34. Westlund, O., Belair-Gagnon, V., Graves, L., Larsen, R., Steensen, S.: What is the problem with misinformation? Fact-checking as a sociotechnical and problem-solving practice. J. Stud. **25**(8), 898–918 (2024)
35. World Economic Forum: Truth at risk: defending facts in the intelligent age, Feb 2025. https://www.weforum.org/stories/2025/02/truth-at-risk-defending-facts-in-the-intelligent-age-ebu-chief/

Synthetic Seduction: Evolving Visual Persuasion in Coordinated Online Gambling Promotion with Generative AI

Fabio Giglietto, Massimo Terenzi, Anwesha Chakraborty, and Giada Marino

1 Introduction

As part of the Vera AI project's broader objective to identify and analyse coordinated networks disseminating harmful content on social media platforms, this chapter offers a focused inquiry into one specific manifestation of such coordinated activity: the promotion of online gambling through visual persuasion. While often perceived as a marginal or less harmful domain, the online gambling ecosystem presents a compelling case of algorithmically optimised manipulation, in which persuasive techniques are deployed at scale to exploit cognitive biases, emotional vulnerabilities, and socio-cultural norms [4].

Drawing upon a network of over 200 coordinated Facebook public groups identified by a global-scale implementation [18] of an existing workflow [16], we examine how gambling-related content circulates through dense and systematic posting behaviours, underpinned by a sophisticated repertoire of visual and semiotic drivers. These include familiar tropes such as aspirational wealth, gamified interfaces, and urgency-based call-to-actions, but also increasingly, synthetic visuals generated by artificial intelligence, which introduce a new aesthetic and affective register into gambling promotion.

This case study contributes to the overarching goals of the project by shedding light on the ways in which coordinated networks mobilise multi-layered persuasive architectures, blending traditional marketing logics with emergent computational techniques. In particular, we interrogate a about the role of generative AI in enhancing or transforming these visual strategies and consider its implications for user manipulation, platform governance, and regulatory frameworks.

F. Giglietto (✉) · M. Terenzi · A. Chakraborty · G. Marino
Department of Communication Sciences, Humanities and International Studies, University of Urbino Carlo Bo, Urbino, Italy
e-mail: fabio.giglietto@uniurb.it

S. Papadopoulos et al. (eds.), *Countering Disinformation in the Era of Generative AI*,
https://doi.org/10.1007/978-3-032-11782-3_4

Methodologically, the chapter adopts an innovative mixed-method approach. We leverage LLMs to produce both denotative and connotative descriptions of over 2300 images extracted from the identified network. These textual representations are subsequently transformed into vector embeddings and clustered to detect recurrent patterns. The resulting clusters are then subjected to a qualitative interpretive analysis aimed at constructing a typology of persuasive visual drivers.

The chapter proceeds as follows. We begin by situating our investigation within relevant theoretical debates concerning digital gambling promotion, coordinated influence operations, and synthetic media. We then detail the methodological pipeline developed within the Vera AI project. The empirical section presents the identified persuasive drivers, with particular attention to the integration of AI-generated content. In the discussion, we consider the broader implications of these findings for computational manipulation, attention economies, and content moderation policies. The chapter concludes with reflections on future research directions and the normative challenges posed by the increasing opacity of algorithmically mediated content of a harmful nature.

2 Theoretical Foundations

Promoting Gambling Through Digital Persuasion in Algorithmic Environments

The contemporary digital environment is increasingly defined by what scholars term the "attention economy," where human attention is the central resource extracted and monetised by platform capitalism [49]. Digital platforms do not merely serve as neutral conduits for content distribution; rather, they actively shape visibility, circulation, and impact through complex algorithmic systems [19]. These algorithmic logics fundamentally reconfigure persuasive communication by enabling new forms of strategic manipulation. In particular, algorithmic amplification creates a feedback loop in which content that elicits high engagement—regardless of its veracity or social value—is prioritised and disseminated more widely [46]. This dynamic gives rise to what has been termed "algorithmic visibility," where success is measured not by the quality or relevance of content but by its capacity to trigger platform-specific engagement mechanisms.

This shift represents a marked departure from the broadcast-era advertising model. Instead of delivering mass communication through linear channels, contemporary platforms use continuous data extraction and algorithmic optimisation to predict and influence human behaviour [57]. These systems also facilitate coordinated manipulation of information flows, enabling the strategic dissemination of content across accounts, platforms, and formats [32]. Unlike traditional propaganda with its centralised and overt messaging, digital manipulation often mimics grassroots activity, masking commercial or political agendas behind a veneer of authenticity.

The resulting "spreadability" of content [24] contributes to the illusion of organic public discourse while reinforcing platform incentives.

A particularly prominent tactic is coordinated sharing—the organised dissemination of content across networks of users, pages, and influencers to simulate grassroots consensus [15]. Unlike conventional advertising, which typically relies on identifiable branding, coordinated sharing draws on the appearance of peer-driven recommendations to promote targeted messages or behaviours. These campaigns often obscure their commercial ties and strategic objectives, making them difficult to detect [20].

This theoretical framework is especially relevant when applied to industries that target vulnerable populations or promote potentially harmful behaviours. The gambling industry, with its well-documented public health implications and sophisticated digital marketing techniques, presents a compelling case. As gambling has expanded digitally, concerns have grown about how it exploits algorithmic infrastructures to circumvent traditional regulatory safeguards and promote risky behaviours. Despite widespread recognition of the public health risks associated with online gambling [48], the industry has rapidly expanded its digital footprint [33], using platform affordances to enhance visibility and user engagement while staying within—or just beyond—the boundaries of existing regulations.

Digital gambling marketing today spans a range of strategies, from traditional promotion of betting websites to more immersive tactics such as user interaction on social media platforms [21]. Facebook and Instagram, for example, enable marketers to insert promotional material into news feeds, stories, and branded pages. Gambling is often linked with sports, entertainment, or cultural events—sometimes even through the creation of branded spectacles—blurring the lines between advertising and social content. These platforms also serve to build online communities and foster brand loyalty [14]. Particularly effective is the integration of gambling into sports fandom, where betting is framed as a natural extension of the spectator experience. Such normalisation is reinforced by metaphors that present gambling as a skill-based activity, akin to training or strategy, which obscures the central role of chance and suggests that expertise can improve outcomes [30].

Targeted marketing based on gender stereotypes is also central to these strategies. While sports betting and poker are primarily marketed to young men, games such as online bingo are more often directed at women. These campaigns frequently rely on gendered imagery and assumptions, portraying men as confident, strategic gamblers and using soft or domestic visual cues to appeal to women [7, 44]. Direct marketing tactics—such as personalised emails, targeted messages, and promotional phone calls—further tailor incentives to drive more frequent and higher-stakes betting [40]. Gambling is routinely depicted as glamorous and rewarding, with risks downplayed and betting normalised as part of everyday life and social interaction [7].

As digital platforms evolve, so do marketing tactics. Increasingly, gambling promotions are embedded within content that appears neutral or educational, making it harder—especially for younger audiences—to recognise them as advertising [41]. E-sports sponsorships, for instance, target young male gamers and help embed gambling within gaming culture [3]. Interactive tools such as polls, contests, and shareable content further enhance engagement and foster a sense of community, although their effectiveness may vary across cultural and regional contexts [29]. While responsible gambling messages are sometimes included in promotional content, they often serve as superficial gestures of corporate responsibility rather than meaningful efforts to mitigate harm [22].

Collectively, these practices disproportionately affect vulnerable groups—particularly young users and individuals with gambling problems—who are especially susceptible to the persuasive force of algorithmically amplified content [13]. The convergence of behavioural targeting, algorithmic distribution, and cultural normalisation has created a digital environment in which harmful behaviours can be promoted at scale, often bypassing regulatory safeguards designed for traditional media. This alignment of platform capitalism, algorithmic mediation, and targeted marketing represents a major shift in how industries shape public behaviour, posing urgent challenges to the adequacy of current public health and regulatory frameworks.

This concern is heightened by the growing convergence of online gambling with digital trading platforms, which similarly raise serious regulatory issues. A study conducted by the Behavioural Insights Team for the Ontario Securities Commission (OSC) examined how investment platforms use gamification to increase user engagement, often without improving long-term financial outcomes [11]. The report identified "gamblification" as a common technique to improve user engagement. The gamblification is particularly problematic, as it incorporates gambling-like mechanics into financial trading, thereby blurring the conceptual boundaries between investing and gambling. These concerns align with warnings from the U.S. Securities and Exchange Commission (SEC) [50], which noted that such features can encourage excessive trading and unsuitable investment decisions, especially among inexperienced users.

Algorithmic Circumvention of Platforms' Advertising Policies and Regulatory Gaps

The strategies outlined above reveal how digital marketing in the gambling industry systematically blurs the boundaries between advertising and organic content, complicating efforts by both platforms and regulators to mitigate gambling-related harm. Within this context, the distinction between paid and unpaid content—central to platform governance—becomes increasingly porous, particularly on Meta's platforms. Meta's advertising policies for gambling are relatively well-defined and restrictive: they require advertisers to seek prior written authorisation for promotional content involving gambling or gaming services that use monetary value as both an entry mechanism and a potential prize. Advertisers must not only obtain explicit approval but also comply with jurisdiction-specific regulations and meet Meta's criteria for audience targeting, including a minimum age threshold of 18 years [35].

However, these restrictions apply primarily to paid advertisements. Meta's policies regarding organic content related to gambling are significantly more permissive.

While the platform formally addresses gambling content in its Community Standards—specifically under the "restricted goods and services" section—it does not prohibit organic posts that promote gambling or social casino games, even when these simulate gambling mechanics using virtual currencies. Instead, Meta employs visibility restrictions, limiting such content to users aged 18 and older. Only explicitly fraudulent or scam-related content is categorically banned.

This asymmetry between paid and organic content governance results in a regulatory grey area where gambling-related material can circulate widely without triggering the oversight mechanisms applied to formal advertising. Algorithmically amplified organic content—often indistinguishable from authentic user posts—can therefore function as a powerful tool for marketing gambling services while evading formal advertising constraints. This dynamic mirrors broader patterns discussed in the previous section, where the affordances of platform architectures enable the spread of persuasive, behaviour-shaping content under the guise of peer-driven engagement.

The relative permissiveness of Meta's policies on organic gambling content opens up a critical space for investigation. It invites a closer look at the specific communicative strategies deployed to promote gambling in ways that appear native to the platform environment. These practices offer insights into how marketers exploit the platform's design and moderation logic to normalise gambling, particularly among vulnerable or high-engagement user groups. Against this backdrop, the following research question guides our inquiry:

RQ1 What are the key drivers of online gambling's organic marketing strategies on Facebook?

AI-Generated Persuasion in Gambling Promotion

The regulatory asymmetries outlined above are further compounded by the growing prevalence of AI-generated content on social media platforms. Emerging influence operations increasingly incorporate synthetic text and imagery designed to mimic organic engagement, further eroding the boundaries between genuine user expression and promotional manipulation [8]. As generative AI becomes more accessible and sophisticated, digital environments are becoming saturated with content that is not only fabricated but also strategically engineered to exploit platform logics and attract engagement at scale.

While existing research has extensively explored the marketing strategies employed by online gambling operators on social media, comparatively little attention has been paid to the deployment of AI-generated promotional materials in this domain. The broader scholarly field investigating AI-generated content for marketing purposes remains nascent, though a growing body of work has begun to trace its use in political disinformation and propaganda campaigns [52]. These studies document how generative AI is employed not just to mislead but to optimise visibility and interaction by mimicking the vernaculars and aesthetic patterns that thrive within social platforms.

Notably, DiResta and Goldstein [8] identified 120 Facebook Pages that had posted at least 50 AI-generated images each. Their analysis highlighted a dual pattern: while some content mirrored typical low-effort clickbait—such as surreal baking images with personalised captions—other examples veered into more bizarre or ideologically charged territory, including images like "Shrimp Jesus" or "Crab Jesus" [26]. These forms of synthetic media attracted massive levels of engagement and, in many cases, were linked to clickfarm operations or promotional links to fraudulent websites. Ferrara [10] has categorised the potential harms associated with such AI-generated content, identifying a broad range of risks including personal deception, financial fraud, misinformation, and sociotechnical manipulation. These tactics often rely on synthetic identities, automated messaging, and misleading visuals to bypass platform moderation while maximising virality.

Beyond empirical concerns, critical scholars have begun to explore the cultural and ideological dimensions of generative AI content. Watkins [53], for instance, has described how the "new aesthetics of fascism" can be reproduced through AI-generated visuals that are seductive in form but regressive in message. Similarly, Meyer's concept of "#PlatformRealism" captures the convergence of meme-driven fascism, neocolonial aesthetics, and influencer grift cultures within a digitally native visual vernacular. Vanicka et al. [51] contribute the notion of the "machinic gaze" to describe how generative systems participate in the reframing of cultural representation itself. These perspectives underscore that AI-generated content operates within a broader sociotechnical system—one shaped not only by platform architecture and algorithmic incentives, but also by emergent aesthetic codes and political imaginaries.

In this wider context, the application of generative AI to gambling promotion remains notably under-researched. Existing literature has largely focused on how AI is deployed within gambling platforms to personalise user experiences and increase engagement (e.g., [39]), rather than how generative AI is used externally to craft and disseminate persuasive content. However, early evidence suggests that online gambling operators have begun leveraging AI-generated imagery on Facebook to attract attention and drive traffic [31]. These developments raise important questions about how such content circulates, how it is visually and rhetorically constructed, and how it may intensify the persuasive strategies already observed in organic gambling promotion.

To address this emerging phenomenon, we propose the following research question:

RQ2 How has the advent of generative AI influenced gambling promotion in terms of (a) content volume and distribution patterns, and (b) the visual execution and intensity of established persuasion drivers?

3 Methodology

Data Gathering

The Discovery of the Network

The network of Facebook groups analysed in this Chapter was discovered through a workflow designed to monitor, detect, and iteratively update known lists of coordinated social media accounts. In this study, we specifically examine coordinated link sharing behaviour—a technique that identifies social media accounts as coordinated when they repeatedly share identical links within very short time periods [17, 55]. The iterative approach of the workflow addresses the dynamic nature of coordinated operations on social media. Rather than providing merely a detailed but static picture of account behaviour, the workflow tracks operations over time, enabling academic researchers, fact-checkers, and civil society organisations to observe how coordinated networks evolve.

The workflow begins with an initial seed list of problematic accounts identified through academic research, verified fact-checking databases, and investigative findings. The first implementation of this workflow was deployed to study the activities of known coordinated accounts leading up to the 2022 Italian election [16]. Building on this experience, the monitoring process was expanded globally, starting with a seed of 1225 coordinated and problematic Facebook public accounts (Pages or public groups). These accounts were identified because they repeatedly coordinated (time window: 14s, percentage edge weight: 0.995) to spread at least four of the 36,091 web pages flagged as false by Meta's third-party fact-checkers between 2017 and 2022 [34].

Between October 2023 and August 2024, this implementation of the workflow (subsequently referred to as "Vera AI alerts") identified 7068 coordinated posts, 10,681 coordinated links, and 2126 new coordinated accounts organised across 17 networks. The operation was discontinued on August 14, 2024, due to the deprecation of CrowdTangle.

This Chapter provides a deep dive into one of the networks discovered by the Vera AI alerts. Composed of 223 public groups, this network is specifically dedicated to sharing posts that promoted gambling activities.

Getting the Posts and Related Multimedia Content (MCL and Images MCL Downloader)

To better understand the gambling promotional strategies employed by these networks, we decided to study the visual content posted by these coordinated groups. To do so, we relied on a new tool developed by Meta with the aim of increasing the platform's transparency. The Meta Content Library (MCL) is an interactive dashboard that allows users to search a real-time public content dataset of posts circulating on Facebook, Instagram, and Threads. Among the different search features, the MCL enables users to upload and manage lists of producers (this is the name used in the tool to refer to a range of social media spaces—from individual profiles to Pages, events, and groups—where posts appear). A subset of the public content created by widely popular producers can be downloaded as a CSV file for further analysis. The CSV contains a set of variables that describe the posts and include a link to the multimedia contents (images, video, reel, etc), eventually embedded in the post.

Using these features, we created a list of producers with our 223 groups. We used this list to search for all the posts (empty query) created by these groups between 13 January 2017 and 7 September 2024. The search on the public content dataset returned over 70 million posts, but only a fraction of these (N = 10,671) met the criteria for inclusion in the downloadable datasets of popular producers (Pages with 15,000 or more likes or followers, Profiles with 25,000 or more followers, and verified Profiles). As of May 2025, at the time of writing this Chapter, among the subset of these groups that remain active, membership sizes range from a minimum of 31,808 to a maximum of 612,736, with an average membership count of approximately 200,000. These figures provide insight into the current scale and potential reach of the producers still active at the time of analysis.

To collect the images embedded in the post, we developed a custom script that automates the process of downloading the multimedia content from the links provided in a CSV obtained from the MCL [47]. The script has been carefully designed to comply with the research data agreement signed by the researchers to secure access to the MCL. The download process is performed entirely client-side on the user's browser, and only authorised users can use these links. A report is also created to preserve the relationship between original posts and the respective downloaded multimedia files.

Using these tools, we collected all 2323 distinct images embedded in the dataset of posts we downloaded from the library.

Using OpenAI's Model to Get a Connotative and Denotative Description of the Images

Automated analysis based on the extraction of features from digital images is not new [56]. However, the advent of Large Language Models capable of automatically describing images is increasingly seen as an alternative promising approach [45]. Leveraging the validation results demonstrating that VLLM-based approaches can improve semantic clustering over CNN-based methods [1], we used OpenAI's gpt-4o-2024-08-06 to generate both a denotative (literal, objective) and connotative (associated feelings, ideas, and cultural meanings) description of our dataset of images (the full prompt and an example of denotative and connotative descriptions are available in the Appendix). The results of the prompt were used without further post-processing. These types of human-AI collaborations for qualitative content analysis are becoming increasingly common in social science research [5, 6, 9]. Scholars have argued that LLMs can perform deductive qualitative coding at a level comparable to and agreeable to human researchers [5]. Large language models (LLMs) can assist in thematic analysis by replicating human-level coding quality while significantly reducing time and labour demands. In particular, LLM-in-the-loop frameworks using in-context learning have shown that models like GPT-3.5 can generate codebooks and perform interpretive tasks comparable to human coders [6]; in our study, we adopt this approach using the more advanced GPT-4o model. To ensure robustness of our analysis, a quarter (n = 85) of our identified 366 connotative and denotative clusters were coded by the four authors until thematic saturation was reached.

Data Analysis

Embedding and Clustering of the Two Sets of Descriptions

Given the final goal of identifying the main drivers used by these groups to promote gambling with visual content, we designed a clustering strategy aimed at taking into account both the connotative and denotative dimensions of the visual elements of our posts.

The strategy starts by transforming both the connotative and denotative descriptions into embeddings using OpenAI's text-embedding-3-small model. The clustering was performed separately on the denotative and connotative descriptions using the procedure described in Fig. 1.

Co-occurrence Matrix of Images Included in the Same Connotative and Denotative Clusters

To identify the most frequently employed drivers for gambling incitement, we constructed a co-occurrence matrix of images that appeared in both connotative and denotative clusters. Our premise is that specific combinations of connotative and denotative descriptions indicate images depicting a particular driver.

We ranked all 366 combinations of connotative and denotative clusters by frequency of assigned images (maximum = 87 images). We then initiated a manual content analysis process to describe the emerging gambling incentive strategies. Combinations containing noise clusters and a single combination of two noise clusters were excluded from the analysis (N = 78).

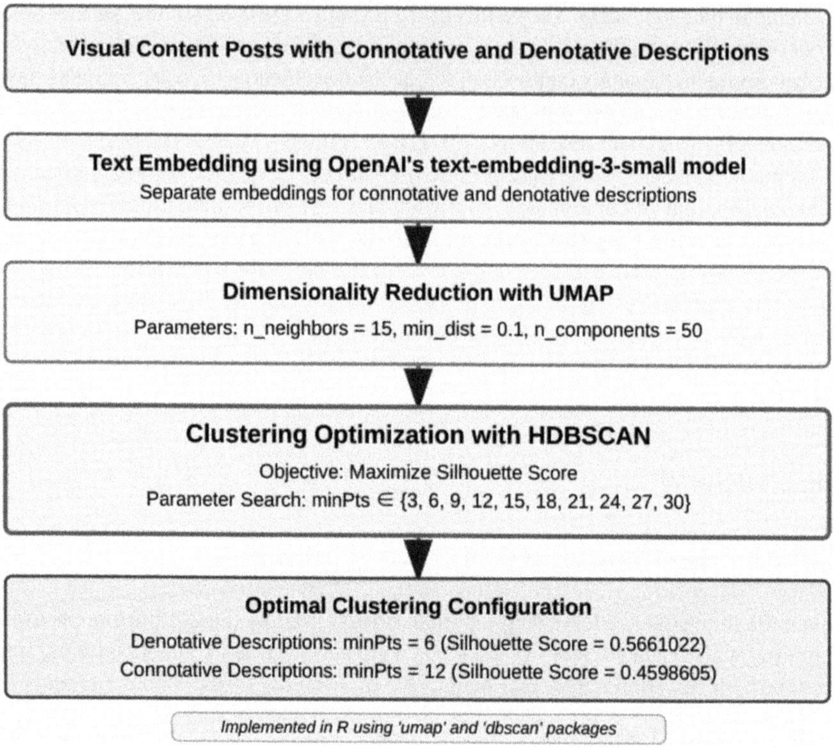

Fig. 1 The analytical workflow .The entire process was performed in R with packages UMAP and HDBSCAN. The clustering process generated 51 clusters for the connotative descriptions and 101 for the denotative descriptions. The noise cluster included 390 and 258 images, respectively

Qualitative Content Analysis of Clusters and Deductive Drivers Identification

To analyse the co-occurrence patterns and deduce the key drivers (RQ1), our team employed a systematic qualitative content analysis approach. All four authors participated in the analytical process, examining each combination of connotative and denotative clusters containing more than six images. In total, 85 such combinations were examined to reach thematic saturation.

The analysis followed an iterative coding procedure until theoretical saturation was reached for each driver, indicated by the reoccurrence of the same gambling driver across multiple combinations. This saturation point signalled that additional sampling would not yield new insights regarding the particular driver.

Each researcher independently analysed 21 cluster combinations, documenting emergent patterns and thematic elements. For each combination, coders were tasked with identifying the underlying gambling driver and formulating a concise descriptive label that captured the essence of the cluster combination.

Through consensus-building discussions, the research team consolidated their individual analyses, resolving any interpretive discrepancies to ensure analytical rigor and intercoder reliability. This collaborative approach enhanced the trustworthiness of the findings while allowing for the nuanced interpretation of visual elements that constitute gambling incentive strategies.

The resulting typology of drivers offers a framework for understanding the visual rhetoric employed to stimulate gambling behaviours across the analysed materials.

Measuring the Impact of Generative AI on Gambling Promotion Strategies

To investigate how generative AI has influenced gambling promotion (RQ2), we employed a mixed-methods approach. For examining content volume changes (RQ2a), we utilised the Meta Content Library API to collect monthly post count estimates from 223 gambling-related Facebook groups identified through the VeraAI Alerts workflow [36]. We analysed data spanning January 2017 through September 2024, with ChatGPT's launch date (November 30, 2022) as our intervention point. Statistical significance was assessed through multiple complementary approaches: two-sample hypothesis tests (t-test, Wilcoxon rank-sum), regression models with interaction terms to capture both level and slope changes, and time series analyses including structural break detection. This allowed us to quantify the magnitude and statistical significance of changes in promotional volume. For analysing how persuasion drivers were executed in AI-generated content (RQ2b), we conducted a qualitative analysis of visual content before and after ChatGPT's introduction. We examined a subset of 2323 images embedded in posts, focusing specifically on how the persuasion drivers identified in RQ1 were being visually rendered in probable AI-generated content. We noted a thematic saturation in the narrative elements of the AI-generated images, as observable in the most viewed posts in the post-ChatGPT period. We analysed elements such as visual style, image composition, colour schemes, character representation, and narrative complexity to determine how generative AI technologies have intensified or transformed the presentation of established persuasion tactics rather than creating entirely new strategies. The top two most viewed such images—which are emblematic of AI-generated visuals from the dataset—are presented in the chapter.

4 Analysis

The Key Visual Drivers

The manual coding of visual content disseminated by gambling-related Facebook pages and groups reveals a sophisticated system of persuasive strategies employed by the owners and administrators of such pages. The visuals do not merely serve an aesthetic function; rather, they operate as carefully planned stimuli designed to capture attention, sustain engagement, and normalise gambling behaviours through multilayered psychological and cultural triggers. In the following paragraphs, we explain the key drivers that we identified in these images that we argue can act as potential triggers for users to engage in online gaming and gambling.

Aspirational Wealth and Hyper-Masculine Status Fantasies

Central to the visual economy perpetuated by these visuals is the deployment of aspirational motifs. In our analysis, aspirational motifs—such as luxury symbols, high-status figures, and narratives of upward mobility—emerge as a recurrent strategy in approximately 55% of the analysed connotative and denotative combinations. This notable prevalence confirms that such motifs are not marginal embellishments, but rather constitute a central visual logic in gambling promotion. Their consistent appearance across different clusters suggests a deliberate effort to frame gambling as a pathway to success, power, and social recognition. Luxury vehicles, premium brands, and high-status objects frequently appear in direct association with gambling-related messaging, constructing a narrative that links betting activities to wealth accumulation, masculine power, and upward social mobility. These images mirror the structure of head-to-head showdowns, linking gambling participation to the excitement of winning against an opponent and the validation provided by public recognition through social media reactions and comments. Such images evoke the dynamics of competition and control, mirroring the logic of gambling itself, where personal risk-taking attitudes are portrayed as paths to financial success and status elevation.

A further dimension of these strategies involves the deliberate use of sexual and physical attractiveness. Women in lingerie or suggestive poses (often Asian models to align with regional beauty standards, see Fig. 2b) are strategically positioned adjacent to bonus offers or jackpot announcements. This aesthetic choice appears recurrent within one of the combinations identified, suggesting a shared ideal of femininity—potentially generated or curated for geographically targeted promotional strategies—in line with the presence of linguistic clusters that also point to geo-specific targeting logics. We can argue that these images depict women in revealing clothing or intimate scenarios to immediately capture attention and enhance the desirability of the gambling context. These visuals are not limited to mere attractiveness but are carefully situated in aspirational, elegant environments—lavish settings, luxury items, and symbols of affluence—that suggest gambling as a conduit to a sophisticated and

(a) (b)

Fig. 2 **a** Side-by-side display of luxury cars used to associate gambling with wealth, competition, and masculine status. **b** Woman in lingerie positioned next to promotional gambling content, exemplifying the use of sexualised femininity to enhance aspirational appeal

rewarding lifestyle. These images appear to reflect the same aspirational masculine imaginary observed in the depiction of luxury cars and competitive scenarios (see Fig. 2a): a symbolic universe where power, control, and success are associated with dominance, ownership, and the capacity to attract and display beauty and wealth. The presence of warm, intimate images, including close-up smiles and body language signalling openness and familiarity, is supposed to foster connections and trust. By combining visual seduction with lifestyle aspiration, these images simultaneously stimulate desire and offer a fantasy narrative in which participation in gambling platforms promises access to wealth, pleasure, and social recognition.

Manufactured Trust Through Transactional Proofs

Speaking of trust, a number of posts shared by these pages include images that can be decoded as manufacturing trust among their core user base. Approximately 37% of the combinations analysed include transactional visuals that function as trust-building devices, reinforcing perceptions of legitimacy through financial documentation. Visual proof-of-payment artifacts, transaction screenshots, and cash-out confirmations are recurrent features. These elements function as performative demonstrations of trustworthiness, using financial documentation to mitigate scepticism and establish platform credibility. The use of recognisable financial intermediaries (such as GCash, which is a well-known payment app in the Philippines) fosters a perception of legitimacy and transparency, while repeated displays of recent and frequent payouts reinforce the illusion of widespread success and collective participation (see

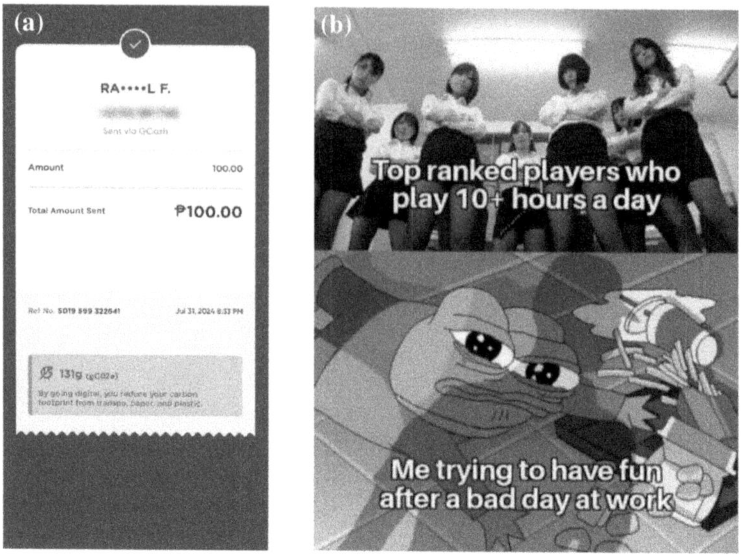

Fig. 3 **a** Mobile payment receipt illustrating the use of micro-transactions in gambling flows. **b** Meme depicting emotional exhaustion and escapist gaming behaviour through ironic imagery

Fig. 3a). This dynamic is further intensified by the integration of humour and social bonding mechanisms. Memes and humorous content referencing gambling losses are deliberately employed to diffuse psychological despair associated with losing money, transforming individual failure into a shared cultural experience that legitimises continued engagement (see Fig. 3b). The underlying psychological strategy is clear: by reframing losses as frequent occurrences, something that is to be seen with a sense of humour, these pages encourage their users to develop the habit of repetitive betting.

The prominence of transaction-based trust inducing drivers in the visual material underlines the platforms' strategic awareness of user scepticism. Screenshots of successful withdrawals, complete with reference numbers and timestamps, are paired with celebratory messages and positive affirmations ("Transfer successful", "Withdrawal completed") to construct a sense of reliability and organisational efficiency. In addition, the frequent depiction of promotional incentives—such as "first deposit bonuses," "rebate systems," and "activity-based rewards"—can be interpreted as a strategy of the pages to cushion the psychological impact of losing by offering additional incentives to continue playing. Progress bars, daily login bonuses, and persistent notifications simulate a sense of gain for the users even when they are losing. This mechanism is well-documented in HCI and gambling research, where interface features such as progress indicators, reward animations, and loss-disguising feedback loops have been shown to reinforce habitual engagement and perceived advancement, even in the absence of actual wins [12, 23]. This, in turn, helps exploit the sunk-cost fallacy, making disengagement increasingly difficult as users invest more time and resources.

Conditioning Through FOMO Strategies

These mechanisms of persuasion are further reinforced by the omnipresence of urgency-inducing design elements. Dynamic countdown timers, flashing "claim" buttons, and time-limited offers create a context of artificial scarcity, exploiting well-documented cognitive biases such as the fear of missing out (FOMO) and immediacy bias [12]. The interface design emulates the slot machine environment, using bright gradients, animated icons, and reward escalation mechanisms to produce continuous reward anticipation cycles (see Fig. 4).

This architecture reflects principles of operant conditioning, a psychological process in which behaviour is shaped and reinforced through repeated exposure to rewards and punishments [25]. In this context, progress indicators, incremental bonuses, and multi-level reward ladders act as reinforcing stimuli that encourage

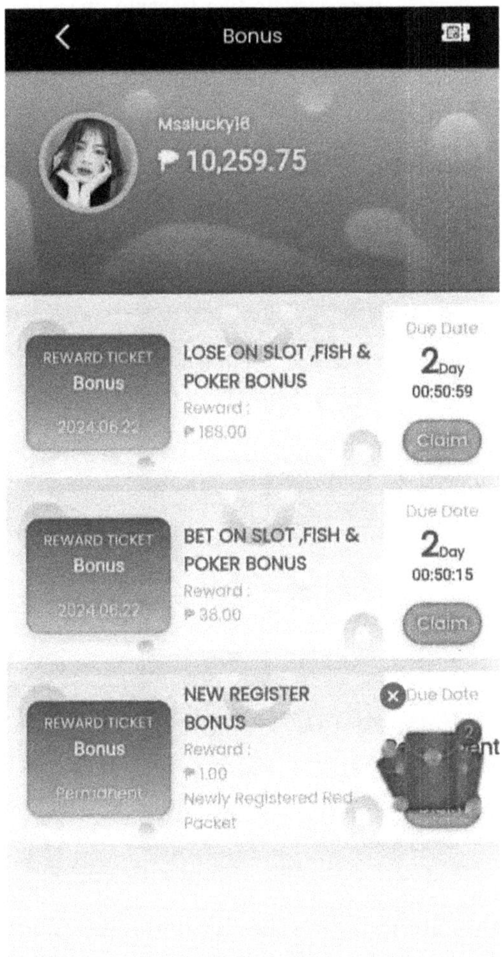

Fig. 4 Countdowns and calls to action prompting users to claim rewards

users to repeat gambling-related actions. This architecture systematically conditions users to engage in repetitive behaviours by alternating between rewards and small, predictable reinforcements, embedding gambling behaviours into habitual digital routines.

Gamification Tactics and Low Entry Barriers

Another important driver utilised by these pages is the deployment of gamification techniques that replicate slot-machine logic in mobile app environments. The presence of spin buttons, multipliers (such as 10× or 20×), visual representations of quests (temples, treasures, pirate adventures), and escalating reward systems contribute to an immersive, overstimulating environment (see Fig. 5a). At the same time, the posts arguably lower cognitive barriers through infantilised design: pastel colour palettes, cartoon-like treasure chest animations, and playful terminologies obscure the underlying financial predation. Such interfaces are designed to make the gambling experience approachable, playful, and seemingly risk-free.

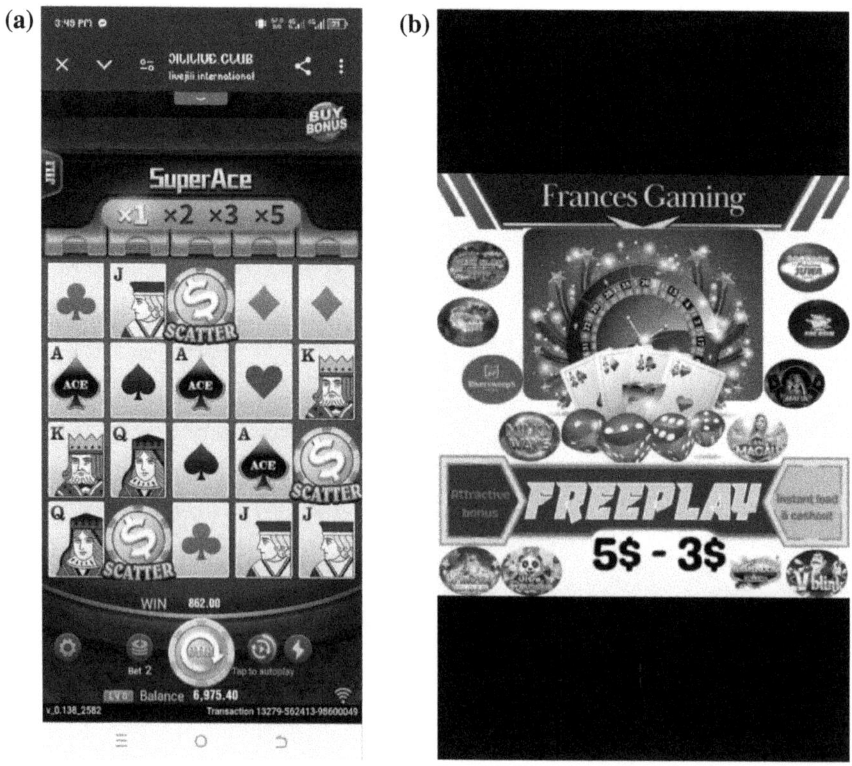

Fig. 5 **a** Interface displaying spin buttons and multipliers, emulating slot-machine mechanics. **b** Promotional content highlighting "free play" incentives, creating an illusion of risk-free gambling to entice users

This is coupled with reward structures that blur the boundary between play and financial commitment. Low-entry incentives, such as "$2 free play" or "₱0.50 bets", are prominently displayed next to screenshots of large winnings, creating the illusion that small investments can yield disproportionately large returns (see Fig. 5b). This psychological mechanism exploits the gambler's fallacy and the illusion of control [54], fostering continued engagement even in the face of repeated losses.

Celebrity and Influencer Endorsements

Another strategic lever is the use of celebrity and influencer endorsements, with public figures lending their credibility and aspirational status to gambling brands (see Fig. 6a). The presence of well-known athletes or media personalities creates the

(a)

(b)

Fig. 6 **a** Promotional collage combining exaggerated winnings and sexualised imagery. **b** Celebrity endorsement leveraging national pride and masculine ideals

illusion of platform legitimacy and appeals to national pride, cultural familiarity, and trust. These figures are often embedded within professionally designed promotional layouts, dressed in branded apparel, or seen posing with items such as microphones, championship belts, or platform logos (see Fig. 6b). Such visual elements strengthen the association between the celebrity's public reputation and the credibility of the gambling service.

In particular, the use of national sports figures leverages affective bonds of national identity and broader masculine ideals of success, discipline, and financial reward. In doing so, the endorsement transfers symbolic capital from the public figure to the gambling brand, situating gambling participation not only as acceptable but as aspirational and even patriotic [27]. The graphic style of these posts also blends corporate polish with emotional appeal: bold fonts, high-contrast colours, and celebratory poses convey excitement while simultaneously offering reassurance through familiarity and trust in the endorser's image.

Exploiting Social Relations

The visual system is embedded in a networked architecture of social relations exploitation. Many images explicitly encourage users to "invite friends" and share content within social groups, turning players into active recruiters and amplifiers of the platform's messaging (see Fig. 7). The convergence of aspirational imagery, emotional manipulation, urgency mechanisms, cultural targeting, gamification, transactional transparency, and viral dissemination strategies reveals a complex, self-reinforcing ecosystem of attention capture and behavioural conditioning.

Fig. 7 Viral recruitment through reward-based sharing and aspirational imagery

Cultural and Linguistic Localisation

Particularly noteworthy and covert is the targeted use of cultural cues and linguistic localisation. 56 clusters show use of Filipino and Urdu languages, integrating gambling promotion with culturally specific symbols, idioms, and social norms. In the case of Filipino-language content, references to group pressure, peer dynamics, and familiar cultural motifs (such as local slang and humour) facilitate the naturalisation of gambling as a community practice. Even more strategically complex is the Urdu-language cluster, which departs from explicit gambling promotion to engage in covert ideological messaging. The imagery in this cluster is dominated by emotionally charged depictions of women in distress, domestic conflicts, and performing traditional roles while the accompanying male figures are distant or downright abusive (see Fig. 8a, b).

This cluster features visual elements—ranging from denotative cues such as tears, physical harm, and abandonment, to connotative framings that evoke narratives of victimhood, betrayal, and the collapse of traditional family values. These semiotic components contribute to an orchestrated effort to exploit collective emotional and moral sensibilities. The visual strategy appears designed to reinforce cultural conservatism and social cohesion around specific ideological axes, while subtly embedding gambling platforms within these broader moral narratives. The repetition of similar scenarios, coupled with moralising captions and traditional symbols, suggests a recurring discursive pattern in which gambling promotion intersects with attempts to shape cultural identity and public sentiment. A summary of the key drivers is presented in Table 1.

At its core, the visual drivers employed by gambling-related social media pages operate as a multifaceted persuasion machine. It combines elements of aspiration, emotion, social bonding, cultural embedding, and behavioural psychology to create a resilient, addictive, and socially reinforced model of user engagement. These pages leverage persuasive design to transform occasional gamblers into daily users. Importantly, what appears as organic user engagement is, in reality, the output of a finely tuned psychological control grid, engineered to bypass cognitive defences through layered emotional conditioning.

LLMs and the Rapid Proliferation of AI-Generated Content in Gambling Groups

Our statistical analysis reveals a transformative shift in the gambling promotion operation following ChatGPT's introduction in November 2022. As illustrated in Fig. 9, the monthly post volumes exhibit a striking exponential growth trajectory after ChatGPT's launch.

This visual evidence is corroborated by statistical testing, which shows mean monthly posts rising from 2121 to 280,952 (13,242% increase) and median posts

Fig. 8 a&b Urdu-language content leveraging emotional distress and cultural conservatism to embed gambling promotion.

(a)

(b)

Table 1 Analysis of key persuasive drivers and illustrative examples

Driver	Key points and examples
Aspirational wealth and hyper-masculine fantasies	Luxury signalling: Mercedes, BMW M-series cars; Rolex watches; cash stacks. Links gambling to wealth/power Competitive framing: "Head-to-head showdowns" mimicking viral challenges; leaderboards Sexualised incentives: Asian models in lingerie adjacent to jackpot ads; women in lavish settings admiring cash, aligned with masculine status tropes
Manufactured trust via transactional proofs	GCash/PayPal receipts: Timestamped "transfer successful" screenshots with reference numbers Humour normalisation: Memes about losses (e.g., "when you lose your salary, but the reload bonus hits") Loss compensation: "First deposit bonuses", "rebate systems"
FOMO and urgency conditioning	Countdown timers: "00:12 left to claim!" Artificial scarcity: "VIP tier" promotions; "7-day offers" Operant conditioning: Progress bars, daily login bonuses, "sunk cost" thermometers
Cultural and linguistic localisation	Filipino targeting: Peer pressure via barkada (group) dynamics; hugot culture humour ("Tropa mong nag-aaya na naman mag-scatter") Urdu moral engineering: Domestic violence imagery; tears/abandonment scenes tied to conservative values
Gamification and low barriers	Slot machine mimicry: Spin buttons, 10×–20× multipliers Infantilised design: Cartoonish treasure chests, pastel colours Micro-incentives: "₱0.50 bets" next to large win screenshots
Celebrity endorsements	Trust transfer: Manny Pacquiao with championship belt imagery ("biggest and most trusted") Sports synergy: Basketball courts in ManilaPlay ads; athlete cameos
Exploiting social relations	Viral recruitment: "Invite 3 friends to unlock gold status!" Shareable badges: "I won!" leaderboards with social media integration

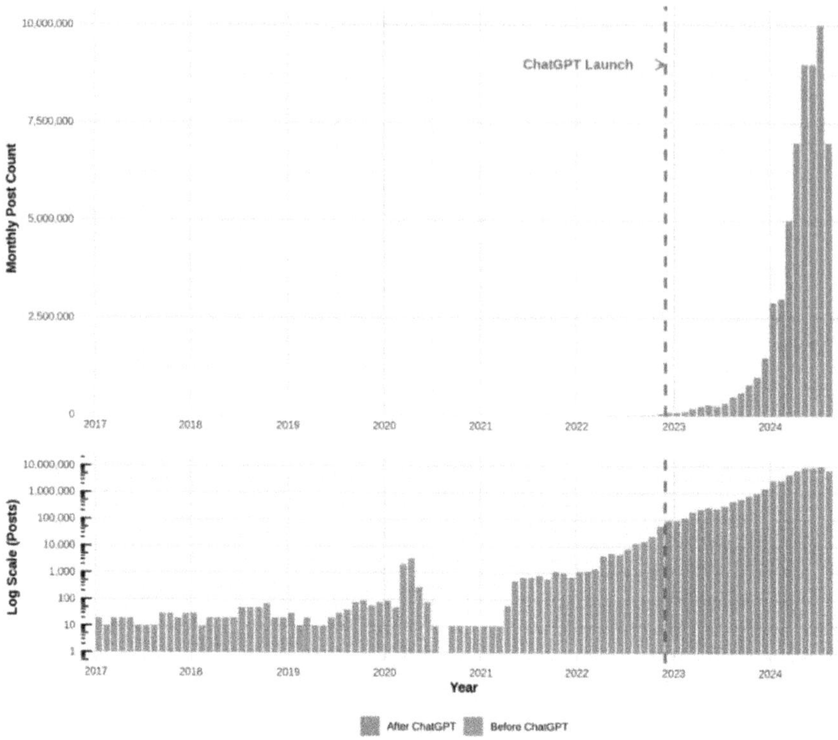

Fig. 9 Evidence of increase in posts since the public launch of ChatGPT [37]

from 30 to 800,000 (2,666,566% increase). Regression analysis confirms this effect was not merely coincidental ($p < 0.0001$), demonstrating both an immediate level increase and a significant acceleration in growth trajectory. The pre-ChatGPT posting trend was essentially flat (154.9 posts per time unit, $p = 0.973$), while the post-ChatGPT slope increased tremendously (481,155 posts per time unit). While this striking temporal correlation is compelling, we should be cautious about attributing direct causality solely to ChatGPT or generative AI technologies. Other factors could have contributed to this exponential growth, including changes in Meta's platform policies, shifts in gambling marketing strategies, or other technological developments occurring during the same timeframe. Nevertheless, the timing, magnitude, and pattern of growth strongly suggest that generative AI technologies likely served as a significant enabler or accelerant for gambling promotion activities, even if not the sole causal factor.

While we cannot directly track how the stylistic attributes of AI-generated visuals evolved over time—due to the ephemeral and reposted nature of most content—we observe a sharp inflection in posting volume and content proliferation following the public launch of ChatGPT and, more broadly, the increasing accessibility of generative tools in early 2023. As illustrated in Fig. 9, the monthly number of posts from the studied network rose from a pre-GPT average of 2121 to peaks exceeding 10 million, with a structural break detected in July 2023. Although we cannot attribute this change solely to the use of generative AI, the scale and timing of this increase strongly suggest that content production became easier and faster, likely enabling the adoption of synthetic media in gambling promotion strategies. Our qualitative analysis of surviving posts [38] from this phase supports this interpretation, showing consistent aesthetic markers associated with automated image generation, albeit without a time-indexed stylistic timeline.

The remaining posts share the core drivers identified in the earlier analysis—such as aspirational wealth, urgency conditioning, gamification, and low-entry incentives—often in intensified or visually polished forms. Prominent among these are messages of "free play" bonuses paired with exaggerated visual cues like oversized buttons, bright gradients, and bold, all-caps typography. The promise of "no deposit," "no task," and "instant cash-out" continues to dominate the promotional language, reinforcing the illusion of effortless and risk-free participation.

What stands out more clearly in this updated corpus is the integration of visual styles that are likely the product of generative AI tools. Several images, particularly those featuring hyper-detailed environments (e.g., shark-infested slot machines, fantasy treasure hunts, stylised royalty) display a surreal, dreamlike quality characterised by exaggerated and fantastical juxtapositions of elements. A number of visual features consistently recurred across the most recent content, allowing us to formulate a plausible attribution of AI-generated origin based on stylistic and compositional patterns. These images frequently displayed hyper realistic lighting gradients, unnaturally smooth surfaces, and near-perfect symmetry—elements rarely achieved through manual production and closely resembling outputs from state-of-the-art diffusion models. Their aesthetic often combined saturated, dreamlike colour schemes with densely layered compositions in which sharks, treasure chests, human figures, and jackpot cues appeared side by side in improbable arrangements. Such symbolic compression, lacking spatial coherence, has become increasingly associated with synthetic generation [2, 42, 43]. Taken together, these recurring features—coupled with the temporal pattern of their proliferation, closely aligned with the public rollout and mass adoption of generative image platforms—support a reasonable, if not forensically verifiable, conclusion: many of the promotional visuals circulated during this period are best understood as synthetic artifacts, produced through automated content generation pipelines rather than conventional photographic or graphic design practices.

A representative example of this stylistic shift can be seen in a promotional image depicting a massive shark emerging from an underwater abyss, surrounded by poker chips and other sharks, with a slot machine placed at the centre. The image advertises "$20 FREE PLAY" with "NO TASKS" in bold, glowing type (see Fig. 10). This visual narrative merges the mechanics of online slots with the visual language of fantasy gaming and high-risk adventure. Its synthetic rendering—high saturation, deep contrast, and fantastical spatial composition—corresponds to the improbable arrangements common to AI-generated images. The imagery not only exploits gamification and FOMO-inducing cues but also creates an immersive spectacle designed

Fig. 10 Post shared by several groups in a coordinated manner on August 6, 2024

to heighten the emotional charge of gambling, positioning it as a thrilling quest for mythical reward. Important to note here that this image, along with its accompanying post, is the second most viewed ostensibly AI-driven image circulated by the studied groups.

Another example features polished, idealised women figures seated at casino tables, holding cards with confident gazes (Fig. 11). Surrounded by soft-focus lighting and a luxurious interior, the image promotes "REDEEMABLE FREEPLAY" and "maximum cashout" with urgent messaging like "Let's start winning." Here, the visual style reflects a post-2022 generative aesthetic—characterised by flawless skin textures, cinematic lighting, and symmetrical composition—elements commonly associated with diffusion-based AI models such as Stable Diffusion and Midjourney, which became widely accessible around the same time as the public release of ChatGPT. While ChatGPT itself was originally text-based, its launch contributed to the broader cultural shift and infrastructural expansion that facilitated the mainstream adoption of generative tools, including those for image production. The convergence of these technologies arguably enabled a new ecosystem of content creation, in which synthetic visual styles became a prominent feature of gambling-related promotional imagery. The image is reflective of multiple persuasion strategies/drivers simultaneously: aspirational wealth, social desirability, manufactured trust via financial terminology, and hyper-masculine fantasies through the figure's overall demeanour. The promotional promise of low-barrier entry reinforces habitual engagement, while the glamourised aesthetic positions gambling as a means to gain wealth and social status. Posts with these images were shared across several fan groups under observation, with many achieving significant engagement. The first variant (see Fig. 11 left) garnered 4.3M views, 160 reactions, 1.1K comments, and 1K shares when posted by "Slots Online" on April 19, 2024. The second variant (see Fig. 11 right) received 3.3M views, 596 reactions, 3.3K comments, and 1.5K shares when posted by "Lucky Game 777" on May 20, 2024. The overall visualisation count for these particular images is in several millions, when one takes into consideration the number of times the posts were shared by different groups of the gambling network.

Fig. 11 Most viewed ostensibly AI-generated posts in the network

These examples point toward an emerging hybrid persuasion strategy: one that fuses previously dominant attention drivers with generative aesthetics to heighten engagement and create a more immersive experience. While human figures—particularly sexualised or influencer-like subjects—continue to appear in select materials, their symbolic function is increasingly paralleled by animated mascots, cartoon avatars, and stylised AI-generated characters. Some of these personas retain emotional appeal, while others intensify immersion through spectacle. In short, the updated visual grammar retains the behavioural hooks of earlier content while experimenting with enhanced visual saturation and narrative density, likely enabled by the expanding accessibility and affordances of AI image-generation tools.

5 Discussion

The analysis presented in this chapter reveals how the visual ecosystem of online gambling promotion on Facebook functions as a multi-layered architecture of persuasion. This ecosystem mobilises a combination of well-established attention drivers—such as aspirational wealth, gamification, and urgency conditioning—and integrates them with emerging aesthetics and scale made possible by generative AI technologies. This hybridisation marks a shift not only in style but in the strategic infrastructure of gambling marketing: from emotional instigation to immersive, semiotic engineering.

Our findings substantiate and extend the existing literature on digital gambling marketing strategies. The use of hyper-masculine fantasies, performative financial trust signals, FOMO tactics, and gamified interfaces aligns with prior research on how online gambling operators construct affective and behavioural pathways to sustain user engagement [14, 21, 30]. The prominence of aspirational wealth imagery directly confirms Deans et al.'s [7] observation that gambling is frequently presented as a glamorous and effortless activity.

However, our visual analysis reveals a more sophisticated application of these principles. Rather than simply portraying gambling as glamorous, the coordinated networks create complete aspirational ecosystems where gambling is positioned as the gateway to an idealised lifestyle. The manufactured trust mechanisms we identified—particularly strategic use of payment receipts—extend Gainsbury's and colleagues' [14] work on how social media platforms foster online communities and strengthen brand loyalty.

In particular, our typology of visual drivers demonstrates that these strategies are not isolated but systematically paired within combinations of denotative and connotative clusters, reinforcing each other and producing what could be described as synergistic instigation tactics. For example, aspirational imagery frequently co-occurs with transaction screenshots and reward interfaces, creating a recursive loop of desire, validation, and behavioural activation. This interweaving suggests a more sophisticated understanding on the part of platform administrators regarding how to engineer emotional immersion and habitual interaction through visual storytelling. We identified additional dimensions specifically adapted for social media contexts, including enhanced aesthetic gamification, narrative-driven gamification, and social-competitive gamification.

Content generated by generative AI tools does not replace previous persuasive elements—it enhances and recombines them in more emotionally potent and cognitively captivating ways, while enabling an unprecedented scale of deployment. By generating hyper-real, surrealistic, or fantastical environments, generative AI extends the semiotic repertoire available to gambling promoters. It allows for the construction of imaginative universes where reward systems are not only emotionally appealing but symbolically elevated. Moreover, AI-generated characters, mascots, and avatars can now serve as emotionally resonant figures in place of influencers or human models. They retain the capacity to simulate intimacy, playfulness, or authority, but without the regulatory mechanisms attached to promoting posts with images of real personalities. This marks a strategic move towards greater use of synthetic figures, potentially circumventing existing guidelines on celebrity endorsements or influencer accountability.

The strategic deployment of generative AI imagery raises pressing concerns for both consumer protection and regulatory frameworks. AI-generated content is not merely novel; it is often designed to evade traditional detection systems, whether human or algorithmic. Its surreal quality makes it harder to classify, while its synthetic nature complicates attribution and accountability. Furthermore, the staggering increase in mean and median monthly posts demonstrates how generative AI has transformed this gambling promotion operation from a modest activity to an industrial-scale operation. This explosive growth, culminating in volumes exceeding ten million monthly posts by 2024, represents a fundamental shift in the information ecosystem surrounding online gambling. The rapid acceleration in the volume of posts raises concerns about platform governance and the limitations of existing transparency tools. Meta Content Library's graphical user interface only permits data collection from popular accounts, significantly restricting comprehensive analysis. While downloading these posts and their multimedia content was instrumental for our methodology, more extensive analysis was constrained by practical limitations. Although the API environment hosted at Somar theoretically enables broader content access, the absence of integrated large language model capabilities and the cumbersome procedures required to use the virtual data enclave prevented us from expanding our analysis to the full dataset.

From a policy standpoint, this suggests an urgent need to redefine what constitutes manipulative content, especially in the context of vulnerable users such as youth [3], problem gamblers [14], or populations targeted through cultural and linguistic localisation. The opacity of AI-generated visuals—both in terms of provenance and intent—introduces what we may call epistemic opacity in the advertising landscape. Users can no longer easily distinguish between organic content, paid promotions, and synthetic manipulations, blurring the thresholds of informed consent and autonomous decision-making.

Additionally, the use of emotional narratives and cultural symbols in AI-generated campaigns—especially in contexts such as the Urdu-language cluster—raises ethical questions about algorithmically optimised exploitation of moral and cultural sensibilities. When gambling is embedded in narratives of victimhood, family breakdown, or economic hardship, the promotional message is no longer just persuasive—it becomes ideologically manipulative.

From a methodological standpoint, this study proposes a hybrid pipeline capable of scaling qualitative analysis across large image datasets. By combining denotative and connotative embeddings, dimensionality reduction, and density-based clustering, we operationalise an approach to detect and create typologies of visual persuasion in a way that is both computationally rigorous and interpretively rich. It is important to acknowledge that our approach has inherent limitations in terms of representativeness. The network analysed represents a specific subset of gambling promotion activities on Facebook and may not be representative of all such activities on the platform. Our discovery method relies on coordination patterns identified through the Vera AI alerts system, which means we may have missed gambling promotion networks that use different coordination tactics or operate below detection thresholds. Additionally, the discovery process was dependent on CrowdTangle, a tool that was deprecated during our study period, potentially limiting our ability to identify new networks or track evolutionary changes in existing ones on Meta platforms. Since the Meta Content Library (MCL) API was launched, we investigated it as a possible alternative. At the time of writing, three limitations prevented us from fully porting our workflow to this environment: the internal MCL ID system is distinct from the one used on Meta platforms, and the clear room environment has restrictions on both task scheduling and data sharing.

The use of LLMs in this study also presents a methodological duality worth noting. On one hand, LLMs allowed us to scale qualitative analysis by generating denotative and connotative image descriptions, which we then clustered and manually coded. This approach offered an efficient and interpretable way to surface visual themes at scale. On the other hand, these same models—when used to generate persuasive visual content—are implicated in the amplification of synthetic persuasion. We thus find ourselves using the very tools under critique. This reflexive position demands an awareness of how LLMs may encode biases, omit culturally specific meanings, or flatten nuance during interpretation. While we attempted to mitigate these effects by manually reviewing a portion of cluster outputs and using a collaborative coding process (see Appendix for the prompts used), future work must continue to critically assess the framing effects and normative assumptions embedded in AI-assisted analysis.

6 Future Directions

Several key directions for future research emerge from our findings. First, while this chapter has documented the prevalence and visual sophistication of AI-generated gambling promotions, it has not measured their *efficacy* in terms of user behaviour. Do synthetic visuals lead to higher engagement, clickthroughs, or gambling frequency compared to human-generated content? Answering this question will require experimental designs such as A/B testing, eye-tracking, or psychological surveys comparing user responses to synthetic versus conventional imagery. Such studies would provide urgently needed insight into whether AI-generated content is simply more prolific, or are also more persuasive.

Second, future work should investigate the algorithmic infrastructures that govern visibility and reach. How do recommendation systems interact with generative content? Are AI-generated gambling posts more likely to be algorithmically amplified? Longitudinal analysis of platform data, ideally with privileged access to backend recommendation logs, could clarify the role of algorithmic curation in the spread of synthetic gambling promotions.

Another critical avenue for future research lies in the domain of platform governance, especially in examining how algorithmic systems—not merely human decisions—shape the visibility and virality of gambling-related content. As our analysis has shown, Meta's regulatory asymmetry between paid advertising and organic content (which, in fact, only seems organic) creates a structural loophole whereby harmful promotional material can proliferate with minimal oversight. This asymmetry is further compounded by what Laufer and Nissenbaum [28] describe as algorithmic amplification: the automated, rule-based processes that determine which content is surfaced, suppressed, or propelled across a platform's user base. Importantly, amplification in this context is not a neutral technical function—it acts as a systemic force capable of displacing traditional mechanisms of social trust and editorial gatekeeping.

This calls for a shift in regulatory focus: rather than concentrating exclusively on moderating "problematic content" after it has appeared, platforms and regulators must interrogate the amplification infrastructures that invisibly prioritise certain types of content—such as visually immersive, AI-generated gambling promotions—while sidelining others. Algorithmic amplification becomes especially problematic when it is mismatched to the platform's stated goals (e.g., user safety or wellbeing) or when it eclipses previously existing, socially embedded forms of information curation and trust-building. In this light, content moderation alone is an insufficient remedy; what is needed is a deeper audit of the amplificatory logic embedded in recommendation systems. Interdisciplinary research efforts should therefore consider how amplification algorithms not only enable but structurally entrench exploitative persuasion architectures in digital environments—and what kinds of accountability mechanisms might address this systemic displacement.

Finally, future interdisciplinary work should investigate further the dual-use nature of generative technologies. As this chapter shows, LLMs and generative image tools can serve both analytical and manipulative functions. Their deployment in social research must be matched with a reflexive awareness of their limitations, assumptions, and social impact. Transparency in model use, clear documentation of interpretive frameworks (such as the prompts provided in Appendix), and continual engagement with ethical debates around AI are essential components of responsible scholarship in this domain.

Appendix

Prompts used for generating connotative and denotative descriptions

Item	Definition and examples	Visual example
Prompt for connotative image description	Description: "Describe the connotative meaning of this image. Avoid phrases like 'the image conveys' or 'the image portrays'. Start the description without any introductory phrases. YOU MUST enclose the description within <desc> and </desc> tags" Example of response: "A vibrant and enticing atmosphere of excitement and opportunity, with elements of chance and luck. The use of bright red and gold colors suggests energy, passion, and a sense of urgency. The presence of playing cards, dice, and a roulette wheel evokes the thrill of gambling and the allure of potential winnings. Phrases like "24/7 OPEN" and "100% LEGIT" imply accessibility and trustworthiness, while "5$ POINTS FREEPLAY" suggests an enticing offer or promotion, encouraging participation and engagement"	

(continued)

(continued)

Item	Definition and examples	Visual example
Prompt for denotative image description	Description: "Describe the denotative meaning of this image. Avoid phrases like 'the image conveys' or 'the image portrays'. Start the description without any introductory phrases. YOU MUST enclose the description within <desc> and </desc> tags" Example of response: "A promotional image for "Frances Gaming" featuring a roulette wheel, playing cards with aces, and red dice. The background is red with star and light effects. Text includes "24/7 OPEN," "100% LEGIT," and "5$ POINTS FREEPLAY." Additional text lists names like "ORIONSTAR," "JUWA," "MILKY WAY," "GAME VAULT," "CASINOWONDERLAND," "FIREKRINE," "RIVERSWEEP," "DOUBLE UP," and "ANDMANYMORE""	

References

1. Arminio, L., Magnani, M., Piqueras, M., Rossi, L., Segerberg, A.: Leveraging VLLMs for visual clustering: image-to-text mapping shows increased semantic capabilities and interpretability. SocArXiv (2024)
2. Bansal, G., Nawal, A., Chamola, V., Herencsar, N.: Revolutionizing visuals: the role of generative AI in modern image generation. ACM Trans. Multimed. Comput. Commun. Appl. **20**, 1–22 (2024). https://doi.org/10.1145/3689641
3. Biggar, B., Zendle, D., Wardle, H.: Targeting the next generation of gamblers? Gambling sponsorship of esports teams. J. Public Health (Oxf.). **45**, 636–644 (2023). https://doi.org/10.1093/pubmed/fdac167
4. Cemiloglu, D., Arden-Close, E., Hodge, S.E., Ali, R.: Explainable persuasion for interactive design: the case of online gambling. J. Syst. Softw. **195**, 111517 (2023). https://doi.org/10.1016/j.jss.2022.111517
5. Chew, R., Bollenbacher, J., Wenger, M., Speer, J., Kim, A.: LLM-assisted content analysis: using large language models to support deductive coding. arXiv [cs.CL] (2023)
6. Dai, S.-C., Xiong, A., Ku, L.-W.: LLM-in-the-loop: leveraging large language model for thematic analysis. arXiv [cs.CL] (2023)
7. Deans, E.G., Thomas, S.L., Daube, M., Derevensky, J., Gordon, R.: Creating symbolic cultures of consumption: an analysis of the content of sports wagering advertisements in Australia. BMC Public Health. **16**, 208 (2016). https://doi.org/10.1186/s12889-016-2849-8
8. DiResta, R., Goldstein, J.A.: How spammers and scammers leverage AI-generated images on Facebook for audience growth. HKS Misinformation Review (2024). https://doi.org/10.37016/mr-2020-151

9. Fan, J., Ai, Y., Liu, X., Deng, Y., Li, Y.: Coding latent concepts: a human and LLM-coordinated content analysis procedure. Commun. Res. Rep. **41**, 324–334 (2024). https://doi.org/10.1080/08824096.2024.2410263
10. Ferrara, E.: GenAI against humanity: nefarious applications of generative artificial intelligence and large language models. J. Comput. Soc. Sci. **7**, 549–569 (2024). https://doi.org/10.1007/s42001-024-00250-1
11. Fleming, T., Passmore, M., Kan, M., Tregebov, S., Salomon-Ballada, S., Callender, L.: Digital engagement practices in retail investing: gamification and other behavioural techniques. Ontario Security Commission (n.d.)
12. Frommel, J., Mandryk, R.L.: Daily quests or daily pests? The benefits and pitfalls of engagement rewards in games. Proc. ACM Hum.-Comput. Interact. **6**, 1–23 (2022). https://doi.org/10.1145/3549489
13. Gainsbury, S.M., King, D.L., Russell, A.M.T., Delfabbro, P., Derevensky, J., Hing, N.: Exposure to and engagement with gambling marketing in social media: reported impacts on moderate-risk and problem gamblers. Psychol. Addict. Behav. **30**, 270–276 (2016). https://doi.org/10.1037/adb0000156
14. Gainsbury, S.M., King, D.L., Abarbanel, B., Delfabbro, P., Hing, N.: Convergence of gambling and gaming in digital media. Online resource. http://pstorage-cqu-2209908187.s3.amazonaws.com/25791314/cqu_15471binb43f68e3c65a4c558a9c39dcbd93ceddbinb43f68e3c65a4c558a9c39dcbd93cedd.2.pdf. Accessed 26 Aug 2025
15. Giglietto, F., Righetti, N., Rossi, L., Marino, G.: It takes a village to manipulate the media: coordinated link sharing behavior during 2018 and 2019 Italian elections. Inf. Commun. Soc. **23**, 867–891 (2020). https://doi.org/10.1080/1369118X.2020.1739732
16. Giglietto, F., Marino, G., Mincigrucci, R., Stanziano, A.: A workflow to detect, monitor, and update lists of coordinated social media accounts across time: the case of the 2022 Italian election. Soc. Media + Soc. **9** (2023). https://doi.org/10.1177/20563051231196866
17. Giglietto, F., Righetti, N., Rossi, L., Marino, G.: Coordinated link sharing behavior as a signal to surface sources of problematic information on Facebook. In: International Conference On Social Media and Society. ACM, New York, NY, USA (2020)
18. Giglietto, F. et al.: Coordinated sharing behaviour detection and disinformation campaign modelling methods. Vera.ai Deliverable 4.2. D4_2_V1_0_013beb034d.pdf (2025). Accessed 24 Dec 2025
19. Gillespie, T.: The relevance of algorithms. In: Media Technologies, pp. 167–194. MIT Press (2014)
20. Gleicher, N.: Head of cybersecurity policy: coordinated inauthentic behavior explained. Meta. https://about.fb.com/news/2018/12/inside-feed-coordinated-inauthentic-behavior/ (2018). Accessed 26 Aug 2025
21. Guillou-Landreat, M., Gallopel-Morvan, K., Lever, D., Le Goff, D., Le Reste, J.-Y.: Gambling marketing strategies and the internet: what do we know? A systematic review. Front. Psychiatry. **12**, 583817 (2021). https://doi.org/10.3389/fpsyt.2021.583817
22. Hernández-Ruiz, A., Gutiérrez, Y.: Analysing the Twitter accounts of licensed sports gambling operators in Spain: a space for responsible gambling? Comunicación y Sociedad. **34**, 65–79 (2021). https://doi.org/10.15581/003.34.4.65-79
23. Hing, N., Cherney, L., Blaszczynski, A., Gainsbury, S.M., Lubman, D.I.: Do advertising and promotions for online gambling increase gambling consumption? An exploratory study. Int. Gambl. Stud. **14**, 394–409 (2014). https://doi.org/10.1080/14459795.2014.903989
24. Jenkins, H., Ford, S., Green, J.: Spreadable Media. New York University Press, New York, NY (2018)
25. King, D.L., Delfabbro, P.H., Griffiths, M.D.: The role of structural characteristics in problematic video game play: an empirical study. Int. J. Ment. Health Addict. **9**, 320–333 (2011). https://doi.org/10.1007/s11469-010-9289-y
26. Koebler, J.: Facebook's algorithm is boosting AI spam that links to AI-generated, ad-laden click farms. 404 Media. https://www.404media.co/facebooks-algorithm-is-boosting-ai-spam-that-links-to-ai-generated-ad-laden-click-farms/ (2024). Accessed 26 Aug 2025

27. Kroon, Å.: Converting gambling to philanthropy and acts of patriotism: the case of "The world's most Swedish gambling company." Discourse Context and Media **34**, 100381 (2020). https://doi.org/10.1016/j.dcm.2020.100381
28. Laufer, B., Nissenbaum, H.: Algorithmic Displacement of Social Trust. Knight First Amendment Institute. https://knightcolumbia.org/content/algorithmic-displacement-of-social-trust (n.d.). Accessed 26 Aug 2025
29. Lindeman, M., Männistö-Inkinen, V., Hellman, M., Kankainen, V., Kauppila, E., Svensson, J., Nilsson, R.: Gambling operators' social media image creation in Finland and Sweden 2017–2020. Nordisk Alkohol Nark. **40**, 40–60 (2023). https://doi.org/10.1177/14550725221111317
30. Lopez-Gonzalez, H., Guerrero-Solé, F., Estévez, A., Griffiths, M.: Betting is loving and bettors are predators: a conceptual metaphor approach to online sports betting advertising. J. Gambl. Stud. **34**, 709–726 (2018). https://doi.org/10.1007/s10899-017-9727-x
31. Marino, G., Giglietto, F., Chakraborty, A., Terenzi, M., Olaniran, S.: Throwing spaghetti, seeing what sticks: iterative deception in digital strategic information operations. AoIR Selected Papers of Internet Research (2025)
32. Marwick, A., Lewis, R.: Media Manipulation and Disinformation Online. Data & Society Research Institute (2017)
33. McCormack, A., Shorter, G.W., Griffiths, M.D.: An empirical study of gender differences in online gambling. J. Gambl. Stud. **30**, 71–88 (2014). https://doi.org/10.1007/s10899-012-9341-x
34. Messing, S., DeGregorio, C., Hillenbrand, B., King, G., Mahanti, S., Mukerjee, Z., Nayak, C., Persily, N., State, B., Wilkins, A.: Facebook Privacy-Protected Full URLs Data Set (2020)
35. Meta: Online gambling and gaming. Meta Transparency Center (2025)
36. Meta Platforms, Inc.: Meta Content Library version v2.0 (2024)
37. Meta Platforms, Inc.: Meta Content Library API version v4.0 (2025)
38. Meta Platforms, Inc.: Meta Content Library version v5.0 (2025)
39. Mihai, F., Aleca, O.E., Iordache, D-M.: AI personalization and its influence on online gamblers' behavior. Behav. Sci. **15**, 779 (2025). https://doi.org/10.3390/bs15060779
40. Russell, A.M.T., Hing, N., Browne, M., Rawat, V.: Are direct messages (texts and emails) from wagering operators associated with betting intention and behavior? An ecological momentary assessment study. J. Behav. Addict. **7**, 1079–1090 (2018). https://doi.org/10.1556/2006.7.2018.99
41. Singer, J., Kufenko, V., Wöhr, A., Wuketich, M., Otterbach, S.: How do gambling providers use the social network twitter in Germany? An explorative mixed-methods topic modeling approach. J. Gambl. Stud. **39**, 1371–1398 (2023). https://doi.org/10.1007/s10899-022-10158-y
42. Smith, A., Hutson, J.: Satirical deepfakes, surreal dreamscapes & nostalgic pixels: the rapid evolution and cultural commentary of AI-aesthetics. ISAR J. Arts Hum. Soc. Sci. **2** (2024)
43. Somaini, A.: Algorithmic images: artificial intelligence and visual culture. Grey Room **74–115** (2023). https://doi.org/10.1162/grey_a_00383
44. Stead, M., Dobbie, F., Angus, K., Purves, R.I., Reith, G., Macdonald, L.: The online bingo boom in the UK: a qualitative examination of its appeal. PLoS One **11**, e0154763 (2016). https://doi.org/10.1371/journal.pone.0154763
45. Stephan, A., Miklautz, L., Sidak, K., Wahle, J.P., Gipp, B., Plant, C., Roth, B.: Text-Guided Image Clustering. arXiv [cs.LG] (2024)
46. Terenzi, M.: Modeling persuasion in social media: a theoretical approach to algorithmic content distribution and manipulation. J. Sociocybernetics **19** (2024). https://doi.org/10.26754/ojs_jos/jos.2024110992
47. Terenzi, M.: MCL media downloader. Zenodo (2025)
48. The Lancet: Problem gambling is a public health concern. Lancet **390**, 913 (2017). https://doi.org/10.1016/S0140-6736(17)32333-4
49. Tufekci, Z.: "Not this one": social movements, the attention economy, and microcelebrity networked activism. Am. Behav. Sci. **57**, 848–870 (2013). https://doi.org/10.1177/0002764213479369

50. U.S. Securities and Exchange Commission: SEC requests information and comment on broker-dealer and investment adviser digital engagement practices, related tools and methods, and regulatory considerations and potential approaches; information and comments on investment adviser use of technology (n.d.)
51. Vanicka, A., Liam, M., Luke, M.: (Re)framing built heritage through the machinic gaze. arXiv [cs.CY] (2023)
52. Wack, M., Ehrett, C., Linvill, D., Warren, P.: Generative propaganda: evidence of AI'S impact from a state-backed disinformation campaign. PNAS Nexus **4**, gaf083 (2025). https://doi.org/10.1093/pnasnexus/pgaf083
53. Watkins, G.: AI: the new aesthetics of fascism. New Socialist https://newsocialist.org.uk/transmissions/ai-the-new-aesthetics-of-fascism/ (2025). Accessed 31 Jul 2025
54. Xu, J., Harvey, N.: Carry on winning: the gamblers' fallacy creates hot hand effects in online gambling. Cognition **131**, 173–180 (2014). https://doi.org/10.1016/j.cognition.2014.01.002
55. Yang, Y., Paudel, R., McShan, J., Hindman, M., Huang, H.H., Broniatowski, D.: Coordinated link sharing on Facebook. Sci. Rep. **15**, 15684 (2025). https://doi.org/10.1038/s41598-025-00233-w
56. Yu, Y., Wang, C., Fu, Q., Kou, R., Huang, F., Yang, B., Yang, T., Gao, M.: Techniques and challenges of image segmentation: a review. Electronics (Basel) **12**, 1199 (2023). https://doi.org/10.3390/electronics12051199
57. Zuboff, S.: Surveillance capitalism or democracy? The death match of institutional orders and the politics of knowledge in our information civilization. Organ. Theory **3**, 263178772211292 (2022). https://doi.org/10.1177/26317877221129290

AI-Generated and Manipulated Media Detection

AI-Based Image Forgery Detection and Localisation

Dimitrios Karageorgiou, Fabrizio Guillaro, Davide Cozzolino, Quentin Bammey, Luisa Verdoliva, and Symeon Papadopoulos

1 Introduction

Over the past decade, remarkable advancements have been made in the development of digital image manipulation tools, fueled by the progress of powerful deep learning methods capable of altering existing images or generating entirely new visual content on demand [116].

Originally, users could manually edit images through software like Photoshop or GIMP, guided by their imagination and creativity, but constrained by their own technical skills and the time needed to perform the editing. The quality of modifications depended heavily on the user's ability to seamlessly integrate and blend new elements into an image, remove undesired objects, and conceal imperfections, often manually operating at a pixel level.

D. Karageorgiou (✉) · S. Papadopoulos
Centre for Research and Technology Hellas (CERTH), Thessaloniki, Greece
e-mail: dkarageo@iti.gr

S. Papadopoulos
e-mail: papadop@iti.gr

F. Guillaro · D. Cozzolino · L. Verdoliva
University of Naples Federico II (UNINA), Naples, Italy
e-mail: fabrizio.guillaro@unina.it

D. Cozzolino
e-mail: davide.cozzolino@unina.it

L. Verdoliva
e-mail: verdoliv@unina.it

Q. Bammey
Ecole Polytechnique Federale de Lausanne (EPFL), Lausanne, Switzerland
e-mail: quentin.bammey@epfl.ch

S. Papadopoulos et al. (eds.), *Countering Disinformation in the Era of Generative AI*,
https://doi.org/10.1007/978-3-032-11782-3_5

Today, what once demanded advanced skills and a significant amount of time, has been disrupted due to the emergence and wide adoption of generative AI technology [42]. AI tools enable the crafting of images of astonishing quality and realism, seamlessly embedding manipulations in the style and lighting conditions of the target image [4, 58, 87, 96]. While not all editing methods rely on foundation models (FMs) [84], the boom of FMs has contributed to the spread of these technologies, making the generation more accessible, user-friendly, and intuitive for users [68].

Thanks to these advancements, users without prior expertise can now create highly realistic images at an unprecedented speed, with little effort and nothing more than simple natural language textual prompts. Beyond artistic expression, these tools are also employed by industries for marketing and entertainment, or in common professional tasks, such as generating compelling visuals for slide decks, promising an increase in productivity [3]. However, similar to the duality of most technological advances, AI also enables malicious use cases, such as deliberately spreading disinformation [29] through the Internet or conducting fraudulent activities such as manipulating identity photos for gaining access to online financial services.

In this landscape, verifying the authenticity of images is crucial for a broad range of sectors, like journalism, finance, or the judiciary. As a response, governments and funding agencies have begun to address these serious threats, on the one hand, by enacting new regulations and, on the other, by launching research programs dedicated to the development of forensic tools capable of countering such attacks. For instance, DARPA—the Defense Advanced Research Projects Agency—has funded two large initiatives aimed at the development of technologies for the digital integrity of multimedia content: the Media Forensics (MediFor) program,[1] and the Semantic Forensics (SemaFor) program.[2] Companies are working to protect users from malicious content as well, by implementing watermarks or markups to the images generated using their own tools,[3] or by providing tools to examine the online history of an image.[4] Nevertheless, despite the several different initiatives, that approach the issue from a wide range of perspectives, a unified approach for verifying image integrity has yet to been described, revealing the inherent complexity of the problem.

Different domains also exhibit diverse requirements regarding image authenticity. For example, judicial cases and criminal investigations usually require confident and justified assessments, due to the severe consequences of errors [5]. Yet, in such scenarios it is both possible to devote significant human labour per case and to assume several aspects of the image acquisition pipeline, e.g. by having direct access to the device that captured an image. Consequenlty, case-specific algorithms can be employed. On the other hand, in the field of open-source intelligence (OSINT) investigations that rely on large amounts of online images, a degree of automation is necessary, as it is not practical for human fact-checkers to rigorously check all the potentially manipulated instances that have been shared online. However, in this latter

[1] https://www.darpa.mil/program/media-forensics.

[2] https://www.darpa.mil/program/semantic-forensics.

[3] https://contentcredentials.org/.

[4] https://blog.google/products/search/about-this-image-google-search/.

case, it is also impossible to make strong prior assumptions about how an image has been obtained and later altered, requiring algorithms with general applicability. Such requirements shape the research directions both in the broader field of multimedia forensics [104] as well as to the tasks of image forgery detection and localisation. The former aims to answer whether an image has been semantically altered, while the latter attempts to find the regions of the image that have been altered.

To tackle the above challenges, adequate discriminative information should be present in the image signal. Literature has established that forgeries leave traces on images, often imperceptible to the naked eye, but detectable with conventional methods or with more recent deep learning approaches [82, 104]. That is because every step in the camera acquisition process generates specific traces, telltale of the source device, which are then disrupted by any subsequent image alterations, such as the introduction of artifacts left by the generative models. Throughout the next paragraphs, we present the types of available artifacts and how AI approaches can be employed for capturing them.

2 The Role of Forensic Clues in the Era of Generative AI

Figure 1 illustrates the common steps employed for the acquisition of a digital image. Each of these steps leaves faint but regular traces that are mostly invisible to the eye. Deviations in the distribution of these traces from their expected behaviour can provide strong evidence of image integrity violation. However, their expected behaviour is often not easy to define due to implementation differences in the image acquisition pipeline across camera models. For instance, Fig. 2 illustrates how the steps performed by the Image Signal Processor of a camera can alter the image. The combination, order, and parameters of these steps depend on the specific camera software.

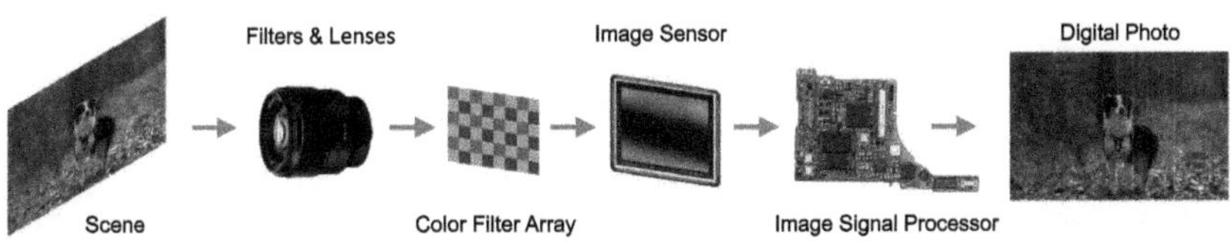

Fig. 1 The fundamental components of the image acquisition pipeline required to capture a real scene. First, optical filters and lenses are used to select and focus the incoming light. A Colour Filter Array (CFA) is then applied to separate the light into red, green, and blue (RGB) components. The image sensor captures this filtered light and outputs a raw image. Finally, the Image Signal Processor (ISP) processes the raw data and converts it into a digital image in a standard format. Figure from Trace [8]

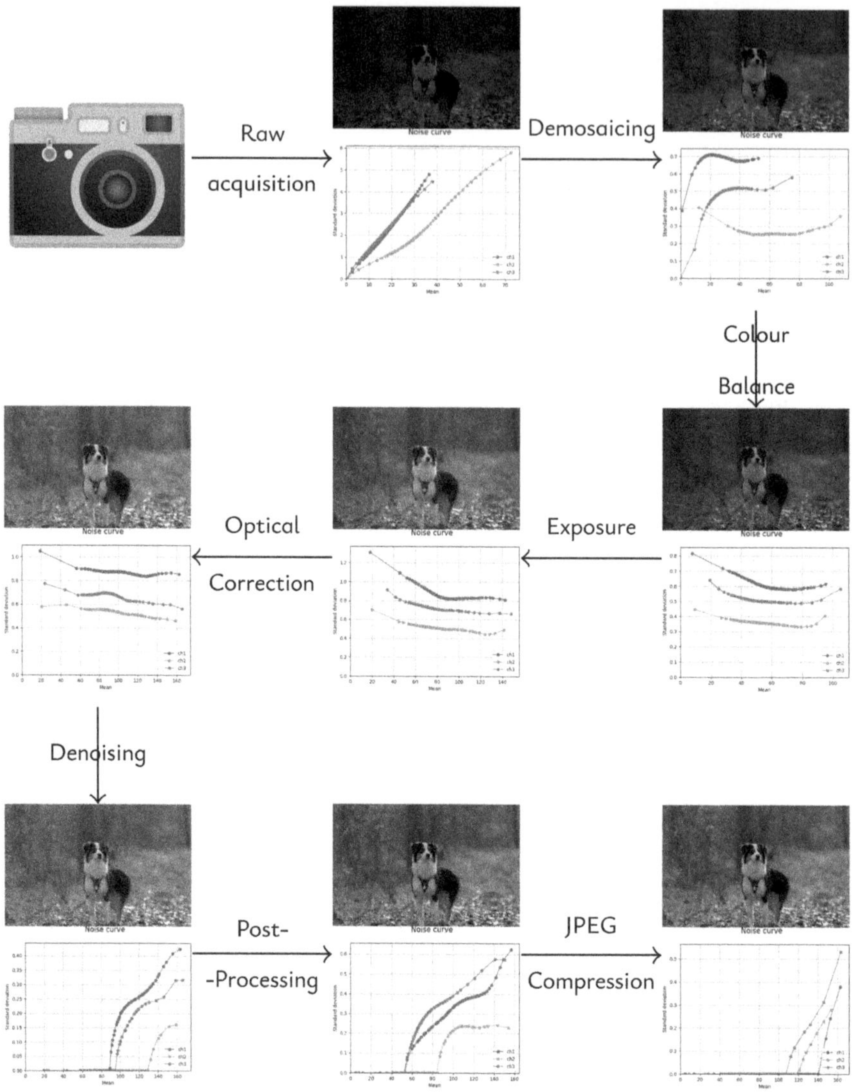

Fig. 2 A simplified illustration of the steps performed by the Image Signal Processor (ISP). These steps leave traces on the image, as can be seen here on the noise curves of the image, which represent the standard deviation of the noise at different intensity levels. Figure adapted from Trace [8]

As discussed in [8], different forensic methods have been proposed, each typically focusing on a specific type of trace. There are *sensor-based* methods [24, 27, 28, 30, 31, 72], *Colour Filter Array (CFA)-based* methods [6, 7, 9–12, 14, 23, 32, 41, 45, 83, 93, 97], and *compression-based* methods [1, 13, 18–20, 22, 73, 74, 85, 90, 102, 106, 114]. In addition, there are *noise-*

based [33, 47, 48, 75, 91, 92] that analyse image noise inconsistencies without focusing on a specific trace.

The clues obtained through the above methods serve multiple forensic interests. Used globally, i.e. at the level of the whole image, they enable linking an image to a pipeline, so as to establish whether an image might have been processed by a specific camera or piece of software [2, 46]. Interestingly, many of these methods can be used locally, to detect inconsistencies among different image regions, i.e. when the traces detected in a particular region are significantly different from traces detected globally [8]. This is typically the case when an object from one image is *spliced* onto another image, a type of forgery that was already common before the generative AI era [37], and has become even easier and more realistic thanks to learning-based methods [54].

These methods can also be directly used, to some extent, to detect images edited with some generative AI models. When an image is altered with such a model, the modified region is regenerated, while the rest of the image remains intact.[5] This means that the traces naturally present in an image will be erased in the forged area, while they will remain intact throughout the rest of the image [67]. Detecting the local absence of traces is a telltale sign of image manipulation.

It must be noted that most of these low-level forensic analysis methods antedate the generative AI era, and thus are not capable of detecting the specific traces left by generative AI models, but instead can detect the absence of traces that should be present in authentic images. For this reason, while they can be used to detect images manipulated through generative AI [52], they will not be able to detail whether the manipulation was done with generative AI tools or conventional ones.

Furthermore, many of these methods can fail to detect traces, or detect inconsistent traces, on specific areas such as saturated, constant, or heavily-textured areas. Should a detection be made in such an area, the evidence should be examined carefully before reaching a decision. However, methods based on specific forensic clues offer the significant advantage of interpretability. In mission critical situations, such as legal proceedings, simply presenting the results of forensic methods is not enough. It is essential to provide an explanation of how, on the basis of which elements, certain conclusions were reached. The detection of alterations of forensic traces is in itself a clear explanation and this is an advantage over data-driven methods, which, due to their black box nature, make it difficult to understand the reason for a particular decision.

3 Forensic Analysis Using AI

Methods based on deep learning, cf. Table 1, often outperform the ones based on handcrafted signal processing pipelines in benchmark datasets, and have rapidly been

[5] Some generative models will actually regenerate the full image [78], rather than just the affected region, with further discussion provided under Sect. 4.

Table 1 State-of-the-art deep learning-based forgery localisation methods

Method	Year	Clues	Inputs	
			High-level	Low-level
Barni2017 [15]	2017	JPEG	–	DWT or DCT
Park2018 [89]	2018	JPEG	–	DCT
RGB-N [118]	2018	Generic	RGB	SRM
EXIF-SC [59]	2018	Camera-based	RGB	–
ManTraNet [108]	2019	Generic	RGB	SRM, Bayar conv.
RRU-Net [17]	2019	Splicing	RGB	–
AdaCFA [9]	2020	Demosaicing	RGB	–
Noiseprint [34]	2020	Camera-based	RGB	–
SPAN [57]	2020	Generic	RGB	SRM, Bayar conv.
CR-CNN [111]	2020	Generic	–	Bayar conv.
MVSS-Net [26]	2021	Generic, splicing	RGB	Bayar conv.
TransForensics [55]	2021	Generic	RGB	–
CAT-Net v2 [65]	2022	Generic, JPEG	RGB	DCT
IF-OSN [109]	2022	Generic	RGB	–
PSCC-Net [71]	2022	Generic	RGB	–
Comprint [79]	2022	JPEG	RGB	–
ObjectFormer [105]	2022	Generic, JPEG	RGB	DCT
SSDA [95]	2022	Generic, splicing	RGB	SRM
TruFor [52]	2023	Camera-based, generic	RGB	Noiseprint++
HiFi-Net [53]	2023	Generic	RGB	LoG
WSCL [115]	2023	Generic	RGB	SRM, Bayar conv.
CFL-Net [88]	2023	Generic	RGB	SRM
SAFL-Net [100]	2023	Generic	RGB	Bayar conv.
APSC-Net [94]	2024	Generic	RGB	–
OMG-Fuser-F [62]	2024	JPEG, camera-based	RGB	DCT, Noiseprint++ [52]
DiffForensics [113]	2024	Mesoscopic	RGB	–

The table presents the type of forensic clues they exploit and their input

established as the state of the art in the field. Yet, such models can suffer from a lack of generalisation. They might fail to detect forgeries different to those on which the model was trained, or detect forgeries for the wrong reasons, such as due to semantic bias in the training data [8], which can lead the model to wrongly incriminate real images as fake. As such, the challenge in image forensics has shifted from building a good theoretical model towards building a suitable training dataset and a proper architecture to enable good generalisation on unseen data.

Deep Learning Methods

Specific Forensic Clues

Many early deep learning approaches focused on the analysis of specific forensic clues [9, 11, 14, 15, 79, 89]. For example, Barni et al. [15] exploits noise residuals rather than working on the RGB image signal, looking for traces left behind by double JPEG compression. A disadvantage of these methods is that the generalisation is still dependent on the diversity of the training set. In an attempt to improve performance in the wild, Park et al. [89] proposed a deep learning approach that considers a large number of JPEG quantisation tables in the training set. Bammey et al. [9, 11, 14] introduced positional learning to analyse the CFA, or mosaic, of an image. As cameras usually sample a single colour per pixel on a fixed pattern, and interpolate missing channels from neighbours, estimating the sampling colour of each pixel can help detect forgeries. They trained a CNN structure to estimate the modulo 2 position of each pixel in an image. As the CNN is translation-invariant and thus inherently blind to each pixel's location, it learns to rely on external clues, such as the artifacts left by demosaicing. At inference, the CNN thus retrieves the correct positional information in authentic images. As tampered images have their CFA-related clues altered in the tampered regions, the CNN fails to detect such positional information, i.e. the forgery is detected as a local error in the CNN output. However, while these recent methods can yield state-of-the-art results on high-quality images, they require them to retain their original resolution and be almost uncompressed, as resampling and JPEG compression quickly erase CFA traces. This limits their utility on social media images, which are often compressed and downsampled.

Generic Forensic Clues

Other methods use generic supervised CNNs instead of looking for specific artifacts. For example, ManTra-Net [108] is an end-to-end fully convolutional network that aims to detect every type of possible local manipulations and features related to local anomalies. SPAN [57] makes use of the attention mechanism at a local level, presenting a Spatial Pyramid Attention Network for forgery detection and localisation. The pyramidal scheme of local self-attention blocks is used to model the relationship between image patches at multiple scales. Both methods are trained on 385 distinct types of manipulation, in order to capture different clues. A segmentation-based approach for image forgery localisation is proposed with RRU-Net [17], in which the learning process is reinforced using both propagation and feedback of the residual in the network. Constrained R-CNN [111] also performs segmentation, proposing a coarse-to-fine architecture for image forgery classification and localisation. The network extracts learnable manipulation features from the image, followed by two stages: the first stage uses an attention region proposal network to extract manipulated regions for coarse manipulation detection, the second for the fine forgery segmentation. Nevertheless, a common issue with methods based on semantic segmentation is their tendency to cluster objects in the image regardless of their authenticity, which could often cause minor false alarms to become well-segmented objects even in pristine images. A more recent method, DiffForensics [113], focuses on the mesoscopic properties of the image rather than focusing on specific noise-based or semantic-based artifacts. Their approach operates in two stages: first a decoder is trained using a self-supervised denoising diffusion scheme, then localisation is refined using edge clue enhancement.

CNN-based methods are typically affected by the issue of global context information. This is often addressed by resizing the image to make processing computationally feasible. However, this is not an option in a tampering localisation scenario, as any process that involves resampling could destroy the fine-grained structure of the image, which contains important forensic traces. A recent approach that aims to solve the global context issue lies in transformer-based architectures [40]. Transformers capture long-range dependencies between sequence elements and support parallel processing, with the attention mechanism tracking correlations among all the input elements (i.e., pixels or patches) to aggregate global information of the input. To discover object-level inconsistencies, [105] uses cross-attention for object-aware tampering localisation. TransForensics [55] performs image forgery localisation using the self-attention mechanism, with a framework consisting of two main components: a dense self-attention encoder, responsible to model global context and rich interactions between patches at different scales, and a dense correction module, used for feature fusion.

Overall, learning-based methods trying to distinguish real and forged regions of images are ultimately limited by the variety and representativeness of the employed training dataset. It is hard for these methods to detect forgeries obtained through other means than what is seen during training, or to operate on images that have undergone processing that significantly differs from that of the training images. Additionally, they are prone to making **semantic detections** [8], i.e. detect objects as forged only because similar objects are often forged in the training dataset. For instance, training a model on datasets where most flags are forged would lead to detecting all flags in new images, no matter whether they are actually forged. This phenomenon is difficult to measure, especially on benchmark datasets that come with given train-test splits, as both sets are usually obtained in very similar ways and follow a very similar distribution.

One-Class Methods

Because of the large variety in potential manipulations, it is often very challenging to build comprehensive training datasets. As such, detectors trained in a supervised setup, are inherently limited to detecting forgeries that were seen during training. Instead of trying to build a training set representative of all possible manipulations, one-class training methods rely on pristine data only. In this way, the machine learning model learns the characteristics of authentic images, treating as anomalies anything that does not conform to this learned model of pristine content. Mayer and Stamm [81], for example, introduced a graph-based representation that models similarity between patches: each vertex represents a patch and the edge between two patches is weighted with a similarity score.

A large set of one-class methods involves the use of a Siamese network [21, 63], which consist in two identical networks that process two separate inputs and provide two outputs, which are then compared using a similarity metric. The twin networks share the same weights to ensure that their parameters are tied and to guarantee that similar images are represented close to each other in the feature space. Mayer et al. [80] adopted this approach by presenting a system that determines if two patches contain the same forensic traces using a score for each pair. The Siamese approach is also used in EXIF-SC [59], which detects splicing by analysing if the image is self consistent, i.e. whether its content could have been produced by a single imaging pipeline. The resulting self-consistency map highlights patches that are not consistent with the imaging pipeline of the rest of the image. Similarly, a one-class approach with Siamese CNN is Noiseprint [34]; this is trained to extract a learned noise residual from an image representing the camera model fingerprint. The Noiseprint is somewhat similar to PRNU [31], but at a model-level rather than a device-level. This CNN is trained with pairs of patches (extracted from the same position) coming from two images captured by either the same camera model or not, adjusting the weights accordingly in a contrastive learning fashion. This process enables the network to suppress the scene content as much as possible. Following [34], Comprint [79] extracts a JPEG fingerprint rather than a camera model one.

Combining Low-Level and High-Level Features

Most methods rely either on the RGB image or on low-level traces, which are usually obtained by suppressing the image content by means of high-pass filters or denoising. The most commonly used filters for the extraction of low-level features are the spatial rich models (SRM) [44], which are often included as a pre-processing step for forensic analysis [57, 88, 95, 108, 115, 118]. Instead, [16] introduces the Bayar convolution, which employs high-pass filters learnt during training. Numerous other works have used such trainable filters to conduct a noise sensitive analysis [26, 57, 100, 108, 111, 115]. Recently, a common effective strategy used for forgery localisation combines high-level features (e.g. the RGB image) and low-level features (e.g. edges, noise residuals, high-pass filtering) to carry out a more comprehensive detection, based on the assumption that they contain complementary information. A pioneering work is the two-branch strategy proposed in [118], which combines the features of the noise and RGB streams through bilinear pooling. Subsequent works also leverage fusion of high and low-level features [26, 52, 53, 57, 62, 65, 88, 95, 100, 105, 108, 115]. A different kind of low-level features are considered in [52], which fuses RGB features with Noiseprint++, a more robust version of the learned noise residual proposed in [34]. Subsequently, [62] also leverages RGB and Noiseprint++ information, together with DCT features.

4 Challenges Posed by Generative AI

The advent of AI-based tools for local image manipulation [98] introduces significant challenges to the image forensics field. As recent studies have shown [78], most existing methods are not sufficient to detect this new type of forgery. It is important to highlight that when using AI-based tools to perform local manipulations, two distinct scenarios arise. In the first scenario, called Splicing (SP) manipulation, the tool only modifies a target area, affecting forensic clues only within that region and leaving the rest of the image intact. In the second scenario, called Fully Regenerating (FR) manipulation, the tool does not directly alter the designated area. Instead, it encodes the image in a latent space, conditionally alters some of its parts without affecting the visual appearance of the rest of the image and finally regenerates the entire image. With respect to detection, these scenarios present two important differences. On the one hand, locating the semantically modified area is more challenging in the FR case, since there is no transition from the pristine to the modified region, as both of them are newly generated [101]. On the other hand, when the entire image is regenerated, manipulations can also be detected using the fully synthetic image detection methods (that will be presented in the next chapter).

In case of splicing manipulations, existing methods based on specific forensic clues, i.e. those that analyse traces left by the image acquisition pipeline, are able also to detect these AI-based alterations, as they can identify any manipulation that locally affects the traces. In contrast, deep learning methods, while often achieving higher performance on conventional manipulations, often struggle with AI-based alterations [49, 78]. The reason is that new manipulations often differ significantly from the data present in training sets used in the development of these methods. Figure 3 illustrates a new form of manipulation along with the result of a state-of-the-art forensic tool. The first two columns show the original image and its new version, expanded at the bottom with new synthetic content. This type of alteration can be easily created using Adobe Photoshop's Generative Expand tool.[6] The third column shows the Noiseprint++ image, a noise residual related to image acquisition forensic traces, which reveals a clear difference between the original and generated regions. Although the TruFor deep learning method [52] exploits Noiseprint++, it fails to localise the expanded region (fourth column) because it was trained using different types of manipulation. However, when TruFor is retrained including this new form of manipulation, it can accurately localise the altered region (last column).

To study the performance of the current image forgery localisation approaches as well as to craft new ones capable of handling these new challenges, suitable datasets are necessary. To this end, Guillaro et al. [52] introduced the CocoGlide benchmark for evaluating the performance of tampering localisation algortihms on splicing-based text-guided manipulations. Later, Mareen et al. [78] considered fully regenerated local manipulations while increasing the scale and diversity of altered images, by introducing the TGIF dataset. To increase the quality of training data, Giak-

[6] https://www.adobe.com/gr_en/products/photoshop/generative-expand.html.

Fig. 3 From left to right: original image, image manipulated using the Generative Expand tool of Adobe Photoshop, its Noiseprint++, localisation map of TruFor, localisation map after retraining

Table 2 Datasets of local image forgeries performed by generative AI

Dataset	Orig. datasets	Orig. images	Inp. images	Inp. models	Inp. pipelines	Double inp.	Type	Resolution
CocoGlide [52]	1	512	512	1	✗	✗	AI	256 × 256
TGIF [78]	1	3,124	74,976	3	✗	✗	AI	Up to 1024p
SAGI-D [49]	3	77,900	95,839	8	5	✓	AI/OR	Up to 2048p

The acronym AI indicates text-guided AI-generated content while OR indicates object removal

oumoglou et al. [49] proposed a pipeline for creating semantically aligned prompts and an uncertainty-guided mechanism for discarding non-realistic images. Training some previously proposed architectures on this latter dataset, also exhibited significant potential on localising tampering on fully regenerated images [49]. An overview of these recently proposed datasets is provided in Table 2.

The use of AI is not limited to the manipulation of conventional photographs; it can also be used to alter biological and medical images, with the risk of falsifying scientific results or compromising medical reports. Forensic methods designed for conventional photographs are often inadequate for these different domains, and developing ad hoc techniques tailored to these domains remains an open challenge [76, 120].

Typically, forensic methods rely on different assumptions about the processing history of the image under analysis. For example, compression-based techniques assume that the manipulated and pristine areas of an image have undergone different compression sequences. Therefore, forensic methods fail when these assumptions do not hold. To increase the chances of detecting manipulations, it is good practice to use several forensic methods based on different assumptions. In such a scenario, a further complication that arises is that different forensic methods, each based on a specific set of assumptions and aimed at exploiting peculiar forensic traces, tend to provide different and even contradictory outputs. In such cases, the burden of finding a meaningful interpretation for these conflicting results and making a sensible decision about the authenticity of an image falls on the forensic analyst. One of the open challenges for future research is how to automate this step as well, using decision fusion techniques that appropriately combine the results of different forensic methods. In this direction, [25] introduced a deep learning architecture to combine the outputs of several tampering localisation algorithms in a single and more robust output, while [99] extended this concept by modeling the attributes of each input using a separate network stream. Recently, [62] highlighted the importance of semantic relationships in effectively interpreting the outputs of image forgery localisation algorithms, and incorporated prior knowledge about them using a large-scale pre-trained instance segmentation network.

5 Research Advances

This section discusses some highlights and advances in the field of image forensics as part of the research efforts in the vera.ai project that aim at building a robust and extensible image verification framework.

Robust and Trustworthhy Image Forgery Localisation

Most methods for detection and localisation of local manipulations exhibit poor performance in the real-world, where images undergo many post-processing steps, like compression and resizing, that attenuate forensic traces. To overcome this problem, we proposed TruFor [52], standing for Trustworthy Image Forensics. This combines both low-level and high-level information (cf. Fig. 4 for an architectural view of the method). From the input RGB image, x, a learned noise-sensitive fingerprint n is extracted (namely *Noiseprint++*), which enhances forensic traces. Both x and n feed a transformer-based cross-modal framework, with a shared encoder that extracts dense features f. These are then processed by two parallel anomaly and confidence decoders to extract an anomaly localisation map l, and a confidence map c. The anomaly decoder relies mostly on Noiseprint++ to localise image areas with anomalous low-level forensic traces and proposes them as possible manipulations. The confidence decoder, trained using true localisation maps, uses the high-level RGB information to associate a reliability score with the selected areas. The two pieces of information, l and c, are processed jointly to decide whether the image is manipulated. Then, they are provided individually to the user for further analysis and to extract a confidence-informed map of image manipulations. Overall, this strategy allows many potential false alarms to be rejected, increasing the reliability and robustness of the method.

Noiseprint++ captures information on the camera model and its editing history. Its extractor learns patch-level self-similarities by means of contrastive learning, obtaining the same fingerprint for patches with similar properties and different noise residuals for patches with different properties (Fig. 5a). To gain robustness, a large variety of editing operations—diverse combinations of resizing, JPEG compression, illumination changes—is introduced, for a total of 512 history pipelines. Figure 5b shows examples of noise fingerprints associated to manipulated images, demon-

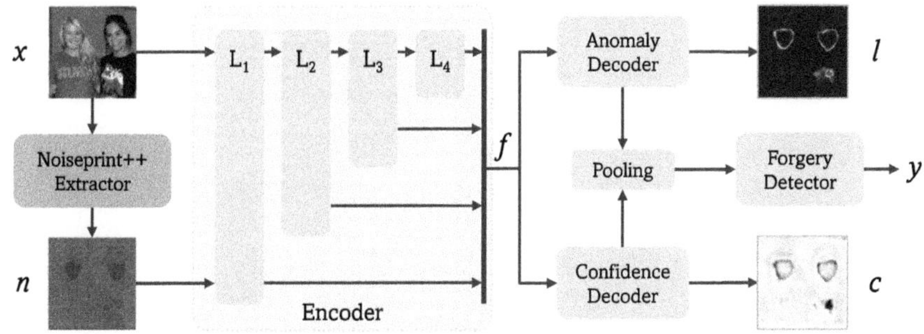

Fig. 4 Overview of the TruFor [52] framework

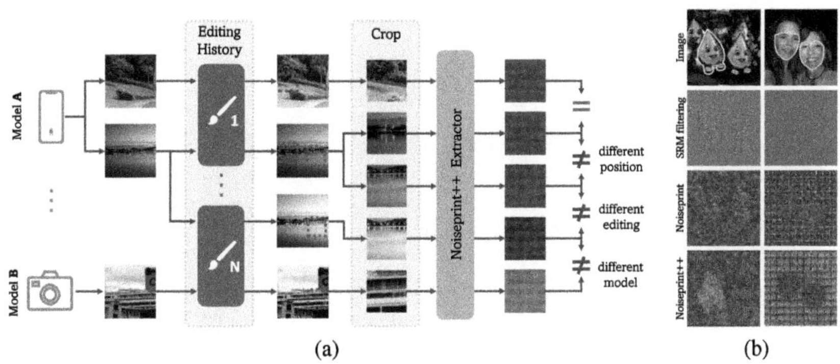

Fig. 5 **a** Noiseprint++ [52] training procedure. **b** A comparison of noise residuals

strating that Noiseprint++ is much better at enhancing forensic artifacts than its previous version, i.e. Noiseprint [34], and other noise residuals, like the spatial rich models [44].

While only pristine images coming from more than 1400 camera models have been used for the training of the Noiseprint++ extractor, both pristine and forged images—including diverse types of manipulations—are leveraged to train the localisation, confidence estimation, and detection networks.

The proposed method has been assessed on datasets that include both conventional (splicing, copy-move and inpainting) [20, 36, 39, 51, 56, 107] as well as deepfake manipulations (GANs and Diffusion Models) [52, 66], for a total of 1.5K fake and 1.5K real images. The evaluation datasets do not contain images seen during training. Table 3 shows the pixel-level localisation performance. TruFor provides the best F1 performance on the average, and it is the best or second best on all datasets, which attests to a remarkable generalisation ability. It performs well also on GAN-based (OpenForensics) and diffusion-based (CocoGlide) local manipulations. Image-level detection results are shown in Table 4 in terms of AUC and Accuracy. TruFor is the best performer on most datasets and has the best average performance. On the contrary, many methods exhibit very poor performance, close to random guessing

Table 3 Pixel-level F1 performance of image forgery localisation

Method	CASIAv1+		Coverage		Columbia		NIST16		DSO-1		VIPP		OpenFor.		CocoGlide		AVG	
	Best	Fixed	Best	Fixed	Best	Fixed	Best	Fixed	Best	Fixed	Best	Fixed	Best	Fixed	Best	Fixed	Best	Fixed
EXIF-SC [59]	0.255	0.106	0.332	0.164	0.880	0.798	0.298	0.227	0.577	0.442	0.424	0.215	0.318	0.175	0.424	0.293	0.437	0.303
CR-CNN [111]	0.538	0.481	0.487	0.391	0.779	0.631	0.363	0.300	0.377	0.289	0.355	0.282	0.143	0.110	0.577	0.447	0.452	0.366
RRU-Net [17]	0.498	0.408	0.339	0.279	0.629	0.575	0.218	0.154	0.360	0.312	0.336	0.272	0.206	0.157	0.504	0.416	0.386	0.322
ManTraNet [108]	0.320	0.180	0.486	0.317	0.650	0.508	0.225	0.172	0.537	0.412	0.373	0.255	0.661	0.551	0.673	0.516	0.491	0.364
SPAN [57]	0.169	0.112	0.428	0.235	0.873	0.759	0.363	0.228	0.390	0.233	0.375	0.223	0.176	0.089	0.350	0.298	0.391	0.272
AdaCFA [9]	0.158	0.128	0.215	0.183	0.587	0.403	0.124	0.106	0.262	0.235	0.210	0.184	0.115	0.098	0.357	0.314	0.254	0.206
CAT-Net v2 [65]	**0.852**	**0.752**	0.582	0.381	**0.923**	**0.859**	0.417	0.308	0.673	0.584	0.672	0.590	**0.947**	**0.899**	0.603	0.434	0.709	0.601
IF-OSN [109]	0.676	0.553	0.472	0.304	0.836	0.753	0.449	0.330	0.621	0.470	0.508	0.403	0.204	0.123	0.589	0.428	0.544	0.421
MVSS-Net [26]	0.650	0.528	0.659	0.514	0.781	0.729	0.372	0.320	0.459	0.358	0.485	0.389	0.225	0.117	0.642	0.486	0.534	0.430
PSCC-Net [71]	0.670	0.520	0.615	0.473	0.760	0.604	0.210	0.113	0.733	0.458	0.309	0.183	0.353	0.105	0.685	0.515	0.542	0.371
Noiseprint [34]	0.205	0.137	0.342	0.229	0.835	0.513	0.345	0.196	0.811	0.439	0.546	0.382	0.675	0.420	0.405	0.318	0.521	0.329
TruFor [52]	0.822	0.737	**0.735**	**0.600**	0.914	**0.859**	**0.470**	**0.399**	**0.973**	**0.930**	**0.746**	**0.693**	0.901	0.827	**0.720**	**0.523**	**0.785**	**0.696**

Results are computed using both the best threshold per image and a fixed threshold (0.5) for all images and datasets
The best value per column is highlighted in bold, and the second best is underlined

Table 4 Image-level AUC and balanced accuracy performance of image forgery detection

Method	CASIAv1+		Coverage		Columbia		NIST16		DSO-1		VIPP		CocoGlide		AVG	
	AUC	Acc	AUC	Acc	AUC	Acc	AUC	Acc	AUC	Acc	AUC	Acc	AUC	Acc	AUC	Acc
EXIF-SC [59]	0.490	0.500	0.498	0.500	0.976	0.506	0.504	0.500	0.764	0.500	0.617	0.500	0.526	0.500	0.625	0.501
CR-CNN [111]	0.670	0.535	0.553	0.510	0.755	0.628	0.737	0.641	0.576	0.535	0.504	0.558	0.589	0.533	0.626	0.563
RRU-Net [17]	0.574	0.488	0.482	0.500	0.583	0.500	0.666	0.500	0.444	0.500	0.534	0.500	0.533	0.503	0.545	0.499
ManTraNet [108]	0.644	0.500	0.760	0.500	0.810	0.500	0.624	0.500	0.874	0.500	0.530	0.500	**0.778**	0.500	0.717	0.500
SPAN [57]	0.480	0.487	0.670	0.605	**0.999**	0.951	0.632	0.597	0.669	0.510	0.580	0.572	0.475	0.491	0.644	0.602
AdaCFA [9]	0.500	0.500	0.500	0.500	0.500	0.500	0.500	0.500	0.500	0.500	0.500	0.500	0.500	0.500	0.500	0.500
CAT-Net v2 [65]	**0.942**	**0.838**	0.680	0.635	0.977	0.803	0.750	0.597	0.747	0.525	0.813	0.565	0.667	0.580	0.797	0.649
IF-OSN [109]	0.735	0.635	0.557	0.510	0.882	0.522	0.658	0.553	0.853	0.505	0.696	0.522	0.611	0.567	0.713	0.545
MVSS-Net [26]	0.932	0.808	0.733	0.545	0.984	0.667	0.579	0.538	0.552	0.485	0.629	0.522	0.654	0.536	0.723	0.586
PSCC-Net [71]	0.869	0.683	0.657	0.550	0.300	0.508	0.485	0.456	0.650	0.543	0.574	0.507	0.777	**0.661**	0.616	0.558
Noiseprint [34]	0.494	–	0.525	–	0.872	–	0.618	–	0.821	–	0.580	–	0.520	–	0.633	–
TruFor [52]	0.916	0.813	**0.770**	**0.680**	0.996	**0.984**	**0.760**	**0.662**	**0.984**	**0.930**	**0.820**	**0.761**	0.752	0.639	**0.857**	**0.781**

The best value per column is highlighted in bold, and the second best is underlined

Table 5 Pixel-level F1 performance (using fixed threshold) on datasets uploaded on Facebook (Fb) and WhatsApp (Wa)

Method	CASIAv1		DSO-1		CocoGlide	
	Fb	Wa	Fb	Wa	Fb	Wa
IF-OSN [109]	0.513	0.524	0.484	0.395	0.406	0.404
CAT-Net v2 [65]	0.681	0.508	0.310	0.247	0.447	0.443
MVSS-Net [26]	0.469	0.444	0.356	0.308	0.347	0.351
TruFor [52]	**0.716**	**0.713**	**0.685**	**0.465**	**0.460**	**0.461**

The best value per column is highlighted in bold

(0.5). This is especially acute for accuracy, which is highly sensitive to the choice of threshold. A robustness analysis on images impaired by compression and resizing has been carried out using datasets uploaded on Facebook and WhatsApp (Table 5). TruFor performs consistently better than all competitors (only the best performers are shown). Figure 6 illustrates some results to provide some more insight into the role of localisation and confidence maps. Two manipulated (left) and two pristine (right) images are shown. In the last image, a false alarm is present in the anomaly map, but the selected region has low confidence (dark in the confidence map) and it is eventually rejected.

Combining Diverse Sources of Forensic Information

Deep learning architectures have enabled recent image forgery detection and localisation approaches to capture a diverse set of forensic artifacts. However, the combination of selected inputs, employed architectural components and training data unavoidably introduce biases towards certain types of artifact. Therefore, any single approach employed in uncontrolled environments, such as the Web, can underperform on images from a significantly different distribution from the modelled one. Solving this issue requires to effectively combine the capabilities of a diverse set of forensic approaches and to conditionally trust the ones whose learned distribution better corresponds to the image being analysed.

In a preliminary work [99] we proposed a multi-stream fusion network to combine the outputs of several image forgery localisation algorithms. Each stream encodes the decision space of a fused algorithm into a common feature space, while a learned bottleneck stage uses an attention mechanism to decide the amount of information to further propagate from each stream. This network exhibited state-of-the-art performance among the popular CASIA [38], IFS-TC [60] and Columbia [86] benchmarks by combining the outputs of a compression [70] and a noise-based algorithm [33], despite each of these algorithms underperforming when employed separately. This provided evidence on the feasibility of the pursued concept.

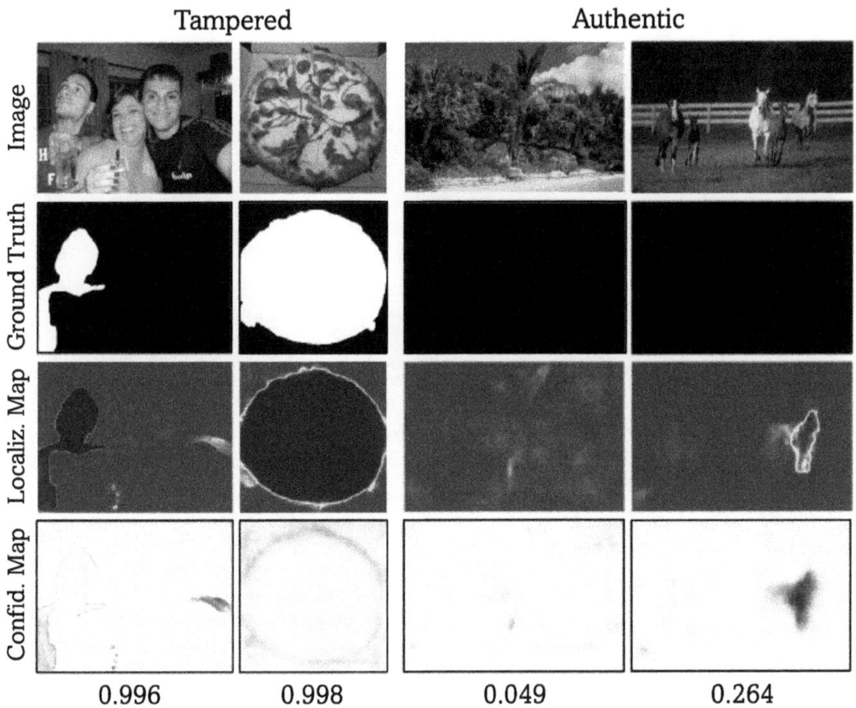

Fig. 6 Manipulated images (left) and pristine images (right). From top to bottom: test image, ground truth, anomaly map, confidence map and image-level score

Recently, in [62] we refined this concept and proposed the Object Mask-Guided Fusion Transformer (OMG-Fuser) approach, to combine an arbitrary number of forensic information sources guided by the image semantics. In particular, it introduced the object-guided transformer for employing prior semantic information regarding the image, obtained from a pre-trained instance segmentation model, by limiting self-attention among image regions depicting the same object. This information is used to analyse each forensic input, captured by a different network stream, at the object level. Then, the token fusion transformer was proposed for combining an arbitrary number of input streams into a comprehensive representation. Finally, a long-range dependencies transformer is employed to integrate this object-level information into an image-level representation, suitable for downstream forensics related tasks, like image forgery detection and localisation. The overview of this architecture is presented in Fig. 7.

The efficacy of the OMG-Fuser architecture was evaluated on combining the outputs of five recent image forgery localisation approaches, i.e. SPAN [57], MVSS-Net [26], CATNet v2 [65], IF-OSN [109] and TruFor [52] that are based on different principles. We refer to this specific score-level fusion implementation as OMG-Fuser$_S$. Seven benchmarks were considered in this evaluation, spanning a broad

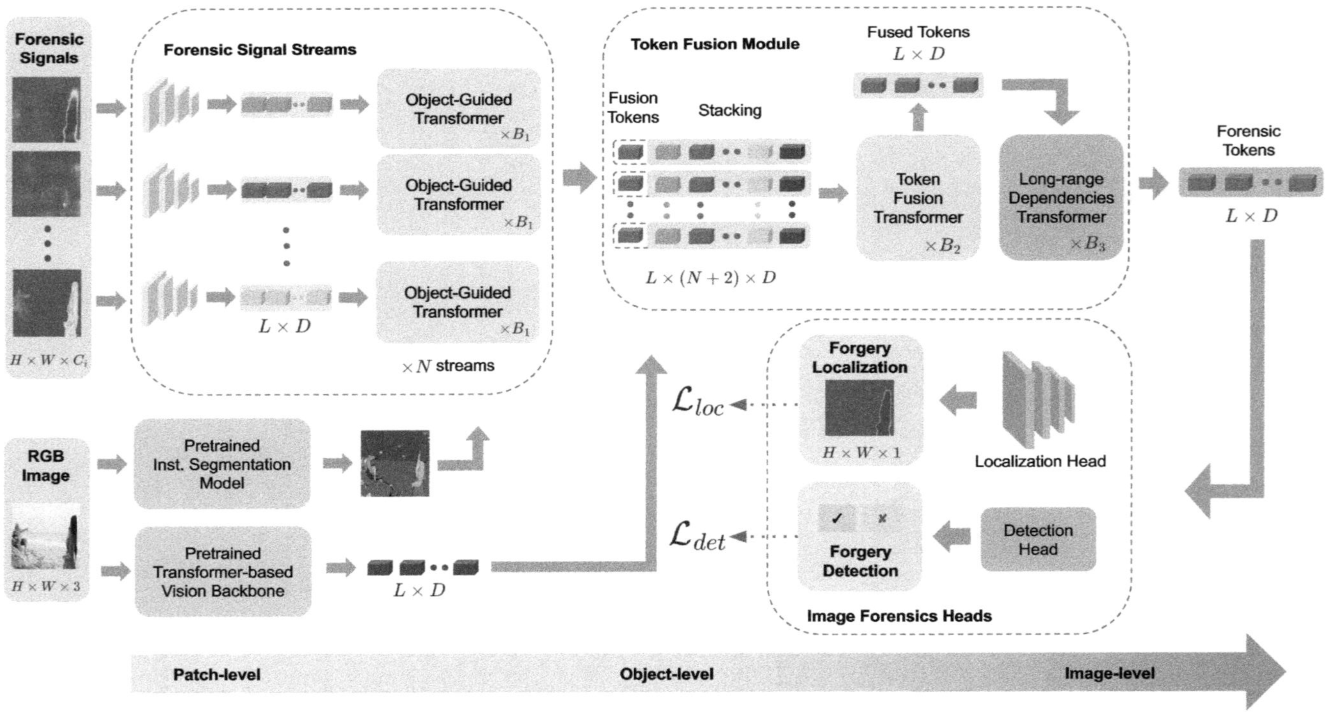

Fig. 7 Overview of OMG-Fuser [62]. Forensic signals are fused into a robust forgery localisation mask and detection score. To achieve that, it combines information from the RGB image and its instance segmentation maps. Each forensic signal and the RGB image are first processed by separate network streams through independent object-guided transformers. Then, the proposed token fusion module fuses the different streams, leading to features with a progressively increasing level of information granularity, from patch-level (in the early stages) to object-level (in intermediate stages) and to image-level (in the final stages). A localisation and a detection head process the extracted forensic tokens to generate the final outputs

range of forgeries, from naive image splicing and copy-move [38, 51, 86, 107, 110] to more sophisticated AI-based image inpaintings [52, 66]. The pixel-level evaluation results are presented in Table 6, while the image-level ones are presented in Table 7. As we see, either previous statistical fusion approaches, like the popular one based on the Dempster–Shafer Theory [43], or naive learnable approaches [25], in many cases perform even worse than a simple averaging operation. This can be attributed to the fact that the former require perfect knowledge about the correlation of the fused signals, something very difficult, if not impossible, to acquire for complex data-driven approaches, while the latter are limited by the variance of the employed training data. Instead, OMG-Fuser, by effectively employing external semantic information from pre-trained segmentation models, provides a consistent performance improvement over previous score-level fusion approaches. Moreover, on the same benchmark, it achieves an absolute improvement of 5.6% on forgery localisation and 8.3% on forgery detection, in terms of AUC, over the best fused algorithm, i.e. TruFor. This highlights its capability to capture complementary information from each of the fused streams, while generalising to forgery types beyond the ones seen during training.

Generation of High-Quality Training Data

Deep learning can be reduced to two key concepts, i.e. data and architectures to model their distribution. As generative models rapidly advance and become capable of producing highly sophisticated and realistic image alterations, any learned detection boundary quickly becomes obsolete. Also, theoretical limitations prevent the existence of any single model capable of indefinitely generalising to unseen challenges [50]. Therefore, effectively combatting the online exploitation of newly introduced generative approaches requires the ability to quickly acquire relevant data of high quality, to model this shifted distribution. While online sources can provide invaluable information to assess the risk of specific types of forgery, solely relying on Web collected data can both lead to noisy ground-truth labels as well as introduce unwanted selection biases.

To reduce such biases while incorporating a representative set of AI-based alterations, we introduced in [78] a pipeline for generating inpaintings starting from a set of authentic images as well as their captions and instance segmentation masks. We considered three generative models, i.e. Stable Diffusion 2 (SD2), Stable Diffusion XL (SDXL) and Adobe Firefly (PS), representative of the early open source models capable of producing high-fidelity imagery, their subsequent counterparts that significantly increased the output resolution, as well as the commercial implementations respectively. We selected the altered region either using the instance segmentation mask or the bounding box of the depicted objects, while both the approaches of splicing (sp) and fully regeneration (fr) are considered. Also, for each case, we generated three inpainted images, using different seeds to the generative models. An overview of this pipeline is presented in Fig. 8. Using this pipeline and employing authentic images and the respective annotations from COCO [69], we generated

Table 6 Comparison of fusion approaches on image forgery localisation

Approach	CASIAv1+		Columbia		Coverage		NIST16		OpenFor.		CocoGl.		DID		Overall	
	F1	AUC	F1	AUC	F1	AUC	F1	AUC	F1	AUC	F1	AUC	F1	AUC	F1	AUC
DST-Fusion [43]	0.753	0.948	0.854	0.935	0.488	0.792	0.147	0.569	0.204	0.507	0.386	0.809	0.249	0.728	0.440	0.756
AVG-Fusion	0.775	0.973	0.876	**0.989**	0.521	0.913	0.185	**0.831**	0.272	0.908	0.428	0.878	0.190	0.905	0.464	0.914
OW-Fusion [25]	0.788	0.970	0.858	0.960	0.477	0.885	0.317	0.744	0.707	0.874	0.480	0.807	0.537	0.902	0.595	0.877
OMG-Fuser$_S$ [62]	**0.851**	**0.981**	**0.929**	0.987	**0.701**	**0.960**	**0.375**	0.821	**0.741**	**0.941**	**0.562**	**0.894**	**0.766**	**0.961**	**0.704**	**0.935**

Pixel-level F1 and AUC scores are presented for each algorithm and dataset
The best value per column is highlighted in bold, and the second best is underlined

Table 7 Comparison of fusion approaches on image forgery detection

Approach	CASIAv1+		Columbia		Coverage		NIST16		CocoGl.		Overall	
	F1	AUC	F1	AUC	F1	AUC	F1	AUC	F1	AUC	F1	AUC
DST-Fusion [43]	0.803	<u>0.938</u>	0.923	0.979	0.690	0.784	0.444	0.751	0.660	<u>0.785</u>	0.704	0.847
OW-Fusion [25]	0.853	0.933	0.801	0.977	0.661	0.724	<u>0.698</u>	0.755	<u>0.693</u>	0.722	0.741	0.822
AVG-Fusion	<u>0.861</u>	0.930	<u>0.945</u>	<u>0.997</u>	<u>0.733</u>	<u>0.807</u>	0.690	<u>0.767</u>	0.692	0.782	<u>0.784</u>	<u>0.857</u>
OMG-Fuser$_S$ [62]	**0.910**	**0.980**	**0.994**	**0.999**	**0.810**	**0.845**	**0.719**	**0.802**	**0.726**	**0.827**	**0.832**	**0.895**

Image-level F1 and AUC scores are presented for each algorithm and dataset
The best value per column is highlighted in bold, and the second best is underlined

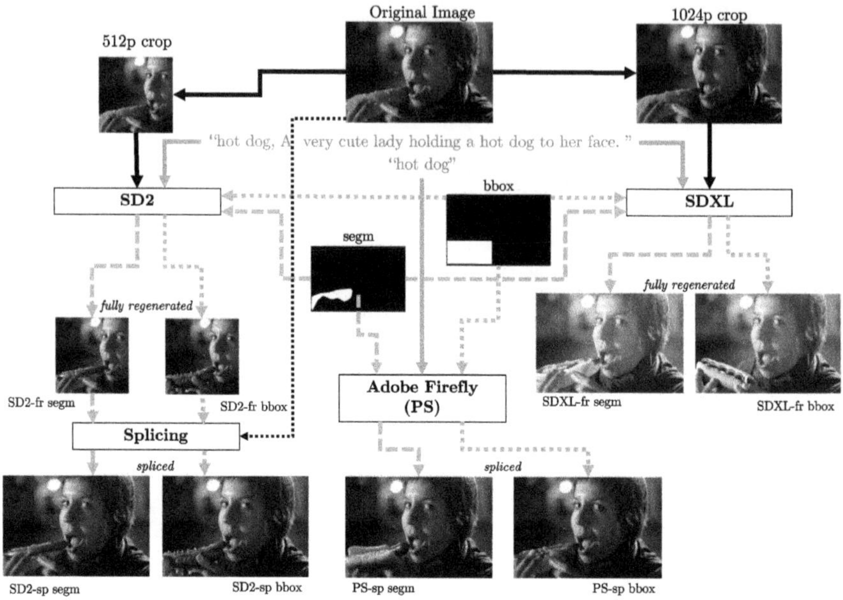

Fig. 8 TGIF [78] dataset creation. The original image is fed to SD2, SDXL, and Adobe Firefly (Photoshop), along with a prompt and a mask (segmentation or bounding box). For SD2, an additional splicing step is performed, which is done automatically in Adobe Firefly, and discarded for SDXL's output. For simplicity, only one variation is illustrated, rather than all three variations that we generated in batch

the Text-Guided Inpainting Forgery (TGIF) dataset and introduced it to the image forensics community.

We employed the TGIF dataset to evaluate the performance of recent pre-trained image forgery localisation models, with the respective pixel-level F1 scores being presented in Table 8. We see that while some of the most sophisticated models exhibit significant localisation performance on splicing-based alterations, all of them catastrophically fail to the case of inpaintings based on full regeneration. The high performance of CAT-Net v2 on the splicing-based alterations, which incorporates a dedicated network branch to capture JPEG-related artifacts, evidences the inability of generative models to reconstruct subtle patterns of the original image. However, distortions introduced to the image signal by popular compression algorithms, suffice to eliminate the discriminative ability of any pre-trained model, irrespective of the type of inpainting. This highlights that, while the network architecture of any detector is a crucial factor towards generalisation, sooner or later, the performance of any model will decrease, under heavy distribution shifts.

Distribution shifts may not only occur due to the introduction of more capable generative models, but also due to the evolution of users' behaviours. Humans usually carefully select the employed prompts and regions to edit as well as perform iterative refinement to create high-quality images. To automate this procedure, in [49] we introduced a model-agnostic generative pipeline, to sample prompts from a distribution that closely aligns with human perception and to evaluate the generated content and discard instances that deviate from such a distribution. This distribution is approximated using pretrained large language and vision-language models, as well as the concepts of Semantically Aligned Object Replacement and Uncertainty-Guided Deceptiveness assessment. The first aims to select prompts and alterations that are plausible to humans, while the latter assesses the potential of a generated image to deceive a human. An overview of this pipeline is presented in Fig. 9.

Table 8 Evaluation of image forgery localisation (IFL) approaches on the TGIF [78] dataset (F1 score)

Method	Uncompressed				JPEG Q80		JPEG Q60		WEBP Q80		WEBP Q60	
	SD2-sp	PS-sp	SD2-fr	SDXL-fr	SD2-sp	PS-sp	SD2-sp	PS-sp	SD2-sp	PS-sp	SD2-sp	PS-sp
PSCC-Net [71]	0.15	0.38	0.05	0.05	–	–	–	–	–	–	–	–
SPAN [57]	0.00	0.00	0.00	0.00	–	–	–	–	–	–	–	–
IF-OSN [109]	0.23	0.36	0.20	0.18	–	–	–	–	–	–	–	–
MVSS-Net [26]	0.07	0.08	0.06	0.09	–	–	–	–	–	–	–	–
Mantranet [108]	0.15	0.56	0.03	0.05	0.08	0.13	0.03	0.04	0.08	0.11	0.09	0.11
CAT-Net v2 [65]	**0.87**	**0.85**	0.04	0.03	0.05	0.07	0.09	0.08	0.13	0.13	0.07	0.07
TruFor [52]	**0.83**	**0.79**	0.19	0.18	0.32	0.44	0.25	0.32	0.24	0.29	0.20	0.23
MMFusion [103]	**0.75**	**0.74**	0.15	0.18	0.35	0.49	0.22	0.32	0.22	0.33	0.19	0.28

Compressed images were only considered for IFL methods and sub-datasets exhibiting decent performance on uncompressed images. The abbreviation *sp* stands for splicing, while *fr* for fully regenerating type of forgery

Decent performing algorithms per column (F1 score above 0.7) are highlighted in bold

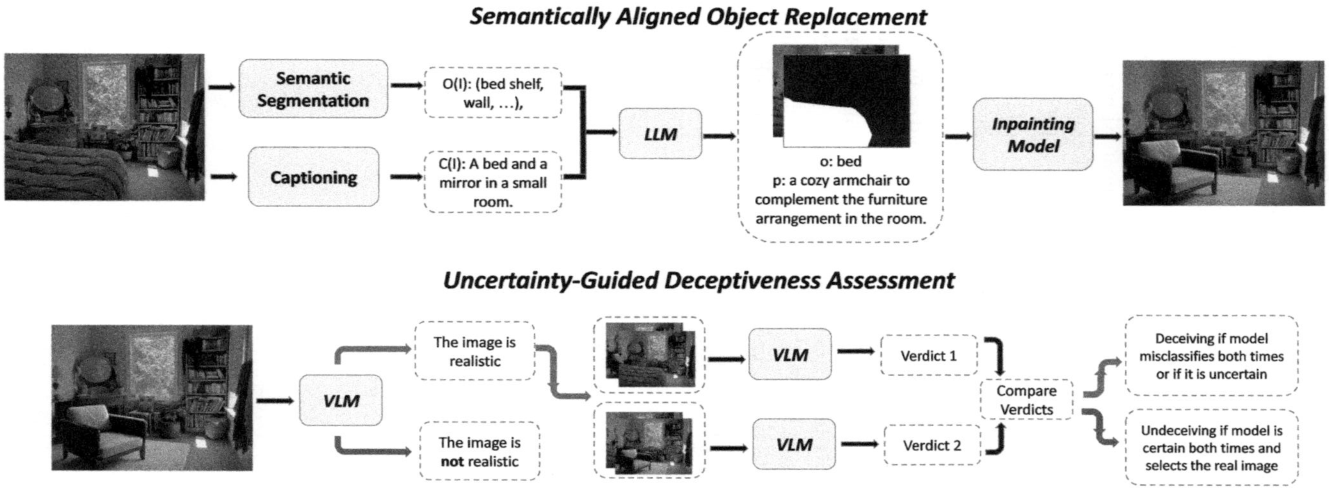

Fig. 9 The first row illustrates SAOR: an input image is processed to identify objects (via labels or segmentation) and generate a caption. The language model selects an object and generates a prompt, which, along with the image and mask, guides the inpainting model to produce the result. The second row depicts UGDA: if the inpainted image passes an initial realism check, it undergoes a second evaluation. The VLM compares the inpainted and original images twice, in reverse order. If the VLM's responses differ (indicating uncertainty) or both favour the inpainted image, it is labelled as deceiving; otherwise, undeceiving

By employing the above process with authentic images from three public collections [35, 64, 69], five inpainting pipelines [61, 77, 112, 117, 119], eight generative models, two distinct LLMs and the ChatGPT-4o VLM, we generated the SAGI-D dataset [49], a diverse collection of 78k authentic images and 96k inpainted ones. This is split in train, validation and test subsets without any shared authentic images among them. Moreover, the test set includes both in- and out-of-domain sub-splits, with the latter also employing a different LLM and a different source of real images. Multiple popular image forgery detection and localisation architectures were trained on this dataset, with the respective accuracy and mean F1 metrics reported in Table 9. Overall, we see that while all the pre-trained models significantly underperform, the retrained versions of architectures like the MMFusion [103] and TruFor [52], exhibit significant performance improvements, even in the challenging out-of-domain case.

Overall, efficient image forgery detection and localisation in the wild, requires a thorough understanding of its generation mechanisms, to enable the design of deep learning architectures that incorporate suitable inductive biases and to train them on representative data collections. However, theoretical limitations related both to the very nature of any digital image as a signal of finite information capacity, as well as to computability boundaries, impose limitations to what can be detected by solely relying on the image signal. Consequently, continuous research is crucial in this "arms race" and, as part of vera.ai, we presented a number of advances aiming at addressing the challenge of AI-based forgery detection and localisation.

Table 9 Evaluation of the SAGI [49] generative pipeline on training forgery detection and localisation models

	Model	Mean F1								Accuracy							
		ID		OOD		SP		FR		ID		OOD		SP		FR	
Original	CAT-Net v2 [65]	0.628		0.537		0.916		0.571		0.598		0.424		0.845		0.399	
	PSCC-Net [71]	0.476		0.476		0.575		0.501		0.599		0.530		0.404		0.334	
	MMFusion [103]	0.573		0.569		0.772		0.407		0.617		0.634		0.629		0.255	
	TruFor [52]	0.464		0.416		0.582		0.222		0.582		0.601		0.410		0.125	
Retrained	CAT-Net v2 [65]	0.989	+ 0.361	0.681	+ 0.144	0.999	+ 0.083	0.999	+ 0.428	0.988	+ 0.390	0.530	+ 0.106	0.999	+ 0.154	0.999	+ 0.600
	PSCC-Net [71]	0.528	+ 0.052	0.640	+ 0.164	0.668	+ 0.093	0.525	+ 0.024	0.634	+ 0.035	0.718	+ 0.188	0.501	+ 0.098	0.356	+ 0.022
	MMFusion [103]	0.934	+ 0.361	0.810	+ 0.241	0.924	+ 0.152	0.898	+ 0.491	0.928	+ 0.311	0.809	+ 0.175	0.859	+ 0.230	0.815	+ 0.560
	TruFor [52]	0.967	+ 0.503	0.929	+ 0.513	0.977	+ 0.495	0.971	+ 0.749	0.962	+ 0.380	0.928	+ 0.327	0.955	+ 0.545	0.944	+ 0.819

Mean F1 is presented for localisation and accuracy for detection. Results include in-domain (ID) and out-of-domain (OOD) performance for spliced (SP) and fully-regenerated (FR) images. ID and OOD columns present performance across forged and real images, while SP and FR specialise on forged images of the corresponding type. Green numbers show improvements over original models. Retraining on this new dataset significantly enhances performance, underscoring the value of semantic alignment for crafting high-quality synthetic data

Acknowledgements This research was supported by the European Union under the Horizon Europe vera.ai project, Grant Agreement number 101070093.

References

1. Agarwal, S., Farid, H.: Photo forensics from JPEG dimples. In: 2017 IEEE Workshop on Information Forensics and Security (WIFS), pp. 1–6 (2017). https://doi.org/10.1109/WIFS.2017.8267641
2. Akshatha, K., Karunakar, A.K., Anitha, H., Raghavendra, U., Shetty, D.: Digital camera identification using PRNU: a feature based approach. Digit. Investig. **19**, 69–77 (2016)
3. Al Naqbi, H., Bahroun, Z., Ahmed, V.: Enhancing work productivity through generative artificial intelligence: a comprehensive literature review. Sustainability **16**(3), 1166 (2024)
4. Avrahami, O., Fried, O., Lischinski, D.: Blended latent diffusion. ACM Trans. Graph. **42**(4) (2023)
5. Bammey, Q., Colom, M., Ehret, T., Gardella, M., Grompone, R., Morel, J., Nikoukhah, T., Perraud, D.: How to reconstruct the history of a digital image, and of its alterations, pp. 1–40 (2022). https://doi.org/10.1002/9781119901808.ch1
6. Bammey, Q., Grompone von Gioi, R., Morel, J.M.: Automatic detection of demosaicing image artifacts and its use in tampering detection. In: 2018 IEEE Conference on Multimedia Information Processing and Retrieval (MIPR), pp. 424–429 (2018). https://doi.org/10.1109/MIPR.2018.00091
7. Bammey, Q., Grompone von Gioi, R., Morel, J.M.: Image forgeries detection through mosaic analysis: the intermediate values algorithm. Image Process. On Line **11**, 317–343 (2021). https://doi.org/10.5201/ipol.2021.355
8. Bammey, Q., Nikoukhah, T., Gardella, M., von Gioi, R.G., Colom, M., Morel, J.M.: Non-semantic evaluation of image forensics tools: methodology and database. In: 2022 IEEE/CVF Winter Conference on Applications of Computer Vision (WACV), pp. 2383–2392 (2022). https://doi.org/10.1109/WACV51458.2022.00244
9. Bammey, Q., von Gioi, R.G., Morel, J.M.: An adaptive neural network for unsupervised mosaic consistency analysis in image forensics. In: 2020 IEEE/CVF Conference on Computer Vision and Pattern Recognition (CVPR), pp. 14182–14192 (2020). https://doi.org/10.1109/CVPR42600.2020.01420
10. Bammey, Q., von Gioi, R.G., Morel, J.M.: Demosaicing to detect demosaicing and image forgeries. In: 2022 IEEE International Workshop on Information Forensics and Security (WIFS), pp. 1–6 (2022). https://doi.org/10.1109/WIFS55849.2022.9975454
11. Bammey, Q., von Gioi, R.G., Morel, J.M.: Forgery detection by internal positional learning of demosaicing traces. In: 2022 IEEE/CVF Winter Conference on Applications of Computer Vision (WACV), pp. 1019–1029 (2022). https://doi.org/10.1109/WACV51458.2022.00109
12. Bammey, Q., von Gioi, R.G., Morel, J.M.: Reliable demosaicing detection for image forensics. In: 2019 27th European Signal Processing Conference (EUSIPCO), pp. 1–5 (2019). https://doi.org/10.23919/EUSIPCO.2019.8903152
13. Bammey, Q.: JADE OWL: JPEG 2000 forensics by wavelet offset consistency analysis. In: 2023 8th International Conference on Image, Vision and Computing (ICIVC), pp. 206–212 (2023). https://doi.org/10.1109/ICIVC58118.2023.10270699
14. Bammey, Q.: A contrario mosaic analysis for image forensics. In: Blanc-Talon, J., Delmas, P., Philips, W., Scheunders, P. (eds.) Advanced Concepts for Intelligent Vision Systems, pp. 222–234. Springer Nature Switzerland, Cham (2023)
15. Barni, M., Bondi, L., Bonettini, N., Bestagini, P., Costanzo, A., Maggini, M., Tondi, B., Tubaro, S.: Aligned and non-aligned double JPEG detection using convolutional neural networks. J. Vis. Commun. Image Represent. 153–163 (2017)

16. Bayar, B., Stamm, M.C.: A deep learning approach to universal image manipulation detection using a new convolutional layer. In: Proceedings of the 4th ACM Workshop on Information Hiding and Multimedia Security, pp. 5–10 (2016)
17. Bi, X., Wei, Y., Xiao, B., Li, W.: RRU-Net: the ringed residual U-Net for image splicing forgery detection. In: Proceedings of the IEEE/CVF Conference on Computer Vision and Pattern Recognition (CVPR) Workshops (2019)
18. Bianchi, T., De Rosa, A., Piva, A.: Improved DCT coefficient analysis for forgery localization in JPEG images. In: 2011 IEEE International Conference on Acoustics, Speech and Signal Processing (ICASSP), pp. 2444–2447 (2011). https://doi.org/10.1109/ICASSP.2011.5946978
19. Bianchi, T., Piva, A.: Detection of nonaligned double JPEG compression based on integer periodicity maps. IEEE Trans. Inf. Forensics Secur. **7**(2), 842–848 (2012). https://doi.org/10.1109/TIFS.2011.2170836
20. Bianchi, T., Piva, A.: Image forgery localization via block-grained analysis of JPEG artifacts. IEEE Trans. Inf. Forensics Secur. **7**(3), 1003–1017 (2012). https://doi.org/10.1109/TIFS.2012.2187516
21. Bromley, J., Guyon, I., LeCun, Y., Säckinger, E., Shah, R.: Signature verification using a "Siamese" time delay neural network. In: Cowan, J., Tesauro, G., Alspector, J. (eds.) Advances in Neural Information Processing Systems, vol. 6. Morgan-Kaufmann (1993)
22. Canh Doan, T.N., Retraint, F., Thai, T.H., Zitzmann, C.: Quality factor estimation of JPEG compressed images. In: 2016 IEEE Global Conference on Signal and Information Processing (GlobalSIP), pp. 104–108 (2016). https://doi.org/10.1109/GlobalSIP.2016.7905812
23. Cao, H., Kot, A.C.: Accurate detection of demosaicing regularity for digital image forensics. IEEE Trans. Inf. Forensics Secur. **4**(4), 899–910 (2009). https://doi.org/10.1109/TIFS.2009.2033749
24. Chakraborty, S., Kirchner, M.: PRNU-based forgery detection with discriminative random fields. In: International Symposium on Electronic Imaging: Media Watermarking, Security, and Forensics (2017)
25. Charitidis, P., Kordopatis-Zilos, G., Papadopoulos, S., Kompatsiaris, I.: Operation-wise attention network for tampering localization fusion. In: 2021 International Conference on Content-Based Multimedia Indexing (CBMI), pp. 1–6. IEEE (2021)
26. Chen, X., Dong, C., Ji, J., Cao, J., Li, X.: Image manipulation detection by multi-view multi-scale supervision. In: Proceedings of the IEEE/CVF International Conference on Computer Vision (ICCV), pp. 14185–14193 (2021)
27. Chen, M., Fridrich, J., Lukàš, J., Goljan, M.: Imaging sensor noise as digital X-ray for revealing forgeries. In: International Workshop on Information Hiding, pp. 342–358 (2007)
28. Chen, M., Fridrich, J., Goljan, M., Lukàš, J.: Determining image origin and integrity using sensor noise. IEEE Trans. Inf. Forensics Secur. **3**(4), 74–90 (2008)
29. Chen, S., Xiao, L., Kumar, A.: Spread of misinformation on social media: what contributes to it and how to combat it. Comput. Hum. Behav. **141**, 107643 (2023)
30. Chierchia, G., Cozzolino, D., Poggi, G., Sansone, C., Verdoliva, L.: Guided filtering for PRNU-based localization of small-size image forgeries. In: IEEE International Conference on Acoustics, Speech and Signal Processing (2014)
31. Chierchia, G., Poggi, G., Sansone, C., Verdoliva, L.: A Bayesian-MRF approach for PRNU-based image forgery detection. IEEE Trans. Inf. Forensics Secur. **9**(4), 554–567 (2014)
32. Choi, C.H., Choi, J.H., Lee, H.K.: CFA pattern identification of digital cameras using intermediate value counting. In: Proceedings of the Thirteenth ACM Multimedia Workshop on Multimedia and Security, MM&Sec'11, pp. 21–26. Association for Computing Machinery, New York, NY, USA (2011). https://doi.org/10.1145/2037252.2037258
33. Cozzolino, D., Poggi, G., Verdoliva, L.: Splicebuster: a new blind image splicing detector. In: 2015 IEEE International Workshop on Information Forensics and Security (WIFS), pp. 1–6. IEEE (2015)
34. Cozzolino, D., Verdoliva, L.: Noiseprint: a CNN-based camera model fingerprint. IEEE Trans. Inf. Forensics Secur. **15**, 144–159 (2020)

35. Dang-Nguyen, D.T., Pasquini, C., Conotter, V., Boato, G.: RAISE: a raw images dataset for digital image forensics. In: Proceedings of the 6th ACM Multimedia Systems Conference, pp. 219–224 (2015)
36. de Carvalho, T.J., Riess, C., Angelopoulou, E., Pedrini, H., de Rezende Rocha, A.: Exposing digital image forgeries by illumination color classification. IEEE Trans. Inf. Forensics Secur. **8**(7), 1182–1194 (2013)
37. Di Martino, J.M., Facciolo, G., Meinhardt-Llopis, E.: Poisson image editing. Image Process. On Line **6**, 300–325 (2016). https://doi.org/10.5201/ipol.2016.163
38. Dong, J., Wang, W., Tan, T.: CASIA image tampering detection evaluation database. In: 2013 IEEE China Summit and International Conference on Signal and Information Processing, pp. 422–426. IEEE (2013)
39. Dong, C., Chen, X., Hu, R., Cao, J., Li, X.: MVSS-Net: multi-view multi-scale supervised networks for image manipulation detection. IEEE Trans. Pattern Anal. Mach. Intell. **45**(3), 3539–3553 (2022)
40. Dosovitskiy, A., Beyer, L., Kolesnikov, A., Weissenborn, D., Zhai, X., Unterthiner, T., Houlsby, N., et al.: An image is worth 16×16 words: transformers for image recognition at scale. In: International Conference on Learning Representations
41. Ferrara, P., Bianchi, T., De Rosa, A., Piva, A.: Image forgery localization via fine-grained analysis of CFA artifacts. IEEE Trans. Inf. Forensics Secur. **7**(5), 1566–1577 (2012). https://doi.org/10.1109/TIFS.2012.2202227
42. Feuerriegel, S., Hartmann, J., Janiesch, C., Zschech, P.: Generative AI. Bus. Inf. Syst. Eng. **66**(1), 111–126 (2024)
43. Fontani, M., Bianchi, T., De Rosa, A., Piva, A., Barni, M.: A framework for decision fusion in image forensics based on Dempster–Shafer theory of evidence. IEEE Trans. Inf. Forensics Secur. **8**(4), 593–607 (2013)
44. Fridrich, J., Kodovsky, J.: Rich models for steganalysis of digital images. IEEE Trans. Inf. Forensics Secur. **7**(3), 868–882 (2012)
45. Gallagher, A.C., Chen, T.: Image authentication by detecting traces of demosaicing. In: 2008 IEEE Computer Society Conference on Computer Vision and Pattern Recognition Workshops, pp. 1–8 (2008). https://doi.org/10.1109/CVPRW.2008.4562984
46. Gardella, M., Musé, P.: Forensic similarity for source camera model comparison. Image Process. On Line **12**, 480–489 (2022). https://doi.org/10.5201/ipol.2022.424
47. Gardella, M., Nikoukhah, T., Li, Y., Bammey, Q.: The impact of JPEG compression on prior image noise. In: ICASSP 2022—2022 IEEE International Conference on Acoustics, Speech and Signal Processing (ICASSP), pp. 2689–2693 (2022). https://doi.org/10.1109/ICASSP43922.2022.9746060
48. Gardella, M., Musé, P., Colom, M., Morel, J.M.: Image forgery detection based on noise inspection: analysis and refinement of the noisesniffer method. Image Process. On Line **14**, 86–115 (2024)
49. Giakoumoglou, P., Karageorgiou, D., Papadopoulos, S., Petrantonakis, P.C.: SAGI: semantically aligned and uncertainty guided AI image inpainting. In: Proceedings of the IEEE/CVF International Conference on Computer Vision (ICCV), pp. 16090–16101 (2025)
50. Goldblum, M., Finzi, M., Rowan, K., Wilson, A.G.: The no free lunch theorem, Kolmogorov complexity, and the role of inductive biases in machine learning. arXiv preprint arXiv:2304.05366 (2023)
51. Guan, H., Kozak, M., Robertson, E., Lee, Y., Yates, A., Delgado, A., Zhou, D., Kheyrkhah, T., Smith, J., Fiscus, J.: MFC datasets: large-scale benchmark datasets for media forensic challenge evaluation. In: IEEE Winter Conference on Applications of Computer Vision (WACV) Workshops, pp. 63–72 (2019)
52. Guillaro, F., Cozzolino, D., Sud, A., Dufour, N., Verdoliva, L.: TruFor: leveraging all-round clues for trustworthy image forgery detection and localization. In: Proceedings of the IEEE/CVF Conference on Computer Vision and Pattern Recognition (CVPR), pp. 20606–20615 (2023)

53. Guo, X., Liu, X., Ren, Z., Grosz, S., Masi, I., Liu, X.: Hierarchical fine-grained image forgery detection and localization. In: Proceedings of the IEEE/CVF Conference on Computer Vision and Pattern Recognition (CVPR), pp. 3155–3165 (2023)
54. Guo, Z., Gu, Z., Zheng, B., Dong, J., Zheng, H.: Transformer for image harmonization and beyond. IEEE Trans. Pattern Anal. Mach. Intell. **45**(11), 12960–12977 (2023). https://doi.org/10.1109/TPAMI.2022.3207091
55. Hao, J., Zhang, Z., Yang, S., Xie, D., Pu, S.: TransForensics: image forgery localization with dense self-attention. In: Proceedings of the IEEE/CVF International Conference on Computer Vision (ICCV), pp. 15055–15064 (2021)
56. Hsu, Y.F., Chang, S.F.: Detecting image splicing using geometry invariants and camera characteristics consistency. In: IEEE International Conference on Multimedia and Expo (ICME), pp. 549–552 (2006)
57. Hu, X., Zhang, Z., Jiang, Z., Chaudhuri, S., Yang, Z., Nevatia, R.: SPAN: spatial pyramid attention network for image manipulation localization. In: Proceedings of the European Conference on Computer Vision (ECCV), pp. 312–328 (2020)
58. Huang, Y., Huang, J., Liu, Y., Yan, M., Lv, J., Liu, J., Xiong, W., Zhang, H., Cao, L., Chen, S.: Diffusion model-based image editing: a survey. IEEE Trans. Pattern Anal. Mach. Intell. (2025)
59. Huh, M., Liu, A., Owens, A., Efros, A.A.: Fighting fake news: image splice detection via learned self-consistency. In: Proceedings of the European Conference on Computer Vision (ECCV) (2018)
60. IFS-TC image forensics challenge. https://signalprocessingsociety.org/newsletter/2013/06/ifs-tc-image-forensics-challenge (2013)
61. Ju, X., Liu, X., Wang, X., Bian, Y., Shan, Y., Xu, Q.: BrushNet: a plug-and-play image inpainting model with decomposed dual-branch diffusion. In: European Conference on Computer Vision, pp. 150–168. Springer (2024)
62. Karageorgiou, D., Kordopatis-Zilos, G., Papadopoulos, S.: Fusion transformer with object mask guidance for image forgery analysis. In: Proceedings of the IEEE/CVF Conference on Computer Vision and Pattern Recognition (CVPR) Workshops, pp. 4345–4355 (2024)
63. Koch, G., Zemel, R., Salakhutdinov, R., et al.: Siamese neural networks for one-shot image recognition. In: ICML Deep Learning Workshop, vol. 2, pp. 1–30. Lille (2015)
64. Kuznetsova, A., Rom, H., Alldrin, N., Uijlings, J., Krasin, I., Pont-Tuset, J., Kamali, S., Popov, S., Malloci, M., Kolesnikov, A., et al.: The open images dataset V4: unified image classification, object detection, and visual relationship detection at scale. Int. J. Comput. Vis. **128**(7), 1956–1981 (2020)
65. Kwon, M.J., Nam, S.H., Yu, I.J., Lee, H.K., Kim, C.: Learning JPEG compression artifacts for image manipulation detection and localization. Int. J. Comput. Vis. **130**(8), 1875–1895 (2022)
66. Le, T.N., Nguyen, H.H., Yamagishi, J., Echizen, I.: OpenForensics: large-scale challenging dataset for multi-face forgery detection and segmentation in-the-wild. In: IEEE/CVF International Conference on Computer Vision (ICCV), pp. 10117–10127 (2021)
67. Li, Y., Gardella, M., Bammey, Q., Nikoukhah, T., Morel, J.M., Colom, M., von Gioi, R.G.: A contrario detection of H.264 video double compression. In: 2023 IEEE International Conference on Image Processing (ICIP), pp. 1765–1769 (2023). https://doi.org/10.1109/ICIP49359.2023.10222775
68. Li, Z., Wu, X., Du, H., Liu, F., Nghiem, H., Shi, G.: A survey of state of the art large vision language models: benchmark evaluations and challenges. In: Proceedings of the Computer Vision and Pattern Recognition Conference, pp. 1587–1606 (2025)
69. Lin, T.Y., Maire, M., Belongie, S., Hays, J., Perona, P., Ramanan, D., Dollár, P., Zitnick, C.L.: Microsoft COCO: common objects in context. In: Computer Vision—ECCV 2014: 13th European Conference, Zurich, Switzerland, 6–12 Sept 2014, Proceedings, Part V 13, pp. 740–755. Springer (2014)
70. Lin, Z., He, J., Tang, X., Tang, C.K.: Fast, automatic and fine-grained tampered JPEG image detection via DCT coefficient analysis. Pattern Recognit. **42**(11), 2492–2501 (2009)

71. Liu, X., Liu, Y., Chen, J., Liu, X.: PSCC-Net: progressive spatio-channel correlation network for image manipulation detection and localization. IEEE Trans. Circuits Syst. Video Technol. **32**(11), 7505–7517 (2022)
72. Lukàš, J., Fridrich, J., Goljan, M.: Detecting digital image forgeries using sensor pattern noise. In: Proceedings of SPIE, pp. 362–372 (2006)
73. Lukás, J., Fridrich, J.: Estimation of primary quantization matrix in double compressed JPEG images. In: Proceedings of Digital Forensic Research Workshop (2003)
74. Luo, W., Huang, J., Qiu, G.: JPEG error analysis and its applications to digital image forensics. IEEE Trans. Inf. Forensics Secur. **5**(3), 480–491 (2010). https://doi.org/10.1109/TIFS.2010.2051426
75. Mahdian, B., Saic, S.: Using noise inconsistencies for blind image forensics. Image Vis. Comput. **27**(10), 1497–1503 (2009)
76. Manjunath, A., Negroni, V., Mandelli, S., Moreira, D., Bestagini, P.: Localization of synthetic manipulations in western blot images. In: IEEE International Workshop on Information Forensics and Security (WIFS), pp. 1–6 (2024). https://doi.org/10.1109/WIFS61860.2024.10810681
77. Manukyan, H., Sargsyan, A., Atanyan, B., Wang, Z., Navasardyan, S., Shi, H.: HD-painter: high-resolution and prompt-faithful text-guided image inpainting with diffusion models. In: The Thirteenth International Conference on Learning Representations (2023)
78. Mareen, H., Karageorgiou, D., Van Wallendael, G., Lambert, P., Papadopoulos, S.: TGIF: text-guided inpainting forgery dataset. In: 2024 IEEE International Workshop on Information Forensics and Security (WIFS), pp. 1–6. IEEE (2024)
79. Mareen, H., Vanden Bussche, D., Guillaro, F., Cozzolino, D., Van Wallendael, G., Lambert, P., Verdoliva, L.: Comprint: image forgery detection and localization using compression fingerprints. In: Pattern Recognition, Computer Vision, and Image Processing. ICPR 2022 International Workshops and Challenges, Montreal, QC, Canada, 21–25 Aug 2022, Proceedings, Part II, pp. 281–299 (2023). https://doi.org/10.1007/978-3-031-37742-6_23
80. Mayer, O., Stamm, M.C.: Forensic similarity for digital images. IEEE Trans. Inf. Forensics Secur. **15**, 1331–1346 (2019)
81. Mayer, O., Stamm, M.C.: Exposing fake images with forensic similarity graphs. IEEE J. Sel. Top. Signal Process. **14**(5), 1049–1064 (2020)
82. Mehrjardi, F.Z., Latif, A.M., Zarchi, M.S., Sheikhpour, R.: A survey on deep learning-based image forgery detection. Pattern Recognit. **144**, 109778 (2023)
83. Milani, S., Bestagini, P., Tagliasacchi, M., Tubaro, S.: Demosaicing strategy identification via eigenalgorithms. In: 2014 IEEE International Conference on Acoustics, Speech and Signal Processing (ICASSP), pp. 2659–2663 (2014). https://doi.org/10.1109/ICASSP.2014.6854082
84. Naveed, H., Khan, A.U., Qiu, S., Saqib, M., Anwar, S., Usman, M., Akhtar N., Barnes N., Mian, A.: A comprehensive overview of large language models. ACM Trans. Intell Syst. Technol. **16**(5), 1–72 (2025)
85. Neelamani, R., de Queiroz, R., Fan, Z., Dash, S., Baraniuk, R.: JPEG compression history estimation for color images. IEEE Trans. Image Process. **15**(6), 1365–1378 (2006). https://doi.org/10.1109/TIP.2005.864171
86. Ng, T.T., Hsu, J., Chang, S.F.: Columbia image splicing detection evaluation dataset. DVMM Laboratory of Columbia University, CalPhotos Digital Library (2009)
87. Nichol, A.Q., Dhariwal, P., Ramesh, A., Shyam, P., Mishkin, P., Mcgrew, B., Sutskever, I., Chen, M.: GLIDE: towards photorealistic image generation and editing with text-guided diffusion models. In: International Conference on Machine Learning, vol. 162, pp. 16784–16804 (2022)
88. Niloy, F.F., Bhaumik, K.K., Woo, S.S.: CFL-Net: image forgery localization using contrastive learning. In: IEEE/CVF Winter Conference on Applications of Computer Vision (WACV), pp. 4642–4651 (2023)
89. Park, J., Cho, D., Ahn, W., Lee, H.K.: Double JPEG detection in mixed JPEG quality factors using deep convolutional neural network. In: Proceedings of the European Conference on Computer Vision (ECCV) (2018)

90. Pevny, T., Fridrich, J.: Detection of double-compression in JPEG images for applications in steganography. IEEE Trans. Inf. Forensics Secur. **3**(2), 247–258 (2008). https://doi.org/10.1109/TIFS.2008.922456
91. Ponomarenko, N.N., Lukin, V.V., Egiazarian, K.O., Astola, J.T.: A method for blind estimation of spatially correlated noise characteristics. In: Astola, J.T., Egiazarian, K.O. (eds.) Image Processing: Algorithms and Systems VIII, vol. 7532, p. 753208. International Society for Optics and Photonics, SPIE (2010). https://doi.org/10.1117/12.847986
92. Ponomarenko, M., Miroshnichenko, O., Lukin, V., Egiazarian, K.: Blind estimation of noise level based on pixels values prediction. Electron. Imaging **34**(14), 152-1 (2022). https://doi.org/10.2352/EI.2022.34.14.COIMG-152
93. Popescu, A., Farid, H.: Exposing digital forgeries in color filter array interpolated images. IEEE Trans. Signal Process. **53**(10), 3948–3959 (2005). https://doi.org/10.1109/TSP.2005.855406
94. Qu, C., Zhong, Y., Liu, C., Xu, G., Peng, D., Guo, F., Jin, L.: Towards modern image manipulation localization: a large-scale dataset and novel methods. In: Proceedings of the IEEE/CVF Conference on Computer Vision and Pattern Recognition (CVPR), pp. 10781–10790 (2024)
95. Rao, Y., Ni, J., Zhang, W., Huang, J.: Towards JPEG-resistant image forgery detection and localization via self-supervised domain adaptation. IEEE Trans. Pattern Anal. Mach. Intell. 1–12 (2022)
96. Rombach, R., Blattmann, A., Lorenz, D., Esser, P., Ommer, B.: Stable diffusion. https://github.com/Stability-AI/stablediffusion (2022)
97. Shin, H.J., Jeon, J.J., Eom, I.K.: Color filter array pattern identification using variance of color difference image. J. Electron. Imaging **26**(4), 043015 (2017). https://doi.org/10.1117/1.JEI.26.4.043015
98. Shuai, X., Ding, H., Ma, X., Tu, R., Jiang, Y.G., Tao, D.: A survey of multimodal-guided image editing with text-to-image diffusion models. arXiv preprint arXiv:2406.14555 (2024)
99. Siopi, M., Kordopatis-Zilos, G., Charitidis, P., Kompatsiaris, I., Papadopoulos, S.: A multi-stream fusion network for image splicing localization. In: International Conference on Multimedia Modeling, pp. 611–622. Springer (2023)
100. Sun, Z., Jiang, H., Wang, D., Li, X., Cao, J.: SAFL-Net: semantic-agnostic feature learning network with auxiliary plugins for image manipulation detection. In: Proceedings of the IEEE/CVF International Conference on Computer Vision (ICCV), pp. 22424–22433 (2023)
101. Tailanian, M., Gardella, M., Pardo, A., Musé, P.: Diffusion models meet image counter-forensics. In: IEEE/CVF Winter Conference on Applications of Computer Vision, pp. 3925–3935 (2024)
102. Taimori, A., Razzazi, F., Behrad, A., Ahmadi, A., Babaie-Zadeh, M.: Quantization-unaware double JPEG compression detection. J. Math. Imaging Vis. **54**, 269–286 (2016)
103. Triaridis, K., Mezaris, V.: Exploring multi-modal fusion for image manipulation detection and localization. In: International Conference on Multimedia Modeling, pp. 198–211. Springer (2024)
104. Verdoliva, L.: Media forensics and deepfakes: an overview. IEEE J. Sel. Top. Signal Process. **14**(5), 910–932 (2020)
105. Wang, J., Wu, Z., Chen, J., Han, X., Shrivastava, A., Lim, S.N., Jiang, Y.G.: ObjectFormer for image manipulation detection and localization. In: Proceedings of the IEEE/CVF Conference on Computer Vision and Pattern Recognition (CVPR) (2022)
106. Wang, Z.F., Zhu, L., Min, Q.S., Zeng, C.Y.: Double compression detection based on feature fusion. In: 2017 International Conference on Machine Learning and Cybernetics (ICMLC), vol. 2, pp. 379–384 (2017). https://doi.org/10.1109/ICMLC.2017.8108951
107. Wen, B., Zhu, Y., Subramanian, R., Ng, T.T., Shen, X., Winkler, S.: COVERAGE—a novel database for copy-move forgery detection. In: IEEE International Conference on Image Processing (ICIP), pp. 161–165 (2016)
108. Wu, Y., AbdAlmageed, W., Natarajan, P.: ManTra-Net: manipulation tracing network for detection and localization of image forgeries with anomalous features. In: Proceedings of the IEEE/CVF Conference on Computer Vision and Pattern Recognition (CVPR) (2019)

109. Wu, H., Zhou, J., Tian, J., Liu, J.: Robust image forgery detection over online social network shared images. In: Proceedings of the IEEE/CVF Conference on Computer Vision and Pattern Recognition (CVPR), pp. 13440–13449 (2022)
110. Wu, H., Zhou, J.: IID-Net: image inpainting detection network via neural architecture search and attention. IEEE Trans. Circuits Syst. Video Technol. **32**(3), 1172–1185 (2021)
111. Yang, C., Li, H., Lin, F., Jiang, B., Zhao, H.: Constrained R-CNN: a general image manipulation detection model. In: 2020 IEEE International Conference on Multimedia and Expo (ICME), pp. 1–6 (2020)
112. Yu, T., Feng, R., Feng, R., Liu, J., Jin, X., Zeng, W., Chen, Z.: Inpaint anything: segment anything meets image inpainting. arXiv preprint arXiv:2304.06790 (2023)
113. Yu, Z., Ni, J., Lin, Y., Deng, H., Li, B.: DiffForensics: leveraging diffusion prior to image forgery detection and localization. In: Proceedings of the IEEE/CVF Conference on Computer Vision and Pattern Recognition (CVPR), pp. 12765–12774 (2024)
114. Zach, F., Riess, C., Angelopoulou, E.: Automated image forgery detection through classification of JPEG ghosts. In: Pinz, A., Pock, T., Bischof, H., Leberl, F. (eds.) Pattern Recognition, pp. 185–194. Springer Berlin Heidelberg, Berlin, Heidelberg (2012)
115. Zhai, Y., Luan, T., Doermann, D., Yuan, J.: Towards generic image manipulation detection with weakly-supervised self-consistency learning. In: Proceedings of the IEEE/CVF International Conference on Computer Vision (ICCV), pp. 22390–22400 (2023)
116. Zhan, F., Yu, Y., Wu, R., Zhang, J., Lu, S., Liu, L., Kortylewski, A., Theobalt, C., Xing, E.: Multimodal image synthesis and editing: the generative AI era. IEEE Trans. Pattern Anal. Mach. Intell. **45**(12), 15098–15119 (2023)
117. Zhang, L., Rao, A., Agrawala, M.: Adding conditional control to text-to-image diffusion models. In: Proceedings of the IEEE/CVF International Conference on Computer Vision, pp. 3836–3847 (2023)
118. Zhou, P., Han, X., Morariu, V.I., Davis, L.S.: Learning rich features for image manipulation detection. In: Proceedings of the IEEE/CVF Conference on Computer Vision and Pattern Recognition (CVPR) (2018)
119. Zhuang, J., Zeng, Y., Liu, W., Yuan, C., Chen, K.: A task is worth one word: learning with task prompts for high-quality versatile image inpainting. In: European Conference on Computer Vision, pp. 195–211. Springer (2024)
120. Zingarini, G., Cozzolino, D., Corvi, R., Poggi, G., Verdoliva, L.: M3DSYNTH: a dataset of medical 3D images with AI-generated local manipulations. In: IEEE International Conference on Acoustics, Speech and Signal Processing (ICASSP), pp. 13176–13180. IEEE (2024)

AI-Generated Image Detection: Challenges and Recent Advances

Christos Koutlis, Riccardo Corvi, Davide Cozzolino, Quentin Bammey, Despina Konstantinidou, Manos Schinas, Dimitrios Karageorgiou, Luisa Verdoliva, and Symeon Papadopoulos

1 Introduction

The field of synthetic image generation has experienced explosive growth during the past decade, mainly driven by the latest advances in deep learning research [5]. Specifically, Generative Adversarial Networks (GAN) [30] revolutionised the field by employing adversarial training to produce increasingly realistic images, and Vari-

C. Koutlis (✉) · D. Konstantinidou · M. Schinas · D. Karageorgiou · S. Papadopoulos
Centre for Research and Technology Hellas (CERTH), Thessaloniki, Greece
e-mail: ckoutlis@iti.gr

D. Konstantinidou
e-mail: dekonstantinidou@iti.gr

M. Schinas
e-mail: manosetro@iti.gr

D. Karageorgiou
e-mail: dkarageo@iti.gr

S. Papadopoulos
e-mail: papadop@iti.gr

R. Corvi · D. Cozzolino · L. Verdoliva
University of Naples Federico II (UNINA), Naples, Italy
e-mail: riccardo.corvi@unina.it

D. Cozzolino
e-mail: davide.cozzolino@unina.it

L. Verdoliva
e-mail: luisa.verdoliva@unina.it

Q. Bammey
Ecole Polytechnique Federale de Lausanne (EPFL), Lausanne, Switzerland
e-mail: quentin.bammey@telecom-paris.fr

LTCI, Télécom Paris, Institut Polytechnique de Paris, Palaiseau, France

S. Papadopoulos et al. (eds.), *Countering Disinformation in the Era of Generative AI*,
https://doi.org/10.1007/978-3-032-11782-3_6

ational Autoencoders (VAE) [44] provide additional capabilities by producing new images that resemble those of their training data distribution. More recently, Diffusion Models (DM) [36], such as Stable Diffusion [66], have achieved remarkable fidelity and diversity by reversing a noise addition process, while transformer models, such as DALL-E [69], have enabled precise text-to-image generation through their understanding of vision-language relationships. These advancements have driven the field towards greater realism, higher resolution, and enhanced user control, while the democratization of this technology via open-source models has reshaped the landscape of visual content creation.

AI-driven image generation technology offers significant benefits through its high creative potential, while at the same time presents significant threats to society [8]. The ease of access to these powerful tools, coupled with the rapid dissemination capabilities of social media, enables their malicious utilization for misleading audiences and carrying out fraudulent activities. In response, the media forensics community has developed several AI-Generated Image Detection (AIGID) approaches for distinguishing among real and synthetic images [55]. These methods often capitalise on the inherent artifacts introduced by generative models [2]. Such artifacts manifest in different forms: some are high-level and visually apparent, such as violations of physical laws or semantic inconsistencies [28, 72], while others are low-level and detectable only through signal and image processing techniques, like subtle discriminative noise patterns [29]. While the former are easier to explain, they are also gradually eliminated by newer generative models that produce highly realistic images. On the other hand, even the most capable generative models have yet to perfectly model the whole frequency spectrum of an image [2]. Handcrafted detection methods [7, 27, 28, 72], while offering transparency, often operate under specific assumptions and constraints, limiting their applicability to particular contexts, such as judicial cases. Conversely, data-driven approaches [19, 41, 47, 83] based on probabilistic modelling excel at efficiently capturing a wider range of artifacts, and this broad scope makes them the preferred choice for "open" use cases like open-source intelligence, albeit with a trade-off of limited transparency and output uncertainty.

A primary objective of AIGID approaches is to achieve generalization to images generated by unseen models, while maintaining robustness to post-processing operations. Also, the data-driven nature of recent works necessitates ample high-quality training data as well as up-to-date and diverse evaluation frameworks. In response, numerous datasets have been developed, pushing the boundaries in terms of scale [14, 94], generative models diversity [62, 83] and semantic alignment [2, 17] between real and fake images, with the later being particularly important for generalization; preventing the learning of contextual biases [33]. Robust generalization though is significantly challenged by shifts in the distribution of fake images, which can quickly render learned detection boundaries obsolete [40]. Furthermore, social media platforms often apply various operations to shared images, such as compression and resizing, which eliminate discriminative features that AIGID models rely on, hindering their ability to generalise to real-world scenarios [25]. Considering that even generative models with minimal architectural differences introduce different artifacts [2, 90] and that the number and variety of social media operations is unknown, maintaining an up-to-date training dataset is too costly, if not impossible. An alternative research direction that has recently emerged considers the distribution of real images to offer an invariant pattern for the task, as it is mostly affected by long-term technological advances (e.g. new cameras, new encoding formats) instead of the introduction of any single generative model. Recent approaches that follow this paradigm aim at modelling the real image distribution, and detect fake images as out-of-distribution samples of this learned model [19, 70]. Crucially, the challenge posed by diverse social media operations, which degrade discriminative features, remains a significant hurdle for both traditional and emerging AIGID methods.

Finally, by its very nature, any digital image constitutes a signal of limited information. Therefore, the distribution of real images, can be naturally defined over a finite set of instances, without known theoretical limitations preventing a finite-capacity generative model to perfectly represent it. Moreover, the image signal may pass through a diverse set of digital and analogue noisy communication channels of limited capacity. Online sharing digital photos of a screen or printed materials are only a few cases that could heavily affect the original image signal, along with any discriminative information it may contain [25]. Such limitations impose lower boundaries to the *aleatoric* uncertainty that any detector solely relying on the image signal can achieve [1]. In practical applications, to counter such issues, the combination of passive AIGID approaches with active mitigation strategies is necessary. Content retrieval approaches [40] as well as the employment of prior knowledge regarding the image semantics [91], can both play a crucial role in countering the malicious exploitation of generative AI.

2 State of the Art Approaches

There has recently been a growing body of research aimed at synthetic image detection. Table 1 lists some of the current state-of-the-art methods. A first approach to achieve robustness to possible impairments is to leverage CNN architectures with a large training set and appropriate augmentation schemes. The importance of a proper augmentation strategy and the variety of the training set has been highlighted in [83], while [17] further supports this. As proposed in [31], a ResNet50 without the first down-sampling layer can better preserve the forensics cues, also showing how the same consideration applies when training on DM generated images. The study also showed how an even stronger augmentation could improve detection generalization, while not improving detection accuracy. Further approaches, improve inference time while preserving detection performance. Lanzino et al. [50] proposes using a Binary Neural Network (BNN) rather than a classic CNN. Their method employs an adapter to convert the RGB image, its FFT magnitude, and the Local Binary Pattern into a suitable input for the BNN. Instead, [9] proposes a patch-based classifier that leverages local image features. The authors propose to divide the image into multiple patches and compute a decision on each. These predictions are then averaged to take a decision at the image level.

Table 1 Reference methods

Acronym [Ref.]	Idea/approach	Training real/fake	#Real (K)	#Fake (K)	Aug.	Test strategy
CNNDetect [83]	High diversity	LSUN [89]/ProGAN	360	360	✓	Global pooling
DMID [17]	No-downsampling	COCO [56], LSUN [89]/latent	180	180	✓	Global pooling
FasterThanLies [50]	Binary Neural Network	COCO [56]/stable	108	542	✓	Resize + cropping
LaDeDa [9]	Local artifacts, patch-based	LSUN [89]/ProGAN	360	360	✓	Resize
LGrad [80]	Gradient-based	LSUN [89]/ProGAN	72	72	✓	Resizing
NPR [79]	Residual	LSUN [89]/ProGAN	72	72		Resizing
DIRE [85]	Inversion	LSUN-Bed [89]/ADM	40	40		Resizing
ZED [19]	Surprise meas., lossless coding	COCO [56]/–	106	–	✓	Global statistics
SPAI [41]	Fourier reconstr. discrepancy	COCO [56], LSUN [89]/latent	180	180	✓	Extracting patches
UniFD [60]	CLIP	LSUN [89]/ProGAN	360	360	✓	Cropping
Raising [18]	CLIP	COCO [56], LSUN [89]/latent	10	10	✓	Resize + crop
DeFake [76]	Prompt-based	COCO [56]/stable diff.	20	20		Resizing
RINE [47]	Intermediate CLIP representation	LSUN [89]/ProGAN	72	72	✓	Crop
C2P-CLIP [78]	Prompt-based	LSUN [89]/ProGAN	72	72	✓	Resize
AIDE [87]	Multiple experts, hybrid features	ImageNet [22]/SD1.4	160	160	✓	Resize
FatFormer [57]	Prompt-based	LSUN [89]/ProGAN	72	72		Resize + cropping
AntifakePrompt [12]	Prompt-based (visual QA)	COCO [56]/Stable3, Stable2 inp	90	60	✓	Cropping
CoDE [4]	Contrastive embeddings	LAION [75]/SD{1.4, 2.1, XL}, DeepFloyd	2300	9200	✓	Cropping
B-Free [33]	Diffusion reconstruction	COCO [56]/SD2.1	51	309	✓	Cropping

For each one we indicate the key idea, the datasets of real and synthetic images used for training, their size, whether or not augmentation is used, and the test strategy

Other methods instead try to exploit the features present in the image to perform the detection and build a classifier (e.g. ResNet50) based on them. Tan et al. [80] uses a pre-trained StyleGAN to use the generator's gradient as an artifact representation, while [79] tries to leverage the artifact left by the up-sampling process by using the difference of the original and interpolated image. Another approach to generate a residual has been proposed by [85], where the method uses as input the reconstruction error of a generative model. The main intuition is that a DM is better suited to fully reconstruct synthetic images, so their error will be smaller than real images. In contrast, [84] identifies fake images by observing how a diffusion model's internal noise predictions and its response to classifier-free guidance reveal characteristic differences between real and generated content. Both [19, 41] try instead to develop methodologies which do not rely on the synthetic data to develop their approach. Using a lossless encoder, [19] evaluates how much the image under test diverges from the model of real images learned. The authors observe that generated images present a bigger shift than the real images. Similarly, [41] first trains a model for the reconstruction of the Fourier spectra in order to learn the distribution of real images. The error in the reconstruction of the spectra is then used to train a classifier.

The final set of approaches for detecting synthetic images primarily leverages large pretrained models, particularly CLIP [67]. Initial explorations, such as that by Ojha et al. [60], demonstrated the efficacy of training a classifier on features extracted from CLIP's vision encoder. Building upon this, [18] showcased CLIP's few-shot learning capabilities, achieving good detection results with as few as 10 pairs of real-fake images. Sha et al. [76] extends this idea by using the features extracted from both the image and its description for binary classification. While these early methods predominantly relied on the final output of the encoder for decision making, [47] introduces a more nuanced perspective, demonstrating that leveraging features from intermediate blocks of CLIP's architecture can enhance detection performance. Further advancements have explored fine-tuning strategies and alternative pretrained models. Tan et al. [78] proposes to fine-tune the image encoder of CLIP using a contrastive learning strategy based on prompts, while [43] show that prompt tuning for CLIP can prove better than linear probing. Yan et al. [87] leverages also the low-level artifacts alongside the features from a ConvNeXt-based OpenCLIP model, via leveraging features extracted using a CNN fed with patches to remove the semantic content. Liu et al. [57] augments the CLIP features by introducing forgery-aware adapters to extract forensics traces in both space and frequency. Chang et al. [12] relies on InstructBLIP instead of CLIP and prompt the model with the question "Is this photo real?", then fine-tune it based on the run. Finally, [4] uses a contrastive loss similar to CLIP (instead of the features from the CLIP encoder) to generate an embedding space where real and fake images are better separated.

3 Datasets

For synthetic image detection, dataset selection is important yet complex. Early, category-specific datasets have evolved with advanced generative models, like Diffusion Models, to include far more diverse images, rendering older, more specialised datasets less representative. Models generally perform best on images from generative models they've been trained on, highlighting the crucial need to understand which evaluation results reflect known models versus true generalization abilities. Similarly, the choice of real images matters; utilising diverse real datasets for testing prevents models from misclassifying genuine images as fake due to overspecialization. Furthermore, neglecting variations in conditioning, generation parameters, and post-processing methods can lead to unpredictable performance on out-of-domain images. Even when training and testing on disjoint parts of the same dataset, shared characteristics can obscure actual real-world performance, emphasising the critical need for carefully curated and diverse datasets for robust evaluation.

Here, we present different datasets for the task of synthetic image detection. Table 2 presents these datasets and their characteristics. One of the first datasets of non-face-specific generated images has been proposed by Wang et al. [83]. It consists of 362,000 images generated with different GANs, paired with real images from ImageNet and LSUN, and targeted to evaluating synthetic image detection tools. With the advent of DMs, new datasets became necessary. DeFake [76] proposed a dataset for both training and testing purposes, featuring images from 4 early DMs. The 2022 IEEE VIP Cup challenge, also for mixed purposes, used images from both GANs and early DMs to train and evaluate new forensic tools. The images in this dataset are particularly challenging, as they are randomly cropped, resized and compressed. A similar post-processing scheme was employed by Corvi et al. [17], with a stronger focus on DM-generated images and designed for use in evaluation. SynthWildX [18], primarily intended for in-the-wild evaluation, has been downloaded from Twitter/X and provides 500 real images and 1500 generated images from 3 Diffusion Models (DALL·E 3, Midjourney and Firefly). As larger datasets were needed for some methods, GenImage [94] proposed a dataset of over a million images including several GANs and DMs, with conditioning limited to only the class names of the ImageNet dataset, thus leading to generated images being limited in variety and complexity. Cifake [6] followed a similar strategy, focusing on Stable Diffusion 1.4 for generation. FakeInversion [10] used reverse image search to match fake images from existing datasets, as well as their own, with real images predating diffusion models, providing a benchmark with in-the-wild real images of various post-processing operations. Finally, to make fair evaluation possible and increase the variety of generation models, Synthbuster [2] introduced a dataset aimed at evaluation, with images generated from 9 DMs, including commercial ones such as Midjourney, Adobe Firefly and DALL·E 2 and 3. Prompts were obtained by textual inversion of the Raise-1k dataset images, followed by manual editing and selection to guarantee the resulting images are as realistic as possible. The images are semantically close to the real images, ensuring that image semantics do not introduce obvious biases in the dataset.

Table 2 Summary of AIGID datasets

Dataset	Synthbuster [2]	SynthWildX [18]	FakeInversion [10]	Cifake [6]	Corvi et al. [17]	GenImage [94]	IEEE VIP CUP [82]	DeFake [76]	Wang et al. [83]
Year	2024	2024	2024	2024	2023	2023	2022	2022	2020
Purpose	Eval.	Eval.	Eval.	Mix.	Eval.	Mix.	Mix.	Mix.	Mix.
Type	Diff.	Diff.	Diff.	Diff.	Both	Both	Both	Diff.	GAN/CNN
# Models	9	3	14	1	10	8	14	4	11
Reals source	Raise-1k [20]	Twitter/X	Reverse image search	CIFAR-10 [48]	ImageNet COCO UCID [73]	ImageNet	FFHQ ImageNet COCO LSUN Vision [77] Raise-1k UCID	COCO Flickr30k [65]	LSUN ImageNet
# Fake	9000	1500	44,100	70,000	16,000	1,331,167	7000	133,236	362,000
# Real	1000	500	44,100	70,000	5000	1,350,000	7000	33,710	362,000
Post-proc.	✗	✓	✗	✗	✓	✗	✓	✗	✗

The datasets differ not only with respect to their generating models and types thereof, but also their purpose (training, testing, or both), the type of generated images and conditioning, as well as the possible conditioning applied to the images

Images were published without any post-processing, thus enabling researchers to apply themselves a variety of processing (including compression, resampling) to test their models' robustness to post-processing.

4 Challenges

Synthetic image detection methods (cf. Sect. 2) have shown remarkable performance when evaluated on publicly available academic benchmarks (cf. Sect. 3) with ample variety of generators, concepts, and image resolutions, highlighting their great potential towards successfully addressing the task. However, there are several scenarios in which those high-performing models face severe challenges [40], such as generalization to data produced from generators significantly different from those used during training, detection of synthetic images after post-processing operations in the wild (e.g. social media platforms), transparency of the decision making process, and biased training data.

Generalization to unseen generators. This is one of the most important objectives of a synthetic image detection method. The typical academic approach to assess generalization is to train on ProGAN data and then test on other types of generators, including GANs, DMs, and even commercial tools such as Midjourney. Li et al. [52] shows that most state-of-the-art approaches struggle to generalise to DMs and commercial tools' data from the GenImage benchmark [94]. Also, [63] conducts cross-generator testing experiments with single generator training, and leave-one-out training and demonstrate that generalization performance significantly drops in both cases but remains acceptable when the training data contain data from generators of similar architecture (e.g., other DMs). Finally, [47] shows that the training data origin has significant impact on generalization. Specifically, generalization to DMs and commercial tools' data from the SynthBuster benchmark [2] is considerably improved when training is conducted on LDM data in comparison to ProGAN data.

Post-processing operations. Moreover, even detectors with great generalization capabilities struggle on the detection of synthetic images that have been subject to operations typically applied in social media. The experimental results provided in [17] show that resizing and compression operations harm the performance of most state-of-the-art detectors rendering their decisions almost random. This is expected if we consider that the low-level synthetic traces of generated images especially those present in high-frequency bands are partially eliminated after such operations. In addition, several papers proposing new AIGID methods provide a pertinent robustness analysis [47, 60, 80, 83] involving blurring, JPEG compression, cropping, noise addition, and resizing, demonstrating the performance of their method under perturbed image scenarios. In most cases, single perturbations (e.g., only blurring) hurt a little their performance, while combining more than one leads to increased performance degradation.

Training data biases. One aspect that is often overlooked is how to properly design the training dataset for the detector, which primarily relies on hidden, unknown traces left by the generator [59, 90]. Bias in the dataset could be exploited by the detector rather than relying on the artifacts left by the generator. Image format issues have shown to create performance issues across various forensics tasks. Grommelt et al. [32] shows that a popular available dataset of synthetic images, GenImage [94], suffers from bias with respect to image. While all synthetic images are generated in lossless format (PNG), real images are usually compressed in a lossy format like JPEG. Therefore, a classifier could learn these inconsistencies in the encoding rather than forensics artifacts. Another such case is exposed in [68] relating to resampling issues: all real images from the LAION dataset were resized to the same resolution while all synthetic images remained unaltered. One further possible bias is semantic bias, which arises when the content of real and synthetic content is not aligned. One possible solution is to generate the synthetic data starting from the real data by either using captions derived from the real images to generate the synthetic ones [2], or by creating the synthetic data from the real data through simulation [92], passing through the autoencoder of a DM [13, 68], or reconstructing the real image using a DM [33].

Transparency. Finally, a major challenge pertains to the transparency with respect to the decision making process of detection models. Methods capable of providing an explanation alongside a decision for an image would increase users' trust in the detector. However, this is an underexplored area in literature. Some methods try to provide an explanation by looking at the areas the detector has focused to make the decision. Bird and Lotfi [6] uses Gradient Class Activation Mapping (Grad-CAM) to explore the areas that the detector focuses on to make its decision, noting that the actual content of the class seems to have little effect. Karageorgiou et al. [41] proposes a spectral reconstruction similarity to capture the difference between real and synthetic images and it introduces a spectral attention scheme to capture the subtle spectral inconsistencies. By overlaying the spectral attention, the authors show that the detectors proposed focus on either semantic inconsistencies or on areas with a high level of detail. In [21], the authors explore the adversarial robustness of both CNN and CLIP based detectors. Interestingly, they show that different detectors focus on different frequencies, with CNN methods focusing on mid to high frequencies while Transformers based focusing on low frequencies. However, while these works provide some insight into the decision making process of the detector, they do not provide a clear explanation, especially to people without technical expertise.

5 AIGID in the Context of vera.ai

Several works addressing AIGID have been conducted in the framework of the vera.ai project. In this section we briefly outline these methods along with representative results. Also, due to constant adaptation to the latest challenges of this domain different evaluation protocols, metrics and datasets have emerged, thus we open this section with a brief pertinent overview. The topics of our AIGID methods can be further grouped in four categories presented in the following sections:

1. Benchmarking and artifact analysis [16, 17, 74]
2. Leveraging foundation model representations [18, 47]
3. Spectral analysis [2, 41, 53]
4. Generalization and in the wild performance [19, 24, 33, 40, 45].

Evolution of Evaluation in AI-Generated Image Detection

The evaluation of synthetic image detection methods has evolved considerably, reflecting the rapid advancements in image generation technologies and the increasing sophistication of detection techniques.

Initially, research primarily focused on Generative Adversarial Networks (GANs), with early methods often trained on datasets like ProGAN and evaluated using accuracy (ACC) and average precision (AP) on benchmarks such as Forensynths [83]. The introduction of diffusion models spurred the development of new datasets, including Diffusion Dataset by UniFD [60] and Synthbuster [2], which maintained ACC and AP as key metrics while adding Area Under the Receiver Operating Characteristic Curve (AUC) for a more comprehensive assessment of model performance.

Later approaches expanded their training paradigms, often utilising Latent Diffusion [71] models and evaluating their robustness against a broader spectrum of advanced generators. This included more recent GAN architectures like GigaGAN [38], diverse diffusion models such as ADM [23] and SDXL [66], and outputs from commercial tools like DALL-E[1] and Adobe Firefly.[2] A crucial aspect of evaluation became robustness assessment, which involved subjecting images to common perturbations like JPEG compression, resizing, blurring, and cropping. While some studies focused on specific perturbations (e.g., only JPEG compression), a more rigorous protocol emerged, applying these distortions to a random 50% subset of samples, both individually and in combination, to simulate real-world degradation. The source of real images also diversified; while many works relied on standard real image sets provided by detection datasets, others incorporated multiple real-world sources to ensure more reliable and generalizable evaluations.

As the field progressed, evaluation extended to even newer generative models like FLUX,[3] and "in-the-wild" evaluations using data from social media platforms gained prominence. Metric suites expanded to include balanced accuracy for imbalanced datasets and negative log-likelihood (NLL), particularly in settings where uncertainty quantification is vital. The emergence of specialised datasets like Chameleon [87],

[1] https://openai.com/index/dall-e-3/.

[2] https://www.adobe.com/products/firefly.html.

[3] https://github.com/black-forest-labs/flux.

GenImage [94], FakeInversion [10], and SynthWildX [18] further enriched evaluation scenarios. Another recent protocol involves assessing performance degradation over time, tracking how detection capabilities are affected by multiple uploads of the same image to social media and the cumulative addition of artifacts. Finally, with the growing concern of misinformation, the evaluation of false positives has become paramount, particularly for fact-checkers, leading to its recent adoption as a critical evaluation metric.

Benchmarking and Artifact Analysis

Here we provide an overview of the vera.ai methods focusing on benchmarking and artifact analysis. Specifically, we report our work on standardising the way AIGID models are evaluated (incl. metrics, evaluation sets and protocol), as well as our analysis on texture-, frequency-, and space-domain artifacts of generated images.

SIDBench: Reliably Assessing Synthetic Image Detection Methods

The performance of synthetic image detection models is fundamental in evaluating their effectiveness and robustness across diverse datasets and image generation techniques. As shown in Section "Evolution of Evaluation in AI-Generated Image Detection", many diverse evaluation protocols have been proposed during the course of the past years. By introducing this benchmarking framework, we aim to standardise the evaluation protocol of detection models on top of identifying strengths and limitations in current approaches. SIDBench [74], at the time of its first release, incorporates 11 state-of-the-art AIGID models identified through a systematic literature review.

- **CNNDet** [83]: A standard ResNet50 [35] architecture pre-trained on ImageNet and fine-tuned on ProGAN generated images with appropriate selection of data augmentations to improve generalization.
- **LGrad** [80]: Uses image gradients, computed using a pre-trained deep network, as features. These are then processed by a standard ResNet50 pre-trained on ImageNet, which is fine-tuned on ProGAN images.
- **DMID** [17]: Similar to CNNDetect, with a modified ResNet50 that avoids down-sampling layers to preserve high frequency fingerprints generated by GANs. It is trained on images generated by ProGAN, Latent Diffusion, and StyleGAN2, with several augmentations for better generalization.
- **FreqDetect** [29]: A standard ResNet50 architecture that employs frequency representations as fingerprints for detecting GAN-generated images, trained on ProGAN.

- **Fusing** [37]: An attention-based approach that fuses global and local ResNet50 embeddings from the whole image and informative patches. It is trained on ProGAN images.
- **GramNet** [58]: A ResNet18 architecture that leverages global image texture representations based on Gram matrices. It is trained on StyleGAN images.
- **NPR** [79]: A ResNet50-based architecture that uses neigh-boring pixel relationships to capture the structural artifacts stemming from up-sampling operations of GANs.
- **UnivFD** [60]: A linear classification layer on top of the last layer features extracted from CLIP's ViT-L/14 image encoder. It is trained on ProGAN images.
- **RINE** [47]: A CLIP-based classifier that leverages the image representations extracted by intermediate Transformer blocks of CLIP's ViT-L/14 image encoder. It is trained on ProGAN and Latent Diffusion images.
- **PatchCraft** [93]: A universal fingerprint is extracted, based on the inter-pixel correlation contrast between regions with high and low texture diversity within an image.

SIDBench uses a range of datasets for evaluation, including ProGAN, StyleGAN, BigGAN, CycleGAN, StarGAN, GauGAN, DeepFakes, and more. It also integrates datasets from recent text-to-image models like LDM and Glide. These help assess model performance on images generated by different generative models. Additionally, it includes the Synthbuster dataset, which contains images from nine different text-to-image models. Tables 3, 4 and 5, present the accuracy and average precision of various detection models across the three datasets.

Evaluation results show that models trained on ProGAN data generally perform well across various GANs, but struggle with DMs like Latent Diffusion and Glide. Among the models, RINE achieved the best performance, with lower variation, while models like GramNet demonstrated high performance in certain cases but struggled with high variation in others. The performance of all models decreased when tested on high-resolution images from the Synthbuster dataset, particularly for more complex models like DALL·E 3 and MidJourney.

In summary, SIDBench provides a systematic framework for evaluating AIGID models, offering insights into their strengths and weaknesses across different generative models. It emphasises the need for thorough evaluation, considering factors like dataset quality, resolution, and model calibration, to better understand real-world application performance.

On the Detection of Synthetic Images Generated by Diffusion Models

This work aims to assess how difficult it is to distinguish DM-generated images from real ones and provide some useful guidelines for further developments. There are two fundamental questions:

- Are DM images characterised by hidden artifacts similar to those observed in GAN images?

Table 3 Forensynths dataset evaluation of models trained on GAN data

Method	Generative Adversarial Networks							DeepFake	Low-level vision		Perceptual loss	
	ProGAN	StyleGAN	StyleGAN2	BigGAN	CycleGAN	StarGAN	GauGAN		SITD	SAN	CRN	IMLE
Accuracy (ACC)												
CNNDetect (prob. 0.5)	**100.00**	73.60	68.00	59.30	80.80	80.90	79.60	50.90	78.06	50.00	87.95	<u>94.35</u>
CNNDetect (prob. 0.1)	78.70	86.90	84.60	52.30	85.65	92.15	78.70	53.55	90.28	50.46	85.95	85.80
LGrad	99.85	89.00	85.10	84.25	87.30	99.40	83.40	52.35	78.89	79.68	53.55	53.55
DMID	**100.00**	**99.10**	<u>90.80</u>	<u>96.80</u>	91.35	99.35	94.00	67.15	**96.11**	56.62	**99.35**	**99.35**
FreqDetect	99.50	90.80	72.30	82.20	79.05	94.40	81.65	63.85	66.39	51.14	59.95	60.05
Fusing	<u>99.90</u>	82.35	80.80	75.70	83.40	91.65	73.95	54.50	82.78	52.51	87.65	89.50
GramNet	**100.00**	82.90	85.65	67.45	74.05	**100.00**	57.55	62.55	72.22	<u>81.51</u>	50.05	50.05
NPR	50.00	50.00	49.95	50.00	49.70	50.00	50.00	54.75	83.06	50.00	50.10	50.05
UniFD	99.85	83.85	75.65	95.05	<u>98.20</u>	96.05	<u>99.45</u>	**100.00**	97.20	97.51	99.29	<u>99.77</u>
RINE	**100.00**	88.00	**94.05**	**99.50**	**99.30**	<u>99.75</u>	**99.60**	**80.30**	<u>90.56</u>	68.26	<u>90.45</u>	91.45
PatchCraft	**100.00**	<u>91.85</u>	89.30	95.25	69.05	**100.00**	71.20	56.15	88.06	**88.58**	50.05	50.05
Average precision (AP)												
CNNDetect (prob. 0.5)	**100.00**	98.49	97.47	88.27	97.03	95.75	98.07	67.08	92.76	63.86	<u>98.94</u>	99.59
CNNDetect (prob. 0.1)	**100.00**	<u>99.62</u>	98.83	84.93	93.88	98.18	89.89	89.56	97.23	70.45	98.49	98.68
LGrad	**100.00**	97.96	98.48	90.90	95.04	**100.00**	94.84	62.44	89.89	84.84	73.01	82.60
DMID	**100.00**	**100.00**	**99.98**	<u>99.78</u>	98.36	<u>99.98</u>	99.75	<u>97.14</u>	<u>99.89</u>	87.19	**100.00**	**99.99**
FreqDetect	**100.00**	98.48	87.72	94.05	85.51	99.57	84.31	72.64	78.08	51.34	81.52	69.68
Fusing	**100.00**	99.24	99.07	88.91	93.48	99.33	88.40	70.24	88.52	77.66	92.40	96.31
GramNet	**100.00**	94.96	<u>99.42</u>	62.04	75.18	**100.00**	54.66	95.09	68.46	81.03	50.18	50.18
NPR	<u>49.66</u>	57.14	62.79	47.87	51.08	49.88	62.85	61.60	93.61	80.67	87.46	95.17
UniFD	**100.00**	97.20	97.51	99.29	<u>99.77</u>	99.49	<u>99.99</u>	82.08	63.84	78.81	97.24	98.76
RINE	**100.00**	99.47	**99.98**	**99.99**	**99.99**	**100.00**	**100.00**	**97.82**	97.20	<u>94.96</u>	97.47	<u>99.67</u>
PatchCraft	**100.00**	98.87	97.61	99.38	84.33	**100.00**	81.76	75.29	**100.00**	**98.54**	59.97	59.89

Best value is highlighted in bold, while second best is underlined

Table 4 Diffusion test set evaluation of models trained on GAN data

Method	Guided	LDM			GLIDE			DALL·E
		200 steps	200 w/ CFG	100 steps	100 27	50 27	100 10	
Accuracy (ACC)								
CNNDetect (prob. 0.5)	52.30	51.10	51.40	51.30	53.30	55.60	54.20	52.50
CNNDetect (prob. 0.1)	62.00	53.85	55.20	55.10	60.30	62.70	61.00	56.05
LGrad	76.10	88.70	<u>90.60</u>	89.70	87.30	89.65	89.35	<u>89.00</u>
DMID	53.85	57.55	59.40	57.60	56.65	58.70	58.85	69.65
FreqDetect	57.65	78.95	76.65	79.25	52.10	53.30	49.65	81.50
Fusing	62.70	53.15	54.25	53.60	60.00	63.10	60.80	53.40
GramNet	<u>79.50</u>	**98.45**	**98.45**	**98.70**	**91.75**	**93.40**	**95.55**	87.75
NPR	50.25	49.95	49.95	49.95	51.55	52.35	51.45	50.00
UniFD	69.65	94.40	74.00	95.00	78.50	79.05	77.90	87.30
RINE	76.10	98.25	88.20	<u>98.60</u>	<u>88.75</u>	<u>92.55</u>	<u>90.70</u>	**95.00**
PatchCraft	**80.50**	<u>91.00</u>	90.05	90.90	78.90	82.40	85.20	85.50
Average precision (AP)								
CNNDetect (prob. 0.5)	68.35	65.92	66.74	65.99	72.03	76.52	73.22	66.26
CNNDetect (prob. 0.1)	77.67	71.16	73.01	72.53	80.51	84.62	82.06	71.30
LGrad	85.27	96.98	<u>97.66</u>	97.23	94.36	96.07	96.59	<u>97.10</u>
DMID	74.57	87.50	89.18	87.77	87.40	90.27	89.34	95.73
FreqDetect	57.11	92.72	90.39	93.11	53.92	55.00	52.22	79.62
Fusing	80.10	75.32	77.08	74.87	83.16	87.91	85.03	86.47
GramNet	79.82	**99.83**	**99.81**	<u>99.84</u>	**99.11**	**99.32**	**99.65**	85.37
NPR	66.51	39.50	42.08	39.18	84.58	89.66	86.96	64.54
UniFD	87.64	<u>99.32</u>	92.50	99.27	95.28	95.56	94.96	93.80
RINE	**96.42**	**99.83**	98.28	**99.87**	<u>98.76</u>	<u>99.24</u>	<u>98.85</u>	**98.86**
PatchCraft	<u>90.63</u>	98.32	97.62	98.41	89.21	92.48	94.41	90.55

Best overall average value is highlighted in bold, while second best is underlined

Table 5 Synthbuster evaluation of models trained on GAN data

Method	Glide	Dall·E 2	Dall·E 3	SD1.3	SD1.4	SD2	SDXL	MJv5	Firefly
Accuracy (ACC)									
CNNDetect (prob. 0.5)	48.15	50.50	**47.40**	47.75	47.80	49.35	49.40	47.90	53.70
CNNDetect (prob. 0.1)	49.75	55.55	45.15	49.80	49.90	49.75	54.20	48.35	53.00
LGrad	**56.55**	38.45	24.85	65.65	66.60	37.35	40.85	37.40	31.45
DMID	49.25	50.80	<u>45.80</u>	49.40	50.05	50.00	47.90	47.10	61.70
FreqDetect	34.30	30.20	34.30	<u>67.85</u>	<u>68.00</u>	33.70	49.30	31.40	64.60
Fusing	52.70	54.20	46.75	50.75	50.85	49.90	49.60	<u>49.30</u>	52.50
GramNet	50.15	57.80	14.40	56.15	56.55	35.95	49.65	35.65	12.25
NPR	45.40	45.45	45.20	45.20	45.20	45.25	45.30	46.15	49.65
UniFD	40.70	**70.95**	34.80	57.85	57.35	<u>63.10</u>	55.45	39.90	<u>78.15</u>
RINE	<u>54.65</u>	<u>70.50</u>	33.50	**72.05**	**71.60**	57.95	<u>59.90</u>	42.85	**79.35**
PatchCraft	52.65	53.05	24.10	67.10	67.35	**68.25**	**71.35**	**53.65**	55.20
Average precision (AP)									
CNNDetect (prob. 0.5)	38.32	51.16	32.74	38.75	39.26	46.95	46.16	36.45	60.77
CNNDetect (prob. 0.1)	48.02	60.72	32.92	47.67	49.14	47.59	56.83	42.26	57.65
LGrad	69.23	41.51	31.89	63.29	65.36	39.11	41.67	39.49	34.71
DMID	49.42	60.13	31.42	52.03	52.98	49.49	43.24	40.35	76.61
FreqDetect	36.79	36.36	**37.83**	<u>82.52</u>	**83.00**	36.88	44.13	35.45	52.30
Fusing	52.80	58.99	32.73	49.02	49.32	49.26	45.70	<u>43.73</u>	59.00
GramNet	50.28	57.08	31.62	55.98	56.50	40.45	48.72	39.66	31.32
NPR	40.45	39.95	32.96	31.68	31.68	33.19	37.51	35.72	48.36
UniFD	**56.60**	**79.85**	30.73	**83.08**	82.92	<u>65.44</u>	**68.31**	40.86	**92.91**
RINE	<u>54.65</u>	<u>70.50</u>	<u>33.50</u>	72.05	71.60	57.95	59.90	42.85	<u>79.35</u>
PatchCraft	48.82	45.79	32.80	79.21	<u>81.35</u>	**79.33**	<u>64.27</u>	**51.06**	44.27

Best overall average value is highlighted in bold, while second best is underlined

- To what extent are current state-of-the-art detectors effective on this type of images?

To answer these questions, a large variety of synthetic images were generated using the most recent generators. The analysis tried to answer if deep learning-based detectors can detect them, not only in ideal conditions but also in the presence of compression and resizing.

To expose the artifacts of DM images we extracted their spatial-domain fingerprints, with the same pipeline used to extract the PRNU pattern. First, the scene content is estimated through a denoising filter and removed from the input image to obtain the so-called noise residual. Then the fingerprint is estimated by averaging a large number of such residuals. Figure 1 shows the Fourier transform of the fingerprints of some popular generators. Strong peaks are clearly visible in the spectra of Latent Diffusion, DALL·E Mini and StyleGAN2, implying the presence of hidden quasi-periodic patterns in the synthetic images, precious for forensic analyses. For other DM architectures, like ADM and DALL·E 2, peaks are much weaker and almost absent, suggesting that these images will be harder to detect.

Table 6 shows the performance of four SotA detectors on images generated by several state-of-the-art generative models including GANs, transformers, and DMs. The ability of detectors to generalise to unseen architectures is of special interest. Detectors are trained on images generated by a single model, and tested on all others. Two cases are considered: (a) training only on ProGAN images; (b) training only on images generated by Latent Diffusion. In both cases, tests are performed on 1000 synthetic images for each model and 5000 real images. Results are reported in terms of area under the receiver-operating curve (AUC) and accuracy at the fixed threshold of 0.5. On uncompressed images (left) detection is very easy, because real images are characterised by JPEG compression artifacts, while synthetic images do not embed such traces. As a result, AUC performance is almost perfect on ProGAN (seen in training) and remains high also for other architectures. Even in this favourable case, accuracy is often unsatisfactory, because the threshold does not work well on images of different origin. On compressed and resized images (right) a performance drop is observed (except for ProGAN, seen in training). Performance is acceptable in terms of AUC, but close to random in terms of accuracy. DALL·E 2 and ADM are the hardest to detect due to their very weak artifacts, as can be seen in Fig. 1. Then, the best performing method [31] is trained on LDM-generated images, and evaluated on the

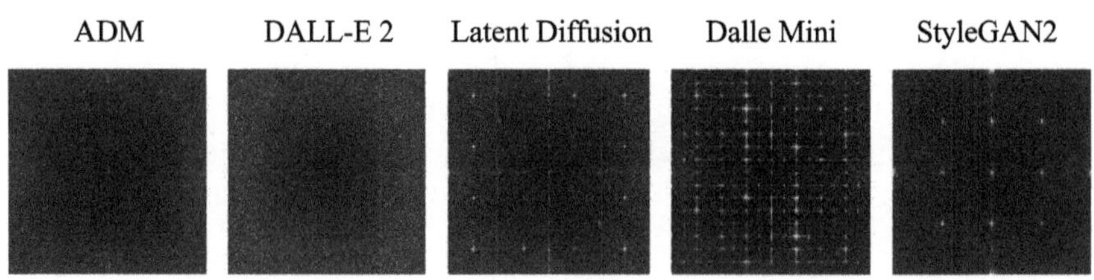

Fig. 1 Fourier amplitude spectra of the artificial fingerprints of some popular generators

Table 6 Comparative analysis of state-of-the-art techniques

	Trained on ProGAN							
	Uncompressed				Resized and compressed			
Acc./AUC%	Spec [92]	PatchFor. [11]	CNNDetect [83]	Grag2021 [31]	Spec [92]	PatchFor. [11]	CNNDetect [83]	Grag2021 [31]
ProGAN	83.5/99.2	64.9/97.6	99.9/100	99.9/100	49.7/48.5	50.4/65.3	99.7/100	99.9/100
StyleGAN2	65.3/72.0	50.2/88.3	74.0/97.3	98.1/99.9	51.8/50.5	50.8/73.6	54.8/85.0	63.3/94.8
StyleGAN3	33.8/4.4	50.0/91.8	58.3/95.1	91.2/99.5	52.9/51.9	50.2/76.7	54.3/86.4	58.3/94.4
BigGAN	73.3/80.5	52.5/85.7	66.3/94.4	95.6/99.1	52.1/52.2	50.5/58.8	55.4/85.9	79.0/99.1
EG3D	80.3/89.6	50.0/78.4	59.2/96.7	99.4/100	58.9/60.6	49.8/81.9	52.1/85.1	56.8/96.6
Taming Tran.	79.6/86.6	50.5/69.4	51.2/66.5	73.5/96.6	49.0/49.1	50.0/64.1	50.5/71.0	56.2/94.3
DALL·E Mini	80.1/88.1	51.5/82.2	51.7/60.6	70.4/95.6	59.1/61.9	50.1/68.7	51.1/66.2	62.3/95.4
DALL·E 2	82.0/93.0	50.0/51.1	50.3/85.8	51.9/94.9	61.8/64.5	49.8/58.3	49.9/46.1	50.0/65.4
GLIDE	73.4/81.9	50.3/96.6	51.1/62.6	58.6/86.4	53.1/52.5	51.0/71.5	50.3/65.9	51.8/90.0
Latent diff.	72.1/78.5	51.8/84.3	51.0/62.5	58.2/91.5	47.9/46.3	50.6/65.2	50.7/69.1	52.4/89.4
Stable diff.	66.8/74.7	50.8/85.0	50.9/65.9	62.1/92.9	46.5/44.5	51.1/77.2	50.7/72.9	58.1/93.7
ADM	55.1/53.3	50.4/87.1	50.6/56.3	51.2/57.4	49.1/49.1	51.0/69.1	50.3/68.1	50.6/77.2
AVG	70.5/75.2	51.9/83.2	59.5/78.6	75.8/92.8	52.7/52.7	50.4/69.2	55.8/75.1	61.5/90.8

All methods were trained only on ProGAN images, and tested both on uncompressed synthetic data (left) and on resized and compressed data (right). Underline indicates that data from the same generative model are used for training and evaluation

Table 7 Results of Grag2021 [31]: trained only on Latent Diffusion (left), fused with Grag2021 trained only on ProGAN (center), with calibration applied after fusion (right)

Acc./AUC%	Trained on Latent Diffusion	Fusion	Calibration
ProGAN	52.0/78.3	90.2/100	99.6/100
StyleGAN2	58.0/85.0	56.6/94.6	85.8/94.6
StyleGAN3	59.5/87.6	55.4/93.9	85.4/93.9
BigGAN	52.9/80.6	59.3/98.5	92.7/98.5
EG3D	65.4/91.8	54.4/97.7	89.6/97.7
Taming Tran.	78.2/97.3	61.5/98.2	92.4/98.2
DALL·E Mini	73.9/97.3	65.9/97.7	90.3/97.7
DALL·E 2	50.3/73.3	50.0/72.2	50.0/72.2
GLIDE	62.5/96.2	52.5/95.9	88.6/95.9
Latent diff.	97.1/99.9	84.9/99.8	97.6/99.8
Stable diff.	99.7/100	92.5/100	99.5/100
ADM	52.9/81.9	50.8/80.6	72.1/80.6
AVG	66.9/89.2	64.5/94.1	87.0/94.1

Underline indicates that data from the same generative model are used for training and evaluation

resized and compressed version of the dataset. Results in Table 7 (left) exhibit excellent performance on all DMs, somewhat lower on GAN generated images. Then, results are reported when fusing the outputs of the networks trained on both datasets (Table 7; centre). Performance improves on GAN images and remains reasonably good on DM images. Accuracy is still very low due to the unsuitable fixed threshold. To improve accuracy, the method has been calibrated using Platt's calibration procedure [64] assuming access to 20 real and 20 synthetic images for each model. Performance (Table 7; right) now improves largely, but the detector still cannot reliably detect images that present artifacts significantly different from those seen during training.

Intriguing Properties of Synthetic Images: From Generative Adversarial Networks to Diffusion Models

In this work, we carried out a systematic study of many image generators of different families, with the aim of discovering the most forensically relevant characteristics of real and generated images. Previous work established the existence of DM fingerprints [17]. This study focuses on their properties by exploiting second-order statistics both in the spatial domain, the image autocorrelation function, and in the frequency domain, the image power spectrum. Figure 2 shows some examples of power spectrum and autocorrelation function (central 65×65 crop) for some generative models. It clearly appears that, just like GAN models, DM-based models

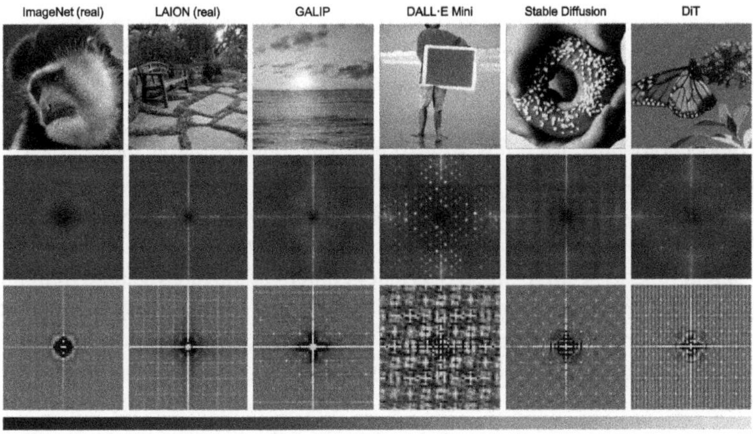

Fig. 2 Examples of real and synthetic images from popular datasets and generators. From left to right: ImageNet (real), LAION (real), GALIP, DALL·E Mini, Stable Diffusion, DiT. For each image we show the average power spectra of the noise residuals in the middle and the autocorrelation in the bottom. Real images embed traces of JPEG compression while all the synthetic images show periodic patterns in the spatial domain

give rise to visible artifacts in the Fourier domain. Moreover, they exhibit anomalous regular patterns in the autocorrelation.

These traces are not only precious for detection, but also help highlight some important issues. In the example of Fig. 2, noise residuals exhibit obvious regular patterns that seem to suggest their artificial origin. However, similar patterns are observed in the residuals of real images used for training. When training images are all JPEG compressed at a given quality factor, the model learns to include the same compression artifacts in the generated images, that is, dataset-related artifacts are transferred in the generated image with the potential to mislead artifact-based detectors.

Then, our evaluation moved towards determining whether the generated images can reproduce the statistical patterns exhibited by natural images. These latter are known to exhibit strong statistical regularities in the frequency domain. Their average power spectrum decays following a square power law. Moreover, the power spectrum is far from isotropic, with energy concentrated especially at the horizontal and vertical orientations and much less at the others. These properties may be useful to detect synthetic images. To analyse possible differences, radial and angular spectra of average noise residuals are computed. The radial spectrum of the ith image is computed by averaging the values of its Fourier transform at distance ρ from the origin, irrespective of the angular direction. Then, an average over 1000 images is taken to characterise the whole source. In our analysis, low frequencies have been discarded to focus on the range $\rho \in 0.2 - 0.5$. In addition, to avoid dataset-specific biases, for a given real source (e.g., ImageNet), the study uses only images that are generated using the very same source as training set. In that way, the resulting differences should be attributable only to the employed generative model. A similar analysis is carried out for the angular spectra where, now, the Fourier transform is averaged on a given angle θ, going from 0 to π, irrespective of the distance from the origin.

Figure 3 compares, for a few widespread real sources, radial spectra of real and corresponding generated images. The former (green) decays with a nearly perfect power law (dashed black). On the contrary, all radial spectra of synthetic sources deviate markedly in one or more frequency ranges from that law. Generally, but not always, real images seem to possess a richer content at the intermediate frequencies. Exceptions are observed only for the FFHQ dataset. However, this is composed of images that have been interpolated, that is low pass filtered, a process that modifies the original spectral content making it resemble that of some synthetic images. Similar considerations hold for radial spectra (Fig. 4). The only exceptions are observed again for the FFHQ dataset and for the same reasons as before. Again, there are significant deviations from the angular spectra of real sources (green). Such deviations can be better appreciated in the plots in the bottom part, showing the square root of the Fisher's discriminant ratios. In this case the real source is represented by the green unit circle. We can see them for both GANs (i.e. StyleGAN-T and BigGAN) and for DMs (i.e. DALL·E 2 and Latent Diffusion). Finally, it is worth noting that the StyleGAN2 and StyleGAN3 models better fit the spectral distribution of real images. For StyleGAN3, this is justified by the development of GAN architectures that were able to avoid the aliasing effect.

Leveraging Foundation Model Representations

Here we provide an overview of the vera.ai methods leveraging foundation model representations. Specifically, CLIP image encoder embeddings are shown to carry discriminative AIGID information which we leverage to build powerful detectors.

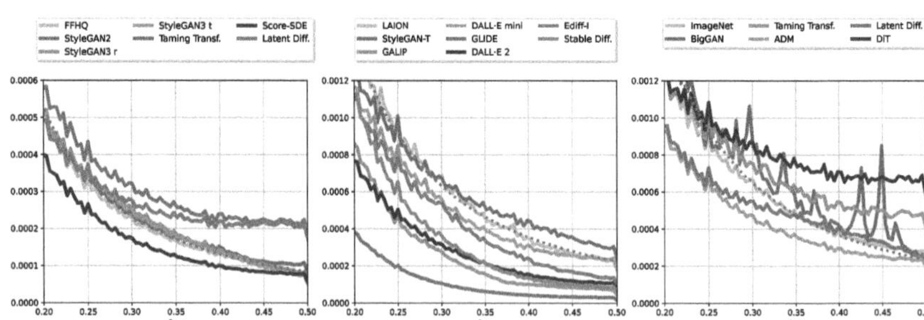

Fig. 3 Radial spectrum power density. Synthetic images are compared with the real images used for training the correspondent model. Real images (green) fit very well the expected theoretical curve (dotted)

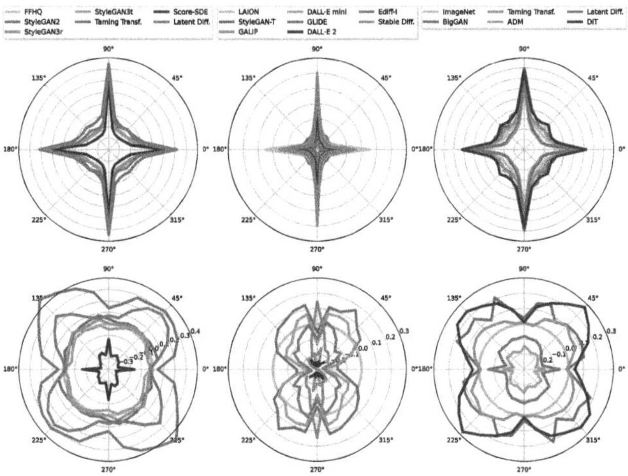

Fig. 4 Angular spectrum power density (top) and the square-root of Fisher's discriminant ratio applied at each direction (bottom)

A CLIP-Based Model Trained on a Small Dataset of Latent Diffusion Generated Images

Most detectors follow a fully supervised approach, where large datasets of real and synthetic images are used to train a deep learning model. The results are very good in lab conditions, when the test images come from the same generators as seen in training. When deployed in the wild, however, a sharp degradation in detection performance is often observed. Most models struggle to generalise to images generated from new sources and also show limited robustness to images impaired by compression and scaling. For example, it has been shown [17] that models trained to detect GAN images perform poorly on DM images and vice versa due to significant differences in the generation processes of these two families. This research explores a method to address these limitations by introducing a universal, untrained detector of AI-generated images, focusing on mitigating the biases introduced by dedicated training sets. To this end, the method leverages large pre-trained vision language models (VLMs) for representation learning. More specifically, features are extracted using Contrastive Language-Image Pre-Training (CLIP) [67], namely CLIP ViT L/14, then, the proposed method employs a lightweight detection strategy that relies on only few examples for each class, and provides excellent results in several challenging situations. The design of the detector consists of the following four steps:

1. collect N real images $R_1 \dots R_N$ with the corresponding captions $t_1 \dots t_N$
2. use the captions to feed a text-driven image generator, $G(\cdot)$, to obtain N synthetic images $F_1 \dots F_N$ with $F_i = G(t_i)$. As such there are N real/fake pairs that share the same textual description

3. feed CLIP with the N real and N fake images and collect the corresponding feature vectors $r_1 \dots r_N$ and $f_1 \dots f_N$ extracted at the output of the next-to-last layer, with $r_i = CLIP(R_i)$ and $f_i = CLIP(F_i)$
4. use these $N + N$ vectors to design a linear SVM classifier.

If the real images have low-quality associated captions, or no caption at all, these are generated by a dedicated tool such as BLIP [51]. Real and fake images are coupled, that is they share the same textual description, to avoid possible semantic biases, which proves beneficial when the number of images is very small, e.g., $N = 10$. The features are extracted from the next-to-last layer rather than the last layer based on the results of preliminary experiments and, likewise, we selected SVM as a classifier experimentally among a set of candidate classifiers.

Several experiments validate the performance of the proposed CLIP-based detector, comparing its performance with that of the most competitive methods. Four versions of the proposed detector are considered, based on $1000(1k)$ or $10{,}000(10k)$ samples, with (+) or without augmentation. In all cases, the samples used to design the SVM classifier come from Latent Diffusion. Tests are conducted on several datasets grouped into three families based on the generation approach, GAN-based, DM-based or unknown. This last family includes images generated by four commercial tools with undisclosed generation process and represents a particularly challenging case. In Table 8, the case of uncorrupted images is considered. All versions of the proposed detector perform very well and are often among the best methods. On average, only the Corvi [17] and Ojha [60] methods are competitive (although inferior). Similar results are observed in Table 9, where the images were corrupted in different ways. In this case, the use of augmentation provides a significant advantage. In extreme synthesis, CLIP features appear to provide a very good representation of the test images, allowing for improved generalization and robustness.

Several further experiments have been conducted to confirm this interpretation. One of the most interesting findings is that CLIP-based features appear to depend only marginally on the high frequencies of the image and more significantly on its mid-frequencies. This is in contrast to most detectors that rely heavily on fine image details of high forensic value. This observation is confirmed by the scatterplot in Fig. 5 that shows on the y-axis the score provided by the proposed method and on the x-axis the score provided by the best CNN-based method [17]. The two scores appear to be largely complementary, paving the way for their possible fusion. A first experiment in this direction is summarised in Table 10 and shows that a direct fusion at the score level provides a significant advantage over each of the two individual scores.

Representations from Intermediate Encoder-Blocks

This work advances AIGID by leveraging the rich representations within foundation models. Rather than relying solely on the final output of these models, the proposed method extracts and utilises information from intermediate layers, which contain cru-

Table 8 Comparison with SotA methods in terms of AUC on uncorrupted images

Method	GAN family					Diffusion family									Commercial tools				AVG
	Pro GAN	Style GAN2	Style GAN3	Style GANT	Giga GAN	Score SDE	ADM	GLIDE	Latent Diff.	Stable Diff.	DeepFl. IF	Ediff-I	DiT	SDXL	DALL· E2	DALL· E3	Midj.	Adobe Firef.	
CNNDetect	100	96.5	98.5	98.9	66.6	32.9	64.3	48.5	59.2	41.5	78.0	64.9	58.6	54.3	64.8	10.9	40.2	84.8	64.6
PatchFor.	92.3	84.5	91.8	91.2	64.7	83.3	74.8	96.2	78.1	62.4	62.7	78.7	83.1	68.4	41.9	52.7	57.8	49.4	73.0
Grag et al.	100	**99.8**	97.5	98.8	82.8	92.1	74.7	62.8	91.9	52.5	69.9	69.6	65.3	58.0	58.3	2.4	43.1	63.5	71.3
Mand et al.	96.2	93.8	**100**	92.6	61.8	99.8	56.5	40.5	70.0	36.8	47.2	65.0	59.1	27.0	14.5	14.7	24.3	36.7	57.6
Liu et al.	100	**99.8**	98.4	98.5	**98.2**	**95.4**	82.5	76.5	**97.6**	77.4	72.2	**98.7**	88.0	31.1	70.4	0.2	40.7	11.8	74.3
DMID	79.4	73.7	50.0	97.1	63.4	65.0	80.7	91.9	100	**100**	**99.9**	85.7	**100**	**100**	69.4	60.8	**100**	**98.0**	84.2
LGrad	100	91.2	83.8	81.8	82.2	80.6	76.9	66.1	81.1	61.5	68.8	74.1	56.2	57.2	58.6	37.9	56.3	40.6	69.7
UniFD	100	93.9	92.3	98.2	96.0	58.4	**86.7**	80.8	85.7	89.5	92.9	80.6	77.8	85.1	**95.2**	36.4	66.2	**97.5**	84.1
DIRE-1	50.6	56.9	47.8	**99.9**	74.1	44.3	75.7	71.4	68.7	39.4	**98.9**	**99.1**	**99.6**	47.1	44.7	47.6	51.0	57.4	65.2
DIRE-2	54.2	52.5	43.0	**99.6**	76.0	41.0	70.1	70.1	69.3	46.9	97.0	98.2	98.3	42.8	41.0	49.6	47.8	43.0	63.3
NPR	100	85.6	77.0	96.4	88.7	91.1	**86.3**	79.3	90.2	64.5	91.6	80.1	78.4	76.7	39.5	48.7	77.0	32.1	76.8
Ours 1k	**98.9**	90.5	85.5	**100**	81.3	89.1	81.1	**99.9**	94.1	87.6	96.5	**98.5**	94.1	87.8	89.0	70.0	73.0	74.4	88.4
Ours 1k+	91.4	80.9	84.0	**99.8**	74.7	84.3	75.2	**99.6**	81.6	89.8	98.0	**99.1**	92.5	88.9	83.6	**93.6**	78.7	85.1	87.8
Ours 10k	**99.8**	91.8	86.8	**100**	83.6	89.0	81.4	**99.9**	94.2	90.7	97.0	**98.7**	95.0	87.4	89.2	77.6	75.3	80.1	**89.8**
Ours 10k+	93.4	87.1	87.6	**99.9**	78.5	89.2	79.9	**99.7**	84.7	91.3	97.9	**99.4**	94.0	90.1	86.3	**92.9**	81.7	87.2	**90.0**

Bold underlines the best performance for each dataset with a margin of 1%

Table 9 Comparison with SotA methods (AUC) on images post-processed by random cropping, resizing and compression

Method	GAN family					Diffusion family									Commercial tools				AVG
	Pro GAN	Style GAN2	Style GAN3	Style GANT	Giga GAN	Score SDE	ADM	GLIDE	Latent Diff.	Stable Diff.	DeepFl. IF	Ediff-I	DiT	SDXL	DALL· E2	DALL· E3	Midj.	Adobe Firef.	
CNNDetect	100	86.6	88.4	61.7	59.2	68.0	65.0	60.6	67.1	55.2	50.3	48.3	55.1	64.5	46.2	27.7	46.7	55.9	61.5
PatchFor.	57.9	51.8	57.0	50.6	53.8	69.0	66.2	83.3	58.8	48.3	61.3	65.0	68.1	63.3	64.3	63.3	59.0	65.1	61.4
Grag et al.	100	**95.4**	**90.9**	94.4	64.4	77.1	77.1	79.8	**84.0**	53.5	50.6	55.6	66.7	66.6	55.2	25.1	48.5	60.2	69.2
Mand et al.	81.1	79.3	87.2	49.1	49.3	64.0	54.8	42.6	52.9	39.4	55.7	54.5	49.8	42.2	47.9	42.3	35.2	53.4	54.5
Liu et al.	64.3	55.1	50.1	57.3	45.4	62.6	51.1	58.6	50.7	58.6	50.9	64.2	53.9	56.0	44.4	61.8	52.6	53.1	55.0
DMID	77.5	74.7	69.4	82.1	66.6	70.4	79.0	93.5	99.3	69.9	60.7	72.1	89.2	61.8	65.9	32.4	51.9	58.1	70.8
LGrad	56.3	58.3	49.8	52.3	43.5	45.9	49.2	42.3	50.4	54.8	40.7	46.4	49.4	53.2	41.8	53.5	50.4	51.8	49.4
UniFD	99.8	75.5	75.4	91.1	**88.5**	79.3	**83.7**	83.3	81.8	75.0	59.9	68.7	70.1	61.8	63.2	41.7	40.6	52.9	71.8
DIRE-1	48.4	42.5	39.1	53.5	54.3	44.1	48.0	44.7	46.1	47.0	66.2	62.8	53.2	47.1	44.6	47.6	51.0	57.4	49.9
DIRE-2	49.3	41.6	38.6	53.8	55.0	44.3	45.1	40.2	45.9	56.4	70.7	72.2	53.0	42.8	40.9	49.7	47.8	43.0	49.5
NPR	54.5	48.5	41.9	54.0	44.8	44.7	46.9	47.2	47.7	55.4	49.6	54.6	50.9	52.8	50.0	67.5	50.8	55.5	51.0
Ours 1k	**85.0**	64.0	66.6	90.2	75.2	74.7	78.1	97.2	77.1	77.6	80.1	86.6	77.5	76.5	77.9	77.4	63.1	70.5	77.5
Ours 1k+	78.7	62.5	68.4	**97.5**	67.9	84.0	74.3	**99.6**	78.2	83.7	94.5	97.1	88.9	**89.6**	81.2	**90.9**	77.6	83.7	83.2
Ours 10k	**85.7**	65.5	68.1	90.5	74.7	75.8	78.4	97.7	77.8	78.1	81.2	87.1	77.2	76.4	78.2	76.4	65.0	72.2	78.1
Ours 10k+	82.8	67.4	70.7	**98.4**	71.9	**85.4**	77.3	**99.7**	80.2	**85.8**	**95.9**	**98.2**	**91.1**	**89.9**	**83.8**	**90.1**	**79.4**	**85.5**	**85.2**

Bold underlines the best performance for each dataset with a margin of 1%

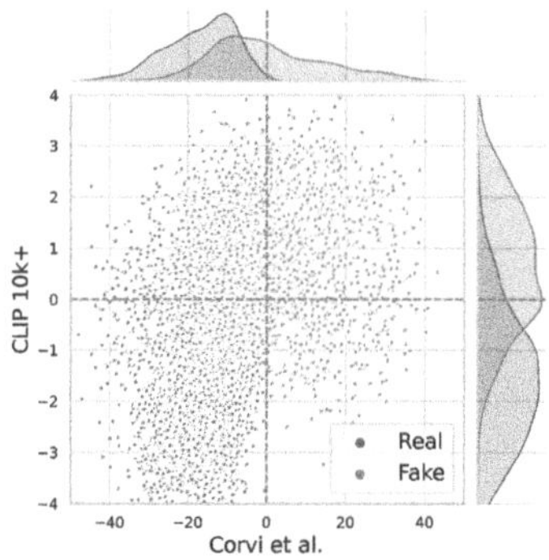

Fig. 5 Scatter plots of CLIP and Corvi et al. scores

Table 10 Performance of CLIP + Corvi fusion

Method	Families of generators			
	GAN	Diffusion	Comm. tools	Average
	AUC/Acc	AUC/Acc	AUC/Acc	AUC/Acc
Corvi et al.	72.7/52.1	91.5/75.1	82.1/62.8	82.1/63.3
Ours 10k	92.4/79.1	92.6/73.3	80.5/52.6	88.5/68.3
Ours 10k+	89.3/74.9	91.8/77.2	87.0/67.3	89.4/73.1
Ours fusion	92.9/80.1	96.9/87.8	88.2/65.3	92.7/77.8
Ours fusion+	89.9/75.5	96.8/88.8	92.3/77.2	93.0/80.5
Corvi et al.	74.0/55.1	77.3/62.1	52.1/50.1	67.8/55.8
Ours 10k	76.9/63.6	81.1/63.7	73.0/52.4	77.0/59.9
Ours 10k+	78.2/69.0	89.3/78.7	84.7/66.4	84.1/71.4
Ours fusion	78.5/66.8	85.1/71.4	72.7/52.6	78.7/63.6
Ours fusion+	79.6/70.8	91.7/80.7	84.5/66.6	85.3/72.7

Top: original images; bottom: compressed/resized images

cial low-level visual cues, in conjunction with the high-level semantic information from the final layer. This approach aims to capture a more comprehensive understanding of image characteristics pertinent to AIGID, enabling more accurate and robust detection of AI-generated images, even those produced by unseen generative models and those that have undergone real world perturbations like compression.

The methodology introduces a novel architecture called RINE for synthetic image detection presented in Fig. 6. It starts by processing input images through the frozen CLIP image encoder, which breaks the images into patches and processes them through a series of Transformer blocks. The key innovation is the extraction of representations from the intermediate layers of this encoder, specifically the classification token from each block, which are then concatenated.

These concatenated representations are fed into a trainable projection network, followed by a Trainable Importance Estimator module. This module learns to assign

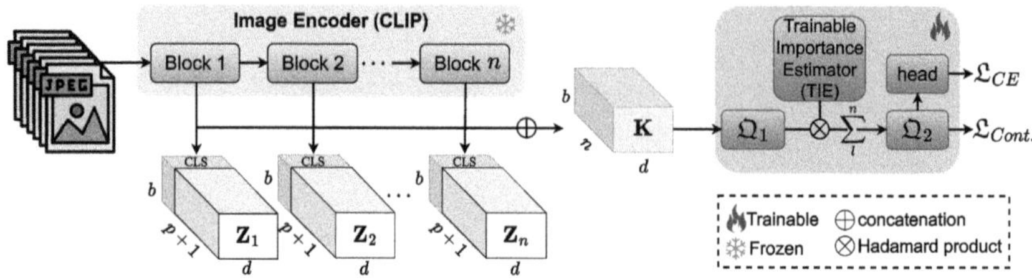

Fig. 6 The RINE architecture

weights to the features from different Transformer blocks, effectively determining their importance for the detection task. The weighted features are then passed through another projection network and a classification head, which outputs the probability of an image being synthetic.

The model is trained using a combination of two loss functions. The first is a standard binary cross-entropy loss, which directly optimises the classification accuracy. The second is a supervised contrastive learning loss, which encourages the model to group similar images (real or synthetic) closer together in the feature space, improving the overall discrimination. A tunable factor controls the influence of the contrastive loss.

The experiments were conducted on a diverse set of datasets, including images generated by various GAN-based models like ProGAN, StyleGAN, BigGAN, and diffusion-based models like DALL-E. The training focused on ProGAN-generated images across different object categories. The testing phase was more comprehensive, utilising 20 different datasets to evaluate the model's generalization capabilities. Hyperparameter tuning was performed to find the optimal settings for factors like the contrastive loss weight, the number of projection network layers, and the dimension of the feature vectors. Data augmentation techniques like blurring, JPEG compression, cropping, and horizontal flipping were applied during training to improve robustness.

The performance of RINE was compared against several state-of-the-art synthetic image detection methods, including ResNet-based approaches, patch-based methods, frequency-based methods, gradient-based methods, and the latest state-of-the-art method based on simple linear probing upon frozen CLIP features (UFD) [60]. The evaluation was performed using Accuracy (ACC) and Average Precision (AP) metrics, with the best models selected based on the combined score of these metrics. The average performance across all test datasets is reported here in Table 11, more detailed evaluation can be found in the paper. RINE outperforms the state-of-the-art by + 10.6 ACC and + 4.5 AP.

Table 11 Average performance, in terms of accuracy (ACC) and average precision (AP), of methods across 20 generators

Method	# classes	AVG ACC	AVG AP
CNNDetect [83]	20	70.2	84.0
Patch-Forensics [11]	–	55.8	74.1
LGrad [80]	1	78.3	86.7
LGrad [80]	2	79.4	86.4
LGrad [80]	4	79.7	85.5
DMID [17]	20	77.6	93.9
UniFD [60]	20	80.9	94.3
RINE [47]	1	90.3	98.6
RINE [47]	2	87.7	98.7
RINE [47]	4	**91.5**	**98.8**

Bold denotes best value per column

Spectral Analysis

Here we provide an overview of the vera.ai methods focusing on spectral analysis. Specifically, these methods leverage distinct artifacts of the frequency spectrum of generated images to detect them.

Towards Spectral Detection of Synthetic Images

Synthetic images are often generated in a latent space, then decoded into images using an autoencoder. Autoencoders include several steps of upsampling, which leave spectral traces in images [54]. Analysing an image's spectrum can help reveal such artifacts, which are telltale signs of generated images.

The most visible spectral sign of generated images comes from peaks in the image spectrum (cf. Fig. 7), as already discussed in Sections "On the Detection of Synthetic Images Generated by Diffusion Models" and "Intriguing Properties of Synthetic Images: From Generative Adversarial Networks to Diffusion Models". Upsampling steps during decoding are usually done by a factor of 2, which causes each upsampling to create peaks in the Fourier transform of the output, corresponding to 2-periodic components. The first upsampling step will create 2-periodic components peaks. The second step upsampling step will shift the 2-periodic components peaks to 4-periodic components and create new 2-periodic components peaks, and so on. Thus, depending on the number of upsampling steps in the decoder, generated images feature peaks of periodicity 2 (one single upsampling step), 4 (2 steps), 8 (3 steps, being the most common), and 16 (4 steps), and any combination thereof in both directions (as well as of a combination of these components with the DC component).

In Synthbuster [2], whose pipeline is described in Fig. 8, we use a high-pass filter to highlight the periodic artifacts. We use the cross-difference filter, which has already been used to detect demosaicing [3] and JPEG compression [15] artifacts.

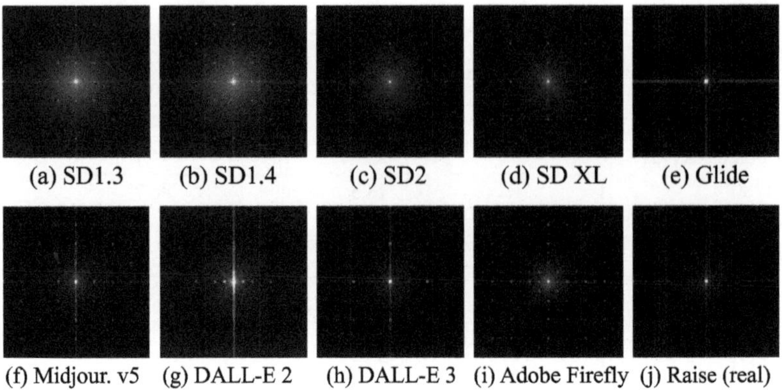

Fig. 7 Spectral signature of several DMs and real images. For each model, 1000 images are filtered through cross-difference. The Fourier transform of their average is then computed to highlight peak regions. The magnitude of the spectra is displayed after a morphological dilation (which is solely done for legibility of the figure, and not used in the methods). With this visualization, one can see the peaks corresponding to components of period 2 (all generative models), 4 and 8 (all but Glide), and 16 (Firefly and DALL·E 2), while these peaks are absent in real images

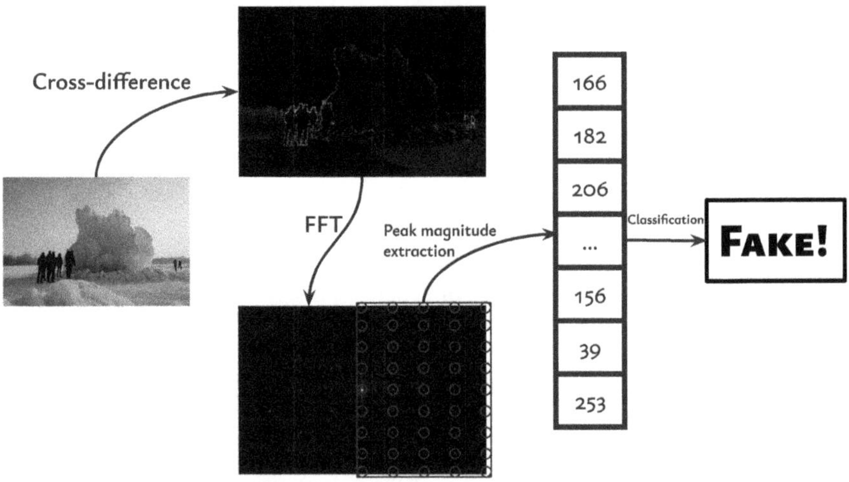

Fig. 8 Pipeline of the Synthbuster [2] method to detect diffusion-model-generated images. Each channel is filtered through cross-difference high-pass filtering, then the magnitude of peak candidate is extracted from the Fourier transform of each filtered channel. A histogram-based boosting tree ensemble is then used to distinguish real from fake images

Let I be a 2-dimensional image, the cross-difference at location (x, y) is defined as

$$C_{x,y} = \left| I_{x,y} + I_{x+1,y+1} - I_{x,y+1} - I_{x+1,y} \right|. \tag{1}$$

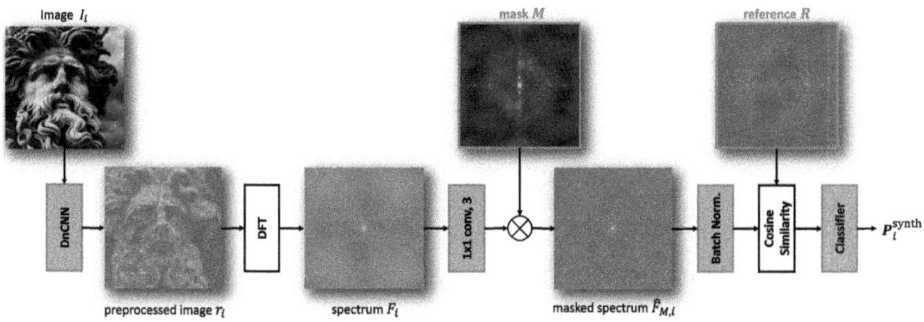

Fig. 9 Pipeline of the MaskSim [53] pipeline to detect generated images. The image is preprocessed with a small convolutional network, then its Fourier transform is computed. The spectrum is further processed with one convolution. A learned mask is applied to the processed spectrum to highlight regions which helps distinguish synthetic images from real ones. The masked spectrum is then normalised, and compared to learned real and fake reference spectra through cosine similarity for classification. The image pre-processing, mask processing, normalization, classifier, as well as the mask and references, are all computed together, end-to-end

This filter dampens the low frequencies in the image and thus increases the visibility of the decoder artifacts. The Fourier transform of the cross-difference is then computed, and normalised by its size. The method then selects the 45 expected peaks, whose corresponding horizontal and vertical periodicities are 0, 2, 4, or 8. The 16-periodic component peaks are ignored, as they were not present in most generative models when this method was designed.

The cross-difference, Fourier transform, and peak extraction is done separately for each channel, then the magnitudes of all extracted peaks are concatenated into 135 values. A histogram-based gradient boosting tree ensemble [42] is then trained to distinguish real from fake images.

The main limitation of this spectral analysis method is that the potential peaks to analyse are hard-coded in the method, thus limiting its generalization to future DMs or resampled images.

To overcome the limitations of Synthbuster, MaskSim [53] removes the hard-coded peak extraction, instead filtering the area with a learned mask that enables the method to select areas that are useful to distinguish real and generated images. This enables capturing not only the peaks, but also variations in the rest of the spectrum that also characterises generated images.

The image is first processed, then its Fourier transform is computed and processed through a single convolution. A learned mask is then applied to the spectrum through pointwise multiplication. This mask selects and weighs to which frequency components the method should be sensitive. The masked spectrum is then batch-normalised, and compared to learned fake and real reference spectra with cosine similarity. A classifier then decides whether the image is considered real or fake. This pipeline is schematised in Fig. 9.

One potential difficulty with detecting synthetic images is due to JPEG compression, as compressed images feature peaks at similar locations. There is thus a risk of incorrectly detecting real, compressed images as synthetic. Synthbuster and

Table 12 The AUC (%) over all the tested classes of synthetic images of the Synthbuster dataset [2] for images without post-processing and JPEG-compressed images at quality factors Q for 90, 80 and 70

Method	No post-processing	Q = 90	Q = 80	Q = 70
UniFD [60]	76.7	76.4	72.5	69.9
CNNDetect [83]	52.1	54.8	55.8	56.6
DMID [17]	82.5	81.2	84.6	86.2
Grag [31]	68.8	64.1	64.4	65.6
PatchFor [11]	29.7	50.1	49.0	48.7
Synthbuster [2]	**98.5**	92.6	91.7	91.3
MaskSim [53]	98.3	**97.9**	**96.6**	**95.5**

Bold denotes best and underline denotes second-best value per column

MaskSim handle compressed images in a different way, as seen in Table 12. Synthbuster naturally handles compressed images, as even though peaks are at the same location, their values are usually different. The tree ensemble is thus able to distinguish generated images from real ones, even in the presence of JPEG compression. MaskSim, on the other hand, is unable to do this fine analysis due to the cosine similarity aggregating the results. However, the mask learns to avoid regions that creates confusion, and will thus avoid using the peaks corresponding to JPEG compression and only use the rest of the area. Its success in distinguishing real from generated images prove that even beyond the peaks, spectral analysis can lead to good detection.

The downside of spectral analysis, though, comes from resampling that may be further applied to images and change the locations of the existing component peaks. Therefore, spectral analysis will need further refinements to be robust to image resampling, as will be explored in Section "Any-Resolution AI-Generated Image Detection by Spectral Learning" through data augmentation.

Any-Resolution AI-Generated Image Detection by Spectral Learning

Recent works have established that AI models introduce spectral artifacts to the generated images [2, 26, 53] (cf. Sections "On the Detection of Synthetic Images Generated by Diffusion Models", "Intriguing Properties of Synthetic Images: From Generative Adversarial Networks to Diffusion Models" and "Towards Spectral Detection of Synthetic Images"). Existing AI-generated image detection methods struggle outside of controlled environments [19, 25], because even minor differences in image generators introduce significant artifacts [2, 81], making it impractical to maintain an exhaustive training dataset due to the vast number of generative models available. To tackle this issue, we introduce the Spectral AI-generated Image detection (SPAI) approach [41] that employs the spectral distribution of real images as a suitable and highly discriminative pattern for the task of synthetic image detection. In particular, we use masked spectral learning for modelling this distribution under a self-supervised setup. This setup employs the pretext task of frequency reconstruction [86], with the objective of reconstructing the filtered out frequencies of an image.

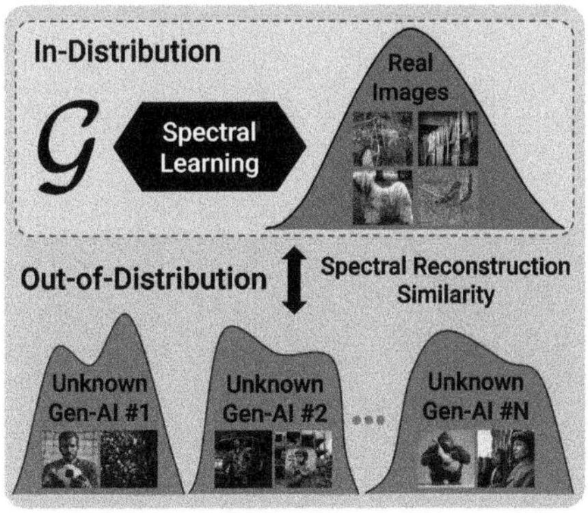

Fig. 10 SPAI employs spectral learning to learn the spectral distribution of real images under a self-supervised setup. Then, using the spectral reconstruction similarity it detects AI-generated images as out-of-distribution samples of this learned model

Then, the spectral reconstruction similarity mechanism is introduced to detect AI-generated images as out-of-distribution samples of this learned spectral model of real images. This formulation is highlighted in Fig. 10.

Capturing subtle traces in images is crucial for effectively distinguishing among real and AI-generated ones [17]. However, most computer vision models, having been designed for semantic-based tasks, cannot efficiently scale to the native resolution of modern photos [88], i.e. several megapixels. Therefore, pre-processing operations are required [45], effectively dropping a significant amount of discriminative information. To utilise all the spectral information present in the image SPAI introduces the spectral context attention to efficiently process any-resolution images without prior pre-processing. It achieves this by combining the most discriminative spectral reconstruction similarity values computed for different patches of the image, according to their spectral context and a learnable spectral reconstruction importance vector. An overview of the SPAI approaches is presented in Fig. 11.

The spectral model is pre-trained on ImageNet [22], while the network components that detect the out-of-distribution samples with respect to it are trained using only the low-resolution images introduced by [17], originating from a single LDM. Nevertheless, as presented in Table 13, it is able to generalise to some of the most advanced generative models, that produce images of very high visual fidelity. In particular, images from 13 recent generative models are considered, covering a broad spectrum of resolutions. In addition, five sources of real images are employed, namely from ImageNet [22], COCO [56], OpenImages [49], RAISE [20] and FODB [34], representing a general collection of online images, an object-focused database, a collection of high-resolution Web images, photos originating from DSLR and smartphone cameras respectively. On average, SPAI improves performance over the previous best approach by 5.5% in terms of AUC, highlighting its efficiency over the previous data-driven approaches that learn explicit discriminative boundaries over some labelled data.

Table 13 Comparison of SPAI against state-of-the-art approaches

Image size approach	< 0.5 MPixels			0.5–1.0 MPixels						> 1.0 MPixels				AVG
	Glide	SD1.3	SD1.4	Flux	DALL·E 2	SD2	SDXL	SD3	GigaGAN	MJv5	MJv6.1	DALL·E 3	Firefly	
NPR [79]	72.2	89.6	60.5	19.8	3.9	12.5	18.1	60.6	83.2	15.3	19.8	97.1	38.0	45.4
Dire [85]	33.3	59.9	61.3	45.7	52.2	68.5	46.9	49.2	36.3	41.9	50.3	65.2	49.9	50.8
CNNDet. [83]	59.2	59.0	61.2	39.8	71.5	57.5	67.4	30.2	73.4	48.8	56.7	23.5	73.4	55.5
FreqDet. [29]	43.6	92.3	92.7	36.5	47.4	42.5	66.5	69.8	63.2	36.9	27.5	42.2	80.9	57.1
Fusing [37]	63.0	62.8	62.2	57.5	76.7	66.9	62.1	38.8	80.4	64.0	74.0	25.2	76.3	62.3
LGrad [80]	76.5	82.4	83.4	74.9	85.7	60.7	70.2	12.7	89.9	69.2	79.6	30.0	42.0	65.9
UniFD [60]	63.3	80.8	81.2	36.3	91.4	84.3	78.3	28.6	86.2	57.1	60.5	31.0	95.5	67.3
GramNet [58]	78.2	83.9	84.3	78.6	85.2	66.7	77.8	19.2	85.0	63.8	84.9	42.9	38.0	68.4
DeFake [76]	86.1	64.2	63.6	90.5	41.4	66.2	52.3	87.7	71.7	67.0	87.5	93.3	39.4	70.1
PatchCr. [93]	78.4	95.7	96.2	86.9	81.8	95.7	96.7	33.8	98.0	79.0	96.1	28.1	79.1	80.4
DMID [17]	73.1	100.0	100.0	97.2	54.3	99.7	99.6	67.9	67.9	99.9	94.4	41.3	90.2	83.5
RINE [47]	95.6	99.9	99.9	93.0	93.0	96.6	99.3	39.1	92.9	96.4	81.2	41.8	82.9	<u>85.5</u>
SPAI (ours)	90.2	99.6	99.6	83.0	91.1	96.5	97.4	75.9	85.4	94.5	84.0	90.2	96.0	**91.0**

Average AUC over 5 sources of real images is reported. Lower values are highlighted in red, while higher values are highlighted in green. Best overall average value is highlighted in bold, while second best is underlined

Generalization and In-the-Wild Performance

Here we provide an overview of the vera.ai methods focusing on improving generalization to unseen generators and concepts, as well as in-the-wild performance and efficiency.

Enhanced Training Using Quality-Aware Sampling

This work focuses on improving the detection of synthetically generated images by incorporating a two-step approach: a sampling strategy based on image quality and a training phase using a CNN architecture [24]. The main contribution lies in the use of quality quantification to construct the training set, which helps detect fake images with greater generalization, especially across different image concepts. In addition to training on a single dataset, a cross-concept training strategy is also proposed, where the model is trained on images from one concept (e.g., human faces) and tested on another (e.g., animals or scenes). This ensures better generalization across diverse image categories.

The methodology introduces a novel approach for synthetic image detection presented in Fig. 12. The first step, the sampling strategy, involves selecting the best generated images for training by quantifying their quality. While traditional metrics like Frechet Inception Distance (FID) and Inception Score (IS) measure the similarity between real and generated images, the proposed method introduces a more tailored approach called Quality Calculation (QC). QC uses a Gaussian Mixture Model (GMM) to model the distribution of real images and then calculates the qual-

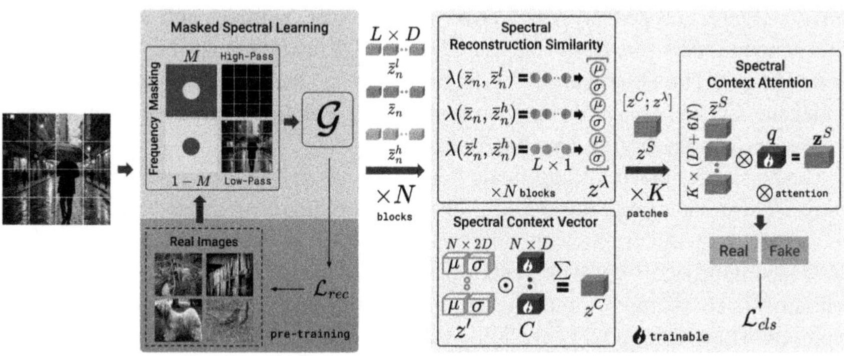

Fig. 11 Overview of the SPAI approach. It learns a model of the spectral distribution of real images under a self-supervised setup using masked spectral learning. Then, it uses the spectral reconstruction similarity to measure the divergence from this learned distribution and detect AI-generated images as out-of-distribution samples of this model. Spectral context vector captures the spectral context under which the spectral reconstruction similarity values are computed, while spectral context attention enables the processing of any-resolution images for capturing subtle spectral inconsistencies

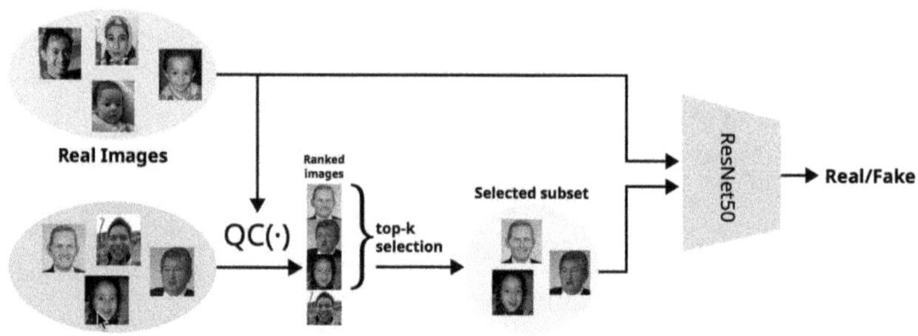

Fig. 12 The synthetically generated images (in the pink ellipsis) are evaluated based on a quality assessment model (QC(·)) trained on real images (in the green ellipse). The top-k generated images are then selected and provided, along with real images, as input to a ResNet50 model, which is trained to discriminate between real and fake images

ity of generated images based on their similarity to this distribution. The QC score ranks the images from highest to lowest quality, unlike FID, which only gives a single scalar value for a set of images. This ranking allows to select the top-k highest-quality images for training the detection model.

The second step involves training a CNN-based classifier to distinguish between real and fake images. The proposed method utilises a ResNet50 model pre-trained on ImageNet, which is fine-tuned on the dataset consisting of high-quality generated images selected through QC and real images. During training, a set of augmentations, including geometric transformations and image compressions, are applied to improve the robustness of the model. The classifier is trained with a binary cross-entropy loss to classify images as real or fake.

The method is evaluated on several publicly available image datasets, including FFHQ, AFHQ, and LSUN, which cover human faces, animals, and various scenes. Pre-trained models like StyleGAN2 and Latent Diffusion are used to generate synthetic images. The effectiveness of the method is evaluated by measuring the Area Under the Curve (AUC) of the detection model, which provides a comprehensive evaluation without relying on a fixed threshold.

The results demonstrate significant improvements in detection performance when using QC for sampling, as seen in Table 14, particularly in cross-concept scenarios, where a model trained on one image concept is evaluated on another. The QC-based approach improves generalization, producing more consistent and reliable models compared to random sampling. Additionally, cross-concept training is explored, where the model is explicitly trained on images from multiple concepts to enhance its adaptability, as well as cross-architecture training, where the model is trained on images from multiple generative model architectures. The performance of the detector is shown to significantly improve when it is trained on a diverse set of generated images, including those produced by StyleGAN2 and LDMs, and evaluated on a range of test sets. The results are shown in Table 15. These further improve detection accuracy when encountering synthetic images from unseen domains.

Table 14 AUC of detection model trained on randomly selected samples or based on the proposed QC score for each concept (Human (H), Animal (A) and Church (C)) and generative model (StyleGAN and Latent Diffusion)

Training	Sampling	$H + H^G$	$A + A^G$	$C + C^G$
StyleGAN2				
$H + H^G$	Random	100.0 ± 0.0	89.1 ± 1.00	77.5 ± 3.42
	QC (ours)	100.0 ± 0.0	**94.8 ± 1.22**	**83.5 ± 0.94**
$A + A^G$	Random	61.8 ± 1.36	100.0 ± 0.0	89.1 ± 0.71
	QC (ours)	**66.4 ± 1.08**	100.0 ± 0.0	86.5 ± 0.15
$C + C^G$	Random	53.7 ± 0.22	58.6 ± 3.51	100.0 ± 0.0
	QC (ours)	**59.4 ± 0.19**	**67.1 ± 0.16**	100.0 ± 0.0
Latent Diffusion				
$H + H^G$	Random	100.0 ± 0.0	64.4 ± 2.31	66.7 ± 0.88
	QC (ours)	100.0 ± 0.0	**74.1 ± 0.68**	**77.5 ± 0.03**
$A + A^G$	Random	52.1 ± 1.47	96.3 ± 0.79	99.7 ± 0.03
	QC (ours)	**56.2 ± 5.13**	**99.6** ± 0.02	99.4 ± 0.02
$C + C^G$	Random	54.2 ± 4.08	96.3 ± 1.19	100.0 ± 0.0
	QC (ours)	**58.5 ± 1.52**	**98.9 ± 0.58**	100.0 ± 0.0

Mean and standard deviation of three training sessions with different seeds are reported. Bold indicates the best performance

Table 15 AUC of detection model when trained on StyleGAN2 (SG) data, Latent Diffusion (LD) data, or both, and evaluated on SG data, LD and both

Test/training	SG	LD	SG + LD
SG	**99.9 ± 0.00**	60.5 ± 1.53	77.3 ± 0.88
LD	59.2 ± 0.29	99.9 ± 0.00	74.6 ± 1.07
SG + LD	**99.9 ± 0.00**	**99.9 ± 0.01**	**99.9 ± 0.00**

Mean and standard deviation of three sessions with different seeds are reported. Bold indicates the best performance

Zero-Shot Detection of AI-Generated Images

The detection of AI-generated images relies traditionally on supervised learning and suffers from poor generalization. Therefore, there is high interest for few-shot and possibly zero-shot methods which require little or no prior knowledge of the target models. Following this line of thinking, the proposal is a zero-shot detector that tells apart real from generated images based on information-theoretic quantities. The idea is to train a model only on real images to learn an accurate statistical model of this single class. Synthetic images from different sources are expected to exhibit different statistics and therefore to be outliers with respect to this model. By selecting appropriate features, they will be easily distinguished from real images. This approach requires no training on synthetic images giving rise to a truly zero-shot detector that can work equally well on all different synthetic sources, including upcoming ones, provided they are not able to perfectly mimic the statistics of real images. The key idea is to use a lossless coder to learn a reliable statistical model of real images. Lossless coding is a mature field of research based on sound information-theoretic concepts. Most lossless image coders work by predicting the value of each pixel based on a suitable known context and then encoding the prediction error. If the image is real, it follows the intrinsic statistical model of real images, and its pixels are not too surprising for the encoder. On the contrary, the pixels of synthetic images happen to exhibit unexpected values thereby causing a coding cost larger than expected. This concept is summarised in Fig. 13.

The method uses a state-of-the-art lossless image coder, the Super-Resolution based lossless Compressor (SReC), which provides a computationally lightweight tool for predicting the probability distribution of image pixels at multiple resolutions. The high-level structure of the zero-shot entropy-based detector (ZED), adapted from SReC, is shown in Fig. 14. The image is subsampled and rounded three times, and its lower resolution versions are used to estimate the probability distribution of all pixels at the next higher resolution, to eventually compute entropy and negative log-likelihood at all levels. These latter quantities are then combined to extract a number of decision statistics considered in the experiments. Images for the tests were collected from publicly available datasets or generated as needed when not publicly available. All datasets include real and synthetic images with similar semantic content, both compressed and uncompressed, to avoid any kind of bias. In particular, if the synthetic image generator was trained on real images from a given dataset, the real images are drawn from the same dataset to verify detection ability, thereby ensuring the absence of unpredictable biases. The real datasets used to this end are LSUN, FFHQ, ImageNet, COCO, LAION, and RAISE, all widely adopted in the community. Results are reported in Table 16 in terms of area under the ROC curve (AUC). For the sake of compactness, the results are averaged on test datasets sharing the same source of real images. The method is compared in its performance with those of the 7 most competitive methods proposed in the recent literature. On the average, only DMID [17] and UniFD [60] perform on par with the proposal, while all other methods are largely inferior. It is also worth reminding that only the proposed

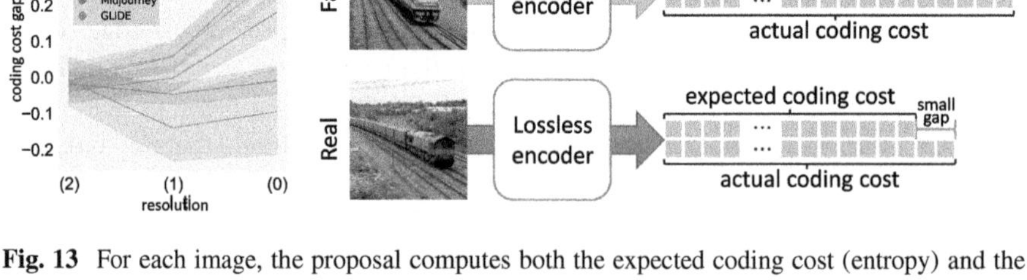

Fig. 13 For each image, the proposal computes both the expected coding cost (entropy) and the actual coding cost (negative log-likelihood). These quantities are expected to be close to one another for real images and further apart for synthetic images. The left box of the figure summarises the different behaviour of decision statistics at various resolution levels for real and synthetic images

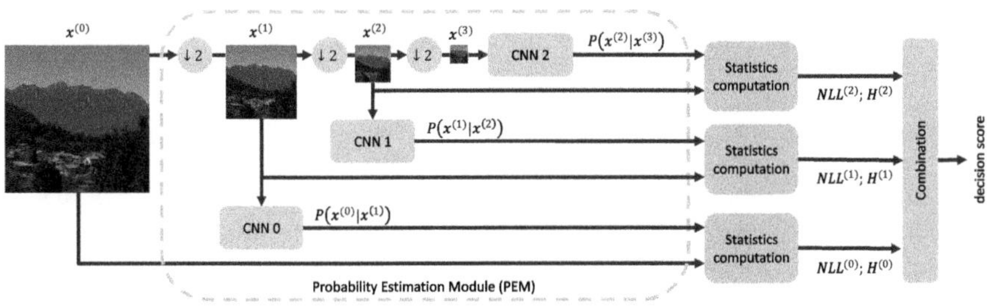

Fig. 14 High-level structure of the proposed zero-shot entropy-based detector. The input image is subsampled and rounded multiple times. Low-resolution images provide the context for predicting pixel at higher resolution. Based on these latter, entropy and negative log likelihood are computed and used for decision

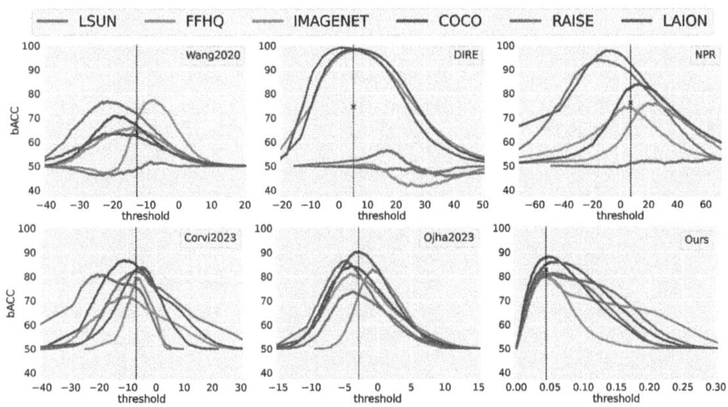

Fig. 15 Balanced accuracy as a function of the detection threshold. For each dataset of real images, the accuracy is averaged over all associated synthetic generators. The dotted vertical line indicates the global optimal threshold, and the "x" symbol the corresponding accuracy. Note that only for the proposed method all peaks are very close, indicating the presence of a single threshold

method is zero-shot, with no training on synthetic images, while DMID [17] and most other methods use intense supervised training and UniFD [60] relies on CLIP features followed by a supervised classifier. Note also that FFHQ and RAISE, the last two real datasets in the table, include only uncompressed images, like all synthetic datasets. In these conditions, where no compression-related bias is possible, the proposed method keeps performing very well, just like with the other datasets. Finally, in Fig. 15, the accuracy is reported as a function of the decision threshold for the best methods. Like before, a separate curve is shown for each source of real images by averaging over the associated synthetic generators. Unlike AUC, the accuracy critically depends on the selection of a good threshold and may decrease dramatically in the absence of some calibration data. Note that only for the proposed ZED method there is a single good threshold that ensures near-optimal accuracy for all datasets.

Table 16 Comparison of ZED with state-of-the-art methods in terms of AUC

Fake data	Real data	Liu2022	DMID	LGrad	DIRE	UniFD	NPR	AEROBLADE	ZED
Diff. GAN		99.5	96.6	**99.5**	49.8	97.4	**100**	43.9	99.5
ADM	S	70.6	80.3	81.1	52.0	88.2	**94.1**	53.1	71.0
StyleGAN2		**99.7**	89.1	**99.8**	58.3	96.7	**100**	30.0	96.5
StarGAN		**99.9**	95.9	73.9	40.4	**99.7**	81.5	84.0	**100**
StyleGAN2	F	**99.9**	58.4	82.7	55.5	91.0	71.3	60.1	88.7
DDPM		22.8	**100**	9.8	23.1	77.7	92.4	81.7	79.6
BigGAN		94.7	83.4	77.2	**99.8**	**99.6**	86.8	51.9	92.6
GigaGAN	I	97.3	50.5	76.4	**99.9**	94.6	82.4	47.5	68.1
ADM		94.4	81.1	72.7	**99.5**	85.3	78.5	80.3	92.1
DiT		88.0	**100**	56.2	**99.6**	77.8	78.4	**99.8**	91.0
GauGAN		**99.7**	83.8	81.6	**99.9**	**100**	89.1	55.1	**99.7**
GigaGAN		**99.6**	90.9	76.7	**99.9**	97.6	95.5	80.6	93.4
GALIP		94.3	87.7	56.7	**100**	98.6	90.7	65.0	99.4
GLIDE		96.3	97.2	81.5	**99.9**	88.8	95.4	98.0	91.1
Stable D. 1.4	C	95.3	**100**	54.7	**99.9**	97.9	76.5	**99.8**	71.4
Stable D. 2		94.2	**100**	62.8	99.3	82.3	89.3	**99.9**	89.1
SDXL		89.3	**100**	89.3	99.5	80.0	99.3	87.9	**99.8**
Deep.-IF		72.2	**99.9**	68.8	98.9	92.9	91.6	81.9	79.4
DALL·E 2		98.9	88.2	78.6	**99.9**	97.1	90.0	59.3	**99.9**
DALL·E 3		99.5	**100**	88.4	**99.9**	86.4	97.7	**99.7**	98.2
DALL·E	L	95.0	98.3	95.2	**99.8**	97.3	**99.5**	24.1	95.4
GLIDE		90.8	86.9	90.3	**100**	95.3	**99.8**	68.7	88.5
GLIDE		56.6	**86.5**	50.6	42.9	72.8	63.3	**87.7**	65.1
Stable D. 1.4		73.4	**100**	50.0	37.6	87.7	43.0	96.9	97.2
Stable D. 2		34.8	**100**	41.4	35.5	89.5	44.0	97.4	95.9
SDXL	R	31.1	**100**	57.2	47.1	85.1	76.7	69.7	99.2
DALL·E 2		70.4	69.4	58.6	44.7	95.2	39.5	32.8	**100**
DALL·E 3		0.2	60.8	37.9	47.6	36.4	48.7	48.3	**78.1**
Midjourney		40.7	**100**	56.3	51.0	66.2	77.0	99.0	98.5
Adobe Firefly		11.8	**98.0**	40.6	57.4	**97.5**	32.1	52.8	80.4
AVG		77.0	89.4	68.2	74.6	88.4	80.1	71.2	**90.0**

Bold underlines the best performance for each row with a margin of 0.5%. For Real data: S = LSUN, F = FFHQ, I = ImageNet, C = COCO, L = LAION, R = RAISE

Evolution of Detection Performance Throughout the Online Lifespan of Synthetic Images

By its very nature, any digital image constitutes a signal of limited information. In order for a passive synthetic image detector to distinguish real from fake images, enough discriminative information should be present in this signal. It can be assumed that such information is added to the signal once, i.e. at generation time. However, after its initial generation, an image may pass through any number of noisy communication channels, either fully digital, or even involving conversion from and to

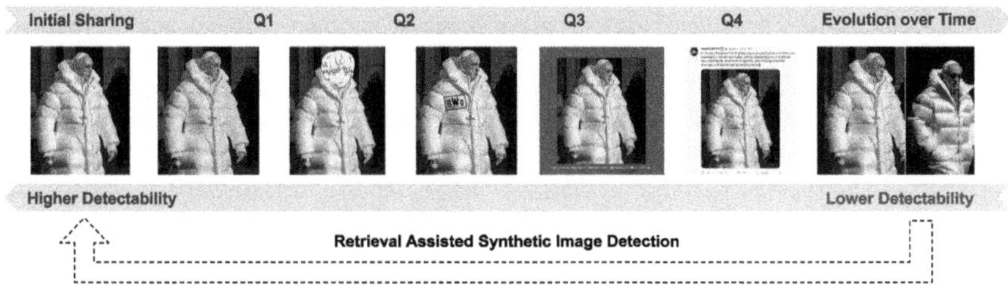

Fig. 16 As derivative copies of a synthetic image are shared online and post-processing operations accumulate, the performance of synthetic image detectors decreases over time. Using retrieval-assisted synthetic image detection, it is feasible to retain the initial detection performance throughout the online lifespan of a synthetic image

analogue format, like in the case of taking snapshots of a screen or printed materials. Ultimately, the signal gets heavily distorted and much of the initial discriminative information is no further distinguishable, inherently increasing the aleatoric uncertainty in deciding whether it is real or fake, solely based on the image signal (Fig. 16).

To mitigate this issue, we observe that while such derivative synthetic images shared online may not contain enough information to discriminate them from real ones, early copies of these same images shared online may be distinguishable with high accuracy [40]. To this end, we propose Retrieval Assisted Synthetic Image Detection (RASID), that attempts to retrieve such early copies, with the intention of exploiting the more discriminative information they may contain. This approach is more robust to distortions of the image signal, as image retrieval approaches primarily employ the semantic information of the image. RASID employs the near-duplicate detection approach introduced in [46] and computes a probability for each image under analysis as the average of the probabilities of its retrieved early copies.

The evaluation of RASID considers 12 different AIGID approaches as well as four groups of images containing 955 unique images, collected from 3070 online sources and spanning an online lifetime from three to ten months. As presented in Table 17 RASID improves performance by 6.7% in terms of balanced accuracy and 7.8% in terms of AUC respectively.

A Bias-Free Training Paradigm for More General AI-Generated Image Detection

Synthetic detectors have a tendency to perform very well in supervised learning benchmarks but fail to generalise to real world situations. This issue could be caused mostly by inadequate training data. In order to overcome this hurdle, this work proposes a bias-free training paradigm where fake images are generated starting from real images to ensure alignment between real and fake images. The proposed pipeline can be seen in Fig. 17. To guarantee that the semantic content of the fake images is perfectly aligned with the real images the conditioning input of the inpainting model

Table 17 RASID vs. Direct detection evaluation. Balanced accuracy (ACC) computed using the equal error rate (EER) threshold and AUC are reported. The performance difference is presented in the last two columns. Improved performance over direct detection is highlighted in green, while a decrease in performance is highlighted in red. The best value per column is highlighted in bold, and the second-best is underlined

Approach	Direct det.		RASID		Diff. (%)	
	ACC	AUC	ACC	AUC	ACC	AUC
GramNet [58]	20.3	15.6	21.8	17.5	7.0	13.0
UniFD [60]	37.4	37.0	41.0	41.7	10.0	13.0
FreqDetect [29]	50.0	51.0	52.2	53.6	4.0	5.0
PatchCraft [93]	54.9	56.0	55.6	56.6	1.0	1.0
NPR [79]	41.6	41.9	57.5	58.4	38.0	39.0
Fusing [37]	57.6	58.6	60.2	61.9	4.0	6.0
CNNDetect [83]	56.7	58.5	59.3	62.3	5.0	7.0
DIRE [85]	50.0	68.6	50.0	67.6	0.0	– 2.0
LGrad [80]	70.1	74.2	71.3	75.7	2.0	2.0
RINE [47]	69.8	73.7	<u>73.2</u>	77.1	5.0	5.0
DeFake [76]	**73.7**	**80.4**	72.9	<u>79.5</u>	– 1.0	– 1.0
DIMD [17]	<u>73.6</u>	<u>79.1</u>	**77.6**	**83.6**	5.0	6.0
				Overall	**6.7**	**7.8**

BA computed using the EER threshold and the AUC metrics are reported

of Stable Diffusion 2.1 is used. The side input is first projected on an intermediate representation, it is then fed to the intermediate layers and, after several denoising steps, the decoder is used to obtain the conditioned image from the embedding vector. The side inputs in the inpainting model used are the reference image, a binary mask of the area to inpaint, and a textual description of the content to add. If the binary mask used is empty the output of the model is a perfect reconstruction of the input. Figure 18 shows how the side inputs can be used to augment the data. Two new versions can be created, one where an object is inpainted with an object of the same type, another one where it is instead replaced with an object from a different one. Beside the fully generated versions, another set of images is obtained by replacing the regenerated background with the original one. The dataset created is then used to train a ViT-based model with four registers pre-trained on the self-supervised learning method DINOv2 [61].

The results comparing the proposed methods with the state of the art can be seen in Table 18. While most methods fail to have good performance especially on newer generators, the proposed method has uniformly good performances regardless of how new the generator is and what the history of the image is.

Table 18 Comparison of B-Free with state-of-the-art methods in terms of balanced accuracy and balanced negative log likelihood (NLL)

bAcc (%)↑/NLL↓	Synthbuster					New generators		WildRF			AVG
	Midjourney	SDXL	DALL·E 2	DALL·E 3	Firefly	FLUX	SD3.5	Facebook	Reddit	Twitter	bAcc↑/NLL↓
CNNDetect	49.5/8.45	49.8/6.90	50.2/5.75	49.5/12.9	50.3/3.66	49.5/10.1	50.0/5.30	50.0/9.84	50.7/6.66	50.1/8.64	50.0/7.83
DMID	**100./0.00**	**99.7/0.01**	50.1/5.99	50.0/7.08	51.0/1.72	63.7/1.27	**99.9/0.01**	87.8/0.52	74.3/1.82	79.1/0.85	75.6/1.93
LGrad	57.7/6.88	58.5/6.81	55.6/7.10	47.9/7.58	47.4/7.50	54.9/7.11	51.9/7.24	66.6/3.74	57.8/4.72	45.7/5.31	54.4/6.40
UniFD	52.4/2.35	68.0/1.15	83.5/0.43	47.3/3.94	90.7/0.24	48.4/3.45	69.3/1.07	48.8/3.06	59.5/1.37	56.0/2.01	62.4/1.91
DeFake	69.7/0.72	76.3/0.56	64.0/0.92	84.9/0.36	72.4/0.63	79.2/0.46	81.2/0.42	66.3/0.89	65.9/0.82	63.4/0.94	72.3/0.67
DIRE	49.7/15.3	49.9/15.3	50.0/15.3	50.0/15.3	49.9/15.3	50.0/15.3	50.0/15.3	51.9/4.98	79.5/2.15	56.7/4.39	53.7/11.9
NPR	44.9/16.6	50.3/16.2	50.2/16.2	0.6/29.9	0.4/47.3	50.3/16.2	50.3/16.2	50.0/32.2	78.3/9.39	51.8/25.2	42.7/22.5
FatFormer	44.4/5.22	66.7/2.76	54.1/3.64	35.9/6.90	60.1/3.59	39.4/6.10	49.1/5.06	54.7/4.54	69.5/2.54	54.8/4.40	52.9/4.48
FasterThanLies	61.3/2.98	71.1/1.79	50.8/5.15	53.5/3.79	55.2/4.40	53.8/4.10	53.7/3.76	46.2/3.32	51.0/3.99	53.9/3.31	55.1/3.66
RINE	54.6/5.03	71.8/1.99	82.2/0.77	45.3/20.5	91.2/0.36	46.7/10.1	81.3/1.22	52.8/6.51	67.7/2.46	56.0/5.23	65.0/5.43
AIDE	57.5/0.95	68.4/0.70	34.9/1.34	33.7/1.38	24.8/2.00	62.9/0.82	63.3/0.82	56.9/0.94	72.1/0.62	57.3/1.01	53.2/1.06
LaDeDa	50.7/24.8	50.7/24.8	50.5/24.8	41.1/25.4	47.4/25.6	50.5/24.8	50.7/24.8	70.3/7.19	74.7/7.93	59.6/9.40	54.6/19.9
C2P-CLIP	52.8/1.10	77.7/0.48	55.6/0.99	63.2/0.73	59.5/0.89	50.1/1.30	60.9/0.93	54.4/0.97	68.4/0.67	57.4/0.91	60.0/0.90
CoDE	76.9/0.82	75.2/0.81	54.6/2.44	73.2/0.98	58.6/2.00	59.8/1.97	67.7/1.27	70.0/0.97	66.1/1.29	70.9/1.01	67.3/1.36
B-Free	**99.6**/0.02	**99.8/0.01**	**95.6/0.10**	**98.2/0.06**	**99.7/0.02**	**92.3/0.19**	98.9/0.04	**95.6/0.14**	**86.2/0.28**	**97.3/0.09**	**96.3/0.10**

Bold underlines the best performance for each column with a margin of 1%

Table 19 Comparison of the proposal with SotA methods in terms of average performance in terms of balanced accuracy and NLL for three additional datasets: GenImage, FakeInversion and SynthWildX

bAcc (%)↑/NLL↓	GenImage	FakeInver.	SynthWildX	AVG
CNNDetect	51.3/7.88	50.9/7.94	50.0/8.08	50.7/7.96
DMID	79.0/1.66	**96.1/0.25**	76.6/0.82	83.9/0.91
LGrad	39.6/7.12	77.2/2.27	46.3/5.53	54.3/4.97
UniFD	65.5/1.31	52.8/2.19	52.5/2.55	56.9/2.02
DeFake	73.7/0.74	63.3/0.95	62.9/0.98	66.6/0.89
DIRE	47.3/6.54	51.8/13.4	52.5/4.60	50.5/8.19
AntifakePrompt	78.5/–	53.9/–	70.8/–	67.8/–
NPR	50.7/25.3	87.0/4.96	49.9/28.2	62.6/19.5
FatFormer	61.5/3.99	59.7/3.45	53.3/4.75	58.2/4.06
FasterThanLies	77.0/1.23	48.6/3.64	50.9/3.40	58.8/2.76
RINE	69.1/2.57	63.6/4.84	56.2/6.07	63.0/4.49
AIDE	60.2/1.01	76.9/0.54	55.0/1.05	64.0/0.86
LaDeDa	50.2/29.2	84.7/3.03	55.1/10.2	63.3/14.1
C2P-CLIP	75.5/0.57	59.6/0.82	57.4/0.91	64.2/0.76
CoDE	71.7/1.43	78.8/0.74	72.3/0.95	74.2/1.04
B-Free (ours)	**89.3/0.27**	86.2/0.32	**95.6/0.14**	**90.4/0.24**

Bold denotes best value per column

In Table 19, the performance is reported on the Unbiased GenImage dataset [94], FakeInversion [10] and SynthWildX [18] as average over all the dataset. Most methods do not achieve good performance on these datasets, especially on SynthWildX where images have been shared over the Web. Finally, recent studies [40] show how the performance of the detectors degrades over time as the image get reposted many times (cf. Section "Evolution of Detection Performance Throughout the Online Lifespan of Synthetic Images"). In Fig. 19, it can be seen that the proposed is the only method that maintains a good performance even after many days that the original image has been posted.

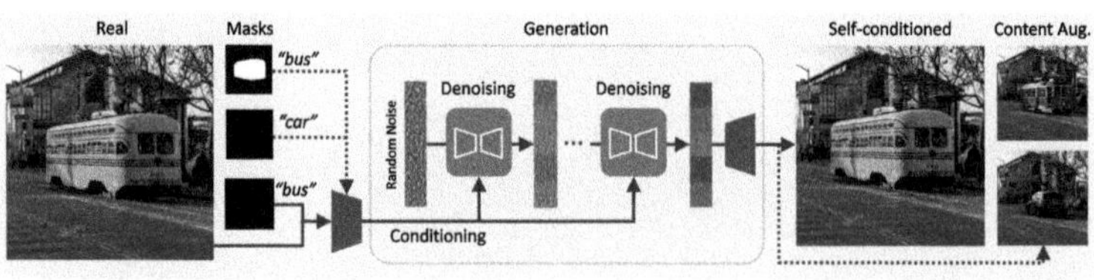

Fig. 17 The pipeline proposed to generate the synthetic images from the real images. The fake images are generated as self reconstructions of real images with augmentation in the form of inpainted versions

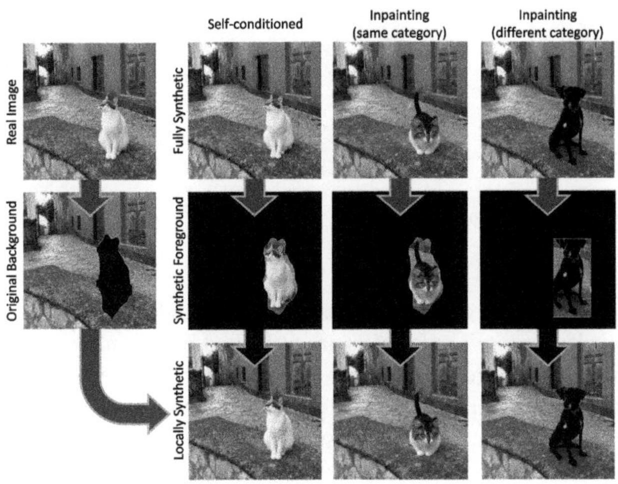

Fig. 18 The content augmentation process. Using the side inputs three different versions can be generated (top row). It is also possible to generate a locally manipulated version by replacing the synthetic background with the original

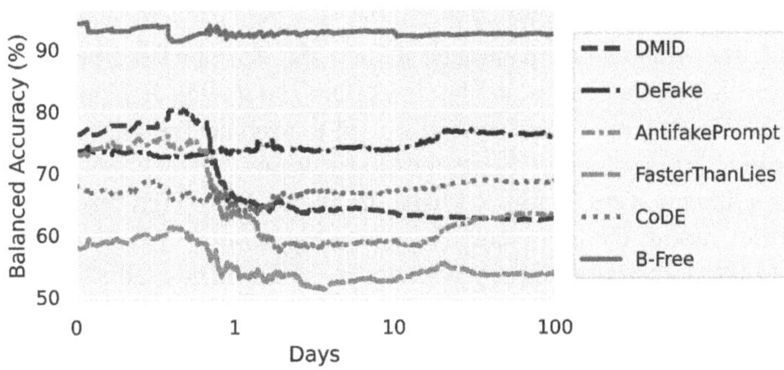

Fig. 19 Results of SotA detectors on viral fake and real images, analysing multiple web-scraped versions of each image. The performance is in terms of balanced accuracy evaluated from the initial online post (log scale). Only detectors with an accuracy over 50% are shown

Texture-Rich Region Selection Cropping

In this study, TextureCrop is introduced, a method designed to enhance AIGID by focusing on texture-rich regions within an image. Traditional AIGID approaches typically resize or centre-crop the image to a fraction of its original size before processing. However, this often results in significant information loss. Some models attempt to process the entire image, but this can be computationally prohibitive. TextureCrop addresses these challenges by selecting and analysing specific regions of the image that contain the most valuable texture information (cf. Fig. 20), optimising both the accuracy and efficiency of detection.

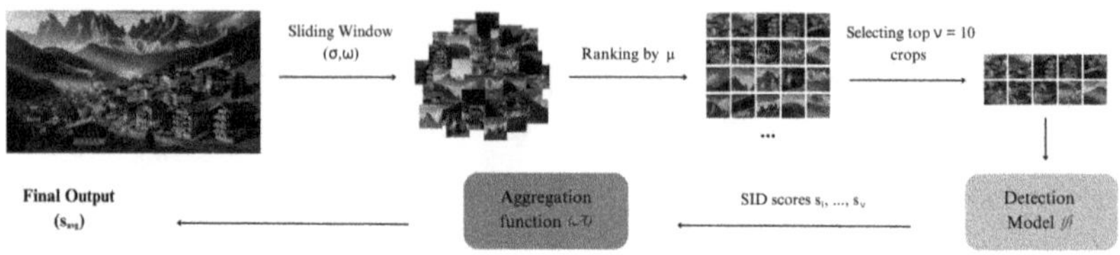

Fig. 20 Overview of the TextureCrop pipeline

To implement this, TextureCrop uses a sliding window technique to divide an image into smaller crops. These crops are evaluated based on their texture, and the most informative ones are selected for further analysis. The method ranks these crops using texture measures, such as Global Histogram Entropy (GHE) [39], which quantifies the randomness in pixel intensity distributions. Crops with higher entropy values, which indicate more complex texture, are prioritised. Once the most relevant crops are identified, the detection model assigns scores to these crops which are then combined to produce a final score that indicates whether the image is real or synthetic.

TextureCrop focuses on a few key parameters to control its effectiveness. The stride parameter determines how far the sliding window moves between crop extractions, while the window size parameter defines the size of each crop. The number of crops selected for analysis is another important factor, with 10 being a commonly chosen value. Lastly, the texture measure used to evaluate the information content of each crop helps in selecting the regions to focus on.

The experiments were conducted using a diverse set of high-resolution images sourced from various datasets, including images generated by GAN-based models like StyleGAN, diffusion-based models such as DALL-E and Stable Diffusion, low-level vision models like SAN and SITD, as well as images collected from real-world environments. The performance of TextureCrop was compared against centre cropping, resizing and ten cropping on several state-of-the-art synthetic image detection methods. The evaluation was performed using Balanced Accuracy (BA), Average Precision (AP) and Area Under the ROC Curve (AUC) metrics. The average performance across all test datasets is reported in Table 20, and a more detailed evaluation can be found in the paper [45]. By prioritising the most texture-rich areas, TextureCrop improves the efficiency of AIGID models and outperforms all the previously used processing methods.

In-the-Wild Implementation of RINE: Enhancing AIGID in Real-World Conditions

The in-the-wild (ITW) implementation of RINE [47] is the result of an analysis of the main aspects that affect performance in the wild. After experimentation, these factors were identified as the backbone, training data, processing method and augmentations. The ITW-RINE model enhances the detection capabilities of synthetic images by

Table 20 Average performance in terms of balanced accuracy (BA), average precision (AP), and area under ROC curve (AUC) of different processing methods across 10 detectors

Method	AVG BA	AVG AP	AVG AUC
CenterCrop	63.50	63.65	67.98
Resizing	55.71	52.39	59.20
TenCrop	64.41	67.24	67.57
TextureCrop	**67.79**	**70.58**	**74.06**

Bold denotes best value per column

Table 21 Performance comparison (ACC/AP) of RINE and ITW-RINE models across three datasets

Model	Synthbuster [2]	Chameleon [87]	ITW-SM	AVG
RINE	87.47/90.45	45.21/39.67	60.33/66.80	64.34/65.64
ITW-RINE	94.90/99.18	78.50/85.51	91.20/98.50	88.20/94.40

building on the foundational principles of the RINE architecture while leveraging a distinct backbone: DINOv2 ViT-L/14 [61] instead of CLIP ViT-L/14. This choice is informed by the backbone ablation studies, which highlighted DINOv2's superior ability to extract fine-grained visual features critical for distinguishing real images from AI-generated content.

The training dataset for the ITW model is significantly augmented beyond the lab-generated images used in the original implementation. It now includes a diverse set of in-the-wild images, ensuring that the model is exposed to realistic and variable conditions. This dual approach—integrating both unprocessed and heavily processed data—further strengthens the model's robustness against real-world perturbations. In place of traditional cropping methods, the ITW implementation adopts the newly proposed texture-cropping strategy [45] (Section "Texture-Rich Region Selection Cropping"), which focuses on extracting regions with high texture information that are indicative of generative artifacts.

This implementation specifically addresses the challenges presented by real-world scenarios, where synthetic images often undergo various transformations and perturbations. To counter these effects, the ITW approach utilises an expanded set of data augmentations. These are designed to create a more varied training set, helping the model generalise better to unseen image variations. The model is trained using a similar configuration as RINE, but with the DINOv2 [61] backbone optimising its performance on challenging real-world but also benchmark datasets.

Performance evaluation of the ITW model is conducted using a variety of metrics, including Accuracy (ACC) and Average Precision (AP) to assess its detection capabilities across different datasets. The ITW implementation demonstrates a significant enhancement in performance over the original RINE method, achieving an average increase of + 23.86% in ACC and + 28.75% in AP across diverse benchmark and real-world datasets. Comprehensive results are summarised in Table 21.

Table 22 FPR comparison of ITW-RINE model using different thresholds across three datasets

Threshold	Synthbuster [2]	Chameleon [87]	ITW-SM	AVG
1% FPR	**0.00**	**7.10**	**1.00**	**2.70**
5% FPR	0.90	15.27	5.00	7.06
0.5	3.20	25.51	13.76	14.16

Bold denotes best value per column

To minimise false positives, which are a critical concern when deploying AIGID models in the wild, a calibration process was implemented using thresholds derived from the ITW-SM calibration dataset, which includes processed social media images. The calibration process fine-tunes the model's predictions, ensuring that results are more reliable. The false positive thresholds were set at 10, 5, and 1%, with corresponding classifications based on the logit scores:

- If the logit is greater than 1% FP rate threshold, the result is classified as strong detection.
- If the logit is between the 5% FP rate and the 1% FP rate threshold, the result is classified as detection.
- If the logit is between the 10% FP rate and the 5% FP rate threshold, the result is classified as inconclusive.
- If the logit is less than 10% FP rate threshold, the result is classified as non-detection.

The additional calibration process significantly improves the model's performance by reducing the false positive rate (FPR). As shown in Table 22, the calibration results in a notable 11.46% drop in false positives when using the 1% threshold across the three datasets. If the 5% threshold is used, the reduction in false positives is 7.10%. This calibration step ensures that the ITW-RINE model not only enhances its ability to detect synthetic content but also improves the reliability of its predictions by minimising false positives.

6 Conclusions

In this chapter we provide a comprehensive overview of the progress in the field of AIGID including recent state-of-the-art methodologies, the evolution of relevant datasets, and current challenges, as well as the pertinent works conducted in the framework of vera.ai.

The explosive growth of AI-driven image generation technology offers significant creative potential, while also presents substantial threats to online information integrity, social trust, and democratic processes due to its potential for malicious use in disinformation campaigns and fraudulent activities. Therefore, there is an urgent need for the development of robust and adaptable detection mechanisms capable of distinguishing between real and synthetic images. AIGID methods capitalise on the artifacts introduced by generative models, which manifest as high-level inconsistencies or low-level subtle noise patterns. While early detection methods focused on handcrafted techniques offering transparency on the models' decisions, the field has shifted towards data-driven approaches that offer broader applicability and high performance. Also, developing reliable AIGID systems involves addressing the challenges of effectively detecting images generated by unseen models and maintaining performance despite post-processing operations common in real-world scenarios, such as those applied by social media platforms.

Within the context of vera.ai, several works have been developed to address AIGID. These works can be categorised into four main areas: benchmarking and artifact analysis; leveraging foundation model representations; spectral analysis; and generalization and in-the-wild performance. Benchmarking efforts have led to the development of SIDBench, a Python framework designed to assess the performance and robustness of AIGID. Also, other two works focusing on artifact analysis reveal the frequency patterns of Diffusion Model generated images providing critical insights on the detector development. Research on leveraging foundation model representations has explored the use of models like CLIP to enhance AIGID. One approach involves training a CLIP-based model on a small dataset of Latent Diffusion generated images, demonstrating that even with limited data, effective detection can be achieved. Furthermore, leveraging representations from intermediate encoder-blocks has shown promise in capturing both low-level visual cues and high-level semantic information for improved detection of AI-generated images. Spectral analysis has also been a key area of focus, with methods like SPAI utilising the spectral distribution of real images to detect synthetic images as out-of-distribution samples. Finally, research on generalization has led to the development of a high-performing zero-shot approach, a method alleviating semantic bias in AIGID datasets, and TextureCrop, an image pre-processing technique that enhances AIGID performance, while research on in-the-wild scenarios has led to the development of a pipeline that enhances RINE's real-world performance and a strategy to mitigate the degradation of detection performance over time by retrieving early copies of synthetic images that contain discriminative information.

Future research should prioritise enhancing generalization to novel generative models, improving robustness against diverse image manipulations, mitigating dataset biases, and increasing the transparency of detection mechanisms. The integration of active mitigation strategies, such as content retrieval and semantic analysis, alongside passive detection methods, is essential for developing comprehensive solutions to counter the malicious use of AI-generated images. In conclusion, the ongoing advancements in AIGID are crucial to address the challenges posed by the rapid evolution of AI-generated imagery, while the continued focus on the key research directions outlined in this chapter will pave the way for more reliable, robust, and trustworthy systems for safeguarding digital content.

Acknowledgements This research was supported by the European Union under the Horizon Europe vera.ai project, Grant Agreement number 101070093.

References

1. Agarwal, S., Varshney, L.R.: Limits of deepfake detection: a robust estimation viewpoint. arXiv preprint arXiv:1905.03493 (2019)
2. Bammey, Q.: Synthbuster: towards detection of diffusion model generated images. IEEE Open J. Signal Process. **5**, 1–9 (2024). https://doi.org/10.1109/OJSP.2023.3337714
3. Bammey, Q., von Gioi, R.G., Morel, J.M.: Reliable demosaicing detection for image forensics. In: 2019 27th European Signal Processing Conference (EUSIPCO), pp. 1–5 (2019). https://doi.org/10.23919/EUSIPCO.2019.8903152
4. Baraldi, L., Cocchi, F., Cornia, M., Baraldi, L., Nicolosi, A., Cucchiara, R.: Contrasting deepfakes diffusion via contrastive learning and global-local similarities. In: European Conference on Computer Vision, pp. 199–216. Springer (2024)
5. Bie, F., Yang, Y., Zhou, Z., Ghanem, A., Zhang, M., Yao, Z., Wu, X., Holmes, C., Golnari, P., Clifton, D.A., et al.: Renaissance: a survey into AI text-to-image generation in the era of large model. IEEE Trans. Pattern Anal. Mach. Intell. (2024)
6. Bird, J.J., Lotfi, A.: CIFAKE: image classification and explainable identification of AI-generated synthetic images. IEEE Access **12**, 15642–15650 (2024). https://doi.org/10.1109/ACCESS.2024.3356122
7. Boháček, M., Farid, H.: A geometric and photometric exploration of GAN and diffusion synthesized faces. In: Proceedings of the IEEE/CVF Conference on Computer Vision and Pattern Recognition, pp. 874–883 (2023)
8. Busacca, A., Monaca, M.A.: Deepfake: creation, purpose, risks. In: Innovations and Economic and Social Changes due to Artificial Intelligence: The State of the Art, pp. 55–68. Springer (2023)
9. Cavia, B., Horwitz, E., Reiss, T., Hoshen, Y.: Real-time deepfake detection in the real-world. arXiv preprint arXiv:2406.09398 (2024)
10. Cazenavette, G., Sud, A., Leung, T., Usman, B.: FakeInversion: learning to detect images from unseen text-to-image models by inverting stable diffusion. In: Proceedings of the IEEE/CVF Conference on Computer Vision and Pattern Recognition (CVPR), pp. 10759–10769 (2024)
11. Chai, L., Bau, D., Lim, S.N., Isola, P.: What makes fake images detectable? Understanding properties that generalize. In: Computer Vision—ECCV 2020: 16th European Conference, Glasgow, UK, 23–28 Aug 2020, Proceedings, Part XXVI 16, pp. 103–120. Springer (2020)
12. Chang, Y.M., Yeh, C., Chiu, W.C., Yu, N.: AntifakePrompt: prompt-tuned vision-language models are fake image detectors. arXiv preprint arXiv:2310.17419 (2023)
13. Chen, B., Zeng, J., Yang, J., Yang, R.: DRCT: diffusion reconstruction contrastive training towards universal detection of diffusion generated images. In: Forty-First International Conference on Machine Learning (2024)
14. Chen, Y., Zou, J.Y.: TWIGMA: a dataset of AI-generated images with metadata from Twitter. Adv. Neural Inf. Process. Syst. **36**, 37748–37760 (2023)
15. Chen, Y.L., Hsu, C.T.: Image tampering detection by blocking periodicity analysis in JPEG compressed images. In: 2008 IEEE 10th Workshop on Multimedia Signal Processing, pp. 803–808. IEEE (2008)
16. Corvi, R., Cozzolino, D., Poggi, G., Nagano, K., Verdoliva, L.: Intriguing properties of synthetic images: from generative adversarial networks to diffusion models. In: Proceedings of the IEEE/CVF Conference on Computer Vision and Pattern Recognition, pp. 973–982 (2023)
17. Corvi, R., Cozzolino, D., Zingarini, G., Poggi, G., Nagano, K., Verdoliva, L.: On the detection of synthetic images generated by diffusion models. In: ICASSP 2023—2023 IEEE International Conference on Acoustics, Speech and Signal Processing (ICASSP), pp. 1–5. IEEE (2023)
18. Cozzolino, D., Poggi, G., Corvi, R., Nießner, M., Verdoliva, L.: Raising the bar of AI-generated image detection with CLIP. In: Proceedings of the IEEE/CVF Conference on Computer Vision and Pattern Recognition, pp. 4356–4366 (2024)
19. Cozzolino, D., Poggi, G., Nießner, M., Verdoliva, L.: Zero-shot detection of AI-generated images. In: European Conference on Computer Vision, pp. 54–72. Springer (2024)

20. Dang-Nguyen, D.T., Pasquini, C., Conotter, V., Boato, G.: RAISE: a raw images dataset for digital image forensics. In: Proceedings of the 6th ACM Multimedia Systems Conference, pp. 219–224 (2015)
21. De Rosa, V., Guillaro, F., Poggi, G., Cozzolino, D., Verdoliva, L.: Exploring the adversarial robustness of clip for AI-generated image detection. In: 2024 IEEE International Workshop on Information Forensics and Security (WIFS), pp. 1–6. IEEE (2024)
22. Deng, J., Dong, W., Socher, R., Li, L.J., Li, K., Fei-Fei, L.: ImageNet: a large-scale hierarchical image database. In: 2009 IEEE Conference on Computer Vision and Pattern Recognition, pp. 248–255. IEEE (2009)
23. Dhariwal, P., Nichol, A.: Diffusion models beat GANs on image synthesis. Adv. Neural Inf. Process. Syst. **34**, 8780–8794 (2021)
24. Dogoulis, P., Kordopatis-Zilos, G., Kompatsiaris, I., Papadopoulos, S.: Improving synthetically generated image detection in cross-concept settings. In: Proceedings of the 2nd ACM International Workshop on Multimedia AI Against Disinformation, pp. 28–35 (2023)
25. Dufour, N., Pathak, A., Samangouei, P., Hariri, N., Deshetti, S., Dudfield, A., Guess, C., Escayola, P.H., Tran, B., Babakar, M., et al.: AMMEBA: a large-scale survey and dataset of media-based misinformation in-the-wild, vol. 1, no. 8. arXiv preprint arXiv:2405.11697 (2024)
26. Durall, R., Keuper, M., Keuper, J.: Watch your up-convolution: CNN based generative deep neural networks are failing to reproduce spectral distributions. In: Proceedings of the IEEE/CVF Conference on Computer Vision and Pattern Recognition, pp. 7890–7899 (2020)
27. Farid, H.: Lighting (in)consistency of paint by text. arXiv preprint arXiv:2207.13744 (2022)
28. Farid, H.: Perspective (in)consistency of paint by text. arXiv preprint arXiv:2206.14617 (2022)
29. Frank, J., Eisenhofer, T., Schönherr, L., Fischer, A., Kolossa, D., Holz, T.: Leveraging frequency analysis for deep fake image recognition. In: Proceedings of the 37th International Conference on Machine Learning, pp. 3247–3258. PMLR (2020). https://proceedings.mlr.press/v119/frank20a.html
30. Goodfellow, I., Pouget-Abadie, J., Mirza, M., Xu, B., Warde-Farley, D., Ozair, S., Courville, A., Bengio, Y.: Generative adversarial nets. Adv. Neural Inf. Process. Syst. **27** (2014)
31. Gragnaniello, D., Cozzolino, D., Marra, F., Poggi, G., Verdoliva, L.: Are GAN generated images easy to detect? A critical analysis of the state-of-the-art. In: 2021 IEEE International Conference on Multimedia and Expo (ICME), pp. 1–6. IEEE (2021)
32. Grommelt, P., Weiss, L., Pfreundt, F.J., Keuper, J.: Fake or JPEG? Revealing common biases in generated image detection datasets. arXiv preprint arXiv:2403.17608 (2024)
33. Guillaro, F., Zingarini, G., Usman, B., Sud, A., Cozzolino, D., Verdoliva, L.: A bias-free training paradigm for more general AI-generated image detection. In: Proceedings of the Computer Vision and Pattern Recognition Conference, pp. 18685–18694 (2024)
34. Hadwiger, B., Riess, C.: The Forchheim image database for camera identification in the wild. In: International Conference on Pattern Recognition, pp. 500–515. Springer (2021)
35. He, K., Zhang, X., Ren, S., Sun, J.: Deep residual learning for image recognition. In: Proceedings of the IEEE Conference on Computer Vision and Pattern Recognition (2015)
36. Ho, J., Jain, A., Abbeel, P.: Denoising diffusion probabilistic models. Adv. Neural Inf. Process. Syst. **33**, 6840–6851 (2020)
37. Ju, Y., Jia, S., Ke, L., Xue, H., Nagano, K., Lyu, S.: Fusing global and local features for generalized AI-synthesized image detection. In: 2022 IEEE International Conference on Image Processing (ICIP), pp. 3465–3469 (2022). https://doi.org/10.1109/ICIP46576.2022.989782
38. Kang, M., Zhu, J.Y., Zhang, R., Park, J., Shechtman, E., Paris, S., Park, T.: Scaling up GANs for text-to-image synthesis. In: Proceedings of the IEEE/CVF Conference on Computer Vision and Pattern Recognition, pp. 10124–10134 (2023)
39. Kapur, J.N., Sahoo, P.K., Wong, A.K.: A new method for gray-level picture thresholding using the entropy of the histogram. Comput. Vis. Graph. Image Process. **29**(3), 273–285 (1985)
40. Karageorgiou, D., Bammey, Q., Porcellini, V., Goupil, B., Teyssou, D., Papadopoulos, S.: Evolution of detection performance throughout the online lifespan of synthetic images. In: European Conference on Computer Vision Workshops (2024)

41. Karageorgiou, D., Papadopoulos, S., Kompatsiaris, I., Gavves, E.: Any-resolution AI-generated image detection by spectral learning. In: Proceedings of the Computer Vision and Pattern Recognition Conference, pp. 18706–18717 (2025)
42. Ke, G., Meng, Q., Finley, T., Wang, T., Chen, W., Ma, W., Ye, Q., Liu, T.Y.: LightGBM: a highly efficient gradient boosting decision tree. Adv. Neural Inf. Process. Syst. **30** (2017)
43. Khan, S.A., Dang-Nguyen, D.T.: Clipping the deception: adapting vision-language models for universal deepfake detection. In: Proceedings of the 2024 International Conference on Multimedia Retrieval, pp. 1006–1015 (2024)
44. Kingma, D.P., Welling, M., et al.: Auto-encoding variational Bayes (2013)
45. Konstantinidou, D., Koutlis, C., Papadopoulos, S.: TextureCrop: enhancing synthetic image detection through texture-based cropping. In: Proceedings of the Winter Conference on Applications of Computer Vision, pp. 1459–1468 (2025)
46. Kordopatis-Zilos, G., Tzelepis, C., Papadopoulos, S., Kompatsiaris, I., Patras, I.: DnS: distill-and-select for efficient and accurate video indexing and retrieval. Int. J. Comput. Vis. **130**(10), 2385–2407 (2022)
47. Koutlis, C., Papadopoulos, S.: Leveraging representations from intermediate encoder-blocks for synthetic image detection. In: European Conference on Computer Vision, pp. 394–411. Springer (2024)
48. Krizhevsky, A., Hinton, G., et al.: Learning multiple layers of features from tiny images (2009)
49. Kuznetsova, A., Rom, H., Alldrin, N., Uijlings, J., Krasin, I., Pont-Tuset, J., Kamali, S., Popov, S., Malloci, M., Kolesnikov, A., et al.: The open images dataset V4: unified image classification, object detection, and visual relationship detection at scale. Int. J. Comput. Vis. **128**(7), 1956–1981 (2020)
50. Lanzino, R., Fontana, F., Diko, A., Marini, M.R., Cinque, L.: Faster than lies: real-time deepfake detection using binary neural networks. In: Proceedings of the IEEE/CVF Conference on Computer Vision and Pattern Recognition (CVPR) Workshops, pp. 3771–3780 (2024)
51. Li, J., Li, D., Xiong, C., Hoi, S.: BLIP: bootstrapping language-image pre-training for unified vision-language understanding and generation. In: International Conference on Machine Learning, pp. 12888–12900. PMLR (2022)
52. Li, O., Cai, J., Hao, Y., Jiang, X., Hu, Y., Feng, F.: Improving synthetic image detection towards generalization: an image transformation perspective. In: Proceedings of the 31st ACM SIGKDD Conference on Knowledge Discovery and Data Mining V. 1, pp. 2405–2414 (2024)
53. Li, Y., Bammey, Q., Gardella, M., Nikoukhah, T., Morel, J.M., Colom, M., von Gioi, R.G.: MaskSim: detection of synthetic images by masked spectrum similarity analysis. In: Proceedings of the IEEE/CVF Conference on Computer Vision and Pattern Recognition, pp. 3855–3865 (2024)
54. Li, Y., Bammey, Q., Gardella, M., Nikoukhah, T., von Gioi, R.G., Colom, M., Morel, J.M.: Image resampling detection via spectral correlation with false alarm control. Authorea Preprints (2025)
55. Lin, L., Gupta, N., Zhang, Y., Ren, H., Liu, C.H., Ding, F., Wang, X., Li, X., Verdoliva, L., Hu, S.: Detecting multimedia generated by large AI models: a survey. arXiv preprint arXiv:2402.00045 (2024)
56. Lin, T.Y., Maire, M., Belongie, S., Hays, J., Perona, P., Ramanan, D., Dollár, P., Zitnick, C.L.: Microsoft COCO: common objects in context. In: Computer Vision—ECCV 2014: 13th European Conference, zurich, Switzerland, 6–12 Sept 2014, Proceedings, Part V 13, pp. 740–755. Springer (2014)
57. Liu, H., Tan, Z., Tan, C., Wei, Y., Wang, J., Zhao, Y.: Forgery-aware adaptive transformer for generalizable synthetic image detection. In: Proceedings of the IEEE/CVF Conference on Computer Vision and Pattern Recognition (CVPR), pp. 10770–10780 (2024)
58. Liu, Z., Qi, X., Torr, P.H.: Global texture enhancement for fake face detection in the wild. In: Proceedings of the IEEE/CVF Conference on Computer Vision and Pattern Recognition, pp. 8060–8069 (2020)

59. Marra, F., Gragnaniello, D., Verdoliva, L., Poggi, G.: Do GANs leave artificial fingerprints? In: 2019 IEEE Conference on Multimedia Information Processing and Retrieval (MIPR), pp. 506–511. IEEE (2019)
60. Ojha, U., Li, Y., Lee, Y.J.: Towards universal fake image detectors that generalize across generative models. In: Proceedings of the IEEE/CVF Conference on Computer Vision and Pattern Recognition, pp. 24480–24489 (2023)
61. Oquab, M., Darcet, T., Moutakanni, T., Vo, H., Szafraniec, M., Khalidov, V., Fernandez, P., Haziza, D., Massa, F., El-Nouby, A., et al.: DINOv2: learning robust visual features without supervision. arXiv preprint arXiv:2304.07193 (2023)
62. Pellegrini, L., Cozzolino, D., Pandolfini, S., Maltoni, D., Ferrara, M., Verdoliva, L., Prati, M., Ramilli, M.: AI-GenBench: a new ongoing benchmark for AI-generated image detection. arXiv preprint arXiv:2504.20865 (2025)
63. Petrzelkova, N., Cech, J.: Detection of synthetic face images: accuracy, robustness, generalization. arXiv preprint arXiv:2406.17547 (2024)
64. Platt, J., et al.: Probabilistic outputs for support vector machines and comparisons to regularized likelihood methods. In: Advances in Large Margin Classifiers, vol. 10, no. 3, pp. 61–74 (1999)
65. Plummer, B.A., Wang, L., Cervantes, C.M., Caicedo, J.C., Hockenmaier, J., Lazebnik, S.: Flickr30k entities: collecting region-to-phrase correspondences for richer image-to-sentence models. In: Proceedings of the IEEE International Conference on Computer Vision, pp. 2641–2649 (2015)
66. Podell, D., English, Z., Lacey, K., Blattmann, A., Dockhorn, T., Müller, J., Penna, J., Rombach, R.: SDXL: improving latent diffusion models for high-resolution image synthesis. arXiv preprint arXiv:2307.01952 (2023)
67. Radford, A., Kim, J., Hallacy, C., Ramesh, A., Goh, G., Agarwal, S., Sastry, G., Askell, A., Mishkin, P., Clark, J., Krueger, G., Sutskever, I.: Learning transferable visual models from natural language supervision. In: Proceedings of the International Conference on Machine Learning (ICML) (2021)
68. Rajan, A.S., Ojha, U., Schloesser, J., Lee, Y.J.: On the effectiveness of dataset alignment for fake image detection. arXiv preprint arXiv:2410.11835 (2024)
69. Ramesh, A., Pavlov, M., Goh, G., Gray, S., Voss, C., Radford, A., Chen, M., Sutskever, I.: Zero-shot text-to-image generation. In: International Conference on Machine Learning, pp. 8821–8831. PMLR (2021)
70. Ricker, J., Lukovnikov, D., Fischer, A.: AEROBLADE: training-free detection of latent diffusion images using autoencoder reconstruction error. In: Proceedings of the IEEE/CVF Conference on Computer Vision and Pattern Recognition, pp. 9130–9140 (2024)
71. Rombach, R., Blattmann, A., Lorenz, D., Esser, P., Ommer, B.: High-resolution image synthesis with latent diffusion models. In: Proceedings of the IEEE/CVF Conference on Computer Vision and Pattern Recognition, pp. 10684–10695 (2022)
72. Sarkar, A., Mai, H., Mahapatra, A., Lazebnik, S., Forsyth, D.A., Bhattad, A.: Shadows don't lie and lines can't bend! generative models don't know projective geometry... for now. In: Proceedings of the IEEE/CVF Conference on Computer Vision and Pattern Recognition, pp. 28140–28149 (2024)
73. Schaefer, G., Stich, M.: UCID: an uncompressed color image database. In: M.M. Yeung, R.W. Lienhart, C.S. Li (eds.) Storage and Retrieval Methods and Applications for Multimedia 2004, vol. 5307, pp. 472–480. International Society for Optics and Photonics, SPIE (2003). https://doi.org/10.1117/12.525375
74. Schinas, M., Papadopoulos, S.: SIDBench: a Python framework for reliably assessing synthetic image detection methods. In: Proceedings of the 3rd ACM International Workshop on Multimedia AI Against Disinformation, pp. 55–64 (2024)
75. Schuhmann, C., Kaczmarczyk, R., Komatsuzaki, A., Katta, A., Vencu, R., Beaumont, R., Jitsev, J., Coombes, T., Mullis, C.: LAION-400M: open dataset of CLIP-filtered 400 million image-text pairs. In: NeurIPS Workshops (2021)

76. Sha, Z., Li, Z., Yu, N., Zhang, Y.: DE-FAKE: detection and attribution of fake images generated by text-to-image generation models. In: Proceedings of the ACM SIGSAC Conference on Computer and Communications Security, pp. 3418–3432 (2023)
77. Shullani, D., Fontani, M., Iuliani, M., Shaya, O.A., Piva, A.: Vision: a video and image dataset for source identification. EURASIP J. Inf. Secur. **2017**(1), 15 (2017)
78. Tan, C., Tao, R., Liu, H., Gu, G., Wu, B., Zhao, Y., Wei, Y.: C2P-CLIP: injecting category common prompt in CLIP to enhance generalization in deepfake detection. In: Proceedings of the AAAI Conference on Artificial Intelligence, Vol. 39, No. 7, pp. 7184–7192 (2024)
79. Tan, C., Zhao, Y., Wei, S., Gu, G., Liu, P., Wei, Y.: Rethinking the up-sampling operations in CNN-based generative network for generalizable deepfake detection. In: Proceedings of the IEEE/CVF Conference on Computer Vision and Pattern Recognition, pp. 28130–28139 (2024)
80. Tan, C., Zhao, Y., Wei, S., Gu, G., Wei, Y.: Learning on gradients: generalized artifacts representation for GAN-generated images detection. In: Proceedings of the IEEE/CVF Conference on Computer Vision and Pattern Recognition, pp. 12105–12114 (2023)
81. Tariang, D., Corvi, R., Cozzolino, D., Poggi, G., Nagano, K., Verdoliva, L.: Synthetic image verification in the era of generative artificial intelligence: what works and what isn't there yet. IEEE Secur. Priv. (2024)
82. Verdoliva, L., Cozzolino, D., Nagano, K.: 2022 IEEE image and video processing cup synthetic image detection (2022). https://grip-unina.github.io/vipcup2022/
83. Wang, S.Y., Wang, O., Zhang, R., Owens, A., Efros, A.A.: CNN-generated images are surprisingly easy to spot... for now. In: Proceedings of the IEEE/CVF Conference on Computer Vision and Pattern Recognition, pp. 8695–8704 (2020)
84. Wang, X., Kalogeiton, V.: Your diffusion model is an implicit synthetic image detector. In: European Conference on Computer Vision, pp. 418–434. Springer (2024)
85. Wang, Z., Bao, J., Zhou, W., Wang, W., Hu, H., Chen, H., Li, H.: DIRE for diffusion-generated image detection. In: Proceedings of the IEEE/CVF International Conference on Computer Vision, pp. 22445–22455 (2023)
86. Xie, J., Li, W., Zhan, X., Liu, Z., Ong, Y.S., Loy, C.C.: Masked frequency modeling for self-supervised visual pre-training. In: The Eleventh International Conference on Learning Representations (2023)
87. Yan, S., Li, O., Cai, J., Hao, Y., Jiang, X., Hu, Y., Xie, W.: A sanity check for AI-generated image detection. arXiv preprint arXiv:2406.19435 (2024)
88. Yao, T., Li, Y., Pan, Y., Mei, T.: HIRI-ViT: scaling vision transformer with high resolution inputs. IEEE Trans. Pattern Anal. Mach. Intell. (2024)
89. Yu, F., Seff, A., Zhang, Y., Song, S., Funkhouser, T., Xiao, J.: LSUN: construction of a large-scale image dataset using deep learning with humans in the loop. arXiv preprint arXiv:1506.03365 (2015)
90. Yu, N., Davis, L.S., Fritz, M.: Attributing fake images to GANs: learning and analyzing GAN fingerprints. In: Proceedings of the IEEE/CVF International Conference on Computer Vision, pp. 7556–7566 (2019)
91. Yu, P., Fei, J., Gao, H., Feng, X., Xia, Z., Chang, C.H.: Unlocking the capabilities of vision-language models for generalizable and explainable deepfake detection. arXiv preprint arXiv:2503.14853 (2025)
92. Zhang, X., Karaman, S., Chang, S.F.: Detecting and simulating artifacts in GAN fake images. In: 2019 IEEE International Workshop on Information Forensics and Security (WIFS), pp. 1–6. IEEE (2019)
93. Zhong, N., Xu, Y., Li, S., Qian, Z., Zhang, X.: PatchCraft: exploring texture patch for efficient AI-generated image detection. arXiv preprint arXiv:2311.12397 (2024)
94. Zhu, M., Chen, H., Yan, Q., Huang, X., Lin, G., Li, W., Tu, Z., Hu, H., Hu, J., Wang, Y.: GenImage: a million-scale benchmark for detecting AI-generated image. Adv. Neural Inf. Process. Syst. **36**, 77771–77782 (2023)

Synthetic Audio Detection

Luca Cuccovillo, Alessandro Pianese, Milica Gerhardt, Davide Cozzolino, Giovanni Poggi, and Patrick Aichroth

1 Introduction

In recent years, speech synthesis technology has undergone remarkable advancements, creating both exciting opportunities and serious challenges.

Synthetic speech is artificially generated speech produced by a computer or an electronic system. We differentiate between text-to-speech (TTS) and voice conversion (VC) algorithms, where TTS generates speech from text, while VC transforms one speaker's voice to sound like another's, preserving the content. In both cases, the resulting synthetic speech was never recorded from a natural speaker, but is produced entirely by computational means.

Speech synthesis traditionally follows a two-stage approach: feature extraction followed by vocoding. In this paradigm, depicted in Fig. 1 and encompassing both TTS and VC solutions, the feature extraction block is used to convert the input text or audio into intermediate acoustic features reflecting the desired spoken content and

L. Cuccovillo (✉) · M. Gerhardt · P. Aichroth
Fraunhofer Institute for Digital Media Technology (IDMT), Ilmenau, Germany
e-mail: luca.cuccovillo@idmt.fraunhofer.de

M. Gerhardt
e-mail: milica.gerhardt@idmt.fraunhofer.de

P. Aichroth
e-mail: patrick.aichroth@idmt.fraunhofer.de

A. Pianese · D. Cozzolino · G. Poggi
University of Naples Federico II (UNINA), Naples, Italy
e-mail: alessandro.pianese@unina.it

D. Cozzolino
e-mail: davide.cozzolino@unina.it

G. Poggi
e-mail: poggi@unina.it

S. Papadopoulos et al. (eds.), *Countering Disinformation in the Era of Generative AI*,
https://doi.org/10.1007/978-3-032-11782-3_7

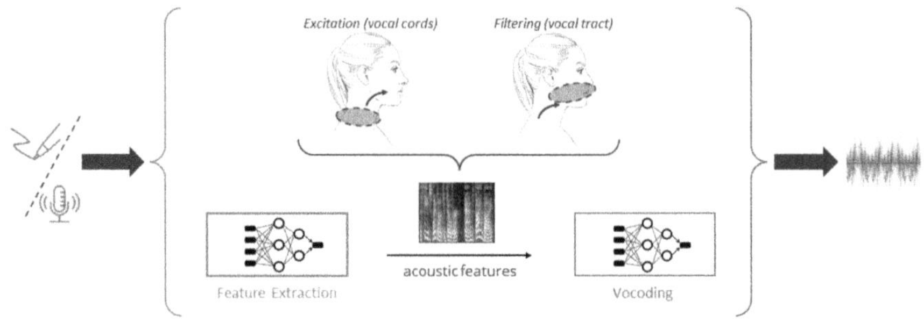

Fig. 1 High level schema of TTS and VC algorithms for speech synthesis

speaker voice, and then a vocoder is used to transform these acoustic features into audible speech waveforms.

A major breakthrough in speech synthesis came in 2017 with Tacotron 2 [1], which marked a shift towards fully neural architectures. Tacotron 2 introduced an encoder-decoder structure where the encoder processes text input through convolutional layers capturing long-term dependencies, while the decoder generates mel-spectrograms frame by frame using attention mechanisms. The revolutionary aspect of Tacotron 2 was the integration of deep neural networks for both the spectrogram prediction and vocoding stages (typically WaveNet [2, 3]), resulting in synthetic speech of unprecedented quality, often indistinguishable from human speech.

Following this milestone, research efforts have concentrated on reducing the required training data and increasing processing efficiency while maintaining or improving speech quality. FastSpeech 2 [4] enhanced speed and robustness by refining acoustic feature modelling, while Glow-TTS [5] introduced a flow-based generative model, enabling parallel sampling and accelerating synthesis. Similarly, VITS (Variational Inference with adversarial learning for end-to-end TTS) [6] unified spectrum prediction and vocoding through a variational autoencoder, and Grad-TTS [7] leveraged diffusion probabilistic models to balance sound quality with inference speed. These advancements have progressively minimised data requirements while maintaining natural-sounding synthetic speech.

Since 2023, state-of-the-art AI systems have made remarkable progress in speech synthesis, particularly in zero-shot voice cloning—where synthetic voices can be generated without extensive training data for specific speakers. Microsoft's VALL-E [8], introduced the concept of using a neural codec language model for TTS, treating TTS as a conditional language model with in-context learning capabilities. This enabled it to synthesise personalised speech with just a 3-second recording of an unseen speaker. Its successor, VALL-E 2 [9], addressed robustness and efficiency through repetition-aware sampling and grouped code modelling techniques, achieving "human parity in zero-shot TTS performance" [9]. Other systems, such as NaturalSpeech 2 [10], incorporated latent diffusion models to achieve expressive prosody and strong zero-shot capabilities. These advances have made high-quality voice synthesis widely accessible, raising concerns about the misuse of such technology.

HARVARD KENNEDY SCHOOL | SHORENSTEIN CENTER ON MEDIA, POLITICS, AND PUBLIC POLICY

Misinformation Review

AUGUST 22, 2024

DOWNLOAD PDF

COMMENTARY

Beyond the deepfake hype: AI, democracy, and "the Slovak case"

BY LLUIS DE NADAL
Sociology Subject Area, University of Glasgow, UK

PETER JANČÁRIK
Seznam.cz, Czechia

Fig. 2 Report on synthetic speech being used to alter elections in Slovakia

The increasing realism of synthetic speech has sparked significant concerns, particularly in journalism and media. The indistinguishability of synthetic voices from natural speech complicates efforts to verify the authenticity of audio content. A prominent example occurred in late 2023 when a synthetic audio clip featuring a political candidate making controversial statements went viral on social media before being identified as AI-generated[1], as also reported by the article in Fig. 2. Such incidents illustrate the potential for synthetic speech to spread misinformation rapidly and undermine public trust in media.

Law enforcement agencies have also raised alarms about the dangers of synthetic speech. A Europol report published in 2022 states that "deepfake technology uses Artificial Intelligence to audio and audio-visual content" and can "convincingly show people saying or doing things they never did, or create personas that never existed" [11]. Law enforcement experts expressed particular concern about "the westernization of social media and the impact of misinformation on public discourse and social cohesion" [11]. The challenge for law enforcement is particularly acute, as people—including officers—typically "trust their own perception to guide them and tell them what is real and what is not" [11]. The increasing sophistication of synthetic media threatens to undermine this fundamental trust mechanism in society.

Recognising these risks, the Automatic Speaker Verification Spoofing and Countermeasures (ASVspoof) community has been actively researching speech synthesis detection solutions since at least 2019. The ASVspoof 2019 [12] initiative compiled a large-scale dataset of synthesised, converted, and replayed speech to assess vulnerabilities in automatic speaker verification systems. The challenge revealed that

[1] https://misinforeview.hks.harvard.edu/article/beyond-the-deepfake-hype-ai-democracy-and-the-slovak-case/.

certain synthetic speech samples were indistinguishable from natural utterances, underscoring the severity of the problem.

Since then, multiple approaches have been proposed for synthetic speech detection, largely driven by the ASVspoof community and kept up-to-date with the latest deep learning advances. Initial sample-based models borrowed from the speaker verification domain [13] were later updated to incorporate increasingly complex applications of attention mechanisms [14, 15]. Nowadays, these algorithms rely on large language models for generic audio processing [16, 17], and will most likely be updated with new editions of the ASVspoof challenge.

Despite the ongoing efforts, however, synthetic speech detection remains an open challenge. The performance of synthetic speech detection systems has not increased at an acceptable rate relative to the advancements in synthesis technology. Many detection systems rely on identifying specific artefacts or patterns, yet as synthesis methods grow more diverse and sophisticated, these markers become obsolete. This persistent gap underscores the pressing need for robust detection tools that can generalise across evolving synthesis techniques.

To address this issue, in the following we will discuss synthetic speech detection with a holistic approach. Section 2 will describe in detail a few key data-driven approaches for synthetic audio detection proposed by the ASVspoof community, highlighting their underlying principles and associated shortcomings. Section 3 will introduce alternative interpretable approaches, designed not to be entirely data-driven, but rather to focus their detection mechanisms on voice properties. Section 4 will then focus on person-centric approaches that enhance long-term generalisation by avoiding the need for constant retraining of detection algorithms. Finally, Section. 5 will address non-technical open challenges, and outline potential solutions that could foster a sustainable ecosystem for future research and development.

2 Data-Driven Analysis for Synthetic Audio Detection

Even though research on speech synthesis dates back several decades, the need for its detection became apparent only in 2017, when Tacotron 2 was able to produce samples of unprecedented quality, often indistinguishable from human speech [1].

The potential implications of misusing this technology for speaker impersonation led to the inclusion of synthetic speech examples in the 2019 edition of an existing anti-spoofing challenge for automatic speaker verification, ubiquitously known as "ASVspoof challenge".

The challenge has included synthetic speech ever since [12, 18, 19], and fuelled research on synthetic audio detection over the years, leading to several data-driven solutions that we are going to summarise in the following.

The first method to introduce a breakthrough in synthetic speech detection was RawNet2, a SincNet architecture designed for speaker identification, which was fine-tuned for synthetic speech detection [13, 20].

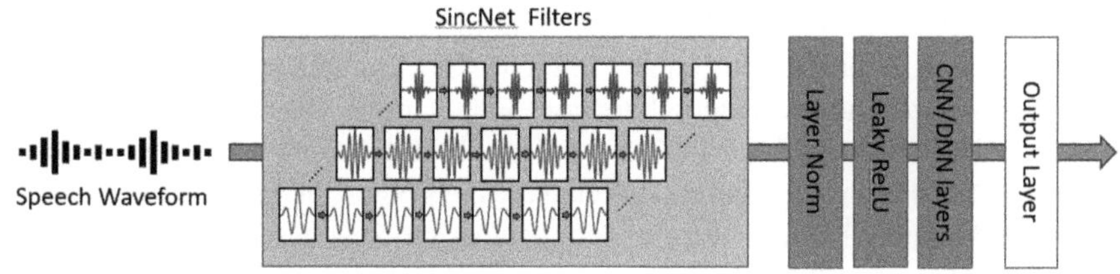

Fig. 3 RawNet2 model for synthetic speech detection [13]

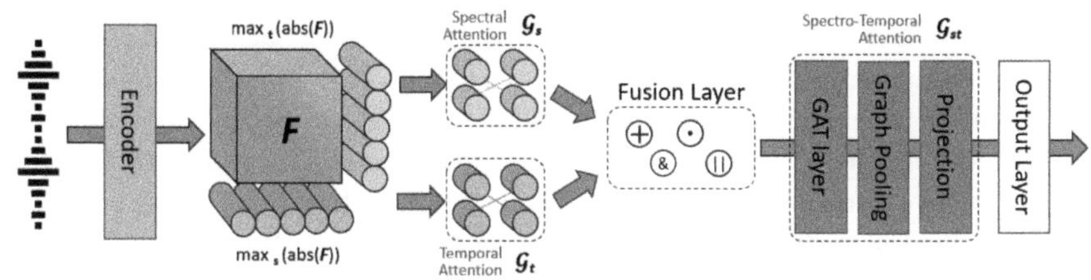

Fig. 4 RawGAT-ST model for synthetic speech detection [15]

The peculiarity of this network is that, starting from raw samples in time domain, it is capable to learn a set of pass-band filters[2] with widths and centre frequencies determined by the desired task—i.e., picked to focus on the parts of the input spectrogram which are relevant for the desired task. A corresponding high-level schema of the underlying SincNet backbone is shown in Fig. 3.

RawNet2 outperformed all other proposals relying on the extraction and analysis of the mel-spectrogram: The mel-spectrogram analysis, albeit being standard procedure, used as input the very same spectral representation that TTS and VC feature extraction models were trained to produce, and was struggling to achieve acceptable results. The decision to learn ad-hoc filter-banks broke this logic and made synthesis detection viable for the first time.

Tak et al. recognised in [15] that different synthesis methods leave specific artefacts in the output audio at different sub-bands. However it is highly impractical to have methods look for something so specific in the sole frequency domain, as it would impact their level of generalisation.

To address this issue, the authors propose to concatenate the RawNet2 encoder with a spectro-temporal (ST) graph attention network (GAT), and named the overall method "RawGAT-ST". With its two branches, one focusing on the spectral domain and the other on temporal one, the model was able to generate features related to different frequency bands at different time locations, substantially improving the generalisation of the bare RawNet2.

The pipeline, also shown in Fig. 4, ends with a fusion block that merges the resulting information from the first two GAT blocks and a final lighter GAT block where the most discriminative nodes are selected before the final classification layer.

[2] Corresponding to cardinal sines $\text{sinc}(x) = \sin(x)/x$, hence the name SincNet.

The potential of graph-based operations was refined by the AASIST model [14], that proposed to modify the fusion and inference blocks of RawGAT-ST in order to model the spectral and the temporal domains jointly, rather than separately.

In RawGAT-ST the spectral and temporal graphs did not interact with each other, and only fused at a late stage before entering the GAT block. In AASIST, instead, the spectral and temporal graphs were joined together by creating edges between their nodes, by means of an heterogeneous stacking graph attention layer.

The authors use three projection vectors for modelling the attention in the heterogeneous graph: one for edges connecting nodes of the temporal graph, one for edges connecting nodes of the spectral graph, and one for edges connecting the nodes of the two different graphs. Moreover, a new "stack node" was introduced to store the relationship between the data from the spectral and temporal domains (Fig. 5).

The additions in AASIST led the network to detect co-occurrence of artefacts *between* the two domains, that the initial fusion block in RawGAT-ST was unable to exploit in full. The further performance gap on the evaluation data, however, came at the cost of an even higher asymmetry between the simplicity of the RawNet2-based spectral encoding, and the complexity of the subsequent analysis stage.

Even though AASIST achieved great results in the ASVspoof 2019 dataset, its authors noticed that the model output would reduce to random guessing for synthetic utterances generated by methods not present in the training set distribution. The lack of generalisation was attributed to passband filters inherited from RawNet2, and by the corresponding excessive focus on a few spectral bands of interest—an issue common to all SincNet-based architecture that could not be solved by revising the sole analysis stage.

The XLSR-AASIST model [16] was proposed to solve the issue by replacing the learnable filterbanks with a wav2vec 2.0 model pretrained to generate cross-lingual speech representations (XLS-R) [21, 22], while leaving the downstream RawNet2 encoder and AASIST graph-based layers intact as in Fig. 6.

Since the XLS-R model was trained for learning robust speech-representation, the use of its embeddings, coupled with the AASIST graph-attention-based post-processing, led to better performance and lower generalisation issues, which in this case could entirely be related to a very unfortunate choice of training material.

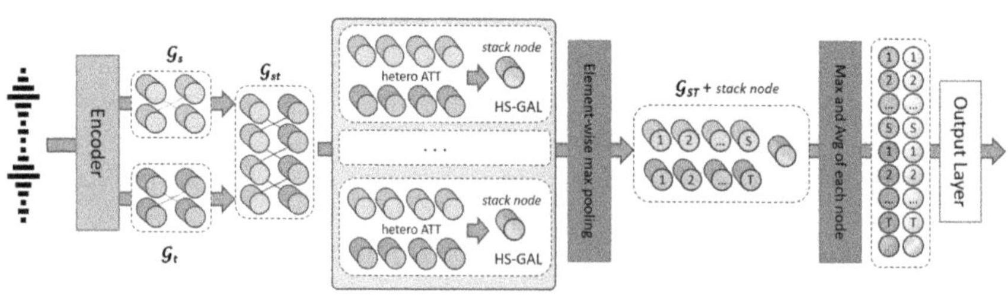

Fig. 5 AASIST model for synthetic speech detection [14]

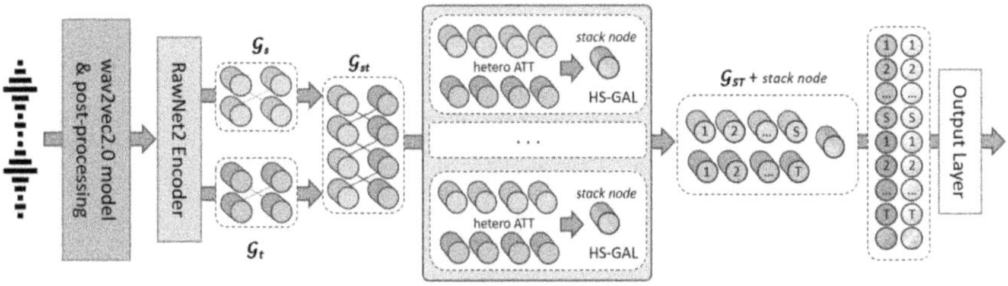

Fig. 6 XLSR-AASIST model for synthetic speech detection [16]

The inclusion of pre-trained general-purpose models in synthetic speech detection pioneered by the XLSR-AASIST model sparked a lot of interest in the synthetic speech detection community.

The XLSR-SLS model [17] is an excellent example of this new paradigm. The authors relied on the wav2vec 2.0 transformer architecture—i.e., a sequence of alternating layers of multi-head self-attention and multi-layer perceptron blocks [23]—and proposed to perform synthetic speech detection by collecting information from all hidden embeddings of each transformer layer, following the idea that for speech related tasks, insightful information can be found not only at the end of the transformer, but also within early and intermediate layers.

Therefore, the authors proposed to condense information across layers by means of a layer-wise weighted sum, with weights determined by a novel module for sensitive layer selection (SLS). The weighted sum was then further processed with a series of max-pooling, fully-connected and softmax layers for reducing the output to a binary decision label (Fig. 7).

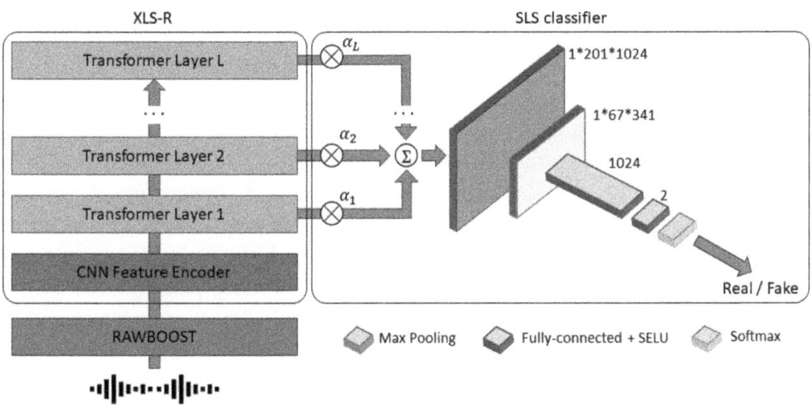

Fig. 7 XLSR-SLS model for synthetic speech detection [17]

All data-driven methods described so far brought significant contributions and advances for the entire audio synthesis detection community, but did not come without important shortcomings.

First and foremost, all these methods lack explainability [24]: They were designed to generically detect "artefacts found in the spectral domain", which were never identified nor understood. The more complex the processing and the more abstract the input speech representation—wav2vec 2.0 embeddings being the epitome of this tendency—the lower the interpretability of the output. This issue has far reaching consequences, starting from lack of trust by journalists involved in the fight against disinformation, and ending with the inadmissibility of such tools in legal proceedings [25, 26].

Moreover, data-driven models are known to strongly relate their outputs to silent intervals in which no speech signal is present [27], with a dramatic performance decrease if silent intervals are missing in the test content. This behaviour is particularity problematic whenever the training data presents hidden biases—e.g., an unequal distribution of silence duration between natural and synthetic examples—and is very evident whenever these models are trained from scratch on curated content.

Further studies relying on trustworthy AI tools have shown that, in addition to focusing on silent intervals, data-driven methods rely on low and high frequency bands in which no speech content is present [28]. The issue is so severe, that test data pre-processed by entirely removing the speech content from it could still be correctly classified as "synthetic speech", based on the sole background noise [29].

Taken together, these characteristics strongly suggest that data-driven methods do not rely on traces left by the feature extraction block, i.e., by the component responsible for converting the input text or audio into a speech characterised by a specific voice. Instead, these data-driven methods appear to rely predominantly on artefacts introduced by the vocoding block, which reconstructs the final waveform by mapping the intermediate representation back to the time domain. Therefore, rather than detecting synthetic speech, the data-driven method presented so far detect "synthetic audio"—and more specifically, neural vocoding traces.

The focus on neural vocoding artefacts inherent in data-driven model started to gain traction, and is being embraced by many recent papers.

Wang and Yamagishi [30], for instance, suggested extracting acoustic features from natural recordings, using several neural vocoders for converting these acoustic features into audio waveforms, and finally treating these audio waveforms as training examples of "synthetic speech".

Sun et al. [31] proposed to use the same self-vocoding paradigm to generate examples for the joint training of a "synthetic speech" detection module and of a vocoder identification module, once again with excellent performance.

Despite their sound and promising methodologies, however, these studies *did not* address synthetic speech detection in the strict sense. If the acoustic features originate from natural recordings, then the definition of synthetic speech—i.e., a signal never recorded from a natural speaker, but produced entirely by computational means—does not hold. Instead, both studies explored an emerging research area named "neural codec detection", which aims to detect traces left by neural vocoding *without* assuming that such traces only occur in synthetic speech.

Moussa et al. [32] were the first to explicitly target the detection of neural encoding traces as a standalone task, clearly separating it from the broader challenge of detecting anomalies created by synthetically-generated acoustic features.

The authors investigated the traces left by several neural codecs with the potential of commercial applications: ©Google's Lyra-V2 [33], ©Meta's EnCodec [34], and ©Descript Inc.'s Improved RVQGAN [35]. Whenever used for self-vocoding natural recordings, all three solutions introduced visible artefacts in the high-frequency domain—i.e., the area in which data-driven networks tend to focus.

These artefacts, clearly visible in Fig. 8, could be detected by applying logistic regression to the Fourier transform of high-pass filtered versions of the input recordings. The outcome, with performance on par with those achievable by deep-learning solutions, was plagued by a lack of generalisability despite the high performance on in-domain test data—yet again, the very same behaviour of much more complex data-driven solutions.

The clear distinction between the two tasks of neural codec detection and synthetic speech detection—i.e., the detection of anomalies created by synthetically-generated acoustic features—is of paramount importance.

The inherent characteristics of data-driven approaches to focus on neural vocoding artefacts is a double-edged sword: As long as these artefacts will only be present in synthetically generated audio content, these algorithms will be able to detect synthetic speech generated with TTS or VC algorithms. However, when neural codecs will become the norm and replace traditional lossy encoders like MP3 and AAC, the purely data-driven solutions introduced so far and their derivative works will all become inapplicable.

Therefore, in the following section we will turn our attention to alternative paradigms. These approaches strived to go beyond a straightforward application of deep-learning principles to audio data, and focused on detection mechanisms designed to detect anomalies in the acoustic features of the speech content, offering a potential pathway to solutions that can withstand the challenge of time.

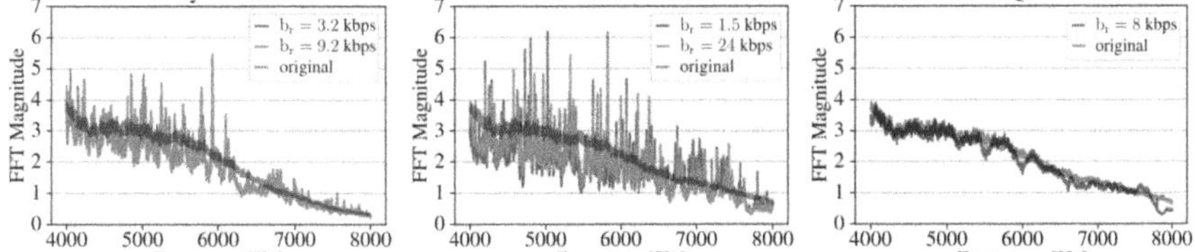

Fig. 8 Neural encoding traces in the high frequencies of self-vocoded recordings

3 Voice-Based Analysis for Explainable Synthetic Speech Detection

The natural tendency of networks for synthetic audio detection to focus on speech-unrelated portions of the input file, and therefore on neural vocoding artefacts, is in essence unavoidable: As long as shortcuts exist, purely data-driven approaches will exploit them rather than performing the desired task, by the principle of least effort [36].

It order to steer the focus of the neural networks out of these shortcuts, it is indeed necessary to step out of black-box solutions, and rather rely on expert models, designed to have an explainable detection mechanism [37].The potential of voice-related features for synthetic speech detection was investigated early on by Attoressi et al. [38].

The authors proposed a novel approach, shown in Fig. 9, in which the detection of synthetic speech was based on two types of embeddings: speaker embeddings describing the timbre of the speaker in the input speech signal, and prosody embeddings describing the corresponding variations in rhythm, pitch and accents.

The proposal was based on the idea that the combination of both embedding types could model both the physiological and the behavioural characteristics of the speaker, thereby leading to a semantically rich representation capable of detecting speech samples generated with both TTS and VC techniques. Furthermore, since both embedding types were expected to be robust towards lossy encoding, the method could inherently handle not only high-quality files, but also low-quality ones found, e.g., on social media.

The extraction of the embeddings was performed using state-of-the-art solutions in 2022, i.e., the ECAPA-TDNN model [39] for speaker verification, and the encoder of the very first prosody-transfer module [40] for Tacotron.

In addition to being mere descriptors, prosodic patterns convey important information about the perceived emotion in an input utterance. Therefore, rather than focusing explicitly on prosodic patterns, Hosler et al. [41] and Conti et al. [42] proposed to base synthetic speech detection on emotion descriptors.

Both approaches are summarised by Fig. 10. As with the analysis of prosodic patterns, the authors relied on existing models for speech emotion recognition to

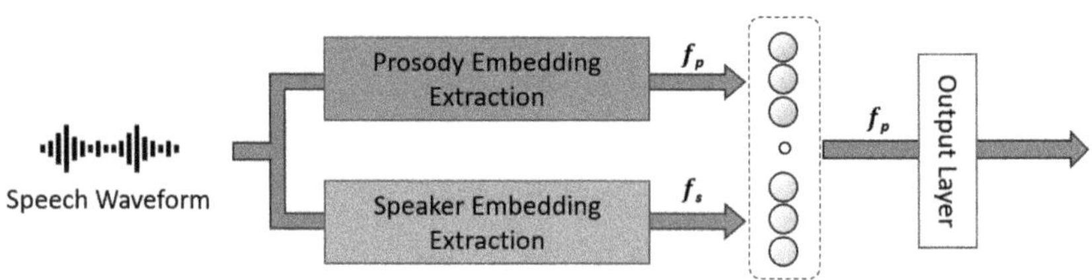

Fig. 9 Synthetic speech detection based on speaker and prosody embeddings [38]

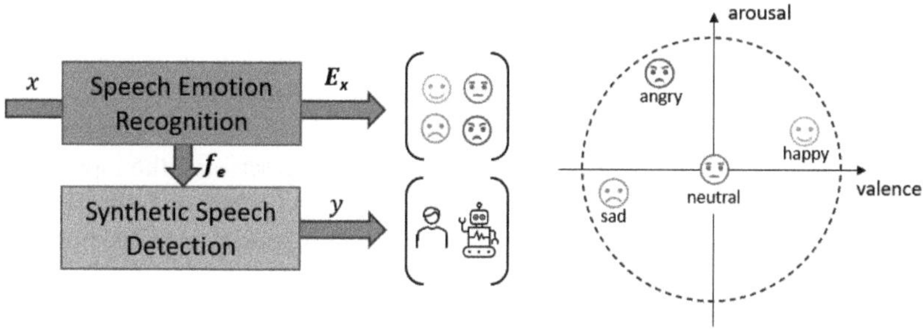

Fig. 10 Synthetic speech detection based on emotion embeddings [41, 42]

generate speech related features, that were then used for the subsequent synthesis detection task. As described in the following, these emotion-related features addressed two semantic levels, the connection of which is also summarised in Fig. 10: the valence-arousal scheme and the categorical emotion labels. The valence-arousal scheme describes an emotion by means of arousal (calm/agitated) and valence (positive/negative feeling) soft indicators, while categorical labels provide a classification with fixed labels such as happiness, sadness, or anger. The combination of these two levels offer a comprehensive approach to emotion modelling, even though they were not used in conjunction in the following works.

Hosler et al. [41] proposed to rely on valence and arousal descriptors, i.e., soft descriptors that in the literature are commonly used to describe human emotions. Aiming at detection of synthetic videos, they proposed to extract these values for both the audio and video stream, and then use a lightweight classifier relying on these values, coupled with concordance indicators between the two domains. The extraction of the emotion embeddings and the final synthesis detection were performed by means of two cascaded LSTM models [43].

Conti et al. [42] refined the emotion-related workflow by focusing solely on the audio. Therefore, they suggested to use as backbone a network trained to discriminate between seven discrete categorical emotions (sadness, fear, disgust, anger, surprise, happiness, neutral), and to use one of its hidden layers as embedding vector to drive the synthetic speech detection. The model used as backbone was a state-of-the-art 3D convolutional recurrent neural network for sentiment analysis [44], and the selected hidden layer was the one that the authors named 'utterance-level emotional representation', i.e., the output of self-attention on an inner LSTM block.

The use of prosodic patterns and emotion descriptors for synthetic speech detection was superseded over the years by the entirely data-driven approaches we described in Section. 2. This shift likely occurred not only due to the sheer performance of data-driven methods, but also because prosody and emotion are key features that all text-to-speech models aim to improve [45]. As a result, models focused solely on these characteristics were at risk of quickly becoming obsolete.

A radical approach to analyse the input speech, with lower risk of colliding with efforts of further research in speech synthesis, was followed in the Speech Formant Analysis Transformer (SFAT-Net) models by L Cuccovillo et al. [46–48].

Starting with the first version of the SFAT-Net in [46], the authors proposed to design and train a neural network focused primarily on describing the input speech, and to treat the detection of synthetic speech as a byproduct of the analysis. Therefore, they proposed to employ a multi-task network with a feature bottleneck, used to autoencode the input spectrogram, then to predict the trajectory of the fundamental frequency (F_0), and finally to determine whether the speech is synthetic or not with an additional prediction layer. The model relied on sequence-to-sequence (seq2seq) transformers architectures, chosen for their strong attention mechanisms [23], which are particularly well suited for tasks such as F_0 estimation, due to the harmonic structure of speech, and spectrogram reconstruction, where the accurate reproduction of harmonic content is critical for minimising reconstruction error.

The model is composed of four primary components: a spectrogram encoder E, a spectrogram decoder D_X, a fundamental frequency decoder D_{F_0}, and a synthesis predictor P. as shown in Fig 13a Inspired by the encoder component of Vision Transformer (ViT) [49], the spectrogram encoder E processes the log-spectrogram of an input speech signal by dividing it into non-overlapping two-dimensional patches. Each patch is flattened and projected into a fixed-dimensional embedding space using a learnable linear transformation. These embeddings are then passed through a sequence of transformer layers that employ multi-head self-attention and feed-forward blocks, computing the final encoded representation y_{enc}.

The spectrogram decoder D_X, aims to reconstruct the original spectrogram from y_{enc}. The encoded sequence is first linearly projected into a new embedding space, via learned projection matrix, and subsequently fed into a decoding transformer T^X. The resulting patch embeddings are then, reshaped and reassembled into a full spectrogram, effectively reverting the operations of the encoder. The model is trained to minimise the mean squared error between the reconstructed and original spectrogram, thereby encouraging the encoded features to preserve detailed acoustic information. A sample reconstructed spectrogram $\hat{X}$ is shown in Fig. 11.

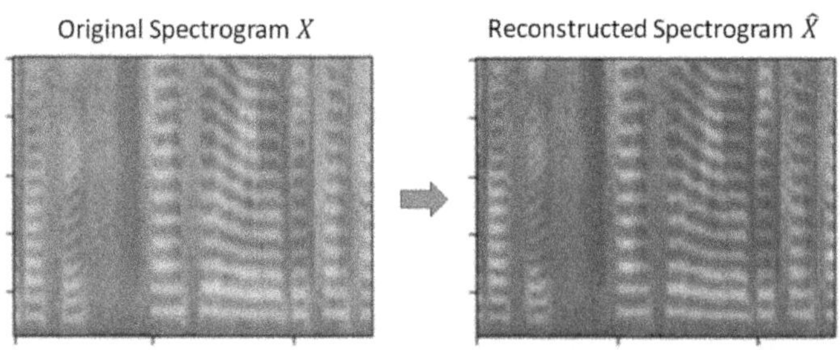

Fig. 11 SFAT-Net: spectrogram reconstruction as output of spectrogram decoder component D_X

The decoder D_{F_0} is dedicated to estimate the fundamental frequency of the input speech. It mirrors the architecture of the spectrogram decoder and performs a regression from the shared encoding y_{enc} to a binary contour matrix that estimates the F_0 trajectory across time and frequency. The ground truth for this task is obtained using the pYin algorithm [50], a pitch estimation method known for its robustness in low-noise environments. To improve stability and reduce sensitivity to minor prediction error, the binary F_0 matrix targets are smoothed using a Gaussian kernel. An example of F_0 contour prediction is depicted in Fig. 12.

The final component, the synthesis predictor P, performs the binary classification task of distinguishing synthetic from natural speech. It begins by projecting the shared encoder output into a new embedding space and appending a class token to the sequence, following the design of ViT classifiers. This extended sequence is processed by a prediction transformer T^P, and the output corresponding to the class token is extracted and passed through a linear classification layer to produce a two-dimensional output vector. This vector represents the probability of the input being synthetic, implicitly capturing energy concentrations in the fundamental frequency and its overtones, which facilitates interpretability of which signal attributes influence the classification decision.

The architecture was later extended in SFAT-Net-2 [47], which updated the bottleneck embeddings by incorporating both the magnitude and phase components of the input signal. These components were coupled via shared positional encodings, reflecting the hypothesis that complexity of phase generation process can lead to anomalies in the phase distribution of synthetic speech, particularly in regions corresponding to vocal formants. To explore this idea, SFAT-Net-2 revised the encoding process from [46] by introducing two separated encoders: E_x for log-magnitude spectrograms and E_ϕ for the phase information, as shown in Fig. 13b. This separation was motivated by the distinct nature of magnitude and phase representations and was considered necessary for learning informative embeddings. Both encoders operate on an unified framing grid and follow the architectural principles introduced in the original SFAT-Net. Their outputs are concatenated to form the joint representation used for the

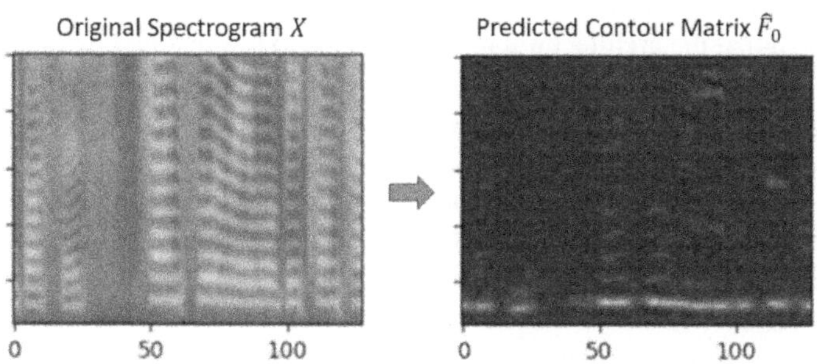

Fig. 12 SFAT-Net: f_0 contour matrix prediction as output of fundamental frequency decoder D_{F_0}

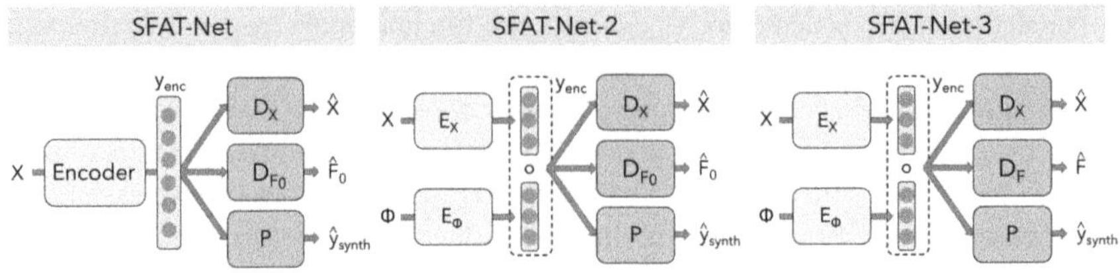

(a) SFAT-Net [17] (b) SFAT-Net-2 [18] (c) SFAT-Net-3 [19]

Fig. 13 SFAT-Net models for synthetic speech detection based on formant analysis

subsequent decoding. Despite maintaining a similar number of parameters and preserving the original bottleneck structure, SFAT-Net-2 outperformed its predecessor, benefiting from the enhanced representation of phase-magnitude interactions.

Building upon this, the most recent evolution, SFAT-Net-3 [48] introduced substantial modifications to the decoding process. Motivated to deepen the analysis of the input signal, SFAT-Net-3 expands its focus beyond the fundamental frequency by incorporating reconstruction of the first and second speech formants, F_1 and F_2. These formants are resonant frequencies produced by the human vocal tract, shaped by its physical configuration—including the throat, mouth, and nasal passages—as air passes through during speech production. In phonetic analysis, F_1 and F_2 are used to characterise linguistic content [51], support speaker identification [52], and describe vocal qualities [53]. The authors hypothesised that just as synthetic speech introduces anomalies in the F_0 distribution, similar irregularities would be detectable in the distributions of F_1 and F_2.

Accordingly, SFAT-Net-3 introduces a new decoder component D_F, illustrated in Fig. 13c, that generalises the role of D_{F_0} to a multi-formant regression task. Rather than estimating only F_0, this decoder maps y_{enc} to a superposition of contour matrices corresponding to F_0, F_1, and F_2. Ground truth annotations for these formants are derived using the Praat software [54], which applies an analysis-by-synthesis strategy for phonetic analysis. Experimental evaluations reported in [48] compared SFAT-Net-3 with its predecessors and with a pure transformer-based baseline. The results demonstrated that the architectural refinements led to lower Equal Error Rate (EER) and higher Area Under the Curve (AUC) scores. Crucially, all versions of SFAT-Net outperformed the baseline, reinforcing the conclusion that multi-task learning focused on specific speech components, such as fundamental frequency and formants, enhances the model's generalisation and detection capabilities.

The core idea at the basis of SFAT-Net models, i.e., to interpret synthesis detection as byproduct of applying attention for performing a speech-related task, might be the key to effectively detect anomalies present in synthetically-generated acoustic features, and therefore to realise synthetic speech detection.

Compared to models for prosody and emotion analysis, SFAT-Net models benefit from an explicit focus on the sheer speech content, without anchoring its detection mechanism to specific defects that are likely to be addressed by future generative models.

Nevertheless, these synthetic speech detectors based on voice analysis still suffer from the need of including annotated synthetic samples in the training procedure: If the training synthetic samples are not representative of the TTS or VC algorithms that might be encountered at test phase, their effectiveness will inevitably be reduced.

A possible solution to this issue is therefore going to be presented in the following section, in which we are going to introduce a training paradigm that overcomes the need for including representative synthetic examples in the training set.

4 POI-Based Analysis for Generalisable Synthetic Speech Detection

As we argued in Section. 3, classical end-to-end supervised methods have difficulty generalising to unseen distributions. Mostly, they learn to recognise artefacts left by the specific synthesis methods used to generate the training samples. In the following, we briefly describe the datasets commonly used to train these models.

ASVspoof 2019 [12] was released within the 2019 automatic speaker verification spoofing and countermeasures challenge, and is the first dataset that addressed the issue of logical access, where audio recordings were digitally manipulated. The dataset comprises 7,355 natural samples and 63,882 synthetic ones, that were generated using 13 different text to speech and voice conversion techniques. It was later expanded with the release of **ASVspoof 2021** [19] which shared the same training partition with its predecessor, but enriched its evaluation by introducing 2,617 additional natural tracks and 589,212 synthetic tracks, specifically focusing on the deepfake detection task rather than the automatic speaker verification (ASV) task.

ASVspoof 5 [55] is the latest iteration of the ASVspoof datasets, with a total of 938,010 synthetic tracks and 239,396 natural ones. In this last release the challenge organizers used up to 32 different combinations of voice conversion/text to speech techniques with two ad-hoc attacks and different kind of background noise. Moreover, in the evaluation tracks the files have been fed through different codecs with variable bitrate and sampling rate at either 8 kHz or 16 kHz.

InTheWild [18] consists of 11,816 synthetic and 19,963 natural audio samples, designed to reflect real-world conditions. It includes recordings from 54 different speaker identities, with natural examples carefully selected to closely match the corresponding synthetic ones in terms of speaker emotion, background noise, duration, and other contextual factors. As the data is collected in uncontrolled real-life environments, no information is available regarding the specific methods used to generate the synthetic audio samples.

With the continuous and rapid progress in this field, these datasets are rapidly becoming obsolete. Their fundamental characteristic of containing synthetic data drawn from a limited set of known generators makes them unsuitable for training tomorrow's forgery detectors. A closed set of synthetic data cannot help address the generalisation problem. It has also been observed that supervised methods sometimes tend to focus on and exploit specific biases in the data, i.e., learn properties that are not truly discriminatory in real-world applications. A well-known example are the ASVspoof 2019 datasets where natural files contain silences that last longer than their synthetic counterparts, allowing models to mistakenly focus on such unreliable details [27]. Finally, even if we limit our focus to existing generators, these training datasets may prove to be poorly suited for analysing recordings distributed online. In fact, synthetic audio generation techniques can be divided into two macro groups with very limited overlap: non-commercial, freely available and open source but requiring a minimum of technical background; and commercial, plug-and-play, but usually closed-source and behind a pay-wall. Researchers mostly adopt non-commercial alternatives due to lack of budget, the need to produce data at scale, and the desire to have good control over the generated data, which is only possible with open-source software. However, malicious actors are more likely to adopt commercial techniques due to their easy-to-use nature and, last but not least, their opacity. This creates an imbalance, since the distribution of audio files found in the wild hardly matches the distribution of academic datasets—another reason why training on such datasets does not ensure good generalisation.

An interesting way to overcome this problem is to rely on one-class detectors, which are trained only on natural samples and do not rely on synthetic ones. With a one-class approach, the goal is to accurately model only the natural class, so that a test sample that does not fit this data distribution is an anomaly and is eventually classified as synthetic. Although conceptually attractive, this approach presents insurmountable challenges: to reliably model the class of all natural recordings, a huge number of natural audio samples would have to be collected under very different conditions and fed into a training pipeline whose cost would quickly become exorbitant.

However, by introducing appropriate domain-related constraints, it is possible to exploit the power of the one-class approach with reasonable costs in terms of data and complexity. This is the case of the person-of-interest (PoI) approach considered here. It is based on the observation that most video manipulations and virtually all audio manipulations break (totally or partially) the natural connection between the person creating the media resource and the video/audio signal representing it. This happens, for example, when a fragment of speech originally produced by identity 'A' is replaced by another fragment generated by a software method. Likewise, when a speech uttered by identity 'B' is regenerated in the style of another identity 'A'. In both cases, we do not need to establish whether the speech under test is natural or synthetic (an extremely challenging problem, as mentioned before), but only whether this speech is naturally generated by the claimed identity 'A'. When this is not the case, the audio under test is considered not to conform to the characteristics of the identity under analysis. With the PoI approach, then, there is no need to model the huge class of natural speech and detect anomalies against it, but only the class of natural speech spoken by the identity creating the audio, a much more achievable task, with anomalies that can stand out much more clearly.

Early examples of this approach can be found in [56–58] where speakers' facial gestures are extracted as reference or training material. However, these methods only apply to videos, excluding the audio domain. The PoI concept was firstly applied to audio in [59]: Instead of designing ad hoc features, such as the facial reference features used in previous work, the authors relied on embeddings produced by existing state-of-the-art speaker verification systems and evaluated their effectiveness in detecting synthetic audio in a PoI framework. Indeed, speaker verification techniques have a long history and are ideal candidates for the one-class approach. First, they are trained on a dataset containing only natural files, ensuring full generalisation capability unlike the supervised method. Furthermore, because no generated data is seen during training, the network cannot be tricked into using the all-too-common shortcuts and biases used by supervised methods. Second, training strategies for speaker verification aim to produce a single embedding per audio file that allows for speaker identification. To do so, these methods use losses that tend to cluster embeddings extracted from recordings with the same speaker. This allows us to reframe the synthetic speech detection problem as a speaker verification problem. That is, the question posed is not "is the recording natural or synthetic", but rather "is the person speaking who they claim to be?"

In the PoI approach, the only new requirement is that a certain number of natural audio samples of the identity under test are available. This assumption is not restrictive at all, since typically there is plenty of useful audio on social networks for "very important people", the favourite victims of these attacks. However, this is often also true for ordinary people, and even when this is not the case, it is reasonable to assume that, to counter the possible attack, the target person will be more than willing to provide reference audio upon request. Therefore, in the following we assume that the *claimed* identity of the speaker is known, and that a reference set $\mathcal{R}$ consisting of genuine audio recordings of the same identity is available. Detection is carried out by comparing the test audio with the reference set, working in the embedding space of the speaker verification model. In more detail, two distinct testing strategies can be considered, illustrated in Fig. 14: Centroid-Based (CB) and Maximum-Similarity (MS).

The Centroid-Based strategy is inspired by the Centroid-Based Metric Learning [60]. First, the centroid of the embedding vectors $\{r_i\}_{i \in \mathcal{R}}$ corresponding to the reference audio samples is computed

$$c = \frac{1}{|\mathcal{R}|} \sum_{i \in \mathcal{R}} r_i . \tag{1}$$

Then, a similarity score

$$s = \rho(x, c) \tag{2}$$

is computed between the centroid and the embedding vector x of the test audio, where $\rho(\cdot, \cdot)$ is the similarity metric used by the speaker verification model. The audio is classified as synthetic whenever this score falls below a predefined threshold.

With the Maximum-Similarity strategy [58, 61], instead, a similarity score

$$s_i = \rho(x, r_i) \tag{3}$$

is computed between the test audio and every single reference sample in $\mathcal{R}$. The final decision statistic is given by the maximum of these scores

$$s = \max_{i \in \mathcal{R}} s_i . \tag{4}$$

With this solution, the test sample needs to be close to only one of the reference audio samples to be considered pristine, and not all of them. This better takes into account the large intra-class variability that can be found, e.g., due to variety of encoding or reverberation conditions in the reference set $\mathcal{R}$, even between different recordings of the same identity. With this decision rule, this framework has proven to be very effective, outperforming both state-of-the-art supervised models and other trained speaker verification networks tested with the same methodology.

In [59] the PoI strategy is implemented on top of a ResNet50 [62] backbone, trained on VoxCeleb2 [63] to extract speaker embeddings that should be very similar for the same speaker. To this end, the loss introduced in [58] is used.

An interesting improvement of the method has been explored in [64], where the main goal is to test whether a pre-trained model can be used as-is to extract discriminative embeddings for deepfake detection. A block diagram of this method is shown in Fig. 15. Overall, the pipeline is very similar to the previous case. However, the ad-hoc trained model is now replaced by a large pre-trained audio model. The intuition was that such a model trained on a very general task with a massive amount of data might be able to produce highly discriminative embeddings for a variety of tasks, including synthetic speech detection.

Four large pre-trained models were compared, shown in Table 1. wav2vec 2.0 XLS-R [21] is the model with the largest number of parameters and number of hours

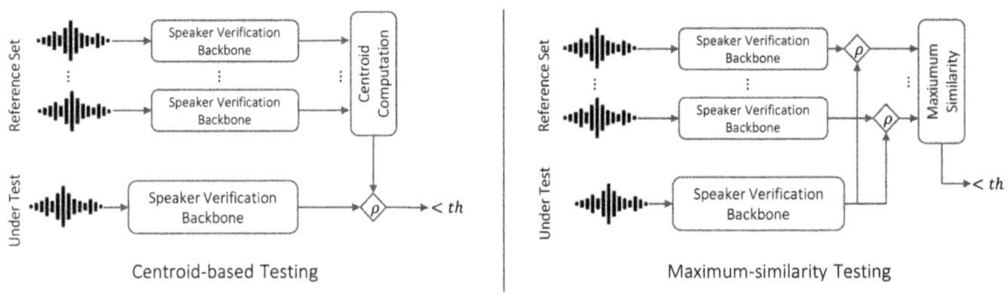

Fig. 14 Basic diagram of the PoI-based speaker verification approach. The left part describes the centroid-based testing strategy where the embedding of the audio under test is compared with the centroid embedding of the reference set and their similarity value is used as classification score. The right part describes the maximum-similarity testing strategy where the embedding of the audio under test is compared with each element of the reference set and the highest similarity value is taken as score

Table 1 Pre-trained models considered in our analysis, along with details on their architecture type, number of parameters, amount of training data (in hours of speech), and training objective—either Speech Recognition (SR) or Latent Representation Learning (LRL)

Model	Network type	Nb. Params	Speech (h)	Task
wav2vec 2.0 XLS-R	CNN + transformer	2B	436K	SR
AudioCLIP	CNN + transformer	134M	5K	LRL
LaionCLAP	Transformer	158M	9K	LRL
BEATs	Transformer	90M	5K	LRL

of audio data in training. It is also the only model trained to perform speech recognition in 128 different languages. All other models were trained on a latent representation learning task, i.e., to produce strong discriminative embeddings. AudioCLIP [65] expands the capabilities of CLIP [66] by adding a third encoder that processes the audio. The number of losses increases to three, one for each pair of encoders. LaionCLAP [67] uses a CLIP-based learning paradigm with the image encoder replaced by an audio encoder, trained on 633,526 text-audio pairs. Finally, BEATs [68] proposes an iterative training strategy where a tokeniser and a self-supervised audio learning model are trained in parallel, each helping to improve the training of the other. Of key importance here is the idea that the tokeniser learns semantic information for each patch of the spectrogram, as with text or image tokens.

Finally, it was observed that all the proposed backbones, except AudioCLIP, were able to provide good embeddings for the task at hand. BEATs proved to be the best performing, achieving almost perfect performance, with an equal error rate of less

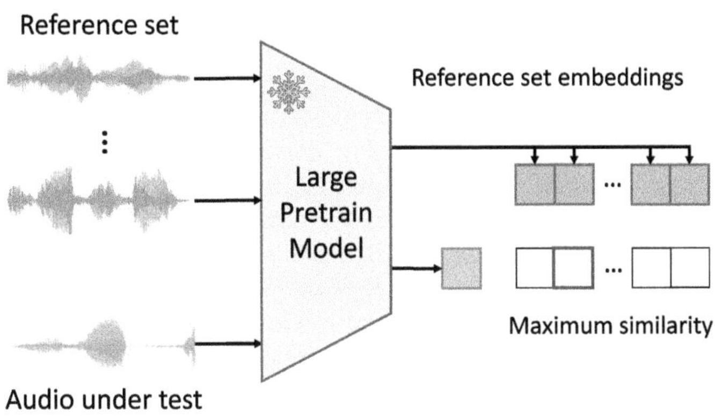

Fig. 15 Making decisions based on large pre-trained models. Audio signals are fed to the model to extract corresponding embeddings. The decision statistic is computed in the latent space as the maximum similarity score between the test audio and the reference audio

than 1%. It was also able to work with a very limited amount of data in the benchmark set, namely just five short samples.

This framework fits very well the task of audio deepfake detection both for its outstanding performance and ease of use. In fact, a pre-trained audio model is more than sufficient to extract the necessary embeddings. However, also this method has its drawbacks. When using supervised models, their output is almost always a binary label that classifies the file as natural or synthetic. Therefore, when used on a natural audio recording, it produces a clear verdict. PoI-based approaches, on the other hand, assign a continuous score ranging from 0 to 1 to each file, i.e. the similarity to the reference set of that identity. This fuzzy score is probably a more honest reading of the problem, but it may be more difficult to accept and explain in certain contexts, such as in a court of law. Furthermore, these models do not have a calibration phase where the ideal threshold for each identity is calculated and then applied to all test files. Calculating this threshold is not a trivial task since there are multiple factors to consider when addressing this problem, such as the quality and quantity of recordings in the reference set.

5 Open Challenges and Path Forward

While speech synthesis technology has advanced rapidly, its detection and responsible integration into digital ecosystems is delayed due to the various unresolved challenges. These challenges are not limited to algorithm design but span legal, economic, perceptual, and societal dimensions. Addressing them requires coordinated, interdisciplinary efforts and sustainable infrastructure.

A central limitation is the lack of high-quality training datasets compliant with the General Data Protection Regulation (GDPR) [69] containing both synthetic and natural speech. Most existing datasets fall short in terms of documentation, consent procedures, or speaker diversity. The Open Dataset of Synthetic Speech (ODSS) [70] is currently the only public resource explicitly designed to meet European data protection standards. However, it remains limited in scale and variety, and has not yet been widely adopted for benchmarking. Its potential impact is further constrained by the absence of standardised evaluation protocols and community-wide agreements on what constitutes fair and meaningful assessment. As long as reproducibility and comparability remain limited by fragmented data and inconsistent evaluation procedures, the field lacks a robust foundation for progress.

Detection methods also face a structural disadvantage. Generative models evolve rapidly and serve a broad range of legitimate applications, while detection efforts are reactive and under-incentivised. However, the barrier to commercial deployment is not the need for continuous updates—on the contrary, regular monitoring and adaptation can form the basis for sustainable, long-term cooperation through subscription-based services, managed detection pipelines, or API-based offerings. The real challenge lies in *misaligned economic incentives and structural free-rider effects*, similar to those observed in other areas of cybersecurity. Organisations may benefit from detection research and services without contributing to their development or upkeep, leading to chronic underinvestment. Moreover, detection responsibility is often diffuse or externalised, further complicating the formation of robust commercial ecosystems.

Access to relevant content for detection and evaluation introduces an additional bottleneck. Effective research, benchmarking, and forensic analysis require timely access not only to the low-quality data reprocessed by online platforms to be served on low-end devices, but on the originally high-quality content and respective metadata provided by the users. While the Digital Services Act (DSA) [71] has introduced legal pathways for researcher access to platform content, practical access remains highly restricted, often bureaucratic, and typically excludes raw data. In parallel, recent platform trends, including stricter API controls and the closure of third-party content access, have reduced transparency and hindered meaningful monitoring. This trajectory contradicts the growing societal need for reliable content verification capabilities and presents a significant challenge to both research and public-interest oversight.

There is also an unresolved tension between scientific openness and security. Publishing detection algorithms enables reproducibility and independent evaluation, but also increases the attack surface by exposing model limitations. Secure evaluation frameworks, coordinated red-teaming efforts, and responsible disclosure practices are needed to reduce this trade-off and ensure safer knowledge sharing.

The mentioned challenges cannot be mitigated by technical solutions alone. In addition to stronger detection, there is a need for regulatory frameworks, economic disincentives for misuse, and promotion of critical thinking at scale. Training individuals to reflect on the credibility, intent, and context of the content they consume becomes increasingly important when intuitive cues such as tone, fluency, or speaker identity are no longer trustworthy.

Progress in this domain therefore depends on building a sustainable and interdisciplinary ecosystem. Key priorities include:

- Targeted funding for dataset creation, benchmark design, and detection system development
- GDPR-compliant data collection pipelines for acquiring natural speech in controlled environments;
- Wider adoption and extension of efforts like ODSS, including its integration into standardised, community-agreed evaluation frameworks
- Incentives for TTS developers to provide labelled outputs and metadata to support the training of synthetic speech detection systems
- Engagement of industry stakeholders, particularly in high-risk domains such as media, finance, and telecommunications
- Development of viable service and licensing models, including detection-as-a-service, integration into media workflows, and hybrid business models
- Improved access to content for research and verification, including raw or high-fidelity media, and enforceable transparency obligations under digital platform regulations

- Public education initiatives to improve societal resilience, including systematic promotion of critical thinking, media literacy, and awareness of cognitive bias

Without addressing these priorities, the reliability of voice as a communication channel will continue to erode. Solutions must be both technically robust and institutionally viable to ensure long-term impact, and realise a sustainable ecosystem paving the way to resilient, future-proof solutions.

Acknowledgements This research was supported by the European Union under the Horizon Europe vera.ai project, Grant Agreement number 101070093, the BMBF news-polygraph project (Grant Agreement number 03RU2U151D), the BMBF SpeechTrust+ project (Grant Agreement number 13N16267), and by the PNRR ICSC National Research Centre for High Performance Computing, Big Data and Quantum Computing (CN00000013), under the NRRP MUR program funded by the NextGenerationEU. This work was also partially supported by SERICS (PE00000014) under the MUR National Recovery and Resilience Plan, funded by the European Union—NextGenerationEU.

References

1. Shen, J., Pang, R., Weiss, R.J., Schuster, M., Jaitly, N., et al.: Natural TTS synthesis by conditioning WaveNet on MEL spectrogram predictions. In: IEEE International Conference on Acoustics, Speech and Signal Processing (ICASSP), pp. 4779–4783 (2018)
2. Tamamori, A., Hayashi, T., Kobayashi, K., Takeda, K., Toda, T.: Speaker-dependent WaveNet vocoder. In: Annual Conference of the International Speech Communication Association (ISCA Interspeech), pp. 1118–1122. Stockholm, Sweden (2017)
3. van den Oord, A., Dieleman, S., Zen, H., Simonyan, K., Vinyals, O., et al.: WaveNet: a generative model for raw audio. In: ISCA Speech Synthesis Workshop (SSW), p. 128 (2016)
4. Ren, Y., Hu, C., Tan, X., Qin, T., Zhao, S., et al.: FastSpeech 2: fast and high-quality end-to-end text to speech. In: International Conference on Learning Representations (ICLR). Online (2021)
5. Kim, J., Kim, S., Kong, J., Yoon, S.: Glow-TTS: A generative flow for text-to-speech via monotonic alignment search. In: Annual Conference on Neural Information Processing Systems (NeurIPS). Online (2020)
6. Kim, J., Kong, J., Son, J.: Conditional variational autoencoder with adversarial learning for end-to-end text-to-speech. In: International Conference on Machine Learning (ICML), pp. 5530–5540. Online (2021)
7. Popov, V., Vovk, I., Gogoryan, V., Sadekova, T., Kudinov, M.: Grad-TTS: a diffusion probabilistic model for text-to-speech. In: International Conference on Machine Learning (ICML), pp. 8D599–8608. Online (2021)
8. Chen, S., Wang, C., Wu, Y., Zhang, Z., Zhou, L., et al.: Neural codec language models are zero-shot text to speech synthesizers. IEEE Trans. Audio, Speech Lang. Process. **33**, 705–718 (2025/2023a)
9. Chen, S., Liu, S., Zhou, L., Liu, Y., Tan, X., et al.: VALL-E 2: Neural Codec Language Models are Human Parity Zero-shot Text to Speech Synthesizers (2024). [Preprint]
10. Shen, K., Ju, Z., Tan, X., Liu, E., Leng, Y., et al.: NaturalSpeech 2: latent diffusion models are natural and zero-shot speech and singing synthesizers. In: International Conference on Learning Representations (ICLR). Vienna, Austria (2024)
11. Europol: Facing Reality? Law Enforcement and the Challenge of Deepfakes, An Observatory Report from the Europol Innovation Lab. Publications Office of the European Union (2022)

12. Wang, X., Yamagishi, J., Todisco, M., Delgado, H., Nautsch, A., et al.: ASVspoof 2019: a large-scale public database of synthesized, converted and replayed speech. Comput. Speech Lang. **64**, 101,114 (2020)
13. Tak, H., Patino, J., Todisco, M., Nautsch, A., Evans, N., et al.: End-to-end anti-spoofing with RawNet2. In: IEEE International Conference on Acoustics. Speech and Signal Processing (ICASSP), pp. 6369–6373. ON, Canada, Toronto (2021)
14. Jung, J.W., Heo, H.S., Tak, H., Shim, H.J., Chung, J.S., et al.: AASIST: Audio anti-spoofing using integrated spectro-temporal graph attention networks. In: IEEE International Conference on Acoustics, Speech and Signal Processing (ICASSP), pp. 6367–6371. Singapore, Singapore (2022)
15. Tak, H., Jung, J., Patino, J., Kamble, M., Todisco, M., et al.: End-to-end spectro-temporal graph attention networks for speaker verification anti-spoofing and speech deepfake detection. In: Automatic Speaker Verification and Spoofing Countermeasures Challenge (ASVspoof), pp. 1–8. Brno, Czech Republic (2021a)
16. Tak, H., Todisco, M., Wang, X., Weon Jung, J., Yamagishi, J., et al.: Automatic speaker verification spoofing and deepfake detection using wav2vec 2.0 and data augmentation. In: The Speaker and Language Recognition Workshop (Odyssey 2022), pp. 112–119. Beijing, China (2022)
17. Zhang, Q., Wen, S., Hu, T.: Audio deepfake detection with self-supervised XLS-R and SLS classifier. In: ACM International Conference on Multimedia, pp. 6765–6773. Melbourne, Australia (2024)
18. Müller, N., Czempin, P., Diekmann, F., Froghyar, A., Böttinger, K.: Does audio deepfake detection generalize? In: Annual Conference of the International Speech Communication Association (ISCA Interspeech), pp. 2783–2787. Incheon, South Korea (2022)
19. Yamagishi, J., Wang, X., Todisco, M., Sahidullah, M., Patino, J., et al.: ASVspoof 2021: accelerating progress in spoofed and deepfake speech detection. In: Automatic Speaker Verification and Spoofing Countermeasures Challenge (ASVspoof), pp. 47–54. Brno, Czech Republic (2021)
20. Ravanelli, M., Bengio, Y.: Speaker recognition from raw waveform with SincNet. In: IEEE Spoken Language Technology Workshop (SLT), pp. 1021–1028. Athens, Greece (2018)
21. Babu, A., Wang, C., Tjandra, A., Lakhotia, K., Xu, Q., et al.: XLS-R: self-supervised cross-lingual speech representation learning at scale. In: Annual Conference of the International Speech Communication Association (ISCA Interspeech). Incheon, South Korea (2022)
22. Baevski, A., Zhou, Y., Mohamed, A., Auli, M.: wav2vec 2.0: a framework for self-supervised learning of speech representations. In: Annual Conference on Neural Information Processing Systems (NeurIPS), pp. 12,449–12,460. Vancouver, BC, Canada (2020)
23. Vaswani, A., Shazeer, N., Parmar, N., Uszkoreit, J., Jones, L., et al.: Attention is all you need. In: International Conference on Neural Information Processing Systems (NeurIPS), pp. 5998–6008 (2017)
24. Cuccovillo, L., Papastergiopoulos, C., Vafeiadis, A., Yaroshchuk, A., Aichroth, P., et al.: Open challenges in synthetic speech detection. In: IEEE International Workshop on Information Forensics and Security (WIFS), pp. 1–6. Shanghai, China (2022)
25. European Union: Regulation (EU) 2024/1689 of the European Parliament and of the Council of 13 June 2024 Laying Down Harmonised Rules on Artificial Intelligence (Artificial Intelligence Act) (2024). http://data.europa.eu/eli/reg/2024/1689/ojj
26. Goodman, B., Flaxman, S.: European Union regulations on algorithmic decision-making and a right to explanation. AI Mag. **38**(3), 50–57 (2017)
27. Zhang, Y., Li, Z., Lu, J., Hua, H., Wang, W., et al.: The impact of silence on speech anti-spoofing. IEEE/ACM Trans. Audio, Speech, Lang. Process. (TASLP) **31**, 3374–3389 (2023)
28. Salvi, D., Bestagini, P., Tubaro, S.: Towards frequency band explainability in synthetic speech detection. In: European Signal Processing Conference (EUSIPCO), pp. 620–624. Helsinki, Finland (2023)
29. Salvi, D., Balcha, T.S., Bestagini, P., Tubaro, S.: Listening between the lines: synthetic speech detection disregarding verbal content. In: IEEE International Conference on Acoustics. Speech, and Signal Processing Workshops (ICASSPW), pp. 883–887. Seoul, South Korea (2024)

30. Wang, X., Yamagishi, J.: Spoofed training data for speech spoofing countermeasure can be efficiently created using neural vocoders. In: IEEE International Conference on Acoustics. Speech and Signal Processing (ICASSP), pp. 1–5. Rhodes Island, Greece (2023)
31. Sun, C., Jia, S., Hou, S., Lyu, S.: AI-synthesized voice detection using neural vocoder artifacts. In: IEEE/CVF Conference on Computer Vision and Pattern Recognition Workshops (CVPRW), pp. 904–912. Vancouver, BC, Canada (2023)
32. Moussa, D., Bergmann, S., Riess, C.: Unmasking neural codecs: forensic identification of AI-compressed speech. In: Annual Conference of the International Speech Communication Association (ISCA Interspeech), pp. 2260–2264. Kos Island, Greece (2024)
33. Kleijn, W.B., Storus, A., Chinen, M., Denton, T., Lim, F.S.C., et al.: Generative speech coding with predictive variance regularization. In: IEEE International Conference on Acoustics. Speech and Signal Processing (ICASSP), pp. 6478–6482. ON, Canada, Toronto (2021)
34. Défossez, A., Copet, J., Synnaeve, G., Adi, Y.: High fidelity neural audio compression. Trans. Mach. Learn. Res. (2023)
35. Kumar, R., Seetharaman, P., Luebs, A., Kumar, I., Kumar, K.: High-fidelity audio compression with improved RVQGAN. In: Annual Conference on Neural Information Processing Systems (NeurIPS), pp. 27,980–27,993. New Orleans, Louisiana, USA (2023)
36. Geirhos, R., Jacobsen, J.H., Michaelis, C., Zemel, R., Brendel, W., et al.: Shortcut learning in deep neural networks. Nat. Mach. Intell. **2**, 665–673 (2020)
37. Ghosh, S., Yu, K., Arabshahi, F., Batmanghelich, K.: Tackling shortcut learning in deep neural networks: an iterative approach with interpretable models. In: International Conference on Machine Learning Workshops (ICMLW). Honolulu, Hawaii, USA (2023)
38. Attorresi, L., Salvi, D., Borrelli, C., Bestagini, P., Tubaro, S.: Combining automatic speaker verification and prosody analysis for synthetic speech detection. In: International Conference on Pattern Recognition (ICPR), pp. 247–263. Montréal, QC, Canada (2022)
39. Desplanques, B., Thienpondt, J., Demuynck, K.: ECAPA-TDNN: emphasized channel attention, propagation and aggregation in TDNN based speaker verification. In: Annual Conference of the International Speech Communication Association (ISCA Interspeech), pp. 3830–3834 (2020)
40. Skerry-Ryan, R., Battenberg, E., Xiao, Y., Wang, Y., Stanton, D., et al.: Towards end-to-end prosody transfer for expressive speech synthesis with Tacotron. In: International Conference on Machine Learning (ICML), pp. 4693–4702. Stockholm, Sweden (2018)
41. Hosler, B., Salvi, D., Murray, A., Antonacci, F., Bestagini, P., et al.: Do deepfakes feel emotions? A semantic approach to detecting deepfakes via emotional inconsistencies. In: IEEE/CVF Conference on Computer Vision and Pattern Recognition Workshops (CVPRW), pp. 1013–1022. Online (2021)
42. Conti, E., Salvi, D., Borrelli, C., Hosler, B., Bestagini, P., et al.: Deepfake speech detection through emotion recognition: a semantic approach. In: IEEE International Conference on Acoustics. Speech and Signal Processing (ICASSP), pp. 8962–8966. Singapore, Singapore (2022)
43. Hochreiter, S., Schmidhuber, J.: Long short-term memory. Neural Comput. **9**(8), 1735–1780 (1997)
44. Chen, M., He, X., Yang, J., Zhang, H.: 3-D convolutional recurrent neural networks with attention model for speech emotion recognition. IEEE Sig. Process. Lett. **25**(10), 1440–1444 (2018)
45. Barakat, H., Turk, O., Demiroglu, C.: Deep learning-based expressive speech synthesis: a systematic review of approaches, challenges, and resources. EURASIP J. Audio, Speech, Music Process. **2024**(1) (2024)
46. Cuccovillo, L., Gerhardt, M., Aichroth, P.: Audio spectrogram transformer for synthetic speech detection via speech formant analysis. In: IEEE International Workshop on Information Forensics and Security (WIFS), pp. 1–6. Nürnberg, Germany (2023)
47. Cuccovillo, L., Gerhardt, M., Aichroth, P.: Audio transformer for synthetic speech detection via formant magnitude and phase analysis. In: IEEE International Conference on Acoustics. Speech and Signal Processing (ICASSP), pp. 4805–4809. Seoul, South Korea (2024a)

48. Cuccovillo, L., Gerhardt, M., Aichroth, P.: Audio transformer for synthetic speech detection via multi-formant analysis. In: IEEE/CVF Conference on Computer Vision and Pattern Recognition Workshops (CVPRW), pp. 4409–4417 (2024b)
49. Dosovitskiy, A., Beyer, L., Kolesnikov, A., Weissenborn, D., Zhai, X., et al.: An image is worth 16×16 words: transformers for image recognition at scale. In: International Conference on Learning Representations (ICLR) (2021)
50. Mauch, M., Dixon, S.: PYIN: a fundamental frequency estimator using probabilistic threshold distributions. In: IEEE International Conference on Acoustics, Speech and Signal Processing (ICASSP), pp. 659–663 (2014)
51. Johnson, K.: Acoustic and Auditory Phonetics, 3d edn. Cambridge University Press (2011/1997)
52. Nolan, F.: The Phonetic Bases of Speaker Recognition. Cambridge University Press (1983)
53. Laver, J.: The Phonetic Description of Voice Quality. Cambridge University Press (1980)
54. Boersma, P., Weenink, D.: Praat: doing phonetics by computer [Computer program] (1992–2022). Version 6.1.09
55. Wang, X., Delgado, H., Tak, H., Jung, J.w., Shim, H.j., et al.: ASVspoof 5: crowdsourced speech data, deepfakes, and adversarial attacks at scale. In: Automatic Speaker Verification and Spoofing Countermeasures Challenge (ASVspoof), pp. 1–8. Kos Island, Greece (2024)
56. Agarwal, S., Farid, H., Gu, Y., He, M., Nagano, K., et al.: Protecting world leaders against deep fakes. In: IEEE Conference on Computer Vision and Pattern Recognition (CVPR) Workshops, pp. 38–45. Long Beach, California, USA (2019)
57. Agarwal, S., Hu, L., Ng, E., Darrell, T., Li, H., et al.: Watch those words: video falsification detection using word-conditioned facial motion. In: IEEE/CVF Winter Conference on Applications of Computer Vision (WACV), pp. 4710–4719. Waikoloa, Hawaii, USA (2023)
58. Cozzolino, D., Rössler, A., Thies, J., Nießner, M., Verdoliva, L.: ID-reveal: identity-aware deepfake video detection. In: IEEE/CVF International Conference on Computer Vision (ICCV), pp. 15,108–15,117. Online (2021)
59. Pianese, A., Cozzolino, D., Poggi, G., Verdoliva, L.: Deepfake audio detection by speaker verification. In: IEEE International Workshop on Information Forensics and Security (WIFS), pp. 1–6. Shanghai, China (2022)
60. Wang, J., Wang, K.C., Law, M.T., Rudzicz, F., Brudno, M.: Centroid-based deep metric learning for speaker recognition. In: IEEE International Conference on Acoustics. Speech and Signal Processing (ICASSP), pp. 3652–3656. Brighton, UK (2019)
61. Cozzolino, D., Pianese, A., Nießner, M., Verdoliva, L.: Audio-visual person-of-interest deepfake detection. In: IEEE/CVF Conference on Computer Vision and Pattern Recognition Workshops (CVPRW), pp. 943–952. Vancouver, BC, Canada (2023)
62. He, K., Zhang, X., Ren, S., Sun, J.: Deep residual learning for image recognition. In: IEEE International Conference on Computer Vision and Pattern Recognition (CVPR), pp. 770–778. Las Vegas, Nevada, USA (2016)
63. Chung, J.S., Nagrani, A., Zisserman, A.: VoxCeleb2: deep speaker recognition. In: Annual Conference of the International Speech Communication Association (ISCA Interspeech), pp. 1086–1090. Hyderabad, India (2018)
64. Pianese, A., Cozzolino, D., Poggi, G., Verdoliva, L.: Training-free deepfake voice recognition by leveraging large-scale pre-trained models. In: ACM Workshop on Information Hiding and Multimedia Security (IH&MMSec), pp. 289–294. Baiona, Spain (2024)
65. Guzhov, A., Raue, F., Hees, J., Dengel, A.: AudioCLIP: extending CLIP to image, text and audio. In: IEEE International Conference on Acoustics. Speech and Signal Processing (ICASSP), pp. 976–980. Singapore, Singapore (2022)
66. Radford, A., Kim, J.W., Hallacy, C., Ramesh, A., Goh, G., et al.: Learning transferable visual models from natural language supervision. In: International Conference on Machine Learning (ICML), pp. 8748–8763. Online (2021)
67. Wu, Y., Chen, K., Zhang, T., Hui, Y., Berg-Kirkpatrick, T., et al.: Large-scale contrastive language-audio pretraining with feature fusion and keyword-to-caption augmentation. In: IEEE International Conference on Acoustics. Speech and Signal Processing (ICASSP), pp. 1–5. Rhodes Island, Greece (2023)

68. Chen, S., Wu, Y., Wang, C., Liu, S., Tompkins, D., et al.: BEATs: audio pre-training with acoustic tokenizers. In: International Conference on Machine Learning (ICML), pp. 5178–5193. Honolulu, Hawaii, USA (2023b)
69. European Union: Regulation (EU) 2016/679 of the European Parliament and of the Council of 27 April 2016 on the Protection of Natural Persons with Regard to the Processing of Personal Data and on the Free Movement of Such Data (General Data Protection Regulation) (2016). http://data.europa.eu/eli/reg/2016/679/2016-05-04
70. Yaroshchuk, A., Papastergiopoulos, C., Cuccovillo, L., Aichroth, P., Votis, K., et al.: An open dataset of synthetic speech. In: IEEE International Workshop on Information Forensics and Security (WIFS), pp. 1–6. Nürnberg, Germany (2023)
71. European Union: Regulation (EU) 2022/2065 of the European Parliament and of the Council of 19 October 2022 on a Single Market for Digital Services and Amending Directive 2000/31/EC (Digital Services Act) (2022). http://data.europa.eu/eli/reg/2022/2065/oj

Video Deepfake Detection: Challenges and Recent Trends

Christos Koutlis, Alessandro Pianese, Davide Cozzolino, Manos Schinas, Stelios Mylonas, Luisa Verdoliva, and Symeon Papadopoulos

1 Introduction

The advent of deepfake technology, driven by the recent advances in deep learning, has enabled the manipulation of digital media such as videos and images with astonishing realism [1]. At its core, deepfake content manipulation relies on sophisticated algorithms that effectively alter facial characteristics or even replace an individual's face altogether. Specifically, Generative Adversarial Networks (GANs) [2] and diffusion models (DMs) [3] have become the most prominent methods, leveraging their ability to learn and replicate complex patterns within visual data to produce highly convincing synthetic content. Also, Variational Auto-Encoders (VAEs) [4] have demonstrated significant capabilities in learning fine-grained representations of facial features, facilitating face manipulation. Traditional image and video pro-

C. Koutlis (✉) · M. Schinas · S. Mylonas · S. Papadopoulos
Centre for Research and Technology Hellas (CERTH), Thessaloniki, Greece
e-mail: ckoutlis@iti.gr

M. Schinas
e-mail: manosetro@iti.gr

S. Mylonas
e-mail: smylonas@iti.gr

S. Papadopoulos
e-mail: papadop@iti.gr

A. Pianese · D. Cozzolino · L. Verdoliva
University of Naples Federico II (UNINA), Naples, Italy
e-mail: alessandro.pianese@unina.it

D. Cozzolino
e-mail: davide.cozzolino@unina.it

L. Verdoliva
e-mail: luisa.verdoliva@unina.it

S. Papadopoulos et al. (eds.), *Countering Disinformation in the Era of Generative AI*,
https://doi.org/10.1007/978-3-032-11782-3_8

cessing techniques, such as warping, blending, and optical flow, remain essential for refining the realism of deepfakes because they address the subtle yet crucial details that deep learning models might struggle to perfectly synthesise (facial alignment, seamless transitions between real and generated parts, temporal consistency across frames). Furthermore, the emerging field of neural radiance fields (NeRFs) [5] contributes by enabling the creation of highly realistic 3D facial rendering, allowing for precise control over appearance and lighting.

Several more specific deepfake manipulation techniques include face-swapping, lip-syncing, face-reenactment, facial attribute manipulation, and fully synthetic face image generation. Face-swapping [6–8] allows the replacement of a person's face with another, creating the illusion of presence within the original scene while maintaining natural head movements and expressions. Lip-syncing [9, 10] extends this manipulation to the auditory domain, enabling the alteration of mouth movements to synchronise with a given audio track, allowing the creation of videos where individuals appear to say things they never did. Face reenactment [11, 12] allows for the transfer of facial expressions and movements from one person to another, effectively animating a target face to mimic the source. This technique can be used to control expressions, head motions and lip movements. Finally, facial attribute manipulation [13, 14] provides control over facial features, allowing the alteration of age, expression, or physical characteristics, thus enabling the creation of entirely fabricated scenarios.

The rapid advancement and widespread accessibility of deepfake technology, coupled with its potential for massive dissemination online, pose significant risks to the integrity of digital information, societal trust, and democratic processes [15]. The growing volume of highly realistic synthetic media erodes people's ability to distinguish truth from falsehood, increasing the feeling of uncertainty. Media manipulation tools can be utilised for malicious purposes such as spreading disinformation, inciting social unrest, and damaging the reputation of individuals or organisations. Furthermore, the psychological impact of deepfakes in cases of non-consensual use can be severe, causing emotional distress and reputation harm. Hence, the need for robust detection tools is paramount to mitigating the adverse consequences of this rapidly evolving technology.

Early deepfake detection methods aimed to identify unnatural patterns in manipulated videos in terms of physiological cues, such as eye blinking, head pose, heart rate, or gaze direction [16–19]. Although the outputs of such approaches are accessible and understandable to wider audiences beyond AI researchers, they have limited practical applicability since they mainly target outdated manipulation techniques, heavily rely on controlled settings (e.g. lightning conditions) and assume video content of sufficient quality and resolution. On the contrary, the majority of current state-of-the-art detection methods rely on data-driven approaches and, specifically, supervised learning to identify generation artifacts [20–22]. These artifacts can manifest as various visual inconsistencies, such as blurring or pixelation in manipulated regions, unnatural skin textures, distorted facial features, inconsistencies in lighting or shadows, and visual noise or glitches introduced during the synthesis process. Some of them are focusing on identifying the temporal inconsistencies that are introduced by many deepfake techniques and may affect lip-sync accuracy [23] or produce inter-frame artifacts [24]. Recent video deepfake detection research is shifting away from traditional frame-based face analysis, focusing more on multimodal detection methods that analyse biometrics and outliers [25] or inconsistencies between the visual and audio modalities [26].

The performance of data-driven deepfake detection methods heavily depends on the employed datasets. One of the major dimensions for datasets is the data modality and the corresponding manipulation techniques they employ. Some datasets contain only visual data and feature face-swapping or face-reenactment manipulations [27–29], while others integrate both visual and auditory components (audio-visual) and focus on lip-syncing [30, 31]. The inclusion of multiple and diverse manipulation methods in a dataset [32] increases its representative power as a benchmark, allowing researchers to evaluate models against a wider range of deepfakes. Another crucial dimension is the dataset's scale, referring both to the number of videos and the number of unique depicted subjects. Larger datasets contain thousands or even millions of manipulated and original videos [30, 33] and feature dozens to hundreds of individuals [27, 30], enabling more robust representation learning. Scene diversity and video quality also vary considerably among datasets. Some of them use paid actors in scripted scenarios [34, 35], providing clean and well-annotated data but often lacking the complexity and variability of real-world content. Others include deepfakes in the wild [36], introducing more challenging conditions such as varied lighting, occlusions, and multi-person cases.

The field of deepfake detection has seen notable progress over the last years, but several challenges remain unresolved. A major issue is the gap between benchmark datasets and performance in the wild, as most datasets lack the compression, resolution changes, and other post-processing transformations typical of video content sourced from the Web and social media. Although data augmentation strategies can help mitigate this issue, it is very challenging to keep up with the continuously evolving and rarely disclosed processing pipelines of online platforms [37]. The employed supervised learning strategies also pose some generalisation issues, since they often rely on manipulation-specific artifacts, causing significant performance drops when encountering previously unseen deepfake techniques [32]. Trustworthiness is another concern, with most models functioning as "black boxes", making it difficult to trust or fully understand their decisions. This lack of transparency is especially problematic in critical domains like journalism [38] or law [39]. Furthermore, deepfake detectors often exhibit demographic bias, performing better on lighter skin tones and male subjects [40]. While there are some efforts to mitigate this, e.g. through balanced datasets and fairness-aware loss functions, these still remain underexplored in current research, which tends to emphasise accuracy over fairness or other trustworthy AI aspects.

2 State of the Art Approaches

In this section we outline the State-of-the-Art in the field of Video Deepfake Detection. Figure 1 illustrates the most prominent research directions along with their strengths and weaknesses.

Detection via Physiological and Biometric Cues

Early deepfake detection methods explored the use of physiological signals as discriminative features for identifying synthetic content. These rely on the assumption that generative models cannot accurately replicate subtle and natural biological signals. One line of research focuses on eye blinking patterns. As demonstrated in [17], authentic human blinking follows a characteristic temporal rhythm and duration that is often absent or irregular in synthetic videos. This method leverages the observation that early deepfake generators typically produced static or unnaturally sparse blinking sequences, though recent advances have made this artifact less prevalent. Beyond eye movements [41], the dynamics of head pose represents another powerful cue. The work in [19] shows that synthetic videos frequently exhibit implausible head

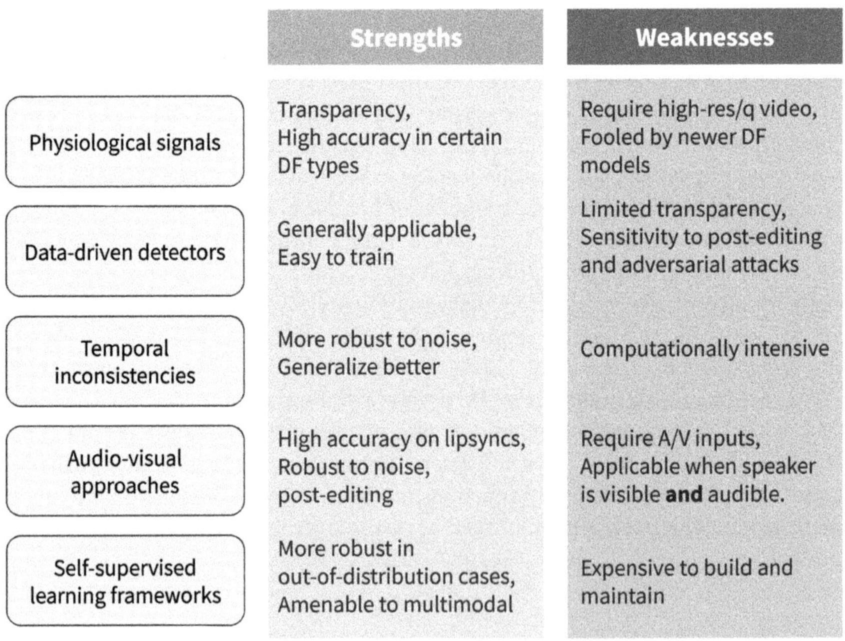

Fig. 1 Video deepfake detection research directions along with corresponding strengths and weaknesses

rotations due to limitations in 3D face modelling. Similarly, facial warping artifacts are exploited in [42] as telltale signs of manipulation.

More sophisticated approaches analyse cardiovascular and other biological signals. For instance, [16, 43] detect inconsistencies in heart rate patterns by analysing subtle colour changes in facial skin. Building on this approach, [44] exploits biological signal inconsistencies across both spatial and temporal domains. A different approach is discussed in [18], proposing a method for detecting deepfakes through the analysis of gaze direction inconsistencies in face videos. Real faces exhibit focused gaze patterns, while fake ones display scattered directions. The method uses a Gaze Analysis Model and a spatial-temporal feature aggregator, enhanced by texture and attribute models.

While such methods offer a high degree of transparency and strong performance against certain classes of deepfakes, they face two key challenges. First, these artifacts can disappear as generative models incorporate more sophisticated physiological modelling (e.g., synthetic heartbeats in [9]). Then, capturing high-quality biological signals often requires controlled lighting or high-resolution video, limiting the applicability of these methods.

Data-Driven Detectors

In the rapidly growing literature on video deepfake detection, a large number of methods rely on supervised training, leveraging extensive datasets of authentic and manipulated videos in order to learn to detect the artifacts introduced by the generation process, hence not only visible errors but also hidden traces related to different noise patterns. When the training data include the same manipulation techniques that characterise test data, these detectors often achieve impressive performance. However, their effectiveness drops when encountering content generated with novel methods not seen during training [29]. Given that this is a rapidly evolving domain, with many new methods constantly being proposed, this latter case may occur frequently. Even assuming that some samples of new types of manipulation are available, it is difficult to continuously re-train the models on larger datasets or even fine-tune them on the new data since this would likely disrupt performance in samples resembling the "old" part of the training set, a phenomenon known as catastrophic forgetting. To face this issue, specific solutions have been proposed in the literature, resorting to few-shot learning or incremental learning [45–47].

As a result, a key challenge concerns the timely and efficient acquisition of samples representing newly emerging manipulation techniques. A straightforward yet effective strategy to mitigate this issue and improve generalisation is the use of data augmentation. While standard augmentation techniques from computer vision, such as flipping, cropping, and contrast enhancement, remain useful, the deepfake detection task requires more targeted operations. In particular, augmentations that simulate real-world degradations introduced by social media platforms, such as lossy compression and rescaling, are essential for enhancing robustness. Additionally, more specialised augmentations, such as face-specific cut-out methods, have been shown to improve generalisation [48]. Another valuable strategy for improving performance and resilience is model ensembling. By aggregating the outputs of multiple models, possibly trained with different architectures, pre-processing pipelines, or input resolutions, it is possible to increase robustness [49].

A major shortcoming of data-driven approaches is their limited transparency. This issue is partially mitigated by methods that attempt to detect specific artifacts or inconsistencies introduced during the manipulation process, offering some insight into the underlying generation mechanisms. One such direction involves the analysis of low-level artifacts introduced by the up-sampling operations commonly used in generative models. These artifacts, often subtle in the spatial domain, become more prominent in the frequency domain, which has led to a number of frequency-based detection approaches [50–52].

Another promising line of work focuses on learning the artifacts produced by blending operations, which are integral to many manipulation pipelines, especially those involving facial compositing [53]. These methods attempt to capture inconsistencies introduced at the boundaries between synthesised and original content. More broadly, attention mechanisms have been employed to improve performance by encouraging networks to focus on informative regions. These mechanisms can highlight relevant spatial and temporal inconsistencies at a low (e.g., texture, noise patterns) or high level (e.g., semantic misalignments) of granularity [24, 37, 54–57]. Despite improving the accessibility and transparency of their decision-making process, these approaches often rely heavily on fine-grained visual cues that are sensitive to video processing operations. Consequently, their performance tends to deteriorate under common scenarios such as video compression, downsampling, or application of post-processing filters. More critically, they are also vulnerable to intentional perturbations, including adversarial attacks and other evasion techniques that deliberately obscure forensic traces [58, 59]. Finally, such approaches will struggle in detection scenarios involving fully generated videos.

Temporal Inconsistencies Analysis

Some video deepfake detection methods specifically exploit temporal inconsistencies [60]. A method is proposed in [24] that consists of two main stages. The first includes a Fully Temporal Convolutional Network, which is designed by reducing the spatial convolution kernel size to 1 while keeping the temporal kernel size intact. The second stage features a Temporal Transformer that captures long-term temporal dependencies. To enhance robustness recent work has shifted toward methods based on higher-level semantic features. A notable example is the approach proposed in [23], which focuses on detecting inconsistencies in lip movements. The method leverages a spatio-temporal architecture pre-trained on a visual speech recognition task, which is subsequently fine-tuned to distinguish between real and manipulated content using mouth embeddings. By grounding detection on semantically meaningful motion patterns, this approach offers greater resilience to low-level noise and compression artifacts, while also increasing transparency.

To exploit inter-frame inconsistencies some other papers leverage optical flow analysis [61, 62] or adopt contrastive learning that operates at both the local and global temporal scales to capture more general and intrinsic temporal inconsistencies between real and fake videos [63]. In [64], it is shown that even when two consecutive frames appear highly similar, subtle unnatural drift and flickering in facial features may still be observed. To exploit these inconsistencies, it is proposed to generate hard negative samples that help the model learn more generalisable features. These are obtained by blending the original image with its frame-by-frame warped version.

Some recent methods rely on pre-trained large vision models for achieving better generalisation [65]. In particular, in [66] the CLIP image encoder is used to identify temporal and spatial artifacts in key facial regions. To this end, a facial component guidance loss is introduced to direct the spatial branch into focusing on skin, nose, eyes, and lips.

Audio-Visual Approaches

The field of deepfake detection has considerably expanded with the emergence of multimodal approaches that jointly analyse audio and video streams. Pioneering works in this domain have primarily focused on identifying inconsistencies between these two modalities, leveraging the inherent limitations of early generation methods. For instance, [67, 68] demonstrated that many methods struggle to synchronise audio and video, hence they are characterised by detectable artifacts. Similarly, [69] proposed learning the natural synchronisation patterns between speech and lip movements as a discriminative feature. A more recent method [70] exploits the biologically intrinsic correlation between lip movements and head postures and proposes a method that identifies subtle temporal inconsistencies between lip movements and audio signals. By mimicking human cognitive processes and focusing on the biological link between the lips and head regions, the approach achieves high accuracy in spotting lip-sync inconsistencies, even in real-world scenarios.

However, the rapid advancement of generative AI can make these approaches obsolete. In fact, modern synthesis techniques are able to produce highly realistic deepfakes with near-perfect lip-sync accuracy, significantly raising the bar for successful detection. This evolution called for more sophisticated multimodal strategies. For example, [71] introduced a framework that extracts and compares emotion-related features across audio and video streams. This principle is also leveraged in [72] that identifies emotion inconsistencies between a speaker's face and voice. Since deepfakes often struggle to generate realistic emotional expressions, the method predicts valence and arousal using LSTM models on audio and video features. These emotion patterns over time are then classified and used to distinguish real from fake videos. In [73], audio-visual inconsistencies across both temporal and spatial dimensions are captured through a temporal-spatial encoder for feature embedding and a multimodal joint decoder that enables joint learning of audio-visual interactions and performs effective fusion of information from both modalities. A cross-modal classifier is then used for robust discrimination of deepfakes based on the alignment between audio and visual cues.

More recent works highlighted the importance of high-quality datasets for deepfake detection. In [74], it is shown that the most widely used audio-video deepfake datasets are characterised by a spurious feature: a brief leading silence at the beginning of fake videos. Using this artifact alone could lead to near-perfect separation between real and fake samples. As a result, many existing audio-only and audio-visual detection models inadvertently exploit this pattern, and suffer from performance collapse when it is removed. To avoid reliance on such spurious correlations, a recent trend is to shift from supervised to unsupervised or self-supervised learning by relying only on real videos to learn aligned audio-visual representations. This approach helps mitigate dataset-specific biases and enhance the robustness of deepfake detection systems. A large-scale and multimodal deepfake dataset comprising 1.3 million audio-visual samples is presented in [75]. The dataset spans 26 languages and includes a diverse range of manipulation scenarios, such as face-swaps, audio spoofing and synchronised audio-video forgeries. To avoid semantic biases, the dataset is carefully curated to ensure a balanced representation of gender and skin tone.

Self-supervised Learning Frameworks

Self-supervised learning is useful to learn meaningful representations from unlabelled data. This approach reduces the need for large labelled datasets and often leads to models that generalise well across different tasks. In deepfake detection, self-supervised learning is especially valuable because it allows models to be trained using only real videos, focusing on natural patterns and avoiding overfitting to artifacts specific to known fake datasets. The method in [76] leverages auxiliary self-supervised tasks tailored for deepfake detection, e.g., forgery region estimation, blending type estimation and blending ratio estimation. The method also uses an adversarial training strategy that dynamically generates the most challenging forgeries. In [77], a facial video masked autoencoder is designed to learn highly robust and generalisable facial embeddings from large-scale, non-annotated facial videos collected from the Web. As auxiliary task, it reconstructs the spatio-temporal details of facial regions focusing on critical areas such as the eyes, nose, mouth, lips, and skin. This reconstruction task leads the model to learn both local and global facial dynamics that are transferable across datasets.

Other works apply self-supervised learning in the context of audio-visual representations. More specifically, the method in [78] looks for anomalies in the audio-visual features using autoregressive models trained only on real videos in order to capture the temporal synchronisation between video frames and audio. The work in [79] proposes a self-supervised audio-visual representation learning framework that leverages the natural correlation between speech audio and facial movements. In this case, joint audio and visual speech representations aim to capture both phonetic (local) and linguistic (global) information. Local dependencies are learned through frame-level alignment between audio and visual features, ensuring precise synchronisation at a fine-grained temporal scale. To model global dependencies, the framework incorporates a masked prediction task, inspired by prior approaches in speech representation learning, allowing the model to understand broader contextual and linguistic patterns across time. A two-stage cross-modal learning framework is proposed in [80] to extract rich and robust cross-modal representations by integrating audio-visual complementary masking with feature fusion. This encourages the model to learn complementary cues from each modality, enhancing its ability to detect subtle inconsistencies representative of manipulated content.

3 Datasets

As deepfake technology continues to evolve, producing ever more realistic fake content, the demand for robust benchmarks that can support the deepfake detection efforts has become increasingly critical. In response to this need, a wide variety of benchmark datasets has emerged, over the last decade, aiming to provide a standardised ground to develop new models and evaluate their accuracy, generalisation and robustness. Each of these datasets comes with its own unique characteristics (either strengths or weaknesses), making the proper dataset selection fundamentally important. Later in this section, we thoroughly describe the most known and widely used datasets in the field, focusing on key aspects such as the underlying video modalities, the employed manipulation techniques, and their differences regarding scale, video content quality or scene diversity. A brief overview of the described datasets can be also found in Table 1.

Visual Deepfake Datasets

Initially, deepfakes were limited to manipulations in the visual domain (primarily face-swaps and face-reenactments) while the audio track remained untouched. This led to the emergence of deepfake datasets specifically designed to target these types of visual-only manipulations. One of the first benchmarks to arise in that field was UADFV [17], which comprised only 98 videos, half real and half fake. The real videos were selected from YouTube, so as to contain at least one eye-blinking event, while the fake ones were generated by swapping the original face in each of the real videos with the face of the actor Nicolas Cage. For their creation, the FakeApp mobile application was used [81]. This dataset is quite limited in terms of both scale and diversity since it features just a single manipulation technique and a single target subject. A larger and more diverse alternative was provided later by the DeepfakeTIMIT dataset [82].

Table 1 Comparison of various visual deepfake detection datasets

Dataset	Year	# Real	# Fake	Data source	# Subjects	Manipulated modality	Manipulation types	Manipulation methods
UADFV [17]	2018	49	49	YouTube	50	V	FS	1
DF-TIMIT [82]	2019	320	640	Actors	32	V	FS	1
FF++ [29]	2019	1000	5000	YouTube	–	V	FS/RE	5
DFD [93]	2019	363	3068	Actors	28	V	FS	–
DFDC [35]	2020	23,654	104,500	Actors	960	AV	FS/AS	8
Celeb-DF [28]	2020	590	5639	YouTube	59	V	FS	1
DeeperForensics-1.0 [92]	2020	50,000	10,000	Actors	100	V	FS	1
WildDeepfake [36]	2020	3805	3509	In-the-wild	–	V	–	–
ForgeryNet [27]	2021	99,630	121,617	Other datasets	5400+	V	FS/RE	8
FakeAVCeleb [31]	2021	500	21,000	YouTube	500	AV	FS/LS/SA	4
KoDF [33]	2021	62,166	175,776	Actors	403	V	FS/RE/LS	6
FFIW10K [94]	2021	10,000	10,000	YouTube	–	V	FS	3
LAV-DF [109]	2022	36,431	99,873	VoxCeleb2	153	AV	LS/SA	2
AV-Deepfake1M [30]	2023	286,721	860,039	VoxCeleb2	2,068	AV	LS/SA	3
DF-platter [105]	2023	764	132,496	YouTube	454	V	FS	3
DF40 [32]	2024	1278	100K+	Other datasets	–	V	FS/RE	23
DeepSpeak [34]	2024	6226	6799	Actors	220	AV	FS/LS/SA	5

FS Face-swap, RE Face-reenactment, AS Audio-swap, LS Lip-sync, SA Synthetic audio

It comprises 640 fake videos created using an adapted version of a GAN-based face-swapping algorithm [83], enhanced with a set of different blending techniques. The face-swapping was applied on 320 real videos of 32 subjects, that were taken from the VidTIMIT database [84], all shot in a controlled environment.

However, the most pivotal development during that period was the introduction of FaceForensics++ (FF++) [29]. This is probably the most well-known dataset in the field and is often considered, even today, the standard choice for training any new method in the literature. It was the first dataset to include deepfakes from multiple manipulation types and from multiple manipulation sources. More specifically, its original version contained a total of 5000 videos, including 1000 real videos from YouTube and 4000 deepfakes produced by applying two face-swap (Deepfakes [85], FaceSwap [86]) and two face-reenactment techniques (Face2Face [87], NeuralTextures [88]) on the set of real videos. It was later enriched by further 1000 synthetic videos produced by the FaceShifter [89] face-swapping model.

According to [90, 91], the three above datasets constitute the first generation of video deepfake datasets. All three suffer from some common drawbacks, such as the low quality of the synthesised faces with some visible boundaries around the face mask, the temporal artifacts between adjacent frames and the limited variability in terms of camera position and lighting conditions. All these factors made the provided deepfakes easily detectable by the human eye, as demonstrated in [92], where participants were asked to rate the realism of various datasets and assigned the lowest scores to all three.

Next generation datasets, such as DFD [93] and DFDC [35] tried to overcome these shortcomings by reducing the visual-level inconsistencies and the limited variability of the previous methods. Both of these datasets were released by major tech companies (DFD by Google and DFDC by Meta) adhering to specific strict requirements regarding the dataset creation. In both cases, all video participants are consenting actors chosen with demographic diversity in mind, e.g. with regard to gender, skin tone, ethnicity, age, and other characteristics. Special emphasis was also placed on diversifying the filming conditions so as to resemble more real-world settings. The different scenarios included, among others, indoor and outdoor filming, different lighting conditions (i.e., day, night), and variability regarding the persons' poses and distances from the camera. Regarding their size, the DFDC can be considered as the first large-scale benchmark, since it contains nearly 1000 subjects and more than 100,000 deepfakes that were created using eight different manipulation techniques, seven of them being face-swaps and only one being an audio-swap. Although DFDC provides audio-visual content and contains manipulations on both modalities, it is inappropriate for audio-visual deepfake detection due to the lack of separate annotations per modality and the quite small proportion of fake audio samples. For that reason, it is mainly used for the evaluation of face-swapping detection algorithms.

Indeed, the human assessment study in [92] indicated that, although these two datasets demonstrate a clear improvement over the first generation, their level of realism still falls short of the desired standards. On the contrary, the two datasets distinguished in this study achieving by far the best scores are Celeb-DF [28] and DeeperForensics-1.0 (DF-1.0) [92]. This can be primarily attributed to the use of advanced, custom face-swapping algorithms developed independently in both studies. In terms of content, Celeb-DF contains in total 6229 videos that feature YouTube interviews of 59 celebrities with a large variation in terms of gender, age, ethnicity, and other aspects such as face sizes, orientations, lighting conditions, and backgrounds. On the other hand, DF-1.0 is considerably larger, featuring 60,000 videos (10,000 manipulated) sourced from 100 paid actors who were filmed in a controlled indoor environment under nine distinct lighting conditions and with eight facial expressions to ensure broad variability. The produced deepfakes were further enhanced with 35 types of perturbations, including compression, blurriness, and transmission errors to resemble real-world settings.

Beyond simply determining whether a video is manipulated or not, it is highly beneficial to localise the forgery, either spatially within individual frames or temporally across the video sequence. The ForgeryNet [27] and FFIW10K [94] datasets support these studies. ForgeryNet provides temporal annotations of the forgeries in each manipulated video, making it suitable for the deepfake temporal localisation task. It is the first large-scale benchmark that contains both face-swaps and face-reenactments with more than 200,000 videos in total. The real videos were sourced from four different audio-visual datasets (CREMA-D [95], RAVDESS [96], VoxCeleb2 [97], AVSpeech [98]), while the fake ones were produced by eight face manipulation techniques, covering a wide range of forgeries including face-swaps (FSGAN [99], Deepfacelab [100], FaceShifter [89]), face transfers (Blendface [101], MMReplacement) and face reenactments (FirstOrderMotion [102], ATVG-Net [103], Talking-head Video [104]). On the other hand, FFIW10K focuses mainly on the spatial localisation of the forgery. Unlike earlier datasets that are mostly single-face, it was designed as a multi-person dataset trying to capture the complexity of real-world videos. Each frame features between one and 15 faces but only a subset of them are actually manipulated. Videos were sourced from YouTube, and face-swapping was performed using three methods: DeepFaceLab [100], FSGAN [99], and FaceSwap [86].

One of the open challenges regarding deepfake detection is the under-representation of various ethnic groups in the existing datasets and the subsequent racial bias issues that may arise from this inconsistency. To mitigate this issue, the DF-Platter dataset, which portrays individuals of Indian ethnicity, was recently proposed [105]. It mainly focuses on advancing the fairness aspects of deepfake detection methods by providing detailed frame annotations with attributes like gender, age, skin tone, resolution, and occlusion. In terms of size, it is another large-scale benchmark containing more than 130,000 face-swaps generated using three different methods (FSGAN [99], FaceSwap [86], FaceShifter [89]). It captures diverse scenarios, including occlusions (spectacles, hats, turbans, hijabs), multiple faces with pose variations, and varying lighting conditions.

The most recent large-scale dataset is DF40 [32] that aims at bridging the gap between video and image deepfake datasets. It features 40 distinct forgery techniques for both video and image modalities. Regarding the video modality, it is undoubtedly the most comprehensive benchmark so far in terms of manipulation types variability, since it contains 23 modern deepfake techniques (10 face-swaps and 13 face-reenactments). It incorporates real data from already established datasets (FF++, Celeb-DF, UADFV) to enable cross-domain evaluation and direct comparison to previous datasets.

Last, special mention should be given to the WildDeepfake (WDF) dataset [36], which contains deepfakes collected directly from real world cases circulating on the Internet. More specifically, it contains 7314 face sequences (3805 real and 3509 deepfakes) extracted from 707 videos collected in the wild. Since the ground-truth labels were not available, the dataset was manually labelled by three human annotators. For the same reason, the manipulation techniques are also unknown. The included video content is quite diverse with events like broadcasts, films, interviews, and talks, with varying backgrounds, environments, lighting conditions, compression rates, resolutions, and video formats. As a result, this dataset is widely regarded as a key benchmark for evaluating the robustness and generalisation capabilities of deepfake detection methods in unconstrained, real-world scenarios.

Audio-Visual Deepfake Datasets

In recent years, breakthroughs in synthetic speech and voice cloning technologies have led to the emergence of highly realistic lip-sync deepfakes, which are challenging for conventional vision-only detectors to identify. Consequently, the rise of multimodal approaches that simultaneously analyse audio and video streams called for the development of corresponding audio-video datasets. One of the first benchmarks in this category is the FakeAVCeleb [31], which contains both video and audio deepfakes with accurate lip-sync. The set of real videos consists of 500 single-face interviews of equally numbered celebrities, collected from YouTube. All individuals in the dataset belong to four major ethnic backgrounds speaking the English language so as to eliminate racial bias issues. 21,000 manipulated videos were generated based on the real videos using three different types of forgeries: face-swapping [99, 106], lip-syncing [9] and voice cloning [107]. The combination of these methods resulted in three different types of deepfakes based on their modality: real-audio with fake-video, fake-audio with real-video, and fake-audio with fake-video.

The first large-scale multimodal dataset was Korean DeepFake Detection (KoDF) [33], which aimed at improving deepfake detection, particularly for Korean subjects, addressing the under-representation of Asian demographics. It comprises 237,942 video clips from 403 participants, with controlled diversity in age, sex, and location. Each participant contributed 150 clips, including scripted speech and scenario-based responses with positive, negative, and neutral emotions. The fake clips were generated using six synthesis models, including face-swapping (FaceSwap [86], DeepFaceLab [100], FSGAN[99]) and face-reenactment via video (FirstOrderMotion [102]) or audio (ATFHP [108], Wav2Lip [9]). All generated clips underwent rigorous quality assessment, ensuring realism and high quality.

The LAV-DF [109] and its successor AV-Deepfake1M [30] are currently among the most widely adopted audio-visual deepfake datasets. Although LAV-DF is considered a large-scale dataset featuring more than 100,000 videos containing 153 unique identities, the size of AV-Deepfake1M is unprecedented, making it the first million-size deepfake benchmark. It contains more than one million videos (most of them deepfakes) corresponding to 1886 h of audio-visual data from 2068 unique subjects captured in diverse background environments. Apart from this difference in size, AV-Deepfake1M explores also the latest open-source state-of-the-art methods to produce lip-synced fake videos of high quality. Such methods are VITS [110] and YourTTS [111] for audio generation and TalkLip [10] for visual content generation (lip-syncing). On the other hand, LAV-DF employs the SV2TTS tool for audio deepfake generation and Wav2Lip [9] for lip-syncing. Another key aspect of both datasets is that their manipulations occur in short segments rather than throughout the entire video making them suitable for the deepfake temporal localisation task. Their primary focus is on content-driven forgeries that alter the sentiment polarity of a video by strategically replacing words in transcripts with their antonyms, leading to significant shifts in meaning. In both cases, videos were sourced from the Vox-Celeb2 dataset [97], ensuring high-quality, English-speaking utterances.

Among the most recently introduced datasets in the field is DeepSpeak [34]. It is a smaller scale dataset of about 44 h total video duration featuring 220 diverse participants and is enhanced with the latest state-of-the-art deepfake techniques. The real videos were crowd-sourced through Prolific, where participants recorded responses to 32 prompts, including scripted, unscripted, and action-based responses. A total of 6799 deepfakes were then generated using three face-swap and two lip-sync models. Face-swap deepfakes replaced the eyebrow-to-chin and cheek-to-cheek region with a new identity using FaceFusion, with variations including default processing, CodeFormer GAN enhancement, and live-stream simulation. Lip-sync deepfakes were created using Wav2Lip [9] and VideoRetalking, aligning speech with mismatched or AI-generated voices. Additionally, audio deepfakes were synthesised using ElevenLabs' voice cloning API.

4 Challenges

The deepfake detection community has made significant progress in addressing the problem introduced by advances in generative technologies. Nevertheless, several open challenges persist, particularly in achieving robust generalisation across diverse real-world conditions and evolving manipulation techniques.

Performance Degradation in Real-World Scenarios

A significant obstacle in video deepfake detection lies in the disparity between academic datasets and real-world conditions. In most publicly available datasets, deepfake videos are typically provided and used in their raw form, directly as produced by the generative models. Furthermore, these datasets often feature uniform video resolutions, formats, and quality levels. This setup fails to accurately reflect the conditions under which deepfakes circulate in the wild—particularly on social media platforms. In real-world scenarios, videos are commonly subjected to complex post-processing pipelines once uploaded to such platforms. These processes include compression, down-scaling, re-encoding at lower bit rates, and other transformations that may obscure or eliminate telltale artifacts of manipulation. Some detection pipelines [112–114] attempt to deal with this issue by applying various data augmentation strategies—such as compression artifacts or perturbations—during training. However, since the exact processing steps used by social media platforms are proprietary and rarely disclosed, it is difficult to replicate their effects precisely. Even when an approximation is achieved, it may only be valid temporarily, as these processing pipelines are subject to frequent updates and changes. A promising direction to address this challenge involves redefining the augmentation strategies employed during training. It is crucial to expose the model to multiple versions of the same video, varying in resolution, codec suite, and compression quality, to encourage focusing of manipulation traces that remain robust under such transformations. Additionally, for multimodal approaches, incorporating augmentations that simulate realistic content overlays—such as embedded text, logos, background music, or speech—is essential. These elements frequently accompany fake videos in real-world scenarios and can interfere with detection if not properly accounted for during training.

Limited Generalisation Across Deepfake Generation Techniques

Another challenge in deepfake detection arises from the inherent limitations of current supervised learning approaches. Most detection pipelines rely on training a model using a dataset composed of both authentic and manipulated videos. While this supervised paradigm often yields near-perfect results during training and evaluation on known data, such performance can be misleading. The root of the issue lies in the tendency of machine learning models to exploit dataset-specific shortcuts to achieve their objective [115]. When the dataset includes deepfakes generated by a finite set of techniques, the model is likely to learn to identify specific artifacts associated with those particular generators, rather than acquiring a generalisable understanding of what constitutes a manipulated video. As a result, the model's performance degrades significantly on deepfakes produced by previously unseen generation methods—often dropping to the level of random guessing. This lack of generalisation is particularly problematic in real-world settings, since it is impractical to anticipate or include all possible generative approaches in the training data. Furthermore, the fast progress of deepfake generation calls for constant retraining of supervised models, incurring high costs and deployment lags. Recent research [25, 116] addresses this problem by training models on real content to improve generalisation and reduce reliance on specific manipulation artifacts. Nonetheless, as long as manipulated data remain part of the training process, even in a limited form, the risk of overfitting to generator-specific traces persists. Thus, achieving seamless generalisation remains a central challenge in the development of reliable deepfake detection systems.

Lack of Trustworthiness

Another significant limitation in current deepfake detection systems is the lack of trustworthiness. Deep neural networks in general operate as "black boxes", providing outputs without offering insights into their decision-making processes. That makes it challenging for humans to understand and subsequently trust these predictions. This opacity is particularly problematic in critical use cases such as those in journalism, legal procedures, and content moderation, where understanding the rationale behind a prediction is essential. Moreover, the lack of transparency limits the ability to understand failures, and detect potential biases, raising concerns about the ethical use of such technologies. Several recent studies on deepfake detection [117–119] address this concern by the use of generic XAI methods such as Grad-CAM [120] or LIME [121]. These approaches typically aim to highlight image regions or features that influence the most the decisions of a detector. However, the impact of this analysis is often evaluated qualitatively on a small number of examples. Overall, a lack of standardised and systematic evaluation remains for assessing the quality and reliability of visual explanations in deepfake detection models.

Fairness and Bias Concerns

An open challenge in deepfake detection is the presence of bias across different demographic groups. Studies have revealed that current deepfake detection models perform inconsistently across demographics, particularly showing higher accuracy for faces with a light skin tone compared to those with darker skin [40]. For instance, the authors in [122] evaluated three popular deepfake detectors, MesoInception4 [123], Xception [29], and Face X-Ray [53], on known datasets like FaceForensics++ [29], and found a significant variation in performance across racial and gender groups. More specifically, females of Asian or African origin were more likely to be misclassified as fake compared to male Caucasian individuals. Another analysis [124] of popular public datasets, such as Celeb-DF [28], FaceForensics++ [29], DeeperForensics-1.0 [92], and DFDC [35], revealed gender imbalance in the datasets and showed that widely used deepfake detectors tend to perform better on males than on females. These biases pose a risk, as deepfakes targeting certain groups may evade detection, highlighting the importance of scrutinising both datasets and detection models to ensure performance across diverse populations. Humans carry their own biases in detecting deepfakes, being more accurate when the demographics of the depicted person match their own, as shown in a recent paper [125]. AI-based Deepfake detection systems may reinforce these existing prejudices. The use of more balanced datasets representative of diverse demographic groups is critical for addressing bias in deepfake detection. Also, no deepfake detection dataset dedicated to assessing fairness exists to date. However, collecting and curating such datasets is often costly and labour-intensive, leading researchers to investigate algorithmic methods to mitigate biases and increase the fairness of AI models. One popular approach involves the development of fairness-aware loss functions that adjust the training process to take into account demographic imbalances. For instance, two recent works [126, 127] follow this approach to optimise models in terms of fairness. Ju et al. [126] introduces different losses that either use or ignore demographic information, while Lin et al. [127] isolates demographic-agnostic forgery features to enhance fairness. However despite these advancements, bias mitigation methodologies remain scarce in the majority of recent studies, as these continue to prioritise and report overall detection performance, often overlooking the critical issues of fairness and bias.

5 Recent Trends in Video Deepfake Detection

Recent research in video deepfake detection is moving away from the traditional paradigm of training frame-based detectors around the detected faces. Two prominent examples of this trend are Person-Of-Interest (POI) forensics [25] focusing on biometrics and outlier detection, and Discourse Modality-information Differentiation (DiMoDif) [26] focusing on local inconsistencies between visual and audio speech. Here, we briefly outline the core components of these methods and present their performance on popular deepfake detection benchmarks. Evaluation is conducted with area under ROC curve (AUC) and accuracy (ACC) for the deepfake detection task, and average precision at p (AP@{0.5,0.75,0.9,0.95}) and average recall at n (AR@{100,50,30,20,10,5}) for the temporal forgery localisation task.

Person-of-Interest Forensics

A fundamentally different paradigm is explored in [128]: training models exclusively on real videos, with the goal of detecting manipulated videos based on their anomalous behaviour. This approach proves particularly effective when the characterisation of pristine faces relies on semantic features, such as soft biometrics, enabling identity-based detection. The key observation is that each person has specific biometric and behavioural characteristics that synthetic generators can hardly reproduce faithfully. Therefore, if the person portrayed in a video does not exhibit the expected characteristics, the video can be assumed to have been generated or manipulated. With this approach, deepfake video detection can be interpreted as a POI-based attribution task. Hence, instead of asking whether the video is real or fake, we pose the question whether the depicted person is really the claimed POI.

Early work in this domain focused on specific face and head movement patterns [129–131], inconsistencies between mouth shape dynamics and spoken phonemes [132], cues related to the specific words uttered by the identity [133], or discrepancies between inner and outer facial regions [134]. However, these methods have notable limitations: they primarily rely on video-only features, occasionally supplemented by video metadata, while neglecting valuable audio cues. Additionally, they require extensive video footage (often spanning several hours) of the identity under test.

To solve this issue, we present a multi-modal Person-of-Interest (POI) deepfake detector, called POI-Forensics. This approach does not require re-training on new identities, and therefore only a few short POI videos are needed at test time, rather than full-length videos. Two dedicated networks are trained to extract audio and video features. In both cases, a contrastive learning paradigm is used to learn the moving face and audio embeddings that are most discriminative for each identity, so that features extracted from videos of the same POI are clustered together and pulled away from features of other POIs. Note that training is carried out exclusively on real talking face video (no deepfakes). Therefore, the detector does not depend on any specific manipulation method and can be expected to easily generalise to new deepfake methods. At test time, the audio and video features of the video under analysis are extracted and compared with the corresponding features extracted from a few reference videos of the POI collected in advance, as depicted in Fig. 2. Suitable similarity indexes are then computed separately for each modality and fused to perform the final decision.

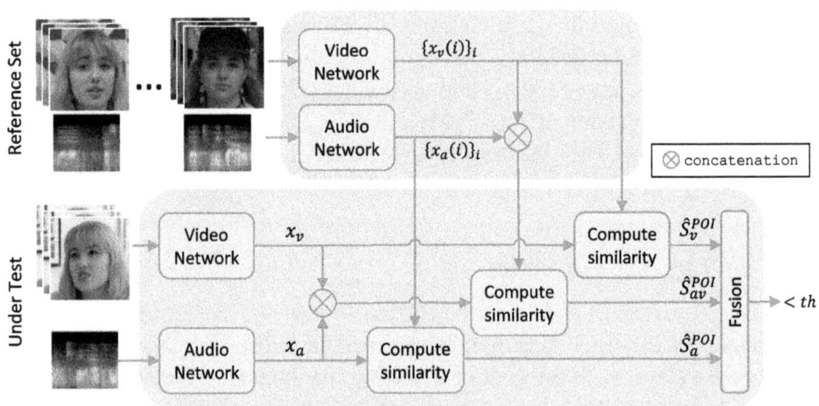

Fig. 2 POI-forensics testing scheme. Audio and video segments are processed to extract their respective embedded feature vectors. These representations are then compared against those derived from a reference set of pristine videos corresponding to the Person of Interest (POI), using three distinct similarity metrics: audio-only, video-only, and joint audio-video indices. Finally, a fusion POI similarity index is computed

We assess the proposed method against state-of-the-art methods on deepfake datasets that provide identity information, namely pDFDC [35], DeepFake-TIMIT [82], FakeAVCelebV2 [31], and KoDF [33]. Methods can be grouped in four categories, (i) frame-based: Seferbekov [48], Real Forensics [116]; (ii) temporal-based: Fully Temporal Convolution Network (FTCN) [24], LipForensics [23]; (iii) based on audio-visual information: MDS-based FD [135], Joint AV [69]; and (iv) identity-based: ICT and ICT-Ref [134], ID-Reveal [131]. To ensure a fair comparison, Seferbekov, FTCN, LipForensics and Real Forensics are all trained on the FaceForensics++ dataset which includes both face-swapping and face reenactment manipulations. MDS-based FD and Joint AV are trained on DFDC that also includes audio manipulations. ICT is trained on MS-Celeb-1M [136], ID-Reveal and POI-Forensics on VoxCeleb2 [97]. The reference set for ICT-Ref, ID-Reveal and the proposed method are built from the same set of pristine videos.

Results are reported in Table 2 in terms of AUC and Accuracy. The top part of the table refers to high-quality (HQ) data, with videos compressed using H.264 coding with factor 23 and original audio tracks. The bottom part is for low-quality (LQ) data, with videos compressed using H.264 coding with factor 40 and 25 fps, and audio tracks compressed using Advanced Audio Coding (AAC) with a sample-rate of 16K and a bit-rate of 48K. In general, all methods have much better performance in terms of AUC than Accuracy, confirming the difficulty in setting a global threshold and the need to properly calibrate each technique to make it work in practical settings. On HQ videos, POI-Forensics outperforms by 2.3% (AUC) and 1.5% (Accuracy) on average the best reference methods (Real Forensics and Seferbekov respectively). MDS-based FD, a supervised audiovisual method, obtains very good performance on pDFDC since it was trained on DFDC, but cannot generalise to other datasets. On LQ videos, the lead of POI-Forensics over all reference methods becomes very large, with an average gain of almost 10% points over the second best in terms of both AUC and Accuracy. In this challenging scenario, only identity-based approaches keep providing good performance.

Discourse Modality-Information Differentiation

Humans combine visual and auditory information for recognition, as shown by cognitive neuroscience [137]. This integration is crucial for speech perception, where the brain predicts utterances using multiple cues. When visual and auditory inputs conflict, the brain registers prediction errors that trigger increased brain activity, indicating heightened cognitive effort to resolve the discrepancies [138]. Drawing inspiration from the human brain's sophisticated multisensory processing, Discourse modality-information differentiation (DiMoDif) [26] aims to emulate the integration of visual and auditory speech-related cues to address the deepfake detection problem.

Specifically, as shown in Fig. 3, the input video $\mathfrak{v} = \{v, a\}$ is first decomposed into its video $v \in \mathbb{R}^{h \times w \times c \times f}$ and audio $a \in \mathbb{R}^s$ streams, with h and w denoting the frame's height and width, c the number of channels, f the number of video frames, and s the

Table 2 Comparison of deepfake detection methods in terms on high-quality (HQ) and low-quality (LQ) videos on pDFDC, DeepfakeTIMIT, FakeAVCelebV2, and KoDF datasets

	AUC/ACC	pDFDC	DF-TIMIT	FakeAVCel.	KoDF	AVG
High quality	Seferbekov	85.5/72.0	95.7/87.6	98.6/95.0	88.4/79.2	92.0/83.5
	FTCN	72.3/63.9	100.0/87.4	84.0/64.9	76.5/63.0	83.2/69.8
	LipForensics	68.7/60.0	98.8/78.0	97.6/83.3	92.9/56.1	89.5/69.3
	Real forensics	85.2/70.4	100.0/99.5	88.3/76.2	95.6/63.1	92.3/77.3
	MDS-based FD	98.0/93.4	56.6/55.8	64.7/61.7	65.3/63.1	71.3/68.5
	Joint AV	53.2/52.8	50.0/50.0	55.1/48.6	49.4/49.2	51.9/50.1
	ICT	77.1/70.7	87.8/77.1	68.2/63.9	62.5/58.9	73.9/67.7
	ICT-ref	87.6/79.8	100.0/94.7	71.9/64.5	79.4/60.3	84.7/74.8
	ID-reveal	91.3/80.4	99.0/92.8	70.2/60.3	87.6/63.7	87.0/74.3
	POI-forensics	95.2/86.7	99.2/85.7	94.1/86.6	89.9/81.1	**94.6/85.0**
Low quality	Seferbekov	62.6/54.0	81.8/71.4	61.7/58.5	79.6/55.9	71.4/59.9
	FTCN	51.3/50.0	78.3/58.9	37.6/42.1	68.4/58.6	58.9/52.4
	LipForensics	46.5/45.8	70.9/62.1	58.3/53.8	85.7/52.3	65.3/53.5
	Real forensics	55.8/57.1	81.1/73.6	52.9/49.2	88.0/56.3	69.4/59.0
	MDS-basedFD	95.6/90.0	52.6/52.2	61.1/58.6	64.6/62.4	68.7/65.8
	Joint AV	53.4/52.5	51.2/50.2	55.2/48.4	50.4/49.6	52.6/50.2
	ICT	72.0/66.4	84.4/74.1	66.9/61.5	61.1/59.3	71.1/65.3
	ICT-ref	82.4/73.8	100.0/96.5	71.2/59.6	78.1/62.3	82.9/73.1
	ID-reveal	86.5/73.9	93.6/75.5	70.8/58.9	85.0/63.8	84.0/68.0
	POI-forensics	93.9/82.0	98.2/76.3	94.4/88.7	89.0/81.5	**93.9/82.1**

number of audio samples. The corresponding visual $\mathbf{v} \in \mathbb{R}^{f \times d_0}$ and audio $\mathbf{a} \in \mathbb{R}^{f \times d_0}$ features are extracted by the lip-reading and speech-to-text predictors proposed in [139] and projected to d dimensions using a lightweight 1D convolutional network with two ReLU-activated layers. Trainable sequence encodings are added, and a separation token is utilised to encode modality information. Positional encoding is applied to all tokens, resulting in the tensor $\mathbf{t}$ that serves as the input to the Transformer encoder $\mathcal{T}$ [140].

Finally, d-dimensional feature pyramids are extracted for all $2 \cdot f$ visual and audio tokens, derived from each of the l layers within the Transformer encoder. Given the importance of short-term inter-modality inconsistency detection for the audio-visual

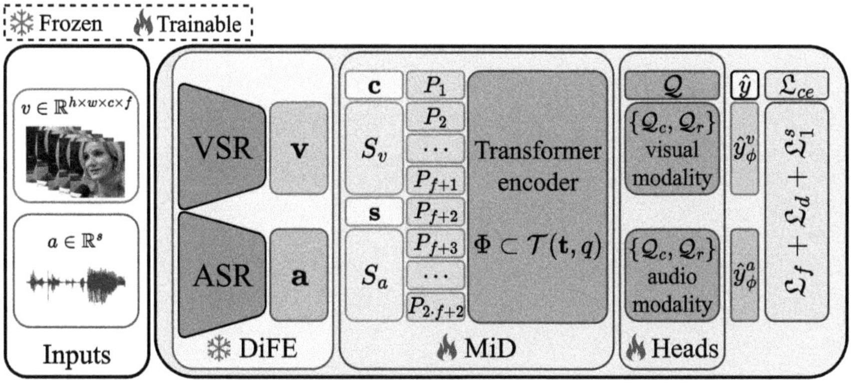

Fig. 3 The DiMoDif architecture. Video and audio streams are processed separately by corresponding speech recognition backbones. The extracted features are projected into a d-dimensional space before feeding them into a transformer encoder. The encoder's local attention mechanism, efficiently identifies short-term inconsistencies between modalities. Finally, dedicated classification and regression heads classify manipulated frames and pinpoint the deepfake's temporal boundaries per modality

deepfake detection task, a local attention mechanism is employed rather than global attention. This choice is not only preferable for capturing local inconsistencies but also significantly improves computational efficiency. Therefore, the Transformer's attention is restricted to a local window of length q surrounding each token. Finally, classification and regression heads provide the probability of frames to be deepfake manipulated along with an estimation for the onset and offset of the deepfake part within a video. For the temporal forgery localisation (TFL) task, a combination of focal loss (for classification, addressing class imbalance), DIoU loss (for regression, maximising overlap), and smooth L1 loss (for boundary distance minimisation) is considered.

Experimental results illustrated in Tables 3 and 4 demonstrate the effectiveness of the method. On LAV-DF, DiMoDif outperforms all competitive approaches with respect to AR@{100,50,20}, is second to best wrt AR@10, and third wrt AP@{0.5,0.75,0.95}. UMMAFormer [147], BA-TFD+ [146] and ActionFormer [145] exhibit similar performance, while the rest of the models have lower localisation abilities. On AV-Deepfake1M, DiMoDif outperforms all competitive approaches across all metrics exhibiting significant performance increase. The proposed method's AR is almost double compared with the second to best, while it exhibits a notable absolute increase of +35.29% and +47.88% in AP at 0.5 and 0.75, respectively.

Table 3 Temporal forgery localisation results on LAV-DF [109]

Method	Modality	AP@0.5	AP@0.75	AP@0.95	AR@100	AR@50	AR@20	AR@10
MDS [141]	$\mathcal{AV}$	12.8	1.6	0.0	37.9	36.7	34.4	32.2
AGT [142]	$\mathcal{V}$	17.9	9.4	0.1	43.2	34.2	24.6	16.7
BMN [143]	$\mathcal{V}$	24.0	7.6	0.1	53.3	41.2	31.6	26.9
BMN (I3D) [143]	$\mathcal{V}$	10.6	1.7	0.0	48.5	44.4	37.1	31.6
AVFusion [144]	$\mathcal{AV}$	65.4	23.9	0.1	63.0	59.3	54.8	52.1
ActionFormer [145]	$\mathcal{V}$	95.3	<u>90.2</u>	<u>23.7</u>	88.4	89.6	90.3	90.4
BA-TFD [109]	$\mathcal{AV}$	76.9	38.5	0.3	66.9	64.1	60.8	58.4
BA-TFD+ [146]	$\mathcal{AV}$	<u>96.3</u>	85.0	4.4	81.6	80.5	79.4	78.8
UMMAFormer [147]	$\mathcal{AV}$	**98.8**	**95.5**	**37.6**	<u>92.4</u>	<u>92.5</u>	<u>92.5</u>	**92.1**
DiMoDif	$\mathcal{AV}$	95.5	87.9	20.6	**94.2**	**93.7**	**92.7**	<u>91.4</u>

Modality denotes the model's input type with $\mathcal{V}$ being visual and $\mathcal{A}$ audio. **Bold** indicates best and <u>underline</u> second to best performance

Table 4 Temporal forgery localisation results on AV-Deepfake1M [30]

Method	Modality	AP@0.5	AP@0.75	AP@0.9	AP@0.95	AR@50	AR@30	AR@20	AR@10	AR@5
Meso4 [123]	$\mathcal{V}$	09.86	06.05	02.22	00.59	38.92	38.91	38.81	36.47	26.91
MesoInception4 [123]	$\mathcal{V}$	08.50	05.16	01.89	00.50	39.27	39.22	39.00	35.78	24.59
EfficientViT [148]	$\mathcal{V}$	14.71	02.42	00.13	00.01	27.04	26.99	26.43	23.90	20.31
TriDet+VideoMAEv2 [149, 150]	$\mathcal{V}$	21.67	05.83	00.54	00.06	20.27	20.23	20.12	19.50	18.18
TriDet+InternVideo [149, 151]	$\mathcal{V}$	29.66	09.02	00.79	00.09	24.08	24.06	23.96	23.50	22.55
ActionFormer+Video MAEv2 [145, 150]	$\mathcal{V}$	20.24	05.73	00.57	00.07	19.97	19.93	19.81	19.11	17.80
ActionFormer+ InternVideo [145, 151]	$\mathcal{V}$	36.08	12.01	01.23	00.16	27.11	27.08	27.00	26.60	25.80
BA-TFD [109]	$\mathcal{AV}$	37.37	06.34	00.19	00.02	45.55	40.37	35.95	30.66	26.82
BA-TFD+ [146]	$\mathcal{AV}$	44.42	13.64	00.48	00.03	48.86	44.51	40.37	34.67	29.88
UMMAFormer [147]	$\mathcal{AV}$	51.64	28.07	7.65	1.58	44.07	43.93	43.45	42.09	40.27
DiMoDif	$\mathcal{AV}$	**86.93**	**75.95**	**28.72**	**5.43**	**81.57**	**80.85**	**80.25**	**78.84**	**76.64**

Modality denotes the model's input type with $\mathcal{V}$ being visual and $\mathcal{A}$ audio. **Bold** indicates best and underline second to best performance

6 Conclusions

This chapter has provided a comprehensive overview of the evolving landscape of video deepfake detection. The state-of-the-art in this field has proposed several methodologies based on advanced supervised and self-supervised deep learning frameworks, leveraging biological cues, and temporal unimodal and multimodal inconsistencies, to identify subtle inconsistencies and artifacts introduced during the manipulation process. Either visual-only or audio-visual datasets are constantly introduced as the generation techniques evolve and have been crucial for training and evaluating such detectors. However, significant challenges remain, including the increasing realism of deepfakes, the difficulty of detection models in generalising across different manipulation techniques and datasets, the inherent model bias and fairness issues, and the robustness of these models against real-world conditions such as compression and adversarial attacks.

Recent trends in deepfake detection research move beyond traditional frame-based face detection approaches. One prominent direction, employs self-supervised learning to recognise audio-visual biometrics of specific individuals and subsequently identify anomalies within a given video with respect to a reference pool of real videos. Another significant trend, focuses on detecting inconsistencies between visual and auditory speech cues, leveraging the inherent human sensitivity to such mismatches.

Acknowledgements This research was supported by the European Union under the Horizon Europe vera.ai project, Grant Agreement number 101070093 and the Horizon Europe AI4Trust project, Grant Agreement number 101070093.

References

1. Pei, G., Zhang, J., Hu, M., Zhang, Z., Wang, C., Wu, Y., Zhai, G., Yang, J., Shen, C., Tao, D.: Deepfake generation and detection: a benchmark and survey. arXiv preprint arXiv:2403.17881 (2024)
2. Goodfellow, I., Pouget-Abadie, J., Mirza, M., Xu, B., Warde-Farley, D., Ozair, S., Courville, A., Bengio, Y.: Generative adversarial nets. Adv. Neural Inf. Process. Syst. **27** (2014)
3. Ho, J., Jain, A., Abbeel, P.: Denoising diffusion probabilistic models. Adv. Neural Inf. Process. Syst. **33**, 6840–6851 (2020)
4. Kingma, D.P., Welling, M., et al.: Auto-Encoding Variational Bayes (2013)
5. Mildenhall, B., Srinivasan, P.P., Tancik, M., Barron, J.T., Ramamoorthi, R., Ng, R.: Nerf: representing scenes as neural radiance fields for view synthesis. Commun. ACM **65**(1), 99–106 (2021)
6. Nirkin, Y., Masi, I., Tuan, A.T., Hassner, T., Medioni, G.: On face segmentation, face swapping, and face perception. In: 2018 13th IEEE International Conference on Automatic Face and Gesture Recognition (FG 2018), pp. 98–105. IEEE (2018)
7. Zhao, W., Rao, Y., Shi, W., Liu, Z., Zhou, J., Lu, J.: Diffswap: high-fidelity and controllable face swapping via 3d-aware masked diffusion. In: Proceedings of the IEEE/CVF Conference on Computer Vision and Pattern Recognition, pp. 8568–8577 (2023)

8. Zhu, Y., Zhao, W., Tang, Y., Rao, Y., Zhou, J., Lu, J.: Stableswap: stable face swapping in a shared and controllable latent space. IEEE Trans. Multimedia (2024)
9. Prajwal, K., Mukhopadhyay, R., Namboodiri, V.P., Jawahar, C.: A lip sync expert is all you need for speech to lip generation in the wild. In: Proceedings of the 28th ACM International Conference on Multimedia, pp. 484–492 (2020)
10. Wang, J., Qian, X., Zhang, M., Tan, R.T., Li, H.: Seeing what you said: talking face generation guided by a lip reading expert. In: IEEE/CVF Conference on Computer Vision and Pattern Recognition, pp. 14653–14662 (2023)
11. Li, W., Zhang, L., Wang, D., Zhao, B., Wang, Z., Chen, M., Zhang, B., Wang, Z., Bo, L., Li, X.: One-shot high-fidelity talking-head synthesis with deformable neural radiance field. In: IEEE/CVF Conference on Computer Vision and Pattern Recognition, pp. 17969–17978 (2023)
12. Yang, K., Chen, K., Guo, D., Zhang, S.H., Guo, Y.C., Zhang, W.: Face2face ρ: real-time high-resolution one-shot face reenactment. In: European Conference on Computer Vision, pp. 55–71. Springer (2022)
13. Ding, Z., Zhang, X., Xia, Z., Jebe, L., Tu, Z., Zhang, X.: Diffusionrig: learning personalized priors for facial appearance editing. In: IEEE/CVF Conference on Computer Vision and Pattern Recognition, pp. 12736–12746 (2023)
14. Jo, Y., Park, J.: SC-FEGAN: face editing generative adversarial network with user's sketch and color. In: IEEE/CVF International Conference on Computer Vision, pp. 1745–1753 (2019)
15. Busacca, A., Monaca, M.A.: Deepfake: creation, purpose, risks. In: Innovations and Economic and Social Changes due to Artificial Intelligence: The State of the Art, pp. 55–68. Springer (2023)
16. Fernandes, S., Raj, S., Ortiz, E., Vintila, I., Salter, M., Urosevic, G., Jha, S.: Predicting heart rate variations of deepfake videos using neural ODE. In: ICCV Workshops (2019)
17. Li, Y., Chang, M.C., Lyu, S.: In ictu oculi: exposing AI created fake videos by detecting eye blinking. In: 2018 IEEE International Workshop on Information Forensics and Security (WIFS), pp. 1–7. IEEE (2018)
18. Peng, C., Miao, Z., Liu, D., Wang, N., Hu, R., Gao, X.: Where deepfakes gaze at? Spatial–temporal gaze inconsistency analysis for video face forgery detection. IEEE Trans. Inf. Forensics Secur. **19**, 4507–4517 (2024)
19. Yang, X., Li, Y., Lyu, S.: Exposing deep fakes using inconsistent head poses. In: IEEE International Conference on Acoustics, Speech and Signal Processing (ICASSP), pp. 8261–8265 (2019)
20. Lin, Y., Song, W., Li, B., Li, Y., Ni, J., Chen, H., Li, Q.: Fake it till you make it: curricular dynamic forgery augmentations towards general deepfake detection. In: European Conference on Computer Vision, pp. 104–122. Springer (2024)
21. Shiohara, K., Yamasaki, T.: Detecting deepfakes with self-blended images. In: Proceedings of the IEEE/CVF Conference on Computer Vision and Pattern Recognition, pp. 18720–18729 (2022)
22. Yan, Z., Zhang, Y., Fan, Y., Wu, B.: UCF: uncovering common features for generalizable deepfake detection. In: Proceedings of the IEEE/CVF International Conference on Computer Vision, pp. 22412–22423 (2023)
23. Haliassos, A., Vougioukas, K., Petridis, S., Pantic, M.: Lips don't lie: a generalisable and robust approach to face forgery detection. In: IEEE Conference on Computer Vision and Pattern Recognition (2021)
24. Zheng, Y., Bao, J., Chen, D., Zeng, M., Wen, F.: Exploring temporal coherence for more general video face forgery detection. In: International Conference on Computer Vision (2021)
25. Cozzolino, D., Pianese, A., Nießner, M., Verdoliva, L.: Audio-visual person-of-interest deepfake detection. In: IEEE/CVF Conference on Computer Vision and Pattern Recognition (CVPR), pp. 943–952 (2023)
26. Koutlis, C., Papadopoulos, S.: DiMoDif: Discourse Modality-Information Differentiation for Audio-Visual Deepfake Detection and Localization. arXiv preprint arXiv:2411.10193 (2024)

27. He, Y., Gan, B., Chen, S., Zhou, Y., Yin, G., Song, L., Sheng, L., Shao, J., Liu, Z.: Forgerynet: a versatile benchmark for comprehensive forgery analysis. In: Proceedings of the IEEE/CVF Conference on Computer Vision and Pattern Recognition, pp. 4360–4369 (2021)
28. Li, Y., Yang, X., Sun, P., Qi, H., Lyu, S.: Celeb-df: a large-scale challenging dataset for deepfake forensics. In: IEEE/CVF Conference on Computer Vision and Pattern Recognition, pp. 3207–3216 (2020)
29. Rossler, A., Cozzolino, D., Verdoliva, L., Riess, C., Thies, J., Nießner, M.: Faceforensics++: learning to detect manipulated facial images. In: IEEE/CVF International Conference on Computer Vision, pp. 1–11 (2019)
30. Cai, Z., Ghosh, S., Adatia, A.P., Hayat, M., Dhall, A., Gedeon, T., Stefanov, K.: AV-Deepfake1M: a large-scale LLM-driven audio-visual deepfake dataset. In: Proceedings of the 32nd ACM International Conference on Multimedia, pp. 7414–7423 (2024)
31. Hasam, K., Shahroz, T., Minha, K., Woo, S.: FakeAVCeleb: a novel audio-video multimodal deepfake dataset. In: Thirty-fifth Conference on Neural Information Processing Systems Datasets and Benchmarks Track (Round 2) (2021)
32. Yan, Z., Yao, T., Chen, S., Zhao, Y., Fu, X., Zhu, J., Luo, D., Wang, C., Ding, S., Wu, Y., Yuan, L.: Df40: toward next-generation deepfake detection. Adv. Neural Inf. Process. Syst. **37**, 29387–29434 (2024)
33. Kwon, P., You, J., Nam, G., Park, S., Chae, G.: Kodf: a large-scale korean deepfake detection dataset. In: Proceedings of the IEEE/CVF International Conference on Computer Vision, pp. 10744–10753 (2021)
34. Barrington, S., Bohacek, M., Farid, H.: Deepspeak dataset v1. 0. arXiv preprint arXiv:2408.05366 (2024)
35. Dolhansky, B., Bitton, J., Pflaum, B., Lu, J., Howes, R., Wang, M., Ferrer, C.C.: The Deepfake Detection Challenge (DFDC) Dataset. arXiv preprint arXiv:2006.07397 (2020)
36. Zi, B., Chang, M., Chen, J., Ma, X., Jiang, Y.G.: Wilddeepfake: a challenging real-world dataset for deepfake detection. In: Proceedings of the 28th ACM International Conference on Multimedia, pp. 2382–2390 (2020)
37. Wang, C., Deng, W.: Representative forgery mining for fake face detection. In: IEEE/CVF Conference on Computer Vision and Pattern Recognition (CVPR) (2021)
38. John-Mathews, J.M.: Some critical and ethical perspectives on the empirical turn of AI interpretability. Technol. Forecast. Soc. Change **174**, 121209 (2022)
39. Deeks, A.: The judicial demand for explainable artificial intelligence. Columbia Law Rev. **119**(7), 1829–1850 (2019)
40. Xu, Y., Terhörst, P., Pedersen, M., Raja, K.: Analyzing fairness in deepfake detection with massively annotated databases. IEEE Trans. Technol. Soc. **5**(1), 93–106 (2024)
41. ad Beibei Liu, M.L., Hu, Y., Wang, Y.: Exposing deepfake videos by tracking eye movements. In: IEEE International Conference on Pattern Recognition (2021)
42. Li, Y., Lyu, S.: Exposing deepfake videos by detecting face warping artifacts. In: IEEE CVPR Workshops (2019)
43. Qi, H., Guo, Q., Juefei-Xu, F., Xie, X., Ma, L., Feng, W., Liu, Y., Zhao, J.: DeepRhythm: exposing deepfakes with attentional visual heartbeat rhythms. In: ACM International Conference on Multimedia, pp. 4318–4327 (2020)
44. Ciftci, U.A., Demir, I., Yin, L.: Fakecatcher: detection of synthetic portrait videos using biological signals. IEEE Transactions on Pattern Analysis and Machine Intelligence, in press (2020)
45. Cheng, J., Yan, Z., Zhang, Y., Hao, L., Ai, J., Zou, Q., Li, C., Wang, Z.: Stacking brick by brick: aligned feature isolation for incremental face forgery detection. In: IEEE/CVF Conference on Computer Vision and Pattern Recognition (CVPR) (2025)
46. Khan, S., Dai, H.: Video transformer for deepfake detection with incremental learning. In: ACM International Conference on Multimedia (2021)
47. Li, C., Huang, Z., Paudel, D.P., Wang, Y., Shahbazi, M., Hong, X., Gool, L.V.: A continual deepfake detection benchmark: dataset, methods, and essentials. In: IEEE/CVF Winter Conference on Applications of Computer Vision (WACV), pp. 1339–1349 (2023)

48. Das, S., Seferbekov, S., Datta, A., Islam, M.S., Amin, M.R.: Towards solving the DeepFake problem: an analysis on improving DeepFake detection using dynamic face augmentation. In: ICCV Workshops (2021)
49. Bonettini, N., Cannas, E., Mandelli, S., Bondi, L., Bestagini, P., Tubaro, S.: Video face manipulation detection through ensemble of CNNs. In: International Conference on Pattern Recognition (ICPR) (2020)
50. Li, J., Xie, H., Li, J., Wang, Z., Zhang, Y.: Frequency-aware discriminative feature learning supervised by single-center loss for face forgery detection. In: IEEE/CVF Conference on Computer Vision and Pattern Recognition (CVPR) (2021)
51. Liu, H., Li, X., Zhou, W., Chen, Y., He, Y., Xue, H., Zhang, W., Yu, N.: Spatial-phase shallow learning: rethinking face forgery detection in frequency domain. In: IEEE/CVF Conference on Computer Vision and Pattern Recognition (CVPR) (2021)
52. Luo, Y., Zhang, Y., Yan, J., Liu, W.: Generalizing face forgery detection with high-frequency features. In: IEEE/CVF conference on Computer Vision and Pattern Recognition (CVPR) (2021)
53. Li, L., Bao, J., Zhang, T., Yang, H., Chen, D., Wen, F., Guo, B.: Face X-ray for more general face forgery detection. In: IEEE/CVF Conference on Computer Vision and Pattern Recognition (CVPR) (2020)
54. Dang, H., Liu, F., Stehouwer, J., Liu, X., Jain, A.: On the detection of digital face manipulation. In: IEEE/CVF Conference on Computer Vision and Pattern Recognition (CVPR) (2020)
55. Zhao, H., Zhou, W., Chen, D., Wei, T., Zhang, W., Yu, N.: Multi-attentional deepfake detection. In: IEEE/CVF Conference on Computer Vision and Pattern Recognition (CVPR) (2021)
56. Zhao, T., Xu, X., Xu, M., Ding, H., Xiong, Y., Xia, W.: Learning self-consistency for deepfake detection. In: IEEE/CVF International Conference on Computer Vision (ICCV), pp. 15023–15033 (2021)
57. Zhu, X., Wang, H., Fei, H., Lei, Z., Li, S.: Face forgery detection by 3d decomposition. In: IEEE/CVF Conference on Computer Vision and Pattern Recognition (CVPR) (2021)
58. Hussain, S., Neekhara, P., Jere, M., Koushanfar, F., McAuley, J.: Adversarial deepfakes: evaluating vulnerability of deepfake detectors to adversarial examples. In: IEEE/CVF Winter Conference on Applications of Computer Vision (WACV) (2021)
59. Neekhara, P., Dolhansky, B., Bitton, J., Ferrer, C.C.: Adversarial threats to deepfake detection: a practical perspective. In: IEEE/CVF Conference on Computer Vision and Pattern Recognition (CVPR) (2021)
60. Güera, D., Delp, E.J.: Deepfake video detection using recurrent neural networks. In: IEEE International Conference on Advanced Video and Signal Based Surveillance (AVSS), pp. 1–6 (2018)
61. Amerini, I., Galteri, L., Caldelli, R., Del Bimbo, A.: Deepfake video detection through optical flow based CNN. In: IEEE/CVF Conference on Computer Vision and Pattern Recognition Workshops (CVPRw) (2019)
62. Saikia, P., Dholaria, D., Yadav, P., Patel, V., Roy, M.: A hybrid CNN-LSTM model for video deepfake detection by leveraging optical flow features. In: International Joint Conference on Neural Networks (IJCNN), pp. 1–7 (2022)
63. Gu, Z., Yao, T., Chen, Y., Ding, S., Ma, L.: Hierarchical contrastive inconsistency learning for deepfake video detection. In: European Conference on Computer Vision, pp. 596–613 (2022)
64. Yan, Z., Zhao, Y., Chen, S., Guo, M., Fu, X., Yao, T., Ding, S., Yuan, L.: Generalizing deepfake video detection with plug-and-play: video-level blending and spatiotemporal adapter tuning. In: IEEE/CVF Conference on Computer Vision and Pattern Recognition (CVPR) (2025)
65. Cui, X., Li, Y., Luo, A., Zhou, J., Dong, J.: Forensics adapter: adapting CLIP for generalizable face forgery detection. In: IEEE/CVF Conference on Computer Vision and Pattern Recognition (CVPR) (2025)
66. Han, Y.H., Huang, T.M., Lo, S.T., Huang, P.H., Hua, K.L., Chen, J.C.: Towards more general video-based deepfake detection through facial feature guided adaptation for foundation model. In: IEEE/CVF Conference on Computer Vision and Pattern Recognition (CVPR) (2025)

67. Korshunov, P., Halstead, M., Castan, D., Graciarena, M., McLaren, M., Burns, B., Lawson, A., Marcel, S.: Tampered speaker inconsistency detection with phonetically aware audio-visual features. In: International Conference on Machine Learning Workshops (ICMLw) (2019)
68. Korshunov, P., Marcel, S.: Speaker inconsistency detection in tampered video. In: European Signal Processing Conference (EUSIPCO) (2018)
69. Zhou, Y., Lim, S.N.: Joint audio-visual deepfake detection. In: International Conference on Computer Vision (2021)
70. Liu, W., She, T., Liu, J., Li, B., Yao, D., Wang, R.: Lips are lying: spotting the temporal inconsistency between audio and visual in lip-syncing deepfakes. Adv. Neural Inf. Process. Syst. **37**, 91131–91155 (2024)
71. Mittal, T., Bhattacharya, U., Chandra, R., Bera, A., Manocha, D.: Emotions don't lie: an audio-visual deepfake detection method using affective cues. In: ACM International Conference on Multimedia (2020)
72. Hosler, B., Salvi, D., Murray, A., Antonacci, F., Bestagini, P., Tubaro, S., Stamm, M.C.: Do deepfakes feel emotions? A semantic approach to detecting deepfakes via emotional inconsistencies. In: IEEE/CVF Conference on Computer Vision and Pattern Recognition (CVPR) Workshops, pp. 1013–1022 (2021)
73. Yang, W., Zhou, X., Chen, Z., Guo, B., Ba, Z., Xia, Z., Cao, X., Ren, K.: Avoid-df: audio-visual joint learning for detecting deepfake. IEEE Trans. Inf. Forensics Secur. **18**, 2015–2019 (2023)
74. Smeu, S., Boldisor, D.A., Oneata, D., Oneata, E.: Circumventing shortcuts in audio-visual deepfake detection datasets with unsupervised learning. IEEE/CVF Conference on Computer Vision and Pattern Recognition (CVPR) (2025)
75. Thakral, K., Ranjan, R., Singh, A., Jain, A., Singh, R., Vatsa, M.: ILLUSION: unveiling truth with a comprehensive multi-modal, multi-lingual deepfake dataset. In: International Conference on Learning Representations (ICLR) (2025)
76. Chen, L., Zhang, Y., Song, Y., Liu, L., Wang, J.: Self-supervised learning of adversarial example: towards good generalizations for deepfake detection. In: IEEE/CVF Conference on Computer Vision and Pattern Recognition (CVPR), pp. 18710–18719 (2022)
77. Cai, Z., Ghosh, S., Stefanov, K., Dhall, A., Cai, J., Rezatofighi, H., Haffari, R., Hayat, M.: MARLIN: masked autoencoder for facial video representation LearnINg. In: IEEE/CVF Conference on Computer Vision and Pattern Recognition (CVPR), pp. 1493–1504 (2023)
78. Feng, C., Chen, Z., Owens, A.: Self-supervised video forensics by audio-visual anomaly detection. In: IEEE/CVF Conference on Computer Vision and Pattern Recognition (CVPR), pp. 10491–10503 (2023)
79. Liang, Y., Yu, M., Li, G., Jiang, J., Li, B., Yu, F., Zhang, N., Meng, X., Huang, W.: SpeechForensics: audio-visual speech representation learning for face forgery detection. In: A. Globerson, L. Mackey, D. Belgrave, A. Fan, U. Paquet, J. Tomczak, C. Zhang (eds.) Advances in Neural Information Processing Systems (NeurIPS), vol. 37, pp. 86124–86144 (2024)
80. Oorloff, T., Koppisetti, S., Bonettini, N., Solanki, D., Colman, B., Yacoob, Y., Shahriyari, A., Bharaj, G.: AVFF: audio-visual feature fusion for video deepfake detection. In: IEEE/CVF Conference on Computer Vision and Pattern Recognition (CVPR), pp. 27102–27112 (2024)
81. Unknown: Fakeapp. https://www.malavida.com/en/soft/fakeapp
82. Korshunov, P., Marcel, S.: Vulnerability assessment and detection of deepfake videos. In: 2019 International Conference on Biometrics (ICB), pp. 1–6. IEEE (2019)
83. Shao-An Lu: faceswap-gan. https://github.com/shaoanlu/faceswap-GAN
84. Sanderson, C., Lovell, B.C.: Multi-region probabilistic histograms for robust and scalable identity inference. In: International Conference on Biometrics, pp. 199–208. Springer (2009)
85. Unknown: Deepfakes Faceswap. https://github.com/deepfakes/faceswap
86. Marek Kowalski: Faceswap. https://github.com/MarekKowalski/FaceSwap
87. Thies, J., Zollhofer, M., Stamminger, M., Theobalt, C., Nießner, M.: Face2face: real-time face capture and reenactment of RGB videos. In: Proceedings of the IEEE Conference on Computer Vision and Pattern Recognition, pp. 2387–2395 (2016)

88. Thies, J., Zollhöfer, M., Nießner, M.: Deferred neural rendering: image synthesis using neural textures. ACM Trans. Graph. (TOG) **38**(4), 1–12 (2019)
89. Li, L., Bao, J., Yang, H., Chen, D., Wen, F.: Faceshifter: Towards High Fidelity and Occlusion Aware Face Swapping. arXiv preprint arXiv:1912.13457 (2019)
90. Altuncu, E., Franqueira, V.N., Li, S.: Deepfake: definitions, performance metrics and standards, datasets, and a meta-review. Front. Big Data **7**, 1400024 (2024)
91. Tolosana, R., Vera-Rodriguez, R., Fierrez, J., Morales, A., Ortega-Garcia, J.: Deepfakes and beyond: a survey of face manipulation and fake detection. Inf. Fusion **64**, 131–148 (2020)
92. Jiang, L., Li, R., Wu, W., Qian, C., Loy, C.C.: Deeperforensics-1.0: a large-scale dataset for real-world face forgery detection. In: Proceedings of the IEEE/CVF Conference on Computer Vision and Pattern Recognition, pp. 2889–2898 (2020)
93. Google: Deepfake Detection (DFD) Dataset. https://research.google/blog/contributing-data-to-deepfake-detection-research (2019)
94. Zhou, T., Wang, W., Liang, Z., Shen, J.: Face forensics in the wild. In: Proceedings of the IEEE/CVF Conference on Computer Vision and Pattern Recognition, pp. 5778–5788 (2021)
95. Cao, H., Cooper, D.G., Keutmann, M.K., Gur, R.C., Nenkova, A., Verma, R.: Crema-D: crowd-sourced emotional multimodal actors dataset. IEEE Trans. Affect. Comput. **5**(4), 377–390 (2014)
96. Livingstone, S.R., Russo, F.A.: The Ryerson audio-visual database of emotional speech and song (RAVDESS): a dynamic, multimodal set of facial and vocal expressions in north American English. PloS One **13**(5), e0196391 (2018)
97. Chung, J.S., Nagrani, A., Zisserman, A.: VoxCeleb2: deep speaker recognition. In: Interspeech (2018)
98. Ephrat, A., Mosseri, I., Lang, O., Dekel, T., Wilson, K., Hassidim, A., Freeman, W.T., Rubinstein, M.: Looking to Listen at the Cocktail Party: A Speaker-Independent Audio-Visual Model for Speech Separation. arXiv preprint arXiv:1804.03619 (2018)
99. Nirkin, Y., Keller, Y., Hassner, T.: Fsgan: subject agnostic face swapping and reenactment. In: Proceedings of the IEEE/CVF International Conference on Computer Vision, pp. 7184–7193 (2019)
100. Liu, K., Perov, I., Gao, D., Chervoniy, N., Zhou, W., Zhang, W.: Deepfacelab: integrated, flexible and extensible face-swapping framework. Pattern Recognit. **141**, 109628 (2023)
101. Shiohara, K., Yang, X., Taketomi, T.: Blendface: re-designing identity encoders for face-swapping. In: Proceedings of the IEEE/CVF International Conference on Computer Vision, pp. 7634–7644 (2023)
102. Siarohin, A., Lathuilière, S., Tulyakov, S., Ricci, E., Sebe, N.: First order motion model for image animation. Adv. Neural Inf. Process. Syst. **32** (2019)
103. Chen, L., Maddox, R.K., Duan, Z., Xu, C.: Hierarchical cross-modal talking face generation with dynamic pixel-wise loss. In: Proceedings of the IEEE/CVF Conference on Computer Vision and Pattern Recognition, pp. 7832–7841 (2019)
104. Fried, O., Tewari, A., Zollhöfer, M., Finkelstein, A., Shechtman, E., Goldman, D.B., Genova, K., Jin, Z., Theobalt, C., Agrawala, M.: Text-based editing of talking-head video. ACM Trans. Graph. (TOG) **38**(4), 1–14 (2019)
105. Narayan, K., Agarwal, H., Thakral, K., Mittal, S., Vatsa, M., Singh, R.: Df-platter: multi-face heterogeneous deepfake dataset. In: Proceedings of the IEEE/CVF Conference on Computer Vision and Pattern Recognition, pp. 9739–9748 (2023)
106. Korshunova, I., Shi, W., Dambre, J., Theis, L.: Fast face-swap using convolutional neural networks. In: Proceedings of the IEEE International Conference on Computer Vision, pp. 3677–3685 (2017)
107. Jia, Y., Zhang, Y., Weiss, R., Wang, Q., Shen, J., Ren, F., Nguyen, P., Pang, R., Lopez Moreno, I., Wu, Y., et al.: Transfer learning from speaker verification to multispeaker text-to-speech synthesis. Adv. Neural Inf. Process. Syst. **31** (2018)
108. Yi, R., Ye, Z., Zhang, J., Bao, H., Liu, Y.J.: Audio-driven talking face video generation with learning-based personalized head pose. arXiv preprint arXiv:2002.10137 (2020)

109. Cai, Z., Stefanov, K., Dhall, A., Hayat, M.: Do you really mean that? Content driven audio-visual deepfake dataset and multimodal method for temporal forgery localization. In: IEEE International Conference on Digital Image Computing: Techniques and Applications (DICTA), pp. 1–10 (2022)
110. Kim, J., Kong, J., Son, J.: Conditional variational autoencoder with adversarial learning for end-to-end text-to-speech. In: International Conference on Machine Learning, pp. 5530–5540. PMLR (2021)
111. Casanova, E., Weber, J., Shulby, C.D., Junior, A.C., Gölge, E., Ponti, M.A.: Yourtts: towards zero-shot multi-speaker tts and zero-shot voice conversion for everyone. In: International Conference on Machine Learning, pp. 2709–2720. PMLR (2022)
112. Stanciu, D.C., Ionescu, B.: Autoencoder-based data augmentation for deepfake detection. In: Proceedings of the 2nd ACM International Workshop on Multimedia AI against Disinformation, pp. 19–27 (2023)
113. Wang, C., Deng, W.: Representative forgery mining for fake face detection. In: Proceedings of the IEEE/CVF Conference on Computer Vision and Pattern Recognition (CVPR), pp. 14923–14932 (2021)
114. Wang, Z., Bao, J., Zhou, W., Wang, W., Li, H.: Altfreezing for more general video face forgery detection. In: Proceedings of the IEEE/CVF Conference on Computer Vision and Pattern Recognition, pp. 4129–4138 (2023)
115. Geirhos, R., Jacobsen, J.H., Michaelis, C., Zemel, R., Brendel, W., Bethge, M., Wichmann, F.A.: Shortcut learning in deep neural networks. Nat. Mach. Intell. **2**, 665–673 (2020)
116. Haliassos, A., Mira, R., Petridis, S., Pantic, M.: Leveraging real talking faces via self-supervision for robust forgery detection. In: IEEE/CVF Conference on Computer Vision and Pattern Recognition (CVPR), pp. 14950–14962 (2022)
117. Malolan, B., Parekh, A., Kazi, F.: Explainable deep-fake detection using visual interpretability methods. In: 2020 3rd International Conference on Information and Computer Technologies (ICICT), pp. 289–293. IEEE (2020)
118. Silva, S.H., Bethany, M., Votto, A.M., Scarff, I.H., Beebe, N., Najafirad, P.: Deepfake forensics analysis: an explainable hierarchical ensemble of weakly supervised models. Forensic Sci. Inter.: Synergy **4**, 100217 (2022)
119. Xu, Y., Raja, K., Pedersen, M.: Supervised contrastive learning for generalizable and explainable deepfakes detection. In: Proceedings of the IEEE/CVF Winter Conference on Applications of Computer Vision (WACV) Workshops, pp. 379–389 (2022)
120. Chattopadhay, A., Sarkar, A., Howlader, P., Balasubramanian, V.N.: Grad-cam++: generalized gradient-based visual explanations for deep convolutional networks. In: 2018 IEEE Winter Conference on Applications of Computer Vision (WACV), pp. 839–847. IEEE (2018)
121. Ribeiro, M.T., Singh, S., Guestrin, C.: Why should i trust you? Explaining the predictions of any classifier. In: Proceedings of the 22nd ACM SIGKDD International Conference on Knowledge Discovery and Data Mining, pp. 1135–1144 (2016)
122. Trinh, L., Liu, Y.: An examination of fairness of AI models for deepfake detection. arXiv preprint arXiv:2105.00558 (2D021)
123. Afchar, D., Nozick, V., Yamagishi, J., Echizen, I.: Mesonet: a compact facial video forgery detection network. In: IEEE International Workshop on Information Forensics and Security (WIFS), pp. 1–7. IEEE (2018)
124. Nadimpalli, A.V., Rattani, A.: Gbdf: gender balanced deepfake dataset towards fair deepfake detection. In: International Conference on Pattern Recognition, pp. 320–337. Springer (2022)
125. Lovato, J., St-Onge, J., Harp, R., Salazar Lopez, G., Rogers, S.P., Haq, I.U., Hébert-Dufresne, L., Onaolapo, J.: Diverse misinformation: impacts of human biases on detection of deepfakes on networks. NPJ Complex. **1**(1), 5 (2024)
126. Ju, Y., Hu, S., Jia, S., Chen, G.H., Lyu, S.: Improving fairness in deepfake detection. In: Proceedings of the IEEE/CVF Winter Conference on Applications of Computer Vision, pp. 4655–4665 (2024)
127. Lin, L., He, X., Ju, Y., Wang, X., Ding, F., Hu, S.: Preserving fairness generalization in deepfake detection. In: Proceedings of the IEEE/CVF Conference on Computer Vision and Pattern Recognition, pp. 16815–16825 (2024)

128. Cozzolino, D., Poggi, G., Verdoliva, L.: Extracting camera-based fingerprints for video forensics. In: CVPR Workshops (2019)
129. Agarwal, S., Farid, H., El-Gaaly, T., Lim, S.N.: Detecting deep-fake videos from appearance and behavior. In: IEEE Workshop on Information Forensics and Security (2020)
130. Agarwal, S., Farid, H., Gu, Y., He, M., Nagano, K., Li, H.: Protecting world leaders against deep fakes. In: CVPR Workshops (2019)
131. Cozzolino, D., Rössler, A., Thies, J., Nießner, M., Verdoliva, L.: ID-reveal: identity-aware DeepFake video detection. In: International Conference on Computer Vision (2021)
132. Agarwal, S., Farid, H., Fried, O., Agrawala, M.: Detecting deep-fake videos from phoneme-viseme mismatches. In: CVPR Workshops (2020)
133. Agarwal, S., Hu, L., Ng, E., Darrell, T., Li, H., Rohrbach, A.: Watch those words: video falsification detection using word-conditioned facial motion. In: IEEE Winter Conference on Applications of Computer Vision (2023)
134. Dong, X., Bao, J., Chen, D., Zhang, T., Zhang, W., Yu, N., Chen, D., Wen, F., Guo, B.: Protecting celebrities from deepfake with identity consistency transformer. In: IEEE Conference on Computer Vision and Pattern Recognition (2022)
135. Chugh, K., Gupta, P., Dhall, A., Subramanian, R.: Not made for each other- audio-visual dissonance-based deepfake detection and localization. In: ACM International Conference on Multimedia (2020)
136. Guo, Y., Zhang, L., Hu, Y., He, X., Gao, J.: MS-Celeb-1M: a dataset and benchmark for large-scale face recognition. In: European Conference on Computer Vision (2016)
137. Stacey, P.C., Kitterick, P.T., Morris, S.D., Sumner, C.J.: The contribution of visual information to the perception of speech in noise with and without informative temporal fine structure. Hear. Res. **336**, 17–28 (2016)
138. Arnal, L.H., Wyart, V., Giraud, A.L.: Transitions in neural oscillations reflect prediction errors generated in audiovisual speech. Nat. Neurosci. **14**(6), 797–801 (2011)
139. Ma, P., Petridis, S., Pantic, M.: Visual speech recognition for multiple languages in the wild. Nat. Mach. Intell. **4**(11), 930–939 (2022)
140. Vaswani, A.: Attention is all you need. Adv. Neural Inf. Process. Syst. (2017)
141. Chugh, K., Gupta, P., Dhall, A., Subramanian, R.: Not made for each other-audio-visual dissonance-based deepfake detection and localization. In: ACM International Conference on Multimedia, pp. 439–447 (2020)
142. Nawhal, M., Mori, G.: Activity graph transformer for temporal action localization. arXiv preprint arXiv:2101.08540 (2021)
143. Lin, T., Liu, X., Li, X., Ding, E., Wen, S.: BMN: boundary-matching network for temporal action proposal generation. In: IEEE/CVF International Conference on Computer Vision (ICCV), pp. 3889–3898 (2019)
144. Bagchi, A., Mahmood, J., Fernandes, D., Sarvadevabhatla, R.K.: Hear Me Out: Fusional Approaches for Audio Augmented Temporal Action Localization. arXiv preprint arXiv:2106.14118 (2021)
145. Zhang, C.L., Wu, J., Li, Y.: Actionformer: localizing moments of actions with transformers. In: European Conference on Computer Vision (ECCV), pp. 492–510. Springer (2022)
146. Cai, Z., Ghosh, S., Dhall, A., Gedeon, T., Stefanov, K., Hayat, M.: Glitch in the matrix: a large scale benchmark for content driven audio-visual forgery detection and localization. Comput. Vis. Image Underst. **236**, 103818 (2023)
147. Zhang, R., Wang, H., Du, M., Liu, H., Zhou, Y., Zeng, Q.: Ummaformer: a universal multimodal-adaptive transformer framework for temporal forgery localization. In: ACM International Conference on Multimedia, pp. 8749–8759 (2023)
148. Coccomini, D.A., Messina, N., Gennaro, C., Falchi, F.: Combining EfficientNet and vision transformers for video deepfake detection. In: International Conference on Image Analysis and Processing, pp. 219–229. Springer (2022)
149. Shi, D., Zhong, Y., Cao, Q., Ma, L., Li, J., Tao, D.: Tridet: temporal action detection with relative boundary modeling. In: IEEE/CVF Conference on Computer Vision and Pattern Recognition (CVPR), pp. 18857–18866 (2023)

150. Wang, L., Huang, B., Zhao, Z., Tong, Z., He, Y., Wang, Y., Wang, Y., Qiao, Y.: Videomae v2: scaling video masked autoencoders with dual masking. In: Proceedings of the IEEE/CVF Conference on Computer Vision and Pattern Recognition, pp. 14549–14560 (2023)
151. Wang, Y., Li, K., Li, Y., He, Y., Huang, B., Zhao, Z., Zhang, H., Xu, J., Liu, Y., Wang, Z., et al.: Internvideo: general video foundation models via generative and discriminative learning. arXiv preprint arXiv:2212.03191 (2022)

AI-Based Tools for Multimodal Disinformation Detection and Analysis

AI-Based Multilingual Credibility Assessment

Olesya Razuvayevskaya, Ivan Srba, Rosanna Milner, and Kalina Bontcheva

1 Credibility Assessment as a Complement to False Information Research

Despite a rising popularity and a corresponding shift of social media platforms towards a short format of multimedia posts (e.g., TikTok or YouTube Shorts), the textual modality still remains largely widespread not only on social media platforms, but also as a means to spread various forms of *false information* (either disinformation or misinformation). The majority of existing solutions to *false information detection*, commonly denoted also as *fake news detection* [1–3], attempts to make a single-label prediction about *content veracity*—either binary (a content is spreading / is not spreading false information) or multiclass (e.g., utilising rating scales used by some fact-checking organisations, such as true, mostly true, mixed, mostly false, false).

Despite indisputable effort and positive outcomes, current solutions for false information detection have been recognised to lack the sufficient accuracy on out-of-distribution data, generalisability and explainability [4–6]. These drawbacks partially relate to a high-level and a single-label (typically binary) nature of this task, which may be too simplified, especially considering a very complex and ambiguous nature of false information spreading in a very dynamic online environment.

O. Razuvayevskaya (✉) · R. Milner · K. Bontcheva
University of Sheffield (USFD), Sheffield, UK
e-mail: o.razuvayevskaya@sheffield.ac.uk

R. Milner
e-mail: rosanna.milner@sheffield.ac.uk

K. Bontcheva
e-mail: k.bontcheva@sheffield.ac.uk

I. Srba
Kempelen Institute of Intelligent Technologies (KInIT), Bratislava, Slovakia
e-mail: ivan.srba@kinit.sk

S. Papadopoulos et al. (eds.), *Countering Disinformation in the Era of Generative AI*,
https://doi.org/10.1007/978-3-032-11782-3_9

Credibility [7] provides an information that is complementary to content veracity. A credible-looking false content may result in a significantly larger negative impact on the general public compared to a false content that can be easily discerned by end users as low credible. Credibility is a multidimensional concept which lacks a universally accepted definition. Different disciplines approach it from varied perspectives and it is often described using related terms such as believability, trustworthiness, and reliability of content or its source [8, 9].

Credibility assessment is a process of determining the credibility level of a target entity. Within the credibility assessment process, a *credibility signal* is any piece of information used as an evidence [7]. This may include measurable features, metadata, or target entity details. Typical examples of textual credibility signals include factuality, subjectivity, bias, persuasion techniques or logical fallacies present in the content, or the detection of machine-generated text.

The two-step approach of credibility assessment—based on detecting and aggregating credibility signals—has several significant advantages. Such credibility signals are flexible, widely-applicable, as well as naturally support better explainability and semi-automatic human-centred AI approaches [10]. Despite these clear advantages, the existing research on automatic credibility assessment and detection of credibility signals can be characterised as highly-fragmented and deserving a larger attention from researchers as well as practitioners [10]. Furthermore, for most credibility signals, existing state-of-the-art methods do not achieve an expected accuracy and generalisability for practical deployment and thus their further improvement introduces many interesting challenges (e.g., a wider adoption of LLMs).

To advance research in area of credibility assessment, within the *vera.ai* project, we contributed with novel methods for *automatic detection of textual credibility signals*. Considering a wide range of stakeholders interested in using such detection (especially media professionals, such as fact-checkers or journalists), we have put a strong focus on *multilinguality* and *practical deployment*, contributing to a larger potential and impact on everyday tasks performed by end users.

Within this chapter, we advocate for strengthening research on credibility assessment and automatic detection of credibility signals. At first, we provide an overview of the current state of the art on credibility signals in written text (Sect. 2). Consequently, we describe three selected examples, showing how we utilise various Natural Language Processing (NLP) approaches, particularly multilingual language models, to automatically detect three categories of credibility signals, namely: (1) framing, (2) genre, and (3) persuasion techniques (Sect. 3). To demonstrate and evaluate the value of automatically-detected credibility signals and credibility assessment in practice, we describe two use cases—the first one providing credibility signals directly to end users by their integration into the *Verification plugin* enhanced within vera.ai project; and the second one utilising credibility signals as features for a classification model performing misinformation detection (Sect. 4). Finally, by building on our own research results achieved within the vera.ai project [10–15] and taking into account the evaluation with end users, we highlight avenues for further impactful research in this area (Sect. 5).

2 Credibility Assessment and Credibility Signals in Written Text

While the credibility of target entity can be assessed directly without any intermediate steps, more common approach is to analyse the target entity for the presence of individual *credibility signals* (serving as a source of evidence) and such signals to aggregate into the final credibility score.

In general, the process of credibility assessment can be done manually or automatically by a *credibility assessment algorithm.* It is typically framed either as: (1) an ordinal classification task (e.g., high/low credibility); or (2) a regression/scoring task (e.g., a credibility score between 0 an 100). In both cases, no standard scales exist.

Credibility signals, as a core element of credibility assessment process, can be broadly classified into content-based and context-based categories [16–18]. Content-based signals stem from the content itself, such as partisanship, emotional appeal, or persuasion techniques. Context-based signals, also known as provenance or meta-information, consider external factors like user statistics, domain reputation, and social engagement metrics [19].

Despite numerous efforts, there is still no standardised categorisation of credibility signals, leading many studies to rely on varied, custom or ad-hoc taxonomies. For example, [20] categorised signals into four groups: (1) message and linguistic features, (2) sources and intentions, (3) structural elements, and (4) network attributes. The Credibility Coalition [18] compiled around 100 signals focused on web page credibility, later refined into 12 categories, including reader behaviour and revenue models. In 2017, it merged into the W3C Credible Web Community Group, which crowdsourced over 200 credibility signals, categorising them by entity type (e.g., claim, text, image, website, creator). Though informal and not yet standardised, this list has influenced various research works [21, 22].

Credibility signals also differ in polarity—some indicate credibility (e.g., citing a source or an authority), while others suggest non-credibility (e.g., emotional or manipulative style). This distinction is crucial when interpreting signals, whether manually or via credibility assessment algorithms [12, 22].

Detection of credibility signals in the (textual) content may require various levels of expertise and resources. Some signals may be less challenging (for a human as well as for an AI-powered method) to assess, e.g., characterising an article title as clickbait. Others may be more challenging or time-consuming, especially when they require reading the whole text and its deeper analysis, such as checking the subjectivity of the text, verifying whether the claims made in the text have been already fact-checked or evaluating the presence of persuasion techniques.

Based on a systematic and extensive literature survey of 175 research papers [10], we identified two streams of ongoing research: (1) first, there are works directly addressing the credibility assessment process, (2) second, there are works automatically detecting one or several (related) categories of credibility signals. While the first stream commonly utilises the terminology of *credibility* and *credibility assessment*,

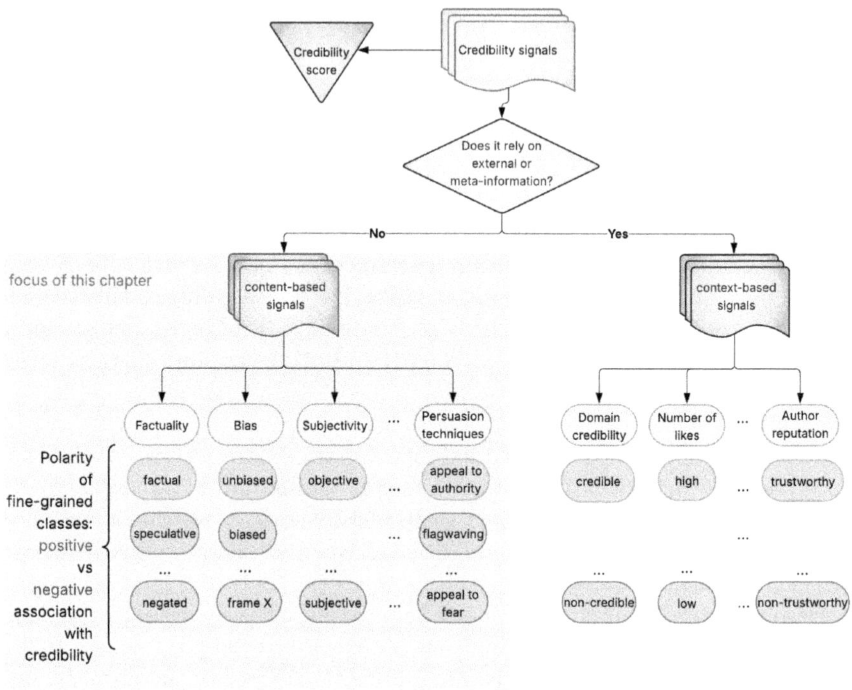

Fig. 1 Summary of the research on credibility signal assessment. Green and red colours indicate the polarity of individual credibility signals. The left side shows the scope of this chapter

the second stream is typically not referring explicitly to a relation with credibility, despite the detected labels have been listed as potential credibility signals (e.g., by [18]). Among the wide range of potential credibility signals, three categories of textual signals have received considerable attention in prior research, namely: (1) factuality, subjectivity and bias, (2) persuasion techniques and logical fallacies, and (3) check-worthy and fact-checked claims. The rest of this section provides a brief overview of such credibility signal categories. For more details, please, refer to the full survey [10].

To enhance the understanding of the relationship between credibility signals and the final credibility assessment, we provide an overview of the signal typology in Fig. 1. As illustrated, these signals can be broadly classified into two principal categories, based on the nature of the information they convey. The primary focus of this chapter is on content-based signals, which are derived exclusively from the textual content, without reference to metadata or external sources. Each category may encompass a range of individual signals, which themselves may exhibit polarity–that is, a positive or negative correlation with perceived credibility.

Credibility assessment. The first group of existing approaches focus specifically on automatic credibility assessment. These works typically address two steps—detection of credibility signals and their aggregation into an overall credibility information. Some approaches—instead of using standard credibility signals—use only shallow features that are approximating such signals (e.g., the length of title).

The research on credibility assessment is heavily influenced by dataset availability, which can be characterised as critically insufficient. There is a general lack of datasets providing annotations of texts with multiple credibility signals or providing general credibility assessment. The datasets that do offer such manual annotations are typically very small in the size (e.g., a dataset containing only 40 samples [18]), or provide only final credibility label (e.g., a dataset of 9,000 Tweets annotated on a binary scale—credible/non-credible [23]).

The approaches for credibility assessment typically consist of three steps: (1) a set of credibility signals is selected; (2) various techniques are employed for their automatic detection; and finally, (3) detected credibility signals are then used to predict an overall credibility or as an input for other tasks, such as information retrieval. Surprisingly, the existing works employ mostly traditional statistical or feature-engineered NLP approaches, while the adoption of LLMs remain limited. One of few works employing LLMs is our own work [12] presented in more detail in Sect. 4.

One prominent example of how such credibility assessment approaches can be practically deployed is the Tanbih [24], a news aggregator that performs media-level and article-level analysis of the news aiming to help users better understand what they are reading. Tanbih displays news grouped into events and generates media profiles that summarise the general factuality of reporting, the degree of propagandistic content, hyper-partisanship, leading political ideology, general frame of reporting, and stance with respect to various claims and topics of a news outlet.

Factuality, subjectivity and bias. In contrast to generally under-researched credibility assessment, there is a considerably larger body of research on three related concepts—factuality, subjectivity and bias. *Factuality*, in the context of credibility analysis, measures the degree of certainty about the occurrence of events, with existing works distinguishing between single event factuality detection (EFD) and document-level event factuality identification (DEFI). *Subjectivity* measures how objective or subjective information is, while *bias* is a more complex characteristic that measures the imbalance in opinions or facts, often linked to ideological favouritism. Bias can involve selective information omission, fact selection, or biased presentation through framing, opinionated reporting, and visual cues.

As our survey [10] shows, the tasks of factuality, subjectivity and bias detection cover various subtasks and task formulations. While subjectivity detection distinguishes between subjective and non-subjective content, certain formulations also perceive it as a sub-task of sentiment analysis. As an example, distinction between neutral and positive/negative sentiment is a type of subjectivity detection task. At the same time, sentiment detection tasks can be seen as a specific case of bias detection.

One of the main challenges for detecting credibility signals within this category is a high diversity in how researchers perceive and address factuality, subjectivity and bias, resulting in many ambiguous definitions and ontologies. This problem, strengthened by the inherent subjective nature of these signals, is also reflected in dataset annotations, causing low inter-annotator agreement [25].

Persuasion techniques and logical fallacies. During the last decade, social media has become a key platform for propagandistic efforts designed to shape public opinion and drive large-scale engagement. To counter this, researchers have developed computational methods for automatically detecting such content [26]. Among propagandistic strategies, the task of automatic detection of *persuasion techniques* and *logical fallacies* has received a particular interest from the NLP research community. The research in this direction is heavily driven especially through the effort of organising multiple shared tasks and data challenges (data science competitions) that have introduced a number of datasets and resulted in a wide range of approaches [27–30].

As our analysis of systems submitted to these shared tasks and data challenges [10] showed, transformer-based models were employed in all top-scoring systems for automatic detection of persuasion techniques due to their ability to capture nuanced contextual information. Unsurprisingly, the larger versions of the models generally outperformed the smaller ones. This observation was also confirmed by our own approach to multilingual persuasion techniques detection (see Sect. 3).

With an exception of few multilingual datasets [30, 31], the majority of available resources remains limited to English or Arabic. Therefore, accurate multilingual persuasion techniques detection remains an open problem.

Check-worthy and fact-checked claims. The assessment of veracity of every piece of online information is a highly costly process. To optimise this task, two key credibility signals play a crucial role in assisting fact-checkers and combating false information [32]: *check-worthiness detection* and *retrieval of previously fact-checked claims*. The first identifies claims that are worth fact-checking due to their significance and public interest [33]. The second, typically following the first, facilitates verification by determining whether a claim has already been fact-checked, using existing fact-checking databases [34], both monolingual and multilingual. While check-worthiness is a content-based signal, fact-check status is context-based, as it relies on external sources for verification.

Similar to the previous category of persuasion techniques and logical fallacies, this category of credibility signals received a lot of research attention from the series of CheckThat! labs [35] organised at CLEF and the most recent SemEval 2025 Task 7 on *Multilingual and Crosslingual Fact-Checked Claim Retrieval* [36]. This led to the release of related datasets and creation of a plethora of diverse solutions.

While the initial approaches to detecting check-worthy claims relied on fine-tuning transformer-based pre-trained models, such as BERT, RoBERTa, DistilBERT, during 2024 edition of CheckThat! lab [35], we witness an adoption of generative LLMs, such as LLama 2 and 3, GPT3.4 and 5, Mixtral and Mistral [35]. For instance, the best performing system for English used Llama2 7b fine-tuned on the original training data by means of the prompts generated by ChatGPT [37].

In case of identification of previously fact-checked claims, the most recent results proposed during the SemEval 2025 Task 7 [36] commonly employ a strategy of fine-tuning the base embedding models in a contrastive learning manner with in-batch negatives (a common negative sampling method which efficiently collects negative samples in batches during training). Further improvements can be obtained by adding hard negatives (i.e., samples that are difficult to distinguish from positive examples), training on diverse subsets, pre-processing (e.g., input text cleaning) and additional post-processing (e.g., re-ranking of retrieved fact-checked claims). The challenging multilingual nature of this task is best to be addressed by training a single model for all languages or on English-translated data.

Challenges and open problems. Following the analysis of 175 research works as well as our own experience in the area of credibility assessment and credibility signal detection, we identified 6 high-level categories of challenges and open problems [10]: (1) research fragmentation and need for integration, (2) adoption and potential of generative LLMs, (3) dataset availability and multilinguality, (4) ethical and legal issues, (5) practical deployment, and (6) multimodal approaches. Within the vera.ai project, we specifically focused on two aspects—*multilinguality* and *practical deployment*, which we considered the most critical in the context of the project. Its strong orientation towards media professionals operating across Europe, tackling the problem for a number of high- as well as low-resource languages, requires models and tools that are capable to function accurately in this highly multilingual environment where input languages are not known in advance. We additionally put a strong focus on practical delivery and integration of the researched solutions. In the following two sections, we provide an in-depth description of how we addressed these challenges and open problems.

3 Automatic Detection of Credibility Signals

In an era of constantly emerging and rapidly evolving false information, automatic detection of misleading content has become a critical area of research. However, training specialised models for this task remains an intractable problem, with the data and the models only becoming available long after the spread of false information, rather than serving as a proactive, preventive measure. Moreover, such systems become outdated very quickly due to the phenomenon known as *concept drift* [38–40] and hence require constant retraining. Additionally, collecting and annotating new data for retraining such models is a costly and resource-intensive process. In the light of these challenges, focusing on the automatic detection of more fine-grained (non)credibility clues has gained prominence as a more explainable and topic-independent approach of identifying certain signals that individually or cumulatively can indicate potential false information.

In this section, we focus on various techniques aimed at automatic detection of credibility signals in the textual content. More specifically, we provide examples of how we approached detection of three categories of credibility signals—(1) *the framing*, (2) *the genre*, and (3) *the persuasion techniques*—in online news in a multilingual setup.

The methods described in this section are trained on the multilingual datasets provided within the *SemEval-2023 Task 3* [30]. The datasets contain news articles in nine languages: English (EN), French (FR), German (DE), Georgian (KA), Greek (EL), Italian (IT), Polish (PL), Russian (RU), and Spanish (ES). Three of the languages

(Georgian, Greek, and Spanish) are "unseen" languages, meaning that no corresponding labelled training data exists in the dataset. Therefore, in order to make predictions on these languages, their test set must either be translated to a seen language, or a multilingual approach capable of supporting zero-shot evaluation must be applied. For the remaining 6 languages, labelled training and validation data is included in the dataset.

Framing Detection

The task of framing detection refers to identifying certain manipulative techniques of presenting information, such as cherry-picking, misinterpreting or highlighting particular facts, in order to shape the perception of the audience. The notion of framing is often seen as a specific case of bias detection [41], which covers various forms of biased presentation, such as opinionated news [30, 42, 43] or visual clues [44] used to distort the perception of information.

Depending on the domain, the task of framing detection can be formulated as a problem of presenting information in a positive, negative or neutral light [45], in terms of a political leaning and orientation [46, 47], or from a perspective of a specific standpoint (healthcare, defense, freedom of speech, etc.) [48]. The latter interpretation of framing can often be confused with the notion of a topic. However, as emphasised by [49], the same topic can often be presented from a variety of perspectives. For example, the topic of *gun violence* can be discussed within the frame of the legal amendments, gun control, mental health or public safety. It is therefore possible to think of a topic as a high-level domain, where each topic can be represented through the lenses of various frames.

For the task of framing detection, we chose the dataset provided by the organisers of the SemEval-2023 Shared Task 3 [30]. The taxonomy of framing considered for this dataset was adopted from the framing definition suggested by [50]. It represents a category-based perspective under which the information is presented, such as *cultural identity*, *economy*, *fairness and equality*, etc. The full list of categories with the number of overall examples in the training set is provided in Table 1. As can be seen, the dataset is highly imbalanced, with the majority of examples available only in English language, and certain frame-language pairs only consisting of 8 articles. The labels were manually assigned by trained annotators based on the pre-defined guidelines. The dataset consists of news articles covering contentious issues such as, immigration and climate change.

Depending on the inference language, our solution for the task consisted of a majority vote ensemble of two types of transformer models, RoBERTa-MUPPET$_{LARGE}$ and XLM-R$_{LARGE}$ [15]. For English and unseen languages, we used an ensemble of monolingual RoBERTa-MUPPET$_{LARGE}$ models. Given the high degree of category skew, we used all of the training data available, by performing the translation of articles in languages other than English into English. For the final inference on non-English languages (Georgian, Spanish and Greek), we applied

Table 1 Distribution of articles in the training set for framing detection task

Frame	Number of articles						Total
	EN	FR	IT	RU	PL	DE	
Crime and punishment	227	12	38	37	32	25	371
External regulation and reputation	121	57	80	32	48	55	393
Morality	203	38	44	17	34	18	354
Legality constitutionality and jurisprudence	203	24	48	24	28	30	357
Health and safety	61	36	55	30	78	54	314
Quality of life	87	21	90	21	46	24	289
Economic	28	50	92	48	86	52	356
Political	235	69	117	33	86	72	612
Cultural identity	31	14	25	8	29	27	134
Policy prescription and evaluation	65	20	82	12	70	41	290
Public opinion	23	18	29	13	46	20	149
Capacity and resources	29	35	71	19	49	56	259
Security and defense	187	64	89	51	69	71	531
Fairness and equality	115	16	37	15	21	22	226
Total	1615	474	897	360	722	567	4635

a ‘translate-test’ approach, i.e., translated the articles in the test set into English. For the remaining languages in the training set (French, German, Italian, Russian, Polish), we used an ensemble of multilingual models (XLM-R$_{LARGE}$) with Pfeiffer bottleneck adapters [51] and task-adaptive pre-training (TAPT) [52]. We found that introducing class weights in the loss function resulted in a better performance on the two least frequent classes (Cultural Identity and Public Opinion), but resulted in a lower performance on better represented frames (such as Political). Therefore, we used an ensemble of models with and without class weights. We additionally applied a set of data cleaning and pre-processing techniques to minimise the amount of irrelevant information and disclaimers. More detailed description of our implementation and hyperparameters can be found in the original paper [15].

The proposed approach was evaluated on multilingual, previously unseen, news articles during our official participation in the shared task. Our method ranked first for English ($F1_{micro} = 57.895$), Greek ($F1_{micro} = 54.630$) and Georgian ($F1_{micro} = 65.421$), second for Russian ($F1_{micro} = 44.144$) and Polish ($F1_{micro} = 64.516$), and third for French ($F1_{micro} = 53.425$), German ($F1_{micro} = 65.251$), and Spanish ($F1_{micro} = 50.829$), placing in top 3 for 8 out of 9 languages. The monolingual ensemble achieved all three of the top-ranking methods.

After the competition, we performed a systematic comparison of mono-and multilingual approaches for each of the languages. Our post-competition results suggest that an even stronger performance could have been achieved for English, Greek and Spanish by training a multilingual model instead. In contrast, the languages for which the multilingual ensemble was applied, could have benefited from a monolingual translate-set approach. Surprisingly, the overall performance on Georgian, an unseen low-resource language, was higher than that on the English test set, even though we applied a monolingual English-only model to infer the results on the unseen language. Details on the competing methods, as well as detailed comparison tables are provided in the summary paper on the shared task [30].

After the competition, we refined the original categorisation by manually combining several semantically close and under-represented frames into one. For example, the “capacity and resources” frame was merged with the “economic” frame due to discussing closely related economic issues and both being under-represented in terms of the number of training examples. Additionally, these two categories had a 62% of article overlap, meaning that 62% of articles were annotated with both of these frames. Similarly, “morality” was defined in the original annotation task as referring to religious and ethical values. We therefore merged it with the under-represented “cultural” frame that had a 42% article overlap and talked about the another dimension of values, associated with cultural background. We re-named the category as “Religious, Ethical and Cultural” to directly reflect different types of values involved. In addition to creating a more interpretable categorisation, such changes helped us to train more robust models due to having a more balanced dataset. This, in turn, ensured the applicability of our method to end user tools. The final categorisation is provided in Table 2 along with the explanation behind each frame.

Table 2 Refined categorisation of framing in news articles

Frame	Description
Economy and resources	Costs, benefits or other financial implications; availability of physical, human or financial resources, and capacity of current systems
Religious, ethical and cultural	Religious or ethical implications; traditions, customs or values in relation to a policy issue
Fairness, equality and rights	Balance or distribution of rights, responsibilities, and resources
Law and justice system	Rights, freedoms, and authority of individuals, corporations, and government
Crime and punishment	Effectiveness and implications of laws and their enforcement
Security, defense and well-being	Threats to welfare of the individual, community, or nation; threats and opportunities for the individual's wealth, happiness, and well-being
Health and safety	Health care, sanitation, public safety
Politics	Considerations related to politics and politicians, including lobbying, elections, and attempts to sway voters; attitudes and opinions of the general public, including polling and demographics; specific politics aimed at addressing problems
International relations	International reputation or foreign policy

Genre Detection

The second category of credibility signals corresponds to genre detection. The notion of information genre typically refers to the differences in the writing style, with certain definitions varying depending on the final task. For example, authors in [53] consider the text genre based on the style used in various information sources, such as research papers, reviews, question answering platforms, news reports and editorials. Some of the definitions further extend this categorisation by introducing specific domains of information (such as financial documents, politics, literature and interviews) [54], as well as specific types of literature (fiction and non-fiction) and legal documents [55]. In the context of news articles, genre can also often be seen as a mixture of the article topics, such as economy, opinion, sports, education, making the notion of the genre synonymous with that of framing [56].

In the context of false information detection, however, the main distinction of our concern is whether the text is written in an objective style or contains manipulative wording. We therefore referred to the definition of genre in sub-task of SemEval-2023 Shared Task 3 [30], where news articles are assigned one of three labels, *objective reporting*, *opinionated* news, or *satirical* news articles. The distribution of data labels is provided in Table 3. In this categorisation, objective reporting is defined by the

Table 3 Distribution of articles in the training set for genre detection task

Genre	Number of articles						Total
	EN	FR	IT	RU	PL	DE	
Opinion	382	103	174	93	104	86	942
Objective reporting	41	43	44	41	25	27	221
Satire	10	11	8	8	15	19	71
Total	433	157	326	142	144	132	1234

inclusion of all relevant facts and viewpoints, avoiding cherry-picking or adopting a particular stance. In contrast, opinionated news often employ propaganda techniques intended to persuade the reader to adopt a specific perspective. Satire, by definition, presents fictional content, typically for humorous or critical effect.

As can be seen, the dataset for genre detection is severely skewed towards the *opinion* genre, with only less than 6% of articles annotated as *satire* and 18% falling into the *reporting* genre. To address this issue, we performed data oversampling with replacement (i.e. by creating copies of existing instances from the minority class, potentially including duplicates, to balance the dataset), which has been empirically proven to be slightly more effective than applying class weighting for this particular task. For a satire class in English, we enriched the data with the satire dataset by [57] and performed oversampling from the external dataset rather than the original one.

Our approach [15] consisted of an ensemble of three fully fine-tuned transformer models and one Houlsby adapter-tuned transformer model [58]. In all four scenarios, we used the multilingual model (mBERT) as the base model [59]. By experimenting with information sampling from various parts of the document, we observed the final few paragraphs of the article to be particularly important for detecting opinionated texts as they tend to contain calls for action and emotional language. Therefore, in the light of the input length limitation of transformer models, we used a concatenation of the sentences sequentially sampled one-by-one from the beginning and the end of the articles.

Our main strategy for maximising the performance on each language was to utilise the validation set in order to detect language-specific optimal checkpoints. As we demonstrate in our paper, in the multilingual training scenario, various languages reach their best performance at different times, making it impossible to achieve the best overall result in a task that requires best performance per individual language. We therefore composed ensembles for each language in the training set by selecting three models with best language-specific checkpoints. For the unseen language inference scenario, we chose the models with the best overall $F1_{macro}$ performance.

We evaluated the proposed approach on previously unseen news articles in various languages as part of the official submission to the shared task. Our system achieved high accuracy on the test set, performing well on both languages included in the training data and those not seen during training. Furthermore, it outperformed several competing approaches. In particular, our solution was ranked joint first for German language ($F1_{macro} = 0.820$), second for Russian ($F1_{macro} = 0.729$) and Georgian ($F1_{macro} = 0.963$), and third for English ($F1_{macro} = 0.784$), Italian ($F1_{macro} = 0.720$) and Polish ($F1_{macro} = 0.764$). Our post-competition results suggest a particularly strong performance of the ensemble approach, achieving better results than each individual multilingual model in 8 out of 9 languages. The benefit of having an ensemble is particularly noteworthy for English, where the performance of the ensemble approach is 25% higher than that of a single fine-tuned multilingual model. Another interesting observation is a high performance achieved for Georgian ($F1_{macro} = 0.963$), despite being a zero-shot prediction on a low-resource language where the transformer models do not have much pre-training data [59]. The lack of the publicly available gold-standard test data prevents us from further analysing the reason behind this. However, given that the results are ranked based on the $F1_{macro}$ scores and the lack of a single *satire* prediction in our final submission, we assume that the test set did not include any of the articles in this genre, which was also the most challenging one to predict given the aforementioned data scarcity and the pragmatic nature of satirical texts. For a thorough comparison of the competing methods, including detailed tables, refer to the shared task summary paper [30].

Persuasion Techniques Detection

Finally, the third selected category of credibility signals, which we addressed in the vera.ai project, corresponds to detection of persuasion techniques (often also referred to as propaganda techniques [60, 61]). Persuasion techniques can be seen as all types of rhetorical means (logos, pathos and ethos, as defined by Aristotle [62]) for making information more convincing, often misleading the reader or discrediting the trustworthiness of the opposing viewpoints. With many classification schemes and datasets suggested during the last decade [10], we chose the most detailed dataset for persuasion technique detection proposed within the SemEval-2023 Task 3 [30]. The annotations classify article paragraphs into zero or more out of 23 persuasion techniques. We present the full statistic about the data set in Table 4. As can be seen from the table, the dataset is highly skewed, with the most striking difference between *Loaded Language*, consisting of 1,809 examples, and *Appeal to Time*, *Questioning the Reputation* and *Appeal to Values* classes having no examples at all for English. Overall, the most frequent technique, *Loaded Language*, is almost 43 times more frequent than the least represented class, *Whataboutism*.

We experimented with two different approaches to address this task.

Method 1: Fine-tuning a large model with carefully calibrated confidence thresholds. As our first approach, we proposed a multilingual system consisting of a single model tackling all languages [11]. Our main strategy was to fine-tune a large pre-trained transformer-based language model. To find the best-performing system, we experimented with different language models and opted for XLM-RoBERTa large due to its performance. We additionally performed hyperparameter tuning and cali-

Table 4 Distribution of articles in the training set for persuasion technique detection task

Persuasion technique	Number of articles						Total
	EN	FR	IT	RU	PL	DE	
Doubt	518	327	882	509	295	288	2819
Repetition	544	92	22	69	13	8	748
Appeal_to_fear-prejudice	310	210	285	54	108	182	1149
Appeal_to_authority	154	76	70	10	41	225	576
Slogans	153	149	54	72	36	87	551
Loaded_language	1809	944	903	641	310	242	4849
False_dilemma-no_choice	122	73	61	28	12	41	337
Flag_Waving	287	37	35	42	68	65	534
Name_calling-labeling	979	428	566	253	475	743	3444
Causal_oversimplification	213	125	50	39	12	33	472
Appeal_to_hypocrisy	40	134	82	103	162	136	657
Obfuscation-vagueness-confusion	18	113	21	19	36	62	269
Exaggeration-minimisation	466	258	143	131	111	157	1266
Red_herring	44	55	23	2	12	30	166
Guilt_by_association	59	130	53	24	94	122	482
Conversation_killer	91	170	178	88	50	121	698
Appeal_to_popularity	15	82	37	8	30	63	235
Straw_man	15	135	51	21	15	15	252
Questioning_the_reputation	0	348	383	303	164	310	1508
Appeal_to_time	0	41	27	28	14	11	121
Whataboutism	16	62	8	7	8	13	114
Appeal_to_values	0	100	131	48	101	73	453
Total	5853	4089	4065	2499	2167	3027	21,700

brated the confidence threshold for the multi-label classification. We also simulated the zero-shot setting on the training data to adjust the confidence threshold and better estimate the performance of our model on the unseen languages (i.e., Georgian, Greek and Spanish).

Furthermore, we experimented with additional configurations, such as translating the data to a single language (English) and using it to fine-tune a monolingual model, applying various text pre-processing strategies, or layer freezing. However, these configurations did not lead to improvements.

Our first method ranked 1st in 6 out of 9 languages(Italian($F1_{micro} = 0.550$), Russian($F1_{micro} = 0.387$), German($F1_{micro} = 0.513$), Polish($F1_{micro} = 0.430$), Greek($F1_{micro} = 0.267$) and Georgian($F1_{micro} = 0.457$)), two of which were the previously unseen languages. For the remaining languages, we achieved 2nd place in Spanish ($F1_{micro} = 0.380$), 3rd for French ($F1_{micro} = 0.432$) and 4th for English ($F1_{micro} = 0.362$). Based on the overall performance across the languages, it became the best performing and the winning solution.

Method 2: Multilingual and monolingual transformer models with class weighting. Our second approach was based on applying class weights and fine-tuning mono- and multi-lingual transformer models [15]. We found that class weights perform significantly better at minimising the effect of data imbalance compared to data oversampling. The main strategy for our training procedure was to introduce the 24th class by assigning the paragraph with no persuasion technique a separate label with a vector of zeros. This contrasts with the baseline models suggested by the organisers which does not consider the irrelevant paragraphs. This approach demonstrated a consistent improvement for all the languages in the dataset.

Our second methods ranked second for English ($F1_{micro} = 0.368$) and third for Italian ($F1_{micro} = 0.538$). It must be noted that the official ranking score for this sub-task was $F1_{micro}$, which means that, given the high data skew, the systems that perform well on the most frequent classes can achieve a very high rank without necessarily being robust overall. If we consider $F1_{macro}$ score instead, the placings of our first approach improve considerably, with the first place for Italian and French and placing in top 3 across all languages except the three unseen ones.

Based on our experiments with both approaches and official ranking on the test set, we made the following main observations:

1. The combination of a high number of predicted classes and multiple languages (including unseen ones) makes the training of monolingual models challenging due to the lack of enough data in a single language. Even though monolingual models trained on all data translated into English language often achieve state-of-the-art or comparable performance on other multilingual tasks, in this case such models are outperformed by the single multilingual model trained on all the data.
2. Since detecting the presence of persuasion techniques is a complex task (even for humans), larger language models perform significantly better. We also recognised the importance of calibrating the confidence thresholds (for seen and unseen languages separately). At the same time, interestingly, many model configurations (pre-processing, layer freezing, etc.) did not improve model performance.

3. We can see a significant difference between F1 micro and macro scores in some of the languages. This difference indicates that our system focuses on the majority classes and struggles with classifying some of the more scarce persuasion techniques within the dataset.

The summary paper on the shared task provides additional details on the competing methods, as well as detailed comparison tables [30].

Additional experiments with prompting LLMs. Besides the two above-mentioned methods submitted to the official leaderboard, we also experimented with zero-shot settings (prompting) as well as few-shot settings (in-context learning) with two large language models (LLMs), namely ChatGPT and Alpaca-30B. We tried two setups: (1) original classification of 23 persuasion techniques; and (2) simplified binary classification whether a provided piece of text contains any persuasion technique.

The results from these additional experiments revealed that for both zero-shot and few-shot settings, both selected LLMs, in both setups were not able to outperform our best performing method (XLM-RoBERTa). We observed a significant difference, for example the performance for fine-grained classification of 23 persuasion techniques, averaged across 6 languages in the training set, achieved F1 performance of 27% and 20% for ChatGPT and Alpaca-30B respectively, while the performance of fine-tuned XLM-RoBERTa large was 49%. The performance gap, despite not as significant, was also present for a simplified binary classification, achieving 64% and 55% for ChatGPT and Alpaca-30B, in contrast to 75% achieved by XLM-RoBERTa large.

This conclusion is in line with a more general finding that when a sufficient amount of training data is available, the performance of specialised (fine-tuned) smaller models can overcome much larger general models (utilised in zero- or few-shot settings), while on average 100 samples is sufficient to achieve break-even performance [63].

The role of persuasion techniques in disinformation narratives. Finally, we explored the use of different frequent persuasion techniques across various disinformation domains [64]. To perform such an analysis, we identified 16 most frequent persuasion techniques from the dataset by [30] and applied the best performing classifier for this task from [14] to various disinformation domains of: Islamic issues [65], COVID-19 [66], Climate change [67], and Russo-Ukrainian war [68]. Our analysis revealed that, while there exist persuasion techniques that are commonly used across various domains, certain types of persuasion are characteristic for the spread of domain-specific narratives. For example, *Appeal to Fear* is very common to spread anti-vaccine disinformation narratives in the context of Covid-19, while pro-Kremlin disinformation actively uses *Flag-waving* (evoking patriotic feelings) and *Appeal to Hypocrisy* by the West in order to spread disinformation.

We further analysed the degree of stylistic adaptation of certain persuasion techniques to various disinformation domains and found specific linguistic patterns. For example, we found that in case of climate change disinformation, the persuasion based on the *Appeal to Authority* is formulated using a more analytic and formal language than in other domains, while *Exaggeration/Minimisation* frequently draws on moral and cultural references. This evidence can assist fact checking journalists in focusing on specific types of propaganda in order to identify disinformation narratives early on.

Improving the Computational Efficiency with PEFT Methods

Following the observation that larger models perform significantly better at the cost of consuming significantly larger computing resources, we performed a follow-up research on how fully fine-tuned solutions for all three categories of credibility signals (used during the SemEval competition) compare in terms of performance as well as computation costs with models utilising parameter-efficient fine-tuning (PEFT) techniques: Adapters and Low-Rank Adaptation (LoRA) [14].

Prior studies demonstrate that PEFT, in addition to being less computationally expensive, can improve the performance on zero-shot cross-lingual classification tasks [69, 70]. Following on this insight, we further performed an extensive comparative study of both computational resources and cross-lingual performance of full fine-tuning (FFT) and PEFT techniques in three training scenarios on three classification tasks corresponding to the credibility signals discussed in this section. In addition, we considered three types of training scenarios: (1) one joint multilingual, and two types of single source language training scenarios; (2) using only the data in English language and translating the test set in the target language into English (English Only); and (3) translating data from other languages into English for both training and testing (English + Translations).

In terms of computational costs, we found that PEFT techniques, while using up to 280 times less trainable parameters and, as a result, requiring up to 44% less training time and a substantially less VRAM, often can reach the same or only marginally lower performance in terms of accuracy. In particular cases, PEFT techniques can even outperform FFT in the multilingual joint training scenario. For example, for the task of persuasion technique detection, LoRA method can reach an $F1_{macro} = 23.7 \pm 6.9$ and $F1_{micro} = 42.9 \pm 9.5$ which even marginally outperforms the fully fine-tuned approach resulting in $F1_{micro} = 23.7 \pm 5.0$ and $F1_{micro} = 41.8 \pm 8.6$. Similarly, the adapter approach can yield a better result for the task of genre detection, resulting in $F1_{micro} = 62.8 \pm 5.7$ compared to $F1_{micro} = 61.7 \pm 7.5$ for the fully fine-tuned model. For cross-lingual zero-shot inference, we found that FFT performs better than PEFT methods in all training scenarios, resulting in $F1_{macro} = 57.1 \pm 2.3$ for the task of genre detection and $F1_{micro} = 55.9 \pm 3.8$ and $F1_{micro} = 35.7 \pm 8.1$ for the tasks of framing and persuasion technique detection respectively. This challenges prior reports on the benefits of this approach for the cross-lingual inference problem.

Explainability of the Models for Credibility Signal Detection

An important aspect towards making our credibility signal detection models useful for fact-checking professionals in a real-world scenario is to provide transparency for our models and methods by displaying specific sentences in content that trigger potential low credibility [71–73]. Since the initial annotations were provided at the article level, it was not feasible to train the models to directly identify the localised presence of individual signals. As a result, we conducted a post-hoc explainability analysis to interpret the models' outputs, i.e. we inferred the rationale behind specific classification decisions after the predictions were made [74, 75]. To achieve this, for each credibility signal in this section, we implemented an explainability method to highlight the sentences that trigger a certain frame, genre or persuasion technique. For this purpose, we utilised the modification of the method for quantifying the attention scores called *attention rollout* [76]. The class-agnostic importance score for each sentence was inferred through a number of steps:

1. Fusing 12 attention heads into 1, resulting in 1 'head' per layer.
2. Aggregating 12 layers, resulting in 1 overall attention pattern. This is achieved by averaging the last n layers, or using attention rollout.
3. Extracting CLS-token attention. This served as the first row of the attention pattern.
4. Calculating average token score per sentence, and highlighting the sentences with the scores above a certain threshold as the most important ones to a certain class.

Additionally, we implement the class-aware explainability scores by fusing the attention heads based on the gradients:

1. We first obtain class-specific gradients via backpropogation. This tells us how important each attention head was to the final class decision.
2. We then fuse attention heads in each layer, weighted by their class-specific importance.
3. After fusing attention heads, the procedure is identical to class-agnostic method.

Figure 2 shows an example of an explainable output of the tool. As can be seen, in this particular case, we chose the frame related to *International Relations*, and the mechanism highlighted the sentence talking about ceasefire agreement between 4 countries.

4 Credibility Signals in Practical Use

This section focuses on two practical use cases in which automatically detected credibility signals can be utilised to tackle false information or to identify reliable trustworthy content. At first, we introduce integration of best-performing solutions

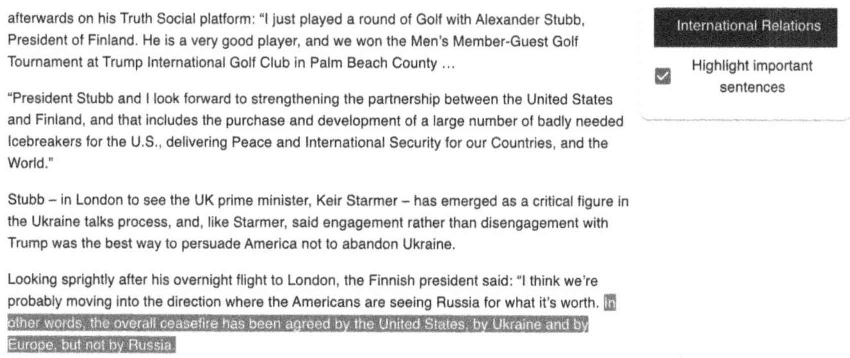

Fig. 2 An example of attention-based explainability for the framing of *International relations*

to credibility signal detection (described in Sect. 3) into the *Verification plugin*[1], where they became directly available as a means of textual content analysis for end users (primarily media professionals). Second, we provide a description of how such credibility signals may serve as features for AI-based misinformation detection. These two use cases demonstrate their broad applicability targeting both human and automatic credibility assessment.

Credibility Assessment in the Verification Plugin

When integrating the research solutions into any kind of user-facing tools, it is necessary to consider various efficiency limitations. Due to the time constraints of running language-specific classifiers in real-time, we opted to use single models instead of ensembles (single mBERT models for genre and persuasion detection and distilled mBERT for framing detection) as a final to-be-deployed solution. We use the same hyperparameters as in the experiments described in the Shared Task paper [15] related to the credibility signals described in Sect. 3.

The first practical use case demonstrates the integration of automatically detected credibility signals into the *Assistant* feature of the *Verification plugin* enhanced in the vera.ai project. The *Verification plugin* is a widely used tool by media professionals as well as general public providing a toolset of various (AI-based) tools ranging from detection of synthetic images, deepfake videos, image manipulation analysis to search engines allowing to retrieve existing fact-checks. The *Assistant* is a part of the *Verification plugin* specifically dedicated to analysis of textual content.

To this end, six credibility signals have been integrated (including ones described in Sect. 3): news framing, news genre, persuasion techniques, subjectivity, machine generated text, and previous fact-checks. To integrate these credibility signals into

[1] https://www.veraai.eu/posts/verification-plugin.

the *Assistant*, the classifiers have been deployed on servers that can be accessed via an endpoint. An API call is performed to send and receive data via the endpoint over the Web. The text is extracted from the page and sent to the endpoints of each of the classifiers using a GET or POST request, depending on what is required for each endpoint. The results are returned asynchronously and each is displayed in the user interface as soon as the *Assistant* has received them.

In terms of user experience, the user can provide a URL for an article or social media post to the *Assistant* and click the "Submit" button. A loading box appears until the first results are returned and displayed in separate tabs. There are tabs inside the "Extracted text" box, and the title of the tabs refers to the credibility signal. The titles are greyed out and unclickable until the results from the API calls have been received and rendered successfully. If there are any errors in the process, the credibility signal title remains greyed out and cannot be clicked, and a service failure warning appears at the beginning of the "Assistant results" section. If successful, the tabs can be clicked and the results are displayed over the extracted text. The results are rendered slightly differently depending on the chosen credibility signal. The first tab "Raw text" refers to the extracted text without any information from the credibility signals. The previous fact-checks results are displayed separately.

The news framing classifier is a multi-label multi-class classifier with nine possible classes for the complete text as listed at the end of Sect. 3. Figure 3 shows how the results are displayed. The left-hand side contains the extracted text with highlighted sentences that have been determined to be important to the classification by the algorithm. The right-hand side contains a threshold slider and a list of the detected classes. For the list of detected classes, only the top three that have a confidence score above 0.8 are displayed. The classifier also indicates which sentences in the text it considers to be most important, which acts as a guide to which parts of the text were most informative to the decision process. The threshold slider changes the sentence importance value threshold from low, showing more sentences, to high, showing less sentences. If no frames are detected, the text "No topics detected" will be displayed to the user.

There are three possible classes for the news genre classifier: opinionated news, objective reporting, and satire, with only one class returned for the overall text. Similarly to the framing detection tab, the left-hand side displays the overall text with highlighted sentences that have been determined to be important to the classification by the algorithm. The right-hand side contains a threshold slider and the single class detected. As with the news framing classifier, the threshold slider changes the sentence importance value threshold from low, showing more sentences, to high, showing less sentences.

For the persuasion technique detection tab, we highlight the paragraphs that the model considers most important when deciding on the class. The 23 possible classes of persuasion technique are listed in Table 4. As a single sentence can have multiple persuasion techniques, the user interface is required to be more informative. The left-hand side shows the relevant sentences highlighted in grey. Hovering over each with the mouse will change the colour to indicate which sentence is currently selected via mouse hover. The pop-up message contains the classes detected. On the right-

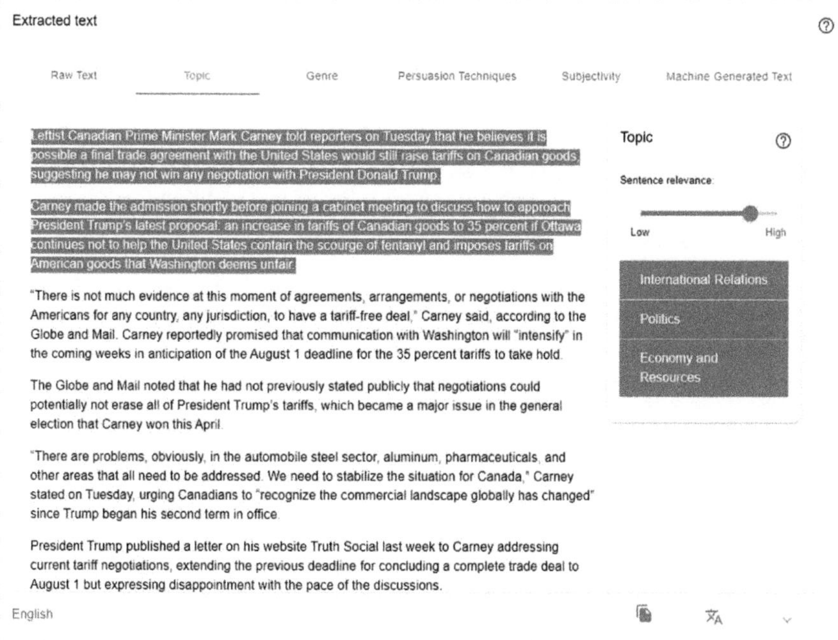

Fig. 3 The credibility signals are displayed in the "Extracted text" section. This figure shows the user interface for the news framing, or topic, classifier result

hand side, a threshold slider is displayed along with the detected classes, and each class is listed with the number of detected sentences. For this credibility signal, each detected class is clickable, which allows the user to see the specific sentences for that class that the model considered particularly important. To return to the previous state with all sentences belonging to all the classes highlighted, the user has to click on the same class twice. The user can change the threshold slider to see more or less detected persuasion techniques given low or high classifier confidence.

The subjectivity classifier tab demonstrates whether there are any subjective sentences within the text. If so, the left-hand side displays the overall text with any sentences labelled as subjective highlighted given the confidence score of the algorithm. The threshold slider on the right-hand side can be varied to see more or less detected subjective sentences detected given low or high classifier confidence, as with the persuasion classifier. The right-hand side also contains the full text score in a gauge format which supports users in making a decision. The full text score is calculated based on the classifier sentence scores.

The machine generated text detection tab returns one of four classes representing scalar ranges: highly likely human written, likely human written, likely machine generated, and highly likely machine generated [77]. The API call to the model can be performed in two ways: by running predictions over 200-word chunks or by running predictions over individual sentences. Both methods provide an overall

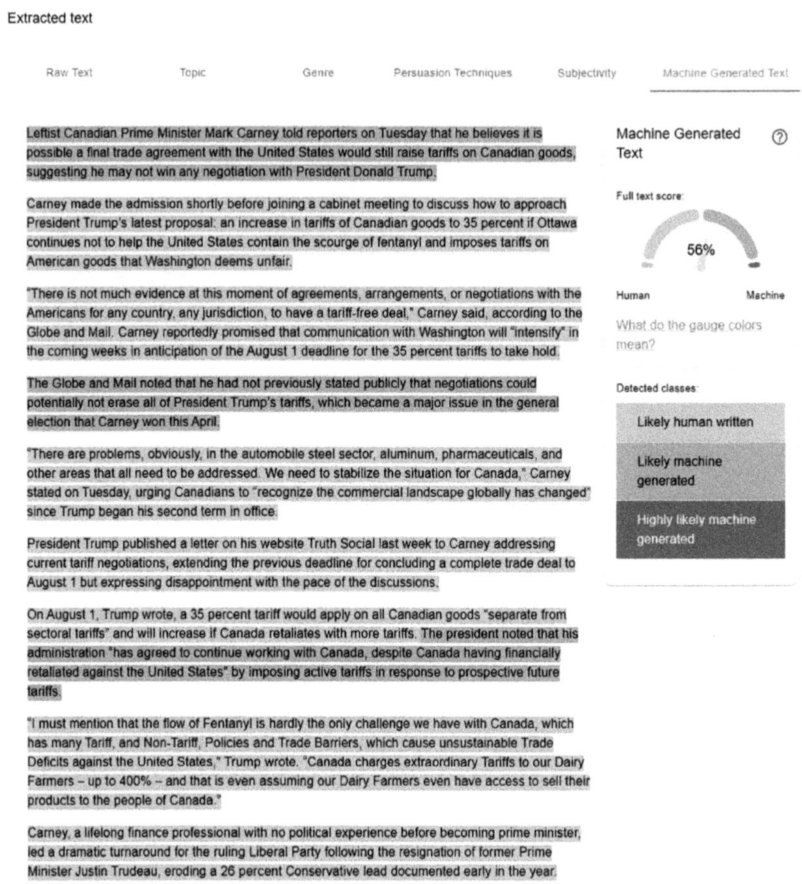

Fig. 4 The machine generated text results are shown with all sentences highlighted depending on the class detected by the classifier. These detected classes are displayed in a list along with the overall score in gauge format so users to see the boundaries between the classes

score. As the inference model is more accurate when run over a 200-word chunk predictions, the two API calls are made to return different information: (1) the call over a 200-word window is used to display the final prediction score, and (2) the sentence-based call is used to provide explainability by highlighting the sentences corresponding to a specific class (similarly to the previous credibility signals). The overall score is given as a percentage value with a class label, and these are presented to the user in a gauge format that allows the user to see where the class decision falls. An example of an interface is provided in Fig. 4.

The previous fact-checks box returns the claims that have previously been fact-checked and that are similar to the text extracted from the provided URL. Claims are scored by the fact-check retrieval mode [78], and only those above a threshold of 0.5 are displayed to the user. The information displayed is the same as within the separate *Fact Check Semantic Search* tool within the *Verification plugin*. This includes the claim text, the title, the rating, the date, the domain of the fact-checker, the text language (with an option for any non-English text to be translated to English) and finally an image for the domain.

Aggregation of Credibility Signals for Misinformation Detection

As discussed above, not all of the credibility signals are equally important for detecting misinformation in a certain domain. It is not straightforward to decide whether the presence of a certain credibility signal shows a potential presence of misinformation, and how many of such signals should be detected to definitively answer whether the input represents misinformation or not. Even if such a deterministic framework existed, training specialised models for the detection of credibility signals is a highly costly process relying on a large amount of annotated data for each individual signal. Collecting such annotations is particularly challenging for longer contents, such as news articles, due to the complexity and the high number of credibility signals.

To address these challenges, we proposed a method that involves applying prompted weak supervision to aggregate the LLM-predicted credibility signals in order to classify text as misinformation or not [79]. We refer to our approach as Prompted weAk Supervision wiTh crEdibility signaLs (Pastel). Within our framework, we identified 19 most frequently used credibility signals proposed in prior studies [22, 80–82], and instructed LLMs to answer whether the signal is present in the input news article. The models were restricted to *Yes*/*No*/*Unsure* answers. The high-level prompt is provided in Fig. 5. For consistency, each of the signals was formulated in such a way that its presence in the article indicates potential lack of credibility. For example, in the case of the *Expert Citation* type of signal, the formulation states that the article *lacks* any expert citation rather than *contains* it.

Upon extracting the credibility signals, we applied the labelling function to infer the labels for individual signals, and trained a weakly supervised model to aggregate individual labels into the final binary prediction (*misinformation* or *non-misinformation*) for the entire article. While the individual labels are expected to be noisy in the lack of gold-standard annotations for individual credibility signals, our approach learns to calibrate the contribution of each labelling function to infer the final weak labels.

We compared our approach with a supervised and zero-shot prediction baselines on four different misinformation datasets. For the supervised models, we opted for fine-tuning two state-of-the-art transformer models (BERT and RoBERTa) previously used to benchmark each of the datasets [83, 84] and one LLM (LLaMa-FT). The version of the LLM used for fine-tuning was kept the same as the version of an LLM used to infer credibility signals. For the unsupervised baseline, we used the

```
### Instruction:
You are a helpful and unbiased news verification assistant. You will be provided with the title and the full body of text of a news article. Then, you will answer further questions related to the given article. Ensure that your answers are grounded in reality, truthful and reliable. You are expected to answer with 'Yes' or 'No', but you are also allowed to answer with 'Unsure' if you do not have enough information or context to provide a reliable answer.

### Input:
{title}
{text}

{question} (Yes/Unsure/No)

### Response:
```

Fig. 5 General prompt from Leite et al. [79] used to infer the presence of each credibility signal. The *question* input presented the definition behind the 19 signals considered

LLM to infer the final label (misinformation or non-misinformation) in a zero-shot manner.

We used the supervised models as an upper bound reference that was specifically fine-tuned on gold-standard labels for each of the datasets. Therefore, it is expected that one of the SOTA models (RoBERTa) demonstrated consistently better results on all four datasets. However, we observed that such an advantage is not consistent across all of the supervised models. For example, in comparison with the fine-tuned BERT model, Pastel approach shows better results on 3 out of 4 datasets despite not having access to gold-standard labels. Surprisingly, the LLaMa-FT model was outperformed by a fine-tuned RoBERTa on all four datasets despite having 70B parameters compared to only up to 150M parameters for RoBERTa. Most importantly, LLaMa-FT model was also outperformed by our zero-shot Pastel method for 3 out of 4 datasets. Finally the comparison between the two unsupervised approaches, LLaMa-ZS and Pastel, showed a consistent significantly better performance for the Pastel approach.

We further explored the generalisation capabilities of our approach by comparing the best performing fine-tuned model, RoBERTa, with Pastel by training the models on one dataset and evaluating on three remaining datasets, resulting in 3 versions and 12 evaluations for each model. Our results demonstrated a striking consistent preference for the Pastel approach across all 12 comparisons. On average, Pastel achieves an $\mathrm{F1}_{macro} = 0.75$ compared to RoBERTa's $\mathrm{F1}_{macro} = 0.46$, which is an increase of 63%. The difference in performances is particularly prominent when the training and test datasets belong to different domains, such as training on the political datasets and evaluation on entertainment articles and vice versa. For example, RoBERTa model fine-tuned on the news data about celebrities and evaluated on a political dataset results in a score of $\mathrm{F1}_{macro} = 0.34$ compared to $\mathrm{F1}_{macro} = 0.80$ for Pastel.

We further analysed the association between each credibility signal and the article's veracity by means of performing Pearson's chi-squared statistical test. We found that all 19 credibility signals show statistically significant association with the veracity of the article for at least one datasets, with the majority of the signals (12) demonstrating such an association for all four datasets.

This study demonstrates the potential of credibility signals, powered with the capabilities of modern LLMs, in overcoming a number of challenges in detecting misinformation:

- LLM-predicted credibility signals eliminate the need for developing costly human annotations for detecting such signals.
- The aggregation of credibility signals in the final prediction provides a more nuanced and explainable approach toward detecting misinformation, similar to the one used by journalists in assessing veracity.
- The weakly supervised aggregation of multiple credibility signals allows to account for potentially noisy and hallucinated answers, outperforming not only a zero-shot binary veracity prediction using LLMs but also the costly fine-tuned performance of LLMs on specialised datasets.
- This approach helps to overcome the generalisation problem of supervised models existing in misinformation research, demonstrating a consistent performance across various domains.

5 Looking Ahead

In this chapter, we have provided a novel approach based on automatic detection of credibility signals, which we adopted to support media professionals within the vera.ai project. While most of past research effort was dedicated to traditional single-label (binary or multiclass) false information detection, we put the emphasis on a complementary approach of credibility assessment and automatic credibility signal detection.

Credibility signals, the core element of credibility assessment, allow two different streams of interpretation. Firstly, they can be manually assessed by human experts (e.g., media professionals) or even general public. This is in line with human-centred AI and pro-active involvement of a human in the process where AI is used to support decision-making instead of trying to replace the human factor completely. To this end, we demonstrated a successful use case of integrating six selected credibility signals into the *Verification plugin*. Secondly, credibility signals can be aggregated as features to perform misinformation detection. In this direction, we presented the second use case in which credibility signals automatically detected by LLMs were combined by means weakly supervised approach to predict content veracity [12]. Our findings revealed that 12 out of the 19 proposed signals exhibit strong associations with veracity across all the evaluated datasets.

Following our extensive and systematic literature survey [10], research outcomes, as well as expertise obtained during practical deployment and usage of credibility signals, we conclude that there is also a number of challenges and open problems related to credibility assessment and automatic detection of textual credibility signals. The first challenge is the *ambiguity and lack of established definitions and taxonomies*, which is characteristic for credibility signals and credibility assessment in general. This causes difficulties for researches who want to get familiar with this domain, incompatibilities in dataset labelling, benchmarking and directly comparing supervised models. This open problem requires a focused multidisciplinary effort that already started but not finalised by standardisation attempts (such as W3C Credible Web community group or Credibility Coalition).

Another challenging aspect is *multilinguality*. Its importance is particularly high when the researched models are being deployed and used by media professionals, who naturally and inevitably work in a highly multilingual environment. For languages lacking annotated datasets, machine translation and zero-shot classification can serve as an alternative. However, joint multilingual training often yields more accurate results. For example, as we showed on the case of persuasion techniques detection [14], monolingual models trained using translated data achieved higher performance on English but not on other languages. Consequently, more diverse multilingual datasets are needed to develop state-of-the-art models and robust evaluation benchmarks.

A related open problem is the *lack of large-enough high-quality (accurately annotated) datasets*. Even despite extensive and commendable effort spent so far (especially as a part of various data challenges and shared tasks), the datasets for providing multiple categories of credibility signals, potentially also with an overall credibility score (which would also be useful for the credibility assessment task), are still lacking. Manual annotation of data is highly challenging due to several mutually interconnected issues, such as a need for sufficient expertise, robust annotation guidelines and prevention of annotators' subjectivity. As illustrated in our overview of credibility assessment methods [10], the majority of resources are focused on English and other widely spoken languages, such as Arabic and Spanish. In contrast, for low- and mid-resource languages, such as Czech or Tamil, there is no coverage across multiple credibility signals. Multilinguality (especially in a case of low-resource languages) is further increasing an already challenging nature of annotation process, by requiring annotators to be fluent in many languages and familiar with a local (societal, cultural, political) norms. Additionally, verifying the correctness of annotations (and an adherence to annotators guidelines) in multilingual data is a complex task. We perceive the most recent LLMs, which already exhibit sufficient language understanding in many high- as well as low-resource languages, as a potential solution for verifying human-annotated samples (by meta evaluation) or even augmenting them (to obtain additional silver-labelled training data).

While credibility signals represent more explainable approaches towards misinformation detection, we also recognise *a need of more explainable and interpretable approaches* for individual credibility signals. Given that such signals serve human experts just as a clue, end users must have a possibility to investigate where and how such signal has been detected. To this end, we adopted an attention-based approach to highlight the most relevant and important spans of the text. Similarly, if an automatic credibility assessment (by combining individual credibility signals) is performed, an appropriate level of explainability and interpretability is needed. This direction represent a large and important avenue for future work.

A well-known challenge is *a diminished out-of-distribution performance*. Due to a more focused nature of individual credibility signals, the decrease of performance on out-of-distribution data seems to be not as dramatic as that for more high-level false information detection tasks. However, it still represents a challenging problem, as we have shown on the example of persuasion technique detection [13]. In a practical real-world deployment, out-of-distribution samples are inevitable, whether it is a different style of content, a different language, a different length of input, or various data/concept drifts, such as large societal events. The credibility assessment approaches should be robust enough to maintain an acceptable performance also in such cases.

Last but not least, the rapid development and expansion of *generative AI will intensify a need for automatic credibility assessment*. The generated text became almost indistinguishable from human-written one [85]. A plethora of available LLMs (commercial as well as open-source ones), therefore, represent a potential threat to be misused for generating credible-looking disinformation content. This is also confirmed by our own research on vulnerabilities of LLMs to be misused to generate highly persuasive disinformation new articles [86] that can even be personalised for different audiences [87]. As we showed, this threat is not only theoretical, but there is also an increasing prevalence of machine-generated text in the fact-checked content starting in 2022, when the first version of the ChatGPT model was released [88] (as is also discussed in Chap. 2 of this book).

Acknowledgements This research was supported by the European Union under the Horizon Europe vera.ai project, Grant Agreement number 101070093, the UK's innovation agency (Innovate UK) grant 10039055 under action number 2020-EU-IA-0282, and by the European Union NextGenerationEU through the Recovery and Resilience Plan for Slovakia under the project No. 09I01-03-V04-00068.

References

1. Hu, B., Mao, Z., Zhang, Y.: An overview of fake news detection: from a new perspective. Fundam. Res. (2024). https://doi.org/10.1016/j.fmre.2024.01.017
2. Shu, K., Sliva, A., Wang, S., Tang, J., Liu, H.: Fake news detection on social media: a data mining perspective. ACM SIGKDD Explor. Newsl. **19**(1), 22–36 (2017). https://doi.org/10.1145/3137597.3137600
3. Zhou, X., Zafarani, R.: A survey of fake news: fundamental theories, detection methods, and opportunities. ACM Comput. Surv. **53**(5), 1–40 (2020). https://doi.org/10.1145/3395046
4. Athira, A.B., Kumar, S.D.M., Chacko, A.M.: A systematic survey on explainable AI applied to fake news detection. Eng. Appl. Artif. Intell. **122**, 106087 (2023). https://doi.org/10.1016/j.engappai.2023.106087

5. Hamed, S.K., Ab Aziz, M.J., Yaakub, M.R.: A review of fake news detection approaches: a critical analysis of relevant studies and highlighting key challenges associated with the dataset, feature representation, and data fusion. Heliyon **9**(10), e20382 (2023). https://doi.org/10.1016/j.heliyon.2023.e20382
6. Suprem, A., Vaidya, S., Pu, C.: Exploring generalizability of fine-tuned models for fake news detection. In: 2022 IEEE 8th International Conference on Collaboration and Internet Computing (CIC), pp. 82–88. IEEE Computer Society (2022). https://doi.org/10.1109/CIC56439.2022.00022
7. Hawke, S.: Technological Approaches to Improving Credibility Assessment on the Web: Final Community Group Report 11 October 2018. https://www.w3.org/2018/10/credibility-tech/
8. Rieh, S.Y., Danielson, D.R.: Credibility: a multidisciplinary framework. Ann. Rev. Inf. Sci. Technol. **41**(1), 307–364 (2007). https://doi.org/10.1002/aris.2007.1440410114
9. Self, C.C., Roberts, C.: Credibility. In: An Integrated Approach to Communication Theory and Research, 3 edn. Routledge (2019)
10. Srba, I., Razuvayevskaya, O., Leite, J.A., Moro, R., Schlicht, I.B., Tonelli, S., García, F.M., Lottmann, S.B., Teyssou, D., Porcellini, V., Scarton, C., Bontcheva, K., Bielikova, M.: A survey on automatic credibility assessment using textual credibility signals in the era of large language models. ACM Trans. Intell. Syst. Technol. (2025). Just Accepted (September 2025). https://doi.org/10.1145/3770077
11. Hromadka, T., Smolen, T., Remis, T., Pecher, B., Srba, I.: KInITVeraAI at SemEval-2023 task 3: simple yet powerful multilingual fine-tuning for persuasion techniques detection. In: A.K. Ojha, A.S. Doğruöz, G. Da San Martino, H. Tayyar Madabushi, R. Kumar, E. Sartori (eds.) Proceedings of the 17th International Workshop on Semantic Evaluation (SemEval-2023), pp. 629–637. Association for Computational Linguistics, Toronto, Canada (2023). https://doi.org/10.18653/v1/2023.semeval-1.86
12. Leite, J.A., Razuvayevskaya, O., Bontcheva, K., Scarton, C.: Weakly Supervised Veracity Classification with LLM-Predicted Credibility Signals (2024). https://arxiv.org/abs/2309.07601
13. Leite, J.A., Razuvayevskaya, O., Scarton, C., Bontcheva, K.: A Cross-Domain Study of the Use of Persuasion Techniques in Online Disinformation (2024). https://arxiv.org/abs/2412.15098
14. Razuvayevskaya, O., Wu, B., Leite, J.A., Heppell, F., Srba, I., Scarton, C., Bontcheva, K., Song, X.: Comparison between parameter-efficient techniques and full fine-tuning: a case study on multilingual news article classification. PLOS ONE **19**(5), 1–26 (2024)
15. Wu, B., Razuvayevskaya, O., Heppell, F., Leite, J.A., Scarton, C., Bontcheva, K., Song, X.: SheffieldVeraAI at SemEval-2023 task 3: mono and multilingual approaches for news genre, topic and persuasion technique classification. In: Ojha, A.K., Doğruöz, A.S., Da San Martino, G., Tayyar Madabushi, H., Kumar, R., Sartori, E. (eds.) Proceedings of the 17th International Workshop on Semantic Evaluation (SemEval-2023), pp. 1995–2008. Association for Computational Linguistics, Toronto, Canada (2023). https://doi.org/10.18653/v1/2023.semeval-1.275
16. Bhuiyan, M.M., Zhang, A.X., Sehat, C.M., Mitra, T.: Investigating differences in crowdsourced news credibility assessment: Raters, tasks, and expert criteria. Proc. ACM Hum.-Comput. Interact. **4**(CSCW2) (2020). https://doi.org/10.1145/3415164
17. Kang, B., O'Donovan, J., Höllerer, T.: Modeling topic specific credibility on twitter. In: Proceedings of the 2012 ACM International Conference on Intelligent User Interfaces, IUI'12, pp. 179–188. Association for Computing Machinery, New York, NY, USA (2012). https://doi.org/10.1145/2166966.2166998
18. Zhang, A.X., Ranganathan, A., Metz, S.E., Appling, S., Sehat, C.M., Gilmore, N., Adams, N.B., Vincent, E., Lee, J., Robbins, M., Bice, E., Hawke, S., Karger, D., Mina, A.X.: A structured response to misinformation: defining and annotating credibility indicators in news articles. In: Companion Proceedings of the The Web Conference 2018, WWW'18, pp. 603–612. International World Wide Web Conferences Steering Committee, Republic and Canton of Geneva, CHE (2018). https://doi.org/10.1145/3184558.3188731

19. Feng, K.K., Ritchie, N., Blumenthal, P., Parsons, A., Zhang, A.X.: Examining the impact of provenance-enabled media on trust and accuracy perceptions. Proc. ACM Human-Comput. Interact. **7**(CSCW2), 1–42 (2023)
20. Molina, M.D., Shyam Sundar, S., Le, T., Lee, D.: Fake news is not simply false information: a concept explication and taxonomy of online content. Am. Behav. Sci. **65**(2), 180–212 (2021). https://doi.org/10.1177/0002764219878224
21. Piccolo, L., Blackwood, A.C., Farrell, T., Mensio, M.: Agents for fighting misinformation spread on twitter: design challenges. In: Proceedings of the 3rd Conference on Conversational User Interfaces, pp. 1–7 (2021)
22. Podgurski, L., Zaczynska, K., Rehm, G.: Evaluating Web Content Using the W3C Credibility Signals (2022). https://doi.org/10.3233/SSW220005
23. El Ballouli, R., El-Hajj, W., Ghandour, A., Elbassuoni, S., Hajj, H., Shaban, K.: CAT: credibility analysis of Arabic content on twitter. In: Habash, N., Diab, M., Darwish, K., El-Hajj, W., Al-Khalifa, H., Bouamor, H., Tomeh, N., El-Haj, M., Zaghouani, W. (eds.) Proceedings of the Third Arabic Natural Language Processing Workshop, pp. 62–71. Association for Computational Linguistics, Valencia, Spain (2017). https://doi.org/10.18653/v1/W17-1308
24. Zhang, Y., Da San Martino, G., Barrón-Cedeño, A., Romeo, S., An, J., Kwak, H., Staykovski, T., Jaradat, I., Karadzhov, G., Baly, R., Darwish, K., Glass, J., Nakov, P.: Tanbih: Get to know what you are reading. In: Padó, S., Huang, R. (eds.) Proceedings of the 2019 Conference on Empirical Methods in Natural Language Processing and the 9th International Joint Conference on Natural Language Processing (EMNLP-IJCNLP): System Demonstrations, pp. 223–228. Association for Computational Linguistics, Hong Kong, China (2019). https://doi.org/10.18653/v1/D19-3038
25. Spinde, T., Richter, E., Wessel, M., Kulshrestha, J., Donnay, K.: What do twitter comments tell about news article bias? Assessing the impact of news article bias on its perception on twitter. Online Soc. Networks Media **37–38**, 100264 (2023)
26. Da San Martino, G., Cresci, S., Barrón-Cedeño, A., Yu, S., Di Pietro, R., Nakov, P.: A survey on computational propaganda detection. In: Proceedings of the Twenty-Ninth International Joint Conference on Artificial Intelligence, IJCAI'20 (2021)
27. Da San Martino, G., Barrón-Cedeño, A., Wachsmuth, H., Petrov, R., Nakov, P.: SemEval-2020 task 11: detection of propaganda techniques in news articles. In: Herbelot, A., Zhu, X., Palmer, A., Schneider, N., May, J., Shutova, E. (eds).: Proceedings of the Fourteenth Workshop on Semantic Evaluation, pp. 1377–1414. International Committee for Computational Linguistics, Barcelona (online) (2020). https://doi.org/10.18653/v1/2020.semeval-1.186
28. Dimitrov, D., Bin Ali, B., Shaar, S., Alam, F., Silvestri, F., Firooz, H., Nakov, P., Da San Martino, G.: SemEval-2021 task 6: detection of persuasion techniques in texts and images. In: Palmer, A., Schneider, N., Schluter, N., Emerson, G., Herbelot, A., Zhu, X. (eds.) Proceedings of the 15th International Workshop on Semantic Evaluation (SemEval-2021), pp. 70–98. Association for Computational Linguistics, Online (2021). https://doi.org/10.18653/v1/2021.semeval-1.7
29. Hasanain, M., Alam, F., Mubarak, H., Abdaljalil, S., Zaghouani, W., Nakov, P., Da San Martino, G., Freihat, A.: ArAIEval shared task: persuasion techniques and disinformation detection in Arabic text. In: Sawaf, H., El-Beltagy, S., Zaghouani, W., Magdy, W., Abdelali, A., Tomeh, N., Abu Farha, I., Habash, N., Khalifa, S., Keleg, A., Haddad, H., Zitouni, I., Mrini, K., Almatham, R. (eds).: Proceedings of ArabicNLP 2023, pp. 483–493. Association for Computational Linguistics, Singapore (Hybrid) (2023). https://doi.org/10.18653/v1/2023.arabicnlp-1.44
30. Piskorski, J., Stefanovitch, N., Da San Martino, G., Nakov, P.: SemEval-2023 task 3: detecting the category, the framing, and the persuasion techniques in online news in a multi-lingual setup. In: Ojha, A.K., Doğruöz, A.S., Da San Martino, G., Tayyar Madabushi, H., Kumar, R., Sartori, E. (eds.) Proceedings of the 17th International Workshop on Semantic Evaluation (SemEval-2023), pp. 2343–2361. Association for Computational Linguistics, Toronto, Canada (2023). https://doi.org/10.18653/v1/2023.semeval-1.317

31. Macagno, F.: Argumentation profiles and the manipulation of common ground. The arguments of populist leaders on twitter. J. Pragmatics **191**, 67–82 (2022). https://doi.org/10.1016/j.pragma.2022.01.022. https://www.sciencedirect.com/science/article/pii/S0378216622000285
32. Guo, Z., Schlichtkrull, M., Vlachos, A.: A survey on automated fact-checking. Trans. Assoc. Comput. Linguist. **10**, 178–206 (2022)
33. Hassan, N., Li, C., Tremayne, M.: Detecting check-worthy factual claims in presidential debates. In: Proceedings of the 24th ACM International on Conference on Information and Knowledge Management, CIKM'15, pp. 1835–1838. Association for Computing Machinery, New York, NY, USA (2015). https://doi.org/10.1145/2806416.2806652
34. Shaar, S., Babulkov, N., Da San Martino, G., Nakov, P.: That is a known lie: detecting previously fact-checked claims. In: Jurafsky, D., Chai, J., Schluter, N., Tetreault, J. (eds.) Proceedings of the 58th Annual Meeting of the Association for Computational Linguistics, pp. 3607–3618. Association for Computational Linguistics, Online (2020). https://doi.org/10.18653/v1/2020.acl-main.332
35. Barrón-Cedeño, A., Alam, F., Chakraborty, T., Elsayed, T., Nakov, P., Przybyła, P., Struß, J.M., Haouari, F., Hasanain, M., Ruggeri, F., Song, X., Suwaileh, R.: The clef-2024 checkthat! lab: check-worthiness, subjectivity, persuasion, roles, authorities, and adversarial obustness. In: Advances in Information Retrieval: 46th European Conference on Information Retrieval, ECIR 2024, Glasgow, UK, March 24–28, 2024, Proceedings, Part V, pp. 449–458. Springer, Berlin, Heidelberg (2024). https://doi.org/10.1007/978-3-031-56069-9_62
36. Peng, Q., Moro, R., Gregor, M., Srba, I., Ostermann, S., Simko, M., Podroužek, J., Mesarčík, M., Kopčan, J., Søgaard, A.: SemEval-2025 task 7: multilingual and crosslingual fact-checked claim retrieval. In: Proceedings of the 19th International Workshop on Semantic Evaluation (SemEval-2025). Association for Computational Linguistics, Vienna, Austria (2025)
37. Li, Y., Panchendrarajan, R., Zubiaga, A.: Factfinders at checkthat! 2024: refining check-worthy statement detection with LLMs through data pruning. In: Faggioli, G., Ferro, N., Galuscáková, P., de Herrera, A.G.S. (eds.) Working Notes of the Conference and Labs of the Evaluation Forum (CLEF 2024), Grenoble, France, 9-12 September, 2024, CEUR Workshop Proceedings, vol. 3740, pp. 520–537. CEUR-WS.org (2024). https://ceur-ws.org/Vol-3740/paper-47.pdf
38. Sarnovský, M., Babič, F.: Concept drift influenced by topic change in data streams from social media. In: 2025 IEEE 23rd World Symposium on Applied Machine Intelligence and Informatics (SAMI), pp. 000337–000340. IEEE (2025)
39. Silva, R.M., Almeida, T.A.: How concept drift can impair the classification of fake news. In: Symposium on Knowledge Discovery, Mining and Learning (KDMiLe), pp. 121–128. SBC (2021)
40. Suryawanshi, S., Goswami, A., Patil, P.: Fakeidca: fake news detection with incremental deep learning based concept drift adaption. Multimedia Tools Appl. **83**(10), 28579–28594 (2024)
41. Waldman, P., Devitt, J.: Newspaper photographs and the 1996 presidential election: the question of bias. J. Mass Commun. Q **75**(2), 302–311 (1998)
42. Entman, R.M.: Framing bias: media in the distribution of power. J. Commun. **57**(1), 163–173 (2007)
43. Soroka, S.N.: The gatekeeping function: distributions of information in media and the real world. J. Polit. **74**(2), 514–528 (2012)
44. Barrett, A.W., Barrington, L.W.: Bias in newspaper photograph selection. Polit. Res. Q. **58**(4), 609–618 (2005)
45. Lecheler, S., Schuck, A.R., De Vreese, C.H.: Dealing with feelings: positive and negative discrete emotions as mediators of news framing effects. Commun.-Eur. J. Commun. Res. **38**(2), 189–209 (2013)
46. Dharshing, S., Hille, S.L., Wüstenhagen, R.: The influence of political orientation on the strength and temporal persistence of policy framing effects. Ecol. Econ. **142**, 295–305 (2017)
47. Mannetti, L., Brizi, A., Giacomantonio, M., Higgins, E.T.: Framing political messages to fit the audience's regulatory orientation: how to improve the efficacy of the same message content. PloS One **8**(10), e77040 (2013)

48. Sheshadri, K., Shivade, C., Singh, M.P.: Detecting framing changes in topical news. IEEE Trans. Comput. Soc. Syst. **8**(3), 780–791 (2021). https://doi.org/10.1109/TCSS.2021.3063108
49. Liu, S., Guo, L., Mays, K., Betke, M., Wijaya, D.T.: Detecting frames in news headlines and its application to analyzing news framing trends surrounding us gun violence. In: Proceedings of the 23rd Conference on Computational Natural Language Learning (CoNLL), pp. 504–514 (2019)
50. Card, D., Boydstun, A., Gross, J.H., Resnik, P., Smith, N.A.: The media frames corpus: annotations of frames across issues. In: Proceedings of the 53rd Annual Meeting of the Association for Computational Linguistics and the 7th International Joint Conference on Natural Language Processing (Volume 2: Short Papers), pp. 438–444 (2015)
51. Pfeiffer, J., Vulić, I., Gurevych, I., Ruder, S.: MAD-X: an adapter-based framework for multi-task cross-lingual transfer. In: Webber, B., Cohn, T., He, Y., Liu, Y. (eds.) Proceedings of the 2020 Conference on Empirical Methods in Natural Language Processing (EMNLP), pp. 7654–7673. Association for Computational Linguistics, Online (2020). https://doi.org/10.18653/v1/2020.emnlp-main.617
52. Gururangan, S., Marasović, A., Swayamdipta, S., Lo, K., Beltagy, I., Downey, D., Smith, N.A.: Don't stop pretraining: adapt language models to domains and tasks. In: Jurafsky, D., Chai, J., Schluter, N., Tetreault, J. (eds.) Proceedings of the 58th Annual Meeting of the Association for Computational Linguistics, pp. 8342–8360. Association for Computational Linguistics, Online (2020). https://doi.org/10.18653/v1/2020.acl-main.740
53. Lee, Y.B., Myaeng, S.H.: Text genre classification with genre-revealing and subject-revealing features. In: Proceedings of the 25th Annual International ACM SIGIR Conference on Research and Development in Information Retrieval, SIGIR '02, pp. 145–150. Association for Computing Machinery, New York, NY, USA (2002). https://doi.org/10.1145/564376.564403
54. Stamatatos, E., Fakotakis, N., Kokkinakis, G.: Automatic text categorization in terms of genre and author. Comput. Linguist. **26**(4), 471–495 (2000)
55. Kessler, B., Nunberg, G., Schütze, H.: Automatic Detection of Text Genre. arXiv preprint cmp-lg/9707002 (1997)
56. Rahman, R.: A benchmark study on machine learning methods using several feature extraction techniques for news genre detection from Bangla news articles and titles. In: Proceedings of the 7th International Conference on Networking, Systems and Security, NSysS'20, pp. 25–35. Association for Computing Machinery, New York, NY, USA (2020). https://doi.org/10.1145/3428363.3428373
57. Golbeck, J., Mauriello, M., Auxier, B., Bhanushali, K.H., Bonk, C., Bouzaghrane, M.A., Buntain, C., Chanduka, R., Cheakalos, P., Everett, J.B., Falak, W., Gieringer, C., Graney, J., Hoffman, K.M., Huth, L., Ma, Z., Jha, M., Khan, M., Kori, V., Lewis, E., Mirano, G., Mohn IV, W.T., Mussenden, S., Nelson, T.M., Mcwillie, S., Pant, A., Shetye, P., Shrestha, R., Steinheimer, A., Subramanian, A., Visnansky, G.: Fake news versus satire: a dataset and analysis. In: Proceedings of the 10th ACM Conference on Web Science, WebSci '18, pp. 17–21. Association for Computing Machinery, New York, NY, USA (2018). https://doi.org/10.1145/3201064.3201100
58. Houlsby, N., Giurgiu, A., Jastrzebski, S., Morrone, B., De Laroussilhe, Q., Gesmundo, A., Attariyan, M., Gelly, S.: Parameter-efficient transfer learning for NLP. In: International Conference on Machine Learning, pp. 2790–2799. PMLR (2019)
59. Devlin, J., Chang, M.W., Lee, K., Toutanova, K.: Bert: pre-training of deep bidirectional transformers for language understanding. In: Proceedings of the 2019 Conference of the North American Chapter of the Association for Computational Linguistics: Human Language Technologies, volume 1 (long and short papers), pp. 4171–4186 (2019)
60. Martino, G., Barrón-Cedeno, A., Wachsmuth, H., Petrov, R., Nakov, P.: Semeval-2020 task 11: Detection of Propaganda Techniques in News Articles. arXiv preprint arXiv:2009.02696 (2020)
61. Martino, G.D.S., Cresci, S., Barrón-Cedeño, A., Yu, S., Di Pietro, R., Nakov, P.: A Survey on Computational Propaganda Detection. arXiv preprint arXiv:2007.08024 (2020)

62. Demirdöğen, Ü.D.: The Roots of Research in (Political) Persuasion: Ethos, Pathos, Logos and the Yale Studies of Persuasive Communications (2010)
63. Pecher, B., Srba, I., Bielikova, M.: Comparing specialised small and general large language models on text classification: 100 Labelled samples to achieve break-even performance. In: Proceedings of the 2025 Conference on Empirical Methods in Natural Language Processing, Suzhou, China, pp. 165–184. Association for Computational Linguistics (2025)
64. Leite, J.A., Razuvayevskaya, O., Scarton, C., Bontcheva, K.: A Cross-Domain Study of the Use of Persuasion Techniques in Online Disinformation. arXiv preprint arXiv:2412.15098 (2024)
65. Hamed, S.K., Ab Aziz, M.J., Yaakub, M.R.: Disinformation detection about Islamic issues on social media using deep learning techniques. Malays. J. Comput. Sci. **36**(3), 242–270 (2023)
66. Patwa, P., Sharma, S., Pykl, S., Guptha, V., Kumari, G., Akhtar, M.S., Ekbal, A., Das, A., Chakraborty, T.: Fighting an infodemic: Covid-19 fake news dataset. In: Combating Online Hostile Posts in Regional Languages During Emergency Situation: First International Workshop, CONSTRAINT 2021, Collocated with AAAI 2021, Virtual Event, February 8, 2021, Revised Selected Papers 1, pp. 21–29. Springer (2021)
67. Diggelmann, T., Boyd-Graber, J., Bulian, J., Ciaramita, M., Leippold, M.: Climate-Fever: A Dataset for Verification of Real-World Climate Claims. arXiv preprint arXiv:2012.00614 (2020)
68. Leite, J.A., Razuvayevskaya, O., Bontcheva, K., Scarton, C.: Euvsdisinfo: a dataset for multilingual detection of pro-kremlin disinformation in news articles. In: Proceedings of the 33rd ACM International Conference on Information and Knowledge Management, pp. 5380–5384 (2024)
69. Chalkidis, I., Fergadiotis, M., Androutsopoulos, I.: Multieurlex—a multi-lingual and multi-label legal document classification dataset for zero-shot cross-lingual transfer. arXiv preprint arXiv:2109.00904 (2021)
70. He, R., Liu, L., Ye, H., Tan, Q., Ding, B., Cheng, L., Low, J.W., Bing, L., Si, L.: On the Effectiveness of Adapter-Based Tuning for Pretrained Language Model Adaptation. arXiv preprint arXiv:2106.03164 (2021)
71. Shin, D.: Why does explainability matter in news analytic systems? Proposing explainable analytic journalism. J. Stud. **22**(8), 1047–1065 (2021). https://doi.org/10.1080/1461670X.2021.1916984
72. Kumar, A., Taylor, J.W.: Feature importance in the age of explainable AI: Case study of detecting fake news and misinformation via a multi-modal framework. Eur. J. Oper. Res. **317**(2), 401–413 (2024)
73. Schmitt, V., Villa-Arenas, L.F., Feldhus, N., Meyer, J., Spang, R.P., Möller, S.: The role of explainability in collaborative human-AI disinformation detection. In: Proceedings of the 2024 ACM Conference on Fairness, Accountability, and Transparency, FAccT'24, pp. 2157–2174. Association for Computing Machinery, New York, NY, USA (2024). https://doi.org/10.1145/3630106.3659031
74. Ribeiro, M.T., Singh, S., Guestrin, C.: Why should i trust you? Explaining the predictions of any classifier. In: Proceedings of the 22nd ACM SIGKDD International Conference on Knowledge Discovery and Data Mining, pp. 1135–1144 (2016)
75. Sydorova, A., Poerner, N., Roth, B.: Interpretable question answering on knowledge bases and text. In: Korhonen, A., Traum, D., Màrquez, L. (eds.) Proceedings of the 57th Annual Meeting of the Association for Computational Linguistics, pp. 4943–4951. Association for Computational Linguistics, Florence, Italy (2019). https://doi.org/10.18653/v1/P19-1488
76. Abnar, S., Zuidema, W.: Quantifying Attention Flow in Transformers. arXiv preprint arXiv:2005.00928 (2020)
77. Macko, D., Moro, R., Srba, I.: Increasing the Robustness of the Fine-Tuned Multilingual Machine-Generated Text Detectors (2025). https://arxiv.org/abs/2503.15128
78. Pikuliak, M., Srba, I., Moro, R., Hromadka, T., Smoleň, T., Melišek, M., Vykopal, I., Simko, J., Podroužek, J., Bielikova, M.: Multilingual previously fact-checked claim retrieval. In: Bouamor, H., Pino, J., Bali, K. (eds.) Proceedings of the 2023 Conference on Empirical

Methods in Natural Language Processing, pp. 16477–16500. Association for Computational Linguistics, Singapore (2023). https://doi.org/10.18653/v1/2023.emnlp-main.1027

79. Leite, J.A., Razuvayevskaya, O., Bontcheva, K., Scarton, C.: Weakly supervised veracity classification with LLM-predicted credibility signals. EPJ Data Sci. **14**(1), 16 (2025)
80. Dufraisse, E., Treuillier, C., Brun, A., Tourille, J., Castagnos, S., Popescu, A.: Don't burst blindly: for a better use of natural language processing to fight opinion bubbles in news recommendations. In: First Workshop on Natural Language Processing for Political Science, pp. 79–85 (2022)
81. Musi, E., Reed, C.: From fallacies to semi-fake news: improving the identification of misinformation triggers across digital media. Discourse Soc. **33**(3), 349–370 (2022)
82. Zhang, A.X., Ranganathan, A., Metz, S.E., Appling, S., Sehat, C.M., Gilmore, N., Adams, N.B., Vincent, E., Lee, J., Robbins, M., et al.: A structured response to misinformation: defining and annotating credibility indicators in news articles. In: Companion Proceedings of the The Web Conference 2018, pp. 603–612 (2018)
83. Goel, P., Singhal, S., Aggarwal, S., Jain, M.: Multi domain fake news analysis using transfer learning. In: 2021 5th International Conference on Computing Methodologies and Communication (ICCMC), pp. 1230–1237. IEEE (2021)
84. Rai, N., Kumar, D., Kaushik, N., Raj, C., Ali, A.: Fake news classification using transformer based enhanced LSTM and BERT. Int. J. Cogn. Comput. Eng. **3**, 98–105 (2022)
85. Sadasivan, V.S., Kumar, A., Balasubramanian, S., Wang, W., Feizi, S.: Can AI-generated text be reliably detected? Stress testing AI text detectors under various attacks. Transactions on Machine Learning Research (2025). https://openreview.net/forum?id=OOgsAZdFOt
86. Vykopal, I., Pikuliak, M., Srba, I., Moro, R., Macko, D., Bielikova, M.: Disinformation capabilities of large language models. In: Ku, L.W., Martins, A., Srikumar, V. (eds.) Proceedings of the 62nd Annual Meeting of the Association for Computational Linguistics (Volume 1: Long Papers), pp. 14830–14847. Association for Computational Linguistics, Bangkok, Thailand (2024). https://doi.org/10.18653/v1/2024.acl-long.793
87. Zugecova, A., Macko, D., Srba, I., Moro, R., Kopál, J., Marcinčinová, K., Mesarčík, M.: Evaluation of LLM vulnerabilities to being misused for personalized disinformation generation. In: Che, W., Nabende, J., Shutova, E., Pilehvar, M.T. (eds.) Proceedings of the 63rd Annual Meeting of the Association for Computational Linguistics (Volume 1: Long Papers), pp. 780–797. Association for Computational Linguistics, Vienna, Austria (2025). https://aclanthology.org/2025.acl-long.38/
88. Macko, D., Ramakrishnan, A.A., Lucas, J.S., Moro, R., Srba, I., Uchendu, A., Lee, D.: Beyond Speculation: Measuring the Growing Presence of LLM-Generated Texts in Multilingual Disinformation (2025). https://arxiv.org/abs/2503.23242

Multimodal Detection of Image Misrepresentation

Stefanos-Iordanis Papadopoulos, Christos Koutlis, Symeon Papadopoulos, and Panagiotis C. Petrantonakis

1 Introduction

Digital technologies have not only accelerated the speed and reach of false information but have also given rise to new, increasingly sophisticated, but now easily accessible, forms of false content [51]. On social media platforms, visual content, such as images and videos, has been found to be far more attention-grabbing and widely shared than plain text, which significantly increases its potential for rapid dissemination and widespread impact [33]. Furthermore, research indicates that pairing a false statement with an image can greatly enhance its persuasiveness, as visual elements tend to convey a sense of credibility and authenticity that bolsters the perceived truth of the message [43]. Given this, a particularly pervasive form of misinformation[1] is multimodal misinformation; false or misleading narratives propagated through the combination of text and images.

[1] In this chapter, we primarily use the term misinformation—false or misleading information shared without the intent to deceive—to avoid making assumptions about the motivations of those disseminating it. However, our working definition and the examples presented may also encompass instances of intentionally spread false information, commonly referred to as disinformation.

S. I. Papadopoulos (✉) · C. Koutlis · S. Papadopoulos
Centre for Research and Technology Hellas (CERTH), Thessaloniki, Greece
e-mail: stefpapad@iti.gr

C. Koutlis
e-mail: ckoutlis@iti.gr

S. Papadopoulos
e-mail: papadop@iti.gr

P. C. Petrantonakis
Aristotle University of Thessaloniki (AUTH), Thessaloniki, Greece
e-mail: ppetrant@ece.auth.gr

S. Papadopoulos et al. (eds.), *Countering Disinformation in the Era of Generative AI*,
https://doi.org/10.1007/978-3-032-11782-3_10

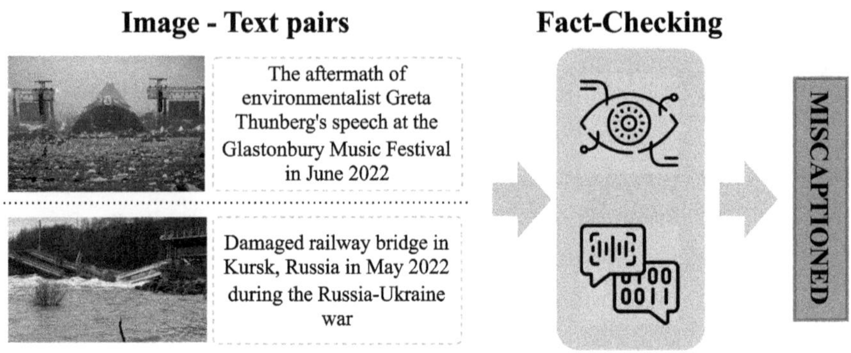

Fig. 1 High-level overview of the image misrepresentation detection process. The figure illustrates sample image-text pairs being processed by a multimodal fact-checking system, and the resulting predictions; "miscaptioned" in both examples. Adapted from the authors' earlier publication [46], with minor modifications

A few examples of multimodal misinformation can be seen in Fig. 1. In the top example, a music festival with littered grounds is accompanied by a caption claiming that the event took place in June 2022 following a speech by environmentalist Greta Thunberg. In reality, while the image does depict the Glastonbury Festival, it was captured in 2015–years before Greta Thunberg became a public figure[2]; in an attempt to frame the environmentalist and her supporters in a negative light. The bottom example shows a collapsed railway bridge over a body of water, with a caption asserting that the incident occurred in Kursk, Russia, during the 2022 Russia-Ukraine war. Although a bridge was indeed damaged in Kursk on that date, this particular image was taken in 2020 in Murmansk, Russia[3]; an effort to misrepresent the severity of the actual event.

Given the scale and rapid spread of misinformation, researchers have increasingly explored automated approaches to assist human fact-checking in their work. Recent efforts have focused on tasks such as claim detection, evidence retrieval, verdict prediction, fact-check article retrieval, and explanation generation [2, 3, 23]. In this chapter, we specifically examine multimodal misinformation detection (MMD), with particular emphasis on the verdict prediction task for decontextualised and miscaptioned images. We provide an overview of relevant literature on MMD datasets and methodologies, discuss key ongoing challenges in the field, and present our research findings and results achieved within the vera.ai project. More specifically, Sect. 2 defines multimodal misinformation as an umbrella term encompassing decontextualised, repurposed, or out-of-context (OOC) images, and miscaptioned (MC) images, and outlines the tasks of both standard and evidence-based MMD. Section. 3 provides an overview of datasets used for MMD, including annotated, weakly-annotated, and synthetic training datasets, and evidence-enhanced datasets. Section 4 delves into

[2] https://www.reuters.com/article/factcheck-glastonbury-greta-idUSL1N2YE1JD.

[3] https://www.reuters.com/article/factcheck-destroyed-bridge-idUSL2N2WU1CM.

detection methodologies, covering modality representation, backbone encoders for feature extraction, modality fusion techniques, and neural network-based approaches that assess either the internal consistency of image-text pairs or integrate external evidence for verification. Section 5 outlines key challenges in MMD, including limited generalisation from models trained on synthetic data, unimodal bias—where unimodal methods outperform multimodal ones due to dataset artifacts—and leaked external evidence, which can hinder the simulation of early misinformation detection. Section 6 provides an overview of our key contributions to the field within the vera.ai research project, including the development of synthetic training datasets, evaluation benchmarks, and methodologies aimed at addressing generalisation, unimodal bias, and evidence reliability challenges in MMD. Finally, Sect. 7 concludes with a summary of our contributions and outlines open research gaps, ongoing challenges, and opportunities for impactful future work in the field.

2 Problem Definition

Let $\mathcal{D} = (I_i, T_i, y_i)_{i=1}^N$ represent a dataset of N image-text pairs, where I_i is an image, T_i is its corresponding text, and y_i is the label indicating the veracity of the pair. The goal of Multimodal Misinformation Detection (MMD) is framed as a classification task $\mathsf{M} : (I, T) \rightarrow \hat{y}$, with M being the mapping function that assigns a predicted label $\hat{y}$ to the given image-text pairs (I, T). While this chapter focuses on image-text pairs, similar formulations can be extended to other modalities—such as video-text or audio-text pairs—for detecting misrepresentation; however, these are beyond the scope of this chapter.

We define multimodal misinformation as an umbrella term that encompasses multiple forms of misleading image-text pairs and introduce two primary variations: out-of-context detection, and miscaptioned image detection. An "Out-Of-Context" (OOC) pair—sometimes referred to as decontextualised or image re-purposing— is defined as a combination of an image I_i^t and a text T_i^x sourced from another image within the truthful sub-set of $\mathcal{D}$ (denoted as $\mathcal{D}^t$), where "x" denotes decontextualisation. On the other hand, a "Mis-Captioned" (MC) image refers to an image whose text T_i^f has been altered to falsely represent its origin, content, or meaning, where "f" signifies the falsehood of the caption. One frequently discussed type of miscaptioning in the literature is Named-Entity Manipulation (NEM), in which named entities—such as people, locations, or dates—are replaced with incorrect or misleading alternatives.

Finally, for the task of evidence-based MMD, we define an enhanced dataset $\mathcal{D}^+ = (I_i, T_i, \mathcal{I}_i^e, \mathcal{T}_i^e, y_i)_{i=1}^N$, where $\mathcal{I}_i^e = [I_{i1}^e, I_{i2}^e, \ldots, I_{iK}^e]$ represents a set of K image-based evidence elements, and $\mathcal{T}_i^e = [T_{i1}^e, T_{i2}^e, \ldots, T_{iZ}^e]$ denotes a set of Z text-based evidence elements; with the task typically being re-defined as $\mathsf{M} : (I, T, \mathcal{I}^e, \mathcal{T}^e) \rightarrow \hat{y}$. These pieces of evidence are linked to the image-caption pair (I_i, T_i) and can be sourced from the Web. Typically external information or images are retrieved by querying search engine APIs (e.g., Google Custom Search) using the textual claim, or by performing reverse image searches (e.g., TinEye) using the image under examination. Other approaches leverage structured knowledge bases, online encyclopedias, or directly access verified content from reputable fact-checking organisations (e.g., Snopes, Reuters) .

3 Datasets

Training machine learning models for MMD using supervised learning relies on the availability of suitable datasets. However, manually annotated datasets are scarce and expensive to produce due to the labor-intensive and time-consuming nature of the annotation process. To mitigate this challenge, researchers have explored three main approaches: collecting high-quality annotated data from fact-checking organisations, leveraging weakly-annotated datasets, and generating synthetic training data. Each approach presents trade-offs in terms of scalability, accuracy, and real-world applicability. Moreover, some datasets incorporate external information from fact-checking articles or Web-retrieved sources to support evidence-based multimodal misinformation detection. The relevant datasets are summarised in Table 1, detailing the number of image-text pairs, the annotation methodology[4], and data sources.

Annotated and Weakly-Annotated Datasets

One attempt at leveraging fact-checking organisations for annotated data is the Fauxtography dataset [83], consisting of image-caption pairs collected from Snopes[5]; 641 labelled as False and 197 as True. To create a more balanced dataset, an additional 395 truthful image-caption pairs were sourced from Reuters. The data were then divided into training and testing sets. Nevertheless, as evidenced by Fauxtography, fact-checking websites offer a relatively limited number of multimodal samples, leading to datasets that lack the scale and diversity needed to train robust MMD models with strong generalisation capabilities. Consequently, most MMD datasets rely on weaker forms of annotations or synthetic data generation to overcome these limitations.

Two widely used datasets in MMD research are the Image Verification Corpus, commonly known as the "Twitter" dataset, and the "Weibo" dataset. The "Twitter" dataset was featured in the MediaEval 2015 and 2016 Verifying Multimedia Use

[4] Wherever possible, we assign specific labels (e.g., OOC, NEM, or MC) to each dataset. However, this is not always straightforward. For instance, while COSMOS is described as an out-of-context dataset, its evaluation set is sourced from Snopes' 'False' and 'Miscaptioned' categories, which more closely align with our definition of miscaptioned images. Similarly, MediaEval Twitter datasets were originally developed for image verification, not explicitly as an MMD tasks. To avoid potential confusion stemming from such ambiguities, we chose not to impose rigid labels in Table 1.

[5] https://www.snopes.com.

Table 1 Overview of image-text-based MMD datasets

Dataset	# Pairs	Construction	Data source
Fauxtography [83]	1233	Annotated	Snopes, reuters
Weibo [27]	9528	Weak annotation	Sina Weibo
Twitter (MediaEval 2015) [10]	15,624	Weak annotation	Twitter
Twitter (MediaEval 2016) [11]	17,857	Weak annotation	Twitter
Fakeddit [42]	680,798	Weak annotation	Reddit
MAIM [26]	239,968	Synthetic (OOC)	Flickr30k, MS COCO
COSMOS (Training set) [6]	200,000	Synthetic (OOC)	News outlets
NewsCLIPpings (Merged) [36]	85,360	Synthetic (OOC)	News outlets
Twitter-COMMs [9]	2,468,592	Synthetic (OOC)	Twitter
MEIR [58]	140,096	Synthetic (NEM)	Flickr
TamperedNews [41]	72,561	Synthetic (NEM)	News outlets
CHASMA [47]	291,782	Synthetic (MC)	News outlets, reddit
FACTIFY [38]	50,000	Weak annotation	Twitter, News/Fact-check articles
NewsCLIPpings+ [1]	85,360	Synthetic (OOC)	News outlets, Search API
COSMOS (Test set) [6]	1700	Annotated	News/Fact-check articles
VERITE (Benchmark) [47]	1000	Annotated	Fact-check articles, Search API [49]

We report the number of image-text pairs, construction strategy (e.g., human-annotated, weakly annotated, or synthetic—either OOC-based or NEM-based, or MisCaptioning (MC) techniques), data source (e.g., social media platforms, news articles, or fact-checking organisations), and whether external evidence is provided for verification. Gray text indicates the presence and source of external evidence included in the dataset

(VMU) challenge [10, 11], compiled through a combination of volunteer efforts and paid micro-workers, consists of user posts collected from Twitter (now X) related to 17 events, including verified incidents and hoaxes. News reports and fact-checking articles were used as supporting evidence to assign ground truth labels. It contains 197 real and 191 misused images, linked to 6,225 real and 9,404 fake tweets, respectively. For the MediaEval 2016 version of the dataset, an additional 998 real tweets and 1,230 fake tweets were included. On the other hand, the "Weibo" dataset [27] includes 19,762 user posts from the Sina Weibo platform containing images related to 73 'real news' events and 73 'fake news' events. For each event, keywords and time spans are extracted, and a query is formed to collect relevant posts through the Weibo search engine. (Note that later studies report only 7,532 user posts for training and 1,996 for testing [44], likely due to deleted posts or broken URLs). While both the Twitter and Weibo datasets have proven to be valuable resources for advancing research on MMD, their limited size is not sufficient to train and test robust detection models. More importantly, the lack of diversity, with only a small number of events represented, restricts the generalisation of models trained on these datasets to real-world misinformation, emerging topics, and new events.

To address the limitations of dataset diversity and scale, the MuMiN dataset was developed as a comprehensive graph dataset linking tweets with users, replies, fact-checked articles, and claims [44]. It contains 21 million tweets spread across 26,000 Twitter threads, linked to 13,000 fact-checked claims covering a wide array of topics and events over a decade. The dataset was built by collecting fact-checked claims from the Google Fact Check Tools, which included 10,920 articles. Using key phrases, the Twitter API was queried to retrieve user posts related to these claims, with posts being no older than three days before the claim date. One of the dataset's strengths is its multilingual nature, supporting 41 languages, making it valuable for global misinformation detection. However, only 6,573 of these posts contain images, while the fact-checked articles lack visual content, limiting the dataset's applicability for research on MMD.

An alternative approach for addressing the challenges of scale and diversity in MMD involved leveraging weak annotations by sourcing data from specific sub-reddits from the forum social network, Reddit, to create the Fakeddit dataset [42]. Labels are assigned based on the originating subreddit, classifying posts into six categories: true, satire, misleading content, manipulated content, false connection, or impostor content (six-way classification); or alternatively grouped into a binary classification of 'misleading' versus 'truthful'. For example, subreddits like *usanews* and *neutralnews* were used for True content, *fakefacts* and *propagandaposters* for Misleading Content, and *theonion* and *fakealbumcovers* for Satire. Of the 1,063,106 total instances, 680,798 contain images, with 413,197 labelled as misleading and 267,601 as truthful. While Fakeddit serves as a valuable large-scale resource, its reliance on automated annotation introduces noise, as subreddit-based labelling may contain inaccuracies or misclassifications, affecting the dataset's reliability.

Synthetic Datasets

Beyond weak annotation, another strategy for constructing MMD datasets involves the use of synthetic, algorithmically generated data. These approaches can be categorised into: decontextualised or out-of-context (OOC) image-caption pairs and named entity manipulation (NEM).

Regarding OOC datasets, early efforts include the Multimodal Information Manipulation (MAIM) dataset, which was constructed using existing image-text pair datasets, Flickr30K and MS COCO. MAIM introduced OOC examples by randomly sampling captions and pairing them with unrelated images to simulate decontextualisation [26], resulting in a dataset of 239,968 image-caption pairs. A similar strategy was later applied in the creation of the COSMOS training dataset, which consists of 200,000 images and 450,000 text samples. Unlike MAIM, COSMOS sources its data from diverse platforms, including 18 news websites, blogs, and social media to increase its relevance for real-world misinformation detection [6]. Nevertheless, pairing an image with a completely random caption often results in easily detectable inconsistencies, making the generated "negative" examples less representative of the nuanced decontextualisation found in real-world misinformation. As a result, models trained on such datasets may struggle to effectively handle real-world cases.

To address this limitation, the NewsCLIPpings dataset was introduced, leveraging VisualNews [34] as its source for image-text pairs, and instead of random sampling, multiple similarity measures were utilised to construct OOC examples more realistically. These include: (1) image-to-text similarity using CLIP [54] embeddings, (2) text-to-text similarity via CLIP embeddings, (3) person matching using S-BERT [57] and Faster R-CNN [19], and (4) scene matching with a ResNet50 [24] classifier trained on Places365 [82]. This approach enhances relevance and cross-modal consistency compared to purely random sampling. The dataset consists of four separate versions based on these methods, along with a final Merged/Balanced version that integrates all four approaches; comprising 85,360 image-text pairs balanced between truthful and OOC samples. To evaluate the quality of the NewsCLIPpings dataset, the authors conducted a human study using 200 balanced samples on Amazon Mechanical Turk. They found that humans' detection accuracy (65.6%) closely matched their model's performance (66.5%) and that human participants were far more accurate on real than falsified samples (96.2% versus 35.0%); underscoring both the inherent difficulty of the task and the plausibility of the synthetically generated mismatches. A similar approach leveraging CLIP-based retrieval to enhance cross-modal relevance was used in constructing the Twitter-COMMs dataset [9], sourcing data from Twitter, focused on misinformation related to Climate, COVID-19, and Military Vehicles.

On the other hand, NEM-based synthetic datasets involve pairing legitimate images with manipulated captions in which named entities—such as people, locations, or events—are altered in a way that misrepresents the image content. To maintain a degree of factual and logical consistency, named entities were replaced using cluster-based retrieval [58] or rule-based substitutions [41]. The Multimodal Entity Image Re-purposing (MEIR) dataset was developed by clustering image-caption pairs based on their semantic and spatial relatedness [58]. This was achieved using GPS coordinates for location proximity, word2vec [37] for textual similarity, and VGG19 [61] (pre-trained on ImageNet) for visual similarity. Within each cluster, named entities of the same type were randomly swapped between captions to generate manipulated samples. The image-text pairs were collected from Flickr, comprising 82,156 truthful samples and 57,940 NEM samples. A similar strategy was employed in the TamperedNews dataset, where named entities were replaced with alternatives of the same type while ensuring contextual consistency—such as maintaining gender when swapping names, selecting geographically proximate locations, or substituting events within the same category (e.g., sports competitions or natural disasters) [41]. The TamperedNews dataset was generated by altering truthful image-text pairs from the BreakingNews dataset, which consists of 72,561 articles.

Evidence-Enhanced Datasets

The above datasets, being annotated, weakly annotated, or synthetic, can be used to train models to identify internal patterns and inconsistencies between image-text pairs. However, internal consistency is not always adequate to detect falsehoods, human fact-checkers require external information, or evidence, to verify information, support or refute a claim. While numerous datasets have been created for text-only evidence-based misinformation detection [5, 7, 31, 68, 70, 78], the use of evidence in MMD remains comparatively underexplored.

The *multimodal fact-checking and explanation generation* (MOCHEG) dataset was introduced as a comprehensive dataset designed to support the full misinformation detection pipeline, including evidence retrieval, verdict prediction, and explanation generation [78]. The dataset comprises 15,601 claims along with 33,880 textual evidence and 12,112 visual evidence. Nevertheless, despite offering both textual and visual evidence, MOCHEG is limited to textual claims rather than multimodal misinformation, limiting its suitability for evidence-based MMD.

On the other hand, the FACTIFY dataset focuses on multimodal evidence entailment, determining whether a combination of images and articles supports, refutes, or provides insufficient evidence for a given claim [38]. It was constructed by collecting tweets from Indian and US news sources, extracting both text and image data from each tweet. Text similarity between tweets from different accounts was evaluated using S-BERT and common word matching, while image similarity was measured using histogram and cosine similarity with a pre-trained ResNet50 model. The tweet pairs were then classified into four categories based on these similarity scores: Support Multimodal, Support Text, Insufficient Multimodal, and Insufficient Text. For the "Refute" category, claims were verified by crawling fact-checking websites, collecting the false claim, its supporting article, and accompanying images. The final dataset contains 50,000 samples, evenly distributed across five categories: Support Multimodal, Support Text, Insufficient Multimodal, Insufficient Text, and Refute. A revised version of FACTIFY was later released, incorporating additional data sources and including satire articles in the "refute" class [66].

A different approach was taken by Abdelnabi et al. [1], who expanded the NewsCLIPpings dataset through automated Web-based evidence retrieval using the Google API. We refer to the evidence-enhanced version of NewsCLIPpings as NewsCLIPpings+ for brevity. The NewsCLIPpings+ dataset consists of 85,360 image-text pairs, evenly distributed between truthful and misleading examples. To gather supporting or refuting evidence, the authors leveraged the textual component T_i to retrieve relevant images ($\mathcal{I}_i^e$) and the visual component I_i to retrieve relevant texts ($\mathcal{T}_i^e$). Each pair is linked to up to 19 textual and 10 visual evidence items, resulting in a total of 146,032 retrieved texts and 736,731 images, all sourced via the Google API. During the evidence collection phase, a language identification tool was used to filter out non-English titles and captions; as a result, with few exceptions, the textual evidence is primarily in English.

4 Methods

The development and training of MMD models for image–text pairs involve several key components. First, ***Modality Representation*** refers to the effective capturing of modality information, as both text and images must be transformed into a representation that can be processed and understood by the AI model. Second, ***Modality Fusion*** involves integrating these representations in a meaningful way to capture cross-modal relationships. Finally, an ***Optimisable Model***, typically a neural network, is required to learn from the fused representations and perform the classification task. A high-level summary of the pipeline and relevant approaches is provided in Fig. 2.

For modality representation, nearly all approaches rely on pre-trained backbone encoders. For textual encoding, early methods utilised models such as TextCNN [30] as used by [71], and word2vec [37] by [29, 64]. Over time, there has been a shift towards more advanced pre-trained language models, including BERT [18] as used by [63, 73], XLNet [77] by [62], RoBERTa [35] by [59], and the Universal Sentence Encoder (USE) [14] by [6]. For visual encoding, researchers have employed convolutional neural networks such as VGG-19 [61] as used by [63, 64, 71, 73] and ResNet-50 [24] by [53], as well as Transformer-based models like Data-efficient Transformers (DeiT) [69] by [79]. More recently, with the rise of large-scale vision-language alignment models like OpenAI's CLIP [54], most studies have transitioned to leveraging these models for both textual and visual representations [1, 36, 40, 81]. Depending on the task, CLIP can be employed in different ways: as a pre-trained encoder without fine-tuning, with end-to-end fine-tuning [36], task-specific fine-tuning [1], or further refined through self-supervised contrastive learning [40].

After extracting modality-specific features using backbone encoders (either pre-trained or fine-tuned), the next step is to effectively combine information from both modalities. Early approaches employed simple concatenation of visual and textual embeddings, followed by a linear classifier [63, 71]. More advanced methods have since introduced sophisticated fusion techniques to enhance cross-modal interactions, strengthening the model's ability to capture consistency or detect inconsistencies between modalities. These include Attention-based Multimodal Bilinear Pooling (AMFB) [32], Bidirectional Cross-modal Fusion (BCMF) [79], MLP-Mixer as a fusion module [28], and Co-Attention mechanisms [73], all of which aim to enhance the integration and alignment of visual and textual information, ultimately improving the performance of the final classification network. For the optimisable model, other approaches have incorporated self-supervised contrastive learning [6], as well as multi-task learning to complement the primary detection objective. Examples include the Event Adversarial Neural Network (EANN), which uses an event discriminator to promote generalisation across events [71], and the Multimodal Variational Autoencoder (MVAE), which reconstructs the input text and image embeddings from a shared latent space using an autoencoder architecture [29].

Recent studies have utilised the NewsCLIPpings+ dataset to incorporate external evidence gathered from the Web, enabling models to evaluate not only the internal consistency of image-text pairs but also their alignment with external sources.

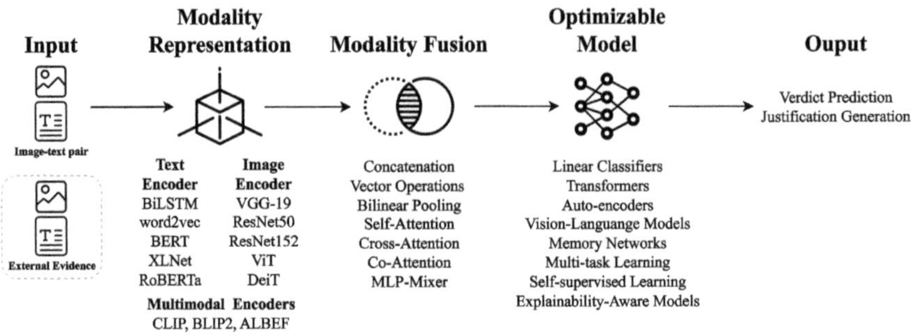

Fig. 2 Overview of the MMD pipeline. The process starts with image-text pairs as input, supplemented with external evidence; if available. Through Modality Representation, modality-specific encoders (e.g., visual and textual) convert the inputs into feature embeddings. These are then integrated via Modality Fusion, combining the information of both modalities. The resulting representations are processed by an Optimisable Model, such as a linear classifier, MLP, or Transformer. The output typically includes a verdict (e.g., truthful or miscaptioned), and may also provide justification, or explanation generation

One such model, the Consistency Checking Network (CCN), assesses both image-to-image evidence and text-to-text evidence consistency using attention-based Memory Networks. CCN leverages ResNet152 for image feature extraction, BERT for text, and a fine-tuned CLIP model (ViT B/32) for multimodal feature fusion. Another approach, the Stance Extraction Network (SEN), builds on the same encoders as CCN but further refines performance by semantically clustering external evidence to determine its stance toward the claim. SEN also integrates co-occurrence information of named entities between the claim text and external evidence [80]. The Explainable and Context-Enhanced Network (ECENet) uses both coarse- and fine-grained attention mechanisms, combining ResNet50, BERT, and CLIP ViT-B/32 for multimodal feature extraction, emphasising the relationship between textual and visual entities to improve overall explanation and contextual understanding [81]. Lastly, SNIFFER focuses on verifying both the internal consistency of image-text pairs and their external consistency with supporting evidence using large visual language models. The model leverages InstructBLIP, which undergoes a two-stage instruction tuning process. First, it refines the model's understanding of generic objects using image captioning data, and then fine-tunes its ability to detect OOC content through task-specific data. SNIFFER employs GPT-4 to generate instruction data that targets inconsistencies, with a focus on named entities in the text and depicted entities in the image, which are extracted using the Google Entity Detection API. This process ultimately produces a unified verdict and explanation.

Methods utilising the NewsCLIPpings+ dataset primarily rely on short texts, such as article titles and image captions, as external information. In contrast, during DE-FACTIFY challenge at AAAI with the FACTIFY2 dataset, which includes full articles as potential evidence, approaches incorporated summarisation tools or top-K sentence retrieval to extract relevant information [65]. Furthermore, similar to NewsCLIPpings+, evidence-based methods on FACTIFY2 leveraged pre-trained encoders like DeBERTa, ViT, and CLIP for modality representation, employed attention mechanisms such as multi-head self-attention or co-attention for fusion, and incorporated additional features like text length and OCR data to enhance performance.

It is important to note that while research on OOC-based and NEM-based datasets and detection methods rarely overlaps directly, many techniques developed for one are likely adaptable to the other. Moreover, a model's output and performance are primarily shaped by the characteristics of the dataset it was trained on, especially how it was constructed and annotated, which largely determine the direction and effectiveness of the detection model.

5 Challenges

Model Generalisation

One notable limitation of synthetic datasets is that, while they attempt to simulate certain characteristics of real-world misinformation—such as manipulated named entities or image-text decontextualisation—they often fail to capture its nuance and variety. As a result, models trained exclusively on synthetic data often struggle to generalise to real-world misinformation. Despite this, most existing studies evaluate their models only on synthetic test sets, which share the same distribution as their training data, limiting insights into real-world applicability. One exception is the COSMOS dataset, which includes a test set of 1,700 annotated samples, with 'Truthful' examples sourced from news outlets and 'False' examples from Snopes [6]. This evaluation benchmark is specifically designed to assess out-of-distribution generalisation, measuring how well models trained on synthetic data perform when faced with real-world misinformation. Originally, the COSMOS test set was structured as triplets $(image, text_1, text_2)$, requiring the model to determine whether both texts are related to the image. However, this setup does not necessarily reflect how misinformation spreads on social media, where misleading content is typically presented as image-text pairs rather than comparative statements. Moreover, $text_2$ from the 'False' class often contains information leakage, as it may either provide the correct caption for the $image$ or explicitly explain why $text_1$ is false. For instance, in one example, $text_1$ states, "Trampoline Bridge across the Seine, Paris" while $text_2$ clarifies, "Photographs purportedly showing a 'trampoline bridge' in Paris are actually concept designs created for an architecture competition". Such cases introduce unintended cues that can make the classification task easier, rendering the dataset unsuitable as a benchmark of actual MMD performance. To better align with real-world misinformation detection, a second task was later introduced in various challenges on 'CheapFake' detection, shifting the focus from $(image, text_1, text_2)$ triplets to $(image, text)$ pairs within the COSMOS dataset [17]. Nevertheless, another challenge with the COSMOS test set is that sourcing truthful data from news outlets and false data from fact-checking organisations may result in significantly different distributions between the two classes, potentially making classification easier by allowing models to rely on dataset biases rather than genuine misinformation detection.

Unimodal Bias

In multimodal learning, unimodal bias occurs when a model disproportionately relies on one modality–the 'dominant' modality–while ignoring or under-utilising information from the other, leading to misleadingly high performance without true multimodal understanding. This issue has been widely studied in various multimodal tasks, such as visual question answering (VQA) [21] and large vision-language models (LVLMs) [15], where models exploit statistical regularities in textual inputs instead of genuinely integrating the visual inputs. However, in the context of MMD, research on unimodal bias remains limited. Recent studies suggest that text manipulations, such as entity substitution in MEIR [58] and TamperedNews [41], can create strong linguistic biases, allowing models to achieve high accuracy without considering the visual modality. For instance, training a text-only model on named entities alone, using the TamperedNews dataset, was shown to perform comparably to full multimodal models [36]. To mitigate this, the NewsCLIPpings dataset was designed to reduce linguistic shortcuts by pairing images with decontextualised captions rather than manipulated named entities. However, this approach does not address model generalisation to real-world misinformation and it primarily addresses one type of multimodal misinformation (OOC) that does not necessarily reflect other types, i.e., miscaptioned images, where falsehoods in the text misrepresent some aspect of the image. Therefore, there is a need for a robust framework that trains MMD models on synthetic data while evaluating their performance on diverse, real-world misinformation, not only OOC but also MC images, while also accounting for unimodal biases.

Leaked Evidence

Evidence-enhanced datasets and evidence-based MMD models incorporate external information to improve verification accuracy, either by retrieving supporting or refuting evidence from the Web or leveraging structured knowledge sources. A critical challenge in this approach is the issue of leaked evidence, which refers to the inclusion of fact-checking articles in the training data [20]. When detection models are trained on such high-quality, human-curated fact-checks, they may become overly reliant on this type of structured information. This creates a major limitation, as fact-checked articles are not immediately available for newly emerging misinformation. Thus, models that depend on leaked evidence may struggle to handle real-world scenarios where misinformation has not yet been addressed by professional fact-checkers, as they have not been trained to independently assess claims based on diverse and unverified evidence. Addressing this issue is essential for building automated fact-checking systems that can generalise beyond previously debunked misinformation and operate reliably in rapidly evolving information environments.

6 MMD in the Context of vera.ai Project

This section provides an overview of our contributions within the scope of the vera.ai project, highlighting key advances in the field of MMD. Specifically, we summarise the development of a framework leveraging synthetic training datasets and evaluation on real-world misinformation to improve model generalisation [46]; the creation of the VERITE benchmark, designed to mitigate unimodal biases in MMD evaluation [47]; the introduction of relevant evidence detection methods to strengthen evidence-based MMD pipelines [49]; an analysis of dataset-specific biases, shortcuts exploited by evidence-based methods for OOC detection [50]; and the proposal of a supervised evidence verification method to address the challenge of leaked and unreliable evidence in evidence-based MMD systems [16].

Synthetic Misinformers

As discussed in Sect. 3, recent MMD models rely on methods that algorithmically generate multimodal misinformation via decontextualisation (OOC) or named entity manipulation (NEM); which we term *Synthetic Misinformers*. However, models trained on synthetic data, were also typically evaluated on synthetic data rather than real-world misinformation, raising concerns about generalisation and assessing progress in the field of MMD. To address this, we proposed an alternative pipeline, illustrated in Fig. 3, that standardises the detection model, optimisation process, and hyperparameter tuning while varying only the training data generated by different *Synthetic Misinformers* while the final evaluation is conducted on a real-world dataset, ensuring a more rigorous assessment of model robustness [46].

We categorised *Synthetic Misinformers* into three types: (1) OOC-based, (2) NEM-based, and (3) hybrid approaches that combine both. To represent these, we used the NewsCLIPpings [36] and MEIR [58] datasets for OOC and NEM, respectively, and explored various approaches using the VisualNews dataset [34], which provides 1.2M truthful image-text pairs from reliable news sources. We ensured a strict training-validation split to prevent overlap. Two examples of OOC- and NEM-based misinformation can be seen in Fig. 4.

- In regards to OOC-based methods, we considered (1) *Random Sampling by Caption* (**RS-C**): randomly samples a text T^x from the corpus for each (I^t, T^t), sim-

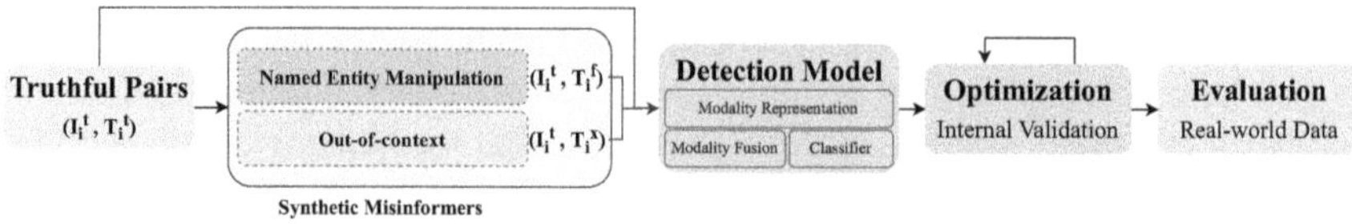

Fig. 3 Overview of the proposed workflow. Truthful image-text pairs from VisualNews are transformed by *Synthetic Misinformers* to generate OOC or NEM samples. The detection model—comprising a backbone encoder (i.e., CLIP ViT-L/14) for modality representation, a modality fusion method (i.e., a Transformer encoder) and classification model—is then trained and validated on synthetic data, and finally, evaluated on real-world, out-of-distribution data (i.e., the COSMOS test set)

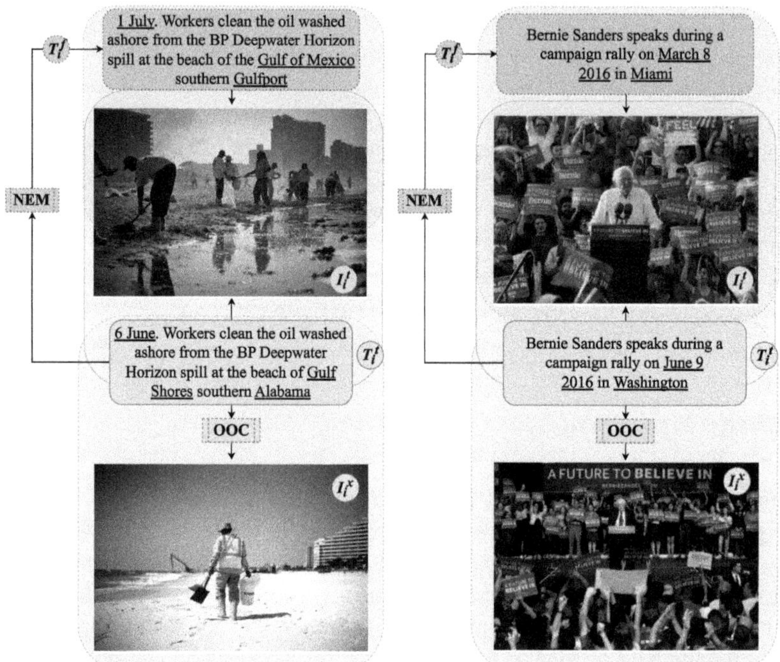

Fig. 4 Training data generated using OOC—and NEM-based *synthetic misinformers* (*CSt-alt* and *CLIP-NESt-alt*)

ilarly to the COSMOS training dataset; (2) *In-topic Random Sampling* (**RSt-C**, **RSt-I**, **RSt-alt**): samples OOC texts or images, or a altering between the two, from the same topic as T^t to increase contextual relevance; (3) *CLIP-based Sampling* (**CSt-C**, **CSt-I**, **CSt-alt**): uses CLIP similarity to find the most similar OOC texts or images within the same topic.

- In regards to NEM-based methods, we considered (1) *Random Entity Swapping* (**R-NESt**): replaces named entities in T^t with randomly selected ones of the same type from the same topic; (2) *CLIP-based Named Entity Swapping* (**CLIP-NESt-**

I, CLIP-NESt-C): finds semantically similar texts via CLIP and swaps named entities of the same type, while preserving contextual relevance.

- Finally, in regards to Hybrid approaches, to better reflect real-world misinformation, we explored methods that blend OOC and NEM. Instead of binary classification, we trained multi-class models that classified samples as *Truthful*, *NEM*, or *OOC* using cross-entropy loss. We tested several combinations, including (1) R-NESt + CSt-alt, (2) R-NESt + NC/T-I, and (3) CLIP-NESt-alt + CSt-alt. While combining OOC and NEM methods typically produce balanced datasets, some hybrid approaches may introduce class imbalance, which we mitigated with random down-sampling.

In regards to the detection model, referred to as **DT-Transformer**, we employed CLIP ViT B/32 and L/14 as backbone encoders [54] for modality representation, a Transformer encoder architecture for attention-based fusion of the modalities, and a classification layer was then used to make the final prediction. The model was optimised using the cross-entropy loss on data generated from one or a combination of *Synthetic Misinformer* methods. The model's hyperparameters were tuned and validated on synthetic validation data, and the model that achieved the highest validation accuracy was then evaluated on the COSMOS test set.

In Table 2, we observe that DT-Transformer consistently outperformed Fine-tuned CLIP [36] across all three NewsCLIpings version, while using a stronger backbone encoder (CLIP ViT-L/14) further boosts performance; achieving up to 77% accuracy on the NC/Bal version. However, as seen in Table 3, when tested on COSMOS, performance dropped significantly, highlighting the challenge of model generalisation. Comparing Synthetic Misinformers, we found that hybrid methods—combining OOC and NEM approaches—performed slightly better than single-method models and that feature-based negative sampling (e.g., *CSt* and *NC*) improves results over random sampling. However, despite these refinements, our models still struggled to detect misleading pairs accurately; the highest accuracy being 59.1%.

Table 2 Comparison of fine-tuned CLIP [36] and DT-Transformer, trained on three versions of the NewsCLIPpings dataset and evaluated on its test set

Dataset	Detector	Encoder	Accuracy
NC/Bal	Fine-tuned CLIP [36]	CLIP ViT-B/32	60.23
NC/Bal	DT-Transformer	CLIP ViT-B/32	65.67
NC/Bal	DT-Transformer	CLIP ViT-L/14	77.09
NC/T-T	Fine-tuned CLIP [36]	CLIP ViT-B/32	69.39
NC/T-T	DT-Transformer	CLIP ViT-B/32	71.63
NC/T-T	DT-Transformer	CLIP ViT-L/14	84.12
NC/T-I	Fine-tuned CLIP [36]	CLIP ViT-B/32	66.98
NC/T-I	DT-Transformer	CLIP ViT-B/32	69.12
NC/T-I	DT-Transformer	CLIP ViT-L/14	80.98

Table 3 Comparison of different *Synthetic misinformers* using the DT-Transformer with CLIP ViT-L/14

Type	Synthetic misinformer	Image-only accuracy	Text-only accuracy	Multimodal accuracy
OOC	RS-C	50.0	50.0	52.2
	RSt-C	50.0	50.0	53.8
	RSt-I	50.2	50.0	52.3
	RSt-alt	50.0	50.0	53.9
	CSt-C	50.0	48.5	53.1
	CSt-I	49.5	50.0	54.7
	CSt-alt	52.3	51.5	55.0
	NC/Bal [36]	50.0	50.0	54.1
	NC/T-T [36]	48.8	50.0	53.7
	NC/T-I [36]	49.2	50.0	55.4
NEM	MEIR [58]	49.4	50.5	53.9
	R-NESt	50.1	58.5	55.7
	CLIP-NESt-C	50.0	58.1	55.3
	CLIP-NESt-I	50.0	54.1	55.2
	CLIP-NESt-alt	50.0	56.7	56.9
Hybrid	R-NESt + CSt-alt	51.8	**59.1**	56.9
	R-NESt + NC/T-I	51.5	57.2	54.4
	CLIP-NESt-alt + CSt-alt	51.3	52.8	<u>58.1</u>

We report accuracy for unimodal (image-only, text-only) and multimodal detectors, evaluated on the COSMOS test set. **Bold** indicates the highest overall accuracy, while <u>underline</u> highlights the best multimodal performance

Critically, we found that text-based models could outperform multimodal ones, exposing a unimodal bias in what is supposed to be a primarily multimodal task. This bias is most evident in NEM-based and Hybrid approaches, likely due to linguistic artifacts introduced by named entity manipulation, as suggested by Luo et al. [36]. However, these approaches also achieve higher performance on the COSMOS test set, raising concerns about the reliability of current datasets and evaluation pipelines for measuring progress in MMD. Moreover, without assessing external evidence or evaluating justification provided by the models, there is a risk that high scores are achieved for the wrong reasons, namely exploiting dataset biases or superficial correlations rather than through genuine multimodal reasoning. This underscores the importance of developing robust training pipelines and evaluation benchmarks that take into account evidence quality and model explainability.

Accounting for Unimodal Bias

In addition to training models on synthetic data and evaluating them on the COSMOS test set, we also examined unimodal bias in the "Twitter" dataset. Here, the image-only DT-Transformer outperformed the multimodal version, achieving 83.7% accuracy compared to 80.5% for the multimodal model. This raised concerns about the suitability of two widely used datasets for MMD. The main concern is that unimodal bias can develop during training due to certain patterns or shortcuts, where models prioritise one modality over the other, if such patterns persist in evaluation benchmarks, they may obscure the presence of unimodal bias in the results and affect assessment of progress in the field. Our hypothesis was that one such problematic pattern contributing to unimodal bias was "asymmetric multimodal misinformation" (AMM), which we contrasted with genuine multimodal misinformation (MM). In AMM, misleading claims are paired with loosely connected images (associative imagery), or manipulated images are accompanied by captions that merely reinforce the false narrative. An example of AMM is shown in Fig. 5c, where a claim about "deceased people turning up to vote" is paired with an image that is loosely related to the claim, used mainly for illustration. In this case, focusing on the dominant modality—whether text or, in some cases, image—would allow a robust detector to identify the misinformation, making the other modality redundant to the detection process. We hypothesise that this asymmetry may contribute to increased unimodal bias. These instances create an imbalance between the modalities, where one modality propagated misinformation, while the other modality plays a minimal or no role. Our estimation is that approximately 41% of COSMOS pairs included associative imagery, 7% reinforcing captions), while only 52% could actually be classified as miscaptioned images, i.e. genuine multimodal misinformation; this partially explains the unimodal bias discussed in Sect. 6.

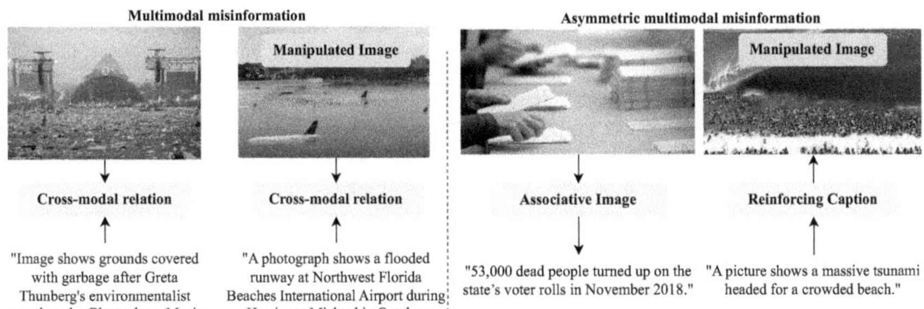

Fig. 5 Examples of multimodal misinformation from VERITE and asymmetric multimodal misinformation from the COSMOS test set

To address the challenge of unimodal bias in MMD model evaluation, we developed the VERification of Image-TExt pairs (VERITE) benchmark [47]. VERITE fills a critical gap by providing real-world, annotated data sourced from fact-checking organisations (Snopes and Reuters) while ensuring the inclusion of only genuine multimodal misinformation, explicitly excluding AMM. The benchmark consists of three categories: True, OOC, and MC, incorporating modality balancing to prevent reliance on a single modality. For each Miscaptioned image from Snopes and Reuters, we also paired the image with its truthful caption and the truthful caption with an OOC image, retrieved via Google API using keywords from the truthful caption—resulting in three pairs from two images and two captions. The data collection process includes strict inclusion criteria, careful selection and refinement of images and captions to eliminate linguistic bias, quality verification, and ensuring misleading alignment in OOC pairs. Figure 6 provides a high-level overview of the data collection process. The final dataset comprises 338 truthful pairs, 338 MC pairs, and 324 OOC pairs.

We then conducted a comparative study, following the approach in Sect. 6, by training DT-Transformer on datasets generated by various synthetic misinformers and evaluating both unimodal (image-only, text-only) and multimodal performance on VERITE. Additionally, we introduced Cross-modal Hard Synthetic MisAlignment (CHASMA), a novel method for generating synthetic training data that maintains the cross-modal relationship between authentic images and misleading, human-written text to create more realistic misinformation pairs. CHASMA utilises a large pre-trained crossmodal alignment model (CLIP) to pair real images from VisualNews [34] with contextually relevant yet deceptive captions from Fakeddit [42]. Unlike NEM-based approaches [58], CHASMA preserves the complex linguistic traits of human-crafted misinformation, including exaggeration, irony, and emotional framing. The final, deduplicated version of CHASMA comprised 145,891 true and 145,891 miscaptioned pairs.

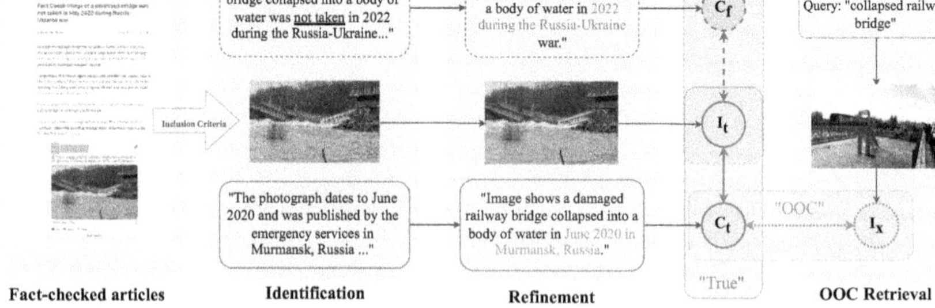

Fig. 6 Overview of the data collection, filtering, and refinement process for constructing the VERITE benchmark, inclusion criteria, selecting and refining images and captions to minimise linguistic bias, ensuring image quality, and retrieving OOC images with misleading alignment

Table 4 DT-Transformer trained and evaluated on separate synthetic datasets, and evaluated on the corresponding synthetic test set

Training dataset	Text-only	Image-only	Multimodal
RSt-alt	50.0	50.0	96.6
CSt-alt	57.4	57.2	75.9
NC/T-T	50.0	53.7	84.3
MEIR	72.2	65.5	73.9
R-NESt	82.6	52.1	91.2
CLIP-NESt-alt	65.5	54.0	70.3
Fakeddit	90.9	90.1	94.5
CHASMA	86.9	60.4	94.3

Table 4 shows the performance of DT-Transformer when trained on separate synthetic datasets and evaluated on their corresponding synthetic test sets. We observe that OOC-based methods exhibit no unimodal bias, with unimodal models making near-random predictions. In contrast, NEM-based approaches, CHASMA, and Fakeddit—where text contains explicit falsehoods—show high text-only accuracy, though never surpassing multimodal performance. Fakeddit also achieves strong image-only results due to its manipulated and humorous images. However, unlike COSMOS, no unimodal model outperforms multimodal ones, indicating that while dataset artifacts contribute to unimodal bias, they do not fully explain it; this highlights that dataset composition—especially the presence of asymmetric multimodal misinformation—plays a key role in amplifying unimodal bias.

Table 5 presents the performance of DT-Transformer trained for multiclass classification by combining the NewsCLIPpings (NC/T-T) dataset to represent OOC and one or two datasets, such as CHASMA and CLIP-NESt, to represent the MC class. The model was evaluated on the VERITE dataset including all three classes. For the True class, we combined truthful samples from all datasets and applied random under-sampling to address class imbalance. The results show that the multimodal DT-Transformer consistently and significantly outperforms its unimodal counterparts in the multiclass setting, indicating that modality balancing helps mitigate unimodal

Table 5 Multiclass classification (three classes) results of DT-Transformer trained on NewsCLIPpings (NC/T-T) combined with one or more MC datasets and evaluated on the VERITE benchmark

MC data	Text-only	Image-only	Multimodal
CLIP-NESt	33.1	33.8	47.7
R-NESt	33.6	34.6	47.7
CHASMA	40.6	37.5	49.0
R-NESt+CHASMA	41.7	33.2	50.0
CLIP-NESt+CHASMA	43.7	34.8	**52.1**

Bold indicates the highest overall accuracy

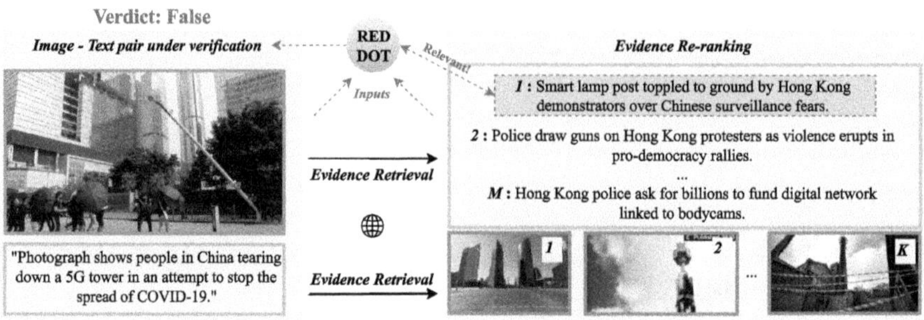

Fig. 7 Visualisation of the verification process for an **image-text** pair using externally sourced *evidence* (**images** and **texts**) retrieved from the Web. The framework first collects and re-ranks external evidence, selecting the most relevant items. RED-DOT then assesses whether the retrieved evidence are relevant or irrelevant to support or contradict the given image-text pair and to finally determine its veracity

bias. Further analysis of binary classification tasks—"True versus OOC" and "True versus MC"—revealed no unimodal bias in the first case. However, in "True versus MC", unimodal and multimodal performance levels were relatively close, though not nearly as skewed as in the COSMOS test set; suggesting that while removing AMM reduces bias, certain distinctive linguistic artifacts in the false texts of MC images remain.

Relevant Evidence Detection

As discussed in Sect. 4, there has been growing interest and progress in evidence-based MMD, particularly in verdict prediction and explanation generation. Nevertheless, existing approaches typically assumed that retrieved content from the Web was relevant and focused on assessing its consistency [1] or stance [80] in relation to the claim under examination. However, we considered that real-world misinformation detection systems must also filter out external information that does not contribute to verifying or refuting a claim. To address this gap, we introduced Relevant Evidence Detection (RED) as an essential step in the MMD pipeline [49]. Our approach included evidence re-ranking, the identification of hard negative samples, and a multi-task learning framework to explicitly assess the relevance of retrieved items. A high-level overview of the RED-DOT architecture can be seen in Fig. 7.

Given a set of K images and Z texts retrieved from the Web for a given image-text pair, we implemented a pre-processing step that ranked evidence based on intra-modal cosine similarity, under the assumption that relevant items exhibit higher similarity than irrelevant ones. To introduce hard negative samples, we incorporated evidence from semantically similar but unrelated image-text pairs, ensuring the model learns to distinguish between truly relevant and irrelevant external information. We then developed the Relevant Evidence Detection Directed Transformer (RED-DOT), which enhances modality fusion by applying element-wise vector operations—addition, multiplication, subtraction, and concatenation—on image-text embeddings. These enriched representations, along with the original image-text pair and retrieved evidence (both relevant and irrelevant), are processed through a Transformer-based architecture similar to DT-Transformer. RED-DOT is trained via multi-task learning, simultaneously optimising for (1) predicting the relevance of each evidence item and (2) determining the final verdict. The model was expected to classify retrieved K images and Z texts as relevant while identifying negatively sampled items (sourced from unrelated claims) as irrelevant, following a weakly supervised learning paradigm. To prevent positional biases, the ordering of external evidence is randomly shuffled during training. We explored multiple RED-DOT variants, including single-stage and dual-stage architectures, as well as different attention mechanisms, such as guided attention. In single-stage learning, the model simultaneously predicts both evidence relevance and the final verdict. Guided attention applies binary cross-entropy loss directly to the attention weights to enhance relevance detection. In contrast, dual-stage learning first identifies relevant evidence, masks irrelevant information, and then makes the final verdict prediction. Additionally, we leveraged various vision-language models (CLIP, ALBEF, and BLIP2) for feature extraction and evidence filtering. For evaluation, we adopt both in-distribution validation (ID-V) on NewsCLIPpings+ and out-of-distribution (OOD) evaluation on VERITE. Furthermore, we introduce Out-Of-Distribution Cross Validation (OOD-CV), employing a 3-fold cross-validation strategy where the model is checkpointed directly on one VERITE fold—enhancing robustness and generalisation to real-world misinformation—before being evaluated on the remaining two folds.

We analysed how the quantity of external evidence impacts performance. Based on the results of Table 6, we observe that using a single piece of re-ranked evidence

Table 6 Variants of RED-DOT (using CLIP ViT B/32) trained with K images and Z texts as external evidence

Method	K, Z = 1	K, Z = 2	K, Z = 4
Baseline (w/o RED module)	<u>70.7</u> (1.5)	65.9 (2.3)	66.4 (2.3)
Single-stage	71.8 (0.1)	<u>72.1</u> (3.7)	67.2 (1.8)
Single-stage + Guided attention	<u>72.6</u> (1.7)	71.9 (3.0)	65.8 (2.7)
Dual-stage + Guided attention	<u>73.6</u> (1.7)	69.9 (2.5)	62.7 (1.7)
Dual-stage + w/ two Transformer encoders	<u>71.3</u> (0.5)	66.5 (2.6)	65.3 (0.7)
Dual-stage	<u>**73.9**</u> (0.5)	70.0 (2.4)	64.7 (1.6)
Mean	**72.3** (1.0)	69.4 (2.8)	65.3 (1.8)

We present accuracy on VERITE ("True versus OOC" classes) along with the standard deviation (in parentheses) for OOD-CV (k-fold=3). The best performance for each method is <u>underlined</u>

($K, Z = 1$) led to the highest accuracy (72.3%) on VERITE (True versus OOC), while adding more evidence led to a decline in performance. Since NewsCLIPpings+ evidence is retrieved from search engines rather than curated by fact-checkers, not all collected items are truly relevant. Increasing K, Z introduces less informative or even misleading evidence, which is still labeled as relevant, adding noise that confuses the model. A similar trend is seen in RED-DOT-Baseline, which does not use irrelevant evidence but still suffers from reduced accuracy with more items. These findings highlighted the benefits of evidence re-ranking, which not only improves detection accuracy by filtering out irrelevant information, but also lowers computational costs by reducing the number of evidence items the model must process.

Dataset-Specific Biases

Research on evidence-based OOC detection has gained significant traction in recent years, with a shift toward increasingly sophisticated architectures; including Transformer-based and memory-augmented networks [1], fine-tuning foundational vision-language models [40], integrating relevant evidence detection modules like RED-DOT, and leveraging instruction tuning and large language models [52]. While these approaches often lead to incremental performance improvements, they also introduce greater computational complexity.

To evaluate progress in the field and identify potential shortcuts exploited by models, we proposed a simple yet effective baseline based on MUltimodal SimilaritiEs (MUSE) [50]. MUSE leverages CLIP-based similarity scores between image-text pairs and their corresponding external evidence. Specifically, we extracted CLIP embeddings for the image, text, top-ranked image evidence, and top-ranked text evidence—re-ranked similarly to our RED-DOT method. We then computed cosine similarity across multiple modalities: (i) image-text pairs under verification, (ii) image-to-image evidence, (iii) text-to-image evidence, (iv) image-to-text evidence, (v) text-to-text evidence, and (vi) image evidence-to-text evidence. This process is illustrated in Fig. 8. The resulting similarity vectors ($S^{v/e}$) were used to train lightweight machine learning classifiers, including Decision Trees (DT), Random Forests (RF), and Multi-layer Perceptrons (MLP), denoted as MUSE-DT, MUSE-RF, and MUSE-MLP, respectively. From a computational standpoint, MUSE is significantly more efficient, requiring only 5,952 FLOPs compared to 2,208,072 FLOPs for RED-DOT—representing a 99.73% reduction in computational cost. Additionally, we also introduced "Attentive Intermediate Transformer Representations" (AITR), which utilises a stack of Transformer encoder layers, each with a varying number of multi-head attention mechanisms. This approach enables the model to analyse the global representation at each Transformer layer and ultimately predict the final verdict. The attention mechanism allows for flexible attention flow, either from a general overview to fine-grained details or vice versa. We integrated the MUSE technique within AITR for enhanced performance.

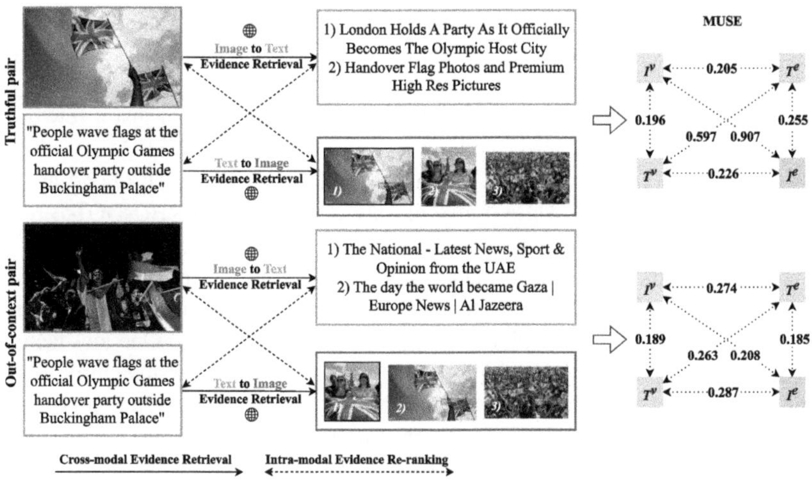

Fig. 8 NewsCLIPpings dataset samples, accompanied by their retrieved and re-ranked evidence, along with the associated multimodal similarity scores. Extracted similarity scores were used to train simple machine learning classifier like decision tree, random forest, and MLP

Table 7 Comparison of evidence-based methods for OOC detection

Method	NewsCLIPpings	VERITE
CCN [1]	84.7	–
SEN [80]	87.1	–
ECENet [81]	87.7	–
SNIFFER [52]	88.4	–
RED-DOT (B/32)	87.8	73.9 (0.5)
RED-DOT (L/14)	90.3	76.9 (5.4)
MUSE-MLP (B/32)	85.4	74.8 (3.8)
MUSE-MLP (L/14)	90.0	80.6 (4.1)
AITR w/ MUSE(B/32)	89.8	76.5 (2.4)
AITR w/ MUSE (L/14)	**93.3**	**82.7** (6.1)

We report "True versus OOC" accuracy along with the standard deviation (in parentheses) on VERITE using the OOD-CV evaluation protocol

In Table 7, we observe that despite its simplicity, MUSE-MLP matched or even outperformed significantly more complex architectures on benchmark datasets like NewsCLIPpings+ and VERITE, while utilising less than 1% of their computational resources. Integrating MUSE within AITR further enhanced performance, establishing a new state-of-the-art performance on both datasets. Our feature importance analysis of MUSE's similarity measures revealed that image-text pair similarity contributes the most to classification accuracy, followed by image-to-image and text-to-text evidence. Additionally, MUSE-MLP maintained strong performance even when trained on just 25% of the NewsCLIPpings training set, while MUSE-RF achieved high accuracy with only 1% of the data—equivalent to just 710 samples. Remarkably, even with as little as 0.1% (71 samples) or 0.05% (36 samples) of the dataset, MUSE-RF's performance did not completely degrade. This suggests that the patterns MUSE-RF relies on are simple enough to be learned from just a few dozen or hundreds of examples. Even without external evidence, MUSE-MLP achieved an accuracy of 80.7% on NewsCLIPpings, surpassing SSDL [40] (71%) and our DT-Transformer (77.1%), while it also closely competes with RED-DOT-Baseline without evidence (81.7%).

Nevertheless, the strong performance of MUSE, despite its simplicity and reliance on similarity-based shortcuts and heuristics, raises concerns about the robustness of current datasets and evaluation protocols for OOC detection. One key factor to consider is that NewsCLIPpings generates OOC samples by mismatching truthful image-text pairs with semantically similar alternatives. By leveraging cross-modal similarities, MUSE could effectively reverse-engineer these misaligned pairs, leading to high accuracy. As a result, MUSE-MLP achieves 81% accuracy without requiring external evidence. Integrating multimodal similarities with external evidence further improved detection accuracy to 90–93%. However, this improvement must be understood in the context of the evidence retrieval process, which involved cross-modal retrieval—where images retrieved text and texts retrieved images—followed by re-ranking based on intra-modal similarity. Given that NewsCLIPpings' truthful image-text pairs originate from major news sources like USA Today, BBC, and The Guardian, the retrieval process often returns the original article or a highly related one, thus, significantly boosting accuracy. In practice, truthful pairs exhibit high similarity scores with retrieved evidence, whereas OOC samples show much lower scores. This heuristic-driven approach resulted in strong performance on NewsCLIPpings but proves relatively less effective on VERITE, where MUSE achieved 80–82% accuracy. Moreover, we observed a notable imbalance, with high accuracy for the Truthful class (90–92%) but substantially lower accuracy for OOC samples (70%). Finally, we found that MUSE and AITR struggled to generalise to the Miscaptioned samples in VERITE, performing at near-random levels. These cases involve images and texts that are closely related but contain critical misrepresentations, such as incorrect people, dates, or events. Since CLIP features and similarity measures fail to capture subtle linguistic nuances, they are ineffective for detecting these discrepancies. These findings raised important questions about the current direction of the field, including the definition of OOC misinformation, dataset construction, and evidence collection methods—topics that will be explored further in Sect. 7.

Evidence Verification

Automated fact-checking pipelines typically rely on external information retrieved from the Web. However, search engine results do not guarantee the credibility or factual accuracy of the retrieved content. With RED-DOT, we re-ranked external information based on relevance. Yet, relevance alone does not prevent unreliable or misleading information from being ranked highly. For more robust fact-checking systems, it is essential to first assess the credibility of the source before passing the retrieved evidence to detection models. Additionally, as discussed in Sect. 5, another critical challenge is the presence of leaked evidence—fact-checked content that may appear in the retrieved evidence during training, leading to unrealistic evaluation settings. Therefore, evidence verification and filtering are crucial pre-processing steps to ensure the reliability of external information and enhance the effectiveness of automated fact-checking pipelines.

To tackle the challenge of unreliable and leaked evidence in automated fact-checking, we developed a supervised evidence verification approach [16]. As part of this effort, we introduced the CREDible, Unreliable, or LEaked (CREDULE) dataset, constructed by modifying, merging, and extending several established datasets that were already annotated and aligned with our criteria. Specifically, MultiFC [7], PUB-HEALTH [31], and Politifact[6] consist of articles collected directly from fact-checking organisations. NELA-GT [45] used credibility scores from Media Bias Fact Check (MBFC) to collect and label articles as reliable, unreliable, or mixed. Meanwhile, the Fake News Corpus[7] and Getting Real About Fake News[8] were assembled by aggregating articles from sources annotated as consistently spreading deceptive or fabricated content. These dataset comprise both short texts (titles) and long texts (full articles). We further processed them by extracting article bodies where necessary and re-balancing class distributions. The final CREDULE dataset comprises 91,632 samples, evenly distributed across three categories: Credible, Unreliable, and Fact-checked (Leaked).

After the creation of CREDULE, our objective was to train an EVidence-Verification Network (EVVER-Net), a classification model capable of identifying credible, unreliable and leaked information retrieved during evidence collection, thus, ensuring that only credible evidence is passed to fact-checking systems (illustrated in Fig. 9). To achieve this, we trained a neural classifier capable of filtering evidence based on its credibility. We experimented with various pre-trained Transformer-based models for both short and long texts, including DeBERTa [25], CLIP [55], T5 [56], LongT5 [22], and Longformer [8]. To further enhance classification, we incorporated domain credibility scores (DCS) from the Media Bias/Fact Check (MBFC) website[9]. Our results showed that, without DCS, the model achieved an accuracy of 79.5% on short texts using DeBERTa embeddings, and 89.0% on long texts with Longformer. When integrating credibility scores, performance improved substantially—91.5% accuracy on short texts with DeBERTa and 94.4% on full articles with Longformer. Note that, in this work, we relied on credibility scores provided by the MBFC organization; for further discussion and potential directions regarding credibility signals, refer to Chap. 9.

---

[6] https://www.kaggle.com/datasets/rmisra/politifact-fact-check-dataset.

[7] https://github.com/several27/FakeNewsCorpus.

[8] https://www.kaggle.com/dsv/911.

[9] https://mediabiasfactcheck.com/.

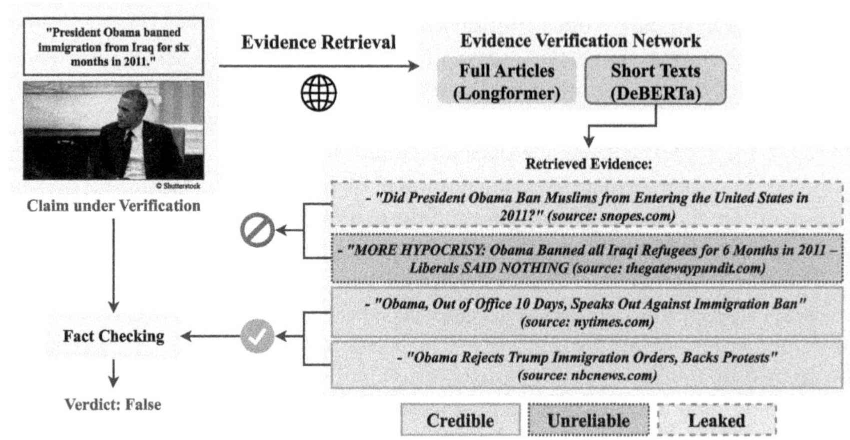

Fig. 9 Overview of the automated fact-checking pipeline incorporating the proposed evidence verification network

Using the trained EVVER-Net, we analysed the external evidence included in several widely-used datasets—namely, LIAR-PLUS [4], FACTIFY [38], MOCHEG [78], and NewsCLIPpings+ [1]. Our analysis reveals that these datasets frequently include evidence that either originates from fact-checking articles themselves (leaked evidence) or stems from unreliable sources. Specifically, 98.5% of LIAR-Plus, 83.6% of MOCHEG, and 95.0% of articles in the "Refute" class of FACTIFY were found to be leaked. Naturally, the use of previously fact-checked information is not inherently problematic. The issue arises when such fact-checked (leaked) evidence is used during the training of evidence-based models intended for early detection—that is, identifying emerging misinformation that has not yet been fact-checked. In this scenario, the model risks learning to rely on high-quality, fact-checked evidence, which will not be available when encountering new, unverified misinformation. This reliance creates unrealistic conditions and undermines the robustness and generalisation ability of evidence-based MMD systems for early detection tasks.

Furthermore, in our analysis, we found that the NewsCLIPpings+ dataset exhibited the lowest proportion of leaked evidence (14.1%), with 64.5% of evidence deemed credible and 21.4% categorised as unreliable. Conversely, the evidence used in RED-DOT and MUSE showed a higher leakage rate of 35.3%, with 42.6% credible and 22.1% unreliable evidence. It is worth noting, however, that both NewsCLIPpings and RED-DOT/MUSE primarily use short texts (article titles) as evidence, which are less likely to leak direct fact-checked information into the model. For instance, excerpts directly sourced from fact-checking articles, such as "[...] But we rated the statement as True" (LIAR-PLUS) or "A satire article [...] intended to be a prank [...]" (FACTIFY) reflect explicit fact-checker judgments and evaluations, effectively revealing the verification outcome within the evidence itself. While informative, such evidence introduces an unrealistic advantage for models designed for early-stage misinformation detection, where fact-checker-verified information would not yet be available. In contrast, short titles like "Does This NASA Photo Show a 'Portal' and 'Wall' on Mars?" (VERITE), do not inherently leak fact-checking information or indicate credibility. However, if these titles were accompanied by the full article content—often containing explicit verification or editorial context—they could similarly introduce leaked or biased information, undermining the intended purpose of evidence-based MMD systems.

7 Conclusions and Future Research

In recent years, multimodal misinformation detection (MMD) has received growing attention from researchers, leading to notable progress in the development of datasets, methodologies, and evaluation protocols. Much of this progress has been driven by efforts to collect and curate large-scale training datasets, both weakly annotated and synthetically generated, as well as by a strong emphasis on evidence-based approaches—motivated by the human fact-checking process, which requires external information to verify claims. Throughout this chapter, we have sought to provide an overview of our contributions to this evolving field in several key ways as part of the vera.ai research project. Specifically, we addressed the challenges of model generalisation and evaluation by proposing a standardised training-evaluation pipeline and by identifying and mitigating unimodal biases in benchmark datasets [46]. We introduced the VERITE benchmark to promote more objective and robust evaluation [47], proposed methods for relevant evidence detection [49] and for evidence verification and filtering [16], and critically examined existing practices by uncovering the prevalence of surface-level artifacts and similarity-based shortcuts in evidence-based MMD systems; highlighting the risks of models relying on shallow cross-modal similarities rather than true factual reasoning [50].

Despite these advancements, it is clear that AI-based MMD remains an extremely challenging and nascent research area. There is still much work to be done to ensure that detection models are robust, trustworthy, and effective in real-world scenarios. One important such limitation is the over-reliance on a narrow definition of out-of-context (OOC) misinformation commonly adopted in the field, defined as the pairing of truthful texts with unrelated images. However, this overlooks the more complex and realistic cases where the text itself may contain falsehoods. We argue for an expanded and more comprehensive definition of multimodal misinformation that includes both OOC and miscaptioned (MC) content; as defined in our VERITE evaluation benchmark. Nevertheless, we caution that the use of manipulated text in MC-based datasets may introduce additional linguistic and unimodal biases [36]. Addressing these biases will require solutions not only at the data level but also through algorithmic interventions, such as bias mitigation techniques explored in prior work [13]. Additionally, we emphasise the need to go beyond current evaluation practices. It is crucial to develop rigorous evaluation tests that assess whether models genuinely reason over factual consistency and logical coherence, rather than exploiting heuristic patterns or superficial similarities—a problem we exposed in our analysis [50].

Another important consideration concerns the over-reliance on synthetic datasets based on simple manipulation rules, such as OOC or Named Entity Manipulation (NEM). While these datasets offer controlled conditions for training, they often lack the complexity and nuance of real-world misinformation. Ideally, large-scale real-world datasets would be the most effective path forward; however, in their absence, AI-generated misinformation datasets, enabled by LVLMs, would offer a promising alternative for exploration. A recent effort to address this gap is our "MisCaption This!" dataset, which consists of LVLM-generated miscaptioned images. Experimental results indicate that models trained on the LVLM-generated data exhibit better generalisation to real-world misinformation, outperforming models trained on traditional OOC-based or NEM-based datasets [48]. However, researchers must proceed with caution, considering the ethical implications and risks of releasing prompts, methods, or tools capable of producing highly realistic and potentially harmful misinformation.

Additionally, the absence of a large-scale dataset of miscaptioned images accompanied by external evidence has limited the community's ability to systematically study this type of misinformation without concerns of leaked evidence. Addressing this gap is a critical step toward more comprehensive and reliable evaluation. One dataset that explicitly addresses the challenge of evidence leakage, as well as the challenges of insufficient evidence and context dependence, is AVERITEC, a collection of 4,568 real-world claims fact-checked by 50 organisations, each annotated with web-sourced external evidence, question–answer pairs, and textual justifications produced through a multi-round human annotation process [60]. Future research should build on such efforts by expanding them to explicitly address the unique challenges of MMD. However, the creation of large-scale training datasets with annotated external evidence remains a significant challenge, given the time and resource demands of human annotation. To address this, automated evidence retrieval pipelines could be developed to collect and filter relevant information from the web, leveraging credibility signals and applying safeguards to prevent temporal leakage. Additionally, contemporary LVLMs also hold potential to assist in both retrieving and filtering external evidence in a scalable manner.

Finally, we encourage future work to expand beyond the current focus on image-text pairs. Misinformation spreads in various forms, including audio, video, and multimodal combinations, which require dedicated research and detection strategies [2, 74]. Similarly, the current landscape is predominantly focused on English-language misinformation. The development of multilingual and cross-lingual MMD methods remains an open and underexplored research direction, essential to tackle misinformation on a truly global scale [39].

Apart from the aforementioned immediate challenges, next-level research could focus on developing end-to-end fact-checking pipelines that encompass claim detection, retrieval of previously fact-checked articles, the collection, filtering, and re-ranking of external information, followed by verdict prediction and explanation generation. LVLMs and Retrieval-Augmented Generation (RAG) approaches could play a central role in such systems by dynamically querying the web in real time, thus emulating human-like fact-checking rather than relying solely on static, pre-trained knowledge. Already, recent works have started incorporating LLMs and LVLMs into the detection pipeline, leveraging their zero-shot and chain-of-thought reasoning abilities for tasks such as evidence retrieval, summarisation, verdict prediction, and justification generation, as seen in frameworks like DEFAME [12], LVLM4FV[72], E2LVLM [67], and LEMMA [75]; all of which report improvements in detection performance and quality of generated explanations.

Future systems may also integrate provenance-aware capabilities to trace the origin and evolution of multimedia content through image forensics, metadata, and reverse image search. Furthermore, interactive, explainable agents could guide users through the verification process, boosting both trust and media literacy. However, these systems would require rigorous safeguards to handle hallucinations, unreliable web data, and feedback loops caused by LLM-generated content polluting online sources. One such recent study simulated the impact of 'polluted' evidence generated by AI models, showing a notable drop in detection performance. To address this, the authors proposed a cross-modal evidence re-ranking method based on claim-evidence reasoning, which effectively filters irrelevant or misleading content and restores performance closer to clean-evidence baselines [76]. Crucially, such tools are not envisioned to replace professional or community-based fact-checking, but rather to augment their efforts; for instance, by prioritising content for human review or offering automated assistance in evidence gathering and monitoring at scale.

In conclusion, while significant progress has been made, MMD research is still in its early stages. Realising the full potential of this field will require continued interdisciplinary efforts, careful methodological choices, and a critical perspective on the limitations and ethical challenges associated with automated misinformation detection.

Acknowledgements This research was supported by the European Union under the Horizon Europe vera.ai project, Grant Agreement number 101070093.

References

1. Abdelnabi, S., Hasan, R., Fritz, M.: Open-domain, content-based, multi-modal fact-checking of out-of-context images via online resources. In: Proceedings of the IEEE/CVF Conference on Computer Vision and Pattern Recognition, pp. 14940–14949 (2022)
2. Akhtar, M., Schlichtkrull, M., Guo, Z., Cocarascu, O., Simperl, E., Vlachos, A.: Multimodal automated fact-checking: a survey. In: Findings of the Association for Computational Linguistics: EMNLP 2023, pp. 5430–5448 (2023)
3. Alam, F., Cresci, S., Chakraborty, T., Silvestri, F., Dimitrov, D., Da San Martino, G., Shaar, S., Firooz, H., Nakov, P., et al.: A survey on multimodal disinformation detection. In: Proceedings of the 29th International Conference on Computational Linguistics, pp. 6625–6643 (2022)
4. Alhindi, T., Petridis, S., Muresan, S.: Where is your evidence: improving fact-checking by justification modeling. In: Thorne, J., Vlachos, A., Cocarascu, O., Christodoulopoulos, C., Mittal,

A. (eds.) Proceedings of the First Workshop on Fact Extraction and VERification (FEVER). Association for Computational Linguistics, Brussels, Belgium, pp. 85–90 (2018). https://doi.org/10.18653/v1/W18-5513. URL https://aclanthology.org/W18-5513
5. Aly, R., Guo, Z., Schlichtkrull, M.S., Thorne, J., Vlachos, A., Christodoulopoulos, C., Cocarascu, O., Mittal, A.: The fact extraction and verification over unstructured and structured information (feverous) shared task. In: Proceedings of the Fourth Workshop on Fact Extraction and VERification (FEVER). Association for Computational Linguistics (2021)
6. Aneja, S., Bregler, C., Nießner, M.: Cosmos: catching out-of-context image misuse using self-supervised learning. In: Proceedings of the AAAI Conference on Artificial Intelligence, vol. 37, pp. 14084–14092 (2023)
7. Augenstein, I., Lioma, C., Wang, D., Lima, L.C., Hansen, C., Hansen, C., Simonsen, J.G.: Multifc: a real-world multi-domain dataset for evidence-based fact checking of claims. In: Proceedings of the 2019 Conference on Empirical Methods in Natural Language Processing and the 9th International Joint Conference on Natural Language Processing (EMNLP-IJCNLP), pp. 4685–4697 (2019)
8. Beltagy, I., Peters, M.E., Cohan, A.: Longformer: the long-document transformer. arXiv preprint arXiv:2004.05150 (2020)
9. Biamby, G., Luo, G., Darrell, T., Rohrbach, A.: Twitter-comms: detecting climate, covid, and military multimodal misinformation. In: Proceedings of the 2022 Conference of the North American Chapter of the Association for Computational Linguistics: Human Language Technologies, pp. 1530–1549 (2022)
10. Boididou, C., Andreadou, K., Papadopoulos, S., Dang Nguyen, D.T., Boato, G., Riegler, M., Kompatsiaris, Y., et al.: Verifying multimedia use at mediaeval 2015. In: MediaEval 2015, vol. 1436. CEUR-WS (2015)
11. Boididou, C., Middleton, S.E., Jin, Z., Papadopoulos, S., Dang-Nguyen, D.T., Boato, G., Kompatsiaris, Y.: Verifying information with multimedia content on twitter: a comparative study of automated approaches. Multimedia Tools Appl. **77**, 15545–15571 (2018). https://doi.org/10.1007/s11042-017-5132-9
12. Braun, T., Rothermel, M., Rohrbach, M., Rohrbach, A.: Defame: dynamic evidence-based fact-checking with multimodal experts. arXiv preprint arXiv:2412.10510 (2024)
13. Cadene, R., Dancette, C., Cord, M., Parikh, D., et al.: Rubi: reducing unimodal biases for visual question answering. Adv. Neural Inform. Process. Syst. **32** (2019)
14. Cer, D., Yang, Y., Kong, S.Y., Hua, N., Limtiaco, N., John, R.S., Constant, N., Guajardo-Cespedes, M., Yuan, S., Tar, C., et al.: Universal sentence encoder for English. In: Proceedings of the 2018 Conference on Empirical Methods in Natural Language Processing: System Demonstrations, pp. 169–174 (2018)
15. Chen, M., Cao, Y., Zhang, Y., Lu, C.: Quantifying and mitigating unimodal biases in multimodal large language models: a causal perspective. In: Findings of the Association for Computational Linguistics: EMNLP 2024, pp. 16449–16469 (2024)
16. Chrysidis, Z., Papadopoulos, S.I., Papadopoulos, S., Petrantonakis, P.: Credible, unreliable or leaked?: Evidence verification for enhanced automated fact-checking. In: Proceedings of the 3rd ACM International Workshop on Multimedia AI against Disinformation, pp. 73–81 (2024)
17. Dang-Nguyen, D.T., Khan, S.A., Riegler, M., Halvorsen, P., Tran, A.D., Dao, M.S., Tran, M.T.: Overview of the grand challenge on detecting cheap fakes at ACM ICMR 2024. In: Proceedings of the 2024 International Conference on Multimedia Retrieval, pp. 1275–1281 (2024)
18. Devlin, J., Chang, M.W., Lee, K., Toutanova, K.: Bert: Pre-training of deep bidirectional transformers for language understanding. In: Proceedings of the 2019 Conference of the North American Chapter of the Association for Computational Linguistics: Human Language Technologies, Vol. 1 (long and short papers), pp. 4171–4186 (2019)
19. Girshick, R.: Fast R-CNN. In: Proceedings of the IEEE International Conference on Computer Vision, pp. 1440–1448 (2015)
20. Glockner, M., Hou, Y., Gurevych, I.: Missing counter-evidence renders NLP fact-checking unrealistic for misinformation. In: Proceedings of the 2022 Conference on Empirical Methods in Natural Language Processing, pp. 5916–5936. (2022)

21. Goyal, Y., Khot, T., Summers-Stay, D., Batra, D., Parikh, D.: Making the V in VQA matter: elevating the role of image understanding in visual question answering. In: Proceedings of the IEEE Conference on Computer Vision and Pattern Recognition, pp. 6904–6913 (2017)
22. Guo, M., Ainslie, J., Uthus, D., Ontanon, S., Ni, J., Sung, Y.H., Yang, Y.: Longt5: efficient text-to-text transformer for long sequences. In: Findings of the Association for Computational Linguistics: NAACL 2022, pp. 724–736. (2022)
23. Guo, Z., Schlichtkrull, M., Vlachos, A.: A survey on automated fact-checking. Trans. Assoc. Comput. Linguist. **10**, 178–206 (2022)
24. He, K., Zhang, X., Ren, S., Sun, J.: Deep residual learning for image recognition. In: Proceedings of the IEEE Conference on Computer Vision and Pattern Recognition, pp. 770–778 (2016)
25. He, P., Liu, X., Gao, J., Chen, W.: Deberta: decoding-enhanced Bert with disentangled attention. arXiv preprint arXiv:2006.03654 (2020)
26. Jaiswal, A., Sabir, E., AbdAlmageed, W., Natarajan, P.: Multimedia semantic integrity assessment using joint embedding of images and text. In: Proceedings of the 25th ACM International Conference on Multimedia, pp. 1465–1471 (2017). https://doi.org/10.1145/3123266.3123385
27. Jin, Z., Cao, J., Zhang, Y., Zhou, J., Tian, Q.: Novel visual and statistical image features for microblogs news verification. IEEE Trans. Multimedia **19**(3), 598–608 (2016)
28. Jing, J., Wu, H., Sun, J., Fang, X., Zhang, H.: Multimodal fake news detection via progressive fusion networks. Inform. Process. Manage. **60**(1), 103120 (2023)
29. Khattar, D., Goud, J.S., Gupta, M., Varma, V.: Mvae: Multimodal variational autoencoder for fake news detection. In: The World Wide Web Conference, pp. 2915–2921 (2019). https://doi.org/10.1145/3308558.3313552
30. Kim, Y.: Convolutional neural networks for sentence classification (2014). URL https://arxiv.org/abs/1408.5882
31. Kotonya, N., Toni, F.: Explainable automated fact-checking for public health claims. In: Proceedings of the 2020 Conference on Empirical Methods in Natural Language Processing (EMNLP), pp. 7740–7754 (2020)
32. Kumari, R., Ekbal, A.: AMFB: attention based multimodal factorized bilinear pooling for multimodal fake news detection. Expert Syst. Appl. **184**, 115412 (2021)
33. Li, Y., Xie, Y.: Is a picture worth a thousand words? an empirical study of image content and social media engagement. J. Mark. Res. **57**(1), 1–19 (2020). https://doi.org/10.1177/0022243719881113
34. Liu, F., Wang, Y., Wang, T., Ordonez, V.: Visual news: benchmark and challenges in news image captioning. In: Proceedings of the 2021 Conference on Empirical Methods in Natural Language Processing, pp. 6761–6771 (2021)
35. Liu, Y., Ott, M., Goyal, N., Du, J., Joshi, M., Chen, D., Levy, O., Lewis, M., Zettlemoyer, L., Stoyanov, V.: Roberta: a robustly optimized Bert pretraining approach. arXiv preprint arXiv:1907.11692 (2019)
36. Luo, G., Darrell, T., Rohrbach, A.: Newsclippings: automatic generation of out-of-context multimodal media. In: Proceedings of the 2021 Conference on Empirical Methods in Natural Language Processing, pp. 6801–6817 (2021)
37. Mikolov, T., Chen, K., Corrado, G., Dean, J.: Efficient estimation of word representations in vector space. arXiv preprint arXiv:1301.3781 (2013)
38. Mishra, S., Suryavardan, S., Bhaskar, A., Chopra, P., Reganti, A.N., Patwa, P., Das, A., Chakraborty, T., Sheth, A.P., Ekbal, A., et al.: Factify: a multi-modal fact verification dataset. In: DE-FACTIFY@ AAAI (2022)
39. Mohtaj, S., Nizamoglu, A., Sahitaj, P., Schmitt, V., Jakob, C., Möller, S.: Newspolyml: multilingual European news fake assessment dataset. In: Proceedings of the 3rd ACM International Workshop on Multimedia AI against Disinformation, pp. 82–90 (2024)
40. Mu, M., Das Bhattacharjee, S., Yuan, J.: Self-supervised distilled learning for multi-modal misinformation identification. In: Proceedings of the IEEE/CVF Winter Conference on Applications of Computer Vision, pp. 2819–2828 (2023)

41. Müller-Budack, E., Theiner, J., Diering, S., Idahl, M., Ewerth, R.: Multimodal analytics for real-world news using measures of cross-modal entity consistency. In: Proceedings of the 2020 International Conference on Multimedia Retrieval, pp. 16–25 (2020). https://doi.org/10.1145/3372278.3390670
42. Nakamura, K., Levy, S., Wang, W.Y.: Fakeddit: a new multimodal benchmark dataset for fine-grained fake news detection. In: Proceedings of the Twelfth Language Resources and Evaluation Conference, pp. 6149–6157 (2020)
43. Newman, E.J., Garry, M., Bernstein, D.M., Kantner, J., Lindsay, D.S.: Nonprobative photographs (or words) inflate truthiness. Psychon. Bull. Rev. **19**, 969–974 (2012). https://doi.org/10.3758/s13423-012-0292-0
44. Nielsen, D.S., McConville, R.: Mumin: a large-scale multilingual multimodal fact-checked misinformation social network dataset. In: Proceedings of the 45th International ACM SIGIR Conference on Research and Development in Information Retrieval, pp. 3141–3153 (2022). https://doi.org/10.1145/3477495.3531744
45. Nørregaard, J., Horne, B.D., Adalı, S.: Nela-gt-2018: a large multi-labelled news dataset for the study of misinformation in news articles. In: Proceedings of the International AAAI Conference on Web and Social Media, vol. 13, pp. 630–638 (2019)
46. Papadopoulos, S.I., Koutlis, C., Papadopoulos, S., Petrantonakis, P.: Synthetic misinformers: generating and combating multimodal misinformation. In: Proceedings of the 2nd ACM International Workshop on Multimedia AI against Disinformation, pp. 36–44 (2023). https://doi.org/10.1145/3592572.3592842
47. Papadopoulos, S.I., Koutlis, C., Papadopoulos, S., Petrantonakis, P.C.: Verite: a robust benchmark for multimodal misinformation detection accounting for unimodal bias. Int. J. Multimedia Inform. Retrieval **13**(1), 4 (2024)
48. Papadopoulos, S.I., Koutlis, C., Papadopoulos, S., Petrantonakis, P.C.: Latent multimodal reconstruction for misinformation detection. arXiv preprint arXiv:2504.06010 (2025)
49. Papadopoulos, S.I., Koutlis, C., Papadopoulos, S., Petrantonakis, P.C.: Red-dot: multimodal fact-checking via relevant evidence detection. IEEE Trans. Comput. Soc. Syst. (2025)
50. Papadopoulos, S.I., Koutlis, C., Papadopoulos, S., Petrantonakis, P.C.: Similarity over factuality: are we making progress on multimodal out-of-context misinformation detection? In: Proceedings of the Winter Conference on Applications of Computer Vision (WACV), pp. 5570–5579 (2025)
51. Paris, B., Donovan, J.: Deepfakes and cheap fakes. United States of America: Data & Society **1** (2019)
52. Qi, P., Yan, Z., Hsu, W., Lee, M.L.: Sniffer: multimodal large language model for explainable out-of-context misinformation detection. In: Proceedings of the IEEE/CVF Conference on Computer Vision and Pattern Recognition, pp. 13052–13062 (2024)
53. Qian, S., Wang, J., Hu, J., Fang, Q., Xu, C.: Hierarchical multi-modal contextual attention network for fake news detection. In: Proceedings of the 44th International ACM SIGIR Conference on Research and Development in Information Retrieval, pp. 153–162 (2021)
54. Radford, A., Kim, J.W., Hallacy, C., Ramesh, A., Goh, G., Agarwal, S., Sastry, G., Askell, A., Mishkin, P., Clark, J., et al.: Learning transferable visual models from natural language supervision. In: International Conference on Machine Learning. PMLR, pp. 8748–8763 (2021)
55. Radford, A., Kim, J.W., Hallacy, C., Ramesh, A., Goh, G., Agarwal, S., Sastry, G., Askell, A., Mishkin, P., Clark, J., et al.: Learning transferable visual models from natural language supervision. In: International Conference on Machine Learning. PMLR, pp. 8748–8763 (2021)
56. Raffel, C., Shazeer, N., Roberts, A., Lee, K., Narang, S., Matena, M., Zhou, Y., Li, W., Liu, P.J.: Exploring the limits of transfer learning with a unified text-to-text transformer. J. Mach. Learn. Res. **21**(1), 5485–5551 (2020)
57. Reimers, N., Gurevych, I.: Sentence-Bert: Sentence embeddings using Siamese Bert-networks. In: Proceedings of the 2019 Conference on Empirical Methods in Natural Language Processing and the 9th International Joint Conference on Natural Language Processing (EMNLP-IJCNLP), pp. 3982–3992 (2019)

58. Sabir, E., AbdAlmageed, W., Wu, Y., Natarajan, P.: Deep multimodal image-repurposing detection. In: Proceedings of the 26th ACM International Conference on Multimedia, pp. 1337–1345 (2018). https://doi.org/10.1145/3240508.3240707
59. Samadi, M., Mousavian, M., Momtazi, S.: Deep contextualized text representation and learning for fake news detection. Inform. Process. Manage. **58**(6), 102723 (2021)
60. Schlichtkrull, M., Guo, Z., Vlachos, A.: Averitec: a dataset for real-world claim verification with evidence from the web. Adv. Neural Inform. Process. Syst. **36**, 65128–65167 (2023)
61. Simonyan, K., Zisserman, A.: Very deep convolutional networks for large-scale image recognition. In: 3rd International Conference on Learning Representations (ICLR 2015). Computational and Biological Learning Society (2015)
62. Singhal, S., Kabra, A., Sharma, M., Shah, R.R., Chakraborty, T., Kumaraguru, P.: Spotfake+: A multimodal framework for fake news detection via transfer learning (student abstract). In: Proceedings of the AAAI Conference on Artificial Intelligence, vol. 34, pp. 13915–13916 (2020)
63. Singhal, S., Shah, R.R., Chakraborty, T., Kumaraguru, P., Satoh, S.: Spotfake: A multi-modal framework for fake news detection. In: 2019 IEEE Fifth International Conference on Multimedia Big Data (BigMM), pp. 39–47. IEEE (2019). https://doi.org/10.1109/BigMM.2019.00-44
64. Song, C., Ning, N., Zhang, Y., Wu, B.: A multimodal fake news detection model based on cross modal attention residual and multichannel convolutional neural networks. Inform. Process. Manage. **58**(1), 102437 (2021)
65. Suryavardan, S., Mishra, S., Chakraborty, M., Patwa, P., Rani, A., Chadha, A., Reganti, A.N., Das, A., Sheth, A.P., Chinnakotla, M., et al.: Findings of factify 2: multimodal fake news detection. In: DE-FACTIFY@ AAAI (2023)
66. Suryavardan, S., Mishra, S., Patwa, P., Chakraborty, M., Rani, A., Reganti, A.N., Chadha, A., Das, A., Sheth, A.P., Chinnakotla, M., et al.: Factify 2: a multimodal fake news and satire news dataset. In: DE-FACTIFY@ AAAI (2023)
67. Tahmasebi, S., Müller-Budack, E., Ewerth, R.: Multimodal misinformation detection using large vision-language models. In: Proceedings of the 33rd ACM International Conference on Information and Knowledge Management, pp. 2189–2199 (2024)
68. Thorne, J., Vlachos, A., Christodoulopoulos, C., Mittal, A.: Fever: a large-scale dataset for fact extraction and verification. In: Proceedings of the 2018 Conference of the North American Chapter of the Association for Computational Linguistics: Human Language Technologies, Vol. 1 (Long Papers), pp. 809–819 (2018)
69. Touvron, H., Cord, M., Douze, M., Massa, F., Sablayrolles, A., Jégou, H.: Training data-efficient image transformers & distillation through attention. In: International Conference on Machine Learning. PMLR, pp. 10347–10357 (2021)
70. Wang, W.Y.: "liar, liar pants on fire": a new benchmark dataset for fake news detection. In: Proceedings of the 55th Annual Meeting of the Association for Computational Linguistics, Vol. 2, Short Papers), pp. 422–426 (2017)
71. Wang, Y., Ma, F., Jin, Z., Yuan, Y., Xun, G., Jha, K., Su, L., Gao, J.: Eann: event adversarial neural networks for multi-modal fake news detection. In: Proceedings of the 24th ACM SIGKDD International Conference on Knowledge Discovery & Data Mining, pp. 849–857 (2018). https://doi.org/10.1145/3219819.3219903
72. Wu, J., Fu, Y., Yu, N., Fu, G.: E2lvlm: evidence-enhanced large vision-language model for multimodal out-of-context misinformation detection. arXiv preprint arXiv:2502.10455 (2025)
73. Wu, Y., Zhan, P., Zhang, Y., Wang, L., Xu, Z.: Multimodal fusion with co-attention networks for fake news detection. In: Findings of the Association for Computational Linguistics: ACL-IJCNLP 2021, pp. 2560–2569 (2021)
74. Xu, Q., Chen, H., Du, H., Zhang, H., Łukasik, S., Zhu, T., Yu, X.: M3a: a multimodal misinformation dataset for media authenticity analysis. Comput. Vis. Image Underst. **249**, 104205 (2024)
75. Xuan, K., Yi, L., Yang, F., Wu, R., Fung, Y.R., Ji, H.: Lemma: towards LVLM-enhanced multimodal misinformation detection with external knowledge augmentation. arXiv preprint arXiv:2402.11943 (2024)

76. Yan, Z., Qi, P., Hsu, W., Lee, M.L.: Mitigating Genai-powered evidence pollution for out-of-context multimodal misinformation detection. arXiv preprint arXiv:2501.14728 (2025)
77. Yang, Z., Dai, Z., Yang, Y., Carbonell, J., Salakhutdinov, R.R., Le, Q.V.: Xlnet: generalized autoregressive pretraining for language understanding. Adv. Neural Inform. Process. Syst. **32** (2019)
78. Yao, B.M., Shah, A., Sun, L., Cho, J.H., Huang, L.: End-to-end multimodal fact-checking and explanation generation: a challenging dataset and models. In: Proceedings of the 46th International ACM SIGIR Conference on Research and Development in Information Retrieval, pp. 2733–2743 (2023)
79. Yu, C., Ma, Y., An, L., Li, G.: BCMF: a bidirectional cross-modal fusion model for fake news detection. Inform. Process. Manage. **59**(5), 103063 (2022). https://doi.org/10.1016/j.ipm.2022.103063
80. Yuan, X., Guo, J., Qiu, W., Huang, Z., Li, S.: Support or refute: analyzing the stance of evidence to detect out-of-context MIS-and disinformation. In: Proceedings of the 2023 Conference on Empirical Methods in Natural Language Processing, pp. 4268–4280 (2023)
81. Zhang, F., Liu, J., Zhang, Q., Sun, E., Xie, J., Zha, Z.J.: Ecenet: explainable and context-enhanced network for muti-modal fact verification. In: Proceedings of the 31st ACM International Conference on Multimedia, pp. 1231–1240 (2023)
82. Zhou, B., Lapedriza, A., Khosla, A., Oliva, A., Torralba, A.: Places: A 10 million image database for scene recognition. IEEE Transactions on Pattern Analysis and Machine Intelligence (2017)
83. Zlatkova, D., Nakov, P., Koychev, I.: Fact-checking meets fauxtography: verifying claims about images. In: Proceedings of the 2019 Conference on Empirical Methods in Natural Language Processing and the 9th International Joint Conference on Natural Language Processing (EMNLP-IJCNLP), pp. 2099–2108 (2019)

Audio-Based Tools for Decontextualisation Detection

Milica Gerhardt, Luca Cuccovillo, Patrick Aichroth, and Jakob Abeßer

1 Introduction: The Case for Audio Tools in Decontextualisation

Decontextualisation refers to the reuse of authentic media content such as images, videos, or audio recordings, outside its original setting, thereby altering or obscuring its intended meaning.[1] Decontextualised material is genuine but presented in a misleading manner, for example by implying a different time, place, or event than the original. While some instances involve unaltered reuse, decontextualisation frequently co-occurs with content-level manipulations such as spatial or temporal cropping, segment reordering, and the insertion of synthetic elements–whether visual overlays, dubbed speech, or background audio. These modifications can serve to enhance narrative coherence, amplify emotional salience, or reduce detectability by forensic tools. Both decontextualisation and manipulation are commonly employed in disinformation campaigns to reinforce false or misleading narratives.

[1] In natural language processing, decontextualisation refers to rewriting a sentence so that it can be understood independently of its original context [11]. In this chapter, we use the term in the inverse sense: detecting when genuine media has been stripped of its context in a way that changes its perceived meaning.

M. Gerhardt (✉) · L. Cuccovillo · P. Aichroth · J. Abeßer
Fraunhofer Institute for Digital Media Technology (IDMT), Ilmenau, Germany
e-mail: milica.gerhardt@idmt.fraunhofer.de

L. Cuccovillo
e-mail: luca.cuccovillo@idmt.fraunhofer.de

P. Aichroth
e-mail: patrick.aichroth@idmt.fraunhofer.de

J. Abeßer
e-mail: jakob.abesser@idmt.fraunhofer.de

S. Papadopoulos et al. (eds.), *Countering Disinformation in the Era of Generative AI*,
https://doi.org/10.1007/978-3-032-11782-3_11

How can such attacks be detected? Two complementary approaches are essential: *provenance analysis* and *context analysis*: *Provenance analysis* traces the origin and transformations of an audio segment. It determines whether a clip has been reused from another source, whether it has undergone technical modifications (e.g. compression, cropping), and how it relates to other known media. This is especially important when verifying if a segment has been selectively extracted from a longer recording, as in the example in Fig. 1. *Context analysis*, on the other hand, assesses whether the content aligns with external contextual information, such as time, location, speaker identity, or intended audience. Even an unaltered audio clip can be used deceptively if it is presented in the wrong context or attributed to the wrong event.

Together, provenance and context analysis address both the technical integrity and the situational plausibility of media content. Neither dimension alone is sufficient: provenance analysis may verify that a clip is authentic and unedited, while context analysis may reveal that it is still being used in a misleading way. Robust detection of decontextualisation therefore requires the joint application of both dimensions.

Decontextualisation can affect all media formats, yet detection tools to date have primarily focused on images. Reverse image search engines, such as Google and TinEye, are widely used to identify reused visual material. For video, keyframes are commonly extracted and subjected to reverse image search. In contrast, no comparable solutions are publicly available for audio–despite its pervasive and persuasive role in communication. Unlike written text, speech conveys not only semantic content but also contextual cues such as speaker identity, emotional tone, and recording conditions. These attributes engage audiences on a more personal and credible level, amplifying the perceived authenticity and emotional resonance of the message. Precisely because of this communicative richness, edits to audio–such as

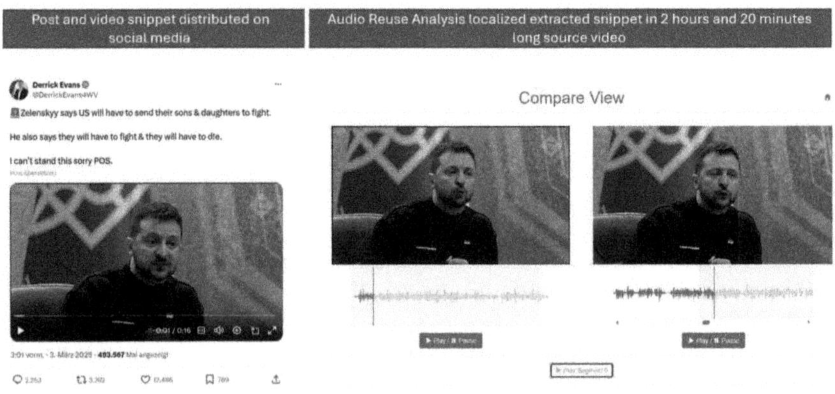

Fig. 1 Left: a tweet disseminating a video clip. Right: results from the audio provenance analysis framework, which successfully localised the matching audio snippet (highlighted in green) within a longer reference recording. By listening to the preceding audio content in the original file, it becomes evident that the disseminated clip was taken out of context, supporting a clear case of decontextualisation.

splicing, overlaying music, or modifying tone–can be highly effective in shaping perception. As a result, such techniques are widely used in professional and user-generated content alike. However, this same potential for enhancing engagement also makes audio particularly vulnerable to misuse: in disinformation contexts, minimal alterations combined with decontextualisation can significantly distort interpretation while preserving surface authenticity.

Despite the importance of audio, it remains underrepresented in content verification research and tool development compared to the visual domain. A main reason for this gap is that audio analysis poses unique challenges. Its inherently temporal structure requires sequential processing, increasing computational complexity relative to static images. Platform-dependent transformations–such as compression, transcoding, or noise filtering–further complicate fingerprinting and matching. Subtle edits, like pitch shifting or time stretching, can profoundly alter the perceived meaning while leaving minimal forensic traces. However, these difficulties are offset by the richness of the modality: audio can convey speaker identity, emotional tone, and environmental cues, making it a powerful yet underexploited channel for identifying decontextualisation and verifying content authenticity.

Building on these observations, this chapter introduces tools for detecting audio decontextualisation. The following sections present how provenance analysis can be used to track reuse, perform clustering, and identify transformations, employing graph-based techniques to reconstruct content lineage and demonstrate their application in real-world scenarios. We then explore contextual audio analysis, showing how environmental sounds and acoustic scenes can provide cues about location and context. The chapter concludes by outlining future directions, including the integration of forensic methods, the use of speech transcripts, and the fusion of provenance and contextual analyses into a unified pipeline for robust decontextualisation detection.

2 Audio Provenance Analysis

Tracing the provenance of audio content presents a significant challenge, particularly when dealing with heterogeneous datasets–collections of media files originating from various internet sources or recording devices, often lacking detailed metadata or content descriptions. In such cases, determining the source(s) of an audio file or identifying the least transformed version is a complex task.

To address these challenges, Audio Provenance Analysis provides a structured method for mapping the relationships between audio files by identifying and analysing reused segments. Formally, the primary objective is to transform a diverse set of files into a "provenance graph", as illustrated in Fig. 2, which also outlines the key steps in this process:

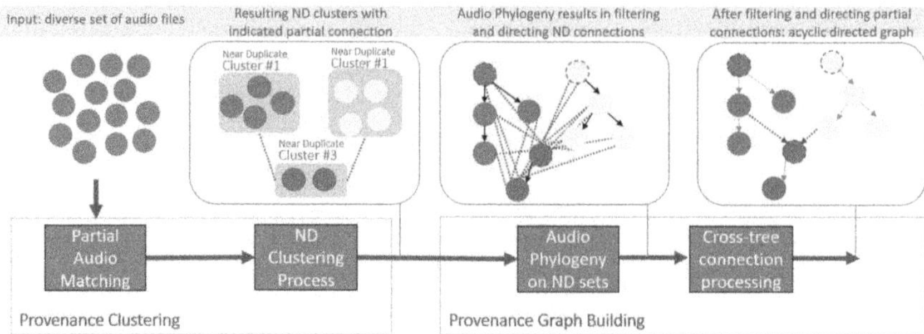

Fig. 2 Detailed workflow of the audio provenance framework proposed by Gerhardt et al. [23]: the framework comprises two main processing blocks—(1) provenance clustering, which performs segment-level partial audio matching and near-duplicate clustering to group related files; and (2) provenance graph building, which first constructs phylogeny trees from near-duplicate clusters (depicted as same-coloured nodes connected by directed solid edges, with tree roots shown using dashed node outlines), then reduces indirect partial connections across trees (dashed links) to a set of directed edges connecting only identified donor files and composition roots

- Identify near-duplicate (ND) audio files within the input dataset,
- Reconstruct their transformation history using directed acyclic graphs (DAGs), where each graph has a single identified root (i.e., the original source) and captures the lineage of reused content. These DAGs are referred to as audio phylogeny trees.
- Detect cross-tree partial content reuse, whenever new audio compositions are formed from audio excerpts taken from one or multiple parents.

Provenance analysis is particularly valuable for journalists and forensic investigators, who frequently need to verify the authenticity of audio content by determining its origin and transformation history. Understanding the lifecycle of an audio file, from initial recording through editing and dissemination on digital platforms, can yield critical insights into potential manipulation, decontextualisation, or misinformation. The task becomes especially complex in large-scale datasets, where manipulated content may contain authentic segments, and identical files may propagate across multiple online platforms. Therefore, distinguishing original from derived versions and identifying applied transformations is critical for verifying content integrity and source attribution.

Gerhardt et al. [23] introduced the first comprehensive study on Audio Provenance Analysis, emphasising the absence of a respective framework in the audio domain. Drawing inspiration from provenance methodologies in image forensics, the authors proposed two foundational tasks for building an effective audio provenance framework: *Provenance Clustering* and *Provenance Graph Building*.

By leveraging these tasks, audio provenance analysis offers a structured approach for tracing content evolution, thereby supporting the detection of misinformation, disinformation, and decontextualisation in digital media. The following sections present the methodologies for provenance clustering and graph construction, as proposed in [23], demonstrating how a heterogeneous audio dataset can be transformed into an acyclic provenance graph.

Provenance Clustering

The goal of Provenance Clustering, illustrated in Fig. 2, is to detect and localise content reuse within an audio collection, forming clusters of near-duplicates and identifying cross-tree connections that indicate segment reuse. As indicated in existing works on image [45, 63] and video provenance analysis [38, 39], accurate and robust matching is crucial for distinguishing near-duplicates and localising matching content segments. An effective method must: (a) robustly detect perceptually identical content, despite common transformations, (b) detect and localise matching segments, and (c) support an unknown and potentially large number of matches.

Existing audio matching techniques are primarily designed for audio identification tasks, where a query is matched against a database to determine its source [5, 8, 12, 13, 21, 29, 30, 57–59, 62]. These methods prioritise global similarity and retrieval speed, making them suitable for large-scale indexing but insufficient for fine-grained segment-level localisation.

The Content-Based Copy Detection (CBCD) task shifts the focus toward localising matches within reference files, assuming that only a portion of the query may match. Several approaches [32, 34, 48, 49, 54] have refined retrieval algorithms to detect sub-sequences. However, these approaches were not designed to detect and localise multiple partial matches, as they often assume one matching segment per file pair and rely on near-duplicate search, voting, or counting strategies. These constraints limit both the granularity and reliability of segment-level match detection.

The partial audio matching method proposed in [41, 42] overcomes these challenges by detecting and localising an unknown number of reused segments, making it an ideal choice for provenance clustering in the Audio Provenance Analysis framework. Accordingly, provenance clustering in the audio domain starts with "Partial Audio Matching" where reused segments between audio files are detected and localised. The subsequent operation is "Near Duplicate Clustering" that according to matching segments, localised in the previous step, identifies near-duplicate clusters of files or partial-duplicate clusters of their segments.

Both operations can be formalised by defining a set of audio files $\mathcal{A} = \{a_i\}$, where each file a_i is represented by a fingerprint F_i. Pairwise fingerprint comparisons yield a set of matching segments:

$$m_{ij}^{(k)} = \left(s_i^{(k)}, s_j^{(k)}, l_{ij}^{(k)}\right), k \in [1, K_{ij}] \quad (1)$$

where s_i and s_j indicate the start of the match in the respective file, l_{ij} its length, and K_{ij} the number of matches detected for the pair of files.

The near-duplicate clustering process determines which partial matching results indicate near-duplicate relationships and organises those files into clusters accordingly. Let $\mathbf{D} = (D_{ij})$ represent a near-duplicates matrix, where

$$D_{ij} = \begin{cases} 1 & (a_i, a_j) \text{ are near-duplicates} \\ 0 & \text{otherwise} \end{cases} \tag{2}$$

and let $\mathbf{P} = \left(P_{ij}\right)$ denote a partial-duplicate matrix in which

$$P_{ij} = \begin{cases} 1 & (a_i, a_j) \text{ are partial-duplicates} \\ 0 & \text{otherwise} \end{cases} \tag{3}$$

Given two files with at least one detected match ($K_{ij} > 0$), they are classified as near-duplicates if the cumulative length of all matching segments exceeds the duration of both files; otherwise, they are considered partial-duplicates, i.e.

$$D_{ij} = \begin{cases} 1 & \sum_{k=1}^{K_i j} l_{ij}^{(k)} > \max(L_i, L_j) - \epsilon \\ 0 & \text{otherwise} \end{cases} \tag{4}$$

$$P_{ij} = \begin{cases} 1 & K_{ij} > 0 \wedge D_{ij} = 0 \\ 0 & \text{otherwise} \end{cases} \tag{5}$$

where ϵ accounts for a small tolerance to minor localisation inaccuracies caused, for example, by background noise or encoding, and L_i, L_j denote the duration (in seconds) of the two audio files.

Provenance Graph Building

The goal of the Provenance Graph Building task, illustrated in Fig. 2, is to reconstruct a directed acyclic graph (DAG) that connects all audio files (nodes) involved in content reuse, while clearly identifying the roots or original sources within this process. The workflow begins with the “Audio Phylogeny on ND Sets” block, which processes clusters of (ND) files and transforms each cluster into a phylogeny tree. In each tree, one root node is identified, and directed edges indicate the inferred provenance—i.e., the sequence of transformations through which near-duplicate files were generated. These trees are individual DAGs where edge direction encodes the content derivation path.

Following the construction of these within-cluster trees, the “Cross-Tree Connection Processing” block addresses partial matches between files belonging to different near-duplicate sets. This step introduces directed edges only where there is sufficient evidence to suggest that a file served as a content donor in the generation of a composite file located in a different tree. As a result, phylogeny trees become interconnected via directed links, forming a larger acyclic graph that reflects both duplication and compositional reuse relationships across the dataset. In the following we provide more details on the methodologies behind these two building blocks and describe the output of the process.

Audio phylogeny aims to uncover the relationships and transformation history among a set of near-duplicate audio items. This process begins by computing a pairwise dissimilarity matrix between all near-duplicate items. The resulting matrix is then used to construct a directed phylogeny tree using the Oriented Kruskal algorithm [16]. This algorithm is an adapted version of the classical Kruskal algorithm, traditionally used for building minimum spanning trees in undirected graphs. The oriented variant, however, is designed to operate on directed graphs, enabling the inference of causal or chronological relationships–thereby identifying likely source (root) file and tracing the direction of transformations across the dataset.

As a core element of provenance graph building, audio phylogeny reconstructs directed graphs within clusters of near-duplicates. Existing approaches range from the computationally intensive methods of Nucci et al. [47], to streamlined transformation detection techniques [43, 61]. More recently, Gerhardt et al. [22] introduced a Deep Neural Network (DNN)-based approach, enhancing both computational efficiency and extensibility.

Unlike manually designed transformation detection functions, the DNN-based method offers seamless expansion by retraining on new data, reducing reliance on manual feature engineering. Given these advantages, the approach from [22] was selected in [23] for graph reconstruction within near-duplicate content sets, forming a key component of the Audio Provenance Analysis system.

Let us denote with $\mathbf{D} = (D_{ij})$ the near-duplicate matrix identified by the clustering algorithm, and with C_n a single cluster of near-duplicates. Prior to phylogeny analysis, the only available information for each pair (i, j) with $a_i, a_j \in C_n$ is that both D_{ij} and D_{ji} are equal and set to one, indicating symmetric near-duplicate status.

The phylogeny analysis, as detailed in [22], yields an asymmetric matrix of edges $\mathbf{E} = (E_{ij})$, where

$$E_{ij} = \begin{cases} 1 & \text{if } \exists \mathcal{T}(\cdot) \, : \, a_j = \mathcal{T}(a_i) \\ 0 & \text{otherwise} \end{cases} \tag{6}$$

with $\mathcal{T}(\cdot)$ representing a content-preserving transformation. Hence, if $E_{ij} = 1$, then a_i is deemed to be a parent of a_j.

To propagate this structure, one can impose $D_{ij} = E_{ij} \forall (a_i, a_j) \in C_n$ and repeat the operation for all near-duplicate clusters within the provenance graph, thus reducing the number of relevant relationships from $|C_n|(|C_n| - 1)/2$ to $|C_n|$.

The final cross-tree connection processing step performs a similar operation to phylogeny analysis, albeit addressing partial matching.

In audio provenance analysis, cross-tree connections occur when two phylogeny trees, T_i and T_j, share at least one common audio segment. This implies that an audio file $\bar{a}_i \in C_i$ from tree T_i was used to generate the root audio file a_{j^*} of tree T_j. The objective of cross-tree connection processing is to identify the donor audio $\bar{a}_{(T_i,T_j)}$ and prune all redundant partial connections, preserving only the transformation link between the donor file and the composition root.

To determine this, the method in [23] first selects the longest matching segment between files in T_i and T_j:

$$\arg\max_{ijk}\left(l_{ij}^{(k)}\right), \quad \forall m_{ij}^{(k)} : (i, j) \in C_i \times C_j. \tag{7}$$

This defines an optimal interval for analysis, to which all files in T_i and T_j are cropped, yielding a new set of cropped near-duplicates, referred to as partial files:

$$\mathcal{P} = \mathcal{P}_i \cup \mathcal{P}_j = \{p_i \in C_i\} \cup \left\{p_j \in C_j\right\}. \tag{8}$$

Next, an audio dissimilarity function diss$(\cdot)$, as introduced in our audio phylogeny framework [22], is applied to compare all elements in $\mathcal{P}_i$ against the cropped root of T_j, e.g. p_{j^*}, and vice versa:

$$D_i^{(j)} = \text{diss}(p_i, p_{j^*}) \quad \forall p_i \in C_i, \tag{9}$$

$$D_j^{(i)} = \text{diss}(p_j, p_{i^*}) \quad \forall p_j \in C_j. \tag{10}$$

The donor audio is selected based on the minimum dissimilarity score:

$$\bar{a}_{(T_i,T_j)} = \begin{cases} a_{i^\dagger} \in C_i & \text{if } \min(D_i^{(j)}) < \min(D_j^{(i)}) \\ a_{j^\dagger} \in C_j & \text{otherwise} \end{cases} \tag{11}$$

where

$$i^\dagger = \arg\min_i(D_i^{(j)}), \quad j^\dagger = \arg\min_j(D_j^{(i)}). \tag{12}$$

Once the donor audio is identified, all non-essential partial connections in the partial-duplicate matrix **P** are pruned, ensuring only the directed connection between $\bar{a}_{(T_i,T_j)}$ and the composition root a_{i^*} or a_{j^*} remains.

The final provenance graph (depicted on the right in Fig. 3) forms a directed acyclic graph, where each tree maintains a single parent node while allowing multiple descendant nodes. Between pairs of trees, only a unique directed connection is permitted from an arbitrary node of the donor tree to the root node of the composition tree, with the result that composition root trees may have multiple inbound partial connections.

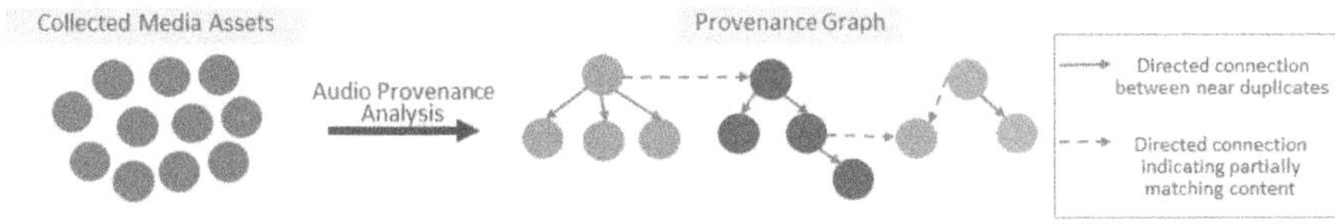

Fig. 3 Provenance analysis summary: from input set to output provenance graph

Real-World Data Experiments

The audio provenance analysis framework described in the previous pages was tested in controlled scenarios using standard metrics, on a dataset that was made publicly available on Zenodo[2]. Evaluation results confirmed the framework's ability to accurately identify original sources even under noisy conditions. However, complete graph reconstruction remains challenging due to variability in reuse patterns and partial transformations.

Evaluation in controlled scenarios, however, is not sufficient to describe if and to which extent provenance analysis could be a useful tool to tackle online disinformation. Therefore, the framework was also tested with real-world data as part of the activities of the vera.ai EU project[3].

Within the project, the framework was used with various datasets to detect disinformation and support early intervention. The following section presents key experiments that illustrate the role of audio analysis in verifying media authenticity and uncovering coordinated sharing behaviour.

Pure Decontextualisation Case

A first real-life investigation addressed a Twitter post showing a video of Joe Biden saying, "We cannot win this re-election; we can only re-elect Donald Trump." The post, available online[4], is also depicted in Fig. 4.

The first step of the investigation involved a keyword search for potential reference files from which this snippet could have been taken to compare and detect signs of manipulation and assess if the original message's context was correctly transmitted. Therefore, we created a reference set comprising all public speeches held in the previous month by Joe Biden for his election race.

The outcome of the matching is depicted in Fig. 5: The provenance analysis framework discovered a match with a reference video from a reliable source, i.e., Biden's very own election committee. The (distorted) audio in the post indeed stemmed from a speech given by Biden, which was however held in Kansas City—and not in St. Louis as reported in the post. A further analysis of the speech transcript, also

[2] https://zenodo.org/records/10960056

[3] vera.ai: VERification Assisted by Artificial Intelligence (https://veraai.eu)

[4] https://twitter.com/DanScavino/status/1236461268594294785

Fig. 4 Social media post with a video under investigation

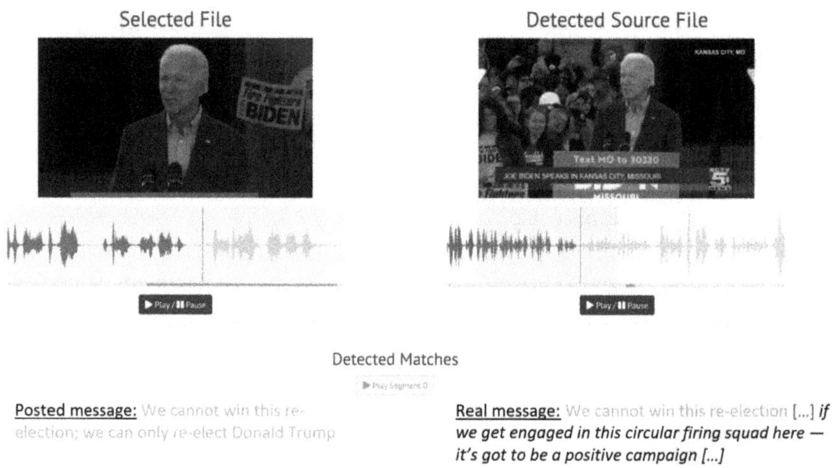

Fig. 5 Examined video on the left and found matching reference video on the right. Audio Provenance Analysis framework accurately localised the matching snippet within the long reference file, which is coloured in green

reported Fig. 5, revealed that the snippet shared on social media deliberately omitted the following assertion from Joe Biden, in which he stated that getting caught in aggressive discussions with the opponent [Donald Trump] would have only held to his re-election.

Therefore, despite the different quality between the audio in the post and the one in the reference sets, provenance analysis was able to identify the original source and to assist decontextualisation detection by media professionals.

Manipulation Detection Via Context Analysis

In this investigation, similar to the previous example, the analysis began with a video that was widely circulated on social media. The post, available online[5], is also depicted in Fig. 6.

Similarly to the first investigation, to determine whether this video shared content with other media files, we conducted a keyword search to compile a dataset of potentially related media. The audio provenance analysis framework was then utilised to compare the social media video against this collected dataset.

The analysis identified a reference video that matched the content of the social media post's video, as shown in Fig. 7. The video in question is displayed on the left, while the reference video from a reputable source, i.e., the White House press office, is on the right. The matched audio segments are highlighted in green and purple. Notably, the waveform of the reference audio (on the right) contains an audio segment between the green and purple portions that is absent in the query video (on the left).

Although initial suspicion might have pointed to decontextualisation, the discovered discrepancy indicated that the viral video had undergone deliberate manipulation. Even though the matched segments did not include the most controversial part of the video–where Biden allegedly continued speaking after leaving the stage–the detection of a missing segment was a crucial clue indicating that further analysis was required.

Therefore, the audio provenance framework played a key role in uncovering this edit, disproving the claim that the viral video was authentic, and casting doubt on the origin of the final portion of the recording.

This case highlighted the value of audio reuse detection, particularly in complex scenarios where it may not be possible to locate all original content online or trace its full provenance. In such instances, content could come from private archives, be artificially generated, or feature voice impersonations, as was suspected in this case.

Coordinated Behaviour Detection

Beyond individual cases of media decontextualisation and manipulation, audio provenance analysis has also been evaluated as a potential tool to support the detection of coordinated sharing behaviour on social media. Coordinated behaviour detection, as described in [25], generally follows a two-step process: First, data is collected to uniquely identify user accounts, the content they share, and the corresponding

[5] https://twitter.com/israelUSAforeve/status/1627778457143857189

Fig. 6 Social media post with a video under investigation

Fig. 7 Example of suspected decontextualisation where, thanks to the audio provenance analysis tools, manipulation was discovered: examined video on the left and found matching reference video on the right. Our audio reuse detection detected and localised two separate matching segments (green and purple), indicating that the query video omits part of the reference recording, supporting the conclusion that it was deliberately manipulated

timestamps; second, these data points are analysed to uncover patterns indicating coordinated activity among multiple accounts. Typically, this second step is carried out using the CoorTweet tool [46, 51]. Crucial to this process is the selection of a suitable similarity indicator that allows for meaningful clustering of shared content.

In the referenced study [25], the similarity indicator used was the presence of identical video descriptions across posts on TikTok. This approach proved highly

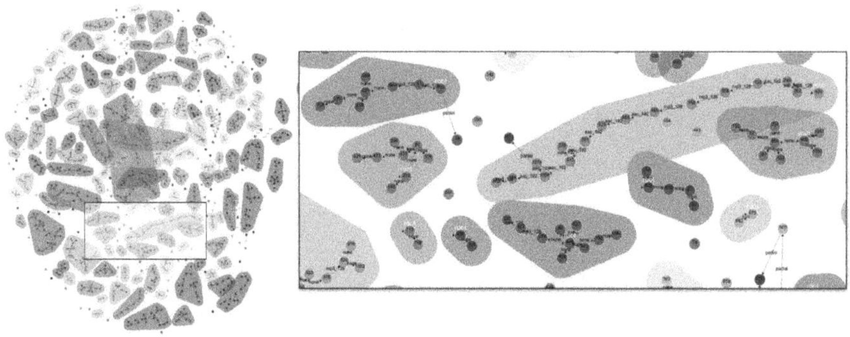

Fig. 8 TikTok experiment: final acyclic graph as output of audio provenance analysis. Single nodes represent individual TikTok videos. When nodes of the same colour represent set of near duplicates, these are illustrated with a bubble. Near duplicates are connected in a directed phylogeny tree with an identified root. Connections between ND trees or individual nodes indicate one or more partial matching segments

effective for identifying coordinated activity in that particular setting. However, it remains agnostic to the actual media content and assumes a specific behaviour (i.e., using the same textual description), which may not generalise across platforms or actor strategies. To address this limitation, we evaluated audio provenance analysis as a content-based similarity metric, capable of uncovering coordination that might not be detectable via metadata alone.

The experiment from [25] began with a dataset of 513 TikTok accounts previously identified as problematic, due to their involvement in suspicious or potentially coordinated activities. These accounts were continuously monitored, and their activity was archived through daily snapshots to enable retrospective analysis. From this dataset, we selected the snapshot from January 8th, 2025 for our experiment.

We downloaded one of the daily snapshots taken on 08.01.2025 in order to detect coordinated networks using one of the following as a similarity indicator: (a) video description as done in [25], or (b) audio ND and partial clusters as result of audio provenance analysis.

We knew that for this dataset coordinated networks were successfully detected using video descriptions, so we used this as a proxy for the ground truth to evaluate our methods using audio ND and partial clusters.

This snapshot contained metadata for 4,034 videos posted by the monitored accounts. At the time of our analysis, 3,993 of these video files were still accessible and were used as the input dataset for audio provenance analysis. The framework identified 1222 (ND) clusters and 1272 partial clusters, resulting in a rich forest of acyclic graphs mapping relationships between reused audio segments. Each graph clearly indicated root files and described derivative nodes through audio transformations, as illustrated in Fig. 8.

To evaluate the usefulness of these audio-based clusters for coordinated behaviour detection, we used three configurations as input to CoorTweet: (a) the original

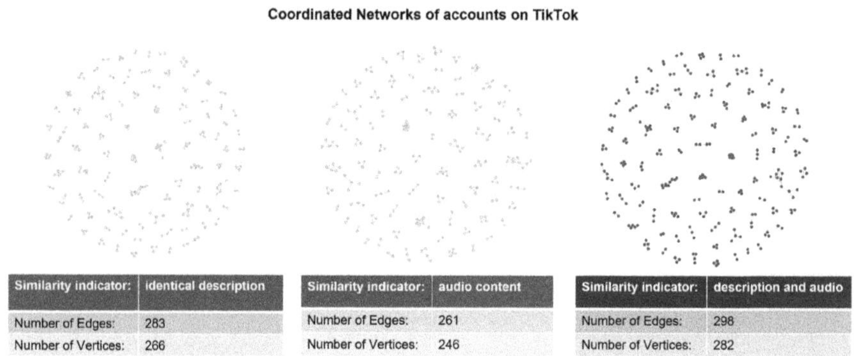

Fig. 9 TikTok experiment: visualising the CooRTweet graph of detected coordinated accounts via: (left) identical titles, (middle) audio ND and partial duplicates, and (right) a combination of identical titles and an audio similarity indication. Each node presents one user account on TikTok

approach based on identical video descriptions (replicating the method from [25]), (b) similarity based on ND and partial audio clusters, and (c) a combination of both indicators. All experiments were run using a time window of 120 seconds to define potential coordination windows. The results of these three approaches are visualised in Fig. 9.

From the Fig. 9, we observe that coordination networks derived from audio content similarity (centre image) closely resemble those detected using textual descriptions (left image), though with a slightly lower number of nodes and edges. This reduction is likely due to audio transformations such as background music overlays or time-stretch effects, which complicate the detection of similarity. Nonetheless, when both similarity indicators were combined (right image), the resulting network contained the highest number of edges and nodes, indicating that audio similarity contributed additional links that would have been missed using description-based matching alone.

These findings suggest that audio provenance analysis is not only a viable content-based similarity metric for detecting coordinated behaviour, but also a complementary one, enhancing metadata-based approaches by revealing additional coordination signals. This capability becomes particularly valuable in environments where textual or metadata clues are obfuscated or inconsistent.

Beyond serving as a similarity indicator, audio provenance analysis supports two further analytical capabilities in the context of coordination detection. First, in cases where a coordinated network is flagged as malicious, the provenance graphs enable the tracing of content propagation through the network. This allows the identification of key source nodes or influencers who may be responsible for initiating or amplifying disinformation (see Fig. 8).

Second, and perhaps more crucially, combining audio provenance analysis with text-based decontextualisation detection introduces a powerful cross-modal approach. When content reuse is confirmed through audio analysis, but the information inferred from the audio contradicts the message conveyed by the accompanying text, this discrepancy becomes a strong indicator of manipulation or coordinated inauthentic behaviour [52]. Such cross-modal inconsistency may point to deliberate intent to mislead, especially in environments where actors attempt to mask disinformation under seemingly authentic multimedia content.

An important element conveyed by both text and audio is contextual information–such as time, location, and the identities of involved actors. In the following section, we therefore turn our focus to the extraction of such contextual cues from the audio signal, with a particular emphasis on location analysis. Incorporating this type of information can enrich audio content with contextual information, offering valuable support for both manual investigations and semi-automated disinformation detection workflows.

3 Audio-Based Contextual Analysis

An important task for newsrooms and investigative journalists is determining whether user-generated content aligns with the context provided—specifically, the people, location, and time. Pinpointing the location of a recording is often crucial, as it enables further verification and analysis, such as consulting local sources to confirm or disprove the context.

Localisation can be achieved with varying levels of precision, ranging from fine-grained geo-tagging of the city through location-specific sounds, to identifying potential countries in which the recording was made, ending up with broad descriptions of the acoustic environment (e.g., indoor, outdoor, or vehicle sounds)—all providing crucial clues for (dis)proving contextual information associated with user-generated content under investigation.

In the following sections, we will explore all three levels of localisation, by proposing a novel algorithm for each level, building on past findings by the Detection and Classification of Acoustic Scenes and Events (DCASE) community, and the respective advancements in both sound event detection (SED) [10, 44] and acoustic scene classification (ASC) [2, 17].

Acoustic Geo-Tagging using Location-Specific Sounds

Location-specific sounds, such as church bells, enhance the understanding of a recording's geographic origin. Originally coined as "soundmarks" in soundscape research [55], these distinctive acoustic landmark sounds contribute to the unique sonic character of a location and enable acoustic geo-tagging (AGT), i.e., the assignment of a specific city (or location within it) to an audio file of unknown origin.

AGT based on "soundmarks" is highly reliable, but difficult in practice: the high geographic specificity of these sounds is counterbalanced by a low frequency in which they occur in real-life user-generated recordings. Therefore, a recent exploratory study [3] investigated the existence of "indicator sounds", i. e., sounds which are characteristic for a specific geolocation, even though not necessarily unique. For example, a car engine sound is more likely to be heard in street traffic than in a natural environment, hence it can act as an indicator sound for outdoor scenes in an urban environment. The underlying assumption of the study is that, if these indicator sounds exist, they might serve as a basis for future AGT works capable of pinpointing the specific city in which a recording took place.

The exploratory study performed its investigation by employing two approaches, based on the TAU 2020 Mobile Urban Acoustic Scenes dataset [31], which provides 64 hours of 10-second-long audio recordings recorded in 10 European capitals and covering 10 acoustic scenes.

In the first approach, a Pretrained Audio Neural Network for Sound Event Detection (PANN SED model) by Kong et al. [37] was used to represent each audio recording using a feature vector of time-averaged probabilities of 527 sound classes, which have been pre-defined in the AudioSet dataset [20]. In order to identify relevant indicator sounds for specific acoustic scenes and cities, several 1 versus N dataset partitions were created where audio recordings from one geo-entity class (e.g., city) are classified against recordings from all other classes. Classification experiments were performed for each dataset partition using a Random Forest classifier and the resulting feature importance values were interpreted as a relevance measure for each sound class for the respective geo-entity. Crucially, the relevance of specific sound events for location detection was not uniformly distributed across cities: Each location could be associated to a subset of events with high relevance—possibly, the "indicator sounds" the study proposed as basis for future work.

In the second approach, two MobileNetV2 models [53] pre-trained for object recognition in natural images were fine-tuned for acoustic scene classification and city classification, respectively, based on Mel spectrograms extracted from the audio recordings. After training both models, the post-hoc explainability method Layer-wise Relevance Propagation (LRP) [7] was used to compute a relevance map for a given input spectrogram, which was further aggregated along frequencies to obtain a relevance function indicating temporal regions of interest for the classifiers. Once again, the existence of "indicator sounds" became evident: Temporal regions of interest for the MobileNetV2 classifiers were clearly associated to specific events among the 527 in the AudioSet dataset, and their distribution was very uneven across cities.

Figure 10 illustrates an example of the most relevant sound classes identified with the first approach (left) and the second approach (right) as a word cloud illustration, in which the importance of the sound categories is indicated by the font size.

Both approaches seem to generally identify relevant sound classes to distinguish indoor, outdoor, and vehicle sound scenes. Naturally, the high number of sound classes considered introduces some redundancy as similar sound classes exist. Due to the 1 versus all paradigm, the first approach naturally focuses on identifying sounds which are specific for particular geo-entities in contrast to others. The second approach provides a more entity-agnostic view and highlights sound classes, which show the largest overall discriminability across multiple geo-entities of the same type.

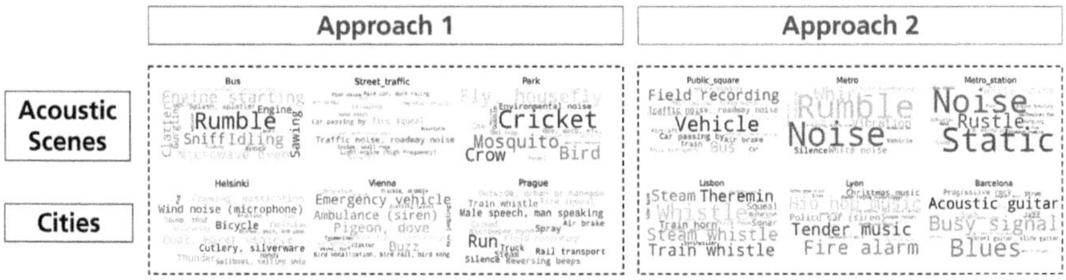

Fig. 10 Selected examples of indicator sounds for three acoustic scene classes and cities for both AGT methods [3]. Font size correlates with sound relevance

For the city classification, the identified sound classes can reveal existing biases in the datasets, as they are typical for the specific recording location but not for the entire city area. For example, Vienna is characterised by siren sounds, Helsinki by water noises, and Barcelona by sounds from street musicians.

The finding from this study underline the potential of "indicator sounds" as valuable cues for acoustic geo-tagging, especially in scenarios where unique soundmarks are absent or rare. The presence of sound events that consistently carry geographic relevance, underline their potential utility as proxies for location-specific acoustic information. These insights open the door for audio-based contextual analysis, e.g., by detecting mismatches between indicator sounds and the claimed or expected location of an audio file under investigation.

Country Detection Via Emergency Siren Analysis

Among possible "sound indicators" with the potential of assisting geo-tagging, siren sounds of emergency vehicles stand out due to their distinctive and loud nature, which makes them clearly audible even in noisy urban environments. The variety of siren sounds across nations is the result of historical preferences and distinct national standards, that arguably might make most of them unique for different geographic regions.

The properties and potential relevance of emergency sirens for geo-tagging were firstly investigated in a preliminary study by Abeßer et al. [4], in which the main focus was the collection of a "Regional Siren Dataset (RSD)" based on siren recordings from 9 countries (Canada, China, France, Germany, India, Italy, Japan, Spain, USA) and 3 types of siren (Ambulance, Firefighters, Police). Figure 11 illustrates the large variety of different pitch contours in siren recordings from this dataset: When analysing the acoustic features of siren sounds, distinct frequency patterns (pitch contours) can be observed, which range from periodic modulation (e.g., American firefighters), over gradual sweeps (e.g., Canadian firefighters), to stable pitch sequences (e.g., German police).

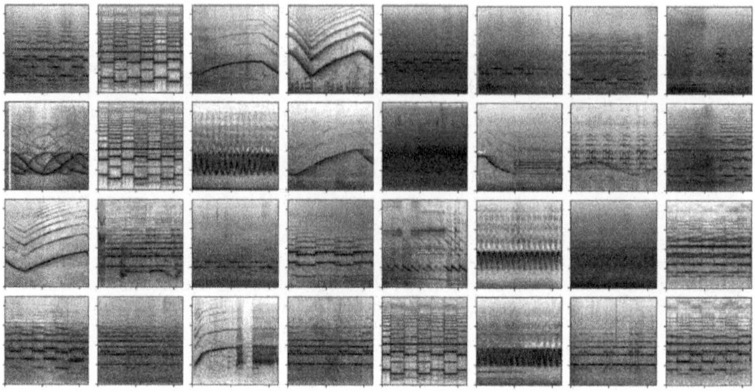

Fig. 11 Selected examples of emergency siren recordings in the RSC dataset. Mel spectrograms are shown highlighting characteristic pitch contours [4]

In a second follow-up study also by Abeßer et al. [1], a novel vision-based approach for pitch contour analysis using a MobileNetV2 model was proposed, and used among other downstream tasks to automatically determine the country of origin of a recording based on the siren sounds within it.

The model was pre-trained in two stages, first on the task of object detection in natural images, followed by pitch contour type classification in audio spectrograms. Synthetic pitch contours of seven contour types (stable, alternating, vibrato, glissando, bend, sawtooth, and triangle) were randomly synthesised. The ranges of contour parameters such as pitch, modulation range, and modulation frequency were chosen to capture pitch contour properties across multiple audio domains, namely speech, music, bioacoustic, and everyday sounds.

After the pre-training stage, the model was fine-tuned and evaluated on eight downstream tasks with relevance to pitch contour classification. The vision-based approach consistently outperforms a baseline approach, which uses the SWIPE pitch tracking method [9] combined with a CNN model, which processes the extracted pitch contours.

The most important downstream task for contextual audio analysis is the classification of the country of origin of the siren sounds in the RSD dataset, for which the model achieves an F-score of 0.72. Figure 12 illustrates the confusion matrix: Siren sounds in France, Canada, Germany, Japan, and USA have the most distinct pitch contours. Overall, the results demonstrate that the vision-based method can capture pitch contour shapes well and is therefore a very useful approach for recognising and classifying siren sounds as acoustic landmarks.

Even though some overlaps among sirens from different countries exist, this analysis can assist in the narrowing down the potential country of origin of a recording, thereby assisting audio-based contextual analysis with information that is valuable both for identifying malicious content and for narrowing down the list of potential countries of origin to a small, more manageable set.

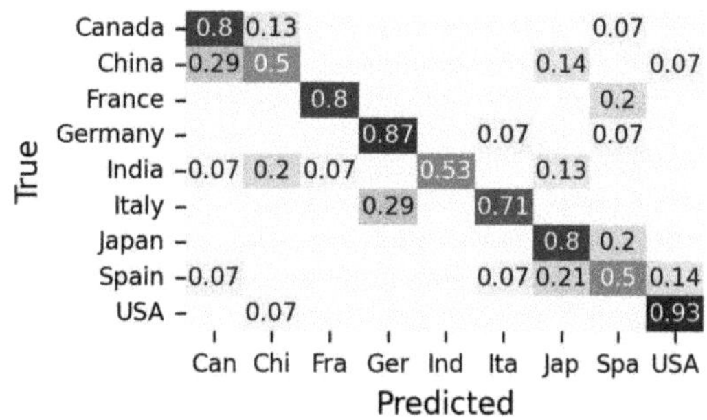

Fig. 12 Confusion matrix for regional siren classification [1]

Audio-Visual Scene Classification

Besides geo-tagging and country-of-origin-detection, a task with potential for contextual analysis is Acoustic Scene Classification (ASC), i. e., the automated process of identifying the type of environment in which an audio recording was made, such as a street, park, subway station, or indoor space, based on its acoustic characteristics.

The task has been thoroughly investigated over the decades by the DCASE research community, which provided several advanced solutions for it [56]. However, its use as a means of decontextualisation detection remains largely unexplored.

Therefore, in this section we are going to focus on a work by Apostolidis et al. [6], a content verification approach in which the authors propose a hybrid deep neural network model trained for joint audio and visual scene classification (AVSC), able to detect misalignment between the geographic scenes detected in the audio and in the visual streams. To enable comparability and reproducibility for future studies on this new task, the study furthermore proposes a novel benchmark dataset and introduces an experimental protocol.

For the ASC task, three types of embeddings are extracted from the audio stream of a given video using pre-trained deep neural networks. The OpenL3 embeddings [14] are derived from a convolutional neural network (CNN) model, which was trained in a self-supervised fashion using an audio-visual correspondence task. The pre-trained Audio Neural Network (PANN) embeddings [37] rely on a CNN model, which has been pre-trained for SED on the AudioSet [20] covering over 2 million audio samples and 527 sound classes. A third embedding representation is extracted using a ResNet model [28], which has been pre-trained for a simplified 3-class ASC task, i. e., indoor-outdoor-vehicle classification. Complementary to the audio analysis, three vision-based embeddings are extracted from the video stream using the vision transformer (ViT) [18], the CLIP (Contrastive Language-Image Pretraining) model [50], as well as a ResNet50 model pre-trained on the Places365 dataset.

The hybrid model includes two input branches to extract single-modality embeddings, several layers for modality fusion, and a final classification head based on two dense layers with dropout to prevent overfitting. In this study, different strategies for modality fusion are evaluated, which combine both concatenation and self-attention layers to better weigh the importance of different elements of the audio-visual embedding representations.

The TAU Urban Audio-Visual Scenes 2021 dataset, which consists of video recordings labelled according to ten urban acoustic environments (e.g., shopping mall, park, airport), is used to first evaluate the scene classification performance based on the two input modalities separately and then using the proposed fusion approach to combine both modalities. In addition to the ten-class taxonomy, a simplified three-class taxonomy is investigated, where videos are classified as indoor, outdoor, or scenes recorded in moving vehicles.

The scene classification performance for the three-class taxonomy is exceptionally high, achieving over 99% accuracy for both individual and fused modalities. For the more challenging ten-class taxonomy, the fusion model that processes both modalities achieves the highest accuracy of 97.2% and outperforms the models processing only audio (78.8 %) or only video (94.3 %).

Based on the audio-visual scene classification dataset, a dataset for the novel visual-audio discrepancy detection (VADD) task is proposed, where audio streams are deliberately swapped between scenes to simulate decontextualised content. Using the three-class taxonomy, a discrepancy is detected, for example, if the audio stream of an outdoor video is replaced by an indoor recording. An ablation study confirmed the importance of the position of self-attention layers in the network architecture. The best-performing model uses a self-attention layer at the end of both audio and vision input branches after concatenating domain-specific embedding vectors.

This work demonstrates that contextual audio tagging can effectively flag decontextualised content by leveraging deep learning techniques for scene classification. The ability to identify cross-modal inconsistencies provides a valuable tool for automated content verification, deepfake detection, and media forensics. The results indicate that ASC achieves near-perfect accuracy in the simplified three-class taxonomy but encounters challenges in a fine-grained distinctions between 10 different scene classes. Unsurprisingly, confusion arises between acoustically and visually similar environments–such as tram versus bus, or airport versus shopping mall. For visual-audio discrepancy detection, the best system achieves an accuracy of 97.2% highlighting the potential of scene classification for detecting decontextualisation in multimedia content. The study underscores the need for alternative feature fusion strategies and contrastive learning approaches to improve performance in complex real-world scenarios.

4 Conclusion and Future Directions

Audio provenance and contextual analysis provide essential tools for identifying manipulated or misleading reuse of media content. In this chapter, we described a framework for provenance analysis, and illustrated how selected contextual clues, such as acoustic scenes and sound events, can support location inference and content verification. However, many more audio-centric clues can potentially be used:

- *Time of recording* via electric network frequency (ENF) analysis can enable timestamp verification [26, 27, 33].
- *Device fingerprinting* via microphone classification can help confirming or challenging claims about the recording source [15, 24, 40].
- *Speaker analysis*, including verification and detection of synthetic speech, can identify and authenticate persons cues [35, 36, 60].
- *Spoken content processing* through ASR and NLP enables comparison between what was said and how that speech is being interpreted or framed.

Together, these methods help answering fundamental contextual questions central to verification and journalistic inquiry: *Who* is speaking? *What* is being said? *When* and *where* was it recorded? *Why* might the statement have been made?

Looking ahead, our objective is to integrate these capabilities into a unified and interpretable decision-making framework that fuses multiple forms of evidence. We propose three parallel analysis pathways, each contributing distinct insights:

- *Linguistic path:* Speech music separation, speaker diarisation and automatic speech recognition create a time-aligned transcript with speaker turns. Combined with original captions or accompanying text, the transcript undergoes NLP processing to extract named entities, locations, timestamps, and thematic cues.
- *Acoustic-context path:* Non-linguistic audio evidence is examined for speaker identity, acoustic scenes, sound events and forensic cues. Additional cues–including ENF traces, microphone characteristics, codec signatures, and distinctive regional sounds–aid in deducing the location, setting, and probable time of recording.
- *Provenance path:* Audio fingerprinting is used to search large reference databases for complete or partial matches. The resulting reuse relationships are structured into directed acyclic graphs via audio provenance analysis, visualising the origin of each recording and the sequence of transformations leading to its current form.

These three analysis paths are merged by a rule-based fusion module, which cross-validates all extracted evidence. Conflicts in time, place, speaker identity, or contextual framing are flagged and contribute to a weighted decontextualisation score. The system then outputs an interpretable decision: including the provenance graph, identified inconsistencies, and triggered rules–offering transparency to investigators and end-users alike.

It is important to note that the applicability of such a framework depends critically on access to relevant content. Without access to the audio, its metadata, and the surrounding context (e.g., associated posts, captions, or claims), such tools cannot operate. This makes regulatory frameworks such as the Digital Services Act [19] essential. They can ensure that platforms provide the necessary data access for verification, while balancing user rights and privacy.

In summary, audio-based contextual analysis has high potential for identifying misleading content—but it only becomes actionable when paired with access, transparency, and system-level enforcement. Without these, even the most advanced tools remain unused.

Acknowledgements This research was supported by the European Union under the Horizon Europe vera.ai project, Grant Agreement number 101070093, the German Ministry of Education and Research BMBF news-polygraph project (Grant Agreement number 03RU2U151D) and by the Deutsche Forschungsgemeinschaft (DFG, German Research Foundation) under Grant Agreement number 350953655 (MU 2686/11-2, AB 675/2-2).

References

1. Abeßer, J., Schwär, S., Müller, M.: Pitch contour exploration across audio domains: a vision-based transfer learning approach (2025). [Preprint]
2. Abeßer, J.: A review of deep learning based methods for acoustic scene classification. Appl. Sci. **10**(6), 1 (2020). https://doi.org/10.3390/app10062020
3. Abeßer, J.: Automatic retrieval of indicator sounds for acoustic geo-tagging. In: Annual Meeting on Acoustics (DAS/DAGA). Copenhagen, Denmark (2025). [Late Poster]
4. Abeßer, J., Mejía, J.M.R., Cuccovillo, L., Aichroth, P.: Siren sounds as acoustic landmarks for content verification. In: Annual Meeting on Acoustics (DAGA). Hannover, Germany (2024). [Late Poster]
5. Anguera, X., Garzon, A., Adamek, T.: MASK: robust local features for audio fingerprinting. In: IEEE International Conference on Multimedia and Expo (ICME). Melbourne, Australia, pp. 455–460 (2012)
6. Apostolidis, K., Abesser, J., Cuccovillo, L., Mezaris, V.: Visual and audio scene classification for detecting discrepancies in video: a baseline method and experimental protocol. In: ACM International Workshop on Multimedia AI Against Disinformation. Phuket, Thailand, pp. 30—-36 (2024)
7. Bach, S., Binder, A., Montavon, G., Klauschen, F., Müller, K.R., Samek, W.: On pixel-wise explanations for non-linear classifier decisions by layer-wise relevance propagation. PLoS ONE **10**(7), 1–46 (2015)
8. Baluja, S., Covell, M.: Audio fingerprinting: combining computer vision & data stream processing. In: IEEE International Conference on Acoustics, Speech and Signal Processing (ICASSP), vol. 2, pp. II–213–II–216 (2007)
9. Camacho, A., Harris, J.G.: A sawtooth waveform inspired pitch estimator for speech and music. J. Acoust. Soc. Am. **124**(3), 1638–1652 (2008)
10. Chan, T.K., Chin, C.S.: A comprehensive review of polyphonic sound event detection. IEEE Access **8**, 103339–73 (2020). https://doi.org/10.1109/ACCESS.2020.2999388
11. Choi, E., Palomaki, J., Lamm, M., Kwiatkowski, T., Das, D., Collins, M.: Decontextualization: making sentences stand-alone. Trans. Assoc. Comput. Linguist. **9**, 447–461 (2021)
12. Cotton, C.V., Ellis, D.P.W.: Audio fingerprinting to identify multiple videos of an event. In: IEEE International Conference on Acoustics. Speech and Signal Processing (ICASSP), pp. 2386–2389. Dallas, TX, USA (2010)
13. Covell, M., Baluja, S.: Known-audio detection using wave print: spectrogram fingerprinting by wavelet hashing. In: IEEE International Conference on Acoustics. Speech, and Signal Processing (ICASSP), vol. 1, pp. 237–240. Honolulu, HI, USA (2007)
14. Cramer, A.L., Wu, H.H., Salamon, J., Bello, J.P.: Look, listen, and learn more: design choices for deep audio embeddings. In: IEEE International Conference on Acoustics. Speech and Signal Processing (ICASSP). Brighton, UK, pp. 3852–3856 (2019)
15. Cuccovillo, L., Aichroth, P.: Open-set microphone classification via blind channel analysis. In: IEEE International Conference on Acoustics. Speech and Signal Processing (ICASSP). Shanghai, China, pp. 2074–2078 (2016)
16. Dias, Z., Rocha, A., Goldenstein, S.: Image phylogeny by minimal spanning trees. IEEE Trans. Inform. Forensics Secur. **7**(2), 774–788 (2012)

17. Ding, B., Zhang, T., Wang, C., Liu, G., Liang, J., Hu, R., Wu, Y., Guo, D.: Acoustic scene classification: a comprehensive survey. Expert Syst. Appl. **238**(121), 902 (2024)
18. Dosovitskiy, A., Beyer, L., Kolesnikov, A., Weissenborn, D., Zhai, X., Unterthiner, T., Dehghani, M., Minderer, M., Heigold, G., Gelly, S., Uszkoreit, J., Houlsby, N.: An image is worth 16x16 words: transformers for image recognition at scale. In: International Conference on Learning Representations (ICLR). Online (2021)
19. European Union: Regulation (EU) 2022/2065 of the European Parliament and of the Council of 19 October 2022 on a single market for digital services and amending directive 2000/31/EC (Digital Services Act) (2022). URL http://data.europa.eu/eli/reg/2022/2065/oj
20. Gemmeke, J.F., Ellis, D.P.W., Freedman, D., Jansen, A., Lawrence, W., Moore, R.C., Plakal, M., Ritter, M.: Audio set: an ontology and human-labeled dataset for audio events. In: IEEE International Conference on Acoustics. Speech and Signal Processing (ICASSP), pp. 776–780. USA, New Orleans, LA (2017)
21. George, J., Jhunjhunwala, A.: Scalable and robust audio fingerprinting method tolerable to time-stretching. In: IEEE International Conference on Digital Signal Processing (DSP). Singapore, Singapore, pp. 436–440 (2015)
22. Gerhardt, M., Cuccovillo, L., Aichroth, P.: Advancing audio phylogeny: a neural network approach for transformation detection. In: IEEE International Workshop on Information Forensics and Security (WIFS). Nürnberg, Germany, pp. 1–6 (2023)
23. Gerhardt, M., Cuccovillo, L., Aichroth, P.: Audio provenance analysis in heterogeneous media sets. In: IEEE/CVF Conference on Computer Vision and Pattern Recognition Workshops (CVPRW). Seattle, WA, USA, pp. 4387–4396 (2024)
24. Giganti, A., Cuccovillo, L., Bestagini, P., Aichroth, P., Tubaro, S.: Speaker-independent microphone identification in noisy conditions. In: European Signal Processing Conference (EUSIPCO). Belgrade, Serbia, pp. 1047–1051 (2022)
25. Giglietto, F., Marino, G., Mincigrucci, R., Stanziano, A.: A workflow to detect, monitor, and update lists of coordinated social media accounts across time: The case of the 2022 Italian election. Soc. Med. Soc. **9**(3)20563051231196866 (2023)
26. Grigoras, C.: Digital audio recording analysis: the electric network frequency (ENF) criterion. Int. J. Speech Lang. Law **12**, 64–76 (2005)
27. Grigoras, C., Cooper, A.J., Michałek, M.: Best practice guidelines for ENF analysis in forensic authentication of digital evidence. European Network of Forensics Science Institutes—Forensic Speech and Audio Analysis Working Group. Issue No. 001 (2009)
28. Grollmisch, S., Cano, E.: Improving semi-supervised learning for audio classification with FixMatch. Electronics **10**(15), 1 (2021)
29. Haitsma, J., Kalker, T.: A highly robust audio fingerprinting system. In: International Conference on Music Information Retrieval (ISMIR). Paris, France, pp. 107–115 (2002)
30. Haitsma, J., Kalker, T.: Speed-change resistant audio fingerprinting using auto-correlation. In: IEEE International Conference on Acoustics. Speech, and Signal Processing (ICASSP), Vol. 4. China, Hong Kong, pp. 728–731 (2003)
31. Heittola, T., Mesaros, A., Virtanen, T.: TAU urban acoustic scenes 2020 mobile, development dataset (2020). URLhttps://doi.org/10.5281/zenodo.3670167. Zenodo
32. Héritier, M., Gupta, V., Gagnon, L., Boulianne, G., Foucher, P.C.S.: CRIM's content-based copy detection system for TRECVID. In: NIST TREC Video Retrieval Evaluation (TRECVID) Conference. Gaithersburg, MD, USA (2009)
33. Huijbregtse, M., Geradts, Z.: Using the ENF criterion for determining the time of recording of short digital audio recordings. In: International Workshop on Computational Forensics (IWCF). The Hague, The Netherlands, pp. 116–124 (2009)
34. Jégou, H., Delhumeau, J., Yuan, J., Gravier, G., Gros, P.: BABAZ: a large scale audio search system for video copy detection. In: IEEE International Conference on Acoustics. Speech and Signal Processing (ICASSP), pp. 2369–2372. Kyoto, Japan (2012)
35. Jung, J., Zhang, W., Shi, J., Aldeneh, Z., Higuchi, T., Gichamba, A., Theobald, B.J., Hussen Abdelaziz, A., Watanabe, S.: ESPnet-SPK: full pipeline speaker embedding toolkit with reproducible recipes, self-supervised front-ends, and off-the-shelf models. In: Annual Conference

of the International Speech Communication Association (Interspeech). Kos Island, Greece, pp. 4278–4282 (2024)
36. Koluguri, N.R., Park, T., Ginsburg, B.: TitaNet: neural model for speaker representation with 1D depth-wise separable convolutions and global context. In: IEEE International Conference on Acoustics. Speech and Signal Processing (ICASSP), pp. 8102–8106. Singapore, Singapore (2022)
37. Kong, Q., Cao, Y., Iqbal, T., Wang, Y., Wang, W., Plumbley, M.D.: PANNs: large-scale pre-trained audio neural networks for audio pattern recognition. IEEE/ACM Trans. Audio Speech Lang. Process. **28**, 2880–2894 (2020)
38. Lameri, S., Bestagini, P., Mellon, A., Milani, S., Rocha, A., Tagliasacchi, M., Tubaro, S.: Who is my parent? Reconstructing video sequences from partially matching shots. In: IEEE International Conference on Image Processing (ICIP). Paris, France, pp. 5342–5346 (2014)
39. Lameri, S., Bestagini, P., Tubaro, S.: Video alignment for phylogenetic analysis. In: European Signal Processing Conference (EUSIPCO). Budapest, Hungary, pp. 2255–2259 (2016)
40. Luo, D., Korus, P., Huang, J.: Band energy difference for source attribution in audio forensics. IEEE Trans. Inform. Forensics Secur. **13**(9), 2179–2189 (2018)
41. Maksimović, M., Aichroth, P., Cuccovillo, L.: Detection and localization of partial audio matches. In: International Conference on Content-Based Multimedia Indexing (CBMI). La Rochelle, France, pp. 1–6 (2018)
42. Maksimović, M., Aichroth, P., Cuccovillo, L.: Detection and localization of partial audio matches in various application scenarios. Multimedia Tools Appl. **80**(1), 22619–22641 (2021)
43. Maksimovic, M., Cuccovillo, L., Aichroth, P.: Phylogeny analysis for MP3 and AAC coding transformations. In: IEEE International Conference on Multimedia and Expo (ICME). Hong Kong, China, pp. 1165–1170 (2017)
44. Mesaros, A., Heittola, T., Virtanen, T., Plumbley, M.D.: Sound event detection: a tutorial. IEEE Signal Process. Mag. **38**(5), 67–83 (2021)
45. Moreira, D., Bharati, A., Brogan, J., Pinto, A., Parowski, M., Bowyer, K.W., Flynn, P.J., Rocha, A., Scheirer, W.J.: Image provenance analysis at scale. IEEE Trans. Image Process. **27**(12), 6109–6123 (2018)
46. Righetti, N.P.B.: CooRTweet: coordinated networks detection on social media. R package version 2.1.0 (2023). URL https://cran.r-project.org/package=CooRTweet
47. Nucci, M., Tagliasacchi, M., Tubaro, S.: A phylogenetic analysis of near-duplicate audio tracks. In: IEEE International Workshop on Multimedia Signal Processing (MMSP). Pula, Italy, pp. 99–104 (2013)
48. Ouali, C., Dumouchel, P., Gupta, V.: A robust audio fingerprinting method for content-based copy detection. In: International Workshop on Content-Based Multimedia Indexing (CBMI). Klagenfurt, Austria, pp. 1–6 (2014)
49. Ouali, C., Dumouchel, P., Gupta, V.: Efficient spectrogram-based binary image feature for audio copy detection. In: IEEE International Conference on Acoustics. Speech and Signal Processing (ICASSP). South Brisbane, QLD, Australia, pp. 1792–1796 (2015)
50. Radford, A., Kim, J.W., Hallacy, C., Ramesh, A., Goh, G., Agarwal, S., Sastry, G., Askell, A., Mishkin, P., Clark, J., Krueger, G., Sutskever, I.: Learning transferable visual models from natural language supervision. In: International Conference on Machine Learning (ICML). Online, pp. 8748–8763 (2021)
51. Righetti, N., Balluff, P.: CooRTweet: a generalized R software for coordinated network detection. Comput. Commun. Res. **7**(1), 1 (2025)
52. Romero-vicente, A., Miguel, R., Sessa, M.: Coordinated inauthentic behavior detection RREE. Tech. rep. EU DisinfoLab (2024)
53. Sandler, M., Howard, A., Zhu, M., Zhmoginov, A., Chen, L.C.: MobileNetV2: inverted residuals and linear bottlenecks. In: IEEE Conference on Computer Vision and Pattern Recognition (CVPR). Salt Lake City, UT, USA, pp. 4510–4520 (2018)
54. Saracoglu, A., Esen, E., Ates, T.K., Acar, B.O., Zubari, U., Ozan, E.C., Ozalp, E., Alatan, A.A., Ciloglu, T.: Content based copy detection with coarse audio-visual fingerprints. In: IEEE International Workshop on Content-Based Multimedia Indexing (CBMI). Chania, Greece, pp. 213–218 (2009)

55. Schafer, R.M.: The Soundscape: Our Sonic Environment and the Tuning of the World. Destiny Books, Rochester, NY, USA (1994)
56. Schmid, F., Primus, P., Heittola, T., Mesaros, A., Martín-Morató, I., Koutini, K., Widmer, G.: Data-efficient low-complexity acoustic scene classification in the dcase 2024 challenge. In: Detection and Classification of Acoustic Scenes and Events Workshop (DCASE). Tokyo, Japan, pp. 136–140 (2024)
57. Schreiber, H., Müller, M.: Accelerating index-based audio identification. IEEE Trans. Multimedia **16**, 1654–1664 (2014)
58. Six, J., Leman, M.: Panako—a scalable acoustic fingerprinting system handling time-scale and pitch modification. In: International Conference on Music Information Retrieval (ISMIR). Taipei, Taiwan, pp. 259–264 (2014)
59. Sonnleitner, R., Widmer, G.: Robust quad-based audio fingerprinting. IEEE/ACM Trans. Audio Speech Lang. Process. **24**(3), 409–421 (2016)
60. Thienpondt, J., Demuynck, K.: ECAPA2: a hybrid neural network architecture and training strategy for robust speaker embeddings. In: IEEE Automatic Speech Recognition and Understanding Workshop (ASRU). Taipei, Taiwan, pp. 1–8 (2023)
61. Verde, S., Milani, S., Bestagini, P., Tubaro, S.: Audio phylogenetic analysis using geometric transforms. In: IEEE Workshop on Information Forensics and Security (WIFS). Rennes, France, pp. 1–6 (2017)
62. Wang, A.: An industrial strength audio search algorithm. In: International Conference on Music Information Retrieval (ISMIR). Washington, D.C., USA, pp. 7–13 (2003)
63. Zhang, X., Sun, Z.H., Karaman, S., Chang, S.F.: Discovering image manipulation history by pairwise relation and forensics tools. IEEE J. Sel. Top. Signal Process. **14**(5), 1012–1023 (2020)

Video Decomposition and Key Visual Elements Extraction and Enhancement

Konstantinos Apostolidis and Vasileios Mezaris

1 Introduction

AI greatly amplifies human analysts' capacity to verify media. It can rapidly process vast amounts of content to analyse metadata, detect manipulated elements, spot subtle clues, and identify inconsistencies. However, while *synthetic* and *deepfake* videos often dominate discussions about misinformation, as discussed in earlier chapters, they represent only part of the problem. Misleading content frequently stems from simpler but effective tactics, including:

- **Digitally altered real videos**: These involve modifying visual or audio elements to distort meaning.
  Example: In May 2019, a video of Speaker Nancy Pelosi was slowed down to make her speech appear slurred, misleading viewers into thinking she was intoxicated.[1]
- **Re-contextualised authentic footage**: Real, unedited videos are falsely presented as depicting a different time, place, or event. The manipulation lies in relocating the footage's meaning by altering its context.
  Example: A video from an August 2020 protest in Minsk was falsely circulated in October 2024 as a far-right demonstration in London, despite visible Belarusian flags and symbols.[2]

---

[1] https://www.reuters.com/article/world/fact-check-drunk-nancy-pelosi-video-is-manipulated-idUSKCN24Z2B1.

[2] https://www.euronews.com/my-europe/2024/11/05/fact-check-belarus-protest-falsely-shared-as-far-right-london-march.

K. Apostolidis · V. Mezaris (✉)
Centre for Research and Technology Hellas (CERTH), Thessaloniki, Greece
e-mail: bmezaris@iti.gr

K. Apostolidis
e-mail: kapost@iti.gr

S. Papadopoulos et al. (eds.), *Countering Disinformation in the Era of Generative AI*,
https://doi.org/10.1007/978-3-032-11782-3_12

- **Misleading framing or captions**: Authentic videos are correctly placed in time and space but are paired with false or deceptive descriptions that misrepresent what is happening.
  Example: In October 2023, a video showing military equipment transport was shared with a caption claiming it depicted U.S. Marines arriving in Israel, falsely implying American ground involvement in the conflict.[3]

It thus becomes clear that relying solely on synthetic video and deepfake detection is not enough for comprehensive media verification, since these advanced tools can miss the broader context behind manipulated narratives and overlook other forms of misleading content.

Video temporal segmentation divides lengthy videos into shorter, semantically coherent snippets, and when combined with keyframe selection techniques, yields a concise set of representative keyframes. These keyframes allow the easy comparison of footage across different sources to determine if content has been repurposed or altered. Furthermore, they provide a solid foundation for additional techniques, like reverse image searches on platforms such as Google Images, Yandex, Bing, or TinEye, which can help trace the source material or locate related content. By focusing on specific visual cues, the detection of key visual elements additionally helps identify whether a video has been reused or digitally altered. Enhancing these detected visual elements further strengthens the verification process by clarifying details critical to confirming a video's authenticity. For example, enhancing a blurred license plate in a disputed video can provide concrete evidence to verify the claims about its content. This enhancement not only improves the visibility of key features but also extracts actionable clues from low-quality frames, effectively flagging content that may have been used out of context.

Technologies such as the above are essential for supporting humans in quickly recognising and countering deceptive narratives. In the following sections, we introduce the Keyframe Selection and Enhancement (KSE) service that leverages advanced video temporal segmentation, representative keyframe extraction, and targeted visual enhancement to the detected critical elements, such as faces and text, providing a streamlined means to aid in the verification of media content.

The proposed framework is designed with a diverse audience in mind, ranging from media verification experts and cybersecurity professionals to law enforcement, intelligence agencies, academics, and researchers. It combines complex AI video analysis methods while at the same time emphasising swift analysis as well as simplicity of use so that even users without deep technical backgrounds can effectively apply these tools.

[3] https://apnews.com/article/israel-hamas-gaza-misinformation-fact-check-e58f9ab8696309305c3ea2bfb269258epar

2 Related Work

To accomplish our goal, we integrate methods from various technology domains. We next present each domain in a structured manner: defining the problem, categorising key methods from the literature, highlighting current state-of-the-art approaches, sharing insights based on our applied experience in media verification, and suggesting possible future directions.

Video Temporal Segmentation

Video temporal segmentation is the process of splitting a video into shorter, non-overlapping segments based on shifts in semantic or visual attributes, so that each segment captures a coherent event or scene, establishing a basis for more effective analysis later on. The process faces challenges such as ambiguous segment types, highly variable content, long-range dependencies, and real-time processing constraints.

Shot Boundary Detection

Shot boundary detection, a core task in temporal segmentation, identifies abrupt transitions (i.e. cuts) and gradual ones (fades, dissolves) by analysing changes in visual content. A shot is defined as a sequence of frames captured continuously by a single camera. Early methods relied on colour histograms, edge detection, statistical measures, and clustering techniques, but more recent approaches use Deep Convolutional Neural Network (CNN) techniques that have set new benchmarks. A notable example is the method of [27], which leverages spatio-temporal CNNs to achieve high accuracy and efficiency in detecting both abrupt and gradual shot transitions at scale, outperforming traditional handcrafted feature-based approaches. The 3D convolutional network presented in Ridiculously Fast Shot Boundary Detection with Fully Convolutional Neural Networks [26] is notable for its high efficiency, even when utilising a single CPU. TransNetV2 [61] is another significant example, introducing transformer-based modules to improve shot boundary detection.

The current state-of-the-art method, AutoShot [104], employs neural architecture search to automatically derive an optimal network tailored for shot boundary detection. AutoShot's performance, robustness, and generalisation have been validated across multiple benchmarks, including the newly introduced SHOT dataset[4], ClipShots[5], BBC Planet Earth shots[6], and RAI[6] datasets.

[4] https://github.com/wentaozhu/AutoShot.

[5] https://github.com/Tangshitao/ClipShots.

[6] https://aimagelab.ing.unimore.it/imagelab/researchActivity.asp?idActivity=19.

Sub-Shot Boundary Detection

Sub-shot boundary detection refines the segmentation process by breaking down shots into finer parts. Sub-shots are defined as visually coherent parts corresponding to specific video capturing activities like camera pan, tilt, zoom, or displacement, which is particularly useful when analysing user-generated videos with diverse and complex motions. This technique captures subtle temporal transitions, such as minor shifts in camera motion or gradual changes in scene content, that do not necessarily qualify as shot changes.

The field has evolved from early approaches based on colour histograms [49] and local descriptors [40], through statistical methods and unsupervised clustering, to the current era of deep CNN-based methods, such as those proposed in [5, 15]. Recent research trends approach sub-shot boundary detection by reframing video temporal segmentation as the identification of perceptually and semantically meaningful event transitions occurring within shots, rather than relying on explicit editing cues. For instance, [25] proposes a Structured Partition of Sequences strategy that explicitly models local temporal context by grouping neighbouring frames into structured segments and learning their relational differences. By comparing structured context representations instead of isolated frames, the method becomes sensitive to subtle changes in motion, interactions, and appearance that are characteristic of sub-shot boundaries.

One recent method that has demonstrated strong performance in temporal sub-shot segmentation tasks is the Temporal Context Aggregation Network (TCANet) [55]. TCANet leverages a multi-scale temporal context aggregation mechanism that combines 1D convolutional layers with self-attention mechanisms, capturing both short-term and long-term dependencies in video sequences. This powerful combination enables TCANet to detect subtle transitions, such as gradual cuts or lighting changes, that traditional methods often overlook.

Although originally designed for temporal action proposal generation, TCANet's multi-scale context aggregation and self-attention mechanisms also excel at detecting subtle sub-shot transitions in video sequences. It achieves an impressive F1 of 92.3% on the RAI dataset and 89.7% on the BBC dataset.

> Through extensive experimentation, we have found that while the concept of a *shot* is more intuitive and easier for human interpretation, *sub-shots* provide a level of granularity that is particularly useful for algorithmic video analysis. Additionally, in the context of short videos or user-generated content where broader segmentation (like shot detection) might miss critical details, sub-shot detection becomes an invaluable tool. This fine-grained segmentation not only enriches the analytical process but also enhances the overall accuracy of video content interpretation.

Looking ahead, efforts will focus on making sub-shot boundary detection more robust across diverse real-world scenarios. Key areas for future research include achieving efficient online or real-time segmentation, which is especially vital for streaming applications, and incorporating multi-modal integration by combining visual, audio, or textual cues. Such advances promise to further refine the segmentation process, making it even more effective and context-aware.

Keyframe Selection

Keyframe selection automatically extracts representative frames from a video sequence that encapsulate its most critical visual and contextual information. This process is vital for video summarisation, indexing, and understanding, as it condenses the video content into essential snapshots. However, two primary challenges arise: first, defining what constitutes a truly representative frame; and second, determining the optimal number of keyframes, ensuring there is neither redundancy from excessive frames nor a risk of overlooking important content by selecting too few.

To address these challenges, several categories of keyframe selection methods have emerged. Heuristic-based methods use temporal or uniform sampling and edge points classification (as in [58, 85]) to pinpoint moments where significant motion changes occur.

Cluster-based methods leverage feature extraction and clustering, for example the Katna Python library[7], which automates keyframe extraction, video compression, and intelligent image cropping. Katna extracts features like colour histograms and employs clustering techniques to group similar frames, selecting the most informative frame from each cluster. Video summarisation–based methods (e.g. DSNet [105]) leverage deep learning to capture temporal dynamics.

Attention-based networks have also been proposed [6]. They use a deep autoencoder with an attention layer to detect keyframes automatically, achieving 77% accuracy on TVSUM dataset[8]. Hybrid approaches further refine the selection process by integrating multiple strategies, for example, [32] fuses multiple visual features and employs a hybrid clustering algorithm combining Fuzzy C-means with artificial hummingbird optimisation to effectively extract keyframes from videos.

The current state-of-the-art in keyframe selection is exemplified by KeyVideoLLM [41]. This method employs a coarse-to-fine framework where a pre-trained Contrastive Language-Image Pre-training (CLIP) model is first used to uniformly sample candidate frames and to embed both the frames and accompanying textual data into a shared semantic space. It then computes the cosine similarity between each frame's visual embedding and a text embedding derived from queries, questions, or answers. By selecting the top-k frames with the highest similarity scores, KeyVideoLLM effectively filters out redundant content while focusing on the most semantically informative frames. This efficiency is reflected in data compression

---

[7] https://github.com/keplerlab/katna.

[8] https://github.com/yalesong/tvsum.

rates of up to approximately 60x, with its robust performance being demonstrated on benchmarks such as ActivityNet[9], MSRVTT[10], MSVD[11], and TGIF[12].

It is important to distinguish keyframe selection from related tasks. Thumbnail selection (e.g. [4]) focuses on choosing a frame that best represents the video to attract viewers, akin to a book cover [66]. In contrast, highlight detection aims to extract the most "exciting" moments based on factors like user engagement and motion intensity [14], while video summarisation condenses a video into a shorter version that captures its main points [3].

Based on our experiments and professional feedback, particularly from journalists involved in media verification tasks, the consensus is that "the more keyframes, the merrier". This feedback indicates that relying on basic visual features to capture significant changes in visual content sufficiently meets the needs of the task in this particular context. While it is crucial to balance the number of keyframes to avoid excessive redundancy and ensure no critical content is omitted, our findings suggest that erring on the side of redundancy is preferable to the risk of missing important details.

Detection of Key Visual Elements

Verifying media authenticity also relies on identifying subtle yet crucial visual clues that, when carefully compiled and highlighted, can then be evaluated by a human expert for their forensic importance. These clues fall into several interconnected categories, each providing unique value in the verification process. Objects of interest, such as vehicles, weapons, or landmarks, can be cross-referenced with known data (e.g. a distinctive road sign or building design) to confirm a video's claimed location and time. Geolocation clues can further enhance verification by enabling the matching of background features, such as landmarks or familiar scenery, to known records or maps. Additionally, digital tampering often leaves traces—artifacts like unnatural lighting, repeated textures, or pixel inconsistencies can expose edits or AI-generated content. Although metadata (e.g. timestamps, camera models) can provide context, it is often stripped by social platforms and, when present, may be unreliable. Watermarks offer stronger provenance clues by linking media to stock platforms or news agencies, though they too can be removed or hidden.

[9] http://activity-net.org/.
[10] https://cove.thecvf.com/datasets/839.
[11] https://www.cs.utexas.edu/~ml/clamp/videoDescription/.
[12] https://raingo.github.io/TGIF-Release/.

Two elements stand out for their universal importance: faces and text regions. Detected faces can facilitate identity verification, while text, such as street signs or timestamps, assists in correlating media with specific times and places. These elements are prioritised for three key reasons. First, they appear in nearly all media types, from social posts to news reports, making them broadly applicable. Second, modern tools like AI-powered face detection and scene text detection enable rapid processing even at scale. Third, they directly address common misinformation tactics, such as falsifying identities or altering contextual details. By integrating automated face and text analysis, verification systems can efficiently flag suspicious content while preserving human oversight for complex cases. This layered approach effectively balances speed and accuracy, which is crucial for countering rapidly spreading disinformation.

Text Detection

Detecting text "in the wild" is crucial for extracting contextual clues like signs or banners. Text detection identifies regions in images containing text, whether printed, handwritten, or part of a scene. This task is complex because real-world text varies widely—it can be curved, rotated, distorted, or placed against cluttered backgrounds. For example, a street sign might be partially hidden by tree branches, or certain characters of a piece of handwritten text could be tilted. Detecting text in these conditions (i.e. "in the wild" detection) requires algorithms able to distinguish characters from similar patterns (like fences or bricks) while handling variations in font, size, and lighting.

Early approaches relied on traditional image processing techniques. Methods like edge detection or connected component analysis (as in [50]) scanned images for sharp contrasts or geometric shapes resembling text. While effective in simple cases, these methods struggled with noisy or complex scenes. Machine learning-based methods improved robustness by using handcrafted features like HOG (Histogram of Oriented Gradients) or SIFT (Scale-Invariant Feature Transform) combined with classifiers such as SVMs [21]. These could better generalise across fonts and backgrounds but still required manual feature engineering. Modern deep learning-based methods revolutionised the field by learning features directly from data. These fall into three main categories:

1. Regression-based methods like EAST [103] predict bounding boxes around text regions in one step, balancing speed and accuracy.
2. Segmentation-based approaches (e.g. [43]) create pixel-level maps of text areas, which are then refined into precise boundaries.
3. Transformer-based models like TrOCR [39] use self-attention to analyse global relationships in images, excelling at irregular text layouts.

Hybrid methods combine these ideas. For instance, Mask TextSpotter [46] integrates detection and recognition into a single network, streamlining the process for arbitrary text shapes. We should note that most deep-learning based detectors are trained primarily on Latin-script datasets, so their out-of-the-box performance can degrade on non-Roman alphabets. To achieve truly script-agnostic detection, models can be fine-tuned or pre-trained on multilingual corpora e.g. ICDAR MLT[13] (9+ languages including Chinese, Japanese, Korean, Arabic, Hindi, Bangla, Hebrew, Thai), IIIT-ILST[14] (with Indic script languages including Hindi, Tamil, Telugu, Malayalam). This ensures proper performance across the full spectrum of scripts encountered in real-world imagery.

The current leader in scene text detection is MixNet [93], which addresses key challenges like small or overlapping text. Its architecture blends CNNs for local detail extraction with transformer modules to model broader context. Two innovations drive its performance: (a) a Feature Shuffle Network (FSNet) that mixes multi-scale features to better capture text of varying sizes, and (b) a Central Transformer Block (CTBlock) that focuses on the centre lines of text regions, improving detection of curved or distorted characters. Tested on benchmarking datasets like Total-Text[15] and MSRA-TD500[16], it achieves top-tier precision and recall, even for text in cluttered or low-contrast environments.

While deep learning dominates research, real-world deployment often requires trade-offs. Regression-based methods like EAST are favoured for speed in mobile apps, while segmentation approaches suit high-precision needs like medical records. Transformer-based models, though powerful, demand more computational resources, thus limiting their use on edge devices. As datasets grow more diverse, future methods will likely focus on lightweight architectures that maintain accuracy without heavy hardware requirements.

Face Detection

Face Detection "in the wild" involves automatically locating human faces in images captured under unconstrained, real-world conditions. Unlike controlled settings, such as studio portraits or passport photos, images "in the wild" display significant variability. A robust face detection system must accurately identify and localise faces regardless of whether they are captured outdoors, in crowds, or on the street, and must handle factors like unpredictable lighting and background interference. Faces can appear from multiple angles, including profile views or partially rotated perspectives, and may be partially occluded by objects (e.g. glasses or masks) or other faces. As a specialised subset of object detection, face detection uses similar techniques,

[13] https://rrc.cvc.uab.es/?ch=12.

[14] https://cvit.iiit.ac.in/research/projects/cvit-projects/iiit-ilst.

[15] https://github.com/cs-chan/Total-Text-Dataset.

[16] http://www.iapr-tc11.org/mediawiki/index.php/MSRA_Text_Detection_500_Database_(MSRA-TD500).

such as convolutional neural networks and region proposal methods, but is fine-tuned to handle the unique challenges posed by facial features. This capability is critical in applications ranging from security and photography to human-computer interaction.

Early methods relied on classical machine learning, using manually designed features to identify faces. The Viola-Jones detector [68], for example, combined Haar-like features (detecting edges or lines) with cascading classifiers to quickly discard non-face regions. While groundbreaking for its time, it struggled with complex scenes. Feature-based methods improved precision by detecting facial landmarks like eyes or nose tips. Techniques like Active Shape Models [16] iteratively adjusted predefined face shapes to match images, refining localisation. However, these still required manual tuning and faltered with diverse poses or lighting. The rise of deep-learning transformed face detection by automating feature learning. Multi-stage detectors like the Multi-task Cascaded Convolutional Network [94] combined face detection and alignment in a cascading process, progressively refining candidate regions. Single-shot detectors such as Single Shot Scale-invariant Face Detector [97] simplified this by processing images in one step, enabling real-time performance without sacrificing accuracy across scales. Recent transformer-based approaches like DETR (DEtection TRansformer) [9] introduced end-to-end detection using self-attention, capturing global relationships for better handling of occluded or distant faces.

Modern systems balance speed and accuracy. The Sample and Computation Redistribution for Efficient Face Detection (SCRFD) model [23] enhances single-stage detection with a multi-scale features aggregating module, improving robustness to poses and low resolution. On the WIDER FACE benchmark, it achieves 95.8% average precision (AP) for easy cases and 91.5% for hard cases, like tiny or heavily obscured faces. The Automatic and Scalable Face Detector (ASFD) [38] takes a different route, using neural architecture search to automate feature aggregation. Its automatic feature enhance module tailors the network to face detection, achieving 96.7% AP on easy cases and maintaining 320 frames per second on high-end GPUs. For resource-constrained settings, lightweight variants like ASFD-D0 offer practical speeds without major accuracy drops. RetinaFace [19] combines multi-task learning with pixel-level supervision. By predicting facial landmarks and using a self-supervised mesh decoder, it refines localisation accuracy, reaching 91.4% AP on hard cases while processing VGA-resolution images in real time on a single CPU core.

DeepFace [63] is frequently cited as a milestone in face verification and demonstrated that deep learning methods could surpass human-level performance. In the paper, it is reported that *"Experiments show that human beings have 97.53% accuracy on facial recognition tasks [on the Labelled Faces in the Wild dataset] whereas those models already reached and passed that accuracy level"*. While current face detection methods have achieved astonishing accuracy on standard benchmarks—sometimes even outperforming average human performance under controlled conditions—there remain significant challenges in truly unconstrained, real-world environments. Detecting tiny faces in crowded scenes or under extreme lighting remains difficult, and biases in training data can lead to uneven performance across demographics. Current research focuses on transformer architectures for better global modelling, self-supervised learning to reduce reliance on labelled data, and efficient designs for edge devices. For example, hybrid models blending CNNs and transformers aim to balance local detail and global context, while techniques like knowledge distillation shrink large models without significant accuracy loss. These advances aim to make face detection more reliable across diverse real-world scenarios.

Grouping of Key Visual Elements

Multi-Object Tracking (MOT) involves detecting and following multiple objects across video frames while maintaining their identities. This task is fundamental for applications such as surveillance and autonomous driving. It faces challenges including occlusions (when objects are partially hidden by others), variations in object appearance (due to lighting, pose, or environmental changes), and complex interactions among objects (such as overlapping paths in crowded scenes). In our work, we extend this concept by grouping detections of similar faces and similar text regions to improve both recognition accuracy and contextual analysis.

MOT approaches vary in their strategies for handling detection and tracking. A common strategy is tracking-by-detection, where objects are first detected in each frame using object detectors like the You-Only-Look-Once (YOLO) family of models (e.g. [70]) or the Faster Region-based CNN (aka Faster R-CNN) [57], and then linked across frames using algorithms such as the Hungarian algorithm [60], an optimisation method that efficiently finds the optimal one-to-one matching between predicted tracks and new detections by minimising a cost matrix. Early examples of MOT methods include Simple Online and Real-time Tracking (SORT) [7], which combines a Kalman filter for predicting object motion with simple data association. For more complex scenarios, global optimisation-based methods analyse the entire video sequence simultaneously, framing tracking as a mathematical optimisation problem. Although these methods excel at handling occlusions, they tend to be slower, making them more suitable for offline processing. Graph-based tracking similarly adopts a holistic view by modelling detections as nodes and their associations as edges, as demonstrated by classic techniques like Multiple Hypothesis Tracking [56]. Recent advances focus on integrating detection and tracking into unified frameworks. For instance, joint detection and tracking methods such as Tracktor perform both tasks in a single step using deep learning. Additionally, deep learning-based trackers like TransTrack[62] use transformer architectures to model long-range dependencies between objects, while re-identification (Re-ID) based methods like Deep SORT [83] combine appearance features with motion models to resolve identity switches in crowded scenes.

Notable MOT approaches include SORT [7], which set a baseline by combining a simple Kalman filter with the Hungarian algorithm for efficient detection association. Building on this, Deep SORT [83] integrated deep appearance features to improve association in challenging scenarios like occlusions and crowded scenes. More recent methods, such as ByteTrack [98], enhance performance by utilising all detections, including low-confidence ones, through a two-stage matching process that significantly reduces false negatives. Meanwhile, FairMOT [101] introduced a unified framework that jointly tackles detection and re-identification with balanced feature learning, offering robust performance for each target. These innovations have set new benchmarks on widely used datasets such as MOT17, achieving high MOTA (Multi-Object Tracking Accuracy) and IDF1 (identity-preservation score) scores while maintaining real-time efficiency.

One of the current state-of-the-art methods is ByteTrack [98] which represents a significant advancement in MOT by addressing a key limitation: many methods discard low-confidence detections (e.g. those from partially occluded objects). ByteTrack employs a two-step process that first matches high-confidence detections to existing tracks and then revisits low-confidence detections to recover missed objects, thereby reducing missed detections. This approach has achieved state-of-the-art results on benchmarks like MOT17, with 80% MOTA and 78% IDF1, all while remaining efficient enough for real-time applications.

MOT methods can generally be grouped into three paradigms based on their priorities:

1. **Detection-and-association**, e.g. SORT [7], emphasising speed and simplicity.
2. **Global optimisation and graph-based**, offering robustness in complex scenarios at the cost of speed.
3. **Integrated frameworks**, e.g. FairMOT [101], balancing detection, tracking, and re-identification features.

Looking ahead, researchers are working to develop lighter and more adaptable models. Transformer-based architectures and self-supervised learning techniques show promise in improving robustness to occlusions and appearance changes. Moreover, domain adaptation methods may help trackers generalise better across diverse environments, from urban traffic to sports broadcasts.

Enhancement of Key Visual Elements

Image enhancement techniques involve a range of methods designed to improve the quality and clarity of images by increasing sharpness, restoring details, and optimising visual appearance. These methods, which are essential across applications from smartphone photography to medical imaging and satellite imagery, leverage advanced algorithms, including super-resolution and deblurring, to recover details and reduce artifacts caused by noise, motion blur, or low resolution.

Image restoration and enhancement methods can be broadly organised into three major categories. First, restoration techniques aim to reverse degradation by removing unwanted noise (denoising), mitigating motion blur (deblurring), eliminating rain streaks (deraining), clearing foggy scenes (dehasing), and upscaling low-resolution images (super-resolution) while recovering fine details; notable works in this area include DeblurGAN [33] and DnCNN (denoising CNN) [95]. Second, some methods focus on sharpening and retouching, boosting contrast and accentuating details to improve overall visual appeal, as demonstrated by methods such as Deep Photo Enhancer [10]. Finally, a third class of enhancement techniques adjusts aesthetic parameters such as brightness, contrast, and color balance to produce more visually pleasing images, with the EnlightenGAN method [31] serving as a characteristic example. Although these methods share the common goal of improving image quality, they differ in their underlying approaches and computational requirements.

Super-Resolution

Super-resolution reconstructs high-resolution images from low-resolution inputs, a task complicated by the fact that many possible high-resolution versions could correspond to a single low-resolution source. The goal is not merely to increase image size, but also to recover lost details, such as textures in medical scans, and fine features in satellite photos. However, this process encounters difficulties since reconstructing missing details accurately is challenging, and upscaling often introduces unwanted artifacts like blurring or unnatural edges. The inherent ambiguity of the task, where multiple valid solutions may exist, necessitates advanced techniques to guide the reconstruction process. Moreover, these methods can be computationally demanding, especially when processing large images or operating in real-time applications.

Super-resolution methods fall into distinct categories based on their approach. Early simple interpolation-based methods, like bicubic interpolation, rely on mathematical formulas to estimate missing pixels but often produce overly smooth results. More advanced example-based methods, such as Sparse Coding Super-Resolution (ScSR) [65, 87], use machine learning to map relationships between low- and high-resolution image patches. Modern approaches rely heavily on neural networks. CNN-based methods, exemplified by the pioneering Super-Resolution Convolutional Neural Network (SRCNN) [20], train convolutional networks to directly predict high-resolution outputs. GAN-based methods like Super-Resolution Generative Adversarial Networks (SRGAN) [35] and Enhanced SRGANs (ESRGAN) [74] improve realism by using a generator network to create details and a discriminator network to assess their authenticity, although this can sometimes reduce traditional quality metrics such as Peak Signal-to-Noise Ratio (PSNR). Recent innovations include transformer-based models, such as the Shifted Window Transformer for Image Restoration (SwinIR) [42], which analyse both local details and global image context using self-attention mechanisms, and diffusion models like the Super-Resolution via Repeated Refinement (SR3) model [59], which gradually refine images through iterative noise reduction.

The current leader in general-purpose super-resolution is SwinIR [42], which combines transformer architecture with shifted window attention to balance local precision and global coherence. On related benchmark datasets such as Urban100 [30] and DIV2K [1], SwinIR outperforms older CNN-based methods in both PSNR and Structural Similarity Index Measure (SSIM) scores, making it versatile for real-world use.

Super-resolution techniques are often adapted to meet specific needs. For face enhancement, methods prioritise preserving identity features such as eyes and facial contours. Face super-resolution methods are typically evaluated using both quantitative metrics (such as PSNR and SSIM) and perceptual metrics like the Learned Perceptual Image Patch Similarity (LPIPS), which measures perceptual similarity by comparing deep features extracted from neural networks [96].

Identity preservation refers to the ability of a super-resolution method to maintain the unique, distinguishing characteristics of an individual's face in the enhanced image, ensuring that the person's identity remains recognisable and consistent with the original low-resolution input. This is often assessed by measuring similarity scores from pre-trained face recognition models (e.g. ArcFace), which help verify that key facial features are accurately retained. Face super-resolution techniques can sometimes generate artificial details that do not accurately preserve the original person's identity, a phenomenon known as face hallucination, where the reconstructed features diverge from true facial characteristics. Thus, for media verification, we have found that moderate upscaling often strikes an optimal balance between detail recovery and computational speed, as excessive enhancement may introduce artifacts without significant quality improvements.

In addition to these quantitative assessments, qualitative evaluation through visual inspection plays a crucial role, as in the case of face super-resolution methods. While metrics like PSNR, SSIM, and LPIPS provide objective measurements, they may not fully capture the perceptual quality and identity fidelity of the super-resolved faces. Human evaluators can identify nuances and artifacts that automated metrics might overlook, such as unnatural textures or subtle distortions in facial features. Therefore, combining quantitative metrics with qualitative analysis ensures a more comprehensive evaluation of the super-resolution method's effectiveness in preserving both the visual quality and the identity information of the face.

Text super-resolution is the process of enhancing low-resolution images that contain textual information by specifically targeting and restoring the fine details and structural features of characters. Unlike standard super-resolution, it employs specialised techniques to preserve legibility and accurately reconstruct character shapes, ensuring that the text remains clear and readable. Recent breakthroughs address challenging cases involving heavily degraded text. For example, the Diffusion Transformer for Text Super-Resolution method [99] combines diffusion models with text-specific guidance to reconstruct intricate strokes in Chinese characters. By separating style restoration (handling colours and backgrounds) from structural accuracy (defining character shapes), it achieves robust results even for blurry or low-quality inputs. Such advances underscore the importance of tailored solutions for specialised super-resolution tasks.

Deblurring

Deblurring aims to recover sharp, detailed images from blurred inputs caused by factors like motion (e.g. shaky cameras) or defocus (e.g. incorrect lens focus). This process is vital for media verification, as blurry frames in videos or images can hide critical details needed to authenticate content, such as faces, text, or environmental clues. Without clear visuals, forensic analysis becomes challenging, potentially allowing manipulated or misleading content to go undetected.

Deblurring methods vary based on input type and underlying algorithms. A primary distinction lies in the number of images used: single-image blind deblurring works with just one blurry input and no prior knowledge of how the blur occurred, while multi-image deblurring combines data from multiple frames (e.g. a burst of photos) to reconstruct sharper results by exploiting variations in blur across frames. Methods can also be grouped by their technical approach. Traditional techniques rely on mathematical models like deconvolution (reversing blur through signal processing) or statistical analysis of blur patterns. These often require manual tuning and struggle with complex blurs. Deep-learning-based methods, in contrast, train neural networks on large datasets of paired blurry/sharp images. Models such as DeblurGAN [33] learn to predict sharp versions directly, while newer architectures like Multi-Stage Progressive Image Restoration (MPRNet) [92] refine results progressively through multiple processing stages.

Most recent breakthroughs include Google's MAXIM [67], a versatile model that combines local and global image analysis using a multi-axis MLP architecture. Built on a UNet-like framework, MAXIM handles multiple enhancement tasks (deblurring, denoising, etc.) in one system. On the GoPro benchmark dataset, specifically the subset for the deblurring task, it achieves PSNR scores around 32dB. However, advanced variants like MAXIM-3S require substantial computational power—22 million parameters and 339 billion FLOPs for one 256×256 image, which scales poorly to full HD video frames.

Despite progress, deblurring remains computationally heavy. Studies [33, 51] show that even modern deep learning models struggle to balance speed and accuracy, especially for high-resolution content. Camera shake, which creates irregular blur patterns, adds complexity by requiring large-scale optimisation [82]. These challenges make real-time deblurring impractical for many applications.

In our video analysis pipeline we deliberately exclude deblurring. While restoring sharpness could theoretically improve detail extraction, the computational cost would drastically slow down processing. By prioritising speed, our system ensures that it can quickly analyse content without waiting for time-consuming enhancements. This approach aligns with our view on real-world needs: in media verification, rapid insights often outweigh marginal gains in visual quality.

3 Proposed Method

The Keyframe Selection and Enhancement (KSE) service is designed to aid the verification of video authenticity by providing a clear and concise visual summary of its content. The service achieves this by isolating critical visual elements, such as faces and text, and enhancing them to facilitate reliable media verification. Figure 1 depicts our high-level workflow. In essence, the service aims to:

1. Segment the video temporally: break the input into shots and sub-shots.
2. Extract representative keyframes: capture each segment's essence to eliminate redundancy.
3. Identify key visual elements: detect faces and text regions in each keyframe.
4. Group key visual elements: group similar faces and text regions for focused analysis.
5. Enhance visual details: apply super-resolution to improve the quality of these elements.

When selecting methods from the literature to include as modules in the KSE service, we applied several criteria. First, we excluded any methods published before 2020 to focus on recent advances and modern architectures. We also prioritised reproducibility by choosing methods with publicly available code and pre-trained models. Pre-trained models significantly simplify deployment, support, and maintenance, eliminating the need to retrain complex architectures from scratch. We also looked at community engagement on platforms like GitHub as a sign that the method is actively maintained and likely to receive long-term support.

In addition to the accuracy metrics reported in the corresponding peer-reviewed publications of the selected methods, we also needed reliable measurements of execution speed, which are often missing or inconsistent due to varying hardware.

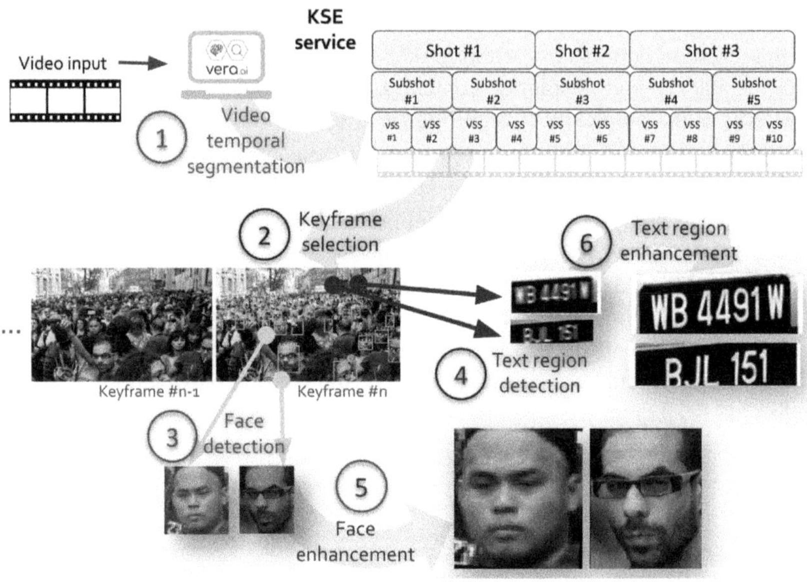

Fig. 1 An overview of the KSE service process: the input video is segmented into shots and subshots, representative keyframes are extracted, and the detected key visual elements (faces and text) are enhanced using super-resolution techniques

Moreover, only a few methods do report metrics such as the Floating Point Operations (FLOPs) counts, required for inference, making it difficult to translate these numbers into real-world performance on specific hardware. To address this, we selected the top-performing methods that met our aforementioned criteria and measured their inference times on the same hardware setup. Thus, by running each method under identical conditions, we were able to calculate an average inference time that provides a practical and fair comparison of computational efficiency.

This approach enabled us to balance accuracy and speed, so that even if one method achieves slightly higher accuracy, we may choose another that offers a better overall trade-off by delivering comparable accuracy with significantly shorter execution times. We further validated these findings by testing with real-world data from journalists and media verification professionals, ensuring that our selection process (based on recency, reproducibility, community support, ease of deployment, and computational efficiency) identifies the most suitable methods for our framework.

Video Temporal Segmentation Method Selection

The selected methods for shot boundary detection that met our criteria are Trans NetV2 [61], Ridiculously Fast Shot Boundary Detection [26], and AutoShot [104].

Table 1 Comparison of the selected video shot boundary detection methods from the literature

Method	F1 (%) on RAI	Average inference time (ms)
TransNetV2 [61]	93.9	5
Ridiculously fast shot boundary detection [26]	88.0	3
AutoShot [104]	95.5	27

TransNetV2 is a deep network architecture designed for rapid shot transition detection; it uses 3D convolutional layers to process spatial and temporal information together and is trained on a large dataset of artificially generated transitions. The method in Ridiculously Fast Shot Boundary Detection employs a simple modular convolutional neural network that achieves well above real-time inference speeds, on a single commodity GPU (e.g. Nvidia GTX 1080). Trained on a dataset of one million frames with automatically generated transitions, it uses a fully convolutional approach along the time axis. AutoShot, the top performer on the ClipShots dataset, is a deep neural network that uses a self-attention mechanism to capture temporal dependencies between frames. It also employs a contrastive loss function to boost the network's ability to differentiate between frames.

Table 1 shows the evaluation scores on the RAI dataset alongside the average inference times, measured by deploying all methods on the same server. The RAI dataset comprises 169 videos from various TV programs, totalling about 24 hours and includes abrupt and gradual transitions, as well as challenging cases like flashes, fast motion, and camera shakes. Although AutoShot achieves a slightly higher F1 of 95.5%, its inference time is significantly slower at 27ms per frame. Conversely, the Ridiculously Fast method delivers the quickest execution (3 ms) but with a lower accuracy of 88%. Overall, TransNetV2, with a 93.9% F1 and a moderate 5 ms inference time, proves to be a well-rounded choice that meets both performance and efficiency requirements. For sub-shot segmentation, we selected Apostolidis et al. method [5] for its sub-millisecond execution and easy pipeline integration. Empirically, it yields coherent sub-shots whose sharpest frames serve reliably as keyframes.

Keyframe Selection Strategy

The proposed keyframe selection approach works by choosing the least blurry frame from each sub-shot as the representative keyframe. This method begins with sub-shot segmentation (using the method in [5]), dividing the video into segments that maintain a consistent visual theme while ensuring clear boundaries between different parts of the video. By selecting the sharpest frame within each sub-shot, the approach directly addresses common quality issues in real-world video capture, such as motion blur and compression artifacts, that can obscure important visual details.

To estimate the blurriness of an image, we use the well-established variance of the Laplacian method [77]. The core idea of this technique is that sharp images exhibit well-defined edges, resulting in a high variance in their Laplacian response, whereas blurry images produce a uniform, low-variance response because their edges are not clearly defined.

This makes the Laplacian variance an effective proxy for perceptual quality, as images with low variance typically contain less useful information for both human viewers and computer vision tasks. Another advantage of this clear and interpretable selection criterion is that it provides transparency compared to black-box neural network decisions. Additionally, the proposed approach is computationally efficient since it avoids the heavy overhead of extensive deep CNN feature extraction by instead using simple DCT-based feature extraction (which transforms small image blocks into their frequency components via the Discrete Cosine Transform) for sub-millisecond image similarity assessment and a straightforward blur metric calculation. With an $O(n)$ complexity compared to the $O(n^2)$ complexity of typical clustering methods, it becomes clear that this approach produces high-quality keyframes while maintaining a high processing speed.

Face Detection Method Selection

We evaluated five top face detectors—RetinaFace, MediaPipe FaceDetector, YOLOv7-Face, TinaFace, and YuNet—against our criteria of accuracy, speed, and ease of deployment. For instance, RetinaFace [18] is a single-stage, dense face localisation approach that performs pixel-wise detection across multiple scales using both extra-supervised and self-supervised multi-task learning. Google MediaPipe's FaceDetector [22], built on BlazeFace, achieves real-time performance that makes it ideal for mobile devices and web browsers. The YOLOv7-Face detector [53] is a tailored extension of the YOLOv7 object detector [70], designed to predict face boxes efficiently with a single network. TinaFace [100] employs a ResNet-50 backbone along with a feature pyramid network and an inception block to generate robust multi-scale feature maps, while YuNet [84] is engineered for mobile GPU inference by using a custom backbone with BlazeBlocks and an innovative anchor scheme to balance detection accuracy and speed.

A detailed comparison of the selected face detection method is presented in Table 2. The YOLOv7 face detector offers a balanced compromise between detection accuracy and speed. While methods like RetinaFace (in both TensorFlow and PyTorch implementations) and TinaFace can deliver marginally higher performance on certain subsets, their inference times (ranging from 50 ms to 87 ms) are notably slower compared to YOLOv7's 18ms inference time. On the other hand, Google MediaPipe and YuNet provide faster inference, but their accuracy, especially on the medium and harder subsets of the WIDER Face dataset, falls short.

Table 2 Comparison of face detection methods from the literature

Method		AP (%) on WIDER face [89]			Average inference time (ms)
		Easy subset	Medium subset	Hard subset	
RetinaFace	Tensorflow	96.9	95.5	88.0	50
	PyTorch	95.5	94.0	84.4	52
Google MediaPipe [22]		90.7	86.5	N/A	4
YOLOv7 face detector [53]		94.7	92.6	82.1	18
TinaFace [100]		95.8	95.3	92.4	87
YuNet [84]		89.9	86.9	69.1	11

Text Detection Method Selection

We identified several state-of-the-art text detection methods from the literature that met our criteria, and after a careful review, we narrowed our focus to three methods. The first one, "Real-Time Scene Text Detection with Differentiable Binarisation and Adaptive Scale Fusion" [44] emphasises real-time performance by integrating a differentiable binarisation module into a segmentation network and adding an adaptive scale fusion module. These enhancements improve scale robustness and help achieve high accuracy even in challenging scenarios. The second one is MixNet ("Toward Accurate Detection of Challenging Scene Text in the Wild") [93] which introduces a hybrid architecture that combines CNNs and Transformers. It utilises a feature shuffle network as its backbone along with a central transformer block, exploiting the one-dimensional manifold constraint of scene text to accurately detect small and challenging text. Finally, the method in "FAST: Faster Arbitrarily-Shaped Text Detector with Minimalist Kernel Representation" [64] focuses on efficiency by using a minimalist kernel representation for modelling arbitrarily shaped text. Its GPU-parallel post-processing efficiently assembles text lines, making it particularly suitable for real-time applications.

In Table 3, a comprehensive overview of text detection results is provided. The FAST method stands out as the most efficient option, achieving an F-Measure of

Table 3 Comparison of text detection methods from the literature

Method	F1(%) on total-text (%)	Average inference time (ms)
MixNet: toward accurate detection of challenging scene text in the wild [93]	90.5	326
Real-time scene text detection with differentiable binarisation and adaptive scale fusion [44]	81.6	256
FAST: faster arbitrarily-shaped text detector with minimalist kernel representation [64]	81.6	174

81.6% with the shortest inference time at 174 ms. Although MixNet delivers a higher accuracy of 90.5%, its significantly slower execution time (326 ms) may not be ideal for real-time applications. Similarly, the Real-Time Scene Text Detection method offers comparable accuracy to FAST but at a longer inference time of 256 ms. Thus, when balancing accuracy and speed, FAST emerges as the preferable choice for scenarios requiring real-time text detection.

Face Super-Resolution Method Selection

We evaluated a broad range of approaches for super-resolution specifically designed for faces, spanning Transformer-based (i.e. CodeFormer [102], RestoreFormer++ [79], MetaF2N [90], Latent Style Guided Transformer-CNN Framework [54]), GAN-based methods (DeblurGAN-v2 [34], HiFaceGAN [86], Real-ESRGAN [73], Progressive Semantic-Aware Style Transformation [13], Generative Facial Prior for Blind Face Restoration [71], SCGAN [29], Face Super Resolution based SRGAN [36], Super-resolution of very low-resolution face images [17], Panini-Net [75]), diffusion-based (Adversarial Training Diffusion Probabilistic Model (AT-DDPM) [52], PseudoGradient Diffusion (PGDiff) [88], Denoising Diffusion Restoration Model (DR2) [72], Diffusion-based Face Image Restoration (DiffBIR) [45], DifFace [91]), and other promising techniques (e.g. Vector Quantised Face Restoration (VQFR) [24], Generative and Controllable Face Super Resolution (GCFSR) [28] and the Spatial-frequency mutual learning of [69]). Diffusion-based methods, despite their impressive image quality, require multiple iterative refinement steps that significantly increase computational demands and inference time. Our experiments on the same test hardware confirmed this, with inference times reaching up to approximately 15 seconds for a 256 $\times$ 256 input image. Given that our framework needs to operate close to real-time, we excluded these methods to ensure a responsive and practical end product.

From the aforementioned extensive pool of state-of-the-art methods, the ones that best met our specified criteria are:

- VQFR [24]: This method leverages a vector-quantised dictionary and a parallel decoder to tackle blind face restoration challenges. By learning a discrete codebook of high-quality facial features, it effectively recovers realistic facial details. A texture warping module further assists in aligning features.
- RestoreFormer [79]: Focused on high-quality blind face restoration, RestoreFormer takes advantage of spatial attention for contextual modelling. Its reconstruction-oriented dictionary of high-quality facial features has shown excellent performance on both synthetic and real-world datasets.
- CodeFormer [102]: Performing blind face restoration as a code prediction task, CodeFormer uses a codebook learned prior to completing the computation, along with a transformer network for code prediction and a decoder to reconstruct the face image.

Table 4 Comparison of face super-resolution methods from the literature

Method	SSIM (%) score on CelebA	Average inference time (ms)
RestoreFormer [79]	85.4	542
VQFR [24]	84.7	617
CodeFormer [102]	83.9	286
FaceFormer [37]	83.2	512
GCFSR [28]	84.3	112

- FaceFormer [37]: Utilising a transformer-based architecture, FaceFormer models both long-range dependencies and local details in face images. It incorporates a multi-scale feature pyramid to capture diverse levels of facial information and uses multi-head attention for effective feature fusion.
- GCFSR [28]: This method employs an encoder-generator architecture with dedicated style modulation and feature modulation modules. It dynamically fuses multi-level encoded features with generated features to reconstruct high-resolution facial images that faithfully preserve identity information without relying on additional facial or GAN priors.

Table 4 details the comparative outcomes of the different face super-resolution methods. Among these contenders, RestoreFormer exhibits the highest visual quality with a SSIM score of 85.4% on the CelebA dataset, though it requires an inference time of 542 ms. VQFR achieves a comparable SSIM of 84.7% but takes slightly longer at 617 ms. Meanwhile, CodeFormer and FaceFormer deliver competitive performance with inference times of 286 ms and 512 ms respectively, making them suitable for applications where speed is critical. Notably, GCFSR provides a balanced performance with a SSIM of 84.3% while achieving a significantly faster average inference time of 112 ms. In our application, we ultimately selected GCFSR due to its fast execution times; because we upscale the face regions only slightly to avoid the face hallucination problem, the extra computational cost of more complex methods is not justified. Furthermore, our visual inspection of results on real-world data confirmed that GCFSR consistently produced clear and faithful reconstructions, reinforcing our choice.

Text Super-Resolution Method Selection

Our candidate methods include: A Text Attention Network for Spatial Deformation Robust Scene Text Image Super-resolution [47], Scene Text Image Super-Resolution in the Wild [78], which is designed for real-world challenges. It uses sequential residual blocks and a boundary-aware loss to handle variable text sizes and complex backgrounds, Text Prior Guided Scene Text Image Super-Resolution [47], which embeds a categorical text prior, sourced from a text recognition model, into the

Table 5 Comparison of text super-resolution methods from the literature

Method	F-Measure (%) on TextZoom	Average inference time (ms)
Scene text telescope [11]	60.1	112
Text prior guided scene text image super-resolution [47]	45.0	89
Scene text image super-resolution in the wild [78]	52.6	92

training process to effectively guide the recovery of high-resolution text images, Text Gestalt: Stroke-Aware Scene Text Image Super-resolution [12], Scene Text Telescope [11], which proposes a text-focused framework using a Transformer-based network to capture both text- and character-level details. A weighted cross-entropy loss helps manage text variations and sharpen features.

After a careful review, the state-of-the-art methods that best met our criteria and were deployed on the same hardware are: (a) Scene Text Telescope, (b) Text Prior Guided Scene Text Image Super-Resolution, and (c) Scene Text Image Super-Resolution in the Wild.

Table 5 offers a detailed breakdown of the performance of the selected text super-resolution methods. Among these, the Scene Text Telescope method stands out by delivering the highest F-Measure of 60.10% while keeping the inference time moderate at 112 ms. Although the other methods are slightly faster, they do so at the expense of accuracy. This balance of reasonable accuracy and high execution speed makes Scene Text Telescope the optimal choice for our application, ensuring clear and legible text in real-world scenarios without undue delays.

Multi-object Tracking Method Selection

Our review of state-of-the-art MOT methods considered several promising candidates. Among them, Observation-Centric SORT (OC-SORT) [8] rethinks the traditional SORT algorithm by employing a purely motion-based, observation-centric approach that achieves exceptional computational efficiency. Building on this, Deep OC-SORT [48] incorporates adaptive re-identification to enhance tracking accuracy in more complex scenarios. SMILEtrack [76] further improves performance by using similarity learning, making it particularly effective in situations with challenging object interactions and appearance variations. Another contender, ByteTrack [98], operates in real time by associating every detection using a lightweight YOLOv5-based detector, cosine similarity, and Kalman filtering. Although methods like BoT-

Table 6 Comparison of multi-object tracking methods from the literature

Method	HOTA (%) on MOT17	Average inference time (ms)
OC-SORT [8]	63.2	1
Deep OC-SORT [48]	64.9	32
SMILEtrack [76]	63.1	72
ByteTrack [98]	63.1	48

SORT [2] and UniTrack [80] were also evaluated, they did not meet our real-time performance requirements as effectively. Therefore, we deployed OC-SORT, Deep OC-SORT, SMILEtrack, and ByteTrack on the same test hardware to obtain precise speed measurements.

Table 6 summarises each method's HOTA (Higher Order Tracking Accuracy) on MOT17 and per-frame inference time, a metric commonly used to evaluate MOT systems. Deep OC-SORT slightly improves tracking accuracy (64.9% HOTA) compared to OC-SORT (63.2% HOTA) but requires 32 ms per frame, whereas OC-SORT achieves an inference time of just 1 ms. SMILEtrack and ByteTrack offer competitive accuracy but at higher computational costs. Given its pure motion-based design, 1 ms per frame latency, and competitive 63.2% HOTA, OC-SORT is our primary choice for real-time tracking.

Implementation Summary

The KSE service builds upon established computer vision research to support verifying a video's authenticity through a systematic pipeline. Here, we detail the specific methods and processing blocks used to implement the service, ensuring a reproducible and efficient pipeline:

1. Video segmentation: The input video undergoes hierarchical temporal segmentation into shots using TransNetV2 [61] and into sub-shots via the method described in [5].
2. Keyframe extraction: Representative keyframes are selected from each sub-shot based on established criteria.
3. Face detection: Facial regions are identified using YOLOv7's specialised face detection module [53].
4. Text detection: Text regions are localised using the FAST (Flexible and Accurate Scene Text Detector) algorithm [64].
5. Face enhancement: Detected faces are processed using the GCFSR super-resolution technique to enhance visual clarity [28].
6. Text enhancement: We apply the Scene Text Telescope [11] text super-resolution method to detected text regions.

7. Result visualisation: The outcomes are presented through an interactive web interface featuring collapsible sections for intuitive analysis.

Performance Optimisation

After establishing the baseline, our focus shifted to making the service more efficient. To reduce redundant processing, we introduced two major optimisations: (a) we group visually similar frames into Visually Similar Sequences (VSS) and select a single optimal frame for performing the detection, and (b) we track object detections across frames, group similar detections, and apply resource-intensive enhancement only to the representative frame of each group.

Our first key improvement comes from applying three levels of temporal fragmentation (into shots, sub-shots, and VSS) which requires accurately assessing the visual similarity between consecutive frames. Initially, we experimented with deep CNN features from pre-trained models such as ResNet, EfficientNet, and GoogLeNet; however, even features from early layers tended to capture high-level semantic information rather than the subtle structural differences we needed. In contrast, the Discrete Cosine Transform (DCT) converts image patches into frequency domain representations using block processing, and by comparing the cosine similarity between the DCT coefficient vectors of consecutive frames, we can quickly and efficiently capture structural similarity, especially in highlighting edge patterns and repetitive structures. Although DCT may not distinguish textures that require higher-level semantic context, its sub-millisecond computation speed and its ability to detect fine structural variations made it the better choice. Additionally, to select the representative frame from each VSS, we assess frame blurriness using the variance of the Laplacian method, ensuring that our chosen keyframe is both clear and informative.

To further optimise computational efficiency when applying enhancement techniques, we group similar detections of key elements (i.e. faces and text regions) before performing any computationally expensive super-resolution. This grouping is achieved using OC-SORT [8], a method that effectively clusters repeated detections across frames. By tracking the same face or text region throughout a video segment, we can apply super-resolution selectively, ensuring that only one representative item per group undergoes enhancement. This strategy minimises computational overhead by reducing the number of images processed with heavy super-resolution, and it ensures that the enhancement is applied to an image with sufficient detail, improving the final quality.

The optimised workflow implements three-tier temporal analysis and grouping of similar detections using MOT techniques, and it follows these steps (text in *emphasis* refers to the newly introduced optimisation steps):

1. Video segmentation into shots, sub-shots, *and VSS*.
2. Keyframe extraction: Representative keyframes are selected from each sub-shot. *Additionally select the least blurry frame of each VSS as its representative.*
3. Face detection: Facial regions are identified *only on the VSS representative frames*.
4. Text detection: Text regions are localised *only on the VSS representative frames*.

5. *Object tracking with OC-SORT for grouping similar detections.*
6. Face enhancement: Detected faces are processed, *with the enhancement process restricted to the best-quality representative of each group of detections.*
7. Text enhancement: We apply the selected text super-resolution method *to the best-quality representative of each group of detections.*
8. Result visualisation: Interactive result presentation through the web interface.

4 Web Service Deployment

The KSE service is deployed as a RESTful web service that requires no installation, fitting seamlessly into existing workflows. Despite using computationally intensive methods, the service is impressively fast, often completing analysis in less time than the video's duration.

The system follows a client-server architecture, consisting of a back-end API and a front-end user interface. The back-end is also integrated into the suite of tools provided by the Verification Plugin enhanced by vera.ai [81], enabling access both through the plugin and the stand-alone interface. Communication is stateless and asynchronous, with each request handled independently. Three types of API calls are supported:

1. *Start Call:* submit a video URL and 32-char user key to receive a session ID.
2. *Status Call:* query session progress, returning status and errors.
3. *Results Call:* fetch final outputs such as keyframes, logs, enhancement results, and visualisation pages.

The web service features a user-friendly interface with three primary components:

1. Landing Page: submit videos via URL or a local file upload (see Fig. 2).
2. Progress Page: monitor analysis status (see Fig. 3).
3. Results Page: view keyframes, face detections, and text enhancements in collapsible panels (see Figs. 4, 5, and 6).

The user interface (UI) allows users to submit a video for analysis, whether available online or stored locally. Once the analysis begins, users can monitor its progress (see Fig. 3) and even submit additional requests while previous ones are still being processed. Upon completion, results are displayed in an interactive interface with three collapsible sections: the first shows selected keyframes (with a yellow line between frames indicating a shot change), and hovering over a keyframe reveals additional details such as timestamps and shot or sub-shot information. The second and third sections display detected faces and text regions, respectively, with pop-ups showing grouped detections. Additional details regarding supported online sources, permitted file types, and data management can be accessed through the "About this tool", "Browser compatibility", and "Disclaimer" buttons on the landing page (Fig. 2), which open additional informational windows.

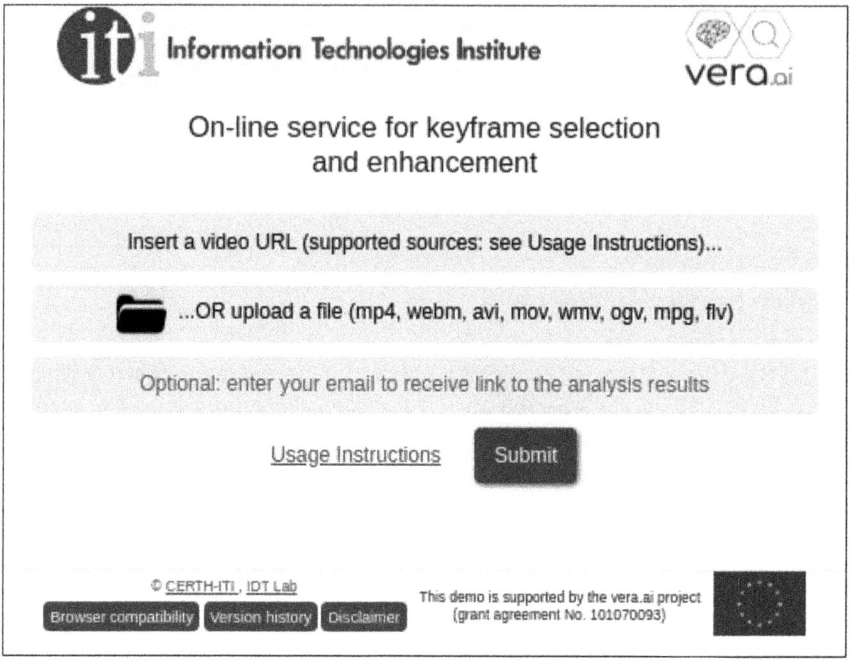

Fig. 2 The landing page of the KSE service's web user interface, where users can submit videos via URL (top text box) or upload a local file (middle text box). Users can optionally submit their email (on the bottom text box) and be notified once the analysis process is completed

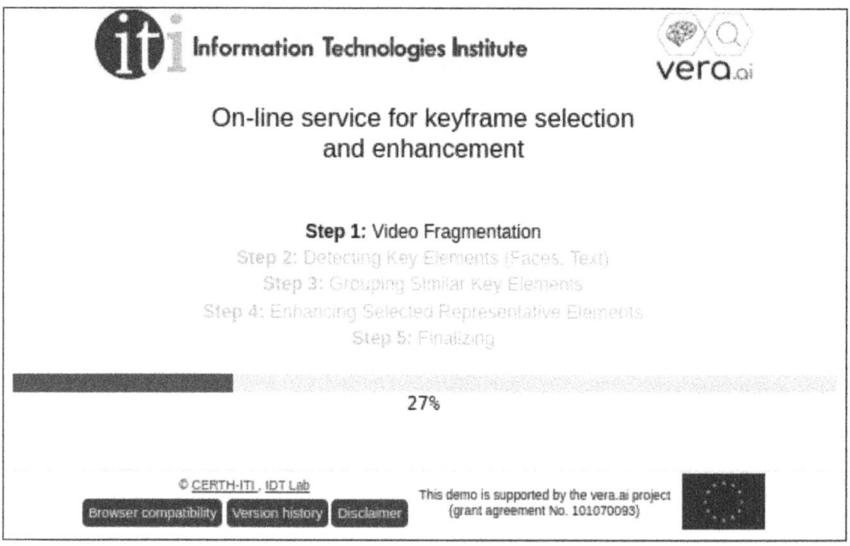

Fig. 3 The progress page of the KSE service's web user interface displaying real-time status updates

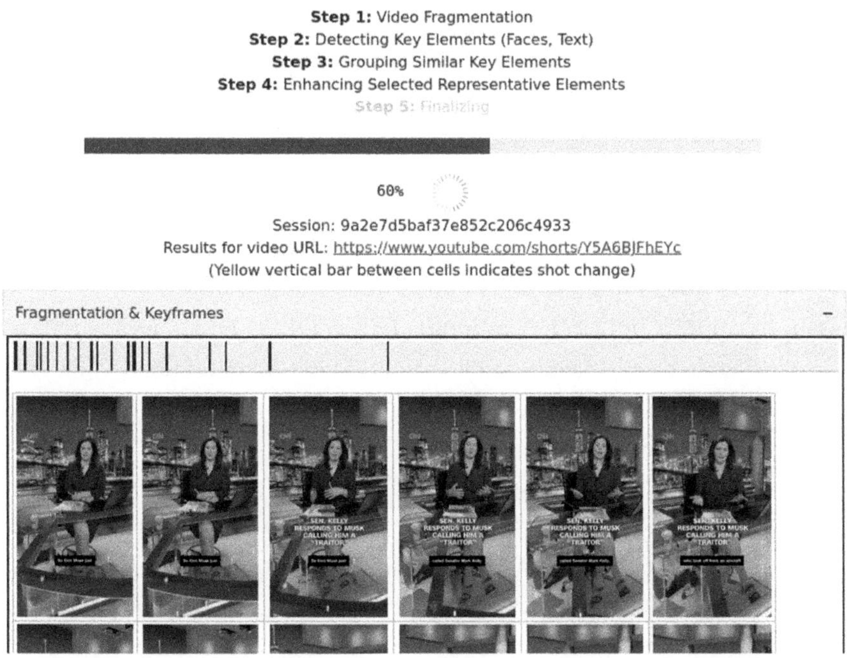

Fig. 4 Illustration of the asynchronous result provisioning in the KSE service's web user interface. The interface displays the fragmentation results, with the "Fragmentation & Keyframes" section expanded to reveal the extracted segments. Meanwhile, the detection and enhancement processes are still in progress, as indicated by the active progress bars. This demonstrates how users can review partial results while the system continues processing in the background

To keep the UI responsive, we display keyframes and shot segmentation immediately upon completion of those stages, while face/text detection and enhancement continue asynchronously (Fig. 4). Users can expand the Fragmentation & Keyframes panel to review results as they arrive, with progress bars indicating ongoing tasks. This design keeps the interface responsive and interactive, enabling users to track progress while minimising perceived waiting times.

Access to the tool is strictly controlled and available only to authorised users with valid keys. However, users can access it via the Verification Plugin enhanced by vera.ai [81]. A public stand-alone version is also available at https://kse.idt.iti.gr. Both interfaces support a wide range of popular online video sources including YouTube, Facebook, Twitter, Instagram, Vimeo, and Dropbox, and accept various video formats such as MP4, WebM, AVI, MOV, and more.

Privacy is a top priority. To protect user data, all submitted videos are automatically deleted immediately after analysis. The system only performs face detection, not full face recognition, so it does not identify individuals. Additionally, all session data is automatically deleted 48 hours after submission.

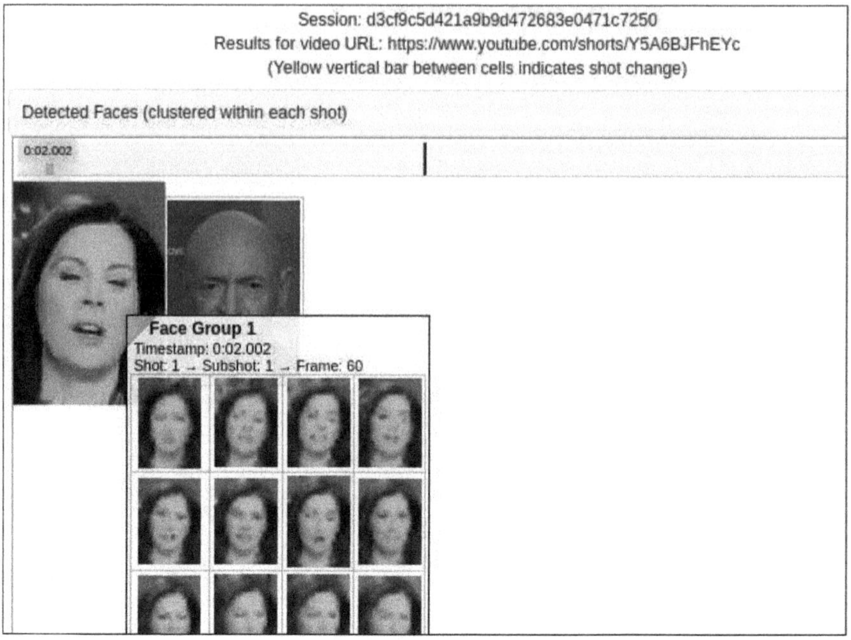

Fig. 5 The KSE service's web user interface with the "Detected Face Regions" collapsible extended

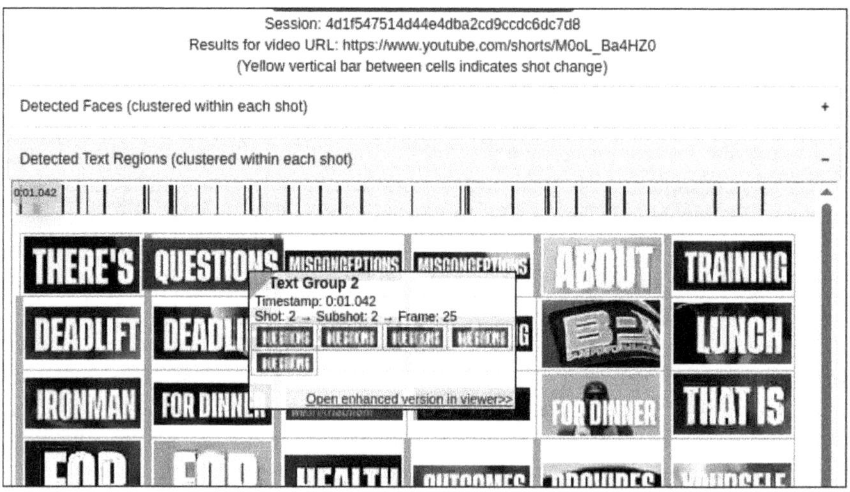

Fig. 6 The KSE service's web user interface with the "Detected Text Regions" collapsible extended

5 Evaluation

This section evaluates two key aspects of our system: its speed and its real-world effectiveness. Speed is critical for ensuring timely performance, while practical effectiveness determines its utility in real-world scenarios. In the following subsections, we first address the speed evaluation, then evaluate accuracy and practical utility, and finally present a real-world use-case analysis.

Speed Evaluation

Recognising that swift performance is essential for the success of the KSE service, we evaluated the baseline and optimised pipelines on five videos of varying lengths (from 83 s to 1193 s) and motion complexity. Our key metric is the ratio of processing time to video duration. Video complexity, influenced by factors such as motion and content dynamics, plays a crucial role in the processing load; longer videos with more complex motion typically require more computational effort. Percentages below 100% indicate faster-than-real-time performance. Table 7 quantitatively compares processing times across various implementations, demonstrating that progressive refinements have greatly reduced processing times.

Table 7 provides a detailed comparison of processing times across various versions of the KSE service, with each score representing the processing time as a percentage of the video duration. It is shown that the baseline pipeline runs at 500–1600% of real time which makes it impractical for real-time applications. Adding VSS segmentation cuts this to 16–220%. Introducing MOT grouping further halves those numbers, and software-level optimisations bring even the hardest case (Test video #5) to just 98% of real time. This progressive reduction from 1623% down to 98% demonstrates the

Table 7 Processing time as a percentage of video duration for successive KSE optimisations

	Test video #1	Test video #2	Test video #3	Test video #4	Test video #5
Video duration (seconds)	991	578	238	1193	83
KSE baseline (%)	523.6	612.8	1023.2	1400.0	1622.7
KSE (VSS) (%)	15.7	92.0	156.8	193.3	219.3
KSE (VSS, MOT) (%)	15.8	51.4	85.3	96.7	106.9
KSE (VSS, MOT, S/W opt.) (%)	14.9	45.9	75.2	81.3	98.4

effectiveness of our optimisation actions, from calculating VSS to employing MOT techniques and implementing further software enhancements.

Accuracy and Practical Utility Evaluation

Besides speed, we also evaluated the system's accuracy and its usefulness for professionals. We evaluated both quantitative performance and practical utility through expert sessions, ensuring our framework excels under controlled metrics and in real-world use. Our system incorporates a variety of methods spanning different domains, each selected after an extensive review of the literature to ensure relevance and applicability (see Tables 1, 2, 3, 4, 5 and 6). Based on the metric evaluations presented in these tables, we carefully selected the top 2–3 performing methods available at present, ensuring that our framework is built on some of the best tools currently achievable. We then corroborated these quantitative findings by visually inspecting the outcomes using real-world data, ensuring that our framework not only performs well under controlled conditions but also in practical, everyday scenarios.

Moreover, our evaluation process included participatory sessions designed to capture the perspective of professionals on KSE. Specifically, we conducted guided sessions with 21 professionals, collecting qualitative feedback over two months and refining it in follow-up remote workshops. This feedback was further discussed during two remote sessions with representatives from the evaluation sessions organising team and the development group. By carefully compiling and analysing several pages of responses, we established that the overall feedback was positive. Testers commended the tool's effectiveness in video verification, text extraction, and intuitive shot change indication, while also suggesting improvements in areas such as face detection and timeline display. All participants reported satisfaction and indicated they would integrate KSE into their workflows, validating both its accuracy and utility.

Real-World Use-Case

To offer a qualitative evaluation in a real-world scenario, we demonstrate how KSE aided in debunking misattributed violence claims through forensic keyframe analysis.

In June 2024, a viral video[17] from X (formerly Twitter) purportedly showing "an illegal immigrant attacking a woman in a German subway station" circulated among far-right networks, accumulating over 2 million views. Although the violent altercation appeared genuine, initial reports were mired in controversy and scepticism. By submitting the video to the KSE service and after experts carefully examined the results, several inconsistencies were revealed:

[17] https://x.com/Nailfreak1/status/1805710338601435236—accessed 28/04/2025.

Fig. 7 Detected face of the alleged "immigrant" in the *Detected Faces* collapsible of the KSE's user interface

1. A brief yet clear keyframe of the mugshot was isolated using the KSE interface (see Figs. 7 and 8). By enhancing the facial details, one can observe that the attacker likely did not belong to the referenced migrant demographic. A reverse image search on the extracted frame revealed multiple verified sources, confirming the suspect's identity and linking him to previous authenticated incidents. While this step was performed manually by experts, KSE significantly streamlined the process by surfacing a suitable, high-quality frame.
2. Experts analysed text from transit maps in the footage. This included terms like "Zona 1" and "Zona 2," which pointed clearly to Barcelona's zonal fare system. An overlay screenshot helped localise the scene. While the interpretation was carried out by human analysts, KSE's automated text extraction dramatically reduced the effort needed.
3. Lastly, based on the enhanced snapshots generated by KSE, experts noted distinctive yellow safety lines on the subway platform—an architectural cue consistent with Barcelona's metro system. This manual visual comparison was not part of KSE's automated capabilities, but the clear contextual frames provided by the system enabled a faster, more confident match.

This qualitative evaluation illustrates KSE's potential as an essential verification tool for journalists. The service reduced verification time through automated evidence compilation, while also confirming external reports that revealed the truth regarding:

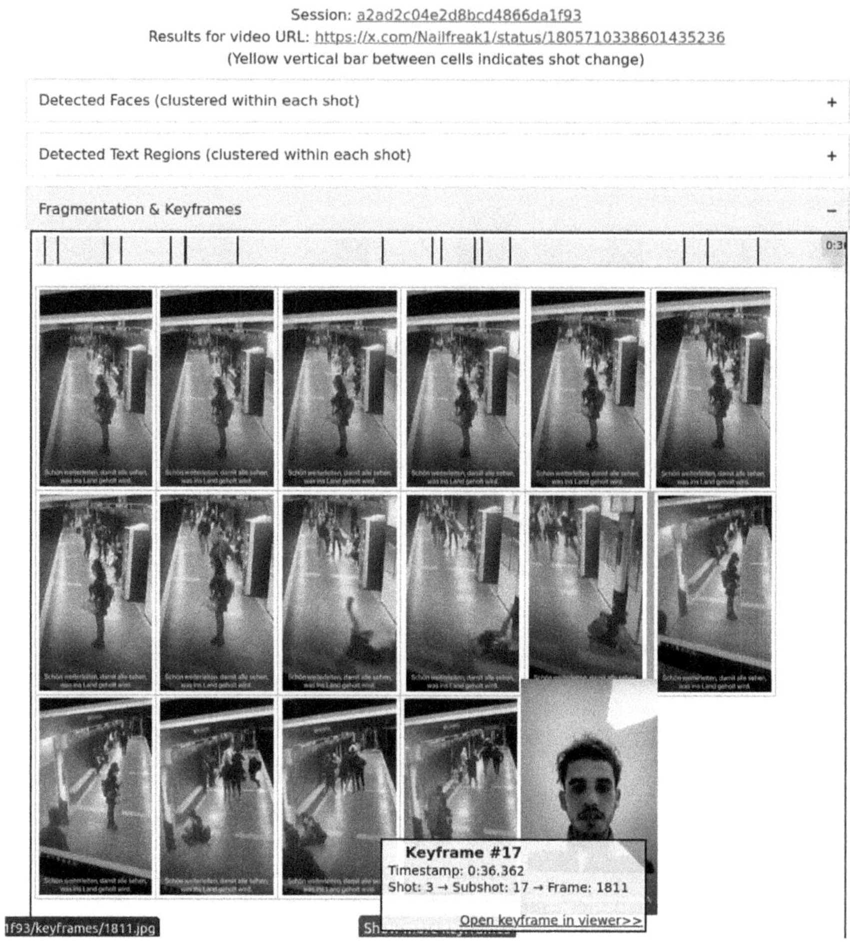

Fig. 8 Detected mugshot of the alleged "immigrant" in the *Fragmentation & Keyframes* collapsible of the KSE's user interface

1. The original location: Spain versus the claimed Germany
2. The attacker's nationality: Spanish versus the "illegal immigrant" claim
3. A temporal mismatch: 2023 footage rebranded as a 2024 event

6 Challenges and Future Directions

Our KSE service faces several challenges that also indicate opportunities for future improvements. Video quality variability remains a major challenge. Heavily compressed or shaky user-generated content often degrades detection accuracy and yields only mediocre enhancement quality. This underscores the need for quality-adaptive pipelines that dynamically adjust processing based on input fidelity.

Computational efficiency is another concern. Although our VSS segmentation and MOT-based selective enhancement optimise performance, further gains could come from model quantisation and lightweight architectures to speed up high-resolution processing.

We also prioritise robust ethical standards throughout our approach. To support transparent verification, we plan to integrate explainable AI (XAI) techniques that will clarify how and why each decision is made. Additionally, we ensure that videos submitted to the service, which may be public videos that contain identifiable individuals, are not stored or otherwise communicated to anyone but the user who submitted each specific video.

Despite these challenges, KSE already meets media verification needs by balancing efficiency and quality. Future work will refine model accuracy, accelerate processing, implement adaptive optimisations, and explore cross-modal analysis and user-feedback-driven enhancements to stay ahead of evolving media threats.

Acknowledgements This research was supported by the European Union under the Horizon Europe vera.ai project, Grant Agreement number 101070093.

References

1. Agustsson, E., Timofte, R.: Ntire 2017 challenge on single image super-resolution: dataset and study. In: Proceedings of the IEEE Conference on Computer Vision and Pattern Recognition Workshops, pp. 126–135 (2017)
2. Aharon, N., Orfaig, R., Bobrovsky, B.Z.: Bot-sort: robust associations multi-pedestrian tracking. arXiv preprint arXiv:2206.14651 (2022)
3. Apostolidis, E., Adamantidou, E., Metsai, A.I., Mezaris, V., Patras, I.: Video summarization using deep neural networks: a survey. Proceed. IEEE **109**(11), 1838–1863 (2021)
4. Apostolidis, E., Balaouras, G., Mezaris, V., Patras, I.: Selecting a diverse set of aesthetically-pleasing and representative video thumbnails using reinforcement learning. In: 2023 IEEE International Conference on Image Processing (ICIP). IEEE, pp. 2460–2464 (2023)
5. Apostolidis, K., Apostolidis, E., Mezaris, V.: A motion-driven approach for fine-grained temporal segmentation of user-generated videos. In: MultiMedia Modeling: 24th International Conference, MMM 2018, Bangkok, Thailand, February 5–7, 2018, Proceedings, Part I 24. Springer, pp. 29–41 (2018)
6. Arslan, S., Tanberk, S.: Key frame extraction with attention based deep neural networks. arXiv preprint arXiv:2306.13176 (2023)
7. Bewley, A., Ge, Z., Ott, L., Ramos, F., Upcroft, B.: Simple online and real time tracking. In: 2016 IEEE International Conference on Image Processing (ICIP). IEEE, pp. 3464–3468 (2016)
8. Cao, J., Pang, J., Weng, X., Khirodkar, R., Kitani, K.: Observation-centric sort: rethinking sort for robust multi-object tracking. In: Proceedings of the IEEE/CVF Conference on Computer Vision and Pattern Recognition, pp. 9686–9696 (2023)

9. Carion, N., Massa, F., Synnaeve, G., Usunier, N., Kirillov, A., Zagoruyko, S.: End-to-end object detection with transformers. In: ECCV (2020)
10. Chen, C., Liu, C., Chen, Q., Koltun, V.: Deep photo enhancer: unpaired learning for image enhancement from photographs. In: Proceedings of the European Conference on Computer Vision (ECCV), pp. 745–760 (2018)
11. Chen, J., Li, B., Xue, X.: Scene text telescope: text-focused scene image super-resolution. In: Proceedings of the IEEE/CVF Conference on Computer Vision and Pattern Recognition, pp. 12026–12035 (2021)
12. Chen, J., Yu, H., Ma, J., Li, B., Xue, X.: Text gestalt: stroke-aware scene text image super-resolution. In: Proceedings of the AAAI Conference on Artificial Intelligence, vol. 36, no. 1, pp. 285–293 (2022)
13. Chen, C., Li, X., Yang, L., Lin, X., Zhang, L., Wong, K.Y.K.: Progressive semantic-aware style transformation for blind face restoration. In: Proceedings of the IEEE/CVF Conference on Computer Vision and Pattern Recognition, pp. 11896–11905 (2021)
14. Papers with code: Highlight detection (2025). https://paperswithcode.com/task/highlight-detection. Accessed: 2025-03-18
15. Cooray, S.H., O'Connor, N.E.: Identifying an efficient and robust sub-shot segmentation method for home movie summarisation. In: 2010 10th International Conference on Intelligent Systems Design and Applications. IEEE, pp. 1287–1292 (2010)
16. Cootes, T.F., Taylor, C.J., Cooper, D.H., Graham, J.: Active shape models-their training and application. Comput. Vis. Image Underst. **61**(1), 38–59 (1995)
17. Dastmalchi, H., Aghaeinia, H.: Super-resolution of very low-resolution face images with a wavelet integrated, identity preserving, adversarial network. Signal Process.: Image Commun. **107**, 116755 (2022)
18. Deng, J., Guo, J., Ververas, E., Kotsia, I., Zafeiriou, S.: Retinaface: single-shot multi-level face localisation in the wild. In: Proceedings of the IEEE/CVF Conference on Computer Vision and Pattern Recognition (CVPR) (2020)
19. Deng, J., Guo, J., Zhou, Y., Yu, J., Kotsia, I., Zafeiriou, S.: Retinaface: single-stage dense face localisation in the wild. arXiv preprint arXiv:1905.00641 (2019). https://arxiv.org/abs/1905.00641
20. Dong, C., Loy, C.C., Tang, X.: Accelerating the super-resolution convolutional neural network. In: Computer Vision–ECCV 2016: 14th European Conference, Amsterdam, The Netherlands, October 11-14, 2016, Proceedings, Part II 14. Springer, pp. 391–407 (2016)
21. Epshtein, B., Ofek, E., Wexler, Y.: Detecting text in natural scenes with stroke width transform. In: CVPR (2010)
22. Google: mediapipe face detection. https://github.com/google/mediapipe/blob/master/docs/solutions/face_detection.md. Accessed: 2025-03-20
23. Guo, J., Deng, J., Lattas, A., Zafeiriou, S.: Sample and computation redistribution for efficient face detection (2021). arXiv preprint arXiv:2105.04714
24. Gu, S., Zhou, Y., Bao, J., Chen, D., Zeng, M., Zhang, Y., Liu, J., Guo, B.: VQFR: blind face restoration with vector-quantized dictionary and parallel decoder. In: Proceedings of the European Conference on Computer Vision (ECCV), pp. 1–17 (2022). https://arxiv.org/abs/2201.09429
25. Gu, X., Li, C., Wang, X., Hong, D., Zhang, L., Luo, T., Wen, L., Fan, H.: Structured context learning for generic event boundary detection (2025). ArXiv preprint arXiv:2512.00475
26. Gygli, M.: Ridiculously fast shot boundary detection with fully convolutional neural networks. In: 2018 International Conference on Content-Based Multimedia Indexing (CBMI). IEEE, pp. 1–4 (2018)
27. Hassanien, A., Elgharib, M., Selim, A., Bae, S.H., Hefeeda, M., Matusik, W.: Large-scale, fast and accurate shot boundary detection through spatio-temporal convolutional neural networks. arXiv preprint arXiv:1705.03281 (2017)
28. He, J., Shi, W., Chen, K., Fu, L., Dong, C.: Gcfsr: a generative and controllable face super resolution method without facial and gan priors. In: Proceedings of the IEEE/CVF Conference on Computer Vision and Pattern Recognition, pp. 1889–1898 (2022)

29. Hou, H., Xu, J., Hou, Y., Hu, X., Wei, B., Shen, D.: Semi-cycled generative adversarial networks for real-world face super-resolution. IEEE Trans. Image. Process. **32**, pp. 1184–1199 (2023)
30. Huang, J., et al.: Urban100 dataset (2010). Available at https://www.kaggle.com/datasets/harshraone/urban100
31. Jiang, Y., Gong, X., Yao, Y., Feng, J.: Enlightengan: deep light enhancement without paired supervision. In: Proceedings of the IEEE Conference on Computer Vision and Pattern Recognition (CVPR), pp. 8244–8253 (2019)
32. Kaur, S., Kaur, L., Lal, M.: An effective key frame extraction technique based on feature fusion and fuzzy-c means clustering with artificial hummingbird. Sci. Rep. **14**(1), 26651 (2024)
33. Kupyn, O., Budzan, V., Mykhailych, M., Mishkin, D., Matas, J.: Deblurgan: blind motion deblurring using conditional adversarial networks. In: Proceedings of the IEEE Conference on Computer Vision and Pattern Recognition, pp. 8183–8192 (2018)
34. Kupyn, O., Martyniuk, T., Wu, J., Wang, Z.: Deblurgan-v2: deblurring (orders-of-magnitude) faster and better. In: Proceedings of the IEEE/CVF International Conference on Computer Vision (ICCV), pp. 8878–8887 (2019)
35. Ledig, C., Theis, L., Huszár, F., Caballero, J., Cunningham, A., Acosta, A., Aitken, A., Tejani, A., Totz, J., Wang, Z., et al.: Photo-realistic single image super-resolution using a generative adversarial network. In: Proceedings of the IEEE Conference on Computer Vision and Pattern Recognition, pp. 4681–4690 (2017)
36. Varma, K., Reddy, G.S., Subramanyam, N.: Face image super resolution using a generative adversarial network. In: 2021 Smart Technologies, Communication and Robotics (STCR), pp. 1–8. IEEE (2021)
37. Li, A., Li, G., Sun, L., Wang, X.: Faceformer: scale-aware blind face restoration with transformers. arXiv preprint arXiv:2207.09790 (2022)
38. Li, J., Zhang, B., Wang, Y., Tai, Y., Zhang, Z., Wang, C., Li, J., Huang, X., Xia, Y.: ASFD: automatic and scalable face detector. In: Proceedings of the 29th ACM International Conference on Multimedia, pp. 2139–2147 (2021)
39. Li, M., Lv, T., Chen, J., Cui, L., Lu, Y., Florencio, D., Zhang, C., Li, Z., Wei, F.: TROCR: transformer-based optical character recognition with pre-trained models. In: Proceedings of the AAAI Conference on Artificial Intelligence, vol. 37, pp. 13094–13102 (2023)
40. Lankinen, J., Kämäräinen, J.K.: Video shot boundary detection using visual bag-of-words. In: VISAPP vol. 1, pp. 788–791 (2013)
41. Liang, H., Li, J., Bai, T., Huang, X., Sun, L., Wang, Z., He, C., Cui, B., Chen, C., Zhang, W.: Keyvideollm: towards large-scale video keyframe selection. arXiv preprint arXiv:2407.03104 (2024)
42. Liang, J., Cao, J., Sun, G., Zhang, K., Van Gool, L., Timofte, R.: Swinir: image restoration using swin transformer. In: Proceedings of the IEEE/CVF International Conference on Computer Vision, pp. 1833–1844 (2021)
43. Liao, M., Wan, Z., Zhang, C., Wang, X., Liu, W., Bai, X.: Real-time scene text detection with differentiable binarization. In: Proceedings of the AAAI Conference on Artificial Intelligence, vol. 34, pp. 11474–11481 (2020)
44. Liao, M., Zou, Z., Wan, Z., Yao, C., Bai, X.: Real-time scene text detection with differentiable binarization and adaptive scale fusion. IEEE Trans. Pattern Anal. Mach. Intell. **45**(1), 919–931 (2022)
45. Lin, X., He, J., Chen, Z., Lyu, Z., Dai, B., Yu, F., Ouyang, W., Qiao, Y., Dong, C.: Diffbir: towards blind image restoration with generative diffusion prior. In: Proceedings of the European Conference on Computer Vision (ECCV) (2024). https://doi.org/10.1007/978-3-031-73202-7_25. arxiv: 2308.15070
46. Lyu, P., Liao, M., Yao, C., Wu, W., Bai, X.: Mask textspotter: an end-to-end trainable neural network for spotting text with arbitrary shapes. In: Proceedings of the European Conference on Computer Vision (ECCV), pp. 67–83 (2018)
47. Ma, J., Guo, S., Zhang, L.: Text prior guided scene text image super-resolution. IEEE Trans. Image Process. **32**, 1341–1353 (2023)

48. Maggiolino, G., Ahmad, A., Cao, J., Kitani, K.: Deep OC-sort: multi-pedestrian tracking by adaptive re-identification. In: 2023 IEEE International conference on image processing (ICIP). IEEE, pp. 3025–3029 (2023)
49. Mas, J., Fernandez, G.: Video shot boundary detection based on color histogram. In: TRECVID (2003)
50. Matas, J., Chum, O., Urban, M., Pajdla, T.: Robust wide-baseline stereo from maximally stable extremal regions. Image Vis. Comput. **22**(10), 761–767 (2004)
51. Nah, S., Hyun Kim, T., Mu Lee, K.: Deep multi-scale convolutional neural network for dynamic scene deblurring. In: Proceedings of the IEEE Conference on Computer Vision and Pattern Recognition, pp. 3883–3891 (2017)
52. Nair, N.G., Mei, K., Patel, V.M.: At-ddpm: restoring faces degraded by atmospheric turbulence using denoising diffusion probabilistic models. In: Proceedings of the IEEE/CVF Winter Conference on Applications of Computer Vision, pp. 3434–3443 (2023)
53. Qi, D.: yolov7-face: yolov7 face detection with landmark. https://github.com/derronqi/yolov7-face (2022)
54. Qi, H., Qiu, Y., Luo, X., Jin, Z.: An efficient latent style guided transformer-CNN framework for face super-resolution. IEEE Trans. Multimedia **26**, 1589–1599 (2023)
55. Qing, Z., Su, H., Gan, W., Wang, D., Wu, W., Wang, X., Qiao, Y., Yan, J., Gao, C., Sang, N.: Temporal context aggregation network for temporal action proposal refinement. In: Proceedings of the IEEE/CVF Conference on Computer Vision and Pattern Recognition, pp. 485–494 (2021)
56. Reid, D.: An algorithm for tracking multiple targets. IEEE Trans. Autom. Control **24**(6), 843–854 (1979)
57. Ren, S., He, K., Girshick, R., Sun, J.: Faster R-CNN: towards real-time object detection with region proposal networks. IEEE Trans. Pattern Anal. Mach. Intell. **39**(6), 1137–1149 (2016)
58. Roberts, R., Lewis, J.P., Anjyo, K., Seo, J., Seol, Y.: Optimal and interactive keyframe selection for motion capture. In: SIGGRAPH Asia 2018 Technical Briefs. Association for Computing Machinery, pp. 1–4 (2018)
59. Saharia, C., Ho, J., Chan, W., Salimans, T., Fleet, D.J., Norouzi, M.: Image super-resolution via iterative refinement. IEEE Trans. Pattern Anal. Mach. Intell. **45**(4), 4713–4726 (2022)
60. Sahbani, B., Adiprawita, W.: Kalman filter and iterative-hungarian algorithm implementation for low complexity point tracking as part of fast multiple object tracking system. In: 2016 6th International Conference on System Engineering and Technology (ICSET). IEEE, pp. 109–115 (2016)
61. Soucek, T., Lokoc, J.: Transnet v2: an effective deep network architecture for fast shot transition detection. In: Proceedings of the 32nd ACM International Conference on Multimedia, pp. 11218–11221 (2024)
62. Sun, P., Cao, J., Jiang, Y., Zhang, R., Xie, E., Yuan, Z., Wang, C., Luo, P.: Transtrack: multiple object tracking with transformer. arXiv preprint arXiv:2012.15460 (2020)
63. Taigman, Y., Yang, M., Ranzato, M., Wolf, L.: Deepface: closing the gap to human-level performance in face verification. In: Proceedings of the IEEE Conference on Computer Vision and Pattern Recognition (CVPR), pp. 1701–1708 (2014)
64. Tang, S., Feng, L., Kuang, Z., Chen, Y., Zhang, W.: Fast video shot transition localization with deep structured models. In: Asian Conference on Computer Vision. Springer, pp. 577–592 (2018)
65. Tang, Y., Yuan, Y., Yan, P., Li, X.: Single-image super-resolution via sparse coding regression. In: 2011 Sixth International Conference on Image and Graphics. IEEE, pp. 267–272 (2011)
66. TechSmith: What are video thumbnails? (2025). https://www.techsmith.com/blog/what-are-video-thumbnails/. Accessed: 2025-03-18
67. Tu, Z., Talebi, H., Zhang, H., Yang, F., Milanfar, P., Bovik, A., Li, Y.: Maxim: Multi-axis MLP for image processing. In: Proceedings of the IEEE/CVF Conference on Computer Vision and Pattern Recognition, pp. 5769–5780 (2022)
68. Viola, P., Jones, M.: Rapid object detection using a boosted cascade of simple features. In: CVPR (2001)

69. Wang, C., Jiang, J., Zhong, Z., Liu, X.: Spatial-frequency mutual learning for face super-resolution. In: Proceedings of the IEEE/CVF Conference on Computer Vision and Pattern Recognition, pp. 22356–22366 (2023)
70. Wang, C.Y., Bochkovskiy, A., Liao, H.Y.M.: YOLOv7: trainable bag-of-freebies sets new state-of-the-art for real-time object detectors. arXiv preprint arXiv:2207.02696 (2022)
71. Wang, X., Li, Y., Zhang, H., Shan, Y.: Towards real-world blind face restoration with generative facial prior. In: Proceedings of the IEEE/CVF Conference on Computer Vision and Pattern Recognition (CVPR), pp. 9168–9178 (2021)
72. Wang, Z., Zhang, Z., Zhang, X., Zheng, H., Zhou, M., Zhang, Y., Wang, Y.: Dr2: diffusion-based robust degradation remover for blind face restoration. In: Proceedings of the IEEE/CVF Conference on Computer Vision and Pattern Recognition, pp. 1704–1713 (2023)
73. Wang, X., Xie, L., Dong, C., Shan, Y.: Real-ESRGAN: training real-world blind super-resolution with pure synthetic data. Proceedings of the IEEE/CVF International Conference on Computer Vision (ICCV) Workshops, pp. 1905–1914 (2021). https://doi.org/10.1109/ICCVW54120.2021.00212.
74. Wang, X., Yu, K., Wu, S., Gu, J., Liu, Y., Dong, C., Qiao, Y., Change Loy, C.: ESRGAN: enhanced super-resolution generative adversarial networks. In: Proceedings of the European Conference on Computer Vision (ECCV) Workshops, pp. 0–0 (2018)
75. Wang, Y., Hu, Y., Zhang, J.: Panini-net: gan prior based degradation-aware feature interpolation for face restoration. In: Proceedings of the AAAI Conference on Artificial Intelligence, vol. 36, no. 3, pp. 2576–2584 (2022)
76. Wang, Y.H., Hsieh, J.W., Chen, P.Y., Chang, M.C., So, H.H., Li, X.: Smiletrack: similarity learning for occlusion-aware multiple object tracking. In: Proceedings of the AAAI Conference on Artificial Intelligence, vol. 38, pp. 5740–5748 (2024)
77. Wang, Z., Bovik, A.C., Sheikh, H.R., Simoncelli, E.P.: Image quality assessment: from error visibility to structural similarity. IEEE Trans. Image Process. **13**(4), 600–612 (2004)
78. Wang, Z., Liao, M., Cheng, Z., Niu, Y., Zhou, J., Bai, X.: Scene text image super-resolution in the wild. In: Proceedings of the IEEE/CVF Conference on Computer Vision and Pattern Recognition, pp. 4404–4413 (2020)
79. Wang, Z., Zhang, Q., Zhang, B., Tai, Y., Li, J., Huang, F., Ma, L., Fan, H., Sun, J., Yang, Y.: Restoreformer++: towards real-world blind face restoration from undegraded key-value pairs. In: Proceedings of the IEEE/CVF Conference on Computer Vision and Pattern Recognition (CVPR), pp. 19523–19532 (2023)
80. Wang, Z., Zhao, H., Li, Y.L., Wang, S., Torr, P., Bertinetto, L.: Do different tracking tasks require different appearance models? Adv. Neural Inform. Process. Syst. **34**, 726–738 (2021)
81. WeVerify project: invid–weverify verification plugin. https://weverify.eu/verification-plugin/ (2025). Accessed: 2025-05-15
82. Whyte, O., Sivic, J., Zisserman, A.: Deblurring shaken and partially saturated images. Int. J. Comput. Vis. **110**, 185–201 (2014)
83. Wojke, N., Bewley, A., Paulus, D.: Simple online and real time tracking with a deep association metric. In: 2017 IEEE International Conference on Image Processing (ICIP). IEEE, pp. 3645–3649 (2017)
84. Wu, W., Peng, H., Yu, S.: Yunet: A tiny millisecond-level face detector. Mach. Intell. Res. **20**(5), 656–665 (2023)
85. Xie, J., Sun, J., Liu, J., Hu, Q.: Key-frame selection strategy based on edge points classification in 2d-to-3d conversion. In: Intelligence Science and Big Data Engineering: 4th International Conference, IScIDE 2013, Beijing, China, July 31–August 2, 2013, Revised Selected Papers 4. Springer, pp. 797–804 (2013)
86. Yang, L., Wang, S., Ma, S., Gao, W., Liu, C., Wang, P., Ren, P.: Hifacegan: face renovation via collaborative suppression and replenishment. In: Proceedings of the 28th ACM International Conference on Multimedia, pp. 1551–1560 (2020)
87. Yang, J., Wright, J., Huang, T.S., Ma, Y.: Image super-resolution via sparse representation. IEEE Trans. Image Process. **19**(11), 2861–2873 (2010)

88. Yang, P., Zhou, S., Tao, Q., Loy, C.C.: PGDIFF: guiding diffusion models for versatile face restoration via partial guidance. arXiv preprint arXiv:2309.10810 (2023). https://arxiv.org/abs/2309.10810
89. Yang, S., Luo, P., Loy, C.C., Tang, X.: Wider face: a face detection benchmark. In: CVPR (2016)
90. Yin, Z., Liu, M., Li, X., Yang, H., Xiao, L., Zuo, W.: Metaf2n: blind image super-resolution by learning efficient model adaptation from faces. In: Proceedings of the IEEE/CVF International Conference on Computer Vision (ICCV), pp. 13033–13044 (2023). https://arxiv.org/abs/2309.08113
91. Yue, Z., Loy, C.C.: Difface: blind face restoration with diffused error contraction. IEEE Transactions on Pattern Analysis and Machine Intelligence (2024)
92. Zamir, S.W., Arora, A., Khan, S., Hayat, M., Khan, F.S., Yang, M.H., Shao, L.: Multi-stage progressive image restoration. In: Proceedings of the IEEE/CVF Conference on Computer Vision and Pattern Recognition, pp. 14821–14831 (2021)
93. Zeng, Y.X., Hsieh, J.W., Li, X., Chang, M.C.: Mixnet: toward accurate detection of challenging scene text in the wild. arXiv preprint arXiv:2308.12817 (2023). https://arxiv.org/abs/2308.12817
94. Zhang, K., Zhang, Z., Li, Z., Qiao, Y.: Joint face detection and alignment using multitask cascaded convolutional networks. IEEE Signal Process. Lett. **23**(10), 1499–1503 (2016). https://doi.org/10.1109/LSP.2016.2603342
95. Zhang, K., Zuo, W., Chen, Y., Meng, D., Zhang, L.: Beyond a gaussian denoiser: residual learning of deep CNN for image denoising. IEEE Trans. Image Process. **26**(7), 3142–3155 (2017)
96. Zhang, R., Isola, P., Efros, A.A., Shechtman, E., Wang, O.: The unreasonable effectiveness of deep features as a perceptual metric. In: Proceedings of the IEEE Conference on Computer Vision and Pattern Recognition, pp. 586–595 (2018)
97. Zhang, S., Cheng, L., Lin, X., Lu, H.: S3fd: single shot scale-invariant face detector. In: ICCV (2017)
98. Zhang, Y., Wang, C., Lin, Z., Cheng, P., Yang, M., Li, S.: Bytetrack: multi-object tracking by associating every detection. arXiv preprint arXiv:2110.06864 (2021). https://arxiv.org/abs/2110.06864
99. Zhang, Y., Zhang, J., Li, H., Wang, Z., Hou, L., Zou, D., Bian, L.: Diffusion-based blind text image super-resolution. In: Proceedings of the IEEE/CVF Conference on Computer Vision and Pattern Recognition, pp. 25827–25836 (2024)
100. Zhao, X., Zhu, X., Lei, Z., Li, S.Z.: Tinaface: strong but simple baseline for face detection. In: arXiv preprint arXiv:2011.13183 (2020)
101. Zhang, Y., Wang, C., Wang, X., Zeng, W., Liu, W.: Fairmot: on the fairness of detection and re-identification in multiple object tracking. Int. J. Comput. Vis. **129**(11), 3069–3087 (2021)
102. Zhou, S., Chan, K.C.K., Li, C., Loy, C.C.: Towards robust blind face restoration with codebook lookup transformer. In: Advances in Neural Information Processing Systems (NeurIPS), pp. 30599–30611 (2022). https://arxiv.org/abs/2206.11253
103. Zhou, X., Yao, C., Wen, H., Wang, Y., Zhou, W., He, Y., Liang, D., Zhang, X.: East: an efficient and accurate scene text detector. In: Proceedings of the IEEE Conference on Computer Vision and Pattern Recognition (CVPR) (2017)
104. Zhu, W., Huang, Y., Xie, X., Liu, W., Deng, J., Zhang, D., Wang, Z., Liu, J.: Autoshot: a short video dataset and state-of-the-art shot boundary detection. arXiv preprint arXiv:2304.06116 (2023). https://arxiv.org/abs/2304.06116
105. Zhu, W., Lu, J., Li, J., Zhou, J.: Dsnet: a flexible detect-to-summarize network for video summarization. IEEE Trans. Image Process. **30**, 948–962 (2020)

Chatbot-Assisted Explainability of AI-Powered Models and Collection of User Feedback

Olesya Razuvayevskaya, Michael Foster, and Kalina Bontcheva

1 The Role of Conversational Agents in Improving User Experience and Collecting Feedback

Powered by the recent advancements in artificial intelligence (AI) and natural language processing (NLP), conversational agents (also known as conversational chatbots, digital assistants or virtual assistants), have become ubiquitous in all aspects of human life. The areas of applications for such agents include but are not limited to automated query answering [27, 105, 115, 116, 137], virtual assistants and personal task managers [63, 92, 112], healthcare assistants for initial symptom-based screening [17, 19, 63, 85] and behavioural intervention [4, 39], mental health support [24, 45], online education [5, 48, 106], hospitality and travel [43, 129], entertainment [30, 37], and recruitment [7, 98]. A specific type of chatbot application area is aimed at collecting user feedback and complaints to improve specialised tools and services [99, 108]. The impact of such assistants is twofold. First, they facilitate an interactive personalised communication, enabling organisations to constantly collect real-time insights efficiently and to reach out to more users as opposed to initiating traditional survey methods [132]. Second, in comparison to the survey methods, conversational agents make the feedback process more implicit, engaging users in dynamic dialogues and adapting to responses in order to clarify information and elicit more detailed and contextually relevant replies, resulting in higher-quality feedback data [57, 99].

O. Razuvayevskaya (✉) · M. Foster · K. Bontcheva
The University of Sheffield (USFD), Sheffield, UK
e-mail: o.razuvayevskaya@sheffield.ac.uk

M. Foster
e-mail: m.foster@sheffield.ac.uk

K. Bontcheva
e-mail: k.bontcheva@sheffield.ac.uk

S. Papadopoulos et al. (eds.), *Countering Disinformation in the Era of Generative AI*,
https://doi.org/10.1007/978-3-032-11782-3_13

Recent studies have demonstrated the effectiveness of conversational agents in collecting and analysing user feedback using deep learning and transfer learning methods. For example, Park et al. [87] introduced a hybrid deep learning-based approach that combines explicit user feedback with the feedback predicted from implicit user messages, highlighting the potential of integrating direct user input into conversational systems. Similarly, Kachuee et al. [56] proposed a self-supervised method using contrastive learning based on the bidirectional encoder representations from transformers (BERT) [33] that averages the pool at the last layers to generate a representation for each session. This approach emphasises an importance of leveraging unlabelled data to enhance feedback collection processes.

In addition to inferring and collecting user feedback, conversational chatbots also play a pivotal role in enhancing user experience by providing explainability within AI systems. Through understandable explanations behind the complex AI decisions, such agents foster explainable artificial intelligence (XAI), providing trust and transparency. XAI methods—also referred to as natural language explanations (NLEs) [18]—can be categorised into *global* and *local* approaches [2, 40], where local explainability enables the explanation generation given the concrete input instance, while the global explainability targets the overall decision making of the model regardless of a particular input. The way explanations are generated can also vary depending on whether they are inferred after the decision is made (*post-hoc explanations*) [96, 110] or at the same time when the decision is made (*self-explanations*) [11]. The latter is typically preferred as a directly interpretable approach that does not require additional operations [29].

Arya et al. [11] further classify the XAI solutions to static and interactive ones, highlighting the importance of adapting explanations to user audiences and domains. Natural language-based XAI represents a subset of interactive explanations, which is closest to human interaction and is shown to be more comprehensible than template-based or graphic explanations [66, 79]. Weitz et al. [120] performed a human study on the benefits of XAI for a machine learning-based speech recognition model which classifies audio keywords. The authors found that the users' trust in the classification model benefited from the additional text output generated by a virtual agent. Similarly, Joshi et al. [54] explored the impact of XAI on the users' perceptions of the vacation booking system by comparing two versions of the system (with high vs. low explainability) among 60 participants. The authors concluded that incorporating explanations within conversational agents significantly increased users' understanding, trust, and acceptance of the system. These findings suggest that empowering the systems' outputs with chatbot-assisted explanations not only clarifies the reasons behind AI decisions but also enhances user engagement and satisfaction.

The rest of this chapter focuses on the role of conversational agents in (i) user feedback collection and their contribution to (ii) explainability in AI systems. We examine their design, implementation, and effectiveness, discussing key challenges such as response biases, user engagement, data quality, and the communication of complex AI decisions. We discuss how by leveraging conversational agents, it is possible to gain deeper insights into user preferences and experiences while simultaneously providing transparent and comprehensible explanations of AI-driven outcomes, ultimately enhancing decision-making and user trust. We provide an overview of various techniques for user intent detection and the role of large language models (LLMs) in generating retrieval-based explanations. In discussing the latter approaches, we emphasise the challenges that arise when evaluating the replies of such models using extrinsic and intrinsic metrics. As a case study, this chapter also provides a description of how LLM-powered conversational agents have been adapted to our work within vera.ai project for enhancing the misinformation detection and verification tools with explainability and enabling user feedback collection. We summarise the methods and evaluation techniques, as well as challenges of preserving user history and handling hallucinations. Finally, we discuss future research directions and challenges that arise with the use of conversational agents in the era of LLMs.

2 User Intent Detection in Conversational Chatbots

The ability of conversational agents to accurately understand and process user input is fundamental to their effectiveness. In this context, the term *user intent* refers to the underlying purpose or goal a user seeks to achieve when interacting with the assistant. The task of *intent recognition* therefore aims to classify user utterances into predefined categories, such as asking the agent to perform a hotel booking or to schedule a meeting. The role of intent recognition in facilitating better user-agent interactions cannot be overstated, as correctly identifying user intent ensures smoother communication and task execution. The task of intent detection is often followed by the *slot-filling* objective, which extracts key parameters or pieces of information necessary to complete the task [113]. For example, in the context of a hotel booking chatbot, the slot-filling task can consist of the detection and extraction of the time, city, price range and the number of guests from the user's request to find suitable hotels. Conversational agents often contain a special type of intent called the *fallback intent* or the default intent indicating that the chatbot failed to recognise the user's utterance or that none of the intents scored above the predefined threshold. In such cases, the chatbot usually returns a default reply to the user, such as "*Sorry, I did not understand your question. Could you try to rephrase it, please?*". Furthermore, the integration of multi-intent recognition models has been a growing area of research, as users may express multiple intents in a single utterance [77].

Early approaches to intent classification primarily relied on supervised learning algorithms such as Support Vector Machines (SVM) [76] and Hidden Markov Models (HMM) [15, 135]. Slot-filling task was typically framed as a sequence-labeling problem, addressed using Conditional Random Fields (CRF) [100] and elastic CRFs (eCRFs), where each slot is encoded into a particular representation through the embedding of its natural language description [28]. The main challenge of these approaches is that they rely on extensive feature engineering and struggle with generalisation to unseen inputs. Recent advances in deep learning have significantly improved the accuracy of intent recognition and slot-filling. During the last decade, Recurrent Neural Networks (RNNs) and Long Short-Term Memory (LSTM) networks became widely adopted for sequence intent classification and slot-filling tasks respectively [60, 94]. More recent state-of-the art approaches, however, involve transformer models and LLMs [10, 82].

In user feedback detection and collection scenarios, intent detection models can, for example, discriminate between positive, negative and neutral feedback [81]. One of the main challenges in training specialised models for intent detection is that in many of the real-world applications, the types of user intents are hard to predict beforehand. To address this challenge, recent studies have explored self-supervised learning methods to detect noisy user feedback. For example, Zhang et al. [136] use multi-task pre-training (MTP) method that jointly optimises a loss function on two sets of data, external labelled data and a target unlabelled data. This allows to detect novel intent categories and expand the original annotation ontology.

The task of slot-filling in user feedback collection scenarios enables the extraction of key attributes such as product name, issue type, and sentiment strength. However, given that the user feedback can often be unstructured and formulated in an implicit way, additional techniques, such as generating clarification questions (CQs) that capture the missing details, may be required [137]. More recently, joint approaches to intent detection and slot-filling were shown to be efficient for both tasks [121]. In particular, transformer-based models such as BERT and generative pre-trained transformers (GPT) have demonstrated state-of-the-art performance in jointly learning intent detection and slot-filling [23].

Despite the above-mentioned advancements, the research on intent recognition and slot-filling remains subject to several ongoing research challenges. One of the challenges stems from the fact that users may provide vague or ambiguous feedback that does not clearly map to a predefined intent category. Zero-shot and few-shot learning techniques are being explored to address this limitation [12, 69]. Such techniques allow to guide the LLMs' responses through prompting either without any examples or with a small number of examples (shots). Another significant challenge is domain adaptation. Many intent classification and slot-filling models are trained on domain-specific datasets, making it difficult for them to generalise across different applications [12]. Transfer learning and meta-learning approaches have been explored to improve cross-domain adaptability [69]. However, these methods often require large-scale pre-training on diverse datasets, which may not always be feasible. Finally, maintaining context across multi-turn dialogues remains a challenge, as intent detection must consider prior conversational history for accuracy [109]. This problem is particularly critical in customer service applications, where contextual understanding plays a major role in successful issue resolution.

In addition to the above-mentioned challenges, real-time processing constraints pose limitations on the complexity of methods applied for intent recognition and slot-filling. Response time was shown to be one of the most important attributes influencing the perception of the chatbots by the users [71, 78]. Many applications, such as virtual assistants and automated customer support systems, require near-instantaneous responses. Deploying computationally expensive deep learning models in production settings necessitates efficient model compression and optimisation techniques [89]. Knowledge distillation, pruning, and quantisation methods have been proposed to reduce the computational burden while maintaining high accuracy [114]. However, the task of balancing model efficiency and accuracy remains an open research problem.

3 Retrieval Augmented Generation for System Explainability

The inherent opacity of many AI models has led to a pressing need for explainability, particularly in user-facing tools. Retrieval-Augmented Generation (RAG) [61] has emerged as a promising approach for enhancing explainability of these systems by leveraging retrieval mechanisms to generate more contextually relevant and transparent explanations. The architecture of RAG-based models consists of two main components: (i) a retrieval module which searches through the available indexed sources to find the evidence closest to the users' encoded questions and ranks them based on the relevance, and (ii) an LLM module which uses the top ranked retrieved documents as a context to generate a concise answer. Thereby, RAG-based models combine the generative capabilities of LLMs with the grounded knowledge from retrieved domain-specific sources, enabling more informative and justifiable responses [61].

The primary applications of RAG models are question answering tasks where users seek more detailed, sourced explanations regarding a certain topic or topics. Unlike traditional generative models, which rely solely on their training data, RAG systems dynamically fetch relevant information from external knowledge bases and published sources, reducing hallucination and improving response fidelity [51]. This capability is particularly useful in domains such as healthcare [6, 9], finance [49, 128], and legal services [46, 122], where accuracy and reliability are paramount. By retrieving verifiable information, RAG-based systems can help end-users comprehend the reasoning behind AI-driven answers, thereby reducing scepticism and promoting informed decision-making.

Another significant application of RAG is in conversational AI systems designed to assist users in understanding complex AI-driven models. RAG can serve as a post-hoc global and local XAI solution (Sect. 1) to provide user-friendly explanations by retrieving pertinent documentation, research papers, or contextual examples [42, 131]. For example, Guttikonda et al. [42] evaluated the effect of RAG-based models with an LLM (Llama-70b) as a generator on three diverse AI-powered tasks, (i) a tool for predicting aerospace manufacturing costs, (ii) a healthcare application for brain tumour type prediction, and (iii) a finance app predicting whether an individual is eligible for the loan. For each of the systems, the authors introduced project documentation and marked down various sections important for providing user explainability. For example, the users of the healthcare system could ask "*How was this classification made?*", and the RAG model would retrieve the relevant parts of the documentation and code in order to explain how the AI model processes images and identifies features for tumour classification.

Despite its advantages, implementing RAG for explainability presents several challenges. One of the main concerns is the quality and relevance of retrieved information. If the retrieval component selects inaccurate or misleading sources, the generated explanations may be counterproductive, leading to misinformation rather than clarity [26, 139]. Ensuring that retrieved documents align with user queries and model decisions is an ongoing research problem that requires careful curation of knowledge bases and advanced retrieval ranking techniques. Adding noise in the form of irrelevant documents was previously shown to improve the retrieval process [26]. Other common techniques include enhancing the initial query by replacing it with search-friendly queries [103], advanced document chunking techniques, metadata annotations to allow better localisation of relevant information, query expansion, applying re-ranking algorithms on top of the retriever, and fine-tuning of embedding models for specialised application domains [102]. As highlighted by Chen et al. [22], despite low confidence in their predictions, RAG models may still generate responses, highlighting a limitation in their ability to accurately reflect uncertainty. To address this issue, the authors propose a counterfactual prompting framework where the quality of the generated answer is challenged by the LLM-generated counterfacts. This allows to ensure that the model refuses to answer questions in case of low confidence in the answer.

Additionally, integrating RAG into real-time systems poses computational challenges, as retrieving and processing external information can introduce latency [47]. The quantised versions of models usually help to achieve efficiency, but at the cost of reduced accuracy [141]. Optimising retrieval efficiency and model inference is essential for maintaining seamless user interactions. Some of the approaches to maximise the retrieval efficiency include the hierarchical caching and dynamic query routing [95], enriching the LLMs with dynamic conditional embeddings, query rewriting using semantic search [88], using Graph Convolutional Networks (GCNs) as retrievers [141], or using cached documents instead of real-time retrievers [20].

Another limitation is the interpretability of RAG-generated responses themselves. The most widespread approach towards the explainability of RAG-based models represents RAGViz, visualising the attentions within the retrieved documents [118]. This approach also enables the comparison of the generated answers with or without certain contexts. Additionally, while RAG provides sourced explanations, the complexity of retrieved documents can sometimes overwhelm end-users, particularly those without technical expertise. The problem of RAG explainability is not limited to the retrieval process, but also to the transparency of the multi-component RAG architectures, including the generation step and misinformation propagation risks [84]. The main challenge in advancing RAG explainability is the lack of standardised datasets and benchmarking metrics for measuring different aspects of XAI in RAG models, as we discuss in depth in Section "Intrinsic Metrics". This problem necessitates the development of highly specialised datasets to evaluate each step of the RAG framework, as we further demonstrate in a real-world RAG model implementation described in Section"RAG for Explanation Generation". In the next section, we provide a detailed overview of the objectives and challenges for developing evaluation frameworks for such models.

4 Metrics for Evaluating the Effectiveness of the RAG-Based Assistants

Evaluating RAG assistants remains complex due to their hybrid architecture. This section discusses the importance of taking into account two types of metrics when evaluating the performance of retrieval-based chatbots (i) intrinsic metrics, which examine the internal quality of retrieval and generation, and (ii) extrinsic metrics, which assess the performance from the perspective of user satisfaction and real-world impact. Figure 1 provides a high-level overview of different dimensions measured within each category and the corresponding metrics associated with those dimensions. In the next two sub-sections, we discuss each of these metrics in detail.

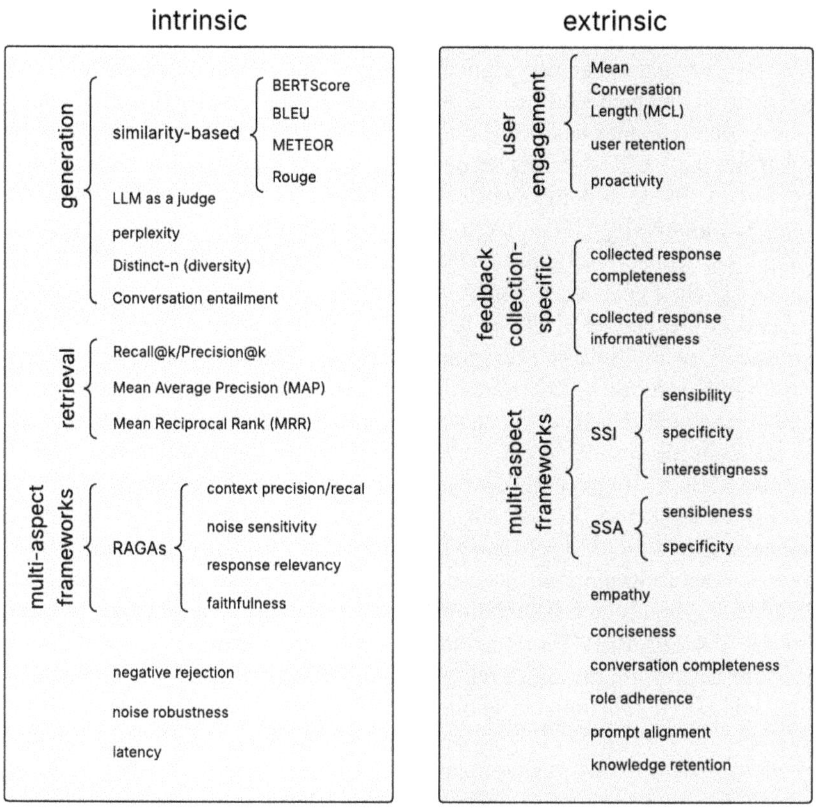

Fig. 1 Overview of evaluation metric types for RAG-based assistants

Intrinsic Metrics

Intrinsic metrics assess the generation quality of conversational agents [31]. While many studies on RAG-based conversational agents rely on standard intrinsic metrics for chatbot evaluation—such as ROUGE, BERTScore, BLEU, and METEOR—to evaluate similarity of their replies with gold-standard responses, these metrics often fall short in capturing the nuanced behaviour of retrieval-augmented models. Moreover, with the rise of LLMs capable of generating highly expressive and coherent replies, traditional n-gram-based metrics have become less relevant, as they tend to favour less expressive, more template-based responses over diverse and nuanced language. As we elaborate further, such surface-level comparisons also do not adequately reflect the system's ability to accurately retrieve, integrate, and ground information. In contrast, more fine-grained intrinsic metrics that target specific stages of the answer generation pipeline—such as retrieval relevance, factual consistency, and source attribution—offer deeper insights into the strengths and limitations of these systems.

The assessment techniques for RAG systems can be broadly categorised into the ones focusing on generation and retrieval. We start by providing an overview of the natural language generation-based metrics. *BLEU (Bilingual Evaluation Understudy)* [86] is a metric that was originally designed for a machine translation task but is widely used for chatbot evaluation. It computes n-gram overlap between generated responses and reference answers, providing a numerical measure of linguistic similarity. However, BLEU does not account for context or dialogue coherence, making it less reliable for open-domain chatbots. *ROUGE (Recall-Oriented Understudy for Gisting Evaluation)* [65] is similar to BLEU, but it emphasises recall over precision, making it particularly useful for evaluating summarisation tasks. ROUGE has been applied to chatbot evaluation, particularly in tasks where response completeness is important. However, like BLEU, ROUGE struggles to capture the nuances of natural conversation, as multiple valid responses may not share exact wording. *METEOR (Metric for Evaluation of Translation with Explicit ORdering)* [13] improves upon BLEU by considering synonym matching, stemming, and word order flexibility. This makes it more suitable for chatbot evaluation in cases where responses can be phrased differently but still convey the same meaning. However, METEOR still suffers from limitations in assessing conversational coherence. *BERTScore* [133] computes cosine similarity between word representations in generated and reference responses, capturing more nuanced meanings. This has proven useful for chatbot evaluation, especially in tasks requiring context awareness and semantic relevance. However, although BERTScore can theoretically range from -1 to 1, it typically falls within a narrow high range, even when comparing substantially different human-written texts [44]. This limits its applicability for making fair and meaningful judgments.

With the rise of LLMs, using them as a judge has become another widespread approach for assessing its own (or other LLMs') generation capabilities [140]. In such settings, LLMs are usually instructed to assess the agent's replies based on a certain scoring system in terms of relevance, fluency or coherence. One group of such scoring systems involves a step-by-step alignment of chain-of-thought (CoT) with a slot-filling paradigm, allowing the LLM to assess outputs in a structured manner (e.g., G-EVAL [67], Portia [64]). Another class of scoring systems, such as TigerScore [52], SELF-J [126] and PHUDGE [32], use human annotations or artificially generated human preference data to align their judgments with human ones. PROMETHEUS is a family of LLMs specifically trained to evaluate other LLMs using a set of fine-grained dimensions [58, 59]. It additionally supports pairwise rankings of the outputs and can perform evaluation of multilingual generated texts [91]. Finally, some of the systems, such as FactScore [80] and FENCE [124], focus on evaluating factual precision of the generating answer though claim-level feedback.

To assess dialogue coherence, *Distinct-n* metrics [62] measure the diversity of generated responses by calculating the ratio of unique n-grams to total n-grams in chatbot outputs. Higher distinct scores indicate less repetitive and more varied responses, which is crucial for avoiding dull and generic chatbot replies. However, excessive diversity may also reduce consistency, leading to incoherent dialogues.

Another essential metric is *Conversational Entailment* [35], which evaluates logical consistency in dialogue by checking whether chatbot responses are entailed by preceding utterances. Conversational entailment is a specific instance of the broader textual entailment detection task. Textual entailment itself is a subcategory of the Natural Language Inference (NLI) task [73], which seeks to determine whether a given hypothesis is entailed by, contradicts, or is neutral with respect to a given premise. In the context of a chatbot, the premise typically corresponds to prior user or system utterances. This helps in detecting contradictions and maintaining consistency, which is especially important in task-oriented dialogue systems.

In the era of LLMs as conversational agents, *Perplexity* has become one of the most useful intrinsic metrics. It measures how well a language model predicts a sequence of words. Lower perplexity indicates that the model assigns higher probabilities to correct word sequences, suggesting better fluency and coherence [16]. The popularity of this metric is also tied to its direct applicability to any piece of text and independence from costly annotated data. However, perplexity does not necessarily correlate with human judgment of conversational quality, as it is only focused on expressiveness, meaning a model can achieve low perplexity by producing generic but uninformative responses.

The retrieval step is typically assessed using standard information retrieval metrics, such as Recall@k/Precision@k, Mean Average Precision (MAP) and Mean Reciprocal Rank (MRR) [125, 130]. *Recall@k/Precision@k* measure how often relevant contexts are retrieved within the top k results, while *MRR* evaluates how quickly the first relevant context appears in the ranked list and *MAP* evaluates the mean of average retriever precisions for each query.

While the generation and retrieval-based metrics assess separate components of the chatbot, they are not always optimal as they do not capture the degree of source attribution for the provided answers [97]. To account for the multidimensional nature of RAG-based assistants, Es et al. [36] proposed a suit of metrics called *RAGAs (Retrieval Augmented Generation Assessment)*. It suggests a 3-tier assessment consisting of (i) context relevance, (ii) faithfulness and (iii) answer relevance. Here, *context relevance* refers to the correctness of the retriever in terms of finding information that is needed to answer the question. It evaluates the precision in terms of the proportion of relevant sentences in the retrieved context. The systems are also penalised for retrieving redundant information. Once the quality of the retriever is evaluated, the framework assesses *faithfulness*, or the degree to which the generated answer is grounded to the contextual data. This is particularly important in the realms of LLMs used as generators, as such models are pre-trained on large amounts of information and are prone to hallucinations. Finally, *answer relevance* addresses the completeness of the answer and its redundancy with regard to the question.

Some other important intrinsic aspects include latency of the retrieval [47], *noise robustness* or the ability of handling irrelevant documents [21], and *negative rejection* or withholding the answers when the questions cannot be directly answered based on the context [21].

Extrinsic Metrics

While intrinsic metrics, discussed in the previous section, assess language generation and retrieval quality, extrinsic evaluation focuses on measuring the chatbot's impact on task completion, user satisfaction, and engagement. These metrics provide a more holistic assessment of chatbot performance in downstream practical settings and are therefore typically reliant on manual human assessment [31].

One of the most widely used extrinsic evaluation metrics is *Sensibility, Specificity, Interestingness (SSI)* [111]. Within this framework, *sensibleness* evaluates whether the chatbot does not contradict previous answers and takes the conversation history into account. Generative LLMs tend to be particularly vulnerable in this regard due to adapting to the user's corrections and new prompts, often contradicting prior responses. However, the system that scores high in terms of sensibleness, typically suffers from repetitiveness and very generic answers. One example is the GenericBot system that always generates fallback answers such as "I don't know" and is nevertheless able to surpass some of the LLMs by scoring over 70% in terms of sensibleness [3]. The latter shortcoming is in turn addressed through *specificity*, or the ability of the model to generate non-generic replies. Finally, *interestingness* is defined as the ability of the chatbot to generate the replies that spark curiosity or grab users' attention.

Conciseness is often considered another important extrinsic metric that assesses the ability to answer user's question in a clear and concise manner as extra verbosity can be very tiring for the end-users and affect their comprehension of the provided information [83, 104]. For example, in the domain of healthcare, conciseness is a crucial requirement for conversational chatbots as it helps users to avoid misunderstanding and wrong interpretations [1]. Conciseness, however, should not be achieved at the cost of *conversation completeness*, or the ability of the agent to thoroughly address all the aspects of user query [14].

The *Sensibleness and Specificity Average (SSA)* metric was introduced by Adiwardana et al. [3] to measure how meaningful and specific a chatbot's responses are in conversation. Unlike n-gram-based intrinsic metrics, SSA aligns more closely with human evaluation.

While concise answers are important for task-specific conversational agents, for the chatbots designed for entertainment or companionship, higher engagement levels and longer replies can be desirable. Engagement metrics, such as *Mean Conversation Length (MCL)* [50] and *user retention* [50, 134], indicate how effectively a chatbot maintains user interest. Engagement can also be measured through repeated interactions, with users returning to the chatbot over time suggesting a positive user experience. Engagement is known to be stimulated by another extrinsic metric called *proactivity* of the chatbot [134]. Pro-active assistants constantly engage the user by means of suggesting to answer the most likely next question of the user, requesting clarifications or posing affirmation questions about the satisfaction of the user with the reply.

The notion of the *empathy* covers various aspects behind the ability to recognise and acknowledge the emotions of the user and exhibit the "humanness" of the interaction. This metric is particularly important for healthcare assistants that need to be compassionate about the users' concerns and issues [1]. Empathetic assistants typically create the impression of a more personalised communication, which is often reflected in users' satisfaction [134].

In cases where the chatbot is prompted to adhere to a specific role profile, *role adherence* is an important metric that estimates whether the agent follows the defined role and uses the injected knowledge and memory for its role [119]. *Knowledge retention* is another important metric that reflects the agents' ability to learn from past interaction and improve over time when answering similar questions [25].

In user feedback collection scenarios, evaluating the chatbot's ability to elicit meaningful insights from users is crucial. In this regard, *response completeness* and *informativeness* are the metrics used to assess whether user feedback is comprehensive and useful. AI-powered survey chatbots, for example, must ensure that user responses contain enough detail to be actionable for decision-making processes [38]. The extrinsic efficiency of such chatbots can further be measured as the number of reactive (provided after the assistant's prompt) and proactive (initiated by the user) feedback points collected by the chatbot.

In the era of LLMs, aligning an LLM's output with the prompt has become another critical extrinsic evaluation metric. This metric reflects the extent to which the model adheres to specific instructions or constraints defined in the prompt [55]. For instance, in RAG models, the prompt may instruct the agent to withhold an answer if no sufficient grounding context is retrieved. In other application domains, alignment may pertain to the model's ability to refuse to generate harmful, biased, or potentially misleading content. Thus, prompt-output alignment serves as a key indicator of both model reliability and responsible behaviour.

As conversational AI continues to evolve, refining extrinsic evaluation methodologies will be essential to ensuring chatbot quality, usability, and real-world effectiveness. Future research should explore hybrid evaluation approaches combining automated assessment with user-driven insights to create a comprehensive framework for chatbot evaluation.

5 Conversational Chatbot for User Feedback Collection and Explanation Generation Within vera.ai

As discussed in Sect. 1, the use of conversational chatbots for collecting user feedback and generating explanations can significantly enhance user experience across a variety of application domains. In this section, we present a concrete use-case scenario in the form of content verification. We first introduce the types of user intents (discussed in Sect. 2) relevant for this real-world scenario and outline the method used to detect these intent types. We then focus on how retrieval-augmented generation (RAG), introduced in Sect. 3, can support the task of explanation generation within this verification plugin setting. To evaluate the system's performance, we explore several intrinsic evaluation metrics—including individual metrics from the RAGAs suite, as well as BERTScore, BLEU, METEOR, and latency—discussed in Section "Intrinsic Metrics". These metrics shed light on different components of the RAG pipeline and help identify performance bottlenecks and areas for improvement.

As a real-world implementation scenario, we describe the work done within vera.ai project to enhance the content verification tools with a conversational chatbot that serves two purposes: (a) collects user feedback to provide a human-in-the-loop opportunity for improving the performance of underlying AI models, and (b) adds explainability about the outputs of those models in a post-hoc global manner (Sect. 1). A particular type of verification tool chosen for this integration concerns various synthetic image detection models that were developed within the vera.ai project and are integrated in a the *Verification plugin*.[1]

Chatbot Architecture

Figure 2 illustrates the high-level architecture of the conversational chatbot for user feedback collection and XAI generation. As can be seen, it consists of two main steps, (i) user intent detection, and (ii) retrieval-augmented generation for the *explanation*-seeking intent. The user intents can be broadly grouped into three main categories: (a) feedback, (b) explanation generation, and (c) state transition interaction.

Here, *greeting* and *end* correspond to the *state transition* intents that signal the chatbot to start or end a new conversation chain with the user respectively. Detecting the *feedback* types of user intents helps the chatbot to collect and store users' suggestions in real-time. For the purpose of the synthetic image detection tools within vera.ai project, three types of user feedback intents are of particular importance: bug,

[1] https://weverify.eu/verification-plugin/.

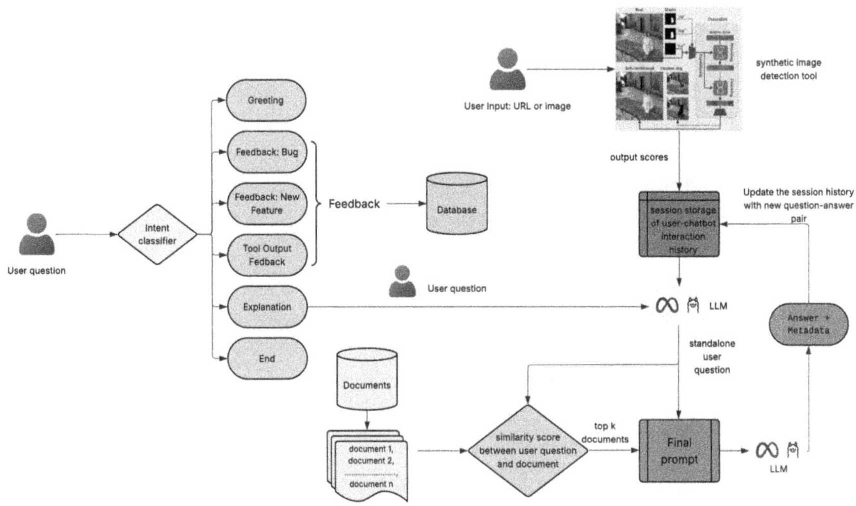

Fig. 2 Chatbot workflow

new feature and feedback about the output of the tool. These three intents can be grouped into one general category of *feedback*, although they concern different types of feedback. Receiving feedback about technical *bugs* or a need for a new *feature* helps to maintain user satisfaction with the functionality of the tools. *Output* type of feedback, on the other hand, is related to collecting new data points for re-training the models behind the detector tool and facilitating a human-in-the-loop approach. When detecting this kind of user intent, the chatbot initiates a series of clarification questions regarding the particular model, input data and the desired output to maximise the quality of the collected data point. In all three cases of user feedback, the chatbot also sends immediate messages to the designated Slack channel.

Finally, when the user intent is detected to be the *explanation* request, the chatbot moves into the RAG mode, where the user question is passed through two parallel processes. First, the question is passed through the LLM along with the current session information which includes (i) prior communication history between the chatbot and the user and (ii) the output of the synthetic image detection tool for the current image submitted by the user. The session history is refreshed when the user submits a new input for analysis. The LLM is then prompted to paraphrase the user question into a standalone question if relevant history is needed to interpret the user question. For example, if the user and the chatbot were previously talking about the output of a ProGAN model, and the user next asks "*Is its accuracy high?*", the LLM would take the prior history into account and return the standalone question: "*Is the accuracy of a ProGAN model high?*". If there is no prior history, the user question is returned as is. Second, the standalone question is translated into a dense representation and compared to the dense representations of individual document chunks (further referred to as *documents* for simplicity). Based on the similarity between the standalone question-document pairs, the documents are then ranked and the top k documents are retrieved. Given the rather straightforward nature of our documentation and user questions, as we show in Section "Document Retrieval", we empirically estimated k = 3 to be the optimal number of retrieved documents, with larger sets resulting in irrelevant information and low precision of the retriever and lower k resulting in a recall decline. The top-k retrieved documents and the standalone question are then passed through the LLM to generate the final answer based on the given context. To facilitate the transparency, the model also returns the metadata in the form of the retrieved documents that support the final answer. As a final step, the user session history is updated with the new question-answer pair.

In the next section we explain the methodology behind the first step of the architecture, the intent classification module of the chatbot.

User Intent Detection

For the user intent detection, we trained a multilingual multilabel model that is able to discriminate between 6 types of user intents. The multilabel definition of the task is essential as users often tend to express several questions as one message.

Method. One of the challenges of training highly-specific intent recognition models is the lack of data. For our task, we manually created a seed dataset of 300 examples of user questions in English along with a sparse vector of associated intents. The dataset was created through consultation sessions with media professionals regarding the types of questions they are most likely to ask when interacting with the tool. We split the data into training (80%), validation (10%) and test (10%) sets, stratified by the intent class. We used the validation set to empirically estimate the optimal threshold for predicting individual intents, which in our case was 0.58. In cases where no intent had a confidence over the defined threshold, the intent with the highest score is used as a prediction.

We experimented with fine-tuning two types of multilingual language models, mBERT-base [90] and XLM-RoBERTa-base [68]. We opted for the base versions of the models due to the importance of latency metric in generating replies. Given that the intent detection step is only the first step towards generating an answer, larger models introduced significant delays that could potentially affect users' satisfaction. Each model was trained for 20 iterations We used with the learning rate of $1e-5$, AdamW optimiser [72] ($\epsilon = 1e-8$) and ReLU activation function in the classifier. For comparison purposes, we trained each model 3 times with various random seeds. Although the training data was only available in English, we benchmarked our models on 6 languages, by translating the test set in English (EN) into German (DE), French (FR), Spanish (ES), Arabic (AR) and Italian (IT) using Google Translate and evaluating how the model performs in zero-shot cross-lingual scenarios.

Results. Table 1 represents the performance of multilingual BERT and RoBERTa models on English and 5 unseen languages. Despite being trained on a relatively small dataset and the complexity of the task in terms of the multiclass multilabel scenario, the models are able to achieve a reliable performance even on complex intents, such as explanation generation or feedback provision. As can be seen, XLM-RoBERTa model is on average outperformed by the mBERT model for the majority of languages despite being significantly larger (270 million parameters compared to 110 million). The two zero-shot cross-lingual scenarios where XLM-RoBERTa demonstrates better average performance are the predictions on French and Spanish. Our error analysis revealed that the significantly lower performance of the mBERT model compared to XLM-RoBERTa on French and Spanish test set is primarily due to its difficulty in recognising implicitly expressed intents, particularly those related to new feature requests and explanation queries. For example, when a user mentions that an image was taken from BBC (a credible news source), mBERT often fails to interpret this as feedback about an incorrect classification by the tool. Similarly, implicit explanation requests—such as a user stating they are unsure about the meaning of certain colours—are frequently misclassified as either new feature requests or bug reports. It is possible that language-specific linguistic features and the limited number of trainable parameters contribute to the difficulty of correctly identifying such implicit intents in French and Spanish by mBERT. However, a more thorough analysis is required to draw definitive conclusions about the underlying causes of this performance gap. Unlike mBERT which performs consistently better on English test data, RoBERTa exhibits better performance on zero-shot languages for certain intent-language pairs. For example, the model's performance in *explanation* intent detection on French and Spanish surpasses that on English despite being trained on English data.

Unsurprisingly, context-independent intents, such as *greeting* and *end* are significantly easier to identify than the task-specific intents that often rely on the specific context or previous interaction history. This is consistent across all the languages and for both models. For example, the user question that states "*This image was downloaded from BBC*" is highly complex in nature due to its implicit intent. It does not explicitly express the dissatisfaction with the models' prediction, but instead mentions the source from which the image is retrieved. To link this statement with the intent to provide feedback about the models' prediction, even a human expert needs to perform a series of inference steps. First, one need to remember a general knowledge fact suggesting that BBC is typically associated with publishing trustworthy media. Additionally, the expert needs to have access to the model's output, which flags the image as synthetic in this case. Such complex reasoning steps are known to be challenging for even LLMs, therefore it is not unusual to observe smaller language models struggling to identify implicit dialogue intents.

Table 1 F1-score (in %) on multilingual data for various types of user intents

Intent type	Multilingual BERT						Multilingual RoBERTa					
	EN	DE	FR	ES	AR	IT	EN	DE	FR	ES	AR	IT
Greeting	100 ± 0.0	98 ± 1.1	99 ± 0.4	100 ± 0.0	99 ± 0.4	99 ± 0.7	100 ± 0.0	100 ± 0.0	98 ± 2.2	99 ± 1.1	100 ± 0.0	94 ± 3.6
Explanation	80 ± 4.1	71 ± 1.9	65 ± 2.9	62 ± 1.8	75 ± 1.7	74 ± 1.6	77 ± 1.9	75 ± 3.8	80 ± 2.6	68 ± 4.7	65 ± 2.1	70 ± 3.2
Bug	92 ± 2.4	65 ± 1.7	68 ± 4.2	60 ± 3.5	79 ± 2.5	81 ± 1.4	79 ± 1.4	60 ± 3.2	73 ± 3.7	79 ± 1.3	70 ± 2.0	69 ± 2.8
New feature	93 ± 1.4	67 ± 2.0	60 ± 1.8	71 ± 1.9	77 ± 2.3	80 ± 1.9	81 ± 1.7	71 ± 1.4	77 ± 2.9	73 ± 1.9	78 ± 3.9	78 ± 3.6
Tool output feedback	84 ± 3.7	69 ± 1.5	72 ± 3.3	65 ± 2.6	73 ± 1.7	82 ± 3.5	83 ± 3.3	69 ± 5.1	71 ± 1.0	80 ± 3.0	80 ± 1.2	81 ± 1.7
End	95 ± 1.5	94 ± 2.4	95 ± 1.6	98 ± 1.1	95 ± 1.0	93 ± 2.2	96 ± 3.1	88 ± 3.7	91 ± 4.4	94 ± 2.5	93 ± 1.7	95 ± 1.3
F1-macro	**89 ± 4.2**	**77 ± 3.1**	77 ± 4.3	76 ± 2.7	**83 ± 2.1**	**85 ± 2.9**	86 ± 3.8	**77 ± 5.2**	**82 ± 4.1**	**82 ± 3.4**	81 ± 2.9	81 ± 3.9

Boldfaced scores demonstrate statistically significant better overall performance of one model compared to the other for a certain language

Given a slight advantage of the mBERT model over the XLM-RoBERTa system, as well as the shorter inference time due to the smaller number of parameters, the best-performing mBERT model was chosen for our final integration. The model is publicly available on HuggingFace.[2]

RAG for Explanation Generation

As illustrated in Fig. 2, if the intent classifier detected the user request to receive an explanation, the chatbot calls a sub-system responsible for retrieval-augmented generation. The generation process consists of three main steps: standalone question generation, document retrieval, and final generation. The rest of this section is therefore structured around these three sub-tasks in the framework flow.

Standalone Question Generation

Incorporating history into RAG systems provides a robust mechanism for improving the quality and relevance of conversational agents, directly influencing the extrinsic metric of sensibility within the SSI framework (Section "Extrinsic Metrics"). By taking into account the conversation history, RAG systems can generate responses that are not only factually grounded but also contextually sensitive and coherent over time.

Method. We implement the conversation history by means of dynamically storing the user-chatbot conversations, accompanied by a unique session identifier, in an SQLLite database. The new session starts when the user submits a new input image for analysis. At each new user question, we retrieve the prior messages that correspond to the current session, and analyse the current question in the context of prior interaction. To do so, we pass the user question and the retrieved conversation history through the LLM in order to formulate the standalone question. We define a *standalone question* as a question that can be understood on its own, without additional context. To generate a standalone question, the LLM is provided with the following prompt:

[2] https://huggingface.co/lesyar/intent_classifier.

Table 2 Performance of various LLMs on the standalone question generation task based on BLEU, METEOR and ROUGE-2 metrics

LLM	BLEU	METEOR	ROUGE-2
Llama-3.2-1B-Instruct	**0.58**	**0.26**	**0.72**
Falcon3-7B-Instruct	0.54	0.19	0.61
Qwen2.5-7B-Instruct-1M	0.48	0.21	0.58
Mistral-7B-Instruct-v0.2	0.55	0.24	**0.72**

The results of the best performing LLMs based on each metric are shown in bold

```
Given the chat history and the latest user ques-
tion which might reference context in the chat
history, formulate a standalone question which
can be understood without the chat history. Do
NOT answer the question, just reformulate it if
needed or otherwise return it as is. If no prior
history is available, just return the user ques-
tion as is.
{history}
{question}
```

Our initial experiments considered the smallest instruction-based versions of open-source families of LLMs, such as Falcon [8], Mistral [53], Llama [34] and Qwen [93]. Our initial experiments demonstrated that the models highly benefited from a few-shot prompting. We therefore added three examples to the prompt that cover the cases of anaphora resolution in a standalone question, a reference to the prior user question, and a reference to a prior chatbot reply. To benchmark the efficiency of generating a standalone question, we manually created a test set of 30 examples, with history and question as an input and the standalone question as an output. Due to the nature of this sub-task, we assumed the conservative n-gram-based metrics to be more indicative of the quality of the output, since the model is not asked to perform an open-ended generation but to paraphrase the provided input using a pre-defined history context. We therefore evaluated the LLMs' performance through BLEU, ROUGE-2 and METEOR scores (Section "Intrinsic Metrics").

Results. Table 2 provides an overview of the model's performance on this task. As can be seen, Llama model consistently outperforms other LLMs despite being the smallest one in terms of the number of parameters (1B compared to 7B for the rest). Our qualitative analysis revealed that Qwen model was more prone to keeping the input unchanged, while Falcon added more of the context that is required to generate a standalone question. All of the models, including Llama, suffered from long history inputs. In cases where the history accounted for more than 5 exchanged question-answer pairs, the models would often either ignore the instruction or fail to account for older history to interpret the question.

Based on our initial evaluation, we chose Llama-3.2-1B-Instruct for both the standalone question and the final answer generation to keep the type of LLM in the final generation chain consistent. The choice of a specific LLM was motivated by several factors, such as the performance on the standalone question generation, latency of generation, and the cost of running and maintaining the LLM. For this implementation, we were constrained by a GPU capacity of 24 GiB and a target generation latency of 7 s or less. These limitations constrained the size of Llama-3 model to up to 7B, as larger versions required higher GPU capacity. Furthermore, we observed that as the model size increased, generation latency also increased—by up to a factor of four—resulting in potential wait times of up to 30 s. Our latency threshold was informed by prior work from Satake et al. [101], which suggested that the preferred response time for users interacting with a conversational chatbot is approximately 1 s. However, it is important to note that this estimate predates the era of transformer models and LLMs, which typically require more time to generate responses—especially in complex settings like ours that involve multiple processing steps. Given this, we allowed for some additional delay beyond the ideal response time.

Document Retrieval

Method. For this sub-task, we generated an indexed database for storing chunks of the documents related to the models behind the synthetic image detection tool and the associated user interface. More specifically, this included the static technical reports with implementation details behind the AI models (model cards) used for synthetic image detection, information about the types of data the models were trained on, associated publications, interpretation of the output scores and information regarding the user interface. As discussed in Sect. 3, metadata annotations were previously shown to be beneficial for retrieval in RAG-based assistants [103]. Therefore, instead of splitting documents into same-length chunks, we annotated the document sections based on the types of information they contain and performed the document split based on markdown headers, with the token overlap of 20 between all the splits. This step is implemented by means of a Langchain framework [75]. The average length of section chunks varied by section type. Dataset description sections averaged 150 tokens, while the sections detailing evaluation procedures were 93 tokens on average. Sections describing model implementation and references averaged 132 and 76 tokens, respectively. Notably, sections discussing interface functionality were the most detailed, with text chunks exceeding 200 tokens on average. We then encoded the document chunks into the `all-mpnet-base-v2` representation [107] and stored the indexed embeddings of the document chunks in a permanent Chroma database.[3] We also implemented the background process that is constantly checking whether some of the source documents were changed or new documents are added to the repository. In case of a change, the database is updated with new embeddings and is re-indexed. This allows to ensure the up-to-dateness of the RAG model, one of the critical extrinsic evaluation criteria [1]. We then use a vector store retriever from

[3] https://www.trychroma.com/.

Table 3 Retriever performance in terms of Recall@k and MRR for different number of retrieved documents and for three types of document search

Number of documents to return	Similarity-based		MMR		Threshold-based	
	Recall@k	MRR	Recall@k	MRR	Recall@k	MRR
k = 1	0.54	0.24	0.56	0.24	0.55	0.25
k = 2	0.76	0.26	0.77	0.26	0.76	0.25
k = 3	0.81	**0.28**	0.85	**0.30**	0.83	**0.29**
k = 4	0.81	0.24	**0.87**	0.28	0.85	**0.29**
k = 5	**0.82**	0.24	**0.87**	0.28	**0.86**	**0.29**

The best performing number of retrieved documents (k) per metric is shown in bold

Langchain to perform a similarity search between the embedded standalone user question and the database contents. We experimented with three types of document search: *similarity-based*, *mmr*, and by calibrating a *similarity score threshold*.

To perform a thorough evaluation of various components of the RAG chatbot, we manually constructed a set of user questions along with up to five document chunks containing the answer to those questions. To construct the dataset, we presented a language model (Llama-3.1-7B) with different sections from the database and asked it to generate sets of questions that could be answered based on the information contained in those sections. We then selected the most relevant question types—those reflecting real-world scenarios—through consultations with media professionals involved in the vera.ai project. Upon construction the test set, we evaluated each of the three search techniques based on the Recall@k and MRR score.

Results. Table 3 shows the results of search algorithm and retrieval length calibration. As can be seen, although, the recall benefits from retrieving more documents, a more balanced MRR metric shows optimal performance for 3 documents. This balance is particularly important for RAG-based systems, as irrelevant contexts can introduce additional noise and decrease factuality during the subsequent generation steps. We also observed the maximal marginal relevance (MMR) [41] algorithm for retrieving relevant document to yield best results. The main advantage of this approach lies in its ability to select chunks of data based on both their relevance to a query and their diversity from previously selected chunks. This helps to avoid situations when the same context is repeated three times during the retrieval step. We therefore proceeded with using 3 document chunks and MMR search type for the retriever in the main implementation.

Final Answer Generation

The final stage of the explanation generation process is to generate the final answer given the prompt along with top 3 retrieved documents and a standalone question generated at the previous step.

Method. We performed a thorough prompt engineering to ensure both extrinsic and intrinsic evaluation criteria, such as minimising the amount of ungrounded information in the reply (Section "Intrinsic Metrics") and encouraging the answer conciseness (Section "Extrinsic Metrics"). We observed that the location of the context in the prompt plays pivotal importance in generating the grounded reply, with the context at the start of the prompt resulting in the LLM ignoring the retrieved documents and generating the answers based on its own pre-training information. At the same time, placing the context and the question at the end of the prompt was causing LLM forgetting particular instructions, specifically about the answer length. It also often resulted in model hallucinations in the form of generating follow-up questions on behalf of the user and answering those questions. This is a novel observation that is contrasting with the conclusions from prior work by Liu et al. [70] who observed that the beginning and the end of the context is the most optimal location for relevant information. Below is the optimal prompt format that was used in our final implementation.

```
You are an assistant chatbot for answering user
queries about the model details and the interface
of the verification plugin for synthetic image
detection. Use the following pieces of retrieved
context to answer the question.
{question}
{context}
If you don't know the answer, just say that you
don't know. Do not output any intermediate steps,
just the final answer. Use three sentences maxi-
mum and keep the answer concise.
```

RAGAs framework (Section "Intrinsic Metrics") provides support for generating a synthetic test set for RAG systems given the task-specific documents by means of creating a knowledge graph and generating the context-grounded questions and answers. When generating questions, it is possible to choose the distribution between one-hop and multi-hop specific and abstract query generation. Here, *one-hop* queries can typically be answered by following from the question to one or more nodes in the context, while *multi-hop* queries rely on more complex reasoning with intermediate nodes between the two target nodes. Such questions require the model to draw an intermediate conclusion(s) that serve as a premise(s) for the final answer. Specific cases of multi-hop QAs may rely on bridging, intersecting or comparing two or more named entities, as well as rely on commonsense reasoning [74]. Within the context of our retrieval-augmented generation (RAG) approach, the model performs a single retrieval step but can potentially draw inferences across the top 3 retrieved documents, analogous to drawing connections between nodes. To illustrate, consider the question:

"Given the accuracy of ProGAN and LDM, is one result more trustworthy than the other?"

To answer this, RAG model would need to extract and integrate the following pieces of information from documentation:

"*ProGAN evaluation (MeVer RINE v1.0): Conducted on over 20 datasets including ProGAN, StyleGAN, StyleGAN2, BigGAN, CycleGAN, and others. Reported average accuracy: 91.5%, AP: 98.8%.*

LDM evaluation (MeVer RINE v1.0): Conducted on the Synthbuster dataset with samples from Midjourney, Firefly, Glide, Stable Diffusion, DALL-E 2, and DALL-E 3. Reported average accuracy: 87.5%, AP: 90.5%. Notably, the model fails at detecting DALL-E 3 images."

The desired response would then be:

"*The average accuracy of the ProGAN method is slightly higher than that of the LDM approach, which adds more credibility to its prediction. However, the two methods are not directly comparable as they were evaluated on different datasets, so the results should be treated as complementary.*"

This example constitutes a multi-hop comparative QA instance [1], where the model retrieves two separate factual statements and compares them along a relevant dimension (accuracy). It additionally infers that the approaches differ across the evaluation dataset dimension, adding nuance to the conclusion. This illustrates how a RAG approach can support multi-hop reasoning despite a single retrieval step, by leveraging the LLM's capacity to synthesise information across retrieved documents.

An example of a single-hop question could be formulated as:

"*Which datasets was the ProGAN method evaluated on?*"

The closest matching information retrieved from the database in response to this question is:

"*ProGAN evaluation (MeVer RINE v1.0): Conducted on over 20 datasets including ProGAN, StyleGAN, StyleGAN2, BigGAN, CycleGAN, and others. Reported average accuracy: 91.5%, AP: 98.8%.*"

And the desired final answer would be:

"*The ProGAN method was evaluated on over 20 datasets, which include ProGAN, StyleGAN, StyleGAN2, BigGAN, and CycleGAN.*"

As can be seen, in contrast to multi-hop reasoning, the answer to the question can be directly inferred from the retrieved text. Both single- and multi-hop queries can be either abstract or specific. Here, *specific* questions target concrete concepts and facts that can be directly extracted from the context. For example: "*What metrics were used to measure the model performance?*" is a specific question in out use case scenario. *Abstract* questions, on the other hand, are challenging for RAG models as they require a high-level analysis of the context and the retrieval of document metadata. An example of an abstract question in our application can be: "*How do you know it is synthetic?*".

In order to perform a better comparison, we generated four types of test examples, with 100 questions and answers in each set: one-hop specific, one-hop abstract,

Table 4 Performance of the model on various types of the test sets based on RAGAs, BERTScore and latency

Question type	Context recall	Faithfulness	Factual correctness	BERTScore	Latency (s)
One-hop specific	0.92	0.89	0.71	0.94	6.2
One-hop abstract	0.72	0.65	0.63	0.87	8.5
Multi-hop specific	0.70	0.77	0.68	0.86	6.2
Multi-hop abstract	0.67	0.54	0.47	0.82	14.3
Joined test set	0.81	0.69	0.59	0.87	8.8
Negative rejection	N/A	0.25	0.21	0.78	7.4

multi-hop specific, and multi-hop abstract. We later manually inspected each of the generated examples and selected 50 in each category that are best fitted to be included in the test set. This allowed us to compile 4 separate test sets, and one joined test set that contains a mixture of 200 question-answer pairs.

Additionally, we wanted to test the model's robustness in terms of negative rejection (Section "Intrinsic Metrics"). For this purpose, we manually created a set of 50 questions that cannot be answered based on the documentation. As a reference answer to each of these questions, we specified "*I don't know*", as this is what the model was instructed to do in such cases.

Results. We evaluated the performance of the system using RAGAs' framework that takes sample documents, user query, reference answers and the model's outputs as an input. Although factual correctness within RAGAs already captures the similarity between the generated answer and the reference, we additionally evaluated the model based on the conventional semantic similarity between just two components, reference answers and model's outputs, using BERTScore (Section "Intrinsic Metrics"). Finally, we measured the average latency in receiving the model's final output (Section "Intrinsic Metrics"). Table 4 demonstrates the model's performance based of various test sets and metrics.

Not surprisingly, specific single-hop types of questions are easier for the model to handle in terms of the retrieval accuracy, groundness to the context and the final generation similarity. On another end of the spectrum, when the question is both abstract and requires multi-hop reasoning to answer, the model struggles to both retrieve relevant documents and to ground the answer to those documents. When comparing the two intermediate cases of questions, multi-hop specific and one-hop abstract, the models performs significantly better in multi-hop specific question answering, both in terms of context-based faithfulness and factual correctness of generation. However, slightly higher context recall is achieved for one-hop abstract question answering. The last observation is surprising given that specific questions are more grounded to the context by definition, and can suggest a significant challenge multi-hop questions pose on a RAG model. In terms of model latency, abstract questions seem to take significantly more time for the model to generate the final answer. It is possible to assume that the reason for this lies in the longer time it takes for the model to retrieve relevant contexts in the absence of high similarity with the question. However, more thorough analysis measuring the latency of each step is needed to definitively answer this question.

For the negative rejection test set, context recall is not applicable, as—by definition—there are no truly relevant documents available to answer the question. However, since the retriever still returns the top 3 most relevant contexts based on similarity, it remains meaningful to compute faithfulness. As expected, faithfulness scores are low in this setting, reflecting the absence of genuinely relevant context. Notably, we also observe low factual correctness, indicating that the LLM often disregards the prompt's instruction to abstain from answering in the absence of sufficient evidence. Instead, it tends to generate a response based on its internal knowledge, highlighting a common challenge in enforcing prompt-aligned behaviour in LLMs (Section "Extrinsic Metrics"). This suggests that stricter mechanisms for negative rejection handling are needed, possibly introducing a threshold for document retrieval and prompting the model to reply "I don't know" in cases when the context is empty.

BERTScore, despite being significantly higher for a single-hop specific question answering task, remains relatively high for all types of questions, including the negative rejection questions for which the RAGAs factuality score is low. This supports the prior reports on the limitations of BERTScore (Section "Intrinsic Metrics") and suggests that similarity-based metrics that are based on dense representation can often be misleading in terms of evaluating the quality of RAG-based models.

Future Extrinsic Evaluation

The chatbot is currently integrated into a real-world synthetic image detection tool, and we plan to gather more statistical data enabling large-scale extrinsic evaluation. With more than 100k users of the verification plugin, over time, it will be possible to calculate the user engagement statistic in terms of the average conversation lengths, the number of collected data points through feedback intents, and the overall frequency of using the chatbot, particularly the number of returning users. In the next section, we describe the details regarding the chatbot integration.

6 Integration of the Human-in-the-Loop Chatbot in a Real-World Verification Tool

We use the chatbot to provide assistance and to collect user feedback for the vera.ai synthetic image detection tool, which is one of several image-analysis tools available in the verification plugin. The interface allows the end users to provide either a URL to an image they wish to analyse or to upload a local file. The tool then employs several machine learning models, each of which provides a score representing how likely it is that the image was synthetically generated by AI. The individual scores are then aggregated into a single overall score which is displayed to the user as a gauge, as illustrated in Fig. 3. The chatbot is used to help users provide feedback on the output of the tool, or ask it clarification questions about the tool's documentation. User inputs and chatbot responses are displayed as "message bubbles", giving the interface a familiar look reminiscent of instant messaging.

When a user submits a message, it is sent through the plugin backend to the chatbot endpoint, along with the session ID. As illustrated in Fig. 2, a two stage process then follows to generate the chatbot response. Firstly, the intent of the user's message is classified. If the intent is to provide a feedback, a stock response is sent back to the user, depending on whether the feedback is a *bug report*, a *new feature request*, or *tool output feedback*. For example, in Fig. 3, the user has informed the chatbot that the image they submitted has, in fact, been generated by AI. In addition to generating a response to the user, the chatbot automatically posts all feedback messages to the tool's feedback Slack channel, along with the email address of the user and the image related to their feedback, so that reports can be followed up. This is illustrated in Fig. 4.

However, if the intent of the user's message is classified as explanation request, the RAG model is called to generate a suitable answer to the user's query. This model generates explanations based on the relevant documents retrieved from the database. As described in Section "Document Retrieval", we implement a background script that continuously monitors the repository for newly added information and re-generates the corresponding representations stored in the database if such change happened. This ensures that the information returned to the end user remains accurate and up-to-date. Once such an answer has been generated, it is passed back to the front-end and displayed to the user. An example of this is shown in Fig. 5.

Since Llama does not keep track of session histories itself, we need to manage this based on pre-defined state transitions in the interface. This raises two important concepts: history and memory. History refers to what is stored in the system and for how long. Memory refers to what is presented to Llama as the context. These two notions deeply intertwined here since an important part of the context passed to Llama also comes from the conversation history.

To keep track of the history, we use a database that indexes messages by their session ID, their sequence in the conversation, and whether they were sent by the human or the chatbot. When a new user message comes through, the entire session history goes into the context passed to Llama. As mentioned in Section"RAG for

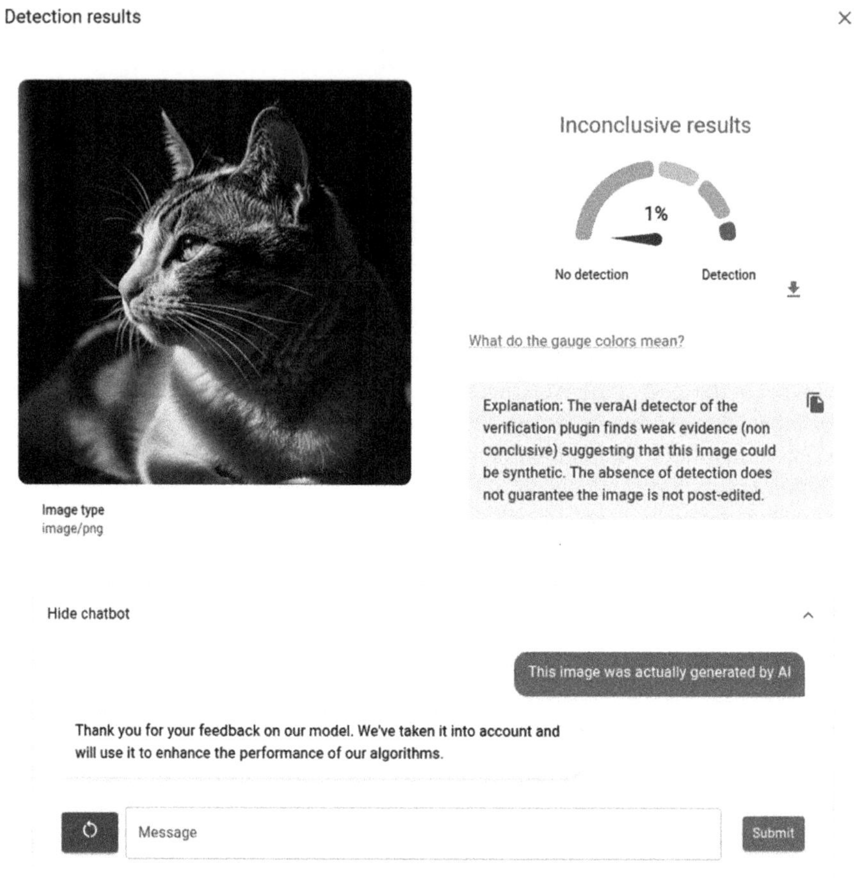

Fig. 3 The chatbot being used to collect feedback of an image of a cat generated by Google Gemini

Fig. 4 Post on the feedback Slack channel with the user's email address, feedback message, and the image

Explanation Generation", an important question here is how to determine that a session is over. One solution would be to simply have one long continuous conversation with the user over the entire time they are logged into the plugin. However, this is

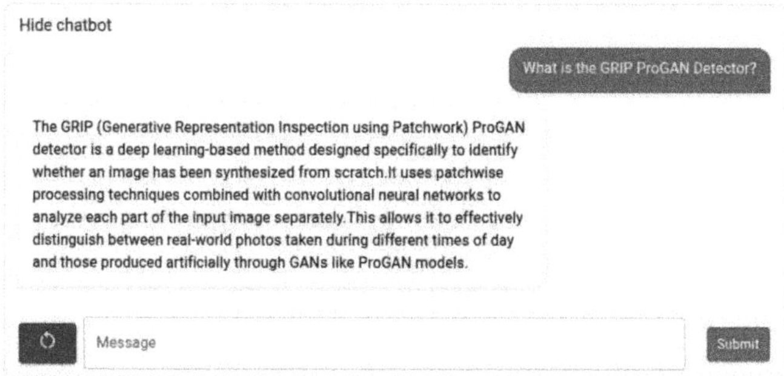

Fig. 5 The chatbot being used to answer questions about the synthetic image detection tools

undesirable for two reasons. Firstly, the chatbot takes longer to respond and requires more resources with a longer session history. Secondly, as time went on, the start of the conversation would become less relevant to newer messages sent by the user. Instead, we begin a new session each time the user submits a new image to the detector. This implicitly means that a session ends when the user closes the browser tab. Additionally, the user can start a new conversation at any time by clicking the "New conversation" button, shown to the left of the message box in Fig. 3, or by sending a goodbye message to the chatbot.

A finished session is recorded in the database, and the corresponding conversations are stored for a certain period as previous chatbot conversations are a good source of data for fine-tuning the chatbot model so that its responses get more relevant over time. This is particularly useful for common problems where similar questions are frequently asked. Older conversations can then be deleted periodically (or on demand) in order to manage the size of the database and to protect user data.

7 Challenges and Future Work

This chapter provided an overview of the potential of retrieval-based conversational agents to effectively collect user feedback regarding the performance of underlying systems while also providing explainability regarding the outputs of those systems. Despite many advancements in this research area in terms of the adoption of LLM, retrieval-augmented generation capabilities and the development of more robust evaluation frameworks, such conversational chatbots continue to face significant challenges related to hallucinations, refusal to perform negative rejection (as was demonstrated in our evaluation in Section "Final Answer Generation"), evaluation, latency, domain adaptability, and other critical aspects that hinder their effectiveness in real-world applications.

As was discussed in this chapter and empirically shown on the example of using BERTScore for the evaluation of our system, traditional text generation metrics like ROUGE, BLEU, or BERTScore are often inadequate for capturing the retrieval faithfulness or factual correctness of the output. While some specialised intrinsic metrics like RAGAs are emerging, this area is still under development, with several frameworks focusing on various aspects. For example, RAGAs evaluates the context recall in a way that is different from traditional retrieval systems, relying on sentence-level relevance of retrieved context. It also does not allow to capture the Precision@k, another important evaluation metric when it comes to information retrieval.

A fundamental limitation of current research on RAG is the retrieval step itself. The relevance of retrieved documents heavily impacts the quality of the generated output. However, retrieval models often struggle with semantic matching, especially when queries and documents use different vocabularies or reasoning styles. This results in noisy contexts, particularly for the simplistic frameworks, like Langchain, that use semantic similarity, MMR or thresholds as the underlying document search mechanisms. Adversarial noise in the form of irrelevant documents is a promising solution to the problem, shown to improve the quality of the retriever [26]. As highlighted by Setti et al. [102], the existing similarity-based search may not be the best approach for RAG altogether as similarity does not often indicate relevance. Future research should focus on developing re-ranking algorithms that are focused on relevance rather than similarity.

While RAG aims to ground LLM outputs in the retrieved contexts, hallucinations, such as generating text not supported by retrieved evidence, remains a critical problem. As was observed in our prompt generation experiments, even in cases of perfect retrieval, LLMs can ignore the context and hallucinate by generating the answer based on the internal knowledge. As shown by Wallat et al. [117], even when presented with correct sources, RAG systems are not faithfully attributing 57% of those citations. This opens doors for future research on a better integration between retrieved information and various generation mechanisms to ensure context attribution and faithfulness.

One of the main reasons behind the disparity between the retrieval recall and faithfulness is the disjoint nature of RAG models. In this regard, joint optimisation of the retriever and generator components offers a potential for future research on RAG. This idea resembles the multi-task learning approach (MTL) that is able to benefit the overall performance on the main task while often also improving the performance on peripheral tasks. Zhang et al. [138] proposed a framework for the joint training of generator and document retriever models, where the retriever is rewarded for extracting the documents with the highest utility for the generation. The authors demonstrate that this approach improves the performance of both retriever and generator components.

As shown in our question-specific evaluation results, while RAG systems perform well in highly specific one-hop question answering tasks, their performance deteriorates significantly when several reasoning hops are needed to reach the final answer. Such models also struggle with abstract questions that are not directly expressed in the factual context. Hierarchical graph-based approaches towards context representation and retrieval can offer a solution for this problem. The structural knowledge can allow retriever to connect semantically distant contexts together in an efficient way, as well as facilitate the retrieval of meta-information when answering abstract questions.

Finally, in the context of tool explainability and feedback collection, there is a great potential in directly embedding tools into AI agents. Over the recent years, the capabilities of LLMs have enabled the emergence of powerful multi-purpose AI agents capable of interacting with external models and Application Programming Interfaces (APIs), planning workflows, storing and recalling information, analysing intermediate results, and even improving the outputs of the tools they invoke [127]. Like most conversational systems, such AI agents typically begin their workflow with an *intent recognition* phase, where the user's query is analysed to determine their underlying request. The identified intent is then passed to a *function selection* module, which selects the most appropriate tool (or a set of tools) to fulfil the request. Subsequently, the agent performs *parameter extraction* or mapping of relevant values from the user's input to the required arguments of the selected functions. During the *function execution* phase, the appropriate tools are invoked with the extracted parameters. The outputs from these tools are then integrated into a coherent and user-friendly response by the em response generation module, which uses the LLM to generate the final answer to the user's query. This modular architecture further enables human-in-the-loop feedback and self-reflection mechanisms, leveraging the LLM's reasoning abilities to assess and improve the performance of individual components. As demonstrated by Wolflein et al. [123], such agents are capable of executing multi-step tasks and performing closed-loop self-improvement by evaluating the tool's outputs for consistency with expected results and iteratively refining the underlying tools or workflows. This direction of research also holds significant promise for verification systems that rely on multiple credibility signals and modalities, such as those being developed within the vera.ai project. It opens up the possibility of allowing users to submit arbitrary questions and input types through a unified interface, rather than navigating a collection of disjoint tools each tied to specific models, resulting in a more coherent user experience.

Acknowledgements This research was supported by the European Union under the Horizon Europe vera.ai project, Grant Agreement number 101070093 and the UK's innovation agency (Innovate UK) grant 10039055 under action number 2020-EU-IA-0282.

References

1. Abbasian, M., Khatibi, E., Azimi, I., Oniani, D., Shakeri Hossein Abad, Z., Thieme, A., Sriram, R., Yang, Z., Wang, Y., Lin, B., et al.: Foundation metrics for evaluating effectiveness of healthcare conversations powered by generative AI. NPJ Digit. Med. **7**(1), 82 (2024)
2. Adadi, A., Berrada, M.: Peeking inside the black-box: a survey on explainable artificial intelligence (XAI). IEEE Access **6**, 52138–52160 (2018). https://doi.org/10.1109/ACCESS.2018.2870052

3. Adiwardana, D., Luong, M.T., So, D.R., Hall, J., Fiedel, N., Thoppilan, R., Yang, Z., Kulshreshtha, A., Nemade, G., Lu, Y., et al.: Towards a human-like open-domain chatbot. arXiv preprint arXiv:2001.09977 (2020)
4. Aggarwal, A., Tam, C.C., Wu, D., Li, X., Qiao, S.: Artificial intelligence-based chatbots for promoting health behavioral changes: systematic review. J. Med. Internet Res. **25**, e40789 (2023)
5. Ait Baha, T., El Hajji, M., Es-Saady, Y., Fadili, H.: The impact of educational chatbot on student learning experience. Educ. Inf. Technol. **29**(8), 10153–10176 (2024)
6. Al Ghadban, Y., Lu, H., Adavi, U., Sharma, A., Gara, S., Das, N., Kumar, B., John, R., Devarsetty, P., Hirst, J.E.: Transforming healthcare education: harnessing large language models for frontline health worker capacity building using retrieval-augmented generation. medRxiv 2023–12 (2023)
7. Albassam, W.A.: The power of artificial intelligence in recruitment: an analytical review of current AI-based recruitment strategies. Int. J. Prof. Bus. Rev. **8**(6), 4 (2023)
8. Almazrouei, E., Alobeidli, H., Alshamsi, A., Cappelli, A., Cojocaru, R., Debbah, M., Goffinet, É., Hesslow, D., Launay, J., Malartic, Q., Mazzotta, D., Noune, B., Pannier, B., Penedo, G.: The falcon series of open language models. https://arxiv.org/abs/2311.16867 (2023)
9. Amugongo, L.M., Mascheroni, P., Brooks, S.G., Doering, S., Seidel, J.: Retrieval augmented generation for large language models in healthcare: a systematic review (2024)
10. Arora, G., Jain, S., Merugu, S.: Intent detection in the age of LLMs. arXiv preprint arXiv:2410.01627 (2024)
11. Arya, V., Bellamy, R.K., Chen, P.Y., Dhurandhar, A., Hind, M., Hoffman, S.C., Houde, S., Liao, Q.V., Luss, R., Mojsilović, A., et al.: One explanation does not fit all: a toolkit and taxonomy of AI explainability techniques. arXiv preprint arXiv:1909.03012 (2019)
12. Atuhurra, J., Kamigaito, H., Watanabe, T., Nichols, E.: Domain adaptation in intent classification systems: a review. arXiv preprint arXiv:2404.14415 (2024)
13. Banerjee, S., Lavie, A.: METEOR: an automatic metric for MT evaluation with improved correlation with human judgments. In: Proceedings of the ACL Workshop on Intrinsic and Extrinsic Evaluation Measures for Machine Translation and/or Summarization, pp. 65–72 (2005)
14. Bedi, S., Cui, H., Fuentes, M., Unell, A., Wornow, M., Banda, J.M., Kotecha, N., Keyes, T., Mai, Y., Oez, M., et al.: MedHELM: holistic evaluation of large language models for medical tasks. arXiv preprint arXiv:2505.23802 (2025)
15. Bhargava, A., Celikyilmaz, A., Hakkani-Tür, D., Sarikaya, R.: Easy contextual intent prediction and slot detection. In: 2013 IEEE International Conference on Acoustics, Speech and Signal Processing, pp. 8337–8341. IEEE (2013)
16. Brown, T., Mann, B., Ryder, N., Subbiah, M., Kaplan, J.D., Dhariwal, P., Neelakantan, A., Shyam, P., Sastry, G., Askell, A., et al.: Language models are few-shot learners. Adv. Neural Inf. Process. Syst. **33**, 1877–1901 (2020)
17. Burle, R., Gundewar, S., Gaurkhede, S., Fulkar, B.: Conversational symptom checker chatbot for disease prediction and suggesting nearby hospitals using machine learning and location services. In: 2025 International Conference on Electronics and Renewable Systems (ICEARS), pp. 775–780 (2025). https://doi.org/10.1109/ICEARS64219.2025.10941338
18. Cambria, E., Malandri, L., Mercorio, F., Mezzanzanica, M., Nobani, N.: A survey on XAI and natural language explanations. Inf. Process. Manage. **60**(1), 103111 (2023)
19. Campos Ferreira, M., Veloso, M., Tavares, J.M.R.S.: A comprehensive examination of user experience in AI-based symptom checker chatbots. In: Duarte, S.P., Lobo, A., Delibašić, B., Kamissoko, D. (eds.) Decision Support Systems XIV. Human-Centric Group Decision, Negotiation and Decision Support Systems for Societal Transitions, pp. 98–108. Springer Nature Switzerland, Cham (2024)
20. Chan, B.J., Chen, C.T., Cheng, J.H., Huang, H.H.: Don't do rag: when cache-augmented generation is all you need for knowledge tasks. arXiv preprint arXiv:2412.15605 (2024)

21. Chen, J., Lin, H., Han, X., Sun, L.: Benchmarking large language models in retrieval-augmented generation. In: Proceedings of the Thirty-Eighth AAAI Conference on Artificial Intelligence and Thirty-Sixth Conference on Innovative Applications of Artificial Intelligence and Fourteenth Symposium on Educational Advances in Artificial Intelligence, AAAI'24/IAAI'24/EAAI'24. AAAI Press (2024). https://doi.org/10.1609/aaai.v38i16.29728
22. Chen, L., Zhang, R., Guo, J., Fan, Y., Cheng, X.: Controlling risk of retrieval-augmented generation: a counterfactual prompting framework. In: Al-Onaizan, Y., Bansal, M., Chen, Y.N. (eds.) Findings of the Association for Computational Linguistics: EMNLP 2024, pp. 2380–2393. Association for Computational Linguistics, Miami, Florida, USA (2024). https://doi.org/10.18653/v1/2024.findings-emnlp.133
23. Chen, Q., Zhuo, Z., Wang, W.: BERT for joint intent classification and slot filling. arXiv preprint arXiv:1902.10909 (2019)
24. Coghlan, S., Leins, K., Sheldrick, S., Cheong, M., Gooding, P., D'Alfonso, S.:To chat or bot to chat: ethical issues with using chatbots in mental health. Digit. Health **9**, 20552076231183542 (2023). https://doi.org/10.1177/20552076231183542
25. Costa, J., Duarte, R.P., Cunha, C., Menoita, J.: Knowledge retention through observation of instant messaging systems. In: Proceedings of the 23rd Pan-Hellenic Conference on Informatics, pp. 105–110 (2019)
26. Cuconasu, F., Trappolini, G., Siciliano, F., Filice, S., Campagnano, C., Maarek, Y., Tonellotto, N., Silvestri, F.: The power of noise: redefining retrieval for rag systems. In: Proceedings of the 47th International ACM SIGIR Conference on Research and Development in Information Retrieval, pp. 719–729 (2024)
27. Cui, L., Huang, S., Wei, F., Tan, C., Duan, C., Zhou, M.: SuperAgent: a customer service chatbot for E-commerce websites. In: Bansal, M., Ji, H. (eds.) Proceedings of ACL 2017, System Demonstrations, pp. 97–102. Association for Computational Linguistics, Vancouver, Canada (2017). https://aclanthology.org/P17-4017/
28. Dai, Y., Zhang, Y., Liu, H., Ou, Z., Huang, Y., Feng, J.: Elastic CRFs for open-ontology slot filling. Appl. Sci. **11**(22) (2021). https://doi.org/10.3390/app112210675
29. Danilevsky, M., Qian, K., Aharonov, R., Katsis, Y., Kawas, B., Sen, P.: A survey of the state of explainable AI for natural language processing. arXiv preprint arXiv:2010.00711 (2020)
30. de Arriba-Pérez, F., García-Méndez, S., González-Castaño, F.J., Costa-Montenegro, E.: Automatic detection of cognitive impairment in elderly people using an entertainment chatbot with natural language processing capabilities. J. Ambient Intell. Humaniz. Comput. **14**(12), 16283–16298 (2023)
31. Deriu, J., Rodrigo, A., Otegi, A., Echegoyen, G., Rosset, S., Agirre, E., Cieliebak, M.: Survey on evaluation methods for dialogue systems. Artif. Intell. Rev. **54**, 755–810 (2021)
32. Deshwal, M., Chawla, A.: PHUDGE: Phi-3 as scalable judge. arXiv preprint arXiv:2405.08029 (2024)
33. Devlin, J., Chang, M.W., Lee, K., Toutanova, K.: BERT: pre-training of deep bidirectional transformers for language understanding. https://arxiv.org/abs/1810.04805 (2019)
34. Dubey, A., Jauhri, A., Pandey, A., Kadian, A., Al-Dahle, A., Letman, A., Mathur, A., Schelten, A., Yang, A., Fan, A., et al.: The Llama 3 herd of models. arXiv e-prints pp. arXiv–2407 (2024)
35. Dziri, N., Kamalloo, E., Mathewson, K., Zaiane, O.R.: Evaluating coherence in dialogue systems using entailment. In: Proceedings of the 2019 Conference of the North American Chapter of the Association for Computational Linguistics: Human Language Technologies, Volume 1 (Long and Short Papers), pp. 3806–3812 (2019)
36. Es, S., James, J., Anke, L.E., Schockaert, S.: RAGAs: automated evaluation of retrieval augmented generation. In: Proceedings of the 18th Conference of the European Chapter of the Association for Computational Linguistics: System Demonstrations, pp. 150–158 (2024)
37. García-Méndez, S., De Arriba-Perez, F., González-Castaño, F.J., Regueiro-Janeiro, J.A., Gil-Castiñeira, F.: Entertainment chatbot for the digital inclusion of elderly people without abstraction capabilities. IEEE Access **9**, 75878–75891 (2021)
38. Gnewuch, U., Morana, S., Heckmann, C., Maedche, A.: Designing conversational agents for energy feedback. In: Designing for a Digital and Globalized World: 13th International

Conference, DESRIST 2018, Chennai, India, 3–6 June 2018, Proceedings 13, pp. 18–33. Springer (2018)

39. Griffin, A.C., Xing, Z., Mikles, S.P., Bailey, S., Khairat, S., Arguello, J., Wang, Y., Chung, A.E.: Information needs and perceptions of chatbots for hypertension medication self-management: a mixed methods study. JAMIA Open **4**(2), ooab021 (2021). https://doi.org/10.1093/jamiaopen/ooab021
40. Guidotti, R., Monreale, A., Ruggieri, S., Turini, F., Giannotti, F., Pedreschi, D.: A survey of methods for explaining black box models. ACM Comput. Surv. **51**(5) (2018). https://doi.org/10.1145/3236009
41. Guo, S., Sanner, S.: Probabilistic latent maximal marginal relevance. In: Proceedings of the 33rd International ACM SIGIR Conference on Research and Development in Information Retrieval, pp. 833–834 (2010)
42. Guttikonda, D., Indran, D., Narayanan, L., Pasarad, T., Sandesh, B.J.: Explainable AI: a retrieval-augmented generation based framework for model interpretability
43. Hanji, S.V., Navalgund, N., Ingalagi, S., Desai, S., Hanji, S.S.: Adoption of AI chatbots in travel and tourism services. In: International Congress on Information and Communication Technology, pp. 713–727. Springer (2023)
44. Hanna, M., Bojar, O.: A fine-grained analysis of BERTScore. In: Proceedings of the Sixth Conference on Machine Translation, pp. 507–517 (2021)
45. Heinz, M.V., Mackin, D.M., Trudeau, B.M., Bhattacharya, S., Wang, Y., Banta, H.A., Jewett, A.D., Salzhauer, A.J., Griffin, T.Z., Jacobson, N.C.: Randomized trial of a generative AI chatbot for mental health treatment. NEJM AI **2**(4), AIoa2400802 (2025). https://doi.org/10.1056/AIoa2400802
46. Hindi, M., Mohammed, L., Maaz, O., Alwarafy, A.: Enhancing the precision and interpretability of retrieval-augmented generation (RAG) in legal technology: a survey. IEEE Access (2025)
47. Hofstätter, S., Chen, J., Raman, K., Zamani, H.: FiD-Light: efficient and effective retrieval-augmented text generation. In: Proceedings of the 46th International ACM SIGIR Conference on Research and Development in Information Retrieval, pp. 1437–1447 (2023)
48. Hwang, G.J., Chang, C.Y.: A review of opportunities and challenges of chatbots in education. Interact. Learn. Environ. **31**(7), 4099–4112 (2023). https://doi.org/10.1080/10494820.2021.1952615
49. Iaroshev, I., Pillai, R., Vaglietti, L., Hanne, T.: Evaluating retrieval-augmented generation models for financial report question and answering. Appl. Sci. **14**(20), 2076–3417 (2024)
50. Irvine, R., Boubert, D., Raina, V., Liusie, A., Zhu, Z., Mudupalli, V., Korshuk, A., Liu, Z., Cremer, F., Assassi, V., et al.: Rewarding chatbots for real-world engagement with millions of users. arXiv preprint arXiv:2303.06135 (2023)
51. Izacard, G., Grave, E.: Leveraging passage retrieval with generative models for open domain question answering. In: Merlo, P., Tiedemann, J., Tsarfaty, R. (eds.) Proceedings of the 16th Conference of the European Chapter of the Association for Computational Linguistics: Main Volume, pp. 874–880. Association for Computational Linguistics, Online (2021). https://doi.org/10.18653/v1/2021.eacl-main.74
52. Jiang, D., Li, Y., Zhang, G., Huang, W., Lin, B.Y., Chen, W.: TIGERScore: towards building explainable metric for all text generation tasks. arXiv preprint arXiv:2310.00752 (2023)
53. Jiang, A.Q., Sablayrolles, A., Mensch, A., Bamford, C., Chaplot, D.S., de las Casas, D., Bressand, F., Lengyel, G., Lample, G., Saulnier, L., Lavaud, L.R., Lachaux, M.A., Stock, P., Scao, T.L., Lavril, T., Wang, T., Lacroix, T., Sayed, W.E.: Mistral 7b. https://arxiv.org/abs/2310.06825 (2023)
54. Joshi, R., Graefe, J., Kraus, M., Bengler, K.: Exploring the impact of explainability on trust and acceptance of conversational agents—a wizard of oz study. In: International Conference on Human-Computer Interaction, pp. 199–218. Springer (2024)
55. Joshi, I., Shahid, S., Venneti, S.M., Vasu, M., Zheng, Y., Li, Y., Krishnamurthy, B., Chan, G.Y.Y.: CoPrompter: user-centric evaluation of LLM instruction alignment for improved prompt engineering. In: Proceedings of the 30th International Conference on Intelligent User Interfaces, pp. 341–365 (2025)

56. Kachuee, M., Yuan, H., Kim, Y.B., Lee, S.: Self-supervised contrastive learning for efficient user satisfaction prediction in conversational agents. arXiv preprint arXiv:2010.11230 (2020)
57. Kim, S., Lee, J., Gweon, G.: Comparing data from chatbot and web surveys: effects of platform and conversational style on survey response quality. In: Proceedings of the 2019 CHI Conference on Human Factors in Computing Systems, CHI '19, pp. 1–12. Association for Computing Machinery, New York, NY, USA (2019). https://doi.org/10.1145/3290605.3300316
58. Kim, S., Shin, J., Cho, Y., Jang, J., Longpre, S., Lee, H., Yun, S., Shin, S., Kim, S., Thorne, J., et al.: Prometheus: inducing fine-grained evaluation capability in language models. In: The Twelfth International Conference on Learning Representations (2023)
59. Kim, S., Suk, J., Longpre, S., Lin, B.Y., Shin, J., Welleck, S., Neubig, G., Lee, M., Lee, K., Seo, M.: Prometheus 2: an open source language model specialized in evaluating other language models. arXiv preprint arXiv:2405.01535 (2024)
60. Kurata, G., Xiang, B., Zhou, B., Yu, M.: Leveraging sentence-level information with encoder LSTM for semantic slot filling. arXiv preprint arXiv:1601.01530 (2016)
61. Lewis, P., Perez, E., Piktus, A., Petroni, F., Karpukhin, V., Goyal, N., Küttler, H., Lewis, M., Yih, W.t., Rocktäschel, T., et al.: Retrieval-augmented generation for knowledge-intensive NLP tasks. Adv. Neural Inf. Process. Syst. **33**, 9459–9474 (2020)
62. Li, J., Galley, M., Brockett, C., Gao, J., Dolan, B.: A diversity-promoting objective function for neural conversation models. arXiv preprint arXiv:1510.03055 (2015)
63. Li, Y., Shibata, H., Takama, Y.: Chatbot-mediated personal daily context modeling upon user story graph. In: 2019 International Conference on Technologies and Applications of Artificial Intelligence (TAAI), pp. 1–6 (2019). https://doi.org/10.1109/TAAI48200.2019.8959867
64. Li, Z., Wang, C., Ma, P., Wu, D., Wang, S., Gao, C., Liu, Y.: Split and merge: aligning position biases in large language model based evaluators. arXiv preprint arXiv:2310.01432 (2023)
65. Lin, C.Y.: ROUGE: a package for automatic evaluation of summaries. In: Text Summarization Branches Out, pp. 74–81 (2004)
66. Lipton, Z.C.: The mythos of model interpretability: in machine learning, the concept of interpretability is both important and slippery. Queue **16**(3), 31–57 (2018)
67. Liu, Y., Iter, D., Xu, Y., Wang, S., Xu, R., Zhu, C.: G-Eval: NLG evaluation using GPT-4 with better human alignment. arXiv preprint arXiv:2303.16634 (2023)
68. Liu, Y., Ott, M., Goyal, N., Du, J., Joshi, M., Chen, D., Levy, O., Lewis, M., Zettlemoyer, L., Stoyanov, V.: RoBERTa: a robustly optimized BERT pretraining approach. arXiv preprint arXiv:1907.11692 (2019)
69. Liu, H., Zhao, S., Zhang, X., Zhang, F., Sun, J., Yu, H., Zhang, X.: A simple meta-learning paradigm for zero-shot intent classification with mixture attention mechanism. In: Proceedings of the 45th International ACM SIGIR Conference on Research and Development in Information Retrieval, SIGIR '22, pp. 2047–2052. Association for Computing Machinery, New York, NY, USA (2022). https://doi.org/10.1145/3477495.3531803
70. Liu, N.F., Lin, K., Hewitt, J., Paranjape, A., Bevilacqua, M., Petroni, F., Liang, P.: Lost in the middle: how language models use long contexts. Trans. Assoc. Comput. Linguist. **12**, 157–173 (2024). https://doi.org/10.1162/tacl_a_00638
71. Lo, C.W., Wang, Y.L.: The effects of response time on older and young adults' interaction experience with chatbot (2024)
72. Loshchilov, I., Hutter, F.: Decoupled weight decay regularization. https://arxiv.org/abs/1711.05101 (2019)
73. MacCartney, B.: Natural Language Inference. Stanford University (2009)
74. Mavi, V., Jangra, A., Jatowt, A., et al.: Multi-hop question answering. Found. Trends® Inf. Retr. **17**(5), 457–586 (2024)
75. Mavroudis, V.: Langchain (2024)
76. Mendoza, M., Zamora, J.: Identifying the intent of a user query using support vector machines. In: International Symposium on String Processing and Information Retrieval, pp. 131–142. Springer (2009)
77. Meng, H., Xin, Z., Liu, T., Wang, Z., Feng, H., Lin, B., Zhao, X., Cao, Y., Sui, Z.: DialogUSR: complex dialogue utterance splitting and reformulation for multiple intent detection.

In: Goldberg, Y., Kozareva, Z., Zhang, Y. (eds.) Findings of the Association for Computational Linguistics: EMNLP 2022, pp. 3214–3229. Association for Computational Linguistics, Abu Dhabi, United Arab Emirates (2022). https://doi.org/10.18653/v1/2022.findings-emnlp.234
78. Milana, F., Costanza, E., Fischer, J.E.: Chatbots as advisers: the effects of response variability and reply suggestion buttons. In: Proceedings of the 5th International Conference on Conversational User Interfaces, CUI '23. Association for Computing Machinery, New York, NY, USA (2023). https://doi.org/10.1145/3571884.3597132
79. Miller, T., Jing, Z.: Explanation in artificial intelligence: insights from the social sciences. Digit. Humanit. Res. **4**(2), 90 (2024)
80. Min, S., Krishna, K., Lyu, X., Lewis, M., Yih, W.t., Koh, P.W., Iyyer, M., Zettlemoyer, L., Hajishirzi, H.: FActScore: fine-grained atomic evaluation of factual precision in long form text generation. arXiv preprint arXiv:2305.14251 (2023)
81. Moradizeyveh, S.: Intent recognition in conversational recommender systems. arXiv preprint arXiv:2212.03721 (2022)
82. Moura, A., Lima, P., Mendonça, F., Mostafa, S.S., Morgado-Dias, F.: On the use of transformer-based models for intent detection using clustering algorithms. Appl. Sci. **13**(8) (2023). https://doi.org/10.3390/app13085178
83. Napoles, C., Van Durme, B., Callison-Burch, C.: Evaluating sentence compression: pitfalls and suggested remedies. In: Proceedings of the Workshop on Monolingual Text-to-Text Generation, pp. 91–97 (2011)
84. Ni, B., Liu, Z., Wang, L., Lei, Y., Zhao, Y., Cheng, X., Zeng, Q., Dong, L., Xia, Y., Kenthapadi, K., et al.: Towards trustworthy retrieval augmented generation for large language models: a survey. arXiv preprint arXiv:2502.06872 (2025)
85. Pan, A., Musheyev, D., Bockelman, D., Loeb, S., Kabarriti, A.E.: Assessment of artificial intelligence chatbot responses to top searched queries about cancer. JAMA Oncol. **9**(10), 1437–1440 (2023). https://doi.org/10.1001/jamaoncol.2023.2947
86. Papineni, K., Roukos, S., Ward, T., Zhu, W.J.: BLEU: a method for automatic evaluation of machine translation. In: Proceedings of the 40th Annual Meeting of the Association for Computational Linguistics, pp. 311–318 (2002)
87. Park, D., Yuan, H., Kim, D., Zhang, Y., Spyros, M., Kim, Y.B., Sarikaya, R., Guo, E., Ling, Y., Quinn, K., et al.: Large-scale hybrid approach for predicting user satisfaction with conversational agents. arXiv preprint arXiv:2006.07113 (2020)
88. Patil, S.G., Ramesh, P., Wan, A., Stoica, I., Shan, Q., Gonzalez, J.E.: Test-time RAG: enhancing long context understanding in LLMs with retrieval-augmented mechanisms
89. Pawlik, L.: How the choice of LLM and prompt engineering affects chatbot effectiveness. Electronics **14**(5) (2025). https://doi.org/10.3390/electronics14050888
90. Pires, T., Schlinger, E., Garrette, D.: How multilingual is multilingual BERT? In: Proceedings of the 57th Annual Meeting of the Association for Computational Linguistics, pp. 4996–5001 (2019)
91. Pombal, J., Yoon, D., Fernandes, P., Wu, I., Kim, S., Rei, R., Neubig, G., Martins, A.F.: M-Prometheus: a suite of open multilingual LLM judges. arXiv preprint arXiv:2504.04953 (2025)
92. Prathiksha, K., Tamizh Malar, S.G., Nivedha, P., Divya, D., Srijayanthi, S.: IntelliAid: a personal assistant chat-bot for enhanced task management. In: 2024 5th International Conference on Electronics and Sustainable Communication Systems (ICESC), pp. 432–436 (2024). https://doi.org/10.1109/ICESC60852.2024.10689912
93. Qwen, Yang, A., Yang, B., Zhang, B., Hui, B., Zheng, B., Yu, B., Li, C., Liu, D., Huang, F., Wei, H., Lin, H., Yang, J., Tu, J., Zhang, J., Yang, J., Yang, J., Zhou, J., Lin, J., Dang, K., Lu, K., Bao, K., Yang, K., Yu, L., Li, M., Xue, M., Zhang, P., Zhu, Q., Men, R., Lin, R., Li, T., Tang, T., Xia, T., Ren, X., Ren, X., Fan, Y., Su, Y., Zhang, Y., Wan, Y., Liu, Y., Cui, Z., Zhang, Z., Qiu, Z.: Qwen2.5 technical report. https://arxiv.org/abs/2412.15115 (2025)
94. Ravuri, S.V., Stolcke, A.: Recurrent neural network and LSTM models for lexical utterance classification. In: Interspeech, pp. 135–139 (2015)

95. Reynolds, A., Corrigan, F.: Improving real-time knowledge retrieval in large language models with a DNS-style hierarchical query rag. Authorea Preprints (2024)
96. Ribeiro, M.T., Singh, S., Guestrin, C.: "Why should I trust you?" Explaining the predictions of any classifier. In: Proceedings of the 22nd ACM SIGKDD International Conference on Knowledge Discovery and Data Mining, pp. 1135–1144 (2016)
97. Roychowdhury, S., Soman, S., Ranjani, H., Gunda, N., Chhabra, V., Bala, S.K.: Evaluation of RAG metrics for question answering in the telecom domain. In: ICML 2024 Workshop on Foundation Models in the Wild
98. Rukadikar, A., Khandelwal, K.: Navigating change: a qualitative exploration of chatbot adoption in recruitment. Cogent Bus. Manag. **11**(1), 2345759 (2024)
99. Sachdeva, A., Kim, A., Dennis, A.R.: Taking the chat out of chatbot? Collecting user reviews with chatbots and web forms. J. Manage. Inf. Syst. **41**(1), 146–177 (2024)
100. Sarikaya, R., Celikyilmaz, A., Deoras, A., Jeong, M.: Shrinkage based features for slot tagging with conditional random fields. In: INTERSPEECH, pp. 268–272 (2014)
101. Satake, S., Kanda, T., Glas, D.F., Imai, M., Ishiguro, H., Hagita, N.: How to approach humans? Strategies for social robots to initiate interaction. In: Proceedings of the 4th ACM/IEEE International Conference on Human Robot Interaction, pp. 109–116 (2009)
102. Setty, S., Thakkar, H., Lee, A., Chung, E., Vidra, N.: Improving retrieval for RAG based question answering models on financial documents. arXiv preprint arXiv:2404.07221 (2024)
103. Shi, Y., Zi, X., Shi, Z., Zhang, H., Wu, Q., Xu, M.: Enhancing retrieval and managing retrieval: a four-module synergy for improved quality and efficiency in RAG systems. arXiv preprint arXiv:2407.10670 (2024)
104. Shichel, Y., Kalech, M., Tsur, O.: With measured words: simple sentence selection for black-box optimization of sentence compression algorithms. In: Proceedings of the 16th Conference of the European Chapter of the Association for Computational Linguistics: Main Volume, pp. 1625–1634 (2021)
105. Singh, D., Suraksha, K., Nirmala, S.: Question answering chatbot using deep learning with NLP. In: 2021 IEEE International Conference on Electronics, Computing and Communication Technologies (CONECCT), pp. 1–6 (2021). https://doi.org/10.1109/CONECCT52877.2021.9622709
106. Sinha, S., Basak, S., Dey, Y., Mondal, A.: An educational chatbot for answering queries. In: Mandal, J.K., Bhattacharya, D. (eds.) Emerging Technology in Modelling and Graphics, pp. 55–60. Springer Singapore, Singapore (2020)
107. Song, K., Tan, X., Qin, T., Lu, J., Liu, T.Y.: MPNet: masked and permuted pre-training for language understanding. Adv. Neural Inf. Process. Syst. **33**, 16857–16867 (2020)
108. Sun, X., Bosch, J.A., De Wit, J., Krahmer, E.: Human-in-the-loop interaction for continuously improving generative model in conversational agent for behavioral intervention. In: Companion Proceedings of the 28th International Conference on Intelligent User Interfaces, pp. 99–101 (2023)
109. Sun, X., Zheng, H., Tang, Z.: Historical information-based intent detection for multiturn dialogue. In: Proceedings of the 8th International Conference on Computing and Artificial Intelligence, ICCAI '22, pp. 566–572. Association for Computing Machinery, New York, NY, USA (2022). https://doi.org/10.1145/3532213.3532299
110. Sydorova, A., Poerner, N., Roth, B.: Interpretable question answering on knowledge bases and text. In: Korhonen, A., Traum, D., Màrquez, L. (eds.) Proceedings of the 57th Annual Meeting of the Association for Computational Linguistics, pp. 4943–4951. Association for Computational Linguistics, Florence, Italy (2019). https://doi.org/10.18653/v1/P19-1488
111. Thoppilan, R., De Freitas, D., Hall, J., Shazeer, N., Kulshreshtha, A., Cheng, H.T., Jin, A., Bos, T., Baker, L., Du, Y., et al.: LaMDA: language models for dialog applications. arXiv preprint arXiv:2201.08239 (2022)
112. Toxtli, C., Monroy-Hernández, A., Cranshaw, J.: Understanding chatbot-mediated task management. In: Proceedings of the 2018 CHI Conference on Human Factors in Computing Systems, CHI '18, pp. 1–6. Association for Computing Machinery, New York, NY, USA (2018). https://doi.org/10.1145/3173574.3173632

113. Tur, G., De Mori, R.: Spoken Language Understanding: Systems for Extracting Semantic Information from Speech. Wiley (2011)
114. Vakili Tahami, A., Ghajar, K., Shakery, A.: Distilling knowledge for fast retrieval-based chat-bots. In: Proceedings of the 43rd International ACM SIGIR Conference on Research and Development in Information Retrieval, SIGIR '20, pp. 2081–2084. Association for Computing Machinery, New York, NY, USA (2020). https://doi.org/10.1145/3397271.3401296
115. Vannala, R., Swathi, S., Puranam, Y.: AI chatbot for answering FAQ's. In: 2022 IEEE 2nd International Conference on Sustainable Energy and Future Electric Transportation (SeFeT), pp. 1–5 (2022). https://doi.org/10.1109/SeFeT55524.2022.9908774
116. Vu, T.L., Tun, K.Z., Eng-Siong, C., Banchs, R.E.: Online FAQ Chatbot for Customer Support, pp. 251–259. Springer Singapore, Singapore (2021). https://doi.org/10.1007/978-981-15-9323-9_21
117. Wallat, J., Heuss, M., de Rijke, M., Anand, A.: Correctness is not faithfulness in rag attributions. arXiv preprint arXiv:2412.18004 (2024)
118. Wang, T., He, J., Xiong, C.: RAGVIZ: diagnose and visualize retrieval-augmented generation. In: Proceedings of the 2024 Conference on Empirical Methods in Natural Language Processing: System Demonstrations, pp. 320–327 (2024)
119. Wang, N., Peng, Z., Que, H., Liu, J., Zhou, W., Wu, Y., Guo, H., Gan, R., Ni, Z., Yang, J., et al.: RoleLLM: benchmarking, eliciting, and enhancing role-playing abilities of large language models. In: Findings of the Association for Computational Linguistics ACL 2024, pp. 14743–14777 (2024)
120. Weitz, K., Schiller, D., Schlagowski, R., Huber, T., André, E.: "Let me explain!": exploring the potential of virtual agents in explainable AI interaction design. J. Multimodal User Interfaces **15**(2), 87–98 (2021)
121. Weld, H., Huang, X., Long, S., Poon, J., Han, S.C.: A survey of joint intent detection and slot filling models in natural language understanding. ACM Comput. Surv. **55**(8), 1–38 (2022)
122. Wiratunga, N., Abeyratne, R., Jayawardena, L., Martin, K., Massie, S., Nkisi-Orji, I., Weerasinghe, R., Liret, A., Fleisch, B.: CBR-RAG: case-based reasoning for retrieval augmented generation in LLMs for legal question answering. In: International Conference on Case-Based Reasoning, pp. 445–460. Springer (2024)
123. Wölflein, G., Ferber, D., Truhn, D., Arandjelović, O., Kather, J.N.: LLM agents making agent tools. arXiv preprint arXiv:2502.11705 (2025)
124. Xie, Y., Zhou, W., Prakash, P., Jin, D., Mao, Y., Fettes, Q., Talebzadeh, A., Wang, S., Fang, H., Rose, C., et al.: Improving model factuality with fine-grained critique-based evaluator. arXiv preprint arXiv:2410.18359 (2024)
125. Xiong, L., Xiong, C., Li, Y., Tang, K.F., Liu, J., Bennett, P., Ahmed, J., Overwijk, A.: Approximate nearest neighbor negative contrastive learning for dense text retrieval. arXiv preprint arXiv:2007.00808 (2020)
126. Ye, H., Ng, H.T.: Self-judge: selective instruction following with alignment self-evaluation. arXiv preprint arXiv:2409.00935 (2024)
127. Yehudai, A., Eden, L., Li, A., Uziel, G., Zhao, Y., Bar-Haim, R., Cohan, A., Shmueli-Scheuer, M.: Survey on evaluation of LLM-based agents. arXiv preprint arXiv:2503.16416 (2025)
128. Yepes, A.J., You, Y., Milczek, J., Laverde, S., Li, R.: Financial report chunking for effective retrieval augmented generation. arXiv preprint arXiv:2402.05131 (2024)
129. Yılmaz, G., Şahin-Yılmaz, A.: An overview of chatbots in tourism and hospitality using bibliometric and thematic content analysis. Worldw. Hosp. Tour. Themes **16**(2), 232–247 (2024)
130. Yu, H., Gan, A., Zhang, K., Tong, S., Liu, Q., Liu, Z.: Evaluation of retrieval-augmented generation: a survey. In: CCF Conference on Big Data, pp. 102–120. Springer (2024)
131. Yuan, J., Sun, S., Omeiza, D., Zhao, B., Newman, P., Kunze, L., Gadd, M.: RAG-Driver: generalisable driving explanations with retrieval-augmented in-context learning in multi-modal large language model. arXiv preprint arXiv:2402.10828 (2024)
132. Zarouali, B., Araujo, T., Ohme, J., De Vreese, C.: Comparing chatbots and online surveys for (longitudinal) data collection: an investigation of response characteristics, data quality, and user evaluation. Commun. Methods Meas. **18**(1), 72–91 (2024)

133. Zhang, T., Kishore, V., Wu, F., Weinberger, K.Q., Artzi, Y.: BERTScore: evaluating text generation with BERT. arXiv preprint arXiv:1904.09675 (2019)
134. Zhang, S., Lu, Y., Liu, J., Yu, J., Qiu, H., Yan, Y., Lan, Z.: Unveiling the secrets of engaging conversations: factors that keep users hooked on role-playing dialog agents. arXiv preprint arXiv:2402.11522 (2024)
135. Zhang, Q., Man, D., Yang, W.: Using HMM for intent recognition in cyber security situation awareness. In: 2009 Second International Symposium on Knowledge Acquisition and Modeling, vol. 2, pp. 166–169. IEEE (2009)
136. Zhang, Y., Zhang, H., Zhan, L.M., Wu, X.M., Lam, A.: New intent discovery with pre-training and contrastive learning. arXiv preprint arXiv:2205.12914 (2022)
137. Zhang, N., Huang, Q., Xia, X., Zou, Y., Lo, D., Xing, Z.: Chatbot4QR: interactive query refinement for technical question retrieval. IEEE Trans. Softw. Eng. **48**(4), 1185–1211 (2022). https://doi.org/10.1109/TSE.2020.3016006
138. Zhang, Y., Sun, S., Gao, X., Fang, Y., Brockett, C., Galley, M., Gao, J., Dolan, B.: RetGen: a joint framework for retrieval and grounded text generation modeling. Proc. AAAI Conf. Artif. Intell. **36**(10), 11739–11747 (2022)
139. Zhao, S., Huang, Y., Song, J., Wang, Z., Wan, C., Ma, L.: Towards understanding retrieval accuracy and prompt quality in RAG systems. arXiv preprint arXiv:2411.19463 (2024)
140. Zheng, L., Chiang, W.L., Sheng, Y., Zhuang, S., Wu, Z., Zhuang, Y., Lin, Z., Li, Z., Li, D., Xing, E., et al.: Judging LLM-as-a-judge with MT-bench and chatbot arena. Adv. Neural Inf. Process. Syst. **36**, 46595–46623 (2023)
141. Zhou, H., Gu, H., Liu, X., Zhou, K., Liang, M., Xiao, Y., Govindan, S., Chawla, P., Yang, J., Meng, X., et al.: The efficiency vs. accuracy trade-off: optimizing RAG-enhanced LLM recommender systems using multi-head early exit. arXiv preprint arXiv:2501.02173 (2025)

www.ingramcontent.com/pod-product-compliance
Ingram Content Group UK Ltd.
Pitfield, Milton Keynes, MK11 3LW, UK
UKHW020911180926
475648UK00002B/16
* 9 7 8 3 0 3 2 1 1 7 8 1 6 *